The Private Side of American History

READINGS IN EVERYDAY LIFE

Second Edition

 I ^{TO} 1877

EDITED BY Gary B. Nash
UNIVERSITY OF CALIFORNIA, LOS ANGELES

UNDER THE GENERAL EDITORSHIP OF
John Morton Blum
YALE UNIVERSITY

Harcourt Brace Jovanovich, Inc.
NEW YORK SAN DIEGO CHICAGO SAN FRANCISCO ATLANTA

ISBN: 0–15–571964–5

Library of Congress Catalog Card Number: 78–71873

Printed in the United States of America

PICTURE CREDITS
COVER Culver Pictures.
7 The Bettmann Archive. **34** The Granger Collection. **51** American Antiquarian
Society. **68** The Bettmann Archive. **98** William L. Clements Library.
127 The New York Historical Society. **155** The Bettmann Archive. **178** The
Granger Collection. **206** The Granger Collection. **231** The Bettmann Archive.
251 The Bettmann Archive. **279** The New York Historical Society. **303** Courtesy
Abby Aldrich Rockefeller Folk Art Collection. **335** The Bettmann Archive.
357 The Bettmann Archive. **380** Culver Pictures. **401** Denver Public Library,
Western History Department. **422** Culver Pictures.

Epigraph on page 401 excerpted from "From an Old House in America." In *Poems,
Selected and New, 1950–1974* by Adrienne Rich, p. 239. New York: W. W. Norton,
1975. Reprinted by permission of the publisher.

Preface

The Private Side of American History, Volume I, is designed to supplement traditional textbooks that emphasize the political and intellectual aspects of history. This collection of readings offers a vivid description of everyday life in rural and urban America, from the colonial period through the third quarter of the nineteenth century. The selections provide a fresh perspective from which to view such vital but often neglected aspects of American history as work; family life, childbirth, child rearing, and sex; education and entertainment; religion; health, disease, and death; and conflicts created by encounters between diverse population groups—Indians and colonists, blacks and whites, and immigrants and established residents.

Arranged in roughly chronological order, the eighteen selections are grouped into four sections, each of which concludes with an annotated bibliography. The headnotes place the subject of each selection in its historical context. A brief introduction to the volume describes the major areas that should be considered in a historical study of everyday life.

For expert assistance and editorial criticism in preparing the manuscript for this book I would like to thank Betty Gerstein and Nola Healy Lynch of Harcourt Brace Jovanovich. William J. Wisneski, also of Harcourt Brace Jovanovich, and Thomas A. Williamson originally suggested the approach to American history reflected in this volume. For scholarly assistance I would like to express my appreciation to the following colleagues: Carol Berkin, The Bernard M. Baruch College of the City University of New York; Robert M. Calhoon, University of North Carolina, Greensboro; David M. Culbert, Louisiana State University; Michael Ebner, Lake Forest College; Thomas R. Frazier, The Bernard M. Baruch College of the City University of New York; James Kettner, University of California, Berkeley; Mary Beth Norton, Cornell University; Robert C. Ritchie, University of California, San Diego; Kathryn Kish Sklar, University of California, Los Angeles; and Daniel Walkowitz, Rutgers University.

GARY B. NASH

Contents

1790–1830
The Early Republic

1830–1877
The Expanding Nation

Topical Table of Contents

Introduction

History has traditionally been written as a record of public rather than private events. The growth of institutions, the election of office-holders, the passage of laws, the conduct of diplomacy and war, the expansion of scientific knowledge, and the process of economic development—these are the major categories employed by historians to reveal the past, as the table of contents of most history textbooks will indicate. Of course any history that did not investigate these topics would be incomplete. But American historians are recognizing that the public aspects of our past reveal far less than we would like to know about how our society and culture developed. For example, though we may understand the forms of government under which the colonies were founded, or the commercial relations between England and her New World colonies, or the rise of schools and colleges in the eighteenth century, we will still comprehend little about the feelings, motivations, and behavior of the great mass of colonizers. In the nineteenth century we may profitably study the Bank War, the building of canals and railroads, the abolitionist crusade, or the evolution of the Whig Party. But the past still will not have come alive because we will know virtually nothing about how people lived, felt, and interacted behind the curtain of public events.

For two reasons, then, the history of public events is lifeless and limited, often unable to move us or re-create a feeling of the past. First, it deals primarily with public figures—the important politicians, business leaders, intellectuals, and military commanders. As many critics have noted recently this kind of historical writing is elitist. It concentrates on the few and ignores the many, assuming that it was the "dynamic," successful handful who led the "passive," ordinary masses. By narrowing our vision in this way, historians indulge in a dangerous assumption about how events and movements occur. They bury from sight the fascinating and important story of all those who lived, worked, and died without leaving a footprint on the public record. Second, the history of public events is as narrow in its understanding of human motivation and behavior as it is in its choice of subjects. It tells us little about the hidden sources of human action and the intimate experiences of life that play such a vital role in public action. The actions of public figures, even the most powerful, have been influenced by their private lives. So to ignore the private side of American history is to cut ourselves off from sources rich with explanatory potential.

The historian-novelist Leo Tolstoy understood both of these failings of traditional history when he wrote *War and Peace*, his great epic of the

Russian people during the Napoleonic Wars. "To study the laws of history," he argued, "we must completely change the subject of our observation, must leave aside kings, ministers, and generals, and study the common infinitesimally small elements by which the masses are moved. No one can say how far it is possible for man to advance in this way toward an understanding of the laws of history; but it is evident that only along that path does the possibility of discovering the laws of history lie." Many would doubt that historical "laws" can be discovered at all. But Tolstoy had hit upon an understanding of how a people or a nation may better be studied. A century later we are beginning to follow his advice. His concern was not only to study "the masses" but also to find the "infinitesimally small elements" that moved all people, whether they numbered among the elite or among the peasantry.

It is primarily to this second question—by what small elements of life are people moved?—that this collection of readings is addressed. Many other books in American history direct our attention to the "forgotten" or "historically voiceless" people of our past—Native Americans, Afro-Americans, Chicanos, women, the poor, the deviant, and so forth. Some of these groups figure prominently in the selections that follow simply because they made up the vast majority of the population. However, the readings have not been selected for this reason, but rather because they deal with the "private side" of American history. They are concerned with the experience of living and the daily aspects of life that mattered most to individual Americans of the past.

What are the "infinitesimally small elements" that are so important to the experience of a society? Very roughly, they are those aspects of life that occupy most of our waking hours today, just as they did the daily rounds of people in the past: *work*—the performance of tasks, whether for pay or not, that consumes the greatest proportion of our time; *learning*—whether transmitted formally in schools or inculcated informally through everyday contact with family, peers, strangers around us, the media, or other sources; *family and sexual relations*—through which the most intimate desires and emotions are expressed and basic needs are fulfilled; *reflection*—whether in the form of religious worship, political or social commitment, or merely daydreaming; *physical preservation*—the simple but vital concern for health and the perpetual struggle against sickness and death; *social relations*—interaction with the world around us, which most often involves no more than conforming to the rules of the community but sometimes involves violence and war against our fellow beings; *public involvement and political action*—by which we express support for or dissatisfaction with elected and appointed officials, institutions and policies, and even forces beyond our ken or control. If studied with care, these areas of human experience, taken together, are profoundly revealing of the life of a society in the past. They apply to the rich and poor, the mighty and humble, male and female, black and white. And though they vary in importance depending upon the era under consideration, all have played important roles at every stage of human history.

It is well to keep in mind that the boundaries between the private dimensions of American life and the better-known history of public events are usually blurred. For example, when men and women took to the streets in pre-Revolutionary Boston they were expressing a private need to be heard in public matters. We can read much about the effects of their actions on English policy and colonial politics but still understand little about how their private lives were touched by participation in violent protest. Similarly, the private and public aspects of history overlap in war. Historians have traditionally told us much about how wars began, how they were fought, and how diplomats drew up treaties to end conflict. But war involves personal trauma and changes the lives of its participants. Conversely, what individuals bring to war in terms of their private makeup affects the outcome. Private and public life mingle everywhere, and only by adding studies of everyday life to the public record can we fully appreciate the richness and complexity of the past.

History is the record of change, so we must be attentive to how the private aspects of American life became transformed on the road from early Jamestown to Watergate. Careful comparison of articles that deal with the same aspect of everyday life in different eras should make this clear. Attitudes toward work among English colonists in the seventeenth century, for example, played an important role in the way society evolved on the Chesapeake, as Edmund Morgan's essay demonstrates. By the early nineteenth century the work attitudes of urbanized, semi-industrial workers within a capitalist system were strikingly different, as the chapter from Alan Dawley's book reveals. The experience of youth, to cite another example, differed greatly between the seventeenth and the nineteenth centuries, as is evident from the studies by John Demos and Joseph Kett included in this collection. Those alterations are of no small importance. Indeed, many historians feel that without understanding changing attitudes toward children and modes of rearing them we can never obtain more than a clouded and incomplete picture of how societies have evolved. Similarly, the daily reality of women's lives in frontier areas in the seventeenth and the nineteenth centuries can be compared in the selection by Lois Green and Lorena Walsh and the one by Johnny Faragher and Christine Stansell. How the private side of life was changed by public events and, conversely, how changes in everyday life molded larger social and political movements are questions students will want to keep in mind as they ponder these essays.

One other reflection on the nature of social change may be useful here. While the same aspects of everyday life in different eras can be studied in many cases, life itself was changing in America as one generation succeeded another. The controlling elements of daily life were replaced or modified, dramatically in some instances, as American society moved from the earliest colonial beginnings to the turbulent nineteenth century. For the first colonists, relations with native inhabitants of eastern North America constituted a new and frightening experience. Invasion of an already inhabited land involved a fearsome contact with a "different" people; it produced violence on a massive scale; and it preoccupied the private thoughts of many men and women whose religiosity compelled them to seek a moral justification for this confrontation of cultures. In the late eighteenth century, as Native American peoples withdrew to the west, this aspect of daily existence diminished except on the frontier. Another dominant concern of everyday life in the colonial period was illness and death. Infant mortality was high, the average lifespan was short, and epidemic diseases were common. Everyone had seen death and few were the families that had not buried several children before they reached adolescence. But intimacy with death waned in the nineteenth century. Medical science conquered many epidemic diseases, the average lifespan increased, and hospitals were created for the sick and dying. The sight and sound of mortal illness and death were gradually placed beyond the experience of most people. While these aspects of private life became less important, others rose in significance. Entertainment assumed far greater importance as working hours were reduced. Political involvement, only an occasional activity for the widely dispersed agricultural population of the eighteenth century, began to pervade the lives of an industrializing, urbanizing, nineteenth-century people. Other examples could be provided. But students will want to make their own calculations of when and how the "infinitesimally small elements" of American society changed, for taking part in the process of exploration is both the surest and the most exciting way of gaining a fuller understanding of the past.

1600–1730
The Colonizers
and
the Colonized

Building No.	Person No.	Source	Authorized By		Date
1650	DWN2	L	S. Koch 713		6/5/80

QTY.	CODE	AID	TITLE
	NASH1		THE PRIVATE SIDE OF AMERICAN HISTORY 2nd Ed. VOL. 1
	NASH2		THE PRIVATE SIDE OF AMERICAN HISTORY 2nd Ed. VOL. 2

The titles below will be shipped when published...

QTY.	CODE	AID	QTY.	CODE	AID	QTY.	CODE	AID

HBJ HARCOURT BRACE JOVANOVICH, INC.
College Department

757 Third Avenue ▪ New York, N.Y. 10017

The First American Boom:
Virginia 1618 to 1630

EDMUND S. MORGAN

Land and labor are indispensable ingredients in the development of all new societies. In North America it was the land of Native Americans and the labor performed by indentured servants and slaves upon which most colonial wealth was built. As many as half of the Europeans who arrived in North America in the seventeenth and eighteenth centuries may have come as indentured servants. As such, they were not free to move where they wanted, marry, or work for themselves. They had "bound out" their labor and their lives for four to seven years to somebody in the colonies whom they had never seen.

Exploitation of indentured labor became the central reality of life in early Virginia. Once the cultivation of tobacco as an export product was successfully established, the colony quickly became an extraordinarily oppressive society. While a few entrepreneurs and plantation owners reaped handsome profits, thousands of indentured servants, most of them men living without women, worked year after year without adequate food or shelter, debilitated by disease and malnutrition, and able to blot out their despair only with alcohol. The wretched lives of ordinary people in Virginia during and after the first tobacco boom were proof of how inherited ideas about work and social relationships could rapidly disintegrate under harsh and isolated conditions. In the absence of the restraining institutions of government and morality that applied in England, the exploiter was rebuked, if at all, only by his own inner murmurings.

One of the most important comparisons the student may wish to make while reading this and the selection by Allan Kulikoff in the next section is between the quality of life of the white indentured servant and that of the black slave. Both servant and slave endured a debilitating and disorienting Atlantic passage; both faced not only physical acclimatization to a new land but psychological adjustment to a new condition; and both were locked into an intimate and oppressive contact with a hitherto unknown master. Of course there were major differences between servitude and slavery. The slave was bound for life and the servant for a limited period. The children of slaves inherited their parents' status, whereas children of servants were born free. And the slave, if freed, faced many more obstacles than the indentured servant who had served his or her time. But the large number of servants who ran away or committed suicide suggests that the conditions of life during the period of bondage may not have been so different for the servant and the slave.

The importance of Virginia far transcended the numbers who went there or the territory they occupied. In their relations with the native inhabitants of the region, in their manner of exploiting labor, and in their redefinition of liberty and authority, Virginians left their mark on all that followed. The Virginians were the first English immigrants to set down permanent roots on the continent, and they provided both models and antimodels for all later colonists. Their imprint, of course, was strongest on the colonial South, but it was not limited to that area.

American historians have always taken delight in the success that followed the introduction of private enterprise in England's first American colonies. Ralph Hamor recorded the spectacular change that came over Virginia with Gov. Thomas Dale's assignment of private gardens to settlers in 1614: "When our people were fedde out of the common store and laboured jointly in the manuring of the ground, and planting corne, glad was the man that could slippe from his labour, nay the most honest of them in a generall businesse, would not take so much faithfull and true paines, in a weeke, as now he will doe in a day, neither cared they for the increase, presuming that howsoever their harvest prospered, the generall store must maintain them, by which meanes we reaped not so much corne from the labours of 30 men, as three men have done for themselves."[1] To which A. L. Rowse adds the comment that comes naturally to all of us: "Well, of course."[2]

Governor Dale's assignment of private gardens in 1614 amounted to only three acres a man, and he gave no one title to the land. But by 1617 a substantial number of colonists had fulfilled their obligations to the Virginia Company and worked entirely for themselves. In the following year the "old planters," those who had come to Virginia before 1616, paying their own way, acquired a hundred acres of land in fee simple. Later settlers paying their own way were to get fifty acres apiece and another fifty for every other person whose way they paid. The Company reached for a new source of profit from the labors of tenants who would be transported to Virginia at Company expense. In seven years, while they lived and worked on Company lands, they would pay rent on a half-and-half, sharecropping basis. And further to encourage immigration and financial investment the Company authorized groups or individual members of the Company to set up "particular plantations" of their own and man them either with servants or with tenants who, like the Company tenants, would work for themselves but give part of their proceeds for a term of years to the men who paid their passage. With the introduction of these new measures in 1618, private enterprise triumphed over the semi-

[1] Ralph Hamor, *A True Discourse of the Present State of Virginia* (Richmond, 1957 [orig. publ. London, 1615]), 17.
[2] *Ibid.*, xvi.

"The First American Boom: Virginia 1618 to 1630," by Edmund S. Morgan. From *William and Mary Quarterly*, 18 (1971):169–98. Reprinted by permission of the author and the publisher.

military work gangs that had kept Virginia going, but barely going, in its first years.[3]

In the six years that followed the triumph of private enterprise, Virginia killed off between three and four thousand Englishmen. An estimated thirty-five hundred to four thousand immigrants increased the population of the colony from about one thousand in 1618 to probably no more than fifteen hundred in 1624.[4] In that year the Virginia Company—itself a private enterprise—was dissolved in disgrace. The royal officials who then took over the government of the colony did not revert to any communal system of work for the colonists. Private enterprise was there to stay. Nevertheless, the failure of the Virginia Company and the staggering death rate suggest that our "Well, of course" to the first successes of private enterprise in the colony is perhaps a little hasty. We need not and should not conclude that allowing men to work for themselves was responsible for the disasters that struck Virginia in the years after 1618. Still, it may be worth inquiring into the way that the incentives of private enterprise operated in the colony during those years, and how those incentives affected the fate of the Company and the later history of the colony.

Modern scholarship has placed the blame for the failure of the Virginia Company on the shoulders of Sir Edwin Sandys, who poured men into Virginia faster than the colony could absorb and support them.[5] Without the capital to equip them properly, Sandys concentrated on getting men across the ocean, not only tenants for the Company's lands but artisans of various kinds to set up production of iron, glass, silk, and ships. Moreover, he encouraged dozens of private investors to establish particular plantations. Ship captains crowded men aboard and dumped them in the colony by hundreds, half dead and without provisions. Most of them died soon after, from malnutrition or from disease aggravated by malnutrition. When the king found out what was happening, he dissolved the Company.

There were of course other well-known reasons for Virginia's troubles, particularly the quarreling among different factions within the Company, the king's desire to maximize his revenues from customs duties on Virginia tobacco, and the Indian massacre of 1622, which alone accounted

---

[3] The classic account of the new program is Wesley F. Craven, *Dissolution of the Virginia Company: The Failure of a Colonial Experiment* (New York, 1932), 47–80.

[4] A list of "the Living and Dead in Virginia," Feb. 16, 1623/4, gives 1,292 persons living. A muster of all the inhabitants made in Jan. and Feb. 1624/5 gives 1,210 persons. The two lists are in the Colonial Office Group, Class 1, Piece 3, Public Record Office. Hereafter cited as C. O. 1/3. Both are printed in John Camden Hotten, *The Original Lists of Persons of Quality . . . and Others who Went from Great Britain to the American Plantations, 1600–1700* (London, 1874), 169–195, 201–265. The muster is also printed in Annie L. Jester and Martha W. Hiden, *Adventurers of Purse and Person, 1607–1625* (Princeton, 1956), 5–69. I suggest 1,500 as a maximum figure, because it seems likely that the persons taking these lists missed a number of people.

[5] Again the authoritative account is Craven, *Dissolution of Virginia Company*. I wish to emphasize that the present article is not intended as a challenge to Craven. It is intended rather as an exploration of developments within the colony that accompanied and aggravated the difficulties resulting from the Sandys program.

for 347 deaths. But there can be no doubt that the big mistake was the transportation to Virginia of such masses of unprepared and unprovisioned settlers, for whom the colonists already there had neither food nor housing. Admitting this much, we may nevertheless press the question why a colony that had been in existence for eleven years in 1618 was unable to provide a welcome for so many helping hands. And since the answer commonly given has centered on the lack of food supplies, it will be appropriate to begin by examining what people who lived at the time said about the scarcity of provisions, considering their statements from the harvest of one year to the harvest of the next.

1619–1620. When George Yeardley arrived as governor in April 1619 to inaugurate the Company's new program, he took over a colony in which the supplies of cattle and corn had been depleted. Yeardley reported that he would devote himself in the coming year to getting a good crop of corn.[6] During that summer, in spite of an epidemic that weakened and killed large numbers, the colony reaped unprecedented harvests, and by the end of September the settlers enjoyed, according to John Pory (no friend of Yeardley), "a marvelous plenty, suche as hath not bene seen since our first coming into the lande."[7] In January 1620 John Rolfe too reported the abundance of corn, and of fish brought from Newfoundland and sturgeon caught in Virginia.[8] According to these leaders of the settlement, Virginians were apparently well fed in the winter of 1619–1620.

1620–1621. I have found no surviving reports about the amount of corn grown in the summer of 1620, but in November Sir Edwin Sandys informed the Company that the settlers no longer wanted English meal sent them. Instead they preferred beads for trade with the Indians.[9] It is evident from other sources too that the colonists were getting corn from the Indians. In December, long after harvest time, George Thorpe observed that "this countrey meandes [i.e., mends, improves] in plentie of victuall everie daie," and he probably meant in supplies obtained from the Indians.[10] By May 1621 Capt. Thomas Nuce, a newcomer, observed that the men sent under his charge lived "very barely for the most part: havinge no other foode but bread and water and such manner of meate as they make of the Mayze: which I would to God I Could say they had in any reasonable plenty." They would have been distressed, he said, if one of their ships had not brought in corn from Chesapeake Bay, where the colony now had "good and free trade" (with the Indians).[11] The winter of 1620-1621 was apparently not a plentiful one, but there was no talk of starvation. In June George Thorpe reported that people were blessed with good health and good hope of a plentiful harvest of all kinds.[12]

---

[6] Susan M. Kingsbury, ed., *The Records of the Virginia Company of London* (Washington, 1906–1935), III, 118–122. Hereafter cited as *Virginia Company Records.*
[7] *Ibid.*, 220; I, 310.
[8] *Ibid.*, III, 241–248.
[9] *Ibid.*, I, 423.
[10] *Ibid.*, III, 417.
[11] *Ibid.*, 455–456.
[12] *Ibid.*, 462.

1621–1622. Again there is no specific report of the harvest. On December 15, 1621, Peter Arondelle, another newcomer, complained of his family's lean diet of one and one-half pints of musty meal a day per man.[13] But the governor and Council reported in January that in the nine ships which had arrived during the autumn, none of the passengers died on the way and all continued in health.[14] A ship from Ireland in November came "soe well furnished with all sortes of provisione, aswell as with Cattle, as wee could wishe all men would follow theire example." [15] If Arondelle's complaint represents a general scarcity in the colony it was not serious enough to lower his enthusiasm for Virginia, because just two weeks later he was writing home about the abundance of cattle and hogs both wild and domestic and observing that "any laborious honest man may in a shorte time become ritche in this Country." [16] The winter of 1621–1622 produced no other surviving complaints of scarcity. There was even some boasting that new immigrants no longer need fear danger from "wars, or famine, or want of convenient lodging and looking to." [17]

Then, on March 22, the Indians struck, killing not only settlers but also much needed cattle. The outlying plantations had to be abandoned. Planting operations had to be curtailed, for corn furnished shelter to lurking Indians.[18] There was no choice but to seek relief from the Indians themselves, not those who had participated in the massacre, but those to the north or south. Various captains were commissioned to get corn from them, by trade if they could, by force if they could not. There was not even a remote possibility that the harvest might be sufficient.

1622–1623. The corn obtained from the Indians and from the settlers' meager crops fell far short of the need, and most Virginians went hungry, as the prices of whatever provisions there were skyrocketed.[19] On July 2, 1623, Delphebus Canne, recently arrived in Virginia from England, regretted not having brought more meal, oatmeal, and peas for sale to the settlers, because "now the land is destitute of food." But he noted that the weather had been good and that people anticipated a large harvest of both corn and tobacco. Moreover, ships were expected daily from Canada and Newfoundland, with enough fish for the whole ensuing year.[20]

1623–1624. Whether the corn crop and the awaited cargoes from the north fulfilled expectations is not clear. In January the governor and Council reported that "the scarsitie this foreruninge yeere hath been greate, and who could expect less, after such a massacre, yett none to our

---

[13] *Ibid.,* 534–535.

[14] *Ibid.,* 582.

[15] *Ibid.,* 587.

[16] *Ibid.,* 589.

[17] Alexander Brown, *The First Republic in America* (Boston, 1898), 464–465.

[18] Edward D. Neill, *Virginia Carolorum* (Albany, 1886), 53; *Virginia Company Records,* III, 613–614; IV, 186, 234.

[19] *Virginia Company Records,* IV, 41–42, 58–62, 89, 231–235. See also Philip A. Bruce, *Economic History of Virginia in the Seventeenth Century* (New York, 1895), II, 6–8.

[20] Delphebus Canne to John Delbridge, July 2, 1623, *Virginia Magazine of History and Biography,* VI (1898–1899), 373–374.

knowledg hath Perished through wante, many seasoned men goinge through theire labours, beside harde marches, which endured the same Comone scarsitie." [21] By April enough provisions had been obtained from the Indians so that the crisis was over.[22]

The reports all reflect some scarcity of food between 1618 and 1624. But only during the year following the massacre was the scarcity acute, and in the winter and spring after the bumper harvest of 1619 there seems to have been no scarcity at all. Yet it is precisely from this winter and spring that we have the most explicit complaints from Virginia about people arriving without adequate provisions. On November 4, 1619, when a hundred Company tenants arrived "lusty and well" on the *Bona Nova,* the governor and Council calculated that the 544 bushels of meal sent with them would last only five and one-half months at two pounds a man per day. Fifty men were therefore parcelled out for a year to private planters.[23] Yet two or three months earlier, when a Dutch ship put in at the colony, the governor and cape merchant, in a famous transaction, bartered Virginia provisions for twenty-odd Negroes, who certainly came ashore unsupplied with anything.[24] It is not recorded that the Negroes were put to work for the Company. The following June, after some four hundred more settlers arrived, Governor Yeardley wrote plaintively to the Company, urging them to send subsequent ships with more provisions, adding that "yf such nombers of people come upon me unexpected, and that at an unhealthfull season and to late to sett Corne I cannott then be able to feed them owt of others labors." In the future, he begged them, they should send men before Christmas (by November 4 perhaps?) with six months' provisions (instead of five and one-half?).[25]

Yeardley's complaints, his purchase of the Negroes, and his disposal of the men from the *Bona Nova* at a time when the colony was reporting an unprecedented abundance, suggest that the problem was not altogether one of whether supplies existed. It was a question of who had them and of who could pay for them. In a year of plenty the governor and Council were unable or unwilling to make use of fifty men without supplies when other Virginians *were* able and willing to do so. The great shortage of supplies, to which we attribute the failure of the Sandys program, was not an absolute shortage in which all Virginians shared and suffered alike. It was a shortage that severely afflicted the Company and its dependents, but it furnished large opportunities for private entrepreneurs,

[21] *Virginia Company Records,* IV, 452.

[22] *Ibid.,* 475. The harvest in the summer of 1624 was plentiful. Gov. Sir Francis Wyatt and Council of Virginia to earl of Southampton and Council and Company of Virginia, Dec. 2, 1624, in W. Noel Sainsbury *et al.,* eds., *Calendar of State Papers, Colonial Series, America and West Indies, 1574–1660* (London, 1860), no. 30 (C. O. 1/3, 102).

[23] *Virginia Company Records,* III, 226, 246; John Smith, *Travels and Works,* ed. Edward Arber (Edinburgh, 1910), II, 542.

[24] *Virginia Company Records,* III, 243. It is perhaps no coincidence that in 1625 Yeardley (governor in 1619) and Abraham Peirscy (cape merchant in 1619) held 15 of the 23 Negroes then in the colony.

[25] *Ibid.,* 299.

and larger ones for Company officials who knew how to turn public distress to private profit.

Throughout the period when too many men were arriving with too few supplies, the established settlers were so eager for more workers that they paid premium wages for them, even when they had to feed as well as pay them. In 1621 the governor and Council set maximum wage rates at three shillings a day for ordinary laborers and four shillings for most skilled craftsmen (joiners got five). If the workman was furnished with food for the day, the rate was only a shilling a day less.[26] These figures amount to three or four times the maximum wages of day labor established by county justices in England, where a man who was fed by his employer generally received about half the wage of one who furnished his own food.[27] Food was comparatively less valuable in Virginia than in England.

Daily wage earners were only one part of Virginia's labor force. An increasing number of workers were servants bound for a period of years. These came at a lower rate, and these were what the planters wanted. It had been common in England for farmers to hire servants by the year, and employers in many trades were required by law to hire their labor by the year.[28] But servants who wanted to go to Virginia were willing to pledge several years' work, usually four to seven years, in return for transportation and maintenance. If a Virginia planter could import a man from England, the cost of his passage to the colony was about six pounds; his provisions and clothes for the voyage and to start him out in the New World might run another four to six pounds.[29] At this rate the cost per year for a servant in Virginia was not much more, and might be less, than in England; for in England too masters had to provide food and shelter and sometimes clothing for their bound servants, and a year's pay for an agricultural worker ran from thirty to fifty shillings in the first decades of the seventeenth century.[30]

Although the planter or entrepreneur who brought a servant to the New World ran the risk of losing his investment through death, Virginia planters evidently shared Edwin Sandys's belief that the rewards outweighed the risks. Despite the fact that bound servants had to be fed,

---

[26] Francis Wyatt, Wyatt Manuscripts, *William and Mary Quarterly*, 2d Ser., VII (1927), 246; *Virginia Company Records*, III, 590. See also the similar rates set in tobacco in Bermuda in 1623 and 1627, J. H. Lefroy, *Memorials of the Discovery and Early Settlement of the Bermudas or Somers Islands 1515–1685* (London, 1877–1879), I, 305.

[27] J. E. T. Rogers, *A History of Agriculture and Prices in England* (Oxford, 1866–1900), VI, 632–633, 692–695; S. A. H. Burne, ed., *The Staffordshire Quarter Sessions Rolls* (Kendal, 1931–   ), V, 259–261, 324–326.

[28] 25 Edw. III, c. 2; 3 Edw. VI, c. 22; 5 Eliz. I, c. 4.

[29] *Virginia Company Records*, III, 499–500; Neill, *Virginia Carolorum*, 109–111; George Reade to Robert Reade, Apr. 24, 1640, *Va. Mag. Hist. Biog.*, XIII (1905–1906), 387; Bruce, *Economic History*, I, 629; William Bullock, *Virginia Impartially Examined . . .* (London, 1649), 49.

[30] See references in note 27 and Calendar of Essex Quarter Sessions (typescript in Essex Records Office, microfilm in University of Wisconsin Library and Yale University Library), XVII, 116.

clothed, and housed, Virginians could not get enough of them. Everybody wanted servants. Even tenants who had been unable to pay their own passage to the colony wanted servants. Richard Berkeley and John Smyth of Nibley received from the tenants at their particular plantation a request for two servants apiece "for their owne pryvate benefit and imploymentes." [31] Indeed, as John Pory put it, "our principall wealth . . . consisteth in servants." [32] And after the Virginia Company had been dissolved, former Governor Yeardley, now representing the interests of the colonists, urged the royal commission in charge of the colony "to advance the Plantacion for the future by sending great number of people." [33]

From what little can be discovered about the value of a man's labor in the soil of Virginia between 1618 and 1624, it is not hard to see why the demand for servants was so high, even in the face of a food scarcity. At the time when Sandys took over the Company and began pouring men into the colony, Virginia had just begun to ship tobacco in quantity to the English market. The prices it brought were considerably lower than those for Spanish tobacco, but high enough to excite the cupidity of every settler. In the colony in 1619 the best grade sold for export at three shillings a pound.[34] In 1623 what reached England was worth no more than half that, and in bartering within the colony it was said to have passed at less than a shilling a pound.[35] In a lawsuit recorded in 1624, it was reckoned at two shillings a pound and in 1625 at three shillings again.[36] The boom lasted until 1629 or 1630 when the price tumbled to a penny a pound.[37] Though it recovered somewhat in ensuing years, it never again reached the dizzy heights of the 1620s. During that decade the profits from tobacco growing were enough to keep everybody scrambling for servants in order to grow as many plants as possible.

The amount of tobacco one man could produce in a year by his own labor varied from place to place, from year to year, and from man to man. In 1619 John Rolfe, who introduced tobacco cultivation in Virginia, estimated that a man could tend four acres of corn and one thousand plants of tobacco.[38] Four years later William Capps, an "old planter," said that a man could tend two thousand plants and that this would make five hun-

---

[31] *Virginia Company Records,* III, 399. At least two Company tenants, Francis Fowler and Thomas Dunthorne, held servants in 1626. See *Minutes of Council* 96, 108, 136, 137.

[32] *Virginia Company Records,* III, 221. It follows that the rising demand ran up the price of servants in Virginia to an amount well above the mere cost of transportation and maintenance.

[33] C. O. 1/3, 227–228; Sir George Yeardley, Propositions touching Virginia, 1625, *Wm. and Mary Qtly.,* 2d Ser., VIII (1928), 162.

[34] *Virginia Company Records,* III, 162. The figure 3d. given here is an obvious misprint for 3s.

[35] *Ibid.,* IV, 264; H. R. McIlwaine, ed., *Journals of the House of Burgesses of Virginia 1619–1658/59* (Richmond, 1915), 24. Hereafter cited as *Journals of Burgesses.*

[36] *Minutes of Council,* 33, 43.

[37] Evidence about the exact time of the collapse is scanty, but see Gov. John Harvey to the Privy Council, May 29, 1630, *Va. Mag. Hist. Biog.,* VII (1899–1900), 382; C. O. 1/8, 17–18; C. O. 1/9, 248–249; C. O. 1/10, 14–17.

[38] Smith, *Works,* II, 541.

dred "weight" (presumably five hundred pounds) of tobacco. He also
maintained that in 1623 three of his boys, whom he calculated as equal to
a man and a half, had produced 3,000 weight of tobacco and 110 barrels
(550 bushels) of corn.[39] Richard Brewster, working with three men, was
said to have grown 2,800 weight of tobacco and 100 bushels of corn.[40]
In 1626 William Spencer testified in court that in 1620 he had overseen
the labor of six or seven men who had produced three or four thousand
weight.[41] The figures differ, perhaps because some of the authors were
boasting, because some men worked harder than others, and because tobacco harvests varied sharply from year to year for reasons beyond human control.[42] But by any calculation the returns from labor invested in
growing tobacco were high. John Pory, after the exceptionally good harvest of 1619, said that one man had cleared £200 sterling by his own
labor and another with six servants had cleared £1,000 sterling. These, he
admitted, were "rare examples, yet possible to be done by others." [43]

　　　Because of the chances of such profits, Jamestown in the last years of
the Virginia Company, while a charnel house, was also the first American
boom town. There was no gold or silver. A man could not make a fortune
by himself. But if he could stay alive and somehow get control of a few
servants and keep them alive, he could make more in a year than he was
likely to make in several in England. And if he could get a large number
of servants, he might indeed make a fortune.
　　　In a boom town not everyone strikes it rich; and even those who
come in from the hills with a pocketful of gold generally give it up in a
hurry—for drink, for women, even for food and clothing at bonanza
prices. Life is cheap, but nothing else is. Those who have what gold will
buy get the gold a good deal easier and faster than the miners who dig it.

[39] *Virginia Company Records*, II, 524; IV, 38.
[40] *Ibid.*, II, 524.
[41] *Minutes of Council*, 99; *Virginia Company Records*, I, 256, 268.
[42] If we may judge from the English customs records of tobacco imported from Virginia, Bermuda, and Maryland, a good year often produced twice the amount of a
poor year and sometimes almost three times the amount. See figures in Neville
Williams, "England's Tobacco Trade in the Reign of Charles I," *Va. Mag. Hist.
Biog.*, LXV (1957), 403–449; Stanley Gray and V. J. Wyckoff, "The International
Tobacco Trade in the Seventeenth Century," *Southern Economic Journal*, VII
(1940), 16–25; Importations of Tobacco, September 29, 1614, to September 29,
1621, "Lord Sackville's Papers respecting Virginia," *American Historical Review*,
XXVII (1921–1922), 526; and Elizabeth B. Schumpeter, *English Overseas Trade
Statistics 1697–1808* (Oxford, 1960), 52–55.
[43] *Virginia Company Records*, III, 221. By the 1640s it was expected that one man's
crop might amount to 1,500 or 2,000 pounds, which at 1619 prices would have
brought from £225 to £300 per man. Bullock, *Virginia Examined*, 63; Samuel
Hartlib, *The Reformed Virginia Silk-worm*, . . . (London, 1655), in Peter Force,
ed., *Tracts and Other Papers Relating Principally to the Origin, Settlement, and
Progress of the Colonies in North America, From the Discovery of the Country to
the Year 1776* (Washington, 1836–1846), III, no. 13, 36; [?], *A Perfect Description
of Virginia* . . . (London, 1649), in *ibid.*, II, no. 8, 4.

And the pleasures and comforts of normal human relationships, the things that gold will not buy, are not to be had at all. Men have come there not to settle down, but to make their pile and move on. But the easy-come, easy-go miner generally carries away as little as he carries in.

So it was in Virginia, where tobacco took the place of gold. Virginia's counterpart of the easy-come, easy-go miner was the small planter who squandered his small crop on the liquor and luxuries that show up in boom towns. "Our Cowe-keeper here of James Citty," wrote John Pory in 1618, "on Sundayes goes acowterd all in freshe flaming silkes and a wife of one that in England had professed the black arte not of a scholler but of a collier of Croydon, wears her rough bever hatt with a faire perle hattband, and a silken suite therto correspondent." [44] The first legislative assembly in Virginia in 1619 felt obliged to pass acts against excess in apparel and also against drunkenness.[45] For it was drink more than clothes that the planters craved. The thirst of Virginians became notorious in England, and the ships that sailed up the James River were heavily freighted with sack and strong waters, even if they neglected to bring more solid fare.[46]

Virginians needed drink, if for nothing else, to solace them for losing the comforts of a settled life. Few were able, like the collier from Croydon, to enjoy the company of a wife. Women were scarcer than corn or liquor in Virginia and fetched a higher price. Seeking to overcome the shortage, the Company dispatched shiploads of maids (for whom prospective husbands were expected to pay), but the numbers were not large enough to alter the atmosphere of transience that pervaded the boom town.[47] The lonely men who pressed aboard every ship in the James River to drown their cares in drink looked on Virginia "not as a place of Habitaciõn but onely of a short sojourninge." [48] They would marry and settle down later somewhere else,

The whole appearance of the settlements, a mere collection of ramshackle hovels, argued that this was only a stopping place. It was a time when Englishmen of all classes were putting up larger and more substantial buildings throughout their own country;[49] and an Englishman's idea of a house was something solid, preferably of brick or stone. If it had to be made of wood, the walls at least should be plastered. Visitors to Virginia rightly judged the intentions of the settlers from the way they were content to live: "Their houses stands scattered one from another, and are

---

[44] *Virginia Company Records*, III, 221.

[45] *Ibid.*, 165.

[46] *Ibid.*, 658, 666; IV, 11, 14, 23, 271–273; Wyatt, A Proclamation Against Drunkennes, Wyatt MSS, *Wm. and Mary Qtly.*, 2d Ser., VII (1927), 247.

[47] *Virginia Company Records*, I, 256, 269, 566; III, 493; IV, 231. By 1624 the total female population by count, including children, was 244 out of 1,292. In 1625 it was 282 out of 1,220. There are 58 living persons of indeterminable sex in the 1624 list and 10 in the 1625 list. Most of these are children, but some are persons with names like Francis. See note 4.

[48] *Ibid.*, I, 566.

[49] W. G. Hoskins, "The Rebuilding of Rural England, 1570–1640," *Past and Present*, No. 4 (Nov., 1953), 44–59.

onlie made of wood, few or none of them beeing framed houses but
punches [posts] sett into the Ground And covered with Boardes so as a
firebrand is sufficient to consume them all." [50] In fact, it did not even take
a firebrand. Virginia "houses" could be kept standing only with difficulty.
At Charles City, where the settlers had considered themselves fortunate
to be released earlier than others from the Company's service, they went
on building "such houses as before and in them lived with continual
repairs, and buildinge new where the old failed." [51] There was no point in
putting up more than a temporary shelter if you did not intend to stay;
and as late as 1626 the governing council admitted that what people looked
for in Virginia was only "a present Cropp, and theire hastie retourne." [52]

The present crop stood in the way of everything else. Although the
government required everyone to plant a certain amount of corn, men
would risk both prosecution and hunger in order to put their time into
tobacco. Even self-preservation came second. After the massacre, when the
government adopted a policy of continuous attack against the Indians, it
was difficult to get men to leave their crops in order to carry on the war
for a few days. When the governor commanded them to go, they would
"Crye out of the loss of Tyme," and when a campaign lasted as long as
two weeks, they would demand "that they might have leave to retourne,
lest it should prove theire utter undoinge." [53] When William Capps, who
had had some experience in Indian fighting, volunteered to lead an expedition of forty men, he found that even the governing council was unwilling to spare them. Capps, whose speech comes through vividly in his
letters, had his own explanation of the reasons for the Council's refusal:
"take away one of my men," he pictures them saying to themselves,
"there's 2000 Plantes gone, thates 500 waight of Tobacco, yea and what
shall this man doe, runne after the Indians? soft, I have perhaps 10, perhaps 15, perhaps 20 men and am able to secure my owne Plantation; how
will they doe that are fewer? let them first be Crusht alitle, and then perhaps they will themselves make up the Nomber for their owne safetie.
Theis I doubt are the Cogitacions of some of our worthier men." [54]

As in other boom towns, a large share of the winnings was carried
away by those who supplied the flaming silks and strong waters, by men
who had even less intention of settling down than the planters. The ships
that anchored in Virginia's great rivers every summer were, as one set-

[50] *Virginia Company Records,* IV, 259.
[51] *Journals of Burgesses,* 33. Planters who had built houses at Kecoughtan on land
   later claimed by the Company were paid from 70 to 100 pounds of tobacco for
   them in 1625. At the maximum valuation of 3s. a pound this would make the best
   house worth £15 (*Minutes of Council,* 41). In spite of the high wages of carpenters
   in Virginia, this was probably no more than half what an English husbandman's
   house might be worth. As late as 1642, Gov. Berkeley was ordered by the Privy
   Council to require everyone with 500 acres to build a brick house "and also not to
   suffer men to build slight cottages as heretofore hath been there used. And to remove from place to place, only to plant Tobacco." Charles I to Sir William Berkeley, Instructions to Berkeley, 1642, *Va. Mag. Hist. Biog.,* II (1894–1895), 284, 287.
[52] *Virginia Company Records,* IV, 572.
[53] *Ibid.,* 451.
[54] *Ibid.,* 38.

tler observed, moving taverns,[55] whose masters, usually private traders, got the greater part of the tobacco that should have been enriching the colonists and the shareholders of the Company. Since the Company had never been able to satisfy the needs of the colonists, it was helpless to prevent them from trading with outsiders, and by 1620 it gave up trying.[56] Thereafter, the most it could do was to invest its dwindling funds in the subcorporations, known as "magazines," through which still hopeful members tried to recoup some of their losses.

A magazine was supposed to turn a profit by exchanging supplies for tobacco or other commodities or for the promise of tobacco when the next crop was in. But somehow the promises were not kept. The floating taverns got the tobacco before it could reach the "cape merchant," as the man in charge of a magazine was known, and all magazines seem to have ended with a loss to the investors in England.[57] There were sometimes as many as seventeen sail of ships to be seen at one time in the James River, and the Virginians swarmed aboard them to drink and carouse and squander their tobacco. Anything that smelled of alcohol would sell, and the governor and Council complained bitterly of the "rates which unconscionable marchantes and maryners doe impose uppon our necessities . . . especyally of rotten Wynes which destroy our bodies and empty our purses." [58] One trader even "boasted that the only sale of fower buttes of wyne would be Sufficyent to clere the whole Vioage." [59]

The private traders from abroad were not the only ones who seized the commercial opportunities of the boom. Complaints reached England against Virginians who got to the ships first and engrossed the commodities most in demand, to resell at monopoly prices.[60] And after the massacre, when corn was at its scarcest, those who had boats and could get a commission from the governor were able to bring back hundreds of bushels from the Chesapeake region, some of it bought, some of it stolen, some of it taken by force from the Indians there. At the price of corn then prevailing in Jamestown, these voyages to the Chesapeake must have been highly profitable, and there were charges that the chief men of the colony were only too willing to prolong the scarcity by discouraging or forbidding the planting of corn. As long as the shortage lasted, "they onely haveinge the means in these extremities to Trade for Corne with the Natives doe hereby engrosse all into their hands and soe sell itt abroad att their owne prizes. . . ." [61] In the winter of 1622–1623 English meal was selling at thirty shillings the bushel and Indian corn at ten to fifteen shillings. By April even Indian corn was at twenty to thirty shillings "and non to bee had but with great men." [62] If thirty shillings a bushel in Virginia meant, as the officers of the colony claimed, only ten pounds of to-

[55] Smith, *Works*, I, 103–104.
[56] *Virginia Company Records*, I, 303; III, 362.
[57] *Ibid.*, II, 52, 218–219; III, 502–505; IV, 14, 23.
[58] *Ibid.*, IV, 453.
[59] *Ibid.*, cf. III, 528, 658–659; IV, 11.
[60] *Ibid.*, III, 504, 703–704; IV, 261.
[61] *Ibid.*, II, 375; IV, 186, 234.
[62] *Ibid.*, IV, 89, 231, 234.

bacco and therefore only ten or fifteen shillings,[63] nevertheless a man who accumulated a thousand bushels of corn on a short trip to the Chesapeake region would be able to trade it for ten thousand pounds of tobacco, worth from five hundred to a thousand pounds sterling.

Although Sir Edwin Sandys had been bent on profit for the Company's investors, profiteering, whether by residents or transients, had been no part of his plans for Virginia. He had hoped to offer a refuge for the underpaid English laborer and at the same time build a community without want and without oppression. Ironically, Virginia suffered both want and oppression, as Sandys's concentration on getting men across the water unwittingly played into the hands of local profiteers who engrossed not only goods but men. Virginia differed from later American boom towns in that success depended not on acquiring the right piece of land but on acquiring men. Land that would grow tobacco was everywhere, so abundant that people frequently did not bother at first to secure patents for the amounts they were entitled to.[64] Instead, men rushed to stake out claims to men, stole them, lured them, fought over them—and bought and sold them, bidding up the prices to four, five, and six times the initial cost.[65] The Company's program obligingly poured men into Virginia for the scramble.

Since the number of older, seasoned servants was limited not only by the high death rate but also by completion of their terms of servitude, it was mainly the newcomers under the Sandys program whose labor enriched the aggressive and enterprising traders and planters. At first sight it might seem that the death rate among the new arrivals (even higher than among men who had survived their first year in the country) was so great as to nullify any advantages to those who sought to exploit them. But the records show that enough of them survived to make up almost the whole labor force and also the vast majority of the population of Virginia by 1625. The muster of inhabitants taken in January and February of that year gives the date of arrival in the colony for 740 of the 1,210 living persons listed.[66] Of the 740, only 110 had come to Virginia before 1618.[67]

---

[63] *Journals of Burgesses*, 24.

[64] This is evident from any comparison of the dates of patents with the dates of transportation of persons for which headrights were claimed. When Abraham Peirsey made his will in Mar. 1626/7, he had not yet taken up land for the servants he had transported since 1620. Neill, *Virginia Carolorum*, 404.

[65] Smith, *Works*, II, 618; *Virginia Company Records*, IV, 235.

[66] See note 4. A convenient breakdown of the information in the muster about numbers of cattle and supplies listed for each household is in "The Virginia Census, 1624–25," *Va. Mag. Hist. Biog.*, VII (1899–1900), 364–367, but this does not analyze dates of arrival or ages and some of the figures are incorrect. The muster was evidently taken by various people who did not all put down the same kinds of information. The dates of arrival are complete for some plantations; others show no dates at all; and still others show dates for some names but not for others. It seems safe to assume that the 740 are roughly typical of the remaining 470, who include, however, a number of children born in the colony.

[67] The rest had come as follows:

   1618: 59
   1619: 78

The muster list also reveals that among the fifteen planters who held ten
or more servants or "men" in 1625, only two servants out of 199 whose
arrival dates are known had come before 1618.[68]

The bondage of the men sent under the Sandys program was of several kinds. The time and produce of the ordinary bound servant belonged
completely to his master. Tenants might live and work independently on
the land of the Company or of some other master, but they had to surrender half of what they earned. There were also "apprentices," often
known as *Duty* boys" from the name of the ship (the *Duty*) on which
some of them were transported. They were bound to serve for seven
years under any planters who would pay ten pounds apiece for them. After their seven years' service, they were to be tenants bound for another
seven years. If, however, a *Duty* boy committed a crime at any time
during the first seven years, his term as a servant was to begin again for
another seven years.[69] Sandys doubtless envisaged the transportation of
these children, taken from the streets of London and sent without their
own consent, as a favor both to them and to those they served: he would
rescue the boys from vice and idleness and at the same time reward the
servant-starved planters, who were to make Virginia prosper.

The role of the *Duty* boys reveals, in fact, the main thrust of Sandys's
plans for Virginia. Sandys was a champion of the rights of Englishmen
against the impositions of the Stuart monarchy. In Virginia he would
enable men to live without the heavy burdens of taxation that the expenses of government imposed on Englishmen, with or without their consent. But his way of doing it was to enlist, with or without consent, the
surplus labor of England. Send men and boys to Virginia, and let them
work there, both for the planters and for the officers of government.
Eventually they would have their freedom and a more prosperous life than
they could have looked forward to in England. Meanwhile they would
enrich everybody else and make possible a government without heavy
taxes, whose officers "should not need to prey upon the people." [70]

For the support of each office of government Sandys persuaded the
Company to allot a tract of land and a quota of tenants to work it for the
incumbent. When a man left an office, he was supposed to turn over both
the land and its tenants to his successor. The amounts were generous.
The governor got three thousand acres and one hundred tenants, the
treasurer and the marshall fifteen hundred acres and fifty tenants apiece,
the vice admiral three hundred acres and twelve tenants.[71] Whenever a

---

1620: 124
1621: 114
1622: 95
1623: 117
1624: 43

[68] I have not counted the few children of servants, but I have included the few wives,
and I have assumed that "men," presumably tenants, were under the control of the
person under whose name they are listed.
[69] *Virginia Company Records*, I, 270–271, 293, 304–307, 411–412, 424, 520; III, 259;
Minutes of Council, 117.
[70] *Virginia Company Records*, IV, 523.
[71] *Ibid.*, I, 256, 268, 454, 549.

new office was created or when the Company wished to reward someone for especially meritorious service, the way to do it was to give him land and tenants.[72] When the secretary was found to be taking high fees for issuing land grants, he was forbidden to charge for his services and given land and tenants instead.[73]

The result of this beneficence was to lay open every surviving tenant sent by the Company to exploitation by any officer who claimed him as part of his quota of tenants. And if an officer did not commandeer him, someone else would. Whether a man came as a servant, as an apprentice, as a tenant, or on his own, he was vulnerable. If death disposed of the master who could rightly claim his labor, an heir, real or fraudulent, would quickly lay hold of him. Or if, having paid his own transportation, he arrived in Virginia with no master but also with no provisions, he was easy prey for anyone who could feed and shelter him. Even if he came sufficiently supplied to set himself up independently, a bad harvest, insurmountable debts, or Indian depredations might force him into the service of a bigger operator. This was particularly true after the massacre, when it was reported that ordinary men who had made a start on their own were obliged, for fear of the Indians, "to forsake their houses (which were very farre scattered) and to joyne themselves to some great mans plantation." [74]

Some planters were not above ransoming captives from the Indians in order to claim their labor. Jane Dickenson and her husband Ralph were tenants of Nicholas Hide when Ralph was killed in the massacre of 1622 and Jane was carried into captivity. After some time Dr. John Pott, the physician who had been sent to Virginia at Company expense, ransomed Jane for two pounds of glass beads. Ten months after her deliverance she complained to the governor and Council that she was held in a servitude that "differeth not from her slavery with the Indians," Dr. Pott alleging that she was "linked to his servitude with a towefold Chaine the one for her late husbands obligation [to Hide] and thother for her ransome, of both which shee hopeth that in Conscience shee ought to be discharged, of the first by her widdowhood, of the second by the law of nations, Considering shee hath already served teen months, tow much for two pound of beades." [75] Other complaints reached London that "divers old Planters and others did allure and beguile divers younge persons and others (ignorant and unskillfull in such matters) to serve them upon intollerable and unchristianlike conditions upon promises of such rewardes and recompense, as they were no wayes able to performe nor ever meant." [76]

Among the worst offenders were the Company's own officials in the colony. In Sandys's shipments of men bound to the Company they had perceived an opportunity for exploiting not only the tenants but the Company itself. The fact that the men arrived without adequate provi-

[72] *Ibid.*, 431; III, 277–280, 313.
[73] *Ibid.*, I, 332–333; II, 94–95, 109.
[74] [?] to Rev. Joseph Mead, Apr. 4, 1623, *Va. Mag. Hist. Biog.*, LXXI (1963), 410.
[75] *Virginia Company Records*, IV, 473.
[76] *Ibid.*, II, 113; see also, II, 442.

sions furnished an excuse for treating tenants as servants.[77] Instead of being seated on Company lands where they could build houses of their own (as the Company's instructions required), the tenants were hired out to private planters, like the fifty men who arrived "lusty and well" on the *Bona Nova*.[78] Although the officers reported that they hired out the sickly rather than the able-bodied, the Company got word that it was the other way round: the strongest men, who might have benefited the Company most, were put to work on private plantations. And "where it is pretended this placinge them with old planters is for theire health, they are so unmercifully used that it is the greatest cause of our Tenntes discontent. . . ."[79] Thus while Company men labored unhappily on the lands of private planters, Company land went uncleared, unfenced, and unplanted. It would be difficult to believe that the Company officials perceived no personal advantage in this situation.

The hiring out of some tenants should have meant more food for those who remained in the Company's care. Apparently, however, the hired men's share of provisions was converted to private uses;[80] and the men who continued as Company tenants were deprived even of the supplies intended for them. Whatever the Company sent, the officers appropriated, and gave the tenants only Indian corn and water,[81] a diet not calculated to speed the recovery of men weakened by a long voyage. But malnutrition and the diseases consequent upon it were not the only reasons for the low productivity of the Company men. According to one dissatisfied London investor, the reason the Company tenants accomplished so little was because "the officers Tenantes were cheifely reguarded and the generall Companies Tenantes the more neglected,"[82] by which he probably meant that the officers made it their business to get a day's work out of their own assigned tenants but not out of the rest. Moreover, John Pory reported to the Company in 1624, the officers were seating the men assigned to their offices "on their private Lands, not upon that [that] belongeth to their office," so that the crop produced on these private lands of the officers "alwaies exceeds yours"; and since the land set aside for officers lay "unmanured [i.e., uncultivated] to any purpose," it would yield little profit to the succeeding officers. The existing ones, Pory added, used the Company's tenants "to row them up and downe, whereby both you and they lose more then halfe."[83]

It is only fair to add that what the Company wanted for Virginia probably could not have been achieved by even the most faithful and assiduous of officers. The Company wanted a stable, diversified society,

---

[77] The officers also cited the lack of housing. But the Company had repeatedly ordered the construction of guest houses to quarter newcomers until they could build houses of their own. The officers in the colony regularly found excuses to evade the orders. *Ibid.*, III, 489, 493, 532.

[78] *Ibid.*, 479, 489. The same hiring out of tenants by those to whom they were entrusted apparently also occurred in Bermuda. Lefroy, *Memorials*, I, 165.

[79] *Virginia Company Records*, III, 489.

[80] *Ibid.*

[81] *Ibid.*, IV, 175.

[82] *Ibid.*, I, 456–457.

[83] Smith, *Works*, II, 571. See also *Virginia Company Records*, III, 479.

where men would make reasonable profits and live ordinary, reasonable lives. It was Virginia's misfortune in the last years of the Company to offer opportunities for profit that were much more than reasonable.

The men who seized the opportunities and captured the labor of Virginia's perishing immigrants are not difficult to identify. In January and February 1625 a muster of the inhabitants indicated the names and numbers of every man's "men" or servants, including both tenants and genuine servants.[84] The fifteen who had ten or more may be taken as the winners in the servant sweepstakes:

Ralph Hamor	10
John Pott	12
Edward Bennett	12
William Epps	13
William Peirce	13
Roger Smith	14
William Barry	15
Francis Wyatt	17
Edward Blaney	17
William Tucker	17
Daniel Gookin	20
Samuel Mathews	23
George Sandys	37
George Yeardley	39
Abraham Peirsey	39

Some of these men may have won fair and square; about several of them we know very little.[85] But the careers of the others make it a question whether we should call them labor barons or robber barons. It would be tedious to pile up the evidence about each of them, but a few simple facts may be suggestive.

[84] See notes 4 and 68. The number of persons employing 10 or more servants in Virginia, with a living population of a little over 1,200 in 1625, was almost as large as in the English county of Gloucestershire in 1608, where the total population was probably more than 50,000 (men aged 20 to 60 amounted to 19,402). See A. J. and R. H. Tawney, "An Occupational Census of the Seventeenth Century," *Economic History Review*, V (1934–1935), 25–64.

[85] Wyatt, who served as governor 1621–1626, and Peirce seem to have made their way without eliciting complaints. Bennett, a Puritan merchant of London and Amsterdam, came to Virginia only after the dissolution of the Company and did not remain. His estate was built up through the efforts of his brother Robert, who sold provisions at prices that drew protests (John B. Boddie, *Seventeenth Century Isle of Wight County, Virginia* [Chicago, 1938], 34–53; *Virginia Company Records*, IV, 453). Gookin too was in Virginia only briefly, though his sons and overseers seem to have done very well for him (Frederick W. Gookin, *Daniel Gookin* [Chicago, 1912], 38–48). Barry and Smith were agents of the Company, and most of the men listed under their names were probably Company tenants and not appropriated to private profit (*Virginia Company Records*, I, 433; *Minutes of Council*, 78, 90).

The frontrunner, Abraham Peirsey, with 39 servants, had been "a verie poore man" when he came to Virginia in 1616 as the cape merchant in charge of the Company's magazine. Although he sold goods at two or three times the prices set by the investors, the magazine under his direction showed a loss, and in 1626 he had not yet paid the investors for the goods sold. But when he died two years later, he "left the best Estate that was ever yett knowen in Virginia." [86] Edward Blaney succeeded Peirsey as cape merchant in 1620. At his death in 1626 he too had not paid for the goods he sold, but he had acquired seventeen servants. He had also succeeded in embezzling a fair amount by marrying a widow and successfully claiming an estate left by a man with the same surname as his wife's first husband, a trick played by a number of quick-witted Virginians at the death of a stranger who happened to bear the same surname.[87] George Sandys, treasurer of the colony, having failed to receive the full quota of tenants assigned to his office, simply appropriated sixteen Company tenants as his servants. Although for some time before his departure for England in 1625 he refused to execute his office (the commission having expired), he continued to hold the tenants in bondage. One of them, listed in the muster as a freeman, wrote to a friend, "he maketh us serve him whether wce will or noe and how to helpe yt we doe not knowe for hee beareth all the sway." [88]

Samuel Mathews was to play a prominent role in the colony in the 1630s and 1640s. He married Peirsey's widow and by 1638 boasted the best estate in the country (Massachusetts Historical Society, *Collections*, 4th Ser., IX [1871], 136n; W. G. Stanard, ed., "Abstracts of Virginia Land Patents," *Va. Mag. Hist. Biog.*, I [1893–1894], 187–188; W. N. Sainbury, ed., "Virginia in 1638–39," *ibid.*, XI [1903–1904], 170–182). Epps, described both as "a mad ranting fellow" and as "a proper yong man," killed another man in a drunken brawl in 1619 and was charged with adultery in 1627. He became a leading figure on the eastern shore, but by 1633 he had moved to St. Christopher (Felix Hull, ed., "The Tufton Manuscripts and the Virginia Connection," *ibid.*, LXV [1957], 313–327; *Virginia Company Records*, III, 121, 242; *Minutes of Council*, 48, 50, 91, 140, 148; Susie M. Ames, ed., *County Court Records of Accomack-Northampton, Virginia 1632-1640* [Washington, 1954], 9, 21, 67, 116, 163–164).

[86] Stanard, ed., "Abstracts," *Va. Mag. Hist. Biog.*, I (1893–1894), 187; Sainsbury, ed., "Virginia in 1638–39," *ibid.*, XI (1903–1904), 175–182; C. O. 1/8, 15–18; *Minutes of Council*, 118; *Virginia Company Records*, I, 333; II, 219. But the estate was appraised at only 60,000 pounds of tobacco, worth at the time a shilling a pound. Success in boom-time Virginia did not necessarily result in lasting wealth.

[87] *Virginia Company Records*, III, 449, 503–504, 526; IV, 106–107, 111, 263–265; *Minutes of Council*, 93, 121. Blaney evidently married the widow of William Powell. The widow brought with her an estate of which her husband had taken possession on the basis of his name after the owner, Capt. Nathaniel Powell, died in the massacre of 1622. Capt. Nathaniel Powell was actually no relation to William Powell, and Nathaniel Powell's surviving brother, Thomas Powell, was trying to recover the estate from Blaney at the time of the latter's death (Petition of Thomas Powell, July 21, 1626, *Va. Mag. Hist. Biog.*, XVI [1907–1908], 30–31; C. O. 1/4, 36).

[88] Lefroy, *Memorials*, I, 264; Gov. Francis West and Council to Privy Council, Mar. 4, 1628, *Va. Mag. Hist. Biog.*, VII (1899–1900), 259; C. O. 1/4, 111. See in general Richard B. Davis, *George Sandys, Poet-Adventurer* (New York, 1955).

William Tucker, who may originally have been a ship captain, probably came to Virginia between 1617 and 1619.[89] Some time before 1622 he was entrusted by John Ferrar and associates with £900 worth of goods to sell in Virginia, for which, like other Virginia factors, he failed to deliver either cash or accounts.[90] He was one of the men commissioned to trade with the Indians for corn in 1622–1623 and was also empowered to negotiate peace with the Pamunkeys of the Potomac River area. His methods of dealing may be judged by his success in poisoning two hundred Pamunkeys with wine brought for that purpose, which he gave them to drink in celebration of the peace treaty he pretended to conclude with them.[91] By 1632 the House of Burgesses was finding his attitude toward his fellow Virginians unsatisfactory and objected to the Privy Council about merchants "who have by needlesse and unprofitable Commodities . . . ingaged the inhabitants in debts of Tobacco, to the value almost of theire ensuinge croppe . . . amonge whome we have good cause to complayne of Captayne *Tucker*, who hath farr exceeded all other marchaunts in the prizes of theire goods. . . ." [92]

Ralph Hamor, though he wrote one of the most effective pamphlets in praise of Virginia, got off to a slow start or else lost heavily in the massacre. In 1623, when other men were already getting rich, George Sandys observed that "Captain Hamor is miserablie poore and necessitie will inforce him to shiftes." [93] The shifts to which he resorted included trading with the Indians and selling English goods at prices that brought accusations of extortion.[94] By 1625, with ten men growing tobacco for him, he was far from poor.

Dr. John Pott seems to have been more assiduous in pursuit of cattle and servants than of his duties as physician. In 1623 George Sandys dismissed him as a mere cipher,[95] but by 1628 he was acting governor. According to his successor, Gov. John Harvey, he took advantage of the position to advance his private interest "by foule and coveteous ways," in particular "by cuting out the markes of other mens neate cattell and markinge them for himselfe with his owne handes, whereby he hath gotten into a greate stock of cattell." Harvey pardoned him because of the col-

---

[89] He invested in the Company in 1617, and in 1619 he represented Kecoughtan in the House of Burgesses, *Virginia Company Records*, III, 58, 154, 535.

[90] *Ibid.*, II, 104.

[91] *Ibid.*, IV, 221–222; Wyatt, Wyatt MSS, *Wm. and Mary Qtly.*, 2d Ser., VII (1927), 206–207.

[92] *Journals of Burgesses*, 55–56. See also Gov. Harvey's complaints against him, Harvey to the Lords Commissioners, May 27, 1632, *Va. Mag. Hist. Biog.*, VIII (1900–1901), 149–150. Tucker was not slow to perceive the danger of Dutch competition to his high profits. He did his best to secure from the government in England a prohibition of Dutch trading in Virginia ([William Tucker], Reasons Against Permitting Dutch Trade to Virginia, Aug., 1633, in *ibid.*, 154; C. O. 1/6, 135, 207–212).

[93] *Virginia Company Records*, IV, 110–111.

[94] Wyatt, Wyatt MSS, *Wm. and Mary Qtly.*, 2 Ser., VII (1927), 204–205, 212, 254; *Minutes of Council*, 48, 132, 135.

[95] *Virginia Company Records*, IV, 110.

ony's need for his services as a physician and because Harvey found his delinquencies to have been in imitation of "the example of a former governor who passed unquestioned for many notable oppressions." [96]

The former governor to whom Harvey referred was probably George Yeardley, who had found Virginia a rewarding environment from the beginning. According to John Pory, when Yeardley arrived there in 1610, he carried with him nothing more valuable than a sword.[97] But when he visited London in 1617, after his first term as governor of Virginia, he was able "out of his meer gettings here" to spend "very near three thousand poundes." Before returning to the colony he got himself knighted, and Londoners observed that "he flaunts it up and down the streets in extraordinary bravery, with fourteen or fifteen fair liveries after him." [98]

Yeardley, when appointed governor in 1618, was assigned three thousand acres of land and one hundred tenants plus thirty more in 1620 to make up for deaths among the first group.[99] When Yeardley gave up the governorship in 1621, he turned over only forty-six tenants. The governor's Council, which now included Yeardley, wrote to the Company in London that "as for the rest of the Tenantes Sir George yardley denieth to make them good, And sayeth that havinge made noe strong Agrement with you at any tyme he holdeth nott him selfe tyed unto yt, And therfore should take it for a matter of great Injustice to bee Compelled therunto." [100] Yeardley, whom William Capps characterized as a "right worthie Statesman, for his own profit," [101] did not give up his tenants, and the records contain accusations against him of detaining servants belonging to other planters and of keeping as a servant a young man whose relatives had paid his way.[102] He remained nevertheless a member of the Council and was again serving as governor when he died in 1627. He was one of those commissioned to trade for corn after the massacre of 1622 and was accused by one settler of discouraging the planting of corn, the word being "that Sir G. Yardlie should provide them Corne if they would provide

[96] Harvey to Lord Dorchester, May 29, to the Privy Council, with enclosures, May 29, 1630, Privy Council to Harvey, with enclosure, Sept. 30, 1630, *Va. Mag. Hist. Biog.*, VII (1899–1900), 378, 381, 382–385. The quotation is on p. 381. See also William W. Hening, ed., *The Statutes at Large; being a Collection of All the Laws of Virginia* . . . (Richmond, 1809–1823), I, 145–146; C. O. 1/6, 36–43; Charles I to Harvey, July 25, Dorchester to Harvey, July 27, 1631, Report of Virginia Commissioners on Dr. Pott's Case, Aug. 20, Memorial in Behalf of Dr. Pott, Aug., 1631, *Va. Mag. Hist. Biog.*, VIII (1900–1901), 33–35; Mass. Hist. Soc., *Collections*, 4th Ser., IX (1871), 143n–144n.

[97] *Virginia Company Records*, III, 221.

[98] *New-England Historical and Genealogical Register*, XXXVIII (1884), 70.

[99] *Virginia Company Records*, I, 268, 332; III, 471.

[100] *Ibid.*, III, 584.

[101] *Ibid.*, IV, 37. Capps's opinion was shared by the earl of Dorset, who blamed the ruin of Southampton Hundred to Yeardley's "being a man wholy adicted to his private." Dorset to Gov. John Harvey, Aug. 1629, Sackville Manuscripts, Library of Congress microfilm (British Manuscripts Project, K334).

[102] *Virginia Company Records*, II, 113, 119; IV, 510–514.

Tobacco."[103] He did, in fact, provide the corn, one thousand bushels in January 1623 alone.[104] At his death Yeardley's estate was apparently valued at only about £10,000.[105] But it is not unlikely that he had already transferred much of what he owned to his wife and children in order to circumvent the litigation that a substantial will often produced.[106]

It seems evident that while the Virginia Company was failing in London a number of its officers in the colony were succeeding. In order to do so they not only rendered less than faithful service to their employers; they also reduced other Virginians to a condition which, while short of slavery, was also some distance from the freedom that Englishmen liked to consider as their birthright. The Company in 1618 had inaugurated a popularly elected representative assembly, but the effective power for at least ten or fifteen years longer remained in the governor and his Council.[107] By no coincidence, the Council consisted almost entirely of the men holding large numbers of servants. Between 1619 and 1627 Hamor, Pott, Smyth, Sandys, Tucker, Mathews, and Yeardley sat on it, while Wyatt and Yeardley took turns in the governor's chair. These men, with a more than average interest in controlling the labor force, were thus enabled to maintain their personal ascendancy not only over their servants but over all lesser men. Whether operating under the Company or, after 1625, under the king, they met every challenge to their authority with a rigor not exceeded by what we know of the earlier absolute government of John Smith or Thomas Dale.

In May 1624, when they discovered that Richard Barnes had uttered "base and detracting" speeches against the governor, they ordered that he "be disarmed, and have his armes broken and his tongue bored through with a awl. shall pass through a guard of 40 men and shalbe butted by every one of them, and att the head of the troope kicked downe and footed out of the fort: that he shalbe banished out of *James Cittye* and the Iland, that he shall not be capable of any priviledge of freedome of the countrey, and that (before he goe out of the Iland) he shall put in suretyes of £200 bond for the good behaviour."[108] When John Heny was reprimanded by Captain Tucker for going aboard a ship contrary to the governor's command, Heny made the mistake of saying, after Tucker had left, that Tucker "would be the death of him as he was of *Robert leyster.*"

[103] *Ibid.*, IV, 186.
[104] *Ibid.*, 9–10.
[105] *Tyler's Quarterly Historical and Genealogical Magazine*, II (1921), 121.
[106] His sons Francis and Argall later cut a large figure in Norfolk and Northampton Counties.
[107] Even the assembly showed itself to be a meeting of masters when the first session, in 1619, adopted measures to secure every man's right to his servants. As protection against servants fraudulently claiming freedom it ordered the establishment of a registry of all servants in the colony and of all that should come in the future, with the dates of expiration of their terms. It also decreed that if a servant, before leaving England, contracted to serve one master in Virginia and then contracted to serve another (who perhaps made a more attractive offer), he should serve two full terms, one with each master (*Virginia Company Records*, III, 167, 171, 174).
[108] *Minutes of Council*, 14.

For these words, reported to the Council, Heny got sixty stripes and had to beg forgiveness of Tucker, pay him one hundred pounds of tobacco, and be imprisoned until he could give bond for good behavior.[109]

Heny's offense came at a time when the Council had also heard of murmurs against their execution of Richard Cornish, a ship master, for sodomy. There is no record of the execution, but some of the testimony in the case was recorded, and there can be no doubt that the execution took place.[110] Afterwards, on a voyage to Canada, one Edward Nevell met up with Cornish's brother, and upon the latter's inquiry as to how the execution came about, Nevell replied "he was put to death through a scurvie boys meanes, and no other came against him." For this statement, made aboard ship off Canada where the governing council of Virginia could scarcely claim jurisdiction, Nevell upon his return to Virginia was required to "stand one the pillory with a paper one his head shewinge the cause of his offence in the markett place, and to loose both his Ears and to serve the Colony for A yeere, And forever to be incapable to be A ffree-man of the Countrey." [111] A month later Thomas Hatch was heard to say in a private house in James City "that in his consyence he thought the said Cornishe was put to death wrongfully." Hatch had the misfortune to be a *Duty* boy, and his seven-year period of service was nearly up. The court therefore ordered that "*Thomas Hatch* for his offence shalbe whipt from the forte to the gallows and from thence be whipt back againe, and be sett uppon the Pillory and there to loose one of his eares, And that his service to Sir *George Yeardley* for seaven yeers Shalbegain [again] from the present dye." [112]

The councillors not only guarded their authority jealously, and perhaps unconstitutionally, but not infrequently they wielded it on their own behalf, participating in decisions that favored their interests. Sandys sat at a meeting in which Luke Eden was seeking payment of twenty bushels of corn due him from Sandys. Whether Eden got the corn is not recorded, but he did get himself fined two hundred pounds of tobacco and laid neck and heels "for his lewd behavior and unreverent speche" toward Sandys in the council chamber.[113] Wyatt participated in a judgment that awarded him a Negro servant "notwithstandinge, any sale by Capt. *Jonnes* to Capt. *Bass*, or any other chaleng by the ships company" (Captain Jones had brought a privateer into the James for provisions and apparently considered the servant part of the ship's booty).[114] Abraham Peirsey sat at a meeting that had Richard Crocker put in the pillory with his ears nailed for saying that Peirsey and Hamor were not fit to sit on the Council because "they deale uppon nothing but extortion." [115] Yeardley sat at a meeting that ordered the execution of a man for killing a calf of Yeardley's

[109] *Ibid.*, 85.
[110] See references to case in *ibid.*, 34, 42, 47, 81, 83, 85.
[111] *Ibid.*, 85.
[112] *Ibid.*, 93.
[113] *Ibid.*, 57.
[114] *Ibid.*, 66–68, 73.
[115] *Ibid.*, 135–136.

and at another meeting that awarded him as tenants all the *Duty* boys who had finished their terms as servants.[116] He also participated in sentencing John Radish to lie neck and heels because Radish "Caryed over Sir *George Yardley* his servants to his house at unsesonable tyme of the night and there gave them Entertainment and made them drunke." [117]

It was apparently not without reason that ordinary men grumbled at the government. In the words of William Tyler, "nether the Governor nor Counsell could or would doe any poore men right, but that they would shew favor to great men and wronge the poore." [118]

It may be contended that severe discipline was necessary in a colony consisting predominantly of lusty young men who had just shaken loose the fetters of home and country. And it must be acknowledged that the men entrusted with government did protect some of the rights of servants. When a master failed to teach an indentured apprentice his trade or when he sought to hold a servant beyond the term of his indenture, the Council might interfere. Dr. Pott was ordered by a meeting at which he was himself present either to teach his apprentice the art of an apothecary (which he was neglecting to do) or else pay him wages.[119]

Nevertheless serious differences made servitude in Virginia more onerous than servitude in England. The ordinary term of service that a man agreed to work in Virginia was not a year but several years; and the wages to which he was entitled had been paid in advance in the form of transportation across the ocean. Almost all servants were therefore in a condition resembling that of the least privileged type of English servant, the parish apprentice, a child who (to relieve the community of supporting him) was bound to service by court order until he was twenty-one or twenty-four, with no obligation on his appointed master's part to teach him a trade or to pay him. In Virginia a master had little reason to treat his servant well in order to obtain a renewal of his services at the expiration of his term, and a servant had little reason to work hard in order to assure being rehired, because men would not bind themselves out for a second long term when they could make more by working for themselves. There was accordingly the more reason for a master to assert his authority in order to get what he considered a full quota of work from his servants. Not surprisingly it was reported in England that Virginians "abuse their servantes there with intollerable oppression and hard usage." [120]

The records are not sufficiently complete to show how extensive the abuse of servants may have been, but there is some evidence that the Council in Virginia (until 1634 the only court) supported masters in severities that would not have been allowed in England. The most extreme example is the case of John and Alice Proctor and their servants Elizabeth Abbott and Elias Hinton, both of whom died after a series of beatings inflicted by the Proctors and by other servants acting under orders from the Proctors.

[116] *Ibid.*, 4–5, 154.
[117] *Ibid.*, 58.
[118] *Ibid.*, 19.
[119] *Ibid.*, 117.
[120] *Virginia Company Records*, II, 422.

Thomas Gates testified that he counted five hundred lashes inflicted on the girl at one time and warned Proctor that he might as well kill her and be done with it. Alice Bennett, who examined her, "'fownd she had been sore beaten and her body full of sores and holes very dangerously raunckled and putrified both above her wast and uppon her hips and thighes." Other witnesses testified that Proctor beat Hinton with a rake. Yet there is no indication that the Proctors were punished.[121] By contrast we find English courts undertaking the work of correcting unruly servants themselves (as the statutes required) and even on occasion forbidding masters to do it.[122] In Virginia, servants who found themselves in the hands of brutal masters like the Proctors had no way out. Some ran away to the Indians and went native, or escaped to the Dutch settlements or to New England. But any Virginian who harbored another man's servant was liable to prosecution, and the records speak often of runaways apprehended and returned to their masters. Even the compassionate witnesses who testified against the Proctors indicated that when the maid came to them for shelter they had instead returned her to her master and mistress in her half-dead condition, with entreaties that *they* pardon *her!*

But whether physically abused or not, Englishmen found servitude in Virginia more degrading than servitude in England. In England the hiring of workers was dignified by laws and customs that gave a servant some control over his own life. He had to give his master three months' notice if he intended to leave at the end of his term, and in order to move from one place to another, he had to have a testimonial that his term of service was finished. But by the same token, a master could not turn away a servant before his term was up and had to give him three months' advance notice that his contract would not be renewed.[123] Once a year, in the petty sessions held by the constables, servants could renew their contracts or make new ones, with the constables recording the transaction. These sessions, usually held in a churchyard, came to be known as hiring fairs and constituted a kind of open labor market where workmen sold their annual services.[124] But in Virginia it was the masters who sold the workmen, and there was no annual hiring fair. Masters bought and sold servants at any time for any period of years covered by their transportation contracts; and during that period a servant might find himself sold without his consent from one master to another. In 1633 a Dutch sea captain found the planters gambling at cards with their servants as stakes.[125] Virginians dealt in servants the way Englishmen dealt in land or chattles.

---

[121] *Minutes of Council,* 22–24.

[122] W. L. Sachse, ed., *Minutes of the Norwich Court of Mayoralty 1630–1631* (Norfolk Record Society, *Publications,* XV [London, 1942]), 90.

[123] 5 Eliz. I, c. 4, paragraphs 4, 7.

[124] Margaret G. Davies, *The Enforcement of English Apprenticeship: A Study in Applied Mercantilism 1563–1642* (Cambridge, Mass., 1956), 191, 196–197, 233. There are records of some of these petty sessions in the typescript calendar of Essex Quarter Sessions. A good contemporary description is in Henry Best, *Rural Economy in Yorkshire in 1641* . . . , ed. Charles Best Robinson (Surtees Society, *Publications,* XXXIII [Durham, 1857]), 134–136.

[125] New-York Historical Society, *Collections,* 2d Ser., III (1857), 36.

This development was a simple outgrowth of the extreme demand for labor in combination with the long terms of service that were exacted for transportation to Virginia. In England itself, after labor became more valuable, the demand produced a certain amount of buying and selling of industrial apprentices. When a man had more apprentices than he needed, he might with the permission of his guild sell an apprentice to another master of the guild.[126] But industrial apprentices were a special case, and the idea of a large-scale market in men, or at least in English men, was shocking to Englishmen. "My Master Atkins," wrote Thomas Best from Virginia in 1623, "hath sold me for a £150 sterling like a damnd slave." [127] This "buying and selling men and boies" had already become a scandal by 1619, when John Rolfe noted that it "was held in *England* a thing most intolerable." [128] Capt. John Smith denounced the "pride, covetousnesse, extortion, and oppression" of men who sold "even men, women and children for who will give most." It would be better, he said, that these profiteers be "made such merchandize themselves, then suffered any longer to use that trade." [129] And in 1625 Thomas Weston refused to carry servants in his ship from Canada to Virginia because "servants were sold heere upp and downe like horses, and therfore he held it not lawfull to carie any." [130]

Other shipmasters were not so scrupulous, and the dissolution of the Virginia Company brought no end to the market in men or to their importation. So much did the planters count on continued importations that the Council during the 1620s awarded as yet unarrived, unknown, and unnamed servants to the victors in lawsuits.[131] A servant, by going to Virginia, became for a number of years a thing, a commodity with a price. Although the government might protect him against continuation in this status beyond the time agreed upon, it was not likely to shorten his term or give him his freedom, even if his master's crimes against him were serious enough to warrant the death penalty. The servant who was the victim of Richard Cornish's homosexual attack did not win his freedom by his master's execution. Even though no other man had a legal claim to his service, the court decreed that he must choose another master, who in return was to compensate the government for the costs of prosecuting Cornish.[132] A servant in Virginia, as long as his term had not expired, was a machine to make tobacco for somebody else.

---

[126] O. Jocelyn Dunlop and Richard D. Denman, *English Apprenticeship & Child Labour; a History* (London, 1912), 57–58, 127–129.

[127] *Virginia Company Records,* IV, 235. If the figure is correct and Atkins bore the initial expense of transportation and support, he must have made a profit of several hundred per cent on the transaction. The original letter does not survive. The quotation is from a contemporary transcript in the Manchester Papers, Nos. 338, 339, Public Record Office, in which it is likely that the scribe erred.

[128] Smith, *Works,* II, 542.

[129] *Ibid.,* 618.

[130] *Minutes of Council,* 82.

[131] *Ibid.,* 63, 134, 155, 160, 170, 181.

[132] *Ibid.,* 47.

"Like a damnd slave," said Thomas Best. To buy and sell servants for a brief period of years was not the same as buying and selling men for life and their unborn children with them. But it was a step in that direction. We can perhaps see, then, in boom-time Virginia not only the fleeting ugliness of private enterprise operating temporarily without check, not only greed magnified by opportunity, producing fortunes for a few and misery for many. We may also see Virginians beginning to move toward a system of labor that treated men as things.

The Seneca Nation of Indians

ANTHONY F. C. WALLACE

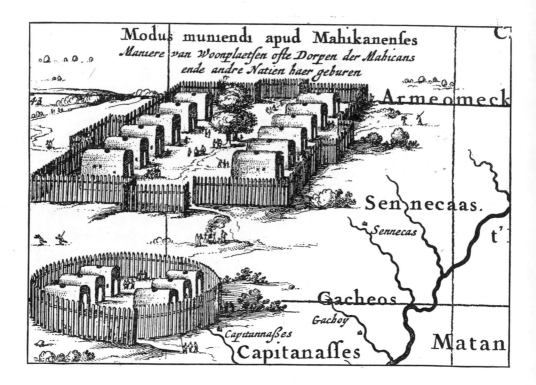

Most Americans have learned their colonial history as if it began with Sir Walter Raleigh at Roanoke Island, continued with the arrival of the Puritans in Massachusetts Bay, and proceeded through the seventeenth and eighteenth centuries with the establishment of thirteen colonies that finally joined in a common effort to protect freedom and other natural rights that were threatened by an autocratic mother country. This is mythological and ethnocentric history because it ignores the central fact of our early development—that for the first two centuries of European presence in North America the colonists were in constant and intimate contact with two other cultural groups, Native Americans and Africans. Our early history is the history of the convergence of three internally diverse peoples—each from a different continent but linked by circumstances and design.

To appreciate this concept we must understand the everyday lives of Native Americans, for there can be no comprehension of "interaction" among three peoples when we know about the culture of only one of them. For another reason also we must understand the everyday lives of "Indians"—the misnomer applied by Columbus to the people he met in the Caribbean in the late fifteenth century and the term used thereafter by European colonizers to describe all of the diverse native inhabitants of two continents. Colonizing Europeans drew upon Indian culture because their survival depended on it. They copied Indian forms of agriculture; incorporated Indian herbal cures into their pharmacology; absorbed Indian political concepts; and, ironically, employed Indian methods of warfare to defeat a people who could not be conquered by European military techniques. Europeans commonly spoke of Indians as "savages," described them as cannibalistic, and talked about raising up "the heathen." Nonetheless, the colonizers borrowed extensively from the Indian cultures they disparaged, as they struggled for a foothold on the eastern edge of the continent.

Anthony Wallace gives us a vivid picture of Seneca culture. Nobody who reads his analysis should fail to understand that while Europeans and Iroquois were in different stages of technological development, each had a culture that served its purposes. That is why the Iroquois—and the point holds for each of the many Indian societies east of the Mississippi River—did not simply abandon their political organization, religious beliefs, kinship arrangements, and methods of child rearing when confronted with invading Europeans who continually pronounced the superiority of their culture. Senecas took from the Europeans what they found useful in strengthening their own society. They rejected the rest. So it was with the French, Dutch, and English who interacted with Senecas. Acculturation was a two-way process, with each society borrowing from the other as it deemed necessary.

By reading sequentially this selection by Wallace and the one by John Demos that follows, students can compare cultural norms that conditioned everyday life in English and Iroquois communities. The concept of masculine domination was ingrained in European culture; the Iroquois matriarchate distributed power and status between the two sexes more evenly. European child rearing was highly authoritarian; the Iroquois method was permissive. Europeans placed the private ownership of property at the center of their scheme of economic and social organization; Iroquois gave it a circumscribed role and emphasized communalism instead.

When Europeans acquired sufficient power to conquer a particular Indian society, they pointed to these cultural differences as proof of Indian "savagery" and thus justified their actions. But their proclamations of disdain cannot hide the fact that the colonizers often envied the Indian's ability to sustain himself in the North American environment, to live a life of simplicity, and to attain, almost without trying, the European goal of community that the colonizers found so elusive.

Another error common to most Americans' views of colonial history is to assume that the history of Indian-white relations is simply the tale of white genocide and the cultural obliteration of Native American ways. It is true that European colonizers were the victors in several centuries of armed clashes, that the Indians were dispossessed of almost all their land, and that by the late nineteenth century the reservation had become the home of most surviving Indian people. But as Wallace shows elsewhere in his book, the Seneca persisted through centuries of contact with European-Americans, continuously adapting their culture in a struggle for cultural as well as physical survival. Their culture is not dead today. It is different; and so is the culture of the Europeans who came to North America. The Senecas' ways of looking at the world around them still influence American culture, perhaps never so much as in the present day when their beliefs concerning the proper relationship between humans and their environment have captured the imagination of a growing number of people. And every reader will note the similarity of "modern" child-rearing practices to those of the Iroquois, who in the seventeenth century were termed "barbarous" by the first settlers.

The world in which Handsome Lake grew to manhood, and in which
he took his place as an active hunter and warrior, was the world of an
unvanquished Indian nation: the Seneca, the most populous and the most
powerful of the confederated Iroquois tribes. They numbered about four
thousand souls, and their tribal territory extended from the upper waters
of the Allegheny and the Susquehanna rivers, on the south, to Lake On-
tario, on the north. The western marches of the Seneca territory were the
shores of Lake Erie. On the east, beyond Seneca Lake, were the Cayuga
people. The other Iroquois tribes—Onondaga, Oneida (and Tuscarora),
and Mohawk—lay successively eastward almost to the Hudson River. The
whole area occupied by the Iroquoian confederacy between the Hudson
River and Lake Erie was compared by the Iroquois themselves to a longhouse compartmented by tribes; and in this longhouse the Seneca were
"the keepers of the western door." They were guardians of that portal
from which Iroquois warriors traditionally issued to attack the western
and southern nations, through which Iroquois hunters passed to exploit
the conquered lands along the Allegheny and Ohio, and on which other
nations, in friendship or in war, must knock before entering the home
country of the confederacy. Their warriors ranged from Hudson's Bay to
the mountains of the Carolinas, and from the Atlantic to the Mississippi,
fighting against members of alien tribes and, on occasion, against the
French and the English; their chiefs and orators sat in council, year after
year, with Europeans in the colonial capitals, working out a *modus vivendi*
with the invaders. To be a Seneca was to be a member of one of the most
feared, most courted, and most respected Indian tribes in North America.

VILLAGERS, WARRIORS, AND STATESMEN

A Seneca village in the eighteenth century was a few dozen houses
scattered in a meadow. No plan of streets or central square defined a neat
settlement pattern. The older men remembered days when towns were
built between the forks of streams, protected by moats and palisades, and
the dwellings within regularly spaced. But these fortified towns were no
longer made, partly because of their earlier vulnerability to artillery and
partly because times had become more peaceful anyway after the close
of the fifty-odd years of war between 1649 and 1701. Now a village was
simply an area within which individual families and kin groups built or
abandoned their cabins at will; such focus as the area had for its several
hundred inhabitants was provided by the council house (itself merely an
enlarged dwelling), where the religious and political affairs of the com-

"The Seneca Nation of Indians." From *The Death and Rebirth of the Seneca* by
Anthony F. C. Wallace, pp. 21–39. Copyright © 1969 by Anthony F. C. Wallace.
Reprinted by permission of Alfred A. Knopf, Inc.

munity were transacted. Year by year the size of a village changed, depending on wars and rumors of war, the shifts of the fur trade, private feuds and family quarrels, the reputation of chiefs, the condition of the soil for corn culture, and the nearness of water and firewood. The same village might, over a hundred years' time, meander over a settlement area ten or fifteen miles square, increasing and decreasing in size, sometimes splitting up into several little settlements and sometimes coalescing into one, and even acquiring (and dropping) new names in addition to the generic name, which usually endured.

The traditional Iroquois dwelling unit was called a longhouse. It was a dark, noisy, smoke-filled family barracks; a rectangular, gable-roofed structure anywhere from fifty to seventy-five feet in length, constructed of sheets of elm bark lashed on stout poles, housing up to fifty or sixty people. The roof was slotted (sometimes with a sliding panel for rainy days) to let out some of the smoke that eddied about the ceiling. There was only one entrance, sometimes fitted with a wooden or bark door on wooden hinges, and sometimes merely curtained by a bearskin robe. Entering, one gazed in the half-light down a long, broad corridor or alleyway, in the center of which, every twelve or fifteen feet, smoldered a small fire. On opposite sides of each fire, facing one another, were double-decker bunks, six feet wide and about twelve feet long. An entire family —mother, father, children, and various other relatives—might occupy one or two of these compartments. They slept on soft furs in the lower bunks. Guns, masks, moccasins, clothing, cosmetic paint, wampum, knives, hatchet, food, and the rest of a Seneca family's paraphernalia were slung on the walls and on the upper bunk. Kettles, braided corn, and other suspendable items hung from the joists, which also supported pots over the fire. Each family had about as much room for permanent quarters as might be needed for all of them to lie down and sleep, cook their meals, and stow their gear. Privacy was not easily secured because other families lived in the longhouse; people were always coming and going, and the fires glowed all night. In cold or wet weather or when the snow lay two or three feet deep outside, doors and roof vents had to be closed, and the longhouses became intolerably stuffy—acrid with smoke and the reeking odors of leftover food and sweating flesh. Eyes burned and throats choked. But the people were nonetheless tolerably warm, dry, and (so it is said) cheerful.

The inhabitants of a longhouse were usually kinfolk. A multifamily longhouse was, theoretically, the residence of a maternal lineage: an old woman and her female descendants, together with unmarried sons, and the husbands and children of her married daughters. The totem animal of the clan to which the lineage belonged—Deer, Bear, Wolf, Snipe, or whatever it might be—was carved above the door and painted red. In this way directions were easier to give, and the stranger knew where to seek hospitality or aid. But often—especially in the middle of the eighteenth century—individual families chose to live by themselves in smaller cabins, only eighteen by twenty feet or so in size, with just one fire. As time went on, the old longhouses disintegrated and were abandoned, and by the middle of the century the Iroquois were making their houses of logs.

Around and among the houses lay the cornfields. Corn was a main food. Dried and pounded into meal and then boiled into a hot mush, baked into dumplings, or cooked in whole kernels together with beans and squash and pieces of meat in the thick soups that always hung in kettles over the fires, it kept the people fed. In season, meats, fresh fruits, herb teas, fried grasshoppers, and other delicacies added spice and flavor to the diet. But the Iroquois were a cornfed people. They consumed corn when it was fresh and stored it underground for the lean winter months. The Seneca nation alone raised as much as a million bushels of corn each year; the cornfields around a large village might stretch for miles, and even scattered clearings in the woods were cultivated. Squash, beans, and tobacco were raised in quantity, too. Domesticated animals were few, even after the middle of the century: some pigs, a few chickens, not many horses or cattle. The responsibility for carrying on this extensive agricultural establishment rested almost entirely on the women. Armed with crude wooden hoes and digging-sticks, they swarmed over the fields in gay, chattering work bees, proceeding from field to field to hoe, to plant, to weed, and to harvest. An individual woman might, if she wished, "own" a patch of corn, or an apple or peach orchard, but there was little reason for insisting on private tenure: the work was more happily done communally, and in the absence of a regular market, a surplus was of little personal advantage, especially if the winter were hard and other families needed corn. In such circumstances hoarding led only to hard feelings and strained relations as well as the possibility of future difficulty in getting corn for oneself and one's family. All land was national land; an individual could occupy and use a portion of it and maintain as much privacy in the tenure as he wished, but this usufruct title reverted to the nation when the land was abandoned. There was little reason to bother about individual ownership of real estate anyway: there was plenty of land. Economic security for both men and women lay in a proper recognition of one's obligation to family, clan, community, and nation, and in efficient and cooperative performance on team activities, such as working bees, war parties, and diplomatic missions.

If the clearing with its cornfields bounded the world of women, the forest was the realm of men. Most of the men hunted extensively, not only for deer, elk, and small game to use for food and clothing and miscellaneous household items, but for beaver, mink, and otter, the prime trade furs. Pelts were the gold of the woods. With them a man could buy guns, powder, lead, knives, hatchets, axes, needles and awls, scissors, kettles, traps, cloth, ready-made shirts, blankets, paint (for cosmetic purposes), and various notions: steel springs to pluck out disfiguring beard, scalp, and body hair; silver bracelets and armbands and tubes for coiling hair; rings to hang from nose and ears; mirrors; tinkling bells. Sometimes a tipsy hunter would give away his peltries for a keg of rum, treat his friends to a debauch, and wake up with a scolding wife and hungry children calling him a fool; another might, with equal improvidence, invest in a violin, or a horse, or a gaudy military uniform. But by and large, the products of the commercial hunt—generally conducted in the winter and often hundreds of miles from the home village, in the Ohio country or down the Susquehanna River—were exchanged for a limited range of European consumer goods, which had become, after five generations of contact with beaver-hungry French, Dutch, and English traders, economic necessities. Many of these goods were, indeed, designed to Indian specifications and manufactured solely for the Indian trade. An Iroquois man dressed in a linen breechcloth and calico shirt, with a woolen blanket over his shoulders, bedaubed with trade paint and adorned with trade armbands and earrings, carrying a steel knife, a steel hatchet, a clay pipe, and a rifled gun felt himself in no wise contaminated nor less an Indian than his stone-equipped great-great-grandfather. Iroquois culture had reached out and incorporated these things that Iroquois Indians wanted while at the same time Iroquois warriors chased off European missionaries, battled European soldiers to a standstill, and made obscene gestures when anyone suggested that they should emulate white society (made up, according to their information and experience, of slaves, cheating lawyers with pen and paper and ink, verbose politicians, hypocritical Christians, stingy tavern keepers, and thieving peddlers).

Behavior was governed not by published laws enforced by police, courts, and jails, but by oral tradition supported by a sense of duty, a fear of gossip, and a dread of retaliatory witchcraft. Theft, vandalism, armed robbery, were almost unknown. Public opinion, gently exercised, was sufficient to deter most persons from property crimes, for public opinion went straight to the heart of the matter: the *weakness* of the criminal. A young warrior steals someone else's cow—probably captured during a raid on a white settlement—and slaughters it to feed his hungry family. He does this at a time when other men are out fighting. No prosecution follows, no investigation, no sentence: the unhappy man is nonetheless severely punished, for the nickname "Cow-killer" is pinned to him, and he must drag it rattling behind him wherever he goes. People call him a coward behind his back and snicker when they tell white men, in his presence, a story of an unnamed Indian who killed cows when he should have been killing men. Such a curse was not generalized to the point of ostracism, however. The celebrated Red Jacket, about whom the "Cow-killer" story was told, vindicated his courage in later wars, became the principal spokesman for his nation, and was widely respected and revered. But he never lost the nickname.[1]

Disputes between people rarely developed over property. Marital difficulties centering around infidelity, lack of support, or personal incompatibility were settled by mutual agreement. Commonly, in case of difficulty, the man left and the woman, with her children, remained with her mother. A few couples remained together for a lifetime; most had several marriages; a few changed mates almost with the season. Men might come to blows during drunken arguments over real or fancied slights to their masculine honor, over politics, or over the alleged mistreatment of their kinfolk. Such quarrels led at times to killings or to accusations of witchcraft. A murder (or its equivalent, the practice of witchcraft) was some-

---

[1] O'Reilly Collection, Vol. XV, d3 (recollections of Thomas Morris), New York Historical Society, New York.

thing to be settled by the victim's kinfolk; if they wished, they might kill the murderer or suspected witch without fear of retaliation from his family (provided that family agreed on his guilt). But usually a known killer would come to his senses, admit himself wrong, repent, and offer retribution in goods or services to the mourning family, who unless exceptionally embittered by an unprovoked and brutal killing were then expected to accept the blood money and end the matter.

Drunkenness was perhaps the most serious social problem. Two Moravian missionaries who visited the Iroquois country in 1750 had the misfortune to reach the Seneca towns at the end of June, when the men were just returning from Oswego, where they had sold their winter's furs, and were beginning to celebrate the start of summer leisure. Hard liquor was dissolving winter's inhibitions and regrets. At Canandaigua, the missionaries, who were guests at the house of a prominent warrior, had just explained the friendly nature of their errand when the rum arrived. "All the town was in a state of intoxication, and frequently rushed into our hut in this condition," complained the white men. "There was every reason to think that fighting might ensue, as there were many warriors among those who were perfectly mad with drink." After a sleepless night the missionaries traveled on, reaching the outskirts of Geneseo on the second of July. "The village," said the observers in surprise, "consisted of 40 or more large huts, and lies in a beautiful and pleasant region. A fine large plain, several miles in length and breadth, stretches out behind the village." But the kegs of rum had anticipated them. "When we caught sight of the town we heard a great noise of shouting and quarreling, from which we could infer that many of the inhabitants were intoxicated, and that we might expect to have an uncomfortable time. On entering the town we saw many drunken Indians, who looked mad with drink. . . ."

Alas, poor Christians! They had to hide in a stuffy garret, without food or water. David, their devoted Indian convert and servant, stole out toward evening with a kettle to fetch his masters some water and was seen. "A troop of drunken women came rushing madly toward him. Some of them were naked, and others nearly so. In order to drive them away he was obliged to use his fists, and deal blows to the right and left. He climbed up a ladder, but when he had scarcely reached the top they seized it and tore it from under his feet." David barely managed to escape "in safety" from these playful Amazons. The missionaries decided not to wait the two days until the liquor ran out to meet the chiefs in council; they bent their prayers to an early departure. They finally managed to escape at dawn by jumping down from an opening in the gable and tiptoeing away. "The Lord watched over us in such a manner that all the drunken savages were in their huts, not a creature to be seen. Even the dogs, numbering nearly 100 in the whole village, were all quiet, wonderful to relate, and not a sound was heard. A dense fog covered the town, so that we could not see 20 steps before us. A squaw stood at the door of the last hut, but she was sober and returned our greeting quietly." [2]

[2] William M. Beauchamp, ed., *Moravian Journals Relating to Central New York, 1745–66* (Syracuse, 1916), 67–84.

But such drunken debauches were only occasional rents in a fabric of polite social behavior. Other missionaries were more favorably impressed than the Moravians. The Seneca, said a Quaker scribe, "appear to be naturally as well calculated for social and rational enjoyment, as any people. They frequently visit each other in their houses, and spend much of their time in friendly intercourse. They are also mild and hospitable, not only among themselves, but to strangers, and good natured in the extreme, except when their natures are perverted by the inflammatory influence of spirituous liquors. In their social interviews, as well as public councils, they are careful not to interrupt one another in conversation, and generally make short speeches. This truly laudable mark of good manners, enables them to transact all their public business with decorum and regularity, and more strongly impresses on their mind and memory, the result of their deliberations." [3]

THE IROQUOIS "MATRIARCHATE"

During the seventeenth and eighteenth centuries Iroquois men earned a reputation among the French and English colonists for being the most astute diplomatically and most dangerous militarily of all the Indians of the Northeast. Yet at the same time the Iroquois were famous for the "matriarchal" nature of their economic and social institutions. After the colonial era came to an end with the victory of the United States in the Revolutionary War, the traditional diplomatic and military role of the Iroquois men was sharply limited by the circumstances of reservation life. Simultaneously, the "matriarchal" character of certain of their economic, kinship, and political institutions was drastically diminished. These changes were codified by the prophet Handsome Lake. As we shall see later in more detail, the changes in kinship behavior that he recommended, and which to a considerable degree were carried out by his followers, amounted to a shift in dominance from the mother-daughter relationship to that of the husband-wife. Handsome Lake's reforms thus were a sentence of doom upon the traditional quasi-matriarchal system of the Iroquois.

The Iroquois were described as matriarchal because of the important role women played in the formal political organization. The men were responsible for hunting, for warfare, and for diplomacy, all of which kept them away from their households for long periods of time, and all of which were essential to the survival of Iroquois society. An expedition of any kind was apt to take months or even years, for the fifteen thousand or so Iroquois in the seventeenth and eighteenth centuries ranged over an area of about a million square miles. It is not an exaggeration to say that the full-time business of an Iroquois man was travel, in order to hunt, trade, fight, and talk in council. But the women stayed at home. Thus, an Iroquois village might be regarded as a collection of strings, hundreds of

---

[3] Halliday Jackson, *Sketch of the Manners, Customs, Religion and Government of the Seneca Indians in 1800* (Philadelphia, 1830), 19.

years old, of successive generations of women, always domiciled in their longhouses near their cornfields in a clearing while their sons and husbands traveled in the forest on supportive errands of hunting and trapping, of trade, of war, and of diplomacy.

The women exercised political power in three main circumstances. First, whenever one of the forty-nine chiefs of the great intertribal League of the Iroquois died, the senior women of his lineage nominated his successor. Second, when tribal or village decisions had to be made, both men and women attended a kind of town meeting, and while men were the chiefs and normally did the public speaking, the women caucused behind the scenes and lobbied with the spokesmen. Third, a woman was entitled to demand publicly that a murdered kinsman or kinswoman be replaced by a captive from a non-Iroquois tribe, and her male relatives, particularly lineage kinsmen, were morally obligated to go out in a war party to secure captives, whom the bereaved woman might either adopt or consign to torture and death. Adoption was so frequent during the bloody centuries of the beaver wars and the colonial wars that some Iroquois villages were preponderantly composed of formally adopted war captives. In sum, Iroquois women were entitled formally to select chiefs, to participate in consensual politics, and to start wars.

Thus the Iroquois during the two centuries of the colonial period were a population divided, in effect, into two parts: sedentary females and nomadic males. The men were frequently absent in small or large groups for prolonged periods of time on hunting, trading, war, and diplomatic expeditions, simultaneously protecting the women from foreign attack and producing a cash crop of skins, furs, and scalps, which they exchanged for hardware and dry goods. These activities, peripheral in a geographical sense, were central to the economic and political welfare of the Six Nations. The preoccupation of Iroquois men with these tasks and the pride they took in their successful pursuit cannot be overestimated. But the system depended on a complementary role for women. They had to be economically self-sufficient through horticulture during the prolonged absences of men, and they maintained genealogical and political continuity in a matrilineal system in which the primary kin relationship (not necessarily the primary social relationship) was the one between mother and daughter.

Such a quasi-matriarchy, of course, had a certain validity in a situation where the division of labor between the sexes required that men be geographically peripheral to the households that they helped to support and did defend. Given the technological, economic, and military circumstances of the time, such an arrangement was a practical one. But it did have an incidental consequence: It made the relationship between husband and wife an extremely precarious one. Under these conditions it was convenient for the marital system to be based on virtually free sexual choice, the mutual satisfaction of spouses, and easy separation. Couples chose one another for personal reasons; free choice was limited, in effect, only by the prohibition of intraclan marriage. Marriages were apt to fray when a husband traveled too far, too frequently, for too long. On his return, drunken quarreling, spiteful gossip, parental irresponsibility, and flagrant infidelity might lead rapidly to the end of the relationship. The husband, away from the household for long periods of time, was apt in his travels to establish a liaison with a woman whose husband was also away. The wife, temporarily abandoned, might for the sake of comfort and economic convenience take up with a locally available man. Since such relationships were, in effect, in the interest of everyone in the long-house, they readily tended to become recognized as marriages. The emotional complications introduced by these serial marriages were supposed to be resolved peacefully by the people concerned. The traveling husband who returned to find his wife living with someone else might try to recover her; if she preferred to remain with her new husband, however, he was not entitled to punish her or her new lover, but instead was encouraged to find another wife among the unmarried girls or wives with currently absent husbands.[4]

THE IDEAL OF AUTONOMOUS RESPONSIBILITY

The basic ideal of manhood was that of "the good hunter." Such a man was self-disciplined, autonomous, responsible. He was a patient and efficient huntsman, a generous provider to his family and nation, and a loyal and thoughtful friend and clansman. He was also a stern and ruthless warrior in avenging any injury done to those under his care. And he was always stoical and indifferent to privation, pain, and even death. Special prominence could be achieved by those who, while adequate in all respects, were outstanding in one or another dimension of this ideal. The patient and thoughtful man with a skin "seven thumbs thick" (to make him indifferent to spiteful gossip, barbed wit, and social pressures generally) might become a sachem or a "distinguished name"—a "Pine Tree" chief. An eloquent man with a good memory and indestructible poise might be a council speaker and represent clan, nation, even the confederacy in far-flung diplomatic ventures. And the stern and ruthless warrior (always fighting, at least according to the theory, to avenge the death or insult of a blood relative or publicly avowed friend) might become a noted war-captain or an official war-chief. The war-captain ideal, open as it was to all youths, irrespective of clan and lineage or of special intellectual qualifications, was perhaps the most emulated.

In the seventeenth century an Onondaga war-captain named Aharihon bore the reputation of being the greatest warrior of the country. He realized the ideal of autonomous responsibility to virtually pathological perfection. Let us note what is told of Aharihon in the *Jesuit Relations*.[5]

---

[4] This section is drawn from a paper entitled "Handsome Lake and the Decline of the Iroquois Matriarchate," which was read at the Wenner-Gren symposium at Burg Wartenstein, Austria, on Kinship and Behavior in the summer of 1966. The concept of dominant kin relationship is developed in Francis L. K. Hsu, "The Effect of Dominant Kinship Relationships on Kin- and Non-Kin Behavior: A Hypothesis," *American Anthropologist*, LXVII (1965), 638–61.

[5] Edna Kenton, ed., *The Indians of North America* (2 vols.; New York, 1927), II, 78–80.

Aharihon was a man of dignified appearance and imposing carriage, grave, polished in manner, and self-contained. His brother had been killed about 1654 in the wars with the Erie, a tribe westward of the Iroquois. As clansman and close relative, he was entitled—indeed obligated—either to avenge his brother's death by killing some Erie people or by adopting a war captive to take his place. Aharihon within a few years captured or had presented to him for adoption forty men. Each of them he burned to death over a slow fire, because, as he said, "he did not believe that there was any one worthy to occupy his |brother's| place." Father Lalemant was present when another young man, newly captured, was given to Aharihon as a substitute for the deceased brother. Aharihon let the young man believe that he was adopted and need have no further fear, and "presented to him four dogs, upon which to hold his feast of adoption. In the middle of the feast, while he was rejoicing and singing to entertain the guests, Aharihon arose, and told the company that this man too must die in atonement for his brother's death. The poor lad was astounded at this, and turned toward the door to make his escape, but was stopped by two men who had orders to burn him. On the fourteenth of February, in the evening, they began with his feet, intending to roast him, at a slow fire, as far up as the waist, during the greater part of the night. After midnight, they were to let him rally his strength and sleep a little until daybreak, when they were to finish this fatal tragedy. In his torture, the poor man made the whole village resound with his cries and groans. He shed great tears, contrary to the usual custom, the victim commonly glorying to be burned limb by limb, and opening his lips only to sing; but, as this one had not expected death, he wept and cried in a way that touched even these Barbarians. One of Aharihon's relatives was so moved with pity, that he advised ending the sufferer's torments by plunging a knife into his breast —which would have been a deed of mercy, had the stab been mortal. However, they were induced to continue the burning without interruption, so that before day he ended both his sufferings and his life." Aharihon's career of death continued without interruption, and by 1663 he was able to boast that he had killed sixty men with his own hand and had burned fully eighty men over slow fire. He kept count by tattooing a mark on his thigh for each successive victim. He was known then as the Captain General of the Iroquois and was nicknamed Nero by the Frenchmen at Montreal because of his cruelty.

The French finally captured him near Montreal, but even in captivity his manner was impressive. "This man," commented Father Lalemant, "commonly has nine slaves with him, five boys and four girls. He is a captain of dignified appearance and imposing carriage, and of such equanimity and presence of mind that, upon seeing himself surrounded by armed men, he showed no more surprise than if he had been alone; and when asked whether he would like to accompany us to Quebec, he deigned only to answer coldly that that was not a question to ask him, since he was in our power. Accordingly he was made to come aboard our Vessel, where I took pleasure in studying his disposition as well as that of an Algonquin in our company, who bore the scalp of an Iroquois but recently slain by him in war. These two men, although hostile enough to

eat each other, chatted and laughed on board that Vessel with great fa-
miliarity, it being very hard to decide which of the two was more skillful
in masking his feelings. I had Nero placed near me at table, where he bore
himself with a gravity, a self-control, and a propriety, which showed
nothing of his Barbarian origin; but during the rest of the time he was
constantly eating, so that he fasted only when he was at table."

But this voracious captain was not renowned among the Onondaga
as a killer only. He was, on the contrary, also a trusted ambassador, dispatched on occasion to Montreal on missions of peace. He was, in a word,
a noted man. He was a killer, but he was not an indiscriminate killer; he
killed only those whom it was his right to kill, tortured only those whom
he had the privilege of torturing, always as an expression of respect for
his dead brother. And although his kinfolk sometimes felt he was a little
extreme in his stern devotion to his brother's memory, they did not feel
that he was any the less a fine man, or that they had a right to interfere
with his impulses; they were willing to entrust the business of peace, as
well as war, to his hand. . . .

With this sort of man serving as an ego-ideal, held up by sanction
and by praise to youthful eyes, it is not remarkable that young men were
ambitious to begin the practice of war. All had seen captives tortured to
death; all had known relatives lost in war whose death demanded revenge
or replacement. The young men went out on practice missions as soon as
they were big enough to handle firearms; "infantile bands, armed with
hatchets and guns which they can hardly carry, do not fail to spread fear
and horror everywhere." [6] Even as late as the middle of the eighteenth
century, Handsome Lake and his brothers and nephews were still busy
at the old business of war for the sake of war. Cornplanter became a noted
war-captain; Blacksnake, his nephew, was one of the official war-chiefs of
the Seneca nation; and Handsome Lake himself took part in the scalping-
party pattern as a young man. But Handsome Lake became a sachem and
later a prophet, and he never gloried in the numbers of men he killed as
his brother Cornplanter (somewhat guiltily) did. "While I was in the use
of arms I killed seven persons and took three and saved their lives," said
Cornplanter. And Blacksnake, in later life, told with relish of his exploits
as a warrior. "We had a good fight there," he would say. "I have killed
how many I could not tell, for I pay no attention to or kept [no] account
of it, it was great many, for I never have it at all my Battles to think about
kepting account what I'd killed at one time. . . ." [7]

The cultivation of the ideal of autonomous responsibility—and the
suppression of its antinomy, dependency—began early in life. Iroquois
children were carefully trained to think for themselves but to act for
others. Parents were protective, permissive, and sparing of punishment;
they encouraged children to play at imitating adult behavior but did not
criticize or condemn fumbling early efforts; they maintained a cool detachment, both physically and verbally, avoiding the intense confronta-

---

[6] Kenton, *Indians of North America*, II, 87–88.
[7] Draper Collection, 16 F 227 ("Cornplanter's Talk"), State Historical Society of
Wisconsin, Madison, Wis.

tions of love and anger between parent and child to which Europeans were accustomed. Children did not so much live in a child's world as grow up freely in the interstices of an adult culture. The gain was an early self-reliance and enjoyment of responsibility; the cost, perhaps, was a life-long difficulty in handling feelings of dependency.

The Seneca mother gave birth to her child in the privacy of the woods, where she retired for a few hours when her time came, either alone or in the company of an older woman who served as midwife and, if the weather was cold, built and tended a fire. She had prepared for this event by eating sparingly and exercising freely, which were believed (probably with good reason) to make the child stronger and the birth easier. The newborn infant was washed in cold water, or even in snow, immediately after parturition and then wrapped in skins or a blanket. If the birth were a normal one, the mother walked back to the village with her infant a few hours afterwards to take up the duties of housewife. The event was treated as the consummation of a healthful process rather than as an illness. The infant spent much of its first nine months swaddled from chin to toe and lashed to a cradleboard. The child's feet rested against a footboard, a block of wood was placed between the heels of a girl to mold her feet to an inward turn. Over its head stretched a hoop, which could be draped with a thin cloth to keep away flies or to protect the child from the cold. The board and its wrappings were often lavishly decorated with silver trinkets and beadwork embroidery. The mother was able to carry the child in the board, suspended against her back, by a tumpline around her forehead; the board could be hung from the limb of a tree while she hoed corn; and it could be converted into a crib by suspending it on a rack of poles laid horizontally on forks stuck in the ground. The mother was solicitous of the child's comfort, nursed it whenever it cried, and loosened it from the board several times a day to change the moss that served as a diaper and to give it a chance to romp. The children, however, tended to cry when released from the board, and their tranquility could often be restored only by putting them back. Babies were seldom heard crying.

The mother's feeling for her children was intense; indeed, to one early observer it appeared that "Parental Tenderness" was carried to a "dangerous Indulgence." [8] Another early writer remarked, "The mothers love their children with an extreme passion, and although they do not reveal this in caresses, it is nevertheless real." [9] Mothers were quick to express resentment of any restraint or injury or insult offered to the child by an outsider. During the first few years the child stayed almost constantly with the mother, in the house, in the fields, or on the trail, playing and performing small tasks under her direction. The mother's chief concern during this time was to provide for the child and to protect it, to "harden" it by baths in cold water, but not to punish. Weaning was not

8 Draper Collection 16 F 32 ("Life of Governor Blacksnake"), State Hist. Soc. of Wis.
9 Milton W. Hamilton, ed., "Guy Johnson's Opinions on the American Indian," *Pennsylvania Magazine of History and Biography*, LXXVII (1953), 320.

normally attempted until the age of three or four, and such control as the child obtained over its excretory functions was achieved voluntarily, not as a result of consistent punishment for mistakes. Early sexual curiosity and experimentation were regarded as a natural childish way of behaving, out of which it would, in due time, grow. Grandparents might complain that small children got into everything, but the small child was free to romp, to pry into things, to demand what it wanted, and to assault its parents, without more hazard of punishment than the exasperated mother's occasionally blowing water in its face or dunking it in a convenient river.

The years between about eight or nine and the onset of puberty were a time of easy and gradual learning. At the beginning of this period the beginnings of the differentiation of the roles of boys and girls were laid down. The girls were kept around the house, under the guidance of their mothers, and assigned to the lighter household duties and to helping in the fields. Boys were allowed to roam in gangs, playing at war, hunting with bows and arrows and toy hatchets, and competing at races, wrestling, and lacrosse. The first successes at hunting were greeted with praise and boasts of future greatness. Sometimes these roaming gangs spent days at a time away from the village, sleeping in the bush, eating wild roots and fruits, and hunting such small game as could be brought down by bow and arrow, blowgun, or snare. These gangs developed into war parties after the boys reached puberty. Among themselves, both in gangs and among siblings of the same family, the children's playgroups were not constantly supervised by parents and teachers, and the children governed themselves in good harmony. Said one close observer, "Children of the same family show strong attachments to each other, and are less liable to quarrel in their youthful days than is generally the case with white children." [10]

The parents usually tried to maintain a calm moderation of behavior in dealing with their children, a lofty indifference alike to childish tantrums and seductive appeals for love. Hardihood, self-reliance, and independence of spirit were sedulously inculcated. When occasion presented itself, fathers, uncles, or other elder kinfolk instructed their sons in the techniques of travel, firemaking, the chase, war, and other essential arts of manhood, and the mothers correspondingly taught their daughters the way to hoe and plant the cornfields, how to butcher the meat, cook, braid corn, and other household tasks. But this instruction was presented, rather than enforced, as an opportunity rather than as a duty. On occasion the parent or other responsible adult talked to the child at length, "endeavoring," as a Quaker scribe gently put it, "to impress on its mind what it ought to do, and what to leave undone." [11] If exhortation seemed inadequate in its effect, the mentor might ridicule the child for doing wrong, or gravely point out the folly of a certain course of action, or even warn him that he courted the rage of offended supernatural beings. Obedience as such was no virtue, however, and blows, whippings, or restraints of any kind, such as restriction to quarters, were rarely imposed, the faults of the child being left to his own reason and conscience to correct as he

[10] Joseph Lafitau, *Moeurs des sauvages Americains* (2 vols., Paris, 1724), I, 393.
[11] Jackson, *Sketch of the Manners,* p. 20.

grew mature. With delicate perception the adults noted that childish faults "cannot be very great, before reason arrives at some degree of maturity." [12]

Direct confrontation with the child was avoided, but when things got seriously out of hand, parents sometimes turned older children over to the gods for punishment. A troublesome child might be sent out into the dusk to meet Longnose, the legendary Seneca bogeyman. Longnose might even be impersonated in the flesh by a distraught parent. Longnose was a hungry cannibal who chased bad children when their parents were sleeping. He mimicked the child, crying loudly as he ran, but the parents would not wake up because Longnose had bewitched them. A child might be chased all night until he submitted and promised to behave. Theoretically, if a child remained stubborn, Longnose finally caught him and took him away in a huge pack-basket for a leisurely meal. And—although parents were not supposed to do this—an unusually stubborn infant *could* be threatened with punishment by the great False Faces themselves, who, when invoked for this purpose, might "poison" a child or "spoil his face." "I remember," recalled a Cayuga woman of her childhood, "how scared I was of the False-faces; I didn't know what they were. They are to scare away disease. They used to come into the house and up the stairs and I used to hide away under the covers. They even crawled under the bed and they made that awful sound. When I was bad my mother used to say the False-faces would get me. Once, I must have been only 4 or 5, because I was very little when I left Canada, but I remember it so well that when I think of it I can hear that cry now, and I was going along a road from my grandfather's; it was a straight road and I couldn't lose my way, but it was almost dark, and I had to pass through some timber and I heard that cry and that rattle. I ran like a flash of lightening and I can hear it yet." [13]

At puberty some of the boys retired to the woods under the stewardship of an old man, where they fasted, abstained from any sort of sexual activity (which they had been free to indulge, to the limit of their powers, before), covered themselves with dirt, and mortified the flesh in various ways, such as bathing in ice water and bruising and gashing the shinbones with rocks. Dreams experienced during such periods of self-trial were apt to be regarded as visitations from supernatural spirits who might grant *orenda*, or magical power, to the dreamer, and who would maintain a special sort of guardianship over him. The person's connection with this supernatural being was maintained through a charm—such as a knife, a queerly shaped stone, or a bit of bone—which was connected with the dream through some association significant to the dreamer. Unlike many other tribes, however, the Iroquois apparently did not require these guardian-spirit visions for pubescent youths. Many youths were said not to have had their first vision until just before their first war party. Furthermore, any man could have a significant dream or vision at any time. Girls too went through a mild puberty ritual, retiring into the woods at first menstruation and paying particular attention to their dreams. With

[12] *Ibid.*
[13] *Ibid.*

the termination of the menstrual period the girl returned to the household; but hereafter, whenever she menstruated, she would have to live apart in a hut, avoiding people, and being careful not to step on a path, or to cook and serve anyone's food, or (especially) to touch medicines, which would immediately lose their potency if she handled them.[14]

The Europeans who observed this pattern of child experience were by no means unfavorably impressed although they were sometimes amazed. They commented, however, almost to a man, from early Jesuit to latter-day Quaker, on a consequence that stood out dramatically as they compared this "savage" maturation with "civilized." "There is nothing," wrote the Jesuit chronicler of the Iroquois mission in 1657, "for which these peoples have a greater horror than restraint. The very children cannot endure it, and live as they please in the houses of their parents, without fear of reprimand or chastisement." [15] One hundred and fifty years later, the Quaker Halliday Jackson observed that "being indulged in most of their wishes, as they grow up, liberty, in its fullest extent, becomes their ruling passion." [16] The Iroquois themselves recognized the intensity of their children's resentment at parental interference. "Some Savages," reported Le Mercier of the Huron, "told us that one of the principal reasons why they showed so much indulgence toward their children, was that when the children saw themselves treated by their parents with some severity, they usually resorted to extreme measures and hanged themselves, or ate of a certain root they call *Audachienrra*, which is a very quick poison." [17] The same fear was recorded among the Iroquois, including the Seneca, in 1657. And while suicides by frustrated children were not actually frequent, there are nevertheless a number of recorded cases of suicide where parental interference was the avowed cause. And *mutatis mutandis*, there was another rationalization for a policy of permissiveness: that the child who was harshly disciplined might grow up, some day, to mistreat his parents in revenge.

This theory of child raising was not taken for granted by the Seneca; on the contrary, it was very explicitly recognized, discussed, and pondered. Handsome Lake himself, in later years, insisted that parents love and indulge their children.

[14] William N. Fenton, "Problems Arising from the Historic Northeastern Position of the Iroquois," *Smithsonian Miscellaneous Collections*, C (1940), 429.
[15] Kenton, *Indians of North America*, II, 90.
[16] Jackson, *Sketch of the Manners*, p. 19.
[17] Kenton, *Indians of North America*, p. 90n.

The Structure of the Household

JOHN DEMOS

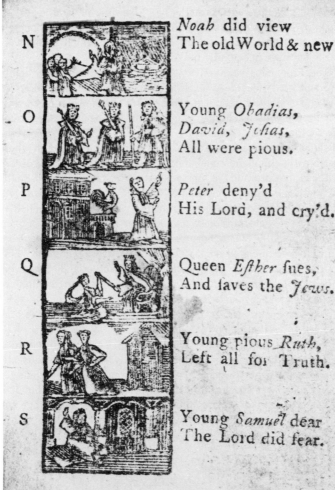

N	*Noah* did view The old World & new
O	Young *Obadias*, *David*, *Jofias*, All were pious.
P	*Peter* deny'd His Lord, and cry'd.
Q	Queen *Esther* sues, And saves the *Jews*.
R	Young pious *Ruth*, Left all for Truth.
S	Young *Samuel* dear The Lord did fear.

For the Puritan settlers of New England, family relationships were of the utmost importance. The nexus between wife and husband, child and parent, sister and brother, and master and servant was essential to the web of human experience. For all but a handful of settlers—trappers, Indian traders, or renegades from "civilization"—family ties provided the framework of life. Coming to a strange environment and confronting conditions that many colonists thought had the potential to drag them down into barbarism, early New Englanders saw the family as the basic building block in erecting a regenerated, godly community. That is why in early New England all single persons were required to live within a family; bachelor living was prohibited because no individual, it was thought, was safe from anarchic impulses if he or she lived outside a family fold. Likewise, all families were required to live within a specified distance of the meetinghouse, because it was the symbol of the larger family to which all individual households must necessarily be subordinate.

The Europeans who settled the New World stood at a point in time where the widespread abuse and abandonment of children were giving way to kindlier treatment and a desire to shape the personalities and mold the wills of children while admitting them to the emotional circle of the family. Puritans, as it has been said, were nine-tenths Englishmen in their cultural traits, and thus the child-parent relationships in a New England community may not have been very different from those that prevailed in the society the Puritans fled. And Englishmen, whether Puritan or Anglican or Catholic, shared much with other western European societies in most of the ways they approached life. Thus the rules governing behavior between man and wife or parent and child in early Massachusetts were not markedly different from those that predominated among Catholics in New France, Quakers in Pennsylvania, or Dutch Reformed in New Netherland. Everywhere, "reciprocal obligations," as John Demos calls them in the following selection, were recognized between different members of the family. These basic elements of the "contract" between members of the family are carefully spelled out by the author.

It is especially important that we attain some precision in our understanding of family relationships in early America, because they form a baseline against which to measure change in later periods. This change came most spectacularly in the twentieth century, but it occurred in other eras of American history as well. Why the change came slowly in some periods and rapidly in others is a question students may wish to ponder.

HUSBANDS AND WIVES

No aspect of the Puritan household was more vital than the relationship of husband and wife. But the study of this relationship raises at once certain larger questions of sex differentiation: What were the relative positions of men and women in Plymouth Colony? What attributes, and what overall valuation, were thought appropriate to each sex?

We know in a general way that male dominance was an accepted principle all over the Western World in the seventeenth century. The fundamental Puritan sentiment on this matter was expressed by Milton in a famous line in *Paradise Lost*: "he for God only, she for God in him;" and there is no reason to suspect that the people of Plymouth would have put it any differently. The world of public affairs was nowhere open to women —in Plymouth only males were eligible to become "freemen." Within the family the husband was always regarded as the "head"—and the Old Colony provided no exceptions to this pattern. Moreover, the culture at large maintained a deep and primitive kind of suspicion of women, solely on account of their sex. Some basic taint of corruption was thought to be inherent in the feminine constitution—a belief rationalized, of course, by the story of Eve's initial treachery in the Garden of Eden. It was no coincidence that in both the Old and the New World witches were mostly women. Only two allegations of witchcraft turn up in the official records of Plymouth,[1] but other bits of evidence point in the same general direction. There are, for example, the quoted words of a mother beginning an emotional plea to her son: "if you would beleive a woman beleive mee. . . ."[2] And why *not* believe a woman?

The views of the Pilgrim pastor John Robinson are also interesting in this connection. He opposed, in the first place, any tendency to regard women as "necessary evils" and greatly regretted the currency of such

---

[1] The first occurred in 1661, in Marshfield. A girl named Dinah Silvester accused the wife of William Holmes of being a witch, and of going about in the shape of a bear in order to do mischief. The upshot, however, was a suit for defamation against Dinah. The Court convicted her and obliged her to make a public apology to Goodwife Holmes. *Records of the Colony of New Plymouth, in New England*, ed. Nathaniel B. Shurtleff and David Pulsifer (Boston, 1855–61), III, 205, 207, 211. The second case (at Scituate, in 1677) resulted in the formal indictment of one Mary Ingham—who, it was said, had bewitched a girl named Mehitable Woodworth. But after suitable deliberations, the jury decided on an acquittal. *Plymouth Colony Records*, V, 223–24.

[2] From a series of depositions bearing on the estate of Samuel Ryder, published in *Mayflower Descendant*, XI, 52. The case is discussed in greater detail below, pp. 165–66.

opinions among "not only heathen poets . . . but also wanton Christians."
The Lord had created both man and woman of an equal perfection, and
"neither is she, since the creation more degenerated than he from the primitive goodness." [3] Still, in marriage some principles of authority were essential, since "differences will arise and be seen, and so the one must give
way, and apply unto the other; this, God and nature layeth upon the
woman, rather than upon the man." Hence the proper attitude of a wife
towards her husband was "a reverend subjection." [4]

However, in a later discussion of the same matter Robinson developed
a more complex line of argument which stressed certain attributes of inferiority assumed to be inherently feminine. Women, he wrote, were
under two different kinds of subjection. The first was framed "in in-
nocency" and implied no "grief" or "wrong" whatsoever. It reflected
simply the woman's character as "the weaker vessel"—weaker, most obviously, with respect to intelligence or "understanding." For this was a gift
"which God hath . . . afforded [the man], and means of obtaining it,
above the woman, that he might guide and go before her." [5] Robinson
also recognized that some men abused their position of authority and oppressed their wives most unfairly. But *even so*—and this was his central
point—resistance was not admissible. Here he affirmed the second kind of
subjection laid upon woman, a subjection undeniably "grievous" but justified by her "being first in transgression." In this way—by invoking the
specter of Eve corrupting Adam in paradise—Robinson arrived in the end
at a position which closely approximated the popular assumption of
woman's basic moral weakness.

Yet within this general framework of masculine superiority there
were a number of rather contrary indications. They seem especially evident in certain areas of the law. Richard B. Morris has written a most interesting essay on this matter, arguing the improved legal status of colonial
women by comparison to what still obtained in the mother country.[6]
Many of his conclusions seem to make a good fit with conditions in
Plymouth Colony. The baseline here is the common law tradition of England, which at this time accorded to women only the most marginal sort
of recognition. The married woman, indeed, was largely subsumed under
the legal personality of her husband; she was virtually without rights to
own property, make contracts, or sue for damages on her own account.
But in the New World this situation was perceptibly altered.

Consider, for example, the evidence bearing on the property rights
of Plymouth Colony wives. The law explicitly recognized their part in the
accumulation of a family's estate, by the procedures it established for the
treatment of widows. It was a basic principle of inheritance in this period
—on both sides of the Atlantic—that a widow should have the use or
profits of one-third of the land owned by her husband at the time of his
death and full title to one-third of his moveable property. But at least in

[3] *The Works of John Robinson,* ed. Robert Ashton (Boston, 1851), I, 236.
[4] *Ibid.,* 239–40.
[5] *Ibid.,* 240.
[6] Richard B. Morris, *Studies in the History of American Law* (New York, 1930),
   Chapter III, "Women's Rights in Early American Law."

Plymouth, and perhaps in other colonies as well, this expressed more than the widow's need for an adequate living allowance. For the laws also prescribed that "if any man do make an irrational and unrighteous Will, whereby he deprives his Wife of her reasonable allowance for her subsistencey," the Court may "relieve her out of the estate, notwithstanding by Will it were otherwise disposed; especially in such case where the Wife brought with her good part of the Estate in Marriage, or hath by her diligence and industry done her part in the getting of the Estate, and was otherwise well deserving." [7] Occasionally the Court saw fit to alter the terms of a will on this acount. In 1663, for example, it awarded to widow Naomi Silvester a larger share of her late husband's estate than the "inconsiderable pte" he had left her, since she had been "a frugall and laborious woman in the procuring of the said estate." [8] In short, the widow's customary "thirds" was not a mere dole; it was her *due*.

But there is more still. In seventeenth-century England women were denied the right to make contracts, save in certain very exceptional instances. In Plymouth Colony, by contrast, one finds the Court sustaining certain kinds of contracts involving women on a fairly regular basis. The most common case of this type was the agreement of a widow and a new husband, made *before* marriage, about the future disposition of their respective properties. The contract drawn up by John Phillips of Marshfield and widow Faith Doty of Plymouth in 1667 was fairly standard. It stipulated that "the said Faith Dotey is to enjoy all her house and land, goods and cattles, that shee is now possessed of, to her owne proper use, to dispose of them att her owne free will from time to time, and att any time, as shee shall see cause." Moreover this principle of separate control extended beyond the realm of personal property. Phillips and widow Doty each had young children by their previous marriages, and their agreement was "that the children of both the said pties shall remaine att the free and proper and onely dispose of theire owne naturall parents, as they shall see good to dispose of them." [9] Any woman entering marriage on terms such as these would seem virtually an equal partner, at least from a legal standpoint. Much rarer, but no less significant, were contracts made by women *after* marriage. When Dorothy Clarke wished to be free of her husband Nathaniel in 1686, the Court refused a divorce but allowed a separation. Their estate was then carefully divided up by contract to which the wife was formally a party.[10] Once again, no clear precedents for this procedure can be found in contemporary English law.

[7] William Brigham, *The Compact with the Charter and Laws of the Colony of New Plymouth* (Boston, 1836), 281.

[8] *Plymouth Colony Records*, IV, 46.

[9] *Ibid.*, 163–64. For another agreement of this type, see *Mayflower Descendant*, XVII, 49 (the marriage contract of Ephraim Morton and Mistress Mary Harlow). The same procedures can be viewed, retrospectively, in the wills of men who had been married to women previously widowed. Thus when Thomas Boardman of Yarmouth died in 1689 the following notation was placed near the end of his will: "the estate of my wife brought me upon marriage be at her dispose and not to be Invintoried with my estate." *Mayflower Descendant*, X, 102. See also the will of Dolar Davis, *Mayflower Descendant*, XXIV, 73.

[10] *Mayflower Descendant*, VI, 191–92.

The specific terms of some wills also help to confirm the rights of women to a limited kind of ownership even within marriage. No husband ever included his wife's clothing, for example, among the property to be disposed of after his death. And consider, on the other side, a will like that of Mistress Sarah Jenny, drawn up at Plymouth in 1655. Her husband had died just a few months earlier, and she wished simply to "Despose of som smale thinges that is my owne proper goods leaveing my husbands will to take place according to the true Intent and meaning thereof." [11] The "smale thinges" included not only her wardrobe, but also a bed, some books, a mare, some cattle and sheep. Unfortunately, married women did not usually leave wills of their own (unless they had been previously widowed); and it is necessary to infer that in most cases there was some sort of informal arrangement for the transfer of their personal possessions. One final indication of these same patterns comes from wills which made bequests to a husband and wife separately. Thus, for example, Richard Sealis of Scituate conferred most of his personal possessions on the families of two married daughters, carefully specifying which items should go to the daughters themselves and which to their husbands.[12] Thomas Rickard, also of Scituate, had no family of his own and chose therefore to distribute his property among a variety of friends. Once again spouses were treated separately: "I give unto Thomas Pincin my bedd and Rugg one paire of sheets and pilloty . . . I give and bequeath unto Joane the wife of the aforsaid Thomas Pincin my bason and fouer sheets . . . I give and bequeath unto Joane Stanlacke my Chest . . . unto Richard Stanlacke my Chest . . . unto Richard Stanlacke my best briches and Dublit and ould Coate." [13]

The questions of property rights and of the overall distribution of authority within a marriage do not necessarily coincide; and modern sociologists interested in the latter subject usually emphasize the process of decision-making.[14] Of course, their use of live samples gives them a very great advantage; they can ask their informants, through questionnaires or interviews, which spouse decides where to go on vacation, what kind of car to buy, how to discipline the children, when to have company in, and so forth. The historian simply cannot draw out this kind of detail, nor can he contrive any substantial equivalent. But he is able sometimes to make a beginning in this direction; for example, the records of Plymouth do throw light on two sorts of family decisions of the very greatest importance. One of these involves the transfer of land, and illustrates further the whole trend toward an expansion of the rights of married women to hold property. The point finds tangible expression in a law passed by the General Court in 1646: "It is enacted &c. That the Assistants or any of them shall have full power to take the acknowledgment of a bargaine and sale of houses and lands . . . And that the wyfe hereafter come in & consent and

[11] *Mayflower Descendant*, VIII, 171.
[12] *Mayflower Descendant*, XIII, 94–96.
[13] *Mayflower Descendant*, IX, 155.
[14] See, for example, Robert O. Blood, Jr., and Donald M. Wolfe, *Husbands and Wives* (Glencoe, Ill., 1960), esp. ch. 2.

acknowledg the sale also; but that all bargaines and sales of houses and lands made before this day to remayne firm to the buyer notwithstanding the wife did not acknowledge the same." [15] The words "come in" merit special attention: the authorities wished to confront the wife personally (and even, perhaps, privately?) in order to minimize the possibility that her husband might exert undue pressure in securing her agreement to a sale.

The second area of decision-making in which both spouses shared an important *joint* responsibility was the "putting out" of children into foster families. For this there was no statute prescribing a set line of procedure, but the various written documents from specific cases make the point clearly enough. Thus in 1660 "An Agreement appointed to bee Recorded" affirmed that "Richard Berry of Yarmouth with his wifes Consent and other frinds; hath given unto Gorge Crispe of Eastham and his; wife theire son Samuell Berry; to bee att the ordering and Disposing of the said Gorge and his wife as if hee were theire owne Child." [16] The practice of formally declaring the wife's consent is evident in all such instances, when both parents were living. Another piece of legal evidence describes an actual deathbed scene in which the same issue had to be faced. It is the testimony of a mother confirming the adoption of her son, and it is worth quoting in some detail. "These prsents Witnesse that the 20th of march 1657–8 Judith the wife of William Peaks acknowlidged that her former husband Lawrence Lichfeild lying on his Death bedd sent for John Allin and Ann his wife and Desired to give and bequeath unto them his youngest son Josias Lichfeild if they would accept of him and take him as theire Child; then they Desired to know how long they should have him and the said Lawrence said for ever; but the mother of the child was not willing then; but in a short time after willingly Concented to her husbands will in the thinge." [17] That the wife finally agreed is less important here than the way in which her initial reluctance sufficed to block the child's adoption, in spite of the clear wishes of her husband.

Another reflection of this pattern of mutual responsibility appears in certain types of business activity—for instance, the management of inns and taverns ("ordinaries" in the language of the day). All such establishments were licensed by the General Court; hence their history can be followed, to a limited degree, in the official Colony Records. It is interesting to learn that one man's license was revoked because he had recently "buryed his wife, and in that respect not being soe capeable of keeping a publicke house." [18] In other cases the evidence is less explicit but still revealing. For many years James Cole ran the principal ordinary in the town of Plymouth, and from time to time the Court found it necessary to censure and punish certain violations of proper decorum that occurred there. In some of these cases Cole's wife Mary was directly implicated. In March

---

[15] Brigham, *The Compact with the Charter and Laws of the Colony of New Plymouth*, 86.
[16] *Mayflower Descendant*, XV, 34.
[17] *Mayflower Descendant*, XII, 134.
[18] *Plymouth Colony Records*, IV, 54.

1669 a substantial fine was imposed "for that the said Mary Cole suffered divers psons after named to stay drinking on the Lords day . . . in the time of publicke worshipp." [19] Indeed the role of women in all aspects of this episode is striking, since two of the four drinking customers, the "divers psons after named," turned out to be female. Perhaps, then, women had considerable freedom to move on roughly the same terms with men even into some of the darker byways of Old Colony life.

The Court occasionally granted liquor licenses directly to women. Husbands were not mentioned, though it is of course possible that all of the women involved were widows. In some cases the terms of these permits suggest retail houses rather than regular inns or taverns. Thus in 1663 "Mistris Lydia Garrett" of Scituate was licensed to "sell liquors, alwaies provided . . . that shee sell none but to house keepers, and not lesse than a gallon att a time;" [20] and the agreement with another Scituate lady, Margaret Muffee, twenty years later, was quite similar.[21] But meanwhile in Middlebury one "Mistress Mary Combe" seems to have operated an ordinary of the standard type.[22] Can we proceed from these specific data on liquor licensing to some more general conclusion about the participation of women in the whole field of economic production and exchange? Unfortunately there is little additional hard evidence on one side or the other. The Court Records do not often mention other types of business activity, with the single exception of milling; and no woman was ever named in connection with this particular enterprise. A few more wills could be cited—for instance, the one made by Elizabeth Poole, a wealthy spinster in Taunton, leaving "my pte in the Iron workes" to a favorite nephew.[23] But this does not add up to very much. The economy of Plymouth was, after all, essentially simple—indeed "underdeveloped"—in most important respects. Farming claimed the energies of all but a tiny portion of the populace; there was relatively little opportunity for anyone, man *or* woman, to develop a more commercial orientation. It is known that in the next century women played quite a significant role in the business life of many parts of New England,[24] and one can view this pattern as simply the full development of possibilities that were latent even among the first generations of settlers. But there is no way to fashion an extended chain of proof.

Much of what has been said so far belongs to the general category of the rights and privileges of the respective partners to a marriage. But what of their duties, their basic responsibilities to one another? Here, surely, is another area of major importance in any assessment of the character of married life. The writings of John Robinson help us to make a start with these questions, and especially to recover the framework of ideals within which most couples of Plymouth Colony must have tried to hammer out

[19] *Plymouth Colony Records,* V, 15.
[20] *Plymouth Colony Records,* IV, 44.
[21] *Plymouth Colony Records,* VI, 187.
[22] *Ibid.,* 141.
[23] *Mayflower Descendant,* XIV, 26.
[24] Elizabeth Anthony Dexter, *Colonial Women of Affairs* (Boston, 1911).

a meaningful day-to-day relationship. We have noted already that Robinson prescribed "subjection" as the basic duty of a wife to her husband. No woman deserved praise, "how well endowed soever otherwise, except she frame, and compose herself, what may be, unto her husband, in conformity of manners." [25] From the man, by contrast, two things were particularly required: "love . . . and wisdom." His love for his wife must be "like Christ's to his church: holy for quality, and great for quantity," and it must stand firm even where "her failings and faults be great." His wisdom was essential to the role of family "head"; without it neither spouse was likely to find the way to true piety, and eventually to salvation.

It is a long descent from the spiritual counsel of John Robinson to the details of domestic conflict as noted in the Colony Records. But the Records are really the only available source of information about the workings of actual marriages in this period. They are, to be sure, a negative type of source; that is, they reveal only those cases which seemed sufficiently deviant and sufficiently important to warrant the attention of the authorities. But it is possible by a kind of reverse inference to use them to reconstruct the norms which the community at large particularly wished to protect. This effort serves to isolate three basic obligations in which both husband and wife were thought to share.

There was, first and most simply, the obligation of regular and exclusive cohabitation. No married person was permitted to live apart from his spouse except in very unusual and temporary circumstances (as when a sailor was gone to sea). The Court stood ready as a last resort to force separated couples to come together again, though it was not often necessary to deal with the problem in such an official way. One of the few recorded cases of this type occurred in 1659. The defendant was a certain Goodwife Spring, married to a resident of Watertown in the Bay Colony and formerly the wife and widow of Thomas Hatch of Scituate. She had, it seems, returned to Scituate some three or four years earlier, and had been living "from her husband" ever since. The Court ordered that "shee either repaire to her husband with all convenient speed, . . . or . . . give a reason why shee doth not." [26] Exactly how this matter turned out cannot be determined, but it seems likely that the ultimate sanction was banishment from the Colony. The government of Massachusetts Bay is known to have imposed this penalty in a number of similar cases. None of the extant records describe such action being taken at Plymouth, but presumably the possibility was always there.

Moreover, the willful desertion of one spouse by the other over a period of several years was one of the few legitimate grounds for divorce. In 1670, for example, the Court granted the divorce plea of James Skiffe "having received sufficient testimony that the late wife of James Skiffe hath unlawfully forsaken her lawfull husband . . . and is gone to Roanoke, in or att Verginnia, and there hath taken another man for to be her husband." [27] Of course, bigamy was always sufficient reason in itself

[25] *The Works of John Robinson*, I, 20.
[26] *Plymouth Colony Records*, III, 174.
[27] *Plymouth Colony Records*, V, 33.

for terminating a marriage. Thus in 1680 Elizabeth Stevens obtained a divorce from her husband when it was proved that he had three other wives already, one each in Boston, Barbadoes, and a town in England not specified.[28]

But it was not enough that married persons should simply live together on a regular basis; their relationship must be relatively peaceful and harmonious. Once again the Court reserved the right to interfere in cases where the situation had become especially difficult. Occasionally both husband and wife were judged to be at fault, as when George and Anna Barlow were "severely reproved for theire most ungodly liveing in contension one with the other, and admonished to live otherwise." [29] But much more often one or the other was singled out for the Court's particular attention. One man was punished for "abusing his wife by kiking her of from a stoole into the fier," [30] and another for "drawing his wife in uncivell manor on the snow." [31] A more serious case was that of John Dunham, convicted of "abusive carriage towards his wife in continuall tiranising over her, and in pticulare for his late abusive and uncivill carryage in endeavoring to beate her in a deboist manor." [32] The Court ordered a whipping as just punishment for these cruelties, but the sentence was then suspended at the request of Dunham's wife. Sometimes the situation was reversed and the woman was the guilty party. In 1655, for example, Joan Miller of Taunton was charged with "beating and reviling her husband, and egging her children to healp her, bidding them knock him in the head, and wishing his victuals might coak him." [33] A few years later the wife of Samuel Halloway (also of Taunton) was admonished for "carryage towards her husband . . . soe turbulend and wild, both in words and actions, as hee could not live with her but in danger of his life or limbs." [34]

It would serve no real purpose to cite more of these unhappy episodes —and it might indeed create an erroneous impression that marital conflict was particularly endemic among the people of the Old Colony. But two general observations are in order. First, the Court's chief aim in this type of case was to restore the couple in question to something approaching tranquility. The assumption was that a little force applied from the outside might be useful, whether it came in the form of an "admonition" or in some kind of actual punishment. Only once did the Court have to recognize that the situation might be so bad as to make a final reconciliation impossible. This happened in 1665 when John Williams, Jr., of Scituate, was charged with a long series of "abusive and harsh carriages" toward his wife Elizabeth, "in speciall his sequestration of himselfe from the marriage bed, and his accusation of her to bee a whore, and that especially in reference unto a child lately borne of his said wife by him denied to bee

28 *Plymouth Colony Records*, VI, 44–45.
29 *Plymouth Colony Records*, IV, 10.
30 *Plymouth Colony Records*, V, 61.
31 *Plymouth Colony Records*, IV, 47.
32 *Ibid.*, 103–4.
33 *Plymouth Colony Records*, III, 75.
34 *Plymouth Colony Records*, V, 29.

legittimate." [35] The case was frequently before the Court during the next two years, and eventually all hope of a settlement was abandoned. When Williams persisted in his "abuses," and when too he had "himself . . . |declared| his insufficiency for converse with weomen," [36] a formal separation was allowed—though not a full divorce. In fact, it may be that his impotence, not his habitual cruelty, was the decisive factor in finally persuading the Court to go this far. For in another case, some years later, a separation was granted on the former grounds alone.[37]

The second noteworthy aspect of all these situations is the equality they seem to imply between the sexes. In some societies and indeed in many parts of Europe at this time, a wife was quite literally at the mercy of her husband—his prerogatives extended even to the random use of physical violence. But clearly this was not the situation at Plymouth. It is, for example, instructive to break down these charges of "abusive carriage" according to sex: one finds that wives were accused just about as often as husbands. Consider, too, those cases of conflict in which the chief parties were of opposite sex but not married to one another. Once again the women seem to have held their own. Thus we have, on the one side, Samuel Norman punished for "strikeing Lydia, the wife of Henery Taylor," [38] and John Dunham for "abusive speeches and carriages" [39] toward Sarah, wife of Benjamin Eaton; and, on the other side, the complaint of Abraham Jackson against "Rose, the wife of Thomas Morton, . . . that the said Rose, as hee came from worke, did abuse him by calling of him lying rascall and rogue." [40] In short, this does *not* seem to have been a society characterized by a really pervasive, and operational, norm of male dominance. There is no evidence at all of habitual patterns of deference in the relations between the sexes. John Robinson, and many others, too, may have assumed that woman was "the weaker vessel" and that "subjection" was her natural role. But as so often happens with respect to such matters, actual behavior was another story altogether.

The third of the major obligations incumbent on the married pair was a normal and exclusive sexual union. As previously indicated, impotence in the husband was one of the few circumstances that might warrant a divorce. The reasoning behind this is nowhere made explicit, but most likely it reflected the felt necessity that a marriage produce children. It is worth noting in this connection some of the words used in a divorce hearing of 1686 which centered on the issue of a man's impotence. He was, according to his wife, "always unable to perform the act of generation." [41] The latter phrase implies a particular view of the nature and significance of the sexual act, one which must have been widely held in this culture. Of course, there were other infertile marriages in the

[35] *Plymouth Colony Records,* IV, 93.
[36] *Ibid.,* 125.
[37] *Plymouth Colony Records,* VI, 191.
[38] *Plymouth Colony Records,* V, 39.
[39] *Ibid.,* 40.
[40] *Plymouth Colony Records,* IV, 11.
[41] *Plymouth Colony Records,* VI, 191.

same period which held together. But perhaps the cause of the problem had to be obvious—as with impotence—for the people involved to consider divorce. Where the sexual function appeared normal in both spouses, there was always the hope that the Lord might one day grant the blessing of children. Doubtless for some couples this way of thinking meant year after year of deep personal disappointment.

The problem of adultery was more common—and, in a general sense, more troublesome. For adultery loomed as the most serious possible distortion of the whole sexual and reproductive side of marriage. John Robinson called it "that most foul and filthy sin, . . . the disease of marriage," and concluded that divorce was its necessary "medicine." [42] In fact, most of the divorces granted in the Old Colony stemmed from this one cause alone. But adultery was not only a strong *prima facie* reason for divorce; it was also an act that would bring heavy punishment to the guilty parties. The law decreed that "whosoever shall Commit Adultery with a Married Woman or one Betrothed to another Man, both of them shall be severely punished, by whipping two several times . . . and likewise to wear two Capital Letters A.D. cut out in cloth and sewed on their uppermost Garments . . . and if at any time they shall be found without the said Letters so worne . . . to be forthwith taken and publickly whipt, and so from time to time as often as they are found not to wear them." [43]

But quite apart from the severity of the prescribed punishments, this statute is interesting for its definition of adultery by reference to a married (or bethrothed) *woman*. Here, for the first time, we find some indication of difference in the conduct expected of men and women. The picture can be filled out somewhat by examining the specific cases of adultery prosecuted before the General Court down through the years. To be sure, the man involved in any given instance was judged together with the woman, and when convicted their punishments were the same. But there is another point to consider as well. All of the adulterous couples mentioned in the records can be classified in one of two categories: a married woman and a married man, or a married woman and a single man. There was, on the other hand, no case involving a married man and a single woman. This pattern seems to imply that the chief concern, the essential element of sin, was the woman's infidelity to her husband. A married man would be punished for his part in this aspect of the affair—rather than for any wrong done to his own wife.

However, this does not mean that a man's infidelities were wholly beyond reproach. The records, for example, include one divorce plea in which the wife adduced as her chief complaint "an act of uncleanes" by her husband with another woman.[44] There was no move to prosecute and punish the husband—apparently since the other woman was unmarried. But the divorce was granted, and the wife received a most favorable settlement. We can, then, conclude the following. The adultery of a wife was

---

[42] *The Works of John Robinson*, I, 241.
[43] Brigham, *The Compact with the Charter and Laws of the Colony of New Plymouth*, 245–46.
[44] *Plymouth Colony Records*, III, 221.

treated as both a violation of her marriage (hence grounds for divorce) *and* an offense against the community (hence cause for legal prosecution). But for comparable behavior by husbands only the former consideration applied. In this somewhat limited sense the people of Plymouth Colony do seem to have maintained a "double standard" of sexual morality.

Before concluding this discussion of married life in the Old Colony and moving on to other matters, one important area of omission should at least be noted. Very little has been said here of love, affection, understanding—a whole range of positive feelings and impulses—between husbands and wives. Indeed the need to rely so heavily on Court Records has tended to weight the balance quite conspicuously on the side of conflict and failure. The fact is that the sum total of actions of divorce, prosecutions for adultery, "admonitions" against habitual quarreling, does not seem terribly large. In order to make a proper assessment of their meaning several contingent factors must be recognized; the long span of time they cover, the steady growth of the Colony's population (to something like 10,000 by the end of the century),[45] the extensive jurisdiction of the Court over many areas of domestic life. Given this overall context, it is clear that the vast majority of Plymouth Colony families never once required the attention of the authorities. Elements of disharmony were, at the least, controlled and confined within certain limits.

But again, can the issue be approached in a more directly affirmative way? Just how, and how much, did feelings of warmth and love fit into the marriages of the Old Colony? Unfortunately our source materials have almost nothing to say in response to such questions. But this is only to be expected in the case of legal documents, physical remains, and so forth. The wills often refer to "my loveing wife"—but it would be foolish to read anything into such obvious set phrases. The records of Court cases are completely mute on this score. Other studies of "Puritan" ideals about marriage and the family have drawn heavily on literary materials—and this, of course, is the biggest gap in the sources that have come down from Plymouth Colony. Perhaps, though, a certain degree of extrapolation is permissible here; and if so, we must imagine that love was quite central to these marriages. If, as Morgan has shown, this was the case in Massachusetts Bay, surely it was also true for the people of Plymouth.[46]

There are, finally, just a few scraps of concrete evidence on this point. As previously noted, John Robinson wrote lavishly about the importance of love to a marriage—though he associated it chiefly with the role of the husband. And the wills should be drawn in once again, especially those clauses in which a man left specific instructions regarding the care of his widow. Sometimes the curtain of legal terms and style seems to

[45] There are three separate investigations dealing with this question: Richard L. Bowen, *Early Rehoboth* (3 vols.; Rehoboth, Mass., 1945), I, 15–24; Joseph B. Felt, "Population of Plymouth Colony," in American Statistical Association *Collections*, I, Pt. ii (Boston, 1845), 143–44; and William Bradford, *Of Plymouth Plantation*, ed. Samuel Eliot Morison (New York, 1952), xi.

[46] See Edmund Morgan, *The Puritan Family* (New York, 1966), esp. 46 ff.

rise for a moment and behind it one glimpses a deep tenderness and concern. There is, for example, the will written by Walter Briggs in 1676.
Briggs's instructions in this regard embraced all of the usual matters—
rooms, bedding, cooking utensils, "lyberty to make use of ye two gardens."
And he ended with a particular request that his executors "allow my said
wife a gentle horse or mare to ride to meeting or any other occasion she
may have, & that Jemy, ye neger, catch it for her." [47] Surely this kind of
thoughtfulness reflected a larger instinct of love—one which, nourished
in life, would not cease to be effective even in the face of death itself.

PARENTS AND CHILDREN

Egalitarianism formed no part of seventeenth-century assumptions
about the proper relationship of parents and children. But at Plymouth
this relationship involved a set of *reciprocal* obligations.

From the standpoint of the child, the Biblical commandment to
"Honor thy father and mother" was fundamental—and the force of law
stood behind it. The relevant statute directed that "If any Childe or
Children above sixteen years old, and of competent Understanding, shall
Curse or Smite their Natural Father or Mother; he or they shall be put
to Death, unless it can be sufficiently testified that the Parents have been
very Unchristianly negligent in the Education of such Children, or so
provoked them by extreme and cruel Correction, that they have been
forced thereunto, to preserve themselves from Death or Maiming." A
corollary order prescribed similar punishment for behavior that was simply "Stubborn or Rebellious"—or indeed, for any sort of habitual disobedience.[48]

The rightful authority of the parents is clear enough here, but it
should also be noted that this authority was limited in several ways. In
the first place, a child less than sixteen years old was excluded from these
prescriptions; he was not mature enough to be held finally responsible
for his actions. Disobedience and disrespect on the part of younger children were surely punished, but on an informal basis and within the family
itself. In such cases, presumably, the purpose of punishment was to form
right habits; it was part of a whole pattern of learning. But for children
of more than sixteen different assumptions applied.[49] Ultimate responsibility could now be imputed, and an offense against one's parents was also
an offense against the basic values of the community. Hence the full
retributive process of the laws might properly be invoked.

The clause relating to "extreme and cruel correction" implied a second limitation on parental power. The child did have the right to protect
his own person from any action that threatened "Death or Maiming."

[47] *Plymouth Colony Records*, VI, 134–35.
[48] Brigham, *The Compact with the Charter and Laws of the Colony of New Ply-
    mouth*, 245.
[49] Sixteen was also the age at which children became fully liable in actions of lying
    and slander. See below, Chapter Ten, for a review of this and other evidence bear-
    ing on adolescence as a "developmental stage."

Finally, it seems significant that the arbiter of *all* such questions was not the parental couple directly involved but rather the constituted authorities of the Colony as a whole. The correct response to gross disobedience in a child was as follows: "his Father and Mother, . . . [shall] lay hold on him, and bring him before the Magistrates assembled in Court, and testifie unto them, that their Son is Stubborn and Rebellious, and will not obey their voice and chastisement." [50] This may sound rather menacing, but it did imply an important kind of negative. The parents shall *not* take matters completely into their own hands. The child shall also have *his* say in Court; and presumably he may try, if he wishes, to show that his behavior was provoked by some cruelty on the part of his parents.

It must be said that only a few cases of youthful disobedience to parents actually reached the Courts, and that these few are not very revealing. Certainly the death penalty was never invoked on such grounds; only once, in fact, was it even mentioned as a possibility. In 1679 "Edward Bumpus for stricking and abusing his parents, was whipt att the post; his punishment was alleviated in regard hee was crasey brained, otherwise hee had bine put to death or otherwise sharply punished." [51] In other instances the Court's function was to mediate between the affected parties or to ratify an agreement which had already been worked out on an informal basis. In 1669, for instance, it heard various testimonies about the "crewell, unnaturall, and extreame passionate carriages" of one Mary Morey toward her son Benjamin, and his own "unbeseeming" response. The situation was described as being so "turbulent . . . that severall of the naighbours feared murder would be in the issue of it." [52] Yet in the end the Court took no action beyond admonishing both principals and making them "promise reformation." Some years earlier Thomas Lumbert of Barnstable complained formally that "Jedediah, his sone, hath carryed stuburnly against his said father," and proposed that the boy be "freed, provided hee doe dispose himselfe in some honest family with his fathers consent." [53] The Court merely recorded this arrangement and decided not to interfere directly unless Jedediah neglected to find himself a good foster home. In sum, then, the role of the Court with regard to specific cases of this type, was quite limited. The laws on the matter should be viewed as expressing broad and basic values rather than an actual pattern of intervention in the day-to-day affairs of Old Colony households. In fact, most parents must have tried to define and enforce their authority very much on an individual basis. Quite likely an appeal to the Courts was a last resort, to be undertaken only with a keen sense of failure and personal humiliation.

The innermost dimensions of these vital intrafamily relationships cannot really be traced. But two particular matters seem noteworthy. Questions of inheritance were more closely intertwined with discipline

[50] Brigham, *The Compact with the Charter and Laws of the Colony of New Plymouth*, 245.
[51] *Plymouth Colony Records*, VI, 20.
[52] *Plymouth Colony Records*, V, 16.
[53] *Plymouth Colony Records*, III, 201.

in that period than is generally the case now. In some of the wills bequests to certain children were made contingent on their maintaining the proper sort of obedience. Thus, for example, Thomas Hicks of Scituate left most of his lands to "my two sonnes Daniell and Samuell upon this proviso that they bee Obedient unto theire mother and carrye themselves as they ought soe as they may live comfortably together but if the one or both live otherwise then they ought and undewtyfully and unquietly with theire Mother . . . then hee that soe carryeth himselfe shall Disinheritt himselte of his pte of this land." [54] The effectiveness of this kind of sanction among the settlers at large is difficult to assess. In many cases, of course, the point was never rendered so explicit as in the will of Thomas Hicks; but it must often have loomed in the background when conflict between parents and children reached a certain degree of intensity.

The same model of filial behavior seems to have obtained for grown as well as for young children, though perhaps in a somewhat attenuated form. In 1663, for example, the Court summoned Abraham Pierce, Jr., "to answere for his abusive speeches used to his father." [55] The younger Pierce was at this time twenty-five years old and married. Another Court case of a different sort involved a question of disputed paternity. Martha, wife of Thomas Hewitt, gave birth shortly—*too* shortly—after their marriage: her husband contended that he could not have been the child's father and so persuaded the Court. Instead suspicion pointed toward Martha's own father, Christopher Winter, raising thereby the awful specter of incest. Among the evidence presented was "Winters acknowlidgment, that after hee had had knowlidge of his said daughters being withchild,—being, as hee said, informed by Hewitt,—hee did not bring them together and enquire into it, nor reprove or beare witnes against her wickednes, as would have become a father that was innosent." [56] Apparently then, a parent would normally continue to concern himself directly in the personal affairs of his children, even when they had become adult and were involved with families of their own. And, by implication, the children should listen to his counsel and respond accordingly.

But if the child owed his parents an unceasing kind of obedience and respect, there were other obligations which applied in the reverse direction. The parent for his part must accept responsibility for certain basic needs of his children—for their physical health and welfare, for their education (understood in the broadest sense), and for the property they would require in order one day to "be for themselves." There were, moreover, legal provisions permitting the community to intervene in the case of parents who defaulted on these obligations. One statute affirmed that when "psons in this Gourment are not able to provide Competent and convenient food and raiment for theire Children," the latter might be taken in hand by local officials and placed in foster families where they would be more "comfortably provided for." [57] Another, more extended

---

[54] *Mayflower Descendant*, XI, 160.
[55] *Plymouth Colony Records*, IV, 47.
[56] *Plymouth Colony Records*, V, 13.
[57] *Plymouth Colony Records*, XI, 111.

set of enactments dealt with the whole educational side of the parental role. Children should be taught to read, "at least to be able duely to read the Scriptures." They should be made to understand "the Capital Laws" and "the main Grounds and Principles of Christian Religion." And they should be trained "in some honest lawful calling, labour or employment, that may be profitable for themselves, or the Country." [58] Parents who neglected any of this were subject to fines; and once again the ultimate recourse of transferring children into new families might be applied if the neglect were habitual. Unfortunately we cannot discover how often these procedures were actually set in motion. The responsibility for specific cases was assigned to local authorities in the various towns, and records of their actions have not survived. But the basic intent behind the laws which covered such matters is clear—and in itself significant.

The obligation to provide a "portion" of property for children when they attained maturity was nowhere expressed in formal, legal terms. But it can certainly be inferred from other types of evidence. Many wills made specific mention of previous bequests to grown children—real or personal property, or both. Deeds of apprenticeship and adoption sometimes included the promise of a portion as one of the essential terms. This responsibility might, it seems, be transferred from a child's natural parents to his new master, but it could not be overlooked altogether. Some men gained the assistance of the government in arranging portions for their young, witness the following type of Court Order: "Libertie is graunted unto Mr. John Alden to looke out a portion of land to accomodate his sons withall." [59] Indeed the fundamental laws of the Colony recognized a special claim to such "accomodation" for "such children as heere born and next unto them such as are heere brought up under their parents and are come to the age of discretion." [60]

More often, however, portions were managed on a purely private basis. One of the rare personal documents to survive from the Old Colony, a letter written by Benjamin Brewster, describes the process as it operated in a particular case: "Being at the hose of Gorge Geres upon the first of may in the yere of our Lord: 1684 then and there was a discourse betwene the aforesayd Geres and his son Jonathan he then being of age to be for him selfe: upon som consederration mofeing the sayd Geres there to he then declared what he would gefe his son Jonathan as the full of his porshon except ypon his sons better behaver should desarve more which was: 130: akers of Land that his father had of Owanneco up in the contre: and: 2: best of 2 yere old: 1: stere of: 4: yer old and a cow." [61]

[58] Brigham, *The Compass with the Charter and Laws of the Colony of New Plymouth*, 270–71.
[59] *Plymouth Colony Records*, III, 120.
[60] Brigham, *The Compact with the Charter and Laws of the Colony of New Plymouth*, 46.
[61] *Mayflower Descendant*, II, 113.

The Planter's Wife:
The Experience of
White Women in
Seventeenth-Century Maryland

LOIS GREEN CARR AND LORENA S. WALSH

Women make up one-half of any society except in unusual circumstances. They play vital roles not only in childbearing and child rearing but also in shaping the economic, political, social, and religious affairs of society. Hence, an appreciation of the productive as well as the reproductive roles of women is crucial to our understanding of the past. Yet only in recent years have historians regarded women as important agents of historical change in America.

Like men, women in colonial America found that much of daily existence was dictated by forces beyond their control. In the early decades of colonization, men greatly outnumbered women and this simple fact ensured that women would be prized in most communities. At the same time, this demographic imbalance subtly influenced men to think of women as commercial articles—valuable for their ability to produce more workers in a labor-short society, to provide sexual gratification in a forbidding and precarious environment, and to transmit the education and refinement that the harshness of frontier life threatened to snuff out. Another brute fact shaping existence was early death. As the following selection shows, it stalked women in the Chesapeake colonies, narrowing their world in ways unfamiliar in their homelands.

While life in early America was "determined" in some ways by demographic and environmental forces, there were areas where women had unusual power to mold the world around them. Although they came in the company of men who held the ideal of subordinate women living out their lives under the direction of husbands and fathers, colonial women proved resilient and resourceful in altering prescribed modes of behavior. Anne Hutchinson of Boston was scourged as a "leper" by the Puritan magistrates for preaching Antinomianism not only because she challenged the religious tenets of the male clergy but because she dared to preach at all. Even after banishment from the colony for her autonomous and heretical behavior she continued her quest. So did hundreds of other women.

We can see in the selection by Carr and Walsh how women's lives in colonial America were partly shaped by their English backgrounds and partly reordered by the exigencies of the New World. The authors show what it meant to immigrate to a malarial climate, to live in a sexually unbalanced world, to be poor and indentured upon arrival, and to enter a society where family formation was stunted. Though Carr and Walsh draw contrasts mainly between women in England and Maryland, students may make their own comparisons between the Chesapeake and New England, where different offshoots of English society were carving out their destinies in the wilderness.

The roots of southern American culture were nourished in the soil of the Chesapeake region. By the late seventeenth century, the planter's wife had secured her place. But she was crossing into new social terrain once more because, as the eighteenth century arrived, white indentured laborers were being replaced by black African slaves. New dynamics of everyday life for the southern woman stemmed from this momentous alteration in the character of the labor force of the South.

Four facts were basic to all human experience in seventeenth-century Maryland. First, for most of the period the great majority of inhabitants had been born in what we now call Britain. Population increase in Maryland did not result primarily from births in the colony before the late 1680s and did not produce a predominantly native population of adults before the first decade of the eighteenth century. Second, immigrant men could not expect to live beyond age forty-three, and 70 percent would die before age fifty. Women may have had even shorter lives. Third, perhaps 85 percent of the immigrants, and practically all the unmarried immigrant women, arrived as indentured servants and consequently married late. Family groups were never predominant in the immigration to Maryland and were a significant part for only a brief time at mid-century. Fourth, many more men than women immigrated during the whole period.[1] These facts—immigrant predominance, early death, late marriage, and sexual imbalance—created circumstances of social and demographic disruption that deeply affected family and community life.

We need to assess the effects of this disruption on the experience of women in seventeenth-century Maryland. Were women degraded by the hazards of servitude in a society in which everyone had left community and kin behind and in which women were in short supply? Were traditional restraints on social conduct weakened? If so, were women more exploited or more independent and powerful than women who remained in England? Did any differences from English experience which we can

---

[1] Russell R. Menard, "Economy and Society in Early Colonial Maryland" (Ph.D. diss., University of Iowa, 1975), 153–212, and "Immigrants and Their Increase: The Process of Population Growth in Early Colonial Maryland," in Aubrey C. Land, Lois Green Carr, and Edward C. Papenfuse, eds., *Law, Society, and Politics in Early Maryland* (Baltimore, 1977), 88–110, hereafter cited as Menard, "Immigrants and Their Increase"; Lorena S. Walsh and Russell R. Menard, "Death in the Chesapeake: Two Life Tables for Men in Early Colonial Maryland," *Maryland Historical Magazine*, LXIX (1974), 211–227. In a sample of 806 headrights Menard found only two unmarried women who paid their own passage ("Economy and Society," 187).

"The Planter's Wife: The Experience of White Women in Seventeenth-Century Maryland," by Lois Green Carr and Lorena S. Walsh. From *William and Mary Quarterly*, 34 (1977):542–71. Reprinted by permission of the authors and the publisher.

observe in the experience of Maryland women survive the transformation from an immigrant to a predominantly native-born society with its own kinship networks and community traditions? The tentative argument put forward here is that the answer to all these questions is Yes. There were degrading aspects of servitude, although these probably did not characterize the lot of most women; there were fewer restraints on social conduct, especially in courtship, than in England; women were less protected but also more powerful than those who remained at home; and at least some of these changes survived the appearance in Maryland of New World creole communities. However, these issues are far from settled, and we shall offer some suggestions as to how they might be further pursued.

Maryland was settled in 1634, but in 1650 there were probably no more than six hundred persons and fewer than two hundred adult women in the province. After that time population growth was steady; in 1704 a census listed 30,437 white persons, of whom 7,163 were adult women.[2] Thus in discussing the experience of white women in seventeenth-century Maryland we are dealing basically with the second half of the century.

Marylanders of that period did not leave letters and diaries to record their New World experience or their relationships to one another. Nevertheless, they left trails in the public records that give us clues. Immigrant lists kept in England and documents of the Maryland courts offer quantifiable evidence about the kinds of people who came and some of the problems they faced in making a new life. Especially valuable are the probate court records. Estate inventories reveal the kinds of activities carried on in the house and on the farm, and wills, which are usually the only personal statements that remain for any man or woman, show something of personal attitudes. This essay relies on the most useful of the immigrant lists and all surviving Maryland court records, but concentrates especially on the surviving records of the lower Western Shore, an early-settled area highly suitable for tobacco. Most of this region comprised four counties: St. Mary's, Calvert, Charles, and Prince George's (formed in 1696 from Calvert and Charles). Inventories from all four counties, wills from St. Mary's and Charles, and court proceedings from Charles and Prince George's provide the major data.[3]

Because immigrants predominated, who they were determined much about the character of Maryland society. The best information so far available comes from lists of indentured servants who left the ports of London, Bristol, and Liverpool. These lists vary in quality, but at the very least they distinguish immigrants by sex and general destination. A place of residence in England is usually given, although it may not represent the emigrant's place of origin; and age and occupation are often noted.

[2] Menard, "Immigrants and Their Increase," Fig. 1; William Hand Browne et al., eds., *Archives of Maryland* (Baltimore, 1883–   ), XXV, 256, hereafter cited as *Maryland Archives.*

[3] Court proceedings for St. Mary's and Calvert counties have not survived.

These lists reveal several characteristics of immigrants to the Chesapeake and, by inference, to Maryland.[4]

Servants who arrived under indenture included yeomen, husbandmen, farm laborers, artisans, and small tradesmen, as well as many untrained to any special skill. They were young: over half of the men on the London lists of 1683–1684 were aged eighteen to twenty-two. They were seldom under seventeen or over twenty-eight. The women were a little older; the great majority were between eighteen and twenty-five, and half were aged twenty to twenty-two. Most servants contracted for four or five years service, although those under fifteen were to serve at least seven years.[5] These youthful immigrants represented a wide range of English society. All were seeking opportunities they had not found at home.

However, many immigrants—perhaps about half [6]—did not leave England with indentures but paid for their passage by serving according to the custom of the country. Less is known about their social characteristics, but some inferences are possible. From 1661, customary service was set by Maryland laws that required four-year (later five-year) terms for men and women who were twenty-two years or over at arrival and longer terms for those who were younger. A requirement of these laws enables us to determine something about age at arrival of servants who came

[4] The lists of immigrants are found in John Camden Hotten, ed., *The Original Lists of Persons of Quality; Emigrants; Religious Exiles; Political Rebels; . . . and Others Who Went from Great Britain to the American Plantations, 1600–1700* (London, 1874); William Dodgson Bowman, ed., *Bristol and America: A Record of the First Settlers in the Colonies of North America, 1654–1685* (Baltimore, 1967 [orig. publ. London, 1929]); C. D. P. Nicholson, comp., *Some Early Emigrants to America* (Baltimore, 1965); Michael Ghirelli, ed., *A List of Emigrants to America, 1682–1692* (Baltimore, 1968); and Elizabeth French, ed., *List of Emigrants to America from Liverpool, 1697–1707* (Baltimore, 1962 [orig. publ. Boston, 1913]). Folger Shakespeare Library, MS, V.B. 16 (Washington, D. C.), consists of 66 additional indentures that were originally part of the London records. For studies of these lists see Mildred Campbell, "Social Origins of Some Early Americans," in James Morton Smith, ed., *Seventeenth-Century America: Essays in Colonial History* (Chapel Hill, N.C., 1959), 63–89; David W. Galenson, "'Middling People' or 'Common Sort'?: The Social Origins of Some Early Americans Reexamined," *William and Mary Quarterly* (forthcoming). See also Menard, "Immigrants and Their Increase," Table 4.1, and "Economy and Society," Table VIII–6; and Lorena S. Walsh, "Servitude and Opportunity in Charles County," in Land, Carr, and Papenfuse, eds., *Law, Society, and Politics in Early Maryland*, 112–114, hereafter cited as Walsh, "Servitude and Opportunity."

[5] Campbell, "Social Origins of Some Early Americans," in Smith, ed., *Seventeenth-Century America*, 74–77; Galenson, "'Middling People' or 'Common Sort'?" *WMQ* (forthcoming). When the ages recorded in the London list (Nicholson, comp., *Some Early Emigrants*) and on the Folger Library indentures for servants bound for Maryland and Virginia are combined, 84.5% of the men (N = 354) are found to have been aged 17 to 30, and 54.9% were 18 through 22. Of the women (N = 119), 81.4% were 18 through 25; 10% were older, 8.3% younger, and half (51.2%) immigrated between ages 20 and 22. Russell Menard has generously lent us his abstracts of the London list.

[6] This assumption is defended in Walsh, "Servitude and Opportunity," 129.

without indentures. A planter who wished to obtain more than four or five years of service had to take his servant before the county court to have his or her age judged and a written record made. Servants aged over twenty-one were not often registered, there being no incentive for a master to pay court fees for those who would serve the minimum term. Nevertheless, a comparison of the ages of servants under twenty-two recorded in Charles County, 1658–1689, with those under twenty-two on the London list is revealing. Of Charles County male servants (N = 363), 77.1 percent were aged seventeen or under, whereas on the London list (N = 196), 77.6 percent were eighteen or over. Women registered in Charles County court were somewhat older than the men, but among those under twenty-two (N = 107), 5.5 percent were aged twenty-one, whereas on the London list (N = 69), 46.4 percent had reached this age. Evidently, some immigrants who served by custom were younger than those who came indentured, and this age difference probably characterized the two groups as a whole. Servants who were not only very young but had arrived without the protection of a written contract were possibly of lower social origins than were servants who came under indenture. The absence of skills among Charles County servants who served by custom supports this supposition.[7]

Whatever their status, one fact about immigrant women is certain: many fewer came than men. Immigrant lists, headright lists, and itemizations of servants in inventories show severe imbalance. On a London immigrant list of 1634–1635 men outnumbered women six to one. From the 1650s at least until the 1680s most sources show a ratio of three to one. From then on, all sources show some, but not great, improvement. Among immigrants from Liverpool over the years 1697–1707 the ratio was just under two and one half to one.[8]

Why did not more women come? Presumably, fewer wished to leave family and community to venture into a wilderness. But perhaps more important, women were not as desirable as men to merchants and planters who were making fortunes raising and marketing tobacco, a crop that requires large amounts of labor. The gradual improvement in the sex ratio among servants toward the end of the century may have been the result of a change in recruiting the needed labor. In the late 1660s the supply of young men willing to emigrate stopped increasing sufficiently to meet the labor demands of a growing Chesapeake population. Merchants who recruited servants for planters turned to other sources, and among these sources were women. They did not crowd the ships arriving in the Chesapeake, but their numbers did increase.[9]

[7] *Ibid.*, 112–114, describes the legislation and the Charles County data base. There is some reason to believe that by 1700, young servants had contracts more often than earlier. Figures from the London list include the Folger Library indentures.
[8] Menard, "Immigrants and Their Increase," Table I.
[9] Menard, "Economy and Society," 336–356; Lois Green Carr and Russell R. Menard, "Servants and Freedmen in Early Colonial Maryland," in Thad W. Tate and David A. Ammerman, eds., *Essays on the Chesapeake in the Seventeenth Century* (Chapel Hill, N.C., forthcoming); E. A. Wrigley, "Family Limitation in Pre-Industrial England," *Economic History Review*, 2d Ser., XIX (1966), 82–109; Michael Drake,

To ask the question another way, why did women come? Doubtless, most came to get a husband, an objective virtually certain of success in a land where women were so far outnumbered. The promotional literature, furthermore, painted bright pictures of the life that awaited men and women once out of their time; and various studies suggest that for a while, at least, the promoters were not being entirely fanciful. Until the 1660s, and to a less degree the 1680s, the expanding economy of Maryland and Virginia offered opportunities well beyond those available in England to men without capital and to the women who became their wives.[10]

Nevertheless, the hazards were also great, and the greatest was untimely death. Newcomers promptly became ill, probably with malaria, and many died. What proportion survived is unclear; so far no one has devised a way of measuring it. Recurrent malaria made the woman who survived seasoning less able to withstand other diseases, especially dysentery and influenza. She was especially vulnerable when pregnant. Expectation of life for everyone was low in the Chesapeake, but especially so for women.[11] A woman who had immigrated to Maryland took an extra risk, though perhaps a risk not greater than she might have suffered by moving from her village to London instead.[12]

The majority of women who survived seasoning paid their transportation costs by working for a four- or five-year term of service. The kind of work depended on the status of the family they served. A female servant of a small planter—who through about the 1670s might have had a servant [13]—probably worked at the hoe. Such a man could not afford to buy labor that would not help with the cash crop. In wealthy families women probably were household servants, although some are occasionally listed in inventories of well-to-do planters as living on the quarters—that is, on plantations other than the dwelling plantation. Such women saved men the jobs of preparing food and washing linen but doubtless also

---

"An Elementary Exercise in Parish Register Demography," *ibid.*, XIV (1962), 427–445; J. D. Chambers, *Population, Economy, and Society in Pre-Industrial England* (London, 1972).

[10] John Hammond, *Leah and Rachel, or, the Two Fruitfull Sisters Virginia and Maryland . . .* , and George Alsop, *A Character of the Province of Mary-land . . . .* in Clayton Colman Hall, ed., *Narratives of Early Maryland, 1633–1684*, Original Narratives of Early American History (New York, 1910), 281–308, 340–387; Russell R. Menard, P. M. G. Harris, and Lois Green Carr, "Opportunity and Inequality: The Distribution of Wealth on the Lower Western Shore of Maryland, 1638–1705," *Md. Hist. Mag.*, LXIX (1974), 169–184; Russell R. Menard, "From Servant to Freeholder: Status Mobility and Property Accumulation in Seventeenth-Century Maryland," *WMQ*, 3d Ser., XXX (1973), 37–64; Carr and Menard, "Servants and Freedmen," in Tate and Ammerman, eds., *Essays on the Chesapeake;* Walsh, "Servitude and Opportunity," 111–133.

[11] Walsh and Menard, "Death in the Chesapeake," *Md. Hist. Mag.*, LXIX (1974), 211–227; Darrett B. and Anita H. Rutman, "Of Agues and Fevers: Malaria in the Early Chesapeake," *WMQ*, 3d Ser., XXXIII (1976), 31–60.

[12] E. A. Wrigley, *Population and History* (New York, 1969), 96–100.

[13] Menard, "Economy and Society," Table VII-5.

worked in the fields.[14] In middling households experience must have varied. Where the number of people to feed and wash for was large, female servants would have had little time to tend the crops.

Tracts that promoted immigration to the Chesapeake region asserted that female servants did not labor in the fields, except "nasty" wenches not fit for other tasks. This implies that most immigrant women expected, or at least hoped, to avoid heavy field work, which English women—at least those above the cottager's status—did not do.[15] What proportion of female servants in Maryland found themselves demeaned by this unaccustomed labor is impossible to say, but this must have been the fate of some. A study of the distribution of female servants among wealth groups in Maryland might shed some light on this question. Nevertheless, we still would not know whether those purchased by the poor or sent to work on a quarter were women whose previous experience suited them for field labor.

An additional risk for the woman who came as a servant was the possibility of bearing a bastard. At least 20 percent of the female servants who came to Charles County between 1658 and 1705 were presented to the county court for this cause.[16] A servant woman could not marry unless someone was willing to pay her master for the term she had left to serve.[17] If a man made her pregnant, she could not marry him unless he could buy her time. Once a woman became free, however, marriage was clearly the usual solution. Only a handful of free women were presented in Charles County for bastardy between 1658 and 1705. Since few free women remained either single or widowed for long, not many were subject to the risk. The hazard of bearing a bastard was a hazard of being a servant.[18]

This high rate of illegitimate pregnancies among servants raises lurid questions. Did men import women for sexual exploitation? Does John Barth's Whore of Dorset have a basis outside his fertile imagination?[19]

14 Lorena S. Walsh, "Charles County, Maryland, 1658–1705: A Study in Chesapeake Political and Social Structure" (Ph.D. diss., Michigan State University, 1977), chap. 4.

15 Hammond, *Leah and Rachel*, and Alsop, *Character of the Province*, in Hall, ed., *Narratives of Maryland*, 281–308, 340–387; Mildred Campbell, *The English Yeoman Under Elizabeth and the Early Stuarts*, Yale Historical Publications (New Haven, Conn., 1942), 255–261; Alan Everitt, "Farm Labourers," in Joan Thirsk, ed., *The Agrarian History of England and Wales, 1540–1640* (Cambridge, 1967), 432.

16 Lorena S. Walsh and Russell R. Menard are preparing an article on the history of illegitimacy in Charles and Somerset counties, 1658–1776.

17 Abbot Emerson Smith, *Colonists in Bondage: White Servitude and Convict Labor in America, 1607–1776* (Chapel Hill, N.C., 1947), 271–273. Marriage was in effect a breach of contract.

18 Lois Green Carr, "County Government in Maryland, 1689–1709" (Ph.D. diss., Harvard University, 1968), text, 267–269, 363. The courts pursued bastardy offenses regardless of the social status of the culprits in order to ensure that the children would not become public charges. Free single women were not being overlooked.

19 John Barth, *The Sot-Weed Factor* (New York, 1960), 429.

In our opinion, the answers are clearly No. Servants were economic investments on the part of planters who needed labor. A female servant in a household where there were unmarried men must have both provided and faced temptation, for the pressures were great in a society in which men outnumbered women by three to one. Nevertheless, the servant woman was in the household to work—to help feed and clothe the family and make tobacco. She was not primarily a concubine.

This point could be established more firmly if we knew more about the fathers of the bastards. Often the culprits were fellow servants or men recently freed but too poor to purchase the woman's remaining time. Sometimes the master was clearly at fault. But often the father is not identified. Some masters surely did exploit their female servants sexually. Nevertheless, masters were infrequently accused of fathering their servants' bastards, and those found guilty were punished as severely as were other men. Community mores did not sanction their misconduct.[20]

A female servant paid dearly for the fault of unmarried pregnancy. She was heavily fined, and if no one would pay her fine, she was whipped. Furthermore, she served an extra twelve to twenty-four months to repay her master for the "trouble of his house" and labor lost, and the fathers often did not share in this payment of damages. On top of all, she might lose the child after weaning unless by then she had become free, for the courts bound out bastard children at very early ages.[21]

English life probably did not offer a comparable hazard to young unmarried female servants. No figures are available to show rates of illegitimacy among those who were subject to the risk,[22] but the female servant was less restricted in England than in the Chesapeake. She did not

[20] This impression is based on Walsh's close reading of Charles County records, Carr's close reading of Prince George's County records, and less detailed examination by both of all other 17th-century Maryland court records.

[21] Walsh, "Charles County, Maryland," chap. 4; Carr, "County Government in Maryland," chap. 4, n. 269. Carr summarizes the evidence from Charles, Prince George's, Baltimore, Talbot, and Somerset counties, 1689–1709, for comparing punishment of fathers and mothers of bastards. Leniency toward fathers varied from county to county and time to time. The length of time served for restitution also varied over place and time, increasing as the century progressed. See Charles County Court and Land Records, MS, L #1, ff. 276–277, Hall of Records, Annapolis, Md. Unless otherwise indicated, all manuscripts cited are at the Hall of Records.

[22] Peter Laslett and Karla Osterveen have calculated illegitimacy ratios—the percentage of bastard births among all births registered—in 24 English parishes, 1581–1810. The highest ratio over the period 1630–1710 was 2.4. Laslett and Osterveen, "Long Term Trends in Bastardy in England; A Study of the Illegitimacy Figures in the Parish Registers and in the Reports of the Registrar General, 1561–1960," *Population Studies*, XXVII (1973), 267. In Somerset County, Maryland, 1666–1694, the illegitimacy ratio ranged from 6.3 to 11.8. Russell R. Menard, "The Demography of Somerset County, Maryland: A Preliminary Report" (paper presented to the Stony Brook Conference on Social History, State University of New York at Stony Brook, June 1975), Table XVI. The absence of figures for the number of women in these places of childbearing age but with no living husband prevents construction of illegitimacy rates.

owe anyone for passage across the Atlantic; hence it was easier for her to marry, supposing she happened to become pregnant while in service. Perhaps, furthermore, her temptations were fewer. She was not 3,000 miles from home and friends, and she lived in a society in which there was no shortage of women. Bastards were born in England in the seventeenth century, but surely not to as many as one-fifth of the female servants.

Some women escaped all or part of their servitude because prospective husbands purchased the remainder of their time. At least one promotional pamphlet published in the 1660s described such purchases as likely, but how often they actually occurred is difficult to determine.[23] Suggestive is a 20 percent difference between the sex ratios found in a Maryland headright sample, 1658–1681, and among servants listed in lower Western Shore inventories for 1658–1679.[24] Some of the discrepancy must reflect the fact that male servants were younger than female servants and therefore served longer terms; hence they had a greater chance of appearing in an inventory. But part of the discrepancy doubtless follows from the purchase of women for wives. Before 1660, when sex ratios were even more unbalanced and the expanding economy enabled men to establish themselves more quickly, even more women may have married before their terms were finished.[25]

Were women sold for wives against their wills? No record says so, but nothing restricted a man from selling his servant to whomever he wished. Perhaps some women were forced into such marriages or accepted them as the least evil. But the man who could afford to purchase a wife —especially a new arrival—was usually already an established landowner.[26] Probably most servant women saw an opportunity in such a marriage. In addition, the shortage of labor gave women some bargaining power. Many masters must have been ready to refuse to sell a woman who was unwilling to marry a would-be purchaser.

If a woman's time was not purchased by a prospective husband, she was virtually certain to find a husband once she was free. Those famous spinsters, Margaret and Mary Brent, were probably almost unique in

[23] Alsop, *Character of the Province*, in Hall, ed., *Narratives of Maryland*, 358.
[24] Maryland Headright Sample, 1658–1681 (N = 625); 257.1 men per 100 women; Maryland Inventories, 1658–1679 (N = 584): 320.1 men per 100 women. Menard, "Immigrants and Their Increase," Table I.
[25] A comparison of a Virginia Headright Sample, 1648–1666 (N = 4,272) with inventories from York and Lower Norfolk counties, 1637–1675 (N = 168) shows less, rather than more, imbalance in inventories as compared to headrights. This indicates fewer purchases of wives than we have suggested for the period after 1660. However, the inventory sample is small.
[26] Only 8% of tenant farmers who left inventories in four Maryland counties of the lower Western Shore owned labor, 1658–1705. St. Mary's City Commission Inventory Project, "Social Stratification in Maryland, 1658–1705" (National Science Foundation Grant GS-32272), hereafter cited as "Social Stratification." This is an analysis of 1,735 inventories recorded from 1658 to 1705 in St. Mary's, Calvert, Charles, and Prince George's counties, which together constitute most of the lower Western Shore of Maryland.

seventeenth-century Maryland. In the four counties of the lower Western Shore only two of the women who left a probate inventory before the eighteenth century are known to have died single.[27] Comely or homely, strong or weak, any young woman was too valuable to be overlooked, and most could find a man with prospects.

The woman who immigrated to Maryland, survived seasoning and service, and gained her freedom became a planter's wife. She had considerable liberty in making her choice. There were men aplenty, and no fathers or brothers were hovering to monitor her behavior or disapprove her preference. This is the modern way of looking at her situation, of course. Perhaps she missed the protection of a father, a guardian, or kinfolk, and the participation in her decision of a community to which she felt ties. There is some evidence that the absence of kin and the pressures of the sex ratio created conditions of sexual freedom in courtship that were not customary in England. A register of marriages and births for seventeenth-century Somerset County shows that about one-third of the immigrant women whose marriages are recorded were pregnant at the time of the ceremony—nearly twice the rate in English parishes.[28] There is no indication of community objection to this freedom so long as marriage took place. No presentments for bridal pregnancy were made in any of the Maryland courts.[29]

The planter's wife was likely to be in her mid-twenties at marriage. An estimate of minimum age at marriage for servant women can be made from lists of indentured servants who left London over the years 1683–1684 and from age judgments in Maryland county court records. If we assume that the 112 female indentured servants going to Maryland and Virginia whose ages are given in the London lists served full four-year terms, then only 1.8 percent married before age twenty, but 68 percent after age twenty-four.[30] Similarly, if the 141 women whose ages were judged in Charles County between 1666 and 1705 served out their terms according to the custom of the country, none married before age twenty-two, and half were twenty-five or over.[31] When adjustments are made for the ages at which wives may have been purchased, the figures drop, but even so the majority of women waited until at least age twenty-four

---

[27] Sixty women left inventories. The status of five is unknown. The two who died single died in 1698. Menard, "Immigrants and Their Increase," Table I.

[28] Menard, "Demography of Somerset County," Table XVII; Daniel Scott Smith and Michael S. Hindus, "Premarital Pregnancy in America, 1640–1971: An Overview," *Journal of Interdisciplinary History*, V (1975), 541. It was also two to three times the rate found in New England in the late 17th century.

[29] In Maryland any proceedings against pregnant brides could have been brought only in the civil courts. No vestries were established until 1693, and their jurisdiction was confined to the admonishment of men and women suspected of fornication unproved by the conception of a child. Churchwardens were to inform the county court of bastardies. Carr, "County Government in Maryland," text, 148–149, 221–223.

[30] The data are from Nicholson, comp., *Some Early Emigrants*.

[31] Charles County Court and Land Records, MSS, C #1 through B #2.

to marry.[32] Actual age at marriage in Maryland can be found for few seventeenth-century female immigrants, but observations for Charles and Somerset counties place the mean age at about twenty-five.[33]

Because of the age at which an immigrant woman married, the number of children she would bear her husband was small. She had lost up to ten years of her childbearing life [34]—the possibility of perhaps four or five children, given the usual rhythm of childbearing.[35] At the same time, high mortality would reduce both the number of children she would bear over the rest of her life and the number who would live. One partner to a marriage was likely to die within seven years, and the chances were only one in three that a marriage would last ten years.[36] In these circumstances, most women would not bear more than three or four children—not counting those stillborn—to any one husband, plus a posthumous child were she the survivor. The best estimates suggest that nearly a quarter, perhaps more, of the children born alive died during their first year and that 40 to 55 percent would not live to see age twenty.[37] Con-

[32] Available ages at arrival are as follows:

Age	under																		
	12	13	14	15	16	17	18	19	20	21	22	23	24	25	26	27	28	29	30
Indentured (1682–1687)			1	1	6	2	9	9	8	29	19	6	5	6	2	3	1	2	3
Unindentured (1666-1705)	8	5	12	4	7	18	16	13	34	9	11	2	1	1					

Terms of service for women without indentures from 1666 on were 5 years if they were aged 22 at arrival; 6 years if 18–21; 7 years if 15–17; and until 22 if under 15. From 1661 to 1665 these terms were shorter by a year, and women under 15 served until age 21. If we assume that (1) indentured women served 4 years; (2) they constituted half the servant women; (3) women under age 12 were not purchased as wives; (4) 20% of women aged 12 or older were purchased; and (5) purchases were spread evenly over the possible years of service, then from 1666, 73.9% were 23 or older at marriage, and 66.0% were 24 or older; 70.8% were 23 or older from 1661 to 1665, and 55.5% were 24 or older. Mean ages at eligibility for marriage, as calculated by dividing person-years by the number of women, were 24.37 from 1666 on and 23.42 from 1661 to 1665. All assumptions except (3) and (5) are discussed above. The third is made on the basis that native girls married as young as age 12.

[33] Walsh, "Charles County, Maryland," chap. 2; Menard, "Demography of Somerset County," Tables XI, XII.

[34] The impact of later marriages is best demonstrated with age-specific marital fertility statistics. Susan L. Norton reports that women in colonial Ipswich, Massachusetts, bore an average of 7.5 children if they married between ages 15 and 19; 7.1 if they married between 20 and 24; and 4.5 if they married after 24. Norton, "Population Growth in Colonial America: A Study of Ipswich, Massachusetts," *Pop. Studies*, XXV (1971), 444. Cf. Wrigley, "Family Limitation in Pre-Industrial England," *Econ. Hist. Rev.*, 2d Ser., XIX (1966), 82–109.

[35] In Charles County the mean interval between first and second and subsequent births was 30.8, and the median was 27.3 months. Walsh, "Charles County, Maryland," chap. 2. Menard has found that in Somerset County, Maryland, the median birth intervals for immigrant women between child 1 and child 2, child 2 and child 3, child 3 and child 4, and child 4 and child 5 were 26, 26, 30, 27 months, respectively ("Demography of Somerset County," Table XX).

[36] Walsh, "Charles County, Maryland," chap. 2.

[37] Walsh and Menard, "Death in the Chesapeake," *Md. Hist. Mag.*, LXIX (1974), 222.

sequently, one of her children would probably die in infancy, and another one or two would fail to reach adulthood. Wills left in St. Mary's County during the seventeenth century show the results. In 105 families over the years 1660 to 1680 only twelve parents left more than three children behind them, including those conceived but not yet born. The average number was 2.3, nearly always minors, some of whom might die before reaching adulthood.[38]

For the immigrant woman, then, one of the major facts of life was that although she might bear a child about every two years, nearly half would not reach maturity. The social implications of this fact are far-reaching. Because she married late in her childbearing years and because so many of her children would die young, the number who would reach marriageable age might not replace, or might only barely replace, her and her husband or husbands as child-producing members of the society. Con-sequently, so long as immigrants were heavily predominant in the adult female population, Maryland could not grow much by natural increase.[39] It remained a land of newcomers.

This fact was fundamental to the character of seventeenth-century Maryland society, although its implications have yet to be fully explored. Settlers came from all parts of England and hence from differing traditions —in types of agriculture, forms of landholding and estate management, kinds of building construction, customary contributions to community needs, and family arrangements, including the role of women. The neces-sities of life in the Chesapeake required all immigrants to make adaptations. But until the native-born became predominant, a securely established Maryland tradition would not guide or restrict the newcomers.

If the immigrant woman had remained in England, she would prob-ably have married at about the same age or perhaps a little later.[40] But the social consequences of marriage at these ages in most parts of England were probably different. More children may have lived to maturity, and

[38] Menard, using all Maryland wills, found a considerably lower number of children per family in a similar period: 1.83 in wills probated 1660–1665; 2.20 in wills pro-bated 1680–1684 ("Economy and Society," 198). Family reconstitution not sur-prisingly produces slightly higher figures, since daughters are often underrecorded in wills but are recorded as frequently as sons in birth registers. In 17th-century Charles County the mean size of all reconstituted families was 2.75. For marriages contracted in the years 1658–1669 (N = 118), 1670–1679 (N = 79), and 1680–1689 (N = 95), family size was 3.15, 2.58, and 2.86, respectively. In Somerset County, family size for immigrant marriages formed between 1665 and 1695 (N = 41) was 3.9. Walsh, "Charles County, Maryland," chap. 2; Menard, "Demography of Somer-set County," Table XXI.

[39] For fuller exposition of the process see Menard, "Immigrants and Their Increase."

[40] P. E. Razell, "Population Change in Eighteenth-Century England. A Reinterpreta-tion," Econ. Hist. Rev., 2d Ser., XVIII (1965), 315, cites mean age at marriage as 23.76 years for 7,242 women in Yorkshire, 1662–1714, and 24.6 years for 280 women of Wiltshire, Berkshire, Hampshire, and Dorset, 1615–1621. Peter Laslett, The World We Have Lost: England before the Industrial Age, 2d ed. (London, 1971), 86, shows a mean age of 23.58 for 1,007 women in the Diocese of Canterbury, 1619–1690. Wrigley, "Family Limitation in Pre-Industrial England," Econ. Hist. Rev., 2d Ser., XIX (1966), 87, shows mean ages at marriage for 259 women in Colyton, Devon, ranging from 26.15 to 30.0 years, 1600–1699.

even where mortality was as high newcomers are not likely to have been the main source of population growth.[41] The locally born would still dominate the community, its social organization, and its traditions. However, where there were exceptions, as perhaps in London, late age at marriage, combined with high mortality and heavy immigration, may have had consequences in some ways similar to those we have found in Maryland.

A hazard of marriage for seventeenth-century women everywhere was death in childbirth, but this hazard may have been greater than usual in the Chesapeake. Whereas in most societies women tend to outlive men, in this malaria-ridden area it is probable that men outlived women. Hazards of childbirth provide the likely reason that Chesapeake women died so young. Once a woman in the Chesapeake reached forty-five, she tended to outlive men who reached the same age. Darrett and Anita Rutman have found malaria a probable cause of an exceptionally high death rate among pregnant women, who are, it appears, peculiarly vulnerable to that disease.[42]

This argument, however, suggests that immigrant women may have lived longer than their native-born daughters, although among men the opposite was true. Life tables created for men in Maryland show that those native-born who survived to age twenty could expect a life span three to ten years longer than that of immigrants, depending upon the region where they lived. The reason for the improvement was doubtless immunities to local diseases developed in childhood.[43] A native woman developed these immunities, but, as we shall see, she also married earlier than immigrant women usually could and hence had more children.[44] Thus she was more exposed to the hazards of childbirth and may have died a little sooner. Unfortunately, the life tables for immigrant women that would settle this question have so far proved impossible to construct.

However long they lived, immigrant women in Maryland tended to outlive their husbands—in Charles County, for example, by a ratio of two

[41] For a brief discussion of Chesapeake and English mortality see Walsh and Menard, "Death in the Chesapeake," *Md. Hist. Mag.*, LXIX (1974), 224–225.

[42] George W. Barclay, *Techniques of Population Analysis* (New York, 1958), 136n; Darrett B. and Anita H. Rutman, " 'Now-Wives and Sons-in-Law': Parental Death in a Seventeenth-Century Virginia County," in Tate and Ammerman, eds., *Essays on the Chesapeake*; Rutman and Rutman, "Of Agues and Fevers," *WMQ*, 3d Ser., XXXIII (1976), 31–60. Cf. Peter H. Wood, *Black Majority: Negroes in Colonial South Carolina from 1670 through the Stono Rebellion* (New York, 1974), chap. 3.

[43] Walsh and Menard, "Death in the Chesapeake," *Md. Hist. Mag.*, LXIX (1974), 211–227; Menard, "Demography of Somerset County."

[44] In Charles County immigrant women who ended childbearing years or died before 1705 bore a mean of 3.5 children (N = 59); the mean for natives was 5.1 (N = 42). Mean completed family size in Somerset County for marriages contracted between 1665 and 1695 was higher, but the immigrant–native differential remains. Immigrant women (N = 17) bore 6.1 children, while native women (N = 16) bore 9.4. Walsh, "Charles County, Maryland," chap. 2; Menard, "Demography of Somerset County," Table XXI.

to one. This was possible, despite the fact that women were younger than men at death, because women were also younger than men at marriage. Some women were widowed with no living children, but most were left responsible for two or three. These were often tiny, and nearly always not yet sixteen.[45]

This fact had drastic consequences, given the physical circumstances of life. People lived at a distance from one another, not even in villages, much less towns. The widow had left her kin 3,000 miles across an ocean, and her husband's family was also there. She would have to feed her children and make her own tobacco crop. Though neighbors might help, heavy labor would be required of her if she had no servants, until—what admittedly was usually not difficult——she acquired a new husband.

In this situation dying husbands were understandably anxious about the welfare of their families. Their wills reflected their feelings and tell something of how they regarded their wives. In St. Mary's and Charles counties during the seventeenth century, little more than one-quarter of the men left their widows with no more than the dower the law required —one-third of his land for her life, plus outright ownership of one-third of his personal property. (See Table I.) If there were no children, a man almost always left his widow his whole estate. Otherwise there were a variety of arrangements. (See Table II.)

During the 1660s, when testators begin to appear in quantity, nearly a fifth of the men who had children left all to their wives, trusting them to see that the children received fair portions. Thus in 1663 John Shircliffe willed his whole estate to his wife "towards the maintenance of herself and my children into whose tender care I do Commend them Desireing

TABLE I

BEQUESTS OF HUSBANDS TO WIVES, ST. MARY'S AND
CHARLES COUNTIES, MARYLAND, 1640 TO 1710

		Dower or Less	
	N	N	%
1640s	6	2	34
1650s	24	7	29
1660s	65	18	28
1670s	86	21	24
1680s	64	17	27
1690s	83	23	28
1700s	74	25	34
Totals	402	113	28

Source: Wills, I–XIV, Hall of Records, Annapolis, Md.

[45] Among 1735 decedents who left inventories on Maryland's lower Western Shore, 1658–1705, 72% died without children or with children not yet of age. Only 16% could be proved to have a child of age. "Social Stratification."

TABLE II

BEQUESTS OF HUSBANDS TO WIVES WITH CHILDREN, ST. MARY'S AND
CHARLES COUNTIES, MARYLAND, 1640 TO 1710

	N	All Estate		All or Dwelling Plantation for Life		All or Dwelling Plantation for Widowhood		All or Dwelling Plantation for Minority of Child		More than Dower in Other Form		Dower or Less or Unknown	
		N	%	N	%	N	%	N	%	N	%	N	%
1640s	3	1	33	33								2	67
1650s	16	1	6	2	13	1	6	1	6	4	25	7	44
1660s	45	8	18	8	18	2	4	3	7	9	20	15	33
1670s	61	4	7	21	34	2	3	3	5	13	21	18	30
1680s	52	5	10	19	37	2	4	2	4	11	21	13	25
1690s	69	1	1	31	45	7	10	2	3	10	14	18	26
1700s	62			20	32	6	10	2	3	14	23	20	32
Totals	308	20	6	101	33	20	6	13	4	61	20	93	30

Source: Wills, I–XIV.

to see them brought up in the fear of God and the Catholick Religion and Chargeing them to be Dutiful and obedient to her." [46] As the century progressed, husbands tended instead to give the wife all or a major part of the estate for her life, and to designate how it should be distributed after her death. Either way, the husband put great trust in his widow, considering that he knew she was bound to remarry. Only a handful of men left estates to their wives only for their term of widowhood or until the children came of age. When a man did not leave his wife a life estate, he often gave her land outright or more than her dower third of his movable property. Such bequests were at the expense of his children and showed his concern that his widow should have a maintenance which young children could not supply.

A husband usually made his wife his executor and thus responsible for paying his debts and preserving the estate. Only 11 percent deprived their wives of such powers. [47] In many instances, however, men also appointed overseers to assist their wives and to see that their children were not abused or their property embezzled. Danger lay in the fact that a second husband acquired control of all his wife's property, including her life estate in the property of his predecessor. Over half of the husbands who died in the 1650s and 1660s appointed overseers to ensure that their wills were followed. Some trusted to the overseers' "Care and

[46] Wills, I, 172.

[47] From 1640 to 1710, 17% of the married men named no executor. In such cases, the probate court automatically gave executorship to the wife unless she requested someone else to act.

good Conscience for the good of my widow and fatherless children."
Others more explicitly made overseers responsible for seeing that "my
said child . . . and the other [expected child] (when pleases God to send
it) may have their right Proportion of my Said Estate and that the said
Children may be bred up Chiefly in the fear of God." [48] A few men—but
remarkably few—authorized overseers to remove children from households of stepfathers who abused them or wasted their property.[49] On the
whole, the absence of such provisions for the protection of the children
points to the husband's overriding concern for the welfare of his widow
and to his confidence in her management, regardless of the certainty of
her remarriage. Evidently, in the politics of family life women enjoyed
great respect.[50]

We have implied that this respect was a product of the experience of
immigrants in the Chesapeake. Might it have been instead a reflection of
English culture? Little work is yet in print that allows comparison of the
provisions for Maryland widows with those made for the widows of
English farmers. Possibly, Maryland husbands were making traditional
wills which could have been written in the communities they left behind.
However, Margaret Spufford's recent study of three Cambridgeshire
villages in the late sixteenth century and early seventeenth century suggests a different pattern. In one of these villages, Chippenham, women
usually did receive a life interest in the property, but in the other two they
did not. If the children were all minors, the widow controlled the property until the oldest son came of age, and then only if she did not remarry.
In the majority of cases adult sons were given control of the property
with instructions for the support of their mothers. Spufford suggests that
the pattern found in Chippenham must have been very exceptional. On
the basis of village censuses in six other counties, dating from 1624 to
1724, which show only 3 percent of widowed people heading households
that included a married child, she argues that if widows commonly controlled the farm, a higher proportion should have headed such households.
However, she also argues that widows with an interest in land would not
long remain unmarried.[51] If so, the low percentage may be deceptive.
More direct work with wills needs to be done before we can be sure that
Maryland husbands and fathers gave their widows greater control of
property and family than did their English counterparts.

Maryland men trusted their widows, but this is not to say that many
did not express great anxiety about the future of their children. They
asked both wives and overseers to see that the children received "some

[48] Wills, I, 96, 69.

[49] *Ibid.*, 193–194, 167, V, 82. The practice of appointing overseers ceased around the
end of the century. From 1690 to 1710, only 13% of testators who made their wives
executors appointed overseers.

[50] We divided wills according to whether decedents were immigrant, native born, or
of unknown origins, and found no differences in patterns of bequests, choice of
executors, or tendency to appoint overseers. No change occurred in 17th-century
Maryland in these respects as a native-born population began to appear.

[51] Margaret Spufford, *Contrasting Communities: English Villagers in the Sixteenth
and Seventeenth Centuries* (Cambridge, 1974), 85–90, 111–118, 161–164.

learning." Robert Sly made his wife sole guardian of his children but admonished her "to take due Care that they be brought up in the true fear of God and instructed in such Literature as may tend to their improvement." Widowers, whose children would be left without any parent, were often the most explicit in prescribing their upbringing. Robert Cole, a middling planter, directed that his children "have such Education in Learning as [to] write and read and Cast accompt I mean my three Sonnes my two daughters to learn to read and sew with their needle and all of them to be keept from Idleness but not to be keept as Comon Servants." John Lawson required his executors to see that his two daughters be reared together, receive learning and sewing instruction, and be "brought up to huswifery." [52] Often present was the fear that orphaned children would be treated as servants and trained only to work in the fields.[53] With stepfathers in mind, many fathers provided that their sons should be independent before the usual age of majority, which for girls was sixteen but for men twenty-one. Sometimes fathers willed that their sons should inherit when they were as young as sixteen, though more often eighteen. The sons could then escape an incompatible stepfather, who could no longer exploit their labor or property. If a son was already close to age sixteen, the father might bind him to his mother until he reached majority or his mother died, whichever came first. If she lived, she could watch out for his welfare, and his labor could contribute to her support. If she died, he and his property would be free from a stepfather's control.[54]

What happened to widows and children if a man died without leaving a will? There was great need for some community institution that could protect children left fatherless or parentless in a society where they usually had no other kin. By the 1660s the probate court and county orphans' courts were supplying this need.[55] If a man left a widow, the probate court—in Maryland a central government agency—usually appointed her or her new husband administrator of the estate with power to pay its creditors under court supervision. Probate procedures provided a large measure of protection. These required an inventory of the movable property and careful accounting of all disbursements, whether or not a man had left a will. William Hollis of Baltimore County, for example, had three stepfathers in seven years, and only the care of the judge of probate prevented the third stepfather from paying the debts of the second with goods that had belonged to William's father. As the judge remarked, William had "an uncareful mother." [56]

Once the property of an intestate had been fully accounted and creditors paid, the county courts appointed a guardian who took charge

[52] Wills, I, 422, 182, 321.

[53] For example, *ibid.*, 172, 182.

[54] Lorena S. Walsh, " 'Till Death Do Us Part': Marriage and Family in Charles County, Maryland, 1658–1705," in Tate and Ammerman, eds., *Essays on the Chesapeake.*

[55] The following discussion of the orphans' court is based on Lois Green Carr, "The Development of the Maryland Orphans' Court, 1654–1715," in Land, Carr, and Papenfuse, eds., *Law, Society, and Politics in Early Maryland*, 41–61.

[56] Baltimore County Court Proceedings, D, ff. 385–386.

of the property and gave bond to the children with sureties that he or she would not waste it. If the mother were living, she could be the guardian, or if she had remarried, her new husband would act. Through most of the century bond was waived in these circumstances, but from the 1690s security was required of all guardians, even of mothers. Thereafter the courts might actually take away an orphan's property from a widow or stepfather if she or he could not find sureties—that is, neighbors who judged the parent responsible and hence were willing to risk their own property as security. Children without any parents were assigned new families, who at all times found surety if there were property to manage. If the orphans inherited land, English common law allowed them to choose guardians for themselves at age fourteen—another escape hatch for children in conflict with stepparents. Orphans who had no property, or whose property was insufficient to provide an income that could maintain them, were expected to work for their guardians in return for their maintenance. Every year the county courts were expected to check on the welfare of orphans of intestate parents and remove them or their property from guardians who abused them or misused their estates. From 1681, Maryland law required that a special jury be impaneled once a year to report neighborhood knowledge of mistreatment of orphans and hear complaints.

This form of community surveillance of widows and orphans proved quite effective. In 1696 the assembly declared that orphans of intestates were often better cared for than orphans of testators. From that time forward, orphans' courts were charged with supervision of all orphans and were soon given powers to remove any guardians who were shown false to their trusts, regardless of the arrangements laid down in a will. The assumption was that the deceased parent's main concern was the welfare of the child, and that the orphans' court, as "father to us poor orphans," should implement the parent's intent. In actual fact, the courts never removed children—as opposed to their property—from a household in which the mother was living, except to apprentice them at the mother's request. These powers were mainly exercised over guardians of orphans both of whose parents were dead. The community as well as the husband believed the mother most capable of nurturing his children.

Remarriage was the usual and often the immediate solution for a woman who had lost her husband.[57] The shortage of women made any woman eligible to marry again, and the difficulties of raising a family while running a plantation must have made remarriage necessary for widows who had no son old enough to make tobacco. One indication of the high incidence of remarriage is the fact that there were only sixty women, almost all of them widows, among the 1,735 people who left probate inventories in four southern Maryland counties over the second half of the century.[58] Most other women must have died while married and therefore legally without property to put through probate.

---

[57] In 17th-century Charles County two-thirds of surviving partners remarried within a year of their spouse's death. Walsh, "Charles County, Maryland," chap. 2.

[58] See n. 26.

One result of remarriage was the development of complex family structures. Men found themselves responsible for stepchildren as well as their own offspring, and children acquired half-sisters and half-brothers. Sometimes a woman married a second husband who himself had been previously married, and both brought children of former spouses to the new marriage. They then produced children of their own. The possibilities for conflict over the upbringing of children are evident, and crowded living conditions, found even in the households of the wealthy, must have added to family tensions. Luckily, the children of the family very often had the same mother. In Charles County, at least, widows took new husbands three times more often than widowers took new wives.[59] The role of the mother in managing the relationships of half-brothers and half-sisters or stepfathers and stepchildren must have been critical to family harmony.

Early death in this immigrant population thus had broad effects on Maryland society in the seventeenth century. It produced what we might call a pattern of serial polyandry, which enabled more men to marry and to father families than the sex ratios otherwise would have permitted. It produced thousands of orphaned children who had no kin to maintain them or preserve their property, and thus gave rise to an institution almost unknown in England, the orphans' court, which was charged with their protection. And early death, by creating families in which the mother was the unifying element, may have increased her authority within the household.

When the immigrant woman married her first husband, there was usually no property settlement involved, since she was unlikely to have any dowry. But her remarriage was another matter. At the very least, she owned or had a life interest in a third of her former husband's estate. She needed also to think of her children's interests. If she remarried, she would lose control of the property. Consequently, property settlements occasionally appear in the seventeenth-century court records between widows and their future husbands. Sometimes she and her intended signed an agreement whereby he relinquished his rights to the use of her children's portions. Sometimes he deeded to her property which she could dispose of at her pleasure.[60] Whether any of these agreements or gifts would have survived a test in court is unknown. We have not yet found any challenged. Generally speaking, the formal marriage settlements of English law, which bypassed the legal difficulties of the married woman's inability to make a contract with her husband, were not adopted by immigrants, most of whom probably came from levels of English society that did not use these legal formalities.

The wife's dower rights in her husband's estate were a recognition of her role in contributing to his prosperity, whether by the property she had brought to the marriage or by the labor she performed in his household. A woman newly freed from servitude would not bring property, but the benefits of her labor would be great. A man not yet prosperous enough to own a servant might need his wife's help in the fields as well

[59] Walsh, " 'Till Death Do Us Part,' " in Tate and Ammerman, eds., *Essays on the Chesapeake*.
[60] *Ibid*.

as in the house, especially if he were paying rent or still paying for land.
Moreover, food preparation was so time-consuming that even if she
worked only at household duties, she saved him time he needed for making
tobacco and corn. The corn, for example, had to be pounded in the
mortar or ground in a handmill before it could be used to make bread,
for there were very few water mills in seventeenth-century Maryland.
The wife probably raised vegetables in a kitchen garden; she also milked
the cows and made butter and cheese, which might produce a salable
surplus. She washed the clothes, and made them if she had the skill. When
there were servants to do field work, the wife undoubtedly spent her
time entirely in such household tasks. A contract of 1681 expressed such
a division of labor. Nicholas Maniere agreed to live on a plantation with
his wife and child and a servant. Nicholas and the servant were to work
the land; his wife was to "Dresse the Victualls milk the Cowes wash for
the servants and Doe allthings necessary for a woman to doe upon the
s[ai]d plantation." [61]

We have suggested that wives did field work; the suggestion is
supported by occasional direct references in the court records. Mary
Castleton, for example, told the judge of probate that "her husband late
Deceased in his Life time had Little to sustaine himselfe and Children but
what was produced out of ye ground by ye hard Labour of her the said
Mary." [62] Household inventories provide indirect evidence. Before about
1680 those of poor men and even middling planters on Maryland's lower
Western Shore—the bottom two-thirds of the married decedents—[63] show
few signs of household industry, such as appear in equivalent English
estates.[64] Sheep and woolcards, flax and hackles, and spinning wheels all
were a rarity, and such things as candle molds were nonexistent. Women
in these households must have been busy at other work. In households
with bound labor the wife doubtless was fully occupied preparing food
and washing clothes for family and hands. But the wife in a household
too poor to afford bound labor—the bottom fifth of the married decedent
group—might well tend tobacco when she could.[65] Eventually, the profits

---

[61] *Maryland Archives*, LXX, 87. See also *ibid.*, XLI, 210, 474, 598, for examples of
allusions to washing clothes and dairying activities. Water mills were so scarce that
in 1669 the Maryland assembly passed an act permitting land to be condemned for
the use of anyone willing to build and operate a water mill. *Ibid.*, II, 211–214. In the
whole colony only four condemnations were carried out over the next 10 years.
Ibid., LI, 25, 57, 86, 381. Probate inventories show that most households had a mortar
and pestle or a hand mill.

[62] Testamentary Proceedings, X, 184–185. Cf. Charles County Court and Land Records, MS, I #1, ff. 9–10, 259.

[63] Among married decedents before 1680 (N = 308), the bottom two-thirds (N =
212) were those worth less than £150. Among all decedents worth less than £150
(N = 451), only 12 (about 3%) had sheep or yarn-making equipment, "Social
Stratification."

[64] See Everitt, "Farm Labourers," in Thirsk, ed., *Agrarian History of England and
Wales*, 422–426, and W. G. Hoskins, *Essays in Leicestershire History* (Liverpool,
1950, 134.

[65] Among married decedents, the bottom fifth were approximately those worth less
than £30. Before 1680 these were 17% of the married decedents. By the end of the

of her labor might enable the family to buy a servant, making greater profits possible. From such beginnings many families climbed the economic ladder in seventeenth-century Maryland.[66]

The proportion of servantless households must have been larger than is suggested by the inventories of the dead, since young men were less likely to die than old men and had had less time to accumulate property. Well over a fifth of the households of married men on the lower Western Shore may have had no bound labor. Not every wife in such households would necessarily work at the hoe—saved from it by upbringing, ill-health, or the presence of small children who needed her care—but many women performed such work. A lease of 1691, for example, specified that the lessee could farm the amount of land which "he his wife and children can tend." [67]

Stagnation of the tobacco economy, beginning about 1680, produced changes that had some effect on women's economic role.[68] As shown by inventories of the lower Western Shore, home industry increased, especially at the upper ranges of the economic spectrum. In these households women were spinning yarn and knitting it into clothing.[69] The increase in such activity was far less in the households of the bottom fifth, where changes of a different kind may have increased the pressures to grow tobacco. Fewer men at this level could now purchase land, and a portion of their crop went for rent.[70] At this level, more wives than before may

---

period, from 1700 to 1705, they were 22%. Before 1680, 92% had no bound labor. From 1700 to 1705, 95% had none. Less than 1% of all estates in this wealth group had sheep or yarn-making equipment before 1681. "Social Stratification."

[66] On opportunity to raise from the bottom to the middle see Menard, "From Servant to Freeholder," *WMQ*, 3d Ser., **XXX** (1973), 37–64; Walsh, "Servitude and Opportunity," 111–133, and Menard, Harris, and Carr, "Opportunity and Inequality," *Md. Hist. Mag.*, LXIX (1974), 169–184.

[67] Charles County Court and Land Records, MS, R #1, f. 193.

[68] For 17th-century economic development see Menard, Harris, and Carr, "Opportunity and Inequality," *Md. Hist. Mag.*, LXIX (1974), 169–184.

[69] Among estates worth £150 or more, signs of diversification in this form appeared in 22% before 1681 and in 67% after 1680. Over the years 1700–1705, the figure was 62%. Only 6% of estates worth less than £40 had such signs of diversification after 1680 or over the period 1700–1705. Knitting rather than weaving is assumed because looms were very rare. These figures are for all estates. "Social Stratification."

[70] After the mid-1670s information about landholdings of decedents becomes increasingly available, making firm estimates of the increase in tenancy difficult. However, for householders in life cycle 2 (married or widowed decedents who died without children of age) the following table is suggestive. Householding decedents in life cycle 2 worth less than £40 (N = 255) were 21% of all decedents in this category (N = 1,218).

	£0–19				£20–39			
	Deced-ents	Land Unkn.	With Land	With Land	Deced-ents	Land Unkn.	With Land	With Land
	N	N	N	%	N	N	N	%
To 1675	10	0	7	70	34	2	29	91
1675 on	98	22	40	53	113	16	64	66

In computing percentages, unknowns have been distributed according to knowns.

have been helping to produce tobacco when they could. And by this time they were often helping as a matter of survival, not as a means of improving the family position.

So far we have considered primarily the experience of immigrant women. What of their daughters? How were their lives affected by the demographic stresses of Chesapeake society?

One of the most important points in which the experience of daughters differed from that of their mothers was the age at which they married. In this woman-short world, the mothers had married as soon as they were eligible, but they had not usually become eligible until they were mature women in their middle twenties. Their daughters were much younger at marriage. A vital register kept in Somerset County shows that some girls married at age twelve and that the mean age at marriage for those born before 1670 was sixteen and a half years.

Were some of these girls actually child brides? It seems unlikely that girls were married before they had become capable of bearing children. Culturally, such a practice would fly in the face of English, indeed Western European, precedent, nobility excepted. Nevertheless, the number of girls who married before age sixteen, the legal age of inheritance for girls, is astonishing. Their English counterparts ordinarily did not marry until their mid- to late twenties or early thirties. In other parts of the Chesapeake, historians have found somewhat higher ages at marriage than appear in Somerset, but everywhere in seventeenth-century Maryland and Virginia most native-born women married before they reached age twenty-one.[71] Were such early marriages a result of the absence of fathers? Evidently not. In Somerset County, the fathers of very young brides—those under sixteen—were usually living.[72] Evidently, guardians were unlikely to allow such marriages, and this fact suggests that they were not entirely approved. But the shortage of women imposed strong pressures to marry as early as possible.

Not only did native girls marry early, but many of them were pregnant before the ceremony. Bridal pregnancy among native-born women was not as common as among immigrants. Nevertheless, in seventeenth-century Somerset County 20 percent of native brides bore children within eight and one half months of marriage. This was a somewhat higher

---

A man who died with a child of age was almost always a landowner, but these were a small proportion of all decedents (see n. 45).

Several studies provide indisputable evidence of an increase in tenancy on the lower Western Shore over the period 1660–1706. These compare heads of households with lists of landowners compiled from rent rolls made in 1659 and 1704–1706. Tenancy in St. Mary's and Charles counties in 1660 was about 10%. In St. Mary's, Charles, and Prince George's counties, 1704–1706, 30–35% of householders were tenants. Russell R. Menard, "Population Growth and Land Distribution in St. Mary's County, 1634–1710" (ms report, St. Mary's City Commission, 1971, copy on file at the Hall of Records); Menard, "Economy and Society," 423; Carr, "County Government in Maryland," text, 605.

[71] Menard, "Immigrants and Their Increase," Table III; n. 40 above.
[72] Menard, "Demography of Somerset County," Table XIII.

percentage than has been reported from seventeenth-century English parishes.[73]

These facts suggest considerable freedom for girls in selecting a husband. Almost any girl must have had more than one suitor, and evidently many had freedom to spend time with a suitor in a fashion that allowed her to become pregnant. We might suppose that such pregnancies were not incurred until after the couple had become betrothed, and that they were consequently an allowable part of courtship, were it not that girls whose fathers were living were usually not the culprits. In Somerset, at least, only 10 percent of the brides with fathers living were pregnant, in contrast to 30 percent of those who were orphans.[74] Since there was only about one year's difference between the mean ages at which orphan and non-orphan girls married, parental supervision rather than age seems to have been the main factor in the differing bridal pregnancy rates.[75]

Native girls married young and bore children young; hence they had more children than immigrant women. This fact ultimately changed the composition of the Maryland population. Native-born females began to have enough children to enable couples to replace themselves. These children, furthermore, were divided about evenly between males and females. By the mid-1680s, in all probability, the population thus began to grow through reproductive increase, and sexual imbalance began to decline. In 1704 the native-born preponderated in the Maryland assembly for the first time and by then were becoming predominant in the adult population as a whole.[76]

This appearance of a native population was bringing alterations in family life, especially for widows and orphaned minors. They were acquiring kin. St. Mary's and Charles counties wills demonstrate the change.[77]

---

[73] *Ibid.*, Table XVII; P. E. H. Hair, "Bridal Pregnancy in Rural England in Earlier Centuries," *Pop. Studies*, XX (1966), 237; Chambers, *Population, Economy, and Society in England*, 75; Smith and Hindus, "Premarital Pregnancy in America," *Jour. Interdisciplinary Hist.*, V (1975), 537–570.

[74] Menard, "Demography of Somerset County," Table XVIII.

[75] Adolescent subfecundity might also partly explain lower bridal pregnancy rates among very young brides.

[76] Menard develops this argument in detail in "Immigrants and Their Increase." For the assembly see David W. Jordan, "Political Stability and the Emergence of a Native Elite in Maryland, 1660–1715," in Tate and Ammerman, eds., *Essays on the Chesapeake*. In Charles County, Maryland, by 1705 at least half of all resident landowners were native born. Walsh, "Charles County, Maryland," chaps. 1, 7.

[77] The proportion of wills mentioning non-nuclear kin can, of course, prove only a proxy of the actual existence of these kin in Maryland. The reliability of such a measure may vary greatly from area to area and over time, depending on the character of the population and on local inheritance customs. To test the reliability of the will data, we compared them with data from reconstituted families in 17th-century Charles County. These reconstitution data draw on a much broader variety of sources and include many men who did not leave wills. Because of insufficient information for female lines, we could trace only the male lines. The procedure compared the names of all married men against a file of all known county residents, asking how many kin in the male line might have been present in the county at the

TABLE III
RESIDENT KIN OF TESTATE MEN AND WOMEN
WHO LEFT MINOR CHILDREN, ST. MARY'S AND CHARLES COUNTIES
1640 TO 1710

A.

	Families N	No Kin % Families	Only Wife % Families	Grown Child % Families	Other Kin % Families
1640–1669	95	23	43	11	23
1670–1679	76	17	50	7	26
1700–1710	71	6	35[a]	25	34[b]

B.

1700–1710					
Immigrant	41	10	37	37	17
Native	30		33[c]	10	57[d]

Notes: [a] If information found in other records is included, the percentage is 30.
  [b] If information found in other records is included, the percentage is 39.
  [c] If information found in other records is included, the percentage is 20.
  [d] If information found in other records is included, the percentage is 70.
  For a discussion of wills as a reliable source for discovery of kin see n. 78.
  Only 8 testators were natives of Maryland before 1680s; hence no effort has
  been made to distinguish them from immigrants.
Source: Wills, I–XIV.

(See Table III.) Before 1680, when nearly all those who died and left families had been immigrants, three-quarters of the men and women who left widows and/or minor children made no mention in their wills of any other kin in Maryland. In the first decade of the eighteenth century, among native-born testators, nearly three-fifths mention other kin, and if we add information from sources other than wills—other probate records, land records, vital registers, and so on—at least 70 percent are found to have had such local connections. This development of local family ties must have been one of the most important events of early Maryland history.[78]

---

time of the married man's death. The proportions for immigrants were in most cases not markedly different from those found in wills. For native men, however, wills were somewhat less reliable indicators of the presence of such kin; when non-nuclear kin mentioned by testate natives were compared with kin found by re-constitution, 29% of the native testators had non-nuclear kin present in the county who were not mentioned in their wills.

[78] Not surprisingly, wills of immigrants show no increase in family ties, but these wills mention adult children far more often than earlier. Before 1680, only 11% of immigrant testators in St. Mary's and Charles counties mention adult children in their wills; from 1700 to 1710, 37% left adult children to help the family. Two facts help account for this change. First, survivors of early immigration were dying in old age. Second, proportionately fewer young immigrants with families were dying, not because life expectancy had improved, but because there were proportionately fewer of them than earlier. A long stagnation in the tobacco economy that

Historians have only recently begun to explore the consequences of the shift from an immigrant to a predominantly native population.[79] We would like to suggest some changes in the position of women that may have resulted from this transition. It is already known that as sexual imbalance disappeared, age at first marriage rose, but it remained lower than it had been for immigrants over the second half of the seventeenth century. At the same time, life expectancy improved, at least for men. The results were longer marriages and more children who reached maturity.[80] In St. Mary's County after 1700, dying men far more often than earlier left children of age to maintain their widows, and widows may have felt less inclination and had less opportunity to remarry.[81]

We may speculate on the social consequences of such changes. More fathers were still alive when their daughters married, and hence would have been able to exercise control over the selection of their sons-in-law. What in the seventeenth century may have been a period of comparative independence for women, both immigrant and native, may have given way to a return to more traditional European social controls over the creation of new families. If so, we might see the results in a decline in bridal pregnancy and perhaps a decline in bastardy.[82]

---

began about 1680 had diminished opportunities for freed servants to form households and families. Hence, among immigrants the proportion of young fathers at risk to die was smaller than in earlier years.

In the larger population of men who left inventories, 18.2% had adult children before 1681, but in the years 1700–1709, 50% had adult children. "Social Stratification."

[70] Examples of some recent studies are Carole Shammas, "English-Born and Creole Elites in Turn-of-the-Century Virginia," in Tate and Ammerman, eds., *Essays on the Chesapeake;* Jordan, "Political Stability and the Emergence of a Native Elite in Maryland," *ibid.;* Lois Green Carr, "The Foundations of Social Order: Local Government in Colonial Maryland," in Bruce C. Daniels, ed., *Town and Country: Essays on the Structure of Local Government in the American Colonies* (Middletown, Conn., forthcoming); Menard, "Economy and Society," 396–440.

[80] Allan Kulikoff has found that in Prince George's County the white adult sex ratio dropped significantly before the age of marriage rose. Women born in the 1720s were the first to marry at a mean age above 20, while those born in the 1740s and marrying in the 1760s, after the sex ratio neared equality, married at a mean age of 22. Marriages lasted longer because the rise in the mean age at which men married —from 23 to 27 between 1700 and 1740—was more than offset by gains in life expectancy. Kulikoff, "Tobacco and Slaves: Population, Economy, and Society in Eighteenth-Century Prince George's County, Maryland" (Ph.D. diss., Brandeis University, 1976), chap. 3; Menard, "Immigrants and Their Increase."

[81] Inventories and related biographical data have been analyzed by the St. Mary's City Commission under a grant from the National Endowment for the Humanities, "The Making of a Plantation Society in Maryland" (R 010585–74–267). From 1700 through 1776 the percentage of men known to have had children, and who had an adult child at death, ranged from a low of 32.8% in the years 1736–1738 to a high of 61.3% in the years 1707–1709. The figure was over 50% for 13 out of 23 year-groups of three to four years each. For the high in 1707–1709 see comments in n. 78.

[82] On the other hand, these rates may show little change. The restraining effect of increased parental control may have been offset by a trend toward increased sexual

We may also find the wife losing ground in the household polity, although her economic importance probably remained unimpaired. Indeed, she must have been far more likely than a seventeenth-century immigrant woman to bring property to her marriage. But several changes may have caused women to play a smaller role than before in household decision-making.[83] Women became proportionately more numerous and may have lost bargaining power.[84] Furthermore, as marriages lasted longer, the proportion of households full of stepchildren and half-brothers and half-sisters united primarily by the mother must have diminished. Finally, when husbands died, more widows would have had children old enough to maintain them and any minor brothers and sisters. There would be less need for women to play a controlling role, as well as less incentive for their husbands to grant it. The provincial marriage of the eighteenth century may have more closely resembled that of England than did the immigrant marriage of the seventeenth century.

If this change occurred, we should find symptoms to measure. There should be fewer gifts from husbands to wives of property put at the wife's disposal. Husbands should less frequently make bequests to wives that provided them with property beyond their dower. A wife might even be restricted to less than her dower, although the law allowed her to choose her dower instead of a bequest.[85] At the same time, children should be commanded to maintain their mothers.

However, St. Mary's County wills do not show these symptoms. (See Table IV.) True, wives occasionally were willed less than their dower, an arrangement that was rare in the wills examined for the period before 1710. But there was no overall decrease in bequests to wives of property beyond their dower, nor was there a tendency to confine the wife's interest to the term of her widowhood or the minority of the oldest son. Children were not exhorted to help their mothers or give them living space. Widows evidently received at least enough property to maintain themselves, and husbands saw no need to ensure the help of children in managing it. Possibly, then, women did not lose ground, or at least not all

---

activity that appears to have become general throughout Western Europe and the United States by the mid-19th century, Smith and Hindus, "Premarital Pregnancy in America," *Jour. Interdisciplinary Hist.*, V (1975), 537–570; Edward Shorter, "Female Emancipation, Birth Control, and Fertility in European History," *American Historical Review*, LXXVIII (1973), 605–640.

[83] Page Smith has suggested that such a decline in the wife's household authority had occurred in the American family by—at the latest—the beginning of the 19th century (*Daughters of the Promised Land: Women in American History* [Boston, 1970], chaps. 3, 4).

[84] There is little doubt that extreme scarcity in the early years of Chesapeake history enhanced the worth of women in the eyes of men. However, as Smith has observed, "the functioning of the law of supply and demand could not in itself have guaranteed status for colonial women. Without a[n] ideological basis, their privileges could not have been initially established or subsequently maintained" (*ibid.*, 38–39). In a culture where women were seriously undervalued, a shortage of women would not necessarily improve their status.

[85] Acts 1699, chap. 41, *Maryland Archives*, XXII, 542.

TABLE IV

BEQUESTS OF HUSBANDS TO WIVES WITH CHILDREN, ST. MARY'S COUNTY, MARYLAND, 1710 TO 1776

	N	All Estate %	All or Dwelling Plantation for Life %	All or Dwelling Plantation for Widowhood %	All or Dwelling Plantation for Minority of Child %	More than Dower in Other Form %	Dower or Less or Unknown %	Maintenance or House Room %
1710–1714	13	0	46	0	0	23	31	0
1715–1719	25	4	24	4	0	28	36	4
1720–1724	31	10	42	0	0	28	23	3
1725–1729	34	3	29	0	0	24	41	3
1730–1734	31	6	16	13	0	29	35	0
1735–1739	27	0	37	4	4	19	37	0
1740–1744	35	3	40	0	3	23	34	0
1745–1749	39	2	31	8	0	31	28	0
1750–1754	43	3	35	7	0	16	40	0
1755–1759	34	3	41	3	0	41	12	0
1760–1764	48	2	46	10	2	13	27	0
1765–1769	45	4	27	11	2	18	33	4
1770–1774	46	4	26	7	0	37	26	0
1775–1776	19	5	32	26	0	5	32	0
Totals	470	3	33	7	1	24	31	1

Source: Wills, XIV–XLI.

ground, within the family polity. The demographic disruption of New World settlement may have given women power which they were able to keep even after sex ratios became balanced and traditional family networks appeared. Immigrant mothers may have bequeathed their daughters a legacy of independence which they in turn handed down, despite pressures toward more traditional behavior.

It is time to issue a warning. Whether or not Maryland women in a creole society lost ground, the argument hinges on an interpretation of English behavior that also requires testing. Either position supposes that women in seventeenth-century Maryland obtained power in the household which wives of English farmers did not enjoy. Much of the evidence for Maryland is drawn from the disposition of property in wills. If English wills show a similar pattern, similar inferences might be drawn about English women. We have already discussed evidence from English wills that supports the view that women in Maryland were favored; but the position of seventeenth-century English women—especially those not of gentle status—has been little explored.[86] A finding of little difference between bequests to women in England and in Maryland would greatly weaken the argument that demographic stress created peculiar conditions especially favorable to Maryland women.

If the demography of Maryland produced the effects here described, such effects should also be evident elsewhere in the Chesapeake. The four characteristics of the seventeenth-century Maryland population—immigrant predominance, early death, late marriage, and sexual imbalance—are to be found everywhere in the region, at least at first. The timing of the disappearance of these peculiarities may have varied from place to place, depending on date of settlement or rapidity of development, but the effect of their existence upon the experience of women should be clear. Should research in other areas of the Chesapeake fail to find women enjoying the status they achieved on the lower Western Shore of Maryland, then our arguments would have to be revised.[87]

[86] Essays by Cicely Howell and Barbara Todd, printed or made available to the authors since this article was written, point out that customary as opposed to free-hold tenures in England usually gave the widow the use of the land for life, but that remarriage often cost the widow this right. The degree to which this was true requires investigation. Howell, "Peasant Inheritance in the Midlands, 1280–1700," in Jack Goody, Joan Thirsk, and E. P. Thompson, eds., *Family and Inheritance: Rural Society in Western Europe, 1200–1800* (Cambridge, 1976), 112–155; Todd, " 'In Her Free Widowhood': Succession to Property and Remarriage in Rural England, 1540–1800" (paper delivered to the Third Berkshire Conference of Women Historians, June 1976).

[87] James W. Deen, Jr., "Patterns of Testation: Four Tidewater Counties in Colonial Virginia," *American Journal of Legal History*, XVI (1972), 154–176, finds a life interest in property for the wife the predominant pattern before 1720. However, he includes an interest for widowhood in life interest and does not distinguish a dower interest from more than dower.

Work is also needed that will enable historians to compare conditions in Maryland with those in other colonies. Richard S. Dunn's study of the British West Indies also shows demographic disruption.[88] When the status of wives is studied, it should prove similar to that of Maryland women. In contrast were demographic conditions in New England, where immigrants came in family groups, major immigration had ceased by the mid-seventeenth century, sex ratios balanced early, and mortality was low.[89] Under these conditions, demographic disruption must have been both less severe and less prolonged. If New England women achieved status similar to that suggested for women in the Chesapeake, that fact will have to be explained. The dynamics might prove to have been different;[90] or a dynamic we have not identified, common to both areas, might turn out to have been the primary engine of change. And, if women in England shared the status—which we doubt—conditions in the New World may have had secondary importance. The Maryland data establish persuasive grounds for a hypothesis, but the evidence is not all in.

[88] Richard S. Dunn, *Sugar and Slaves: The Rise of the Planter Class in the English West Indies, 1624–1713* (Chapel Hill, N.C., 1972), 326–334. Dunn finds sex ratios surprisingly balanced, but he also finds very high mortality, short marriages, and many orphans.

[89] For a short discussion of this comparison see Menard, "Immigrants and Their Increase."

[90] James K. Somerville has used Salem, Massachusetts, wills from 1660 to 1770 to examine women's status and importance within the home ("The Salem [Mass.] Woman in the Home, 1660–1770," *Eighteenth-Century Life,* I [1974]), 11–14). See also Alexander Keyssar, "Widowhood in Eighteenth-Century Massachusetts: A Problem in the History of the Family," *Perspectives in American History,* VIII (1974), 83–119, which discusses provisions for 22 widows in 18th-century Woburn, Massachusetts. Both men find provisions for houseroom and care of the widow's property enjoined upon children proportionately far more often than we have found in St. Mary's County, Maryland, where we found only five instances over 136 years. However, part of this difference may be a function of the differences in age at widowhood in the two regions. Neither Somerville nor Keyssar gives the percentage of widows who received a life interest in property, but their discussions imply a much higher proportion than we have found of women whose interest ended at remarriage or the majority of the oldest son.

Savage War

FRANCIS JENNINGS

C. Smith taketh the King of Pamavnkee prisoner 1608

Violence, or the threat of violence, was a primary fact of life for almost every European colonizer in America. That is why almost every free white male between sixteen and sixty was required to serve in the colonial militia. Eternal readiness to ward off hostile forces was everybody's responsibility, and therefore military service became a key element of everyday life.

It is a mistake, however, to accept the notion that the ever-present threat of violence originated in hostile Indians. For most European colonizers, violence was a state of mind before it was a physical reality. Even before they arrived in North America, the English carried in their minds a split image of the Native American. On the one hand, the native people were seen as brutish, even cannibalistic, inhabitants of "a savage wilderness" that threatened chaos on every side and could drag "civilized" men down to the level of beasts. On the other hand, the Indians were pictured as winsome, if ignorant, creatures living in an Arcadia that had long filled the dreams of Europeans.

It was the negative side of this split image that quickly prevailed in most minds. Land was the key to English settlement in North America, and it was logical to assume that the native occupiers of the land would not willingly give it up. The stereotype of a hostile, heathen "savage," which quickly dominated colonial thinking about Native Americans, was linked to the problem of land. Seeing Indians in this way helped assuage the guilt that inevitably arose when Europeans, whose culture was based on the concept of private property, embarked on a campaign to dispossess another people of the land that sustained them. To typecast the Indian as a "savage" was to justify European seizure of the land. Moreover, as Richard Slotkin has shown, English colonizers, especially Puritans, developed the belief that through heroic but violent conquest of the New World "wilderness" and its inhabitants corrupt Europeans could experience renewal and purification.

This cast of mind helped bring Massachusetts to war with neighboring Indians before the colony was seven years in existence. The charter of the colony pronounced that the "principall ende of this plantacion" was to "wynn and incite the natives of [the] country, to the knowledge and obedience of the onlie true God and Savior of mankinde." But violence, not preaching, became the instrument most frequently employed in Puritan relations with the Indians. The destruction rather than the conversion of the indigenous people, who came to be thought of as Satan's disciples, became the dominant fact of seventeenth-century Indian-European relations. From the extermination of the Pequots in 1637, which served the economic purpose of opening up rich new lands for the growing population of Massachusetts and the psychological purpose of establishing Puritan "order" over Indian "chaos," armed conflict with Native Americans was an integral part of the colonial experience. "The Indian wars," writes Slotkin, in his book **Regeneration Through Violence: The Mythology of the American Frontier,** "became the distinctive event of American history, the unique national experience."

The keepers of the past in every society ordinarily attempt to justify the violence that their people have initiated or participated in. Americans, especially, have never imagined themselves a warlike people. Their mission has been to create, not to conquer and kill. So we celebrate our military victories over aggressor nations but feel the need to justify violence on our own shores. This disavowal of rapacious impulses seemed especially necessary for the English colonizers because they pictured themselves entering an earthly paradise—a New World— where the war, brutality, and degradation that had haunted Europe would be left behind. Thus, "savage warfare," as Francis Jennings explains in this selection, must have originated with somebody else.

Myth contrasts civilized war with savage war by accepting the former as a rational, honorable, and often progressive activity while attributing to the latter the qualities of irrationality, ferocity, and unredeemed retrogression. Savagery implies unchecked and perpetual violence. Because war is defined as organized violence between politically distinct communities, some writers have questioned whether savage conflicts really qualify for the dignity of the name of war. By whatever name, savage conflicts are conceived to be irrational because they supposedly lack point or objective beyond the satisfaction of sadistic appetites that civilization inhibits, and savages are ferocious through the force of these appetites.

These images are by-products of the master myth of civilization locked in battle with savagery. Civilized war is the kind *we* fight against *them* (in this case, Indians), whereas savage war is the atrocious kind that they fight against us. The contrast has been sustained by means of biased definition on the one hand and tendentious description on the other. Savage war has been dismissed as mere "vengeance" or "feud," and writers have made it seem incomparably more horrible than civilized war by dwelling upon the gory details of personal combat, massacre, and torture on the Indian side while focusing attention diversely on the goals and strategy of wars on the European side.

Still another circumstance has contributed to the myth. Indian governments held jurisdiction over relatively small territories, and there were a great many of them. No supreme power existed to suppress conflicts; the tribes settled their differences themselves by negotiation or struggle.

"Savage War." From *The Invasion of America: Indians, Colonialism, and the Cant of Conquest* by Francis Jennings. (Copyright 1975 The University of North Carolina Press.) Published for the Institute of Early American History and Culture.

With so many possible combinations of interest groups, statistical odds dictated frequent intertribal conflicts. European governments, in comparison, extended over larger territories, and thus the possible number of international wars was statistically a good deal less. Furthermore, European society may have deferred some "organized" warfare, not by abolishing violence, but by internalizing much of it. Nearly all the violence of Indian society expressed itself intertribally in the form of war, but internal violence in the European states required a vast apparatus for its suppression, the means of which were also violent: Londoners could always find sadistic entertainment at Tyburn or the Tower, and the gaolers buried more prisoners than they discharged. There were also means of violent struggle between nation-states other than declared war; Sir Francis Drake sacked Spanish towns in time of peace, and pirates were ever present on all the seas. We tend to glorify these "sea dogs" instead of putting them on the same low level as Indian raiders, but the victims in both cases went through much the same experiences. If we focus entirely on internal order, the Indian village was a peaceful place compared to the European town. If we focus instead on relations between polities, the nation-states were under tighter controls than the tribes.[1] It seems to me that a proper comparison should include both internal and external relations and should examine the total level of violence in each society, its forms and motives, and the methods used to control and direct it. From this perspective aboriginal Indian society appears to have been far less violent than seventeenth-century European society. The wasting wars so prominent among Indians in historic times were a factor of adaptation to European civilization.

Indian tribes were internally more peaceful than European nations partly because of the kin-oriented sanctions pervading Indian villages, as distinct from the greater impersonality of European social relationships, and partly because Indian custom defined and punished fewer crimes than European law. If there is merit in the argument that psychological aggressions are the cause of social violence (and, like most psychological explanations, this one permits large flights of fancy), then the aggressive feelings of Indians were vented mostly upon persons outside the protection of kin obligation—that is to say, outside the clan and tribe. The same customary sanctions were notably tolerant of many sorts of behavior that Europeans classed as crime, especially regarding deviant sexual and religious conduct. There was no crime of fornication or "unnatural vice" among Indians, nor was there any heresy as that was defined by European law.[2] All sex relations except rare cases of rape were personal matters outside the jurisdiction of sachem and council, and religious *belief* was totally personal. Although participation in rituals was expected, the punishment for withdrawal was limited to public obloquy; in extreme cases the offender might be bewitched or poisoned by the tribal powwow, but such acts were clandestine. Indians knew nothing of the whole class of

[1] [J. H.] Kennedy, *Jesuit and Savage in New France*, [Yale Historical Publications, Miscellany, L (New Haven, Conn., 1950),] 114–115, 130.
[2] Fornication and adultery comprised most of colonial New England's court load. Edmund Morgan, "The Puritans and Sex," *New England Quarterly*, XV (1942), 596.

offenses called by European lawyers "crimes without victims." When one considers the floggings, jailings, hangings, torture, and burnings inflicted by European states for the multitude of crimes that did not even exist in Indian society, one becomes painfully aware that an incalculably great proportion of European violence against persons was inflicted by the very agencies whose ostensible function was to reduce violence. In due course "civil society" would seek to tranquilize its communities by emulating savage toleration of human variety, but even today this has still only begun.

Of crimes common to both societies, murder requires special notice. It was conceived of differently by Indian and European and was therefore punished by different processes. In Europe murder was an offense against the state; among Indians it was an offense against the family of the victim. European law demanded the murderer's life as atonement to the state; Indian custom made his life forfeit to his victim's family. In Europe the state apprehended the murderer; among Indians it was the family's obligation to do so. European observers tagged the Indian custom "revenge" and blathered much about the savagery revealed by it. Yet, as compared to the state's relentlessness, the tribe provided an institution carefully and precisely designed to stanch the flow of blood. The obligation of blood for blood could be commuted into a payment of valuable goods by the murderer's own kinsfolk to the relatives of his victim.[3] This custom (which had been known centuries earlier in Anglo-Saxon England as *wergild*) was a widespread stabilizer of Indian societies, forestalling the development of obligatory revenge into exterminating feuds. Although the term *feud* has been used freely by the condemners of savage society, Marian W. Smith has been unable to find the phenomena properly denoted by it. "True feud," she remarks, "in its threat of continued violence between particular groups, is surprisingly rare in the New World."[4]

Europeans understood the *wergild* custom and used it themselves in their dealings with Indians, but only unilaterally. Europeans would pay blood money to avert Indian revenge for the killing of an Indian, but Indians were not permitted to buy absolution for the killing of a European. In the latter case the Europeans demanded the person of the accused Indian for trial in a European court.[5] In the event of nonapprehension of

[3] [Daniel] Gookin, "Historical Collections [of the Indians of New England . . . ," (1674), in Massachusetts Historical Society, *Collections*], 1st Ser., 149; Elisabeth Tooker, *An Ethnography of the Huron Indians, 1615–1649*, Smithsonian Institution, Bureau of American Ethnology, Bulletin 190 (Washington, D.C., 1964), 28; "Penn to Free Society of Traders, 1683;" [Albert Cook] Myers, ed., *Narratives of Early Pennsylvania [West New Jersey, and Delaware, 1630–1707*, Original Narratives of Early American History (New York, 1912)], 236; [George S.] Snyderman, *Behind the Tree of Peace*, in [*Pennsylvania Archaeologist*], XVIII (1948), 31; David H. Corkran, *The Creek Frontier, 1540–1783*, Civilization of the American Indian Series (Norman, Okla., 1967), 26.

[4] Marian W. Smith, "American Indian Warfare," New York Academy of Sciences, *Transactions*, 2d Ser., XIII (June 1951), 352.

[5] [Bruce G.] Trigger, "Champlain Judged by His Indian Policy: [A Different View of Early Canadian History]," *Anthropologica*, N.S., XIII (1971), 96–97; *A Relation*

the suspected culprit, mass retribution might be visited upon his village or tribe.[6] The savagery of revenge, therefore, was simply a semantic function of its identification with an Indian; European revenge was civilized justice.

When Indians stirred abroad they were safe in their own territory and in those of tribes with whom they were at peace. The hospitality trait so prominent in all the tribes guaranteed to the traveler not only security but also shelter, sustenance, and sometimes sexual entertainment, all free of charge. Europeans traveling through Indian territory received the same treatment.[7] But travelers in seventeenth-century Europe risked life and property on every highway and in many inns, and they paid for all they got.

The violence and horrors of civil war were rare among Indians, probably because they tolerated secession, while England underwent the Puritan Revolution and France the Catholic-Hugenot agonies, to say nothing of dynastic upheavals by the score. Nor were there class wars or riots in Indian society. Nor did aboriginal Indians experience drunken orgies with their attendant tumults until rum and brandy were poured into the villages from Europe. Thereafter, however, drunken rage became a recurring menace everywhere.

When all this has been said, there still remains the problem of conflict between the tribes. The traditional conception of savage war depicts it as so unrelenting and frightful as to be incapable of proper comparison with the purposeful and disciplined processes of civilized war. No less an authority than A. L. Kroeber has attributed to the east coast Indians of North America a kind of "warfare that was insane, unending, continuously attritional, from our point of view." It was nightmarish—"so integrated into the whole fabric of Eastern culture, so dominantly emphasized within it, that escape from it was well-nigh impossible. Continuance in the system became self-preservatory. The group that tried to shift its

of Maryland (1635), in Clayton Colman Hall, ed., *Narratives of Early Maryland, 1633–1684*, Original Narratives of Early American History (New York, 1910), 88–90; minutes, Jan. 27, 1672, and Lovelace to Salisbury, Jan. 27, 1672, in Victor Hugo Paltsits, ed., *Minutes of the Executive Council of the Province of New York: Administration of Francis Lovelace, 1668–1673* (Albany, N.Y., 1910), I, 156–157, II, 756–757.

6 John Smith, *Generall Historie of Virginia*, in [Edward] Arber and [A. G.] Bradley, eds., *[The] Travels and Works of [Captain John] Smith, [President of Virginia, and Admiral of New England, 1580–1631* (Edinburgh, 1910),] II, 538–539.

7 [Robert] Beverley, *[The] History [and Present State of Virginia (1705)]*, ed. [Louis B.] Wright [(Chapel Hill, N.C., 1947)], 186–189; Corkran, *Creek Frontier*, 23–25; [Lewis Henry] Morgan, *League of the [Ho-De-No-Sau-Nee,] Iroquois* [(Rochester, N.Y., 1851)], 327–329; [Roger] Williams, *[A Key into the Language of America: Or, An help to the Language of the Natives in that part of America, called New England . . . (1643)]*, ed. [James Hammond] Trumbull, Narragansett Club, [*Publications*, I (Providence, R.I., 1866)], chap. 11; [John] Heckewelder, *[An] Account of the [History, Manners, and Customs of the] Indian Nations, [Who Once Inhabited Pennsylvania and the Neighbouring States (1819),]* ed. [William C.] Reichel, [Historical Society of Pennsylvania,] *Memoirs*, XII [(Philadelphia, 1881)], 148–149.

values from war to peace was almost certainly doomed to early extinction." [8] This harsh indictment would carry more weight if its rhetoric were supported by either example or reference. The only example that comes to mind in support of Kroeber is the Lenape mission of the Moravian church in the mid-eighteenth century. The Indians of that mission took their Christianity seriously, became absolute pacifists, and were unresistingly massacred. But their experience does not quite illustrate Kroeber's point, for their killers were not other Indians but backcountry Euramerican thugs, also Christian after a fashion, who were rather less ready to attack the old-fashioned pagan sort of Indian that fought back. [9]

Kroeber's implication of heavy casualties in aboriginal warfare is contradicted by seventeenth-century reports of Europeans with attitudes as diverse as those of Roger Williams and Captain John Underhill. From his observation post among the warring Narragansett and Pequot Indians, Williams saw that their fighting was "farre lesse bloudy and devouring than the cruell Warres of Europe." [10] Underhill was contemptuous of what Williams approved. He sneered at the Indian warriors who called off a battle after inflicting only a few deaths, and he reported complacently the Narragansetts' protest against his English-style war that "slays too many men." [11]

Imagined dogmas about warriors' lethal accomplishments have led sober scholars into impossible contradictions. For instance, Harold E. Driver has remarked, on the one hand, that "the greed, cupidity, deceit, and utter disregard of Indian life on the part of most of the European conquerors surpassed anything of the kind that the Indian cultures had been able to produce on their own in their thousands of years of virtual independence from the Old World." But Driver has also written, in conformity to savagery mythology, that "no young man ever thought of getting married or of being accepted as an adult citizen until he had slain an enemy and brought back a scalp to prove it." [12] The mathematical implications of the latter statement are wondrous. To demonstrate what it would mean in practice, let us imagine a situation in which two villages are perpetually raiding each other as they would be obliged to do in order to qualify their males for manhood and matrimony. Assuming that the age of eighteen is the threshold of manhood, we find that all of the eighteen-year-old men of one village achieve the right to marry by killing off an equal number of males in the other village. The total population of both villages would thus be reduced annually by the total number of eighteen-year-old men (at least this is so if the eighteen-year-olds from the two villages avoided killing each other). This is the minimum implica-

[8] [Alfred Louis] Kroeber, [*Cultural and Natural Areas of*] *Native North America,* [University of California Publications in American Archaeology and Ethnology, XXXVIII (Berkeley and Los Angeles, 1939)], 148.
[9] Edmund De Schweinitz, *The Life and Times of David Zeisberger* (Philadelphia, 1870), chap. 35.
[10] Williams, *Key,* ed. Trumbull, Narragansett Club, *Pubs.,* I, 204.
[11] John Underhill, *Newes from America; or, A New and Experimentall Discoverie of New England* . . . (London, 1638), 26, 42–43.
[12] Harold E. Driver, *Indians of North America* (Chicago, 1961), 384, 370.

tion of one coup per warrior. If some braves showed more than minimum enthusiasm and skill, the whole process would be speeded up accordingly. Such a process would lead inexorably, year by year, not just to a low level of population, but to total extinction. The thing is impossible, of course, and so is the dogma on which it is predicated. Clearly there were young men in Indian society who got married before they ever killed anyone, and the mathematics imply that a lot of old Indian men also died without having killed. What really made an Indian youth a citizen of his community was an initiation ritual, and the process has been observed and reported thousands of times. William Penn reported that young Delawares were permitted to marry "after having given some Proofs of their Manhood by a good return of Skins" and that almost all of them were wed before they reached nineteen years of age.[13] Among the Delawares, therefore, a man could marry when he could demonstrate the ability to support a family. How many Euramerican parents have drilled that notion into their offspring? That the young Indian could gain prestige and status by killing and scalping is undeniable, and that many youngsters itched for such fame is as plain as the enlistment of European mercenaries for pay and plunder. But universal generalizations should be grounded in some minimum quantity of evidence and common sense.

Suppose it be argued that the disastrous demographic implications just presented are fallacious because warriors might diffuse the population loss by taking scalps from women and children. Deductively such an objection might have merit if not for the inductive evidence available. Contact-era Europeans agreed that, with few exceptions that occurred in the confusion of battle, Indians killed only men.[14] The cultural imperative may have been a survival trait rather than pure sentiment, because one reason for sparing these noncombatants was to assimilate them into the victorious tribe, thus to enlarge and strengthen it.[15] Some tribes were observed to begin war for the specific purpose of augmenting their female population.[16] Whatever the motive, the merciful custom was universal in regard to women and children.

Treatment of captured men was more varied. Early southern accounts

---

13 "Penn to Free Society of Traders, 1638," Myers, ed., *Narratives of Early Pennsylvania*, 231.
14 [Gabriel] Sagard, [*The*] *Long Journey to the* [*Country of the*] *Hurons* [(1632)], ed. [George M.] Wrong, trans. [H. H.] Langton, [Champlain Society Publications, XXV (Toronto, 1939),] 140; [Adriaen] Van der Donck, [*A*] *Description of* [*the*] *New Netherlands* [(2d ed., 1656), trans. Jeremiah Johnson,] in [New-York Historical Society, *Collections*], 2d Ser., I [(New York, 1841)], 211; John Smith, [*A*] *Map of Virginia* [(1612),] in [Philip L.] Barbour, ed., [*The*] *Jamestown Voyages* [*under the First Charter, 1606–1609*, Hakluyt Society Publications, CXXXVI–CXXXVII (Cambridge, 1969)], II; 372; Heckewelder, *Account of the Indian Nations*, ed. Reichel, in Hist. Soc. Pa., *Memoirs*, XII, 337–339; David Pietersz. de Vries, *Short Historical and Journal notes Of several Voyages made in the four parts of the World, namely, Europe, Africa, Asia, and America* (1655), trans. Henry C. Murphy, in N.-Y. Hist. Soc., *Colls.*, 2d Ser., III (New York, 1857), 116.
15 Snyderman, *Behind the Tree of Peace*, in *Pa. Archaeol.*, XVIII (1948), 13–15.
16 John Smith, *Map of Virginia*, in Barbour, ed., *Jamestown Voyages*, II, 360.

indicate that all male prisoners were put to death except the chiefs.[17] By the seventeenth century torture of men was practiced fairly extensively, although some doubt exists about how widespread this trait had been at an earlier time. An ameliorating custom decreed the sparing of a large proportion of male captives, however. Again, the custom may have arisen out of the dire pressures of population decline, in this case pinpointed on particular families. Women among the victors, who had lost a husband or kinsman, held unchallengeable individual right to "adopt" a prisoner in his place, and the man so chosen became immediately assimilated into the tribe as well as the family. (In our terminology he was naturalized as well as adopted.[18]) Perhaps the most famous example of the custom is Pocahontas's rescue of John Smith, although Smith rejected assimilation at the first opportunity to escape. Not every European captive followed Smith's example. It was a constant crying scandal that Europeans who were adopted by Indians frequently preferred to remain with their Indian "families" when offered an opportunity to return to their genetic kinsmen.[19]

The adoption custom grew in importance with the intensification of war during the macrocontact era. Of all the Indians, the Iroquois, who are generally agreed to have been the most militaristic and to have suffered the most debilitating casualties, seem to have practiced adoption more than any other tribe. At one time adoptees constituted two-thirds of the Iroquois Oneidas.[20] The Senecas adopted whole villages of Hurons after the breakup of the Huron "nation" under Iroquois attack,[21] and various Iroquois tribes struggled for possession of Susquehannocks after the latter's dispersal under attack from Maryland and Virginia.[22]

Still another Indian custom served (aboriginally) to reduce the deadliness of war. Indians refrained from the total war that involved systematic destruction of food and property—until its use by Europeans roused the

[17] *Ibid.*, II, 361; [Marc] Lescarbot, [*The*] *History of New France* [(1618)], trans. [W. L.] Grant, [introduction by H. P. Biggar, Champlain Society Publications, I, VII, XI (Toronto, 1907–1914),] I, 88.

[18] Morgan, *League of the Iroquois*, 341–344; Snyderman, *Behind the Tree of Peace*, in *Pa. Archaeol.*, XVIII (1948), 18; Heckewelder, *Account of the Indian Nations*, ed. Reichel, in Hist. Soc. Pa., *Memoirs*, XII, 217–218; [Cadwallader] Colden, [*The*] *History of [the] Five [Indian] Nations [Depending on the Province of New-York in America* (Ithaca, N.Y., 1958 [orig. publ. 1727–1747])], Pt. I, chap. I, 8; [Woodbury] Lowery, [*The*] *Spanish Settlements [within the Present Limits of the United States, 1513–1561* (New York, 1959 [orig. publ. 1901–1905])], I, 37.

[19] [Philip L.] Barbour, *Pocahontas [and Her World* (Boston, 1970)], 23–25. I thank James Axtell for providing an advance copy of his article "The White Indians of Colonial America," [*William and Mary Quarterly*], 3d Ser., XXXII (1975), 55–88. This is the first objective treatment, to my knowledge, of the European prisoners who refused repatriation.

[20] Letter of Jacques Bruyas, Jan. 21, 1668, [Reuben Gold] Thwaites, ed., [*The*] *Jesuit Relations [and Allied Documents: Travels and Explorations in New France, 1610–1791* (Cleveland, Ohio, 1896–1901)], LI, 123.

[21] Letter of Jacques Fremin, n.d. ("Relation of 1669–1670"), *ibid.*, LIV, 81–83.

[22] [Francis] Jennings, "Glory, Death, and Transfiguration," [American Philosophical Society, *Proceedings*], CXII (1968), 40.

Indians to reprisal.[23] In this respect, as in so many others, the English continued a tradition of long standing from their devastations in Ireland.[24] Burning villages and crops to reduce Irish tribesmen to subjection under Elizabeth I led naturally enough to using the same tactics against the tribesmen of Virginia.[25] A "relation" of 1629 tells how the Virginia colonists compelled a hostile Indian chief to seek peace, "being forc't to seek it by our continuall incursions upon him and them, by yearly cutting downe, and spoiling their corne." [26] The same practice was used everywhere in North America when Indian guerrilla tactics prevented Europeans from gaining victory by decisive battle.[27] According to Indian logic, such destruction doomed noncombatants as well as warriors to die of famine during a winter without provisions.

These remarks are not intended to suggest that Indians of precontact days were gentle pacifists whom the Europeans seduced to evil warlike ways. On the contrary, all evidence points to a genuinely endemic state of sporadic intertribal violence. Had this base not been present, Europeans could not so readily have achieved hegemony by playing off one tribe against another. But the dispersion of violence tells nothing of its intensity. What is especially at issue here is the significance of the data in comparison with the phenomena of war in European society. As the history of feudal Europe well exemplifies, endemic war does not necessarily imply, although it may be associated with, population decline. The fact is unlovely, but growth in human societies is demonstrably compatible with bellicosity, up to a critical level of mortality. We have no difficulty in perceiving this rule at work in, say, ancient Greece; yet we deny that the rule applied to Amerindians when we attribute to them a savage kind of war that supposedly was incomparably more continuous, more widespread, more integral to cultural values, and more senseless in the long view than the dedicated vocation of backward but civilized Sparta —or of Athens, for that matter. To show the falsity of these absolute antitheses is a primary objective here. Indians could be and often were as stupid and vicious as Europeans, which is to say that they belonged to the same human species. They were never so much more devoted than Europeans to killing each other that their uniquely violent natures or cultures doomed their societies to perpetual stagnation.

To discover the nature of aboriginal Indian war requires a skeptical and analytical approach not only to European sources but to Indian

[23] Minutes, Aug. 26, 1645, [David] Pulsifer, ed., *Acts of [the Commissioners of the] United Colonies [of New England* (in Nathaniel E. Shurtleff and David Pulsifer, eds., *Records of the Colony of New Plymouth in New England*, IX–X [Boston, 1859])], I, 44.

[24] For the practice of Richard II in the late 14th century, see [J. F.] Lydon, [*The] Lordship of Ireland [in the Middle Ages* (Toronto, 1972)], 234.

[25] *Encyclopaedia Britannica*, 11th ed., s.v. "Ireland (History from the Anglo-Norman Invasion)."

[26] Capt. William Perse "Relation," Aug. 1629, C.O. 1/5, Pt. 1, fol. 69, [Public Record Office].

[27] E.g., the French foray against the Mohawks in 1666. [E. B.] O'Callaghan, ed., [*The Documentary History of the State of New-York* (Albany, N.Y., 1849–1851)], I, 70.

sources as well. Like old tales in other cultures, Indian "traditions" were of several sorts: some preserved the memory of historical events, and others were invented to amuse or edify. Wendell S. Hadlock has shown how legends diffused rapidly, being adapted to the local settings of different tribes so that "a single occurrence in history has been told in varying ways so as to appear like many incidents." [28] Sometimes one may doubt whether the "single occurrence" ever did happen anywhere.

One genre of such legends, dealing with the "grasshopper war," has been interpreted by chroniclers in its multiple manifestations as literal fact demonstrating the terrible carnage that Indians would wreak over such trivial causes as a children's quarrel about possession of a grasshopper. That grasshopper hopped over a lot of territory. He spilled the same mythical blood by gallons from the Micmacs of Newfoundland to the Shawnees, Lenape, and Tuscaroras of western Pennsylvania. The story seems to have been in the same class as Aesop's fables. Whatever may have been its remote origins, it diffused so widely because of its didactic utility rather than its historical reality. Hadlock associated it with a table of similar stories that "are not so much an explanation of a war incident as philosophical explanations of tribal fission." [29]

To Frank G. Speck it was fiction, and Speck's interpretation implies bittersweet irony as to how the Indian myth was absorbed and transformed in the European myth of savagery: "In the 'grasshopper war' legend we have an example of the type of Algonkian moral teaching with which the ethnologist has long been familiar. Need the moralist point out that its clarified motive is to portray the consequences of grown-ups taking over the disputes of children, the curse of partisanship in disputes of a trivial nature, the abomination of giving way to emotional impulses? The myth is a great composition for the lesson it carries extolling self-restraint and the virtues of deliberation before taking action that may lead to disastrous outcome." [30]

By the transforming power of the savagery myth, a fable denouncing war's irrationality was converted into evidence of the real existence of widespread irrational bellicosity. The Indian could not even preach against war without convicting himself of obsessive love for it. By the same logic Quakers would be the most militaristic of Euramericans.

Historical sources strongly suggest that aboriginal war among the hunting Indians of the cold north differed markedly from the wars carried on by the agricultural tribes farther south. During most of the year the hunters lived dispersed in family bands that were occupied full-time in making a living. Opportunity to organize concerted tribal wars existed briefly during the summer months when the bands congregated at tribal

[28] Wendell S. Hadlock, "War among the Northeastern Woodland Indians," *American Anthropologist*, N.S., XLIX (1947), 217–218.

[29] Wendell S. Hadlock, "The Concept of Tribal Separation as Rationalized in Indian Folklore," *Pa. Archaeol.*, XVI (1946), 84–88.

[30] Frank G. Speck, "The Grasshopper War in Pennsylvania: An Indian Myth That Became History," *Pa. Archaeol.*, XII (1942), 34. See also C. E. Schaeffer, "The Grasshopper or Children's War—A Circumboreal Legend?" *ibid.*, XII (1942), 60–61; John Witthoft, "The Grasshopper War in Lenape Land," *ibid.*, XVI (1946), 91–94.

centers and had some leisure. Wars could then be organized, but they were sporadic, individualistic affairs.[31] A Jesuit observer condemned both the Indians' motives and scale of operations with a succinct phrase—"their war is nothing but a manhunt"—and narrated how a war party of thirty men dwindled to fifteen who returned home satisfied after they had taken the scalps of three unoffending members of a friendly tribe.[32] In Europe such waylaying would have been called brigandage rather than war.

Farming Indians operated on a larger scale and under the direction of tribal purposes and policies. Their more complex culture provided a variety of motives. Sometimes they fought to gain territory, although apparently not in the fashion of European empire building; when Indians fought for territory as such, they wanted to displace its occupants rather than to subject them. Lands thus made available might be occupied by the victors, left empty for use as hunting grounds, or kept as a protective buffer against distant enemies.[33]

Sometimes, it seems, agricultural Indians fought to achieve dominance —to make the defeated tribe confess the victor's preeminence. The symbol of such acknowledgment was the payment of tribute. Because the tributary role has been much confused, it needs a moment of special attention. First, tribute should be distinguished from plunder. When the Niantics raided Long Island's Montauks for wampum in 1638, they were after loot.[34] When the Iroquois Five Nations—the Mohawks among them— required wampum from the Lenape of the Delaware Valley in the eighteenth century, they wanted ceremonial recognition of a confederate relationship in which the Iroquois were superior.[35] Several contrasts mark the difference. Loot was seized by a raiding party; tribute was presented by a diplomatic mission. Loot's value increased precisely in accordance with quantity; tribute's value was primarily symbolic, secondarily quantitative. The taking of loot was a one-sided transaction; the presentation of tribute was reciprocated by a counter presentation of wampum to confirm the tributary agreement.

The last difference was especially important, because tribute sym-

---

[31] Hadlock, "War among Northeastern Indians," *Am. Anthro.*, N.S., XLIX (1947), 211–214.

[32] Andre Richard, "Relation of 1661–1662," Thwaites, ed., *Jesuit Relations*, XLVII, 221–239.

[33] Occupation: Pequot displacement of Niantics. [Frederick Webb] Hodge, ed. *Handbook of [American Indians North of Mexico*, Smithsonian Institution, Bureau of American Ethnology, Bulletin 30 (Washington, D.C., 1907–1910)], s.v. "Pequot." Hunting grounds: Five Nations displacement of tribes around Lake Erie. Five Nations deed, July 19, 1701, [in E. B. O'Callaghan and Berthold Fernow, eds., *Documents Relative to the Colonial History of the State of New York* (Albany, N.Y., 1856–1887),] IV, 908, [hereafter cited as *N.Y. Col. Docs.*]. Buffer lands: Hadlock, "War among Northeastern Indians," *Am. Anthro.*, N.S., XLIX (1947), 217.

[34] [Benjamin F.] Thompson, [*The*] *History of Long Island*, [2d ed. (New York, 1843)], I, 89–90.

[35] Minutes, May 19, 1712, [in Samuel Hazard, ed., *Minutes of the Provincial Council of Pennsylvania . . .* (Harrisburg, Pa., 1838–1853),] II, 546; draft minutes of treaty, Sept. 15, 1718, Logan Papers, XI, 7, and Sassoonan's speech, Aug. 7, 1741, Records of the Provincial Council and Other Papers, boxed manuscripts, fol. 1740–1749, both in Hist. Soc. Pa., Philadelphia.

bolized subordinate alliance rather than subjection and thus entailed obligation on the part of the superior tribe as well as the tributary. In essence the alliance entitled the tributary to freedom from molestation by its patron and to protection by the patron against attack by a third party. In return the tributary was expected to give ceremonial deference on all occasions, to allow free passage through its territory by members of the patron tribe, and to permit or encourage the recruitment of its own young men to join the patron's war parties. This sort of mutual obligation can be identified in the historic period, but it does not appear that all tributary relationships were the same; there seem to have been grades and degrees of obligation,[36] and the word *tribute* was also applied to payments of wampum or other valuable goods in the nature of a toll. For instance, English officials agreed to pay tribute to the Illinois tribes in 1764 for the privilege of unobstructed passage through the tribes' territory, and the Indians knew perfectly well that the English were not submitting or subjecting themselves by the payments.[37]

It may be said quite positively that a tributary tribe did not necessarily give up title to its lands when it presented tribute. After the defeat of the upper Hudson Mahicans by the Mohawks in 1628, the Mahicans offered tribute as a means of purchasing peace, but they also sold land to the Dutch without Mohawk objection, and after two years of tribute payment they "got drunk and lost the pouch [of wampum]." Mohawk sachem Joseph Brant, who told the story, commented that the Mohawks did not "take it hard" when payment ceased.[38] Four decades later, when the Executive Council of New York considered purchase of land from the "Wickerscreek" (Wecquaesgeek) tribe, the council had to consider whether the Wickerscreeks could deliver good title, "now they are beaten off" by the Mohawks. The Indians replied that the Mohawks would not "have any pretence to their Land, although being at Warre they would destroy their Persons, and take away their Beavers and Goods." [39]

The "sales" by dominant tribes like the Pequots and Iroquois of their rights in tributaries' territory were in the nature of quitclaims, without prejudice to the tributaries' retained rights of habitation and enjoyment. The Pequots quit their own claims to the Connecticut Valley and per-

[36] Snyderman, *Behind the Tree of Peace*, in Pa. *Archaeol.*, XVIII (1948), 33; Anthony F. C. Wallace, *King of the Delawares: Teedyuscung, 1700–1763* (Philadelphia, 1949), 195–196, and his "Political Organization," *Southwestern Journal of Anthropology*, XIII (1957), 308–309; Beverley, *History of Virginia*, ed. Wright, 174; [Regina] Flannery, [*An*] *Analysis of Coastal Algonquin Culture*, [Catholic University of America Anthropological Series, VII (Washington, D.C., 1939),] 117–118; [Francis] Jennings, "[The Constitutional] Evolution of [the] Covenant Chain," Am. Phil. Soc., *Procs.*, CXV, (1971), 90–94.

[37] Gen. Thomas Gage to Johnson, May 28, 1764, [in James Sullivan et al., eds., *The Papers of Sir William Johnson* (Albany, N.Y., 1921–1965),] IV, 433–434, [hereafter cited as *Sir William Johnson Papers*]; Johnson to Gage, June 9, 1764, *ibid.*, XI, 223.

[38] Douglas W. Boyce, ed., "A Glimpse of Iroquois Culture History through the Eyes of Joseph Brant and John Norton," Am. Phil. Soc., *Procs.*, CXVII (1973), 290; Bruce G. Trigger, "The Mohawk-Mahican War (1624–28): The Establishment of a Pattern," *Canadian Historical Review*, LII (1971), 281.

[39] Minutes, Oct. 30, 1671, Paltsits, ed., *Minutes of Council of N.Y.*, I, 105.

mitted Englishmen to settle there, but after the English evicted a tributary chief, the Pequots attacked in reprisal.[40] When the Iroquois were bribed by Pennsylvanians in the eighteenth century to "quit" a claim they had never made to the Delaware Valley, the swindle ruptured their confederacy.[41]

The customary situation was summarized by General Thomas Gage in the course of his systematic correspondence on Indian affairs with Sir William Johnson. Gage's confidential letter also clarifies the English motives that often led to the muddying of the formal records. "It is asserted as a general Principle that the Six Nations having conquered such and such Nations, their Territorys belong to them, and the Six Nations being the Kings Subjects which by treaty they have acknowledged themselves to be, those Lands belong to the King. I believe it is for our Interest to lay down such principles especially when we were squabbling with the French about Territory, and they played us off in the same stile of their Indian Subjects, and the right of those Indians." Gage went on to define the Indian customs as he privately understood them. "I never heard that Indians made War for the sake of Territory like Europeans, but that Revenge, and an eager pursuit of Martial reputation were the Motives which prompted one Nation to make War upon another. If we are to search for truth and examine her to the Bottom, I dont imagine we shall find that any conquered Nation ever formaly ceded their Country to their Conquerors, or that the latter ever required it. I never could learn more, than that Nations have yielded, and acknowledged themselves subjected to others, and some ever have wore Badges of Subjection." [42]

Gage's remark refers to the most frequently mentioned motive for Indian war—behavior that is almost invariably termed *revenge*. Like most effective propaganda language, the term has a referent in reality, and also like most propaganda, it distorts that referent in the mere naming of it. Our English word implies an act of retaliation intended to inflict suffering upon an enemy and performed in part for the emotional satisfaction that the avenger will achieve from contemplation of that suffering. (Who has not hated the villainous Iago?) Revenge connotes ferocity—personal, unrestrained by charity or mercy or any of the nobler impulses of humanity —in short, savagery. The actual phenomenon in Indian society to which this name has been given did not conform to these connotations. As it manifested itself intratribally, we have already noticed revenge as an obligatory retaliation for murder, together with the commutation custom by which the obligation might be discharged in lieu of blood for blood.[43]

---

[40] See chaps. 12 and 13 [of Jennings, *Invasion of America*].

[41] [Francis] Jennings, "[The] Delaware Interregnum," [*Pennsylvania Magazine of History and Biography*], LXXXIX (1965), 174–198; [Anthony] F. C. Wallace, [*The*] *Death and Rebirth of the Seneca* [(New York, 1970)], 154.

[42] Gage to Johnson, Oct. 7, 1772, *Sir William Johnson Papers*, XII, 994–995.

[43] See the description by missionary Francesco Bressani (1653) who remarked, "it is the public that gives satisfaction for the crimes of the individual, whether the culprit be known or not. In fine, the crime alone is punished, and not the criminal; and this, which elsewhere would appear an injustice, is among them a most efficacious means for preventing the spread of similar disorders." Thwaites, ed., *Jesuit Relations*, XXXVIII, 273–287, quote at p. 277.

Intertribal retaliation for wrongs done or fancied (a real omnipresent occurrence) was also bound up in motives and restraints imposed by custom and social purpose, including commutation by payment between tribes as well as between families. As Marian W. Smith has noted, such retaliations bear "a legalistic tinge. They serve as mechanisms for righting the balance of sanctions in the society, and the reprisal is seen as justified, in view of the fact that it reestablishes the validity of customs which had been violated." [44]

Smith wrote in the formal language of the twentieth-century scholar. A seventeenth-century Lenape Indian phrased the "justified reprisal" idea—which in Europe might readily have been classed as "just war"—in simpler language when he told a Pennsylvanian, "We are minded to live at Peace: If we intend at any time to make War upon you, we will let you know of it, and the Reasons why we make War with you; and if you make us satisfaction for the Injury done us, for which the War is intended, then we will not make War on you. And if you intend at any time to make War on us, we would have you let us know of it, and the Reasons for which you make War on us, and then if we do not make satisfaction for the injury done unto you, then you make make War on us, otherwise you ought not to do it." To one looking back from the twentieth century this sounds quaintly moralistic. In the era of total "preventive" war, what is one to make of "otherwise you ought not to do it"? [45]

Marian W. Smith identifies a "mourning-war" complex of traits correlating to the northern distribution of maize agriculture. By implication she makes it a development of the revenge trait, but her definition is brief and unenlightening: it is "an elaborate socio-religious complex relating individual 'emotion' to social reintegration through group activity and sanctioned homicide." [46] This seems more to describe what happens psychologically to a tribe after it has gone to war than to explain the reasons for its choosing to fight a particular foe at a certain time and place; further, it could as well apply to the nations of World War II as to aboriginal Indians.[47] Pursued to their logical assumptions, such psycho-

[44] M. W. Smith, "American Indian Warfare," N.Y. Acad. Sciences, *Trans.*, 2d Ser., XIII (1951), 352. See also the discussion of revenge in Snyderman, *Behind the Tree of Peace*, in *Pa. Archaeol.*, XVIII (1948); A. F. C. Wallace, *Death and Rebirth of the Seneca*, 44–48; Heckewelder, *Account of the Indian Nations*, ed. Reichel, in Hist. Soc. Pa., *Memoirs*, XII, 175–176; Tooker, *Ethnography of the Huron Indians*, 28; [John A.] Lawson, [A] *New Voyage to Carolina* [(1709), March of America Facsimile Series, No. 35 (Ann Arbor, Mich., 1966)], 199; Driver, *Indians of North America*, 354.

[45] Thomas Budd, *Good Order Established in Pennsilvania & New-Jersey in America* (1685), March of America Facsimile Series, No. 32 (Ann Arbor, Mich., 1966), 33.

[46] M. W. Smith, "American Indian Warfare," N.Y. Acad. Sciences, *Trans.*, 2d Ser., XIII (1951), 359.

[47] See W. W. Newcomb, Jr., "Toward an Understanding of War," in Gertrude E. Dole and Robert L. Carneiro, eds., *Essays in the Science of Culture in Honor of Leslie A. White* (New York, 1960), 322–324, and Newcomb, "A Reexamination of the Causes of Plains Warfare," *Am. Anthro.*, LII (1950), 328–329.

logical explanations of war, primitive or modern, take one ultimately to a neo-Calvinist faith in the innate depravity/bellicosity of man, a position both unwarranted by science and vicious in effect and, ultimately, a self-fulfilling prophecy that stultifies investigation of the empirical sources of war and thus guarantees war's perpetuation. We shall do better to stick with Smith's genuine insight into Indian war as a means of reestablishing the validity of violated customs; it raises questions that can be answered historically.

In sum, the motives for aboriginal war appear to have been few, and the casualties slight. Contact with Europeans added new motives and weapons and multiplied casualties. The trade and dominance wars of the macrocontact era were indeed beyond the sole control of aboriginal cultural and political institutions, because they were bicultural wars, the motives and promptings for which originated in colony and empire as well as in tribe. These wars were truly attritional for Indians—appallingly so—but they were the result of civilization's disruption of aboriginal society rather than the mere outgrowth of precontact Indian culture.

Most discussions of Indian war have probably concerned themselves less with the Indians' motives than with their manner of fighting. Every "frontier" history abounds with tales of grim figures skulking through the woods, striking from ambush, spreading havoc and desolation, and culminating their horrors with scalping, torture, and cannibalism. In many instances the tales are verifiable, and no attempt will be made here to palliate their horrors. But when atrocity is singled out as a quality exclusive to tribesmen (Indians or others), myth is being invoked against evidence—indeed against the sorrowful experience of our own twentieth century and our own "highest" civilization of all time. The Indians of the macrocontact era, and presumably their aboriginal ancestors also, undoubtedly showed plenty of ferocity when aroused; what will be argued here is that the records of European war of the same era display the same quality in ample measure also. There were no Indians in Ireland when Cromwell's armies made it a wilderness, nor were there Indians with Wallenstein and Tilly during the Thirty Years' War in central Europe. If savagery was ferocity, Europeans were at least as savage as Indians.

Many of the aspects of so-called savage war were taught to Indians by European example. As to torture, for example, a systematic examination of the documents of the early contact era, published by Nathaniel Knowles in 1940, found no references to torturing by Indians of the southeast coast region "until almost 200 years after white contact." Knowles added, "It seems even more significant that there are no expressions by the early explorers and colonizers indicating any fear of such treatment. The Europeans were only too willing in most cases to call attention to the barbarity of the Indians and thus justify their need for either salvation or extermination." [48] Among the northeastern Indians,

[48] Nathaniel Knowles, "The Torture of Captives by the Indians of Eastern North America," Am. Phil. Soc., *Procs.*, LXXXII (1940), 202. This is a systematic study fundamental to any study of torture in North America. Knowles remarked that Ponce de Leon in 1613 had met a Florida Indian who understood the Spanish lan-

Knowles found that deliberate torture, as distinct from simple brutality (i.e., unplanned and unorganized cruelty), had not been practiced in aboriginal times except by the Iroquois, who associated it with the practice of ritual cannibalism. These usages seem to have been derived from an ancient complex of customs connected with human sacrifice and perhaps tracing back to similar practices in Mexico. Iroquois torture secondarily served as a terrorist device to keep surrounding tribes in fear, but its usefulness for this purpose declined as some neighbors adopted the same trait in reprisal, much as the southern Indians had retaliated against such European tortures as burning at the stake.[49] After describing the torture of an Iroquois prisoner by Samuel de Champlain's allies, Marc Lescarbot remarked, "I have not read or heard tell that any other savage tribe behaves thus to its enemies. But someone will reply that these did but repay the Iroquois who by similar deeds have given cause for this tragedy."[50] Lescarbot stated positively that "our sea-coast Indians" did not practice torture, and his modern translator added a note of confirmation.[51] Although some Indians practiced the ritual cannibalism that Europeans had sublimated many centuries earlier into symbolic acts of "communion," other Indians abominated man-eating as much as the Europeans themselves. Algonquian speakers used a contemptuous epithet meaning "man-eaters" to refer to their Iroquois neighbors: it took the forms of Mengwe, Mingo, Maqua, and finally, in English, Mohawk.[52]

Europeans and Indians differed in the publicity given to torture. Europeans burnt heretics and executed criminals in ingeniously agonizing ways, but much European torture was inflicted secretly for the utilitarian purpose of extracting confessions from suspects. Public or private, European torture was performed by specialists appointed by governmental authority, whereas torture among Indians was a spectacle for popular participation as well as observation. It seems reasonable to infer that comparably painful practices in the two societies were sharply distin-

guage, "thus making it apparent that the atrocious cruelty of the Spanish for some twenty years in the West Indies had become known to the inhabitants of the mainland prior to the discovery of the continent by the whites" (p. 156). Knowles cites the speculation of Lowery that the Floridians' resistance to the Spaniards indicated "they had learned somewhat of the treatment they were to expect at the hands of such conquerors." Lowery, *Spanish Settlements*, I, 144–145. In 1642 the Canadian Jesuit martyr Father Isaac Jogues wrote, "*Never till now* had the Indian [torture] scaffold beheld French or other Christian captives." *NY. Col. Docs.*, XIII, 581 (emphasis added).

[49] Knowles, "Torture," Am. Phil. Soc., *Procs.*, LXXXII (1940), 190–191, 213, 215; Heckewelder, *Account of the Indian Nations*, ed. Reichel, in Hist. Soc. Pa., *Memoirs*, XII, 343.

[50] Lescarbot, *History of New France*, trans. Grant, III, 13–15.

[51] *Ibid.*, III, 20–21.

[52] [Allen W.] Trelease, *Indian Affairs in [Colonial] New York: [The Seventeenth Century* (Ithaca, N.Y., 1960)], 41. But see a dissenting meaning for "Mohawk" given by Mohawk sachem Joseph Brant who held that it came from the Mahican word *munkwas*, meaning "fish dryed." Brant may have been a little sensitive on the subject. Boyce, ed., "Glimpse of Iroquois Culture History," Am. Phil. Soc., *Procs.*, CXVII (1973), 291.

guished in European minds by what was conceived as their relative law-fulness. Torture by commission of civil authority was merely execution of the law, often highly approved as a means of preserving order, but torture by a self-governing rabble was savagery. The *Encyclopaedia Britannica* has noted that the name of torture has been historically used "especially" for the modes of inflicting pain "employed in a legal aspect by the civilized nations of antiquity and of modern Europe." [53] In such a context the remark of seventeenth-century friar Louis Hennepin becomes ironic: "We are surprised at the cruelty of tyrants and hold them in horror: but that of the Iroquois is not less horrible." [54]

Plenty of sadism was evident in both cultures. Indians vented it directly upon the person of their victim, hacking and slashing at his body democratically with their own hands. Even old women would satisfy some horrid lust by thrusting firebrands at his genitals or chewing off the joints of his fingers. Their culture sanctioned what they did in the same way that local and regional cultures in nineteenth- and twentieth-century America sanctioned somewhat similar practices by white suprema-cists at lynching parties. In the more authoritarian seventeenth century the European populace in general was not allowed to participate except as spectators in the tortures prescribed for condemned persons. When we consider that crowds brought their lunch along to be enjoyed during such entertainments as disemboweling and slow immolation, we may wonder about the significance of the cultural difference. We have no way of knowing how many Europeans were prevented from soaking their own hands in blood only by the state's armed guards. Equally we have no way of knowing how many of the persons in an Indian village were active participants in the grim sport of torture, or how many just looked on. The diverse qualities of character that we recognize as distinguishing one European or Euramerican from another are ignored or denied among Indians. Savages are homogeneously cruel.

In America, Europeans sometimes turned captives over to allied Indians for torture in order to make hostility between two tribes irrevo-cable. Their own complicity was not felt keenly enough to shame the Europeans into silence; after having thus condemned a victim they would sometimes fastidiously deplore the sadistic appetites of the Indian torturers who were carrying out the Europeans' own desires.[55] One French officer, after "prudently" consigning an old Onondaga to the torture in 1696, considered that the *victim's* taunting defiance "will be found perhaps to flow rather from ferociousness, than true valour." [56]

[53] *Encyclopaedia Britannica*, 11th ed., s.v. "torture."
[54] Louis Hennepin, *A Description of Louisiana* (1683), trans. John Gilmary Shea, March of America Facsimile Series, No. 30 (Ann Arbor, Mich., 1966), 311–312.
[55] Heckewelder, *Account of the Indian Nations*, ed. Reichel, in Hist. Soc. Pa., *Memoirs*, XII, 343–344; *Dictionary of Canadian Biography*, I (1966), s.v. "Buade de Frontenac et de Palluau, Louis de." Sir William Johnson followed the same practice but masked it under euphemisms. For example, he told Cadwallader Colden, Mar. 16, 1764, "I was obliged to *give* them People 5 Prisoners for their good behaviour." To General Gage, on the same day, Johnson wrote that the Indians had "kept" the five prisoners. *Sir William Johnson Papers*, IV, 365, 368–369. (emphasis added).
[56] O'Callaghan, ed., *Doc. Hist. of N.-Y.*, I, 334.

One thing is not in doubt: as befitted its greater progress in technology, Europe had designed a variety of implements for the specific purpose of creating agony, not merely death, in human bodies. Their function was to make pain excruciating—a word that itself commemorates one of the pioneering inventions in that field and recalls its connection with European worship. Indians never achieved the advanced stage of civilization represented by the rack or the Iron Maiden. They simply adapted instruments of everyday utility to the purposes of pain. It may be worth a moment to reflect on the cultural traits imaged in the specialized torture technology of Europe. Something more than sudden emotional impulse will have to be taken into account.

I have an impression that about midway through the seventeenth century the outlook toward torture began to change in opposite directions among the two peoples. It seems to me from general reading that European attitudes toward mutilation of the human body began to run negative. The old delight in hacking enemies' corpses in the public square and exposing their heads on palings went out of fashion—gradually and with conspicuous exceptions such as the displays made of sachem Philip and "squaw sachem" Weetamoo in "King Philip's War." [57] Slowly the use of torture for extracting information from political prisoners came under disapproval and ultimately under official ban. At the same time, torture was increasing among Indians as trade wars multiplied and European conflicts dragged Indian allies along. It is easy to understand why the Europeans, who were apparently trying to overcome their own worst traits, should have found relief and a sense of superior righteousness by rejecting torture and cruelty as things foreign to their own best impulses and therefore to civilization per se. No one dreamed at the time that the increase of torture by Indians could have come as the result of exposure to the uplifting influence of Europe, but the idea seems more credible nowadays after the revelations of German and Russian secret police practices, French policy in Algiers, Mississippi justice, and the ministrations of nice young American boys in Vietnam.

Every day brings revelations of secret tortures committed as deliberate instrumentation of governmental policy. Today's newspaper leads off an article with this paragraph: "Amnesty International, the organization dedicated to assisting political prisoners, has charged that torture as a systematic weapon of control is being used by almost half the world's governments and is spreading rapidly." The civilized world's response to this information is symbolized by the United Nations Educational, Scientific, and Cultural Organization. UNESCO withdrew from Amnesty International the offer of its facilities because the torture report implicated more than 60 of UNESCO's 125 member countries. [58] Clearly civilization is not a homogeneous whole, whatever it may otherwise be. Nor was it in the seventeenth century.

Apart from torture, some Europeans have domineered over Indians,

---

[57] [Samuel G.] Drake, *Biography and History of the Indians* [*of North America from its First Discovery* . . . , 11th ed. (Boston, 1856)], 189–190, 227.

[58] *New York Times*, Dec. 16, 1973: "64 Nations Charged in Report as Users of Torture."

when they could, with a reign of terror functioning through indiscriminate cruelty. In early Virginia the curtain was opened briefly on the reality behind self-serving and self-glorifying reports when Englishmen slew twelve Chickahominy Indians without cause and by treachery. Relatives of the victims retaliated against ten colonists and then fled into the woods. The rest of the villagers, abused by both sides, "much feared the English would be revenged on them"—a fear they had unquestionably been taught by the swaggering Virginians. Grand sachem Opechancanough "saved" the village from causeless slaughter, and incidentally revealed the motive behind the English menaces, by ceding the village to the colonists.[59] On a larger scale, after the much-provoked Virginia Indians rebelled in 1622, English writers fumed against the Indian massacre even as English soldiers multiplied their vengeance massacres beyond counting. Virginian Dr. John Pott became "the Poysner of the Savages thear" in some sort of episode so shocking that the earl of Warwick insisted it was "very unfitt" that Pott "should be imployed by the State in any business." But Pott became governor.[60]

Virginia was not exceptional. Puritan New England initiated its own reign of terror with the massacres of the Pequot conquest. David Pieterszoon de Vries has left us an unforgettable picture of how Dutch mercenaries acted, under orders of New Netherland's Governor Willem Kieft, to terrorize Indians into paying tribute.

About midnight, I heard a great shricking, and I ran to the ramparts of the fort, and looked over to Pavonia. Saw nothing but firing, and heard the shrieks of the Indians murdered in their sleep. . . . When it was day the soldiers returned to the fort, having massacred or murdered eighty Indians, and considering they had done a deed of Roman valour, in murdering so many in their sleep; where infants were torn from their mother's breasts, and hacked to pieces in the presence of the parents, and the pieces thrown into the fire and in the water, and other sucklings being bound to small boards, and then cut, stuck, and pierced, and miserably massacred in a manner to move a heart of stone. Some were thrown into the river, and when the fathers and mothers endeavoured to save them, the soldiers would not let them come on land, but made both parents and children drown—children from five to six years of age, and also some old and decrepit persons. Many fled from this scene, and concealed themselves in the neighbouring sedge, and when it was morning, came out to beg a piece of bread, and to be permitted to warm themselves; but they were murdered in cold blood and tossed into the water. Some came by our lands in the country with their hands, some with their legs cut off, and some holding their entrails in their arms, and others had such horrible cuts, and gashes, that worse than they were could never happen.

[59] John Smith, *Generall Historie of Virginia*, in Arber and Bradley, eds., *Travels and Works of Smith*, II, 528, 538–539.
[60] See [Wesley Frank] Craven, "Indian Policy in Early Virginia," *WMQ*, 3d Ser., I (1944), 73; Warwick to Sec. Conway, Aug. 9, 1624, C.O. 1/3, 94; C.O. 1/5, Pt. 2, fol. 206, Public Record Office.

And the sequel: "As soon as the Indians understood that the Swannekens [Dutch] had so treated them, all the men whom they could surprise on the farm-lands, they killed; but we have never heard that they have ever permitted women or children to be killed." [61]

Indians have often been charged with senseless bloodlust in their fighting, even to the point of treacherously murdering people who had befriended them. The variety of friendship claimed for the victims of such murders should always be investigated in particular detail. The purported friend often turns out to be no more than someone who lived close to the Indians in order to exploit them more efficiently than he could from a distance—his "friendship" is proved by nothing more than his toleration of their persons—or one who warded off other exploiters in order to preserve his own monopoly. For reasons of space and proportion, the subject cannot be fully discussed here, but examples can be cited of real discrimination by Indians in favor of persons that they recognized as friends. David de Vries, himself one such person, was able, after Kieft's massacre, to walk alone, unmenaced and unscathed, in the midst of the very Indians whose kinsfolk had been treated so cruelly. [62] The most startling example is to be found in eighteenth-century Pennsylvania, where the entire Religious Society of Friends, whose members were settled the length and breadth of the colony, was excepted from the raids of the Seven Years' War. In 1758 the Yearly Meeting held at Burlington for New Jersey and Pennsylvania recorded its "Thankfulness for the peculiar favour extended and continued to our Friends and Brethren in profession, none of whom have as we have yet heard been Slain nor carried into Captivity." In consideration of Indian willingness to reciprocate benevolence, the Yearly Meeting displayed an unusual form of racist thinking: it urged all Friends to show their gratitude practically by freeing their slaves. [63]

Indian war, like European war, changed with time and circumstance. The guerrilla raids of small war parties became more common after the introduction of firearms made massed attack suicidal. Firearms also reduced the value of stockades around villages even as they had destroyed the invulnerability of walled castles in Europe. The most militaristic of Indians, the Iroquois, adapted to fighting with guns by casting aside their encumbering wooden and leather body armor to gain greater mobility. The naked warrior of the savage stereotype became real enough, but among the Iroquois, at least, he was the product of acculturation rather than an aboriginal prototype. [64]

The influence of European contact on Indian warfare is quite plain. In New England, for instance, until the Pequot conquest, the tribes

[61] De Vries, *Voyages*, in N.-Y. Hist. Soc., *Colls.*, 2d Ser., III, 115–116.
[62] *Ibid.*, 116–120.
[63] Minutes, 1758, Minutes of the Yearly Meeting Held at Burlington for New Jersey and Pennsylvania, Manuscripts, Bk. A3, 121, Department of Records, Philadelphia Yearly Meeting, Society of Friends, 302 Arch St., Philadelphia.
[64] Keith F. Otterbein, "Why the Iroquois Won: An Analysis of Iroquois Military Tactics," *Ethnohistory*, XI (1964), 57–59; Snyderman, *Behind the Tree of Peace*, in *Pa. Archaeol.*, XVIII (1948), 75–77.

marched to war en masse, but the Pequots recognized that such tactics would be futile against English firepower. They therefore approached the Narragansetts to propose joint harassment of the English rather than confrontation. They would kill livestock, waylay travelers, and ambush isolated farmers. The Narragansetts rejected this proposal in favor of an English alliance and later fought a battle against the Mohegans with the traditional tactics of a large army; but when they were finally forced into open violence against the English in "King Philip's War," they adopted the Pequots' proposed guerrilla tactics, to New England's great distress. Cultural change in response to the contact situation was not one-sided, however. While Pequots and Narragansetts changed traditional tactics to cope with English colonials, the Englishmen were also modifying ancient military wisdom to meet the needs created by Indian guerrilla war. In James Axtell's words, "From these opponents the English gradually learned to fight 'Indian-style,' an ability that once again spelled the difference between their destruction and survival in the New World."[65]

Customs and practices changed from decade to decade, even in regard to the trait of scalping, which, while apparently Indian in origin, did not exist among many Indian tribes in the early seventeenth century. It seems to have been adopted in New England, for example, as a convenient way to collect provincial bounties for heads without having to lug about the awkward impedimenta attached to the scalps.[66]

Both Indians and Englishmen took heads as trophies and put them on show, and the practice of paying bounties for heads was well established among Englishmen. It had been conspicuous in the wars in Ireland in the thirteenth and fourteenth centuries.[67] In the sixteenth century Sir Humphrey Gilbert had terrorized the Irish by ordering that "the heddes of all those (of what sort soever thei were) which were killed in the daie, should be cutte off from their bodies and brought to the place where he incamped at night, and should there bee laied on the ground by eche side of the waie ledyng into his owne tente so that none could come into his tente for any cause but commonly he must passe through a lane of heddes which he used *ad terrorem.* . . . [It brought] greate terrour to the people when thei sawe the heddes of their dedde fathers, brothers, children, kinsfolke, and freinds. . . ."[68]

As Europeans taught Indians many of the traits of "savage" war, so also their intrusion into Indian society created new situations to which the Indians responded by cultural change on their own initiative. The attritional warfare of the macrocontact era did indeed justify A. L. Kroeber's indictment of having become so integrated in the culture that escape from it had become impossible, but it was not the aboriginal culture that took such a grim toll. It was instead a culture in which European

[65] [William] Bradford, *Of Plymouth Plantation,* [*1620–1647*], ed. [Samuel Eliot] Morison [(New York, 1952)], 294–295, 330–331; James Axtell, "The Scholastic Philosophy of the Wilderness," *WMQ*, 3d Ser., XXIX (1972), 340.

[66] Hodge, ed., *Handbook of N. Am. Indians,* s.v. "scalping."

[67] Lydon, *Lordship of Ireland,* 195.

[68] [Nicholas P.] Canny, "[The] Ideology of English Colonization: [From Ireland to America]," *WMQ*, 3d Ser., XXX (1973), 582.

motives and objectives of war multiplied war's occasions and casualties. Four different kinds of war took place in the macrocontact era: European versus European, Indian versus Indian, intermixed allies versus other allies, and, rarely, European versus Indian. In all of them the influence of European political or economic institutions is apparent. Many of the Indian versus Indian combats were really European wars in which the Indians unconsciously played the role of expendable surrogates. The curbs and restraints of aboriginal custom held no power over Europeans, and particular tribes were in various states of dependency or "ambipendency" with regard to particular colonies. Continual European initiatives and pressures for war created a *macrocontact* system in which tribal bellicosity was indeed self-preservatory for particular groups in particular circumstances, even though it worked general calamity upon the whole of Indian society.

There were no innate differences between Indians and Europeans in their capacity for war or their mode of conducting it. Their differences were matters of technology and politics.[69] Only a few generations before the invasion of America, Europeans had conducted war according to feudal rules very different from those of the nation-state but startlingly similar in many respects to the practices of Indian war. Admittedly Indian society was not class-stratified like feudal society, and the Indian warrior differed from the feudal knight by being an all-purpose man who turned his hand to peasant occupations between battles. Clearly, also, Indians did not build or besiege castles, or fight with metal weapons and armor. But let not reality disappear behind the knight's armor plate; there was a naked warrior within. From childhood he had received special training in the use of arms, and he spent much time in strenuous sports that would strengthen and condition his body for war. So did the Indian. Both were hunters, and in the hunt both maintained their skill in the use of weapons. Like the Indian the medieval knight hunted for food as well as for sport and training; and, as with the Indian's hunting territories, unauthorized persons were forbidden to hunt in the knight's domain.[70]

A special purification ritual admitted the European esquire into the status of warrior; so also for the Indian, although in his case the ritual was also an ordeal. Knight and warrior mobilized for war in similar ways:

---

[69] The only extended discussion seems to be one without visible virtues: Henry Holbert Turney-High, *Primitive War: Its Practice and Concepts* (Columbia, S.C., 1949). This is an unreliable, superficial, Colonel Blimp sort of repetitive dogma and slippery semantics. The author repeatedly expresses his contempt of the social sciences and declares that any noncommissioned officer knows more than all the social scientists. He hastens to add that he was himself a commissioned officer.

[70] A. F. C. Wallace has erroneously extrapolated the American custom of freedom to hunt on unposted lands back into European times, and the error is repeated by Vaughan; but hunting in Europe was stringently limited to the nobility and to "stinted" limits of rights in commons for the lower orders. Wallace, "Political Organization [and Land Tenure among the Northeastern Indians, 1600–1830]," *Southwest. Jour. of Anthro.*, XIII (1957), 312, n. 7; [Alden T.] Vaughan, *New England Frontier: [Puritans and Indians, 1620–1675* (Boston, 1965)], 108; E. C. K. Gonner, *Common Land and Inclosure* (London, 1912), 14–16.

the knight responded, if he felt like it, to the call of a lord to whom he had commended himself as vassal; the warrior responded, if he felt like it, to the invitation of an admired chief. No warrior was conscripted against his will. In neither case was there a bureaucracy to recruit and organize a fighting force; such loyalty as existed was that of man to man and family to family. Naturally enough, such soldiers knew nothing of Prussian discipline. Knights and warriors were free men fighting in wars and battles of their own choosing, unlike the hireling standing armies of the nation-state, who accepted orders with their wages.

One of the most striking parallels between the customs of feudal knights and those of Indian warriors was a code of behavior that in Europe is called chivalry. The sparing of women and children in Indian warfare fits snugly into the doctrines of chivalry avowed by feudal knights (and even practiced by them when the women and children were of their own religion). The practice was abandoned by the more rational or efficient killing machines organized by the nation-states; chivalry belonged to the knights, and the knights belonged to the Middle Ages. Chivalry, in short, was barbarous.

Perhaps an opportunity exists here to use the parallel between America and Europe to learn more about Europe. A customary explanation of chivalry's rise has been that the sweet moan of minnesingers and troubadours softened the hearts and manners of the great hulks on horseback. This lacks persuasion. Indians had a different sort of explanation for their own variety of chivalry: they needed to rebuild their declining populations. Feudal Europe was a time of population uncertainty, and the damsels spared by gallant knights were prime breeding stock—a fact sometimes put to test by the knights. In this respect the Indians seem to have been the more chivalrous, for they were observed everywhere to refrain from sexual molestation of female prisoners; they took the women and girls, untouched, back to the captors' villages for assignment to families as wives and daughters.[71] The knight, however, though he served the public interest by preserving his prisoners' lives, served himself also by demanding ransom.

Knight and warrior both gave first allegiance to their kin. This reservation of loyalty from the monopoly demanded by the nation-state was the unforgivable sin that has roused nationalists to denounce the special barbarity of feudal Europe and the special savagery of Indian America. That all war is cruel, horrible, and socially insane is easy to demonstrate, but the nationalist dwells upon destiny, glory, crusades, and other such claptrap to pretend that his own kind of war is different from and better than the horrors perpetrated by savages. This is plainly false. The qualities of ferocity and atrocity are massively visible in the practices of European and American powers all over the world, quite recently in the assaults of the most advanced civilized states upon one another.

[71] Hodge, ed., *Handbook of N. Am. Indians*, s.v., "captives"; Heckewelder, *Account of the Indian Nations*, ed. Reichel, in Hist. Soc. Pa., *Memoirs*, XII, 339–340.

Suggestions for Further Reading

The everyday lives of colonizing Europeans in the seventeenth century are disclosed in a variety of recent work in American history. For ideas about the New World and what immigrants might have expected to find, see Howard Mumford Jones, *O Strange New World: American Culture, The Formative Years** (New York, 1964); Richard Slotkin, *Regeneration Through Violence: The Mythology of the American Frontier, 1600–1860** (Middletown, Conn., 1973); Louis B. Wright, *The Colonial Search for a Southern Eden* (University, Ala., 1953); and Henri Baudet, *Paradise on Earth: Thoughts on European Images of Non-European Man,* trans. Elizabeth Wentholt (New Haven, Conn., 1965).

Attitudes toward work are discussed in Keith Thomas, "Work and Leisure in Pre-Industrial Society," *Past and Present* 29 (1964): 50–66, and David Bertelson, *The Lazy South* (New York, 1967).

Family relations—including attitudes toward sex, love, marriage, and familial rights and responsibilities—are discussed in Edmund S. Morgan, *The Puritan Family: Religion and Domestic Relations in Seventeenth-Century New England** (New York, 1966) and *Virginians at Home; Family Life in the Eighteenth Century** (Williamsburg, Va., 1952); Philip J. Greven, Jr., *Four Generations: Population, Land, and Family in Colonial Andover, Massachusetts** (Ithaca, N.Y., 1970); and John Demos, "Families in Colonial Bristol, Rhode Island: An Exercise in Historical Demography," *William and Mary Quarterly* 25 (1968):40–57. For attitudes toward child rearing see Joseph Illick, "Child-rearing in 17th-Century England"; and John F. Walzer, "A Period of Ambivalence: Eighteenth-Century Childhood," in Lloyd deMause, ed., *The History of Childhood* (New York, 1974), pp. 303–350 and 351–382.

The daily lives of colonial women are discussed in Mary Ryan, *Womanhood in America from Colonial Times to the Present* (New York, 1975), chs. 1–2; Ben Barker-Benfield, "Anne Hutchinson and the Puritan Attitude toward Women," *Feminist Studies,* 1 (1972): 65–96; Julia C. Spruill, *Women's Life and Work in the Southern Colonies* (Chapel Hill, N.C., 1938); and Mary S. Benson, *Women in Eighteenth-Century America* (New York, 1935).

For Indian cultures of the Northeast Woodlands at the time of European arrival, the literature is vast. For a general introduction the student may consult Gary B. Nash, *Red, White, and Black: The Peoples of Early America** (Englewood Cliffs, N.J., 1974), and Francis Jennings, *The Invasion of America: Indians, Colonialism, and the Cant of Conquest* (Chapel Hill, N.C., 1975). Also valuable

* Available in paperback edition.

are Harold Fey and D'Arcy McNickle, *Indians and Other Americans: Two Ways of Life Meet** (New York, 1959), and Kenneth Macgowan and Joseph A. Hester, Jr., *Early Man in the New World** (Garden City, N.Y., 1962).

In studying early attitudes toward the Indians and the conflict that resulted, Richard Slotkin, *Regeneration Through Violence*, is indispensable. Also of great value are Roy Harvey Pearce, *Savagism and Civilization: A Study of the Indian and the Idea of Civilization** (Baltimore, 1953), and Wilcomb E. Washburn, *The Governor and the Rebel: A History of Bacon's Rebellion in Virginia** (Chapel Hill, N.C., 1957).

Other insights into the daily lives of the earliest colonists can be gleaned from David E. Stannard, *The Puritan Way of Death* (New York, 1977); David H. Flaherty, *Privacy in Colonial New England* (Charlottesville, Va., 1972); Darrett B. Rutman, *Husbandmen of Plymouth: Farms and Villages of the Old Colony, 1620–1692* (Boston, 1967); and from John Barth's marvelously revealing novel about early life on the Chesapeake, *The Sot-Weed Factor** (Garden City, N.Y., 1960).

1730–1790
Creating a Nation

The Beginnings of the
Afro-American Family
in Maryland

ALLAN KULIKOFF

It is commonly assumed that African slaves, brought to European colonies in North and South America, were simply fitted into a closed system of forced labor where they lived out their lives—cowed, brutalized, and de-Africanized. The historical focus has been on the slave system fashioned by slave owners: the black codes they enacted, their treatment of slaves, and the economic development they directed. But the slaves themselves are often forgotten as active participants in a cultural process. How did they experience life in an environment vastly different from their native one? To what degree did they adopt the norms of white colonial society? How did they respond to the loss of freedom and to the separation from all that was familiar in their own society? To what extent did they fashion a new Afro-American culture that blended their traditional mores with those of their European masters? Only by posing questions of this kind can we study the lives of slaves rather than the lives of the masters who held the power of life and death over their human property.

Over the last few decades many historical analyses of slavery have been written in response to the thesis of Stanley Elkins that plantation slavery in North America was a uniquely brutal and closed system of forced labor. In the English colonies, Elkins argues, masters were unrestrained by the institutions of church, law, and government that mediated between slave and master in the Spanish and Portuguese colonies. Ironically, a far more repressive and dehumanizing system of slavery developed in the more "enlightened" and "modern" environment of English North America than in the more "feudalistic" and "authoritarian" milieu of Latin America. Racial lines were more strictly drawn in the English colonies, manumission of slaves was less frequent, and freed slaves had less opportunity to attain any worthy status than in New Spain or Brazil.

Developed at length in Elkins's book **Slavery: A Problem in American Institutional and Intellectual Life,** this postulation of the differences in slave behavior in different colonies has generated almost two decades of sharp debate that has greatly furthered slave studies. But only in the last few years have historians begun to probe the daily lives of slaves in eighteenth-century America. This new work tells us that, though kept in bondage, slaves were far from passive. They were not stripped of their identities; they were rarely emotionally attached to their masters; they seldom forgot their African culture. Instead, they were locked into a dynamic relationship with their owners in which, despite the grotesquely uneven distribution of power, they demonstrated extraordinary ingenuity in setting limits on the master's ability to coerce them. However brutal the power held over them, slaves were actively and continuously involved in carving out psychological "space" for themselves. Survival was their immediate goal, but freedom was their ultimate hope.

Within the argument about the slave experience, the nature of the Afro-American family has a special importance. One of the casualties of the American system of chattel slavery, according to sociologists and historians, was the black family. American slavery, we have been told, was at its worst in denying slaves even the most basic human right of family association. By splitting up husbands and wives or parents and children, by sexually exploiting black women, and by refusing to grant marriage rights to their slaves, white slave masters unremittingly assaulted the black family.

Historians have recently questioned these views about the disintegration of the African family in its American slave setting. They have found that slaveowners could not obliterate slave family life without threatening the efficient and profitable management of the plantation. Often they encouraged slaves to live together and take up the role of parents, for masters found that slaves were more dutiful and productive when tied to spouses and offspring. If not concerned about the morality of their slaves, they were interested in maximizing the output of labor and minimizing insubordination. Also, slaves themselves refused to give up the right to family association. Though strictly confined within the "peculiar Institution," they still managed to forge affective ties. Overcoming formidable obstacles, slaves fashioned intimate bonds between man and woman, parent and child. It is this fascinating struggle among American slaves to create a family life that is revealed in the following selection.

Sometime in 1728, Harry, a recently imported African, escaped from his master in southern Prince George's County, Maryland, and joined a small black community among the Indians beyond the area of white settlement. The following year, Harry returned to Prince George's to urge his former shipmates, the only "kinfolk" he had, to return there with him. Over forty years later, another Harry, who belonged to John Jenkins of Prince George's, ran away. The Annapolis newspaper reported that "he has been seen about the Negro Quarters in *Patuxent*, but is supposed to have removed among his Acquaintances on Potomack; he is also well acquainted with the Negroes at Clement Wheeler's Quarter on Zekiah, and a Negro Wench of Mr. Wall's named Rachael; a few miles from that Quarter is his Aunt, and he may possibly be harboured thereabouts." [1]

These two incidents, separated by two generations, are suggestive. African Harry ran away *from* slavery to the frontier; Afro-American Harry ran *to* his friends and kinfolk spread over a wide territory. The Afro-American runaway could call on many others to hide him, but the African had few friends and seemingly, no wife. These contrasts raise many questions. How did Afro-Americans organize their families in the

"The Beginnings of the Afro-American Family in Maryland," by Allan Kulikoff. Reprinted from *The American Family in Social-Historical Perspective*, Michael Gordon, ed. (New York: St. Martin's Press, 1978). Originally printed, in a somewhat longer version, in *Law, Society, and Politics in Early Maryland*, Carr, Land, and Papenfuse, eds. (Baltimore: Johns Hopkins University Press, 1977), copyright © 1977 by Hall of Records Commission of the State of Maryland.

Chesapeake colonies during the eighteenth century? Who lived in slave households? How many Afro-American fathers lived with their wives and children? What was the impact of arbitrary sale and transfer of slaves upon family life? How did an Afro-American's household and family relationships change through the life cycle?

This paper attempts to answer these questions.[2] While literary documents by or about slaves before 1800, such as runaway narratives, WPA freed-slave interviews, black autobiographies, or detailed travel accounts are very infrequently available to historians of colonial slave family life, they can gather age and family data from probate inventories, personal information from runaway advertisements, and depositions in court cases. These sources, together with several diaries and account books kept by whites, provide a great deal of material about African and Afro-American family life in the Chesapeake region.

Almost all the blacks who lived in Maryland and Virginia before 1780 were slaves. Because his status precluded him from enjoying a legally secure family life, a slave's household often excluded important family members. Households, domestic groups, and families must therefore be clearly distinguished. A household, as used here, is a coresidence group that includes all who shared a "proximity of sleeping arrangements," or lived under the same roof. Domestic groups include kin and nonkin, living in the same or separate households, who share cooking, eating, childrearing, working, and other daily activities. Families are composed of people related by blood or marriage. Several distinctions are useful in defining the members of families. The immediate family include husband and wife or parents and children. Near kin include the immediate family and all other kin, such as adult brothers and sisters or cousins who share the same house or domestic tasks with the immediate family. Other kinfolk who do not function as family members on a regular basis are considered to be distant kin.[3]

The process of family formation can perhaps best be understood as an adaptive process. My ideas about this process owe much to a provocative essay by Sidney Mintz and Richard Price on Afro-American culture. Blacks learned to modify their environment, learned from each other how to retain family ties under very adverse conditions, and structured their expectations about family activities around what they knew the master would permit. If white masters determined the outward bounds of family activities, it was Africans, and especially their descendants, who gave meaning to the relationships between parents and children, among siblings, and with more distant kinfolk. As a result, black family structure on the eve of the Revolution differed from both African and white family systems.[4]

Africans who were forced to come to the Chesapeake region in the late seventeenth and early eighteenth centuries struggled to create viable families and households, but often failed. They suffered a great loss when they were herded into slave ships. Their family and friends, who had given meaning to their lives and structured their place in society, were left behind and they found themselves among strangers. They could never recreate their families and certainly not devise a West African kinship system in the Chesapeake. The differences between African communities were too great. Some Africans lived in clans and lineages, others did not; some traced their descent from women but others traced descent from men; mothers, fathers, and other kin played somewhat different roles in each community; initiation ceremonies and puberty rites, forbidden marriages, marriage customs, and household structures all varied from place to place.[5]

Though African immigrants did not bring a unified West African culture with them to the Chesapeake colonies, they did share important beliefs about the nature of kinship. Africans could modify these beliefs in America to legitimate the families they eventually formed. They saw kinship as the principal way of ordering relationships between individuals. Each person in the tribe was related to most others in the community. The male was father, son, and uncle; the female was mother, daughter, and aunt to many others. Because their kinship system was so extensive, Africans included kinfolk outside the immediate family in their daily activities. For example, adult brothers or sisters of the father or mother played an important role in childrearing and domestic activities in many African societies.[6]

Secondly, but far less certainly, African immigrants may have adapted some practices associated with polygyny, a common African marital custom. A few men on the Eastern Shore of Maryland in the 1740s, and perhaps others scattered elsewhere, lived with several women. However, far too few African women (in relation to the number of men) immigrated to make polygynous marriages common. Nevertheless, the close psychological relationship between mothers and children, and the great social distance between a husband and his various wives and children found in African polygynous societies might have been repeated in the Chesapeake colonies. In any event, African slave mothers played a more important role than fathers in teaching children about Africa and about how to get along in the slave system. Both African custom and the physical separation of immigrant men and women played a role in this development.[7]

Africans faced a demographic environment hostile to most forms of family life. If African men were to start families, they had to find wives, and that task was difficult. Most blacks lived on small farms of less than 11 slaves; and the small black population was spread thinly over a vast territory. Roads were rudimentary. Even where concentrations of larger plantations were located, African men did not automatically find wives. Sex ratios in southern Maryland rose from 125 to 130 (men per 100 women) in the mid-seventeenth century to about 150 in the 1710s and 1720s, and to around 180 in the 1730s. In Surry County, Virginia, the slave sex ratio was about 145 in the 1670s and 1680s, but over 200 in the 1690s and 1700s. Wealthy slaveowners did not provide most of their African men with wives; the larger the plantation, the higher the sex ratio tended to be.[8]

Africans had competition for the available black women. By the 1690s, some black women were natives, and they may have preferred Afro-American men. White men were also competitors. Indeed, during the seventeenth and early eighteenth centuries, white adult sex ratios were as high (or higher) than black adult sex ratios. At any period whites possessed a monopoly of power and some of them probably took slave women as their common-law wives. African men competed for the remaining black women who were mostly recently-enslaved Africans. These immigrant women often waited two or three years before marrying. Since the number of women available to African men was so small, many probably died before they could find a wife. In 1739 African men planned an uprising in Prince George's County partly because they could not find wives.[9]

Foreign-born male slaves in Maryland and Virginia probably lived in a succession of different kinds of households. Newly imported Africans had no black kin in the Chesapeake. Since sex ratios were high, most of these men probably lived with other, unrelated men. African men may have substituted friends for kin. Newly enslaved Africans made friends with their nearest shipmates during the middle passage, and after their arrival in Maryland, some of them lived near these men. New Negroes could live with other recent African immigrants because migration from Africa occurred in short spurts from the 1670s to the late 1730s. The high sex ratios of large plantations indicate that wealthy men bought many of these Africans. Even if his shipmates lived miles away, the new immigrant could share the experiences of others who had recently endured the middle passage.[10]

Despite the difficulties, most Africans who survived for a few years eventually found a wife. In societies with high sex ratios, women tend to marry young, but men have to postpone marriage. This increases the opportunity of older men to marry by reducing the sexual imbalance. (That is, there are as many younger women as older men.) By the 1690s, large numbers of Afro-American women entered their midteens and married Afro-American and African men.[11] Because the plantations were small, and individual farm sex ratios likely to be uneven, the wives and children of married African men very often lived on other plantations. These men still lived mainly with other unrelated men, but at least they had begun to develop kin ties.[12] A few African men lived with their wives and children, and some limited evidence suggests that the longer an African lived in the Chesapeake, the more likely he was to live with his immediate family.[13]

Unlike most African men, African women commonly lived with their children. Some African women may have been so alienated that they refused to have children, but the rest bore and raised several offspring, protected by the master's reluctance to separate very young children from their mothers. Since the children were reared by their mothers and eventually joined them in the tobacco fields, these households were domestic groups although incomplete as families.[14]

A greater proportion of African women than African men lived with both spouses and children. These opportunities usually arose on large plantations. There was such a surplus of men on large plantations that African women who lived on them could choose husbands from several African or Afro-American men. The sex ratio on large plantations in Prince George's during the 1730s, a period of heavy immigration, was

249. This shortage of women prevented most recently arrived African men from finding a wife on the plantation. For them the opportunity to live with a wife and children was rare. More Africans probably lived with their immediate families in the 1740s; immigration declined, large planters bought more African women, and the sex ratio on big plantations fell to 142.[15]

Because African spouses were usually separated, African mothers reared their Afro-American children with little help from their husbands. Even when the father was present, the extended kin so important in the lives of African children was missing. Mothers probably taught them the broad values they brought from Africa and related the family's history in Africa and the Chesapeake. When the children began working in the fields, they learned from their mothers how to survive a day's work and how to get along with master and overseer.

Each group of Africans repeated the experiences of previous immigrants. Eventually, more and more Afro-American children matured and began families of their own. The first large generation of Afro-Americans in Maryland probably came of age in the 1690s; by the 1720s, when the second large generation had matured, the black population finally began increasing naturally.[16]

The changing composition of the black population combined with other changes to restructure Afro-American households and families. Alterations in the adult sex ratio, the size of plantations, and black population density provided black people with opportunities to enjoy a more satisfying family life. The way masters transferred slaves from place to place limited the size and composition of black households, but Afro-American family members separated by masters managed to establish complex kinship networks over many plantations. Afro-Americans used these opportunities to create a kind of family life that differed from African and Anglo-American practices.

Demographic changes led to more complex households and families. As the number of adult Africans in the population decreased, the sex ratio in Maryland declined to between 100 and 110 by the 1750s. This decline gave most men an opportunity to marry by about age thirty. The number of slaves who lived on plantations with more than twenty blacks increased; the density of the black population in tidewater Maryland and Virginia rose; the proportion of blacks in the total population of Prince George's County, in nearby areas of Maryland, and throughout tidewater Virginia rose to half or more by the end of the century; and many new roads were built. The number of friends and kinfolk whom typical Afro-Americans saw every day or visited with regularity increased, while their contact with whites declined because large areas of the Chesapeake became nearly black counties.[17]

How frequently masters transferred their Afro-American slaves, and where they sent them, affected black household composition. Surviving documents do not allow a systematic analysis of this point, but several conclusions seem clear. First, planters kept women and their small children together but did not keep husbands and teenage children with their immediate family. Slaveowner after slaveowner bequeathed women and

their "increase" to sons or daughters. However, children of slaveowners
tended to live near their parents; thus, even when members of slave
families were so separated, they remained in the same neighborhood.[18]
Secondly, Afro-Americans who lived on small farms were transferred
more frequently than those on large plantations. At their deaths small
slaveowners typically willed a slave or two to their widows and to each
child. They also frequently mortgaged or sold slaves to gain capital. If a
slaveowner died with many unpaid debts, his slaves had to be sold.[19]
Finally, relatively few blacks were forced to move long distances. Far
more blacks were affected by migrations of slaves from the Chesapeake
region to the new Southwest in the nineteenth century than by long-
distance movement in the region before the Revolution.[20] These points
should not be misunderstood. Most Afro-Americans who lived in Maryland or Virginia during the eighteenth century experienced separations
from members of their immediate families sometime in their lives. Most,
however, were able to visit these family members occasionally.

These changes led to a new social reality for most slaves born in the
1750s, 1760s, and 1770s. If unrelated people and their progeny stay in a
limited geographic area for several generations, the descendants of the
original settlers must develop kin ties with many other people who live
nearby. Once the proportion of adult Africans declined, this process
began. African women married and had children; the children matured
and married. If most of them remained near their first homes, each was
bound to have siblings, children, spouses, uncles, aunts, and cousins living
in the neighborhood. How these various kinspeople were organized into
households, families, and domestic groups depended not only upon the
whims of masters but also upon the meaning placed on kinship by the
slaves themselves.

The process of household and family formation and dissolution was
begun by each immigrant woman who lived long enough to have children.
The story of Ann Joice, a black woman who was born in Barbados, taken
to England as a servant, and then falsely sold into slavery in Maryland in
the 1670s, may have been similar to that of other immigrant women once
she became a slave. The Darnall family of Prince George's owned Ann
Joice. She had seven children with several white men in the 1670s and
1680s; all remained slaves the rest of their lives. Three of her children
stayed on the Darnall home plantation until their deaths. One was sold
as a child to a planter who lived a few miles away; another was eventually
sold to William Digges, who lived about five miles from the Darnall farm.
Both the spatial spread and the local concentration of kinfolk continued
in the next generation. Peter Harbard, born between 1715 and 1720, was
the son of Francis Harbard, who was Ann Joice's child. Peter grew up
on the Darnall farm, but in 1737 he was sold to George Gordon, who lived
across the road from Darnall. As a child, Peter lived with or very near his
grandmother Ann Joice, his father, and several paternal uncles and aunts.
He probably knew his seven cousins(father's sister's children), children of
his aunt Susan Harbard, who lived on William Digges's plantation. Other
kinfolk lived in Annapolis but were too far away to visit easily.[21]

As Afro-American slaves were born and died, and as masters sold or bequeathed their slaves, black households were formed and reformed, broken and created. Several detailed examples can illustrate this process. For example, Daphne, the daughter of Nan, was born about 1736 on a large plantation in Prince George's owned by Robert Tyler, Sr. Until she was two, she lived with her mother, two brothers, and two sisters. In 1738, Tyler died and left his slaves to his wife, children, and grand-children. All lived on or near Tyler's farms. Three of Daphne's siblings were bequeathed to granddaughter Ruth Tyler, who later married Morde-cai Jacob, her grandfather's next-door neighbor. Daphne continued to live on the Tyler plantation. From 1736 to 1787, she had six different masters, but she still lived where she was born. Daphne lived with her mother until her mother died, and with her ten children until 1779. Children were eventually born to Daphne's daughters; these infants lived with their mothers and near their maternal grandmother. When Robert Tyler III, Robert senior's grandson and Daphne's fifth master, died in 1779, his will divided Daphne's children and grandchildren between his son and daughter. Daphne was thus separated from younger children, born be-tween 1760 and 1772. They were given to Millicent Beanes, Robert III's daughter, who lived several miles away. Daphne continued to live on the same plantation as her four older children and several grandchildren. An intricate extended family of grandmother, sons, daughters, grandchildren, aunts, uncles, nieces, nephews, and cousins resided in several households on the Tyler plantation in 1778, and other more remote kinfolk could be found on the neighboring Jacob farm.[22]

Family separations might be more frequent on smaller plantations. Rachael was born in the late 1730s and bore ten children between 1758 and 1784. As a child she lived on the plantation of Alexander Magruder; a large slaveowner in Prince George's; before 1746, Alexander gave her to his son Hezekiah, who lived on an adjoining plantation. Hezekiah never owned more than ten slaves, and when he died in 1769, he owned only two—including one willed to his wife by her brother. Between 1755 and 1757, he mortgaged nine slaves, including Rachael, to two merchants. In 1757, Samuel Roundall (who lived about five miles from the Magruders) seized Rachael and six other slaves mortgaged to him. This and subsequent transfers can be seen on Figure 1. In 1760 Roundall sold Rachael and her eldest daughter to Samuel Lovejoy, who lived about nine miles from Roundall. At the same time, four other former Magruder slaves were sold: two to planters in Lovejoy's neighborhood, one to a Roundall neigh-bor, and one to a planter living at least fifteen miles away in Charles County. Rachael's separation from friends and family members continued. In 1761, her eldest child was sold at age three to George Stamp, a neighbor of Lovejoy. By the time Samuel Lovejoy died in 1762, she had two other children. She and her youngest child went to live with John Lovejoy, Samuel's nephew and near-neighbor, but her second child, about age two, stayed with Lovejoy's widow. Her third child was sold at age six, but Rachael and her next seven children lived with John Lovejoy until at least 1787.[23]

These three examples suggest how Afro-American households and families developed in the eighteenth century. Husbands and wives and

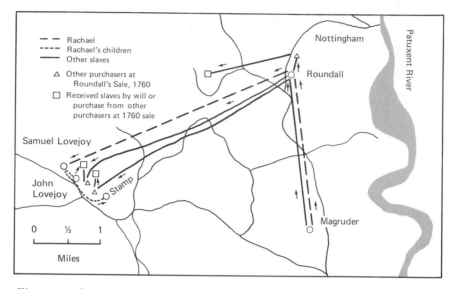

Figure 1   Sale and Later Transfer of Hezekiah Magruder's Slaves, 1755–1780

parents and children were frequently separated by the master's transfers of family members. At the same time, as generation followed generation, households, or adjacent huts, became increasingly complex, and sometimes included grandparents, uncles, aunts, or cousins, as well as the immediate family. Since other kin lived on nearby or distant plantations, geographically concentrated (and dispersed) kinship networks that connected numbers of quarters emerged during the pre-Revolutionary era.

How typical were the experiences suggested by the examples? How were families organized into households and domestic groups on large and small quarters? Data from three large planter's inventories taken in 1759, 1773–1774, and 1775, and from a Prince George's census of 1776 permit a test of the hypotheses concerning changes in household structure, differences between large and small units, and the spread of kinfolk across space. Table I details household structure on large quarters of over twenty and Table II shows the kinds of households on small farms. About half of all slaves probably lived on each plantation type.[24] This evidence provides a good test, because by the 1770s most Afro-Americans could trace a Chesapeake genealogy back to immigrant grandparents or great-grandparents.[25]

Kinfolk (immediate families and near kin) on large plantations were organized into three kinds of residence groups. Most of the slaves of some quarters were interrelated by blood or marriage. Domestic groups included kinfolk who lived on opposite sides of duplex slave huts and who shared a common yard and eating and cooking arrangements. Finally, most households included members of an immediate family.

The kinship structure of large plantations is illustrated by a household inventory taken in 1773–1774 of 385 slaves owned by Charles Carroll of Carrollton on thirteen different quarters in Anne Arundel County. Because

TABLE I

AFRO-AMERICAN HOUSEHOLD STRUCTURES ON THREE LARGE PLANTATIONS
IN PRINCE GEORGE'S AND ANNE ARUNDEL COUNTIES,
MARYLAND, 1759–1775

| Household Type | Percentage in Household Type | | | | Percentage Total in Household Types |
	Males 15+	Females 15+	Children 0–9	Children 10–14	
Husband-wife-children	40	43	55	44	47
Mother-children	2	17	22	10	14
Mother-children-other kin	4	14	8	13	9
Siblings	7	4	6	12	7
Husband-wife-children-other kin	2	2	2	2	2
Father-children	5	0	3	5	3
Husband-wife	2	2	0	0	1
Three generation	1	2	2	3	2
Unknown or mixed	36	16	3	12	15
Total percentage	99	100	101	101	100
Number people	142	129	178	77	526

Sources: PG Inventories, GS No. 1, f. 73 (1759; James Wardrop's, 32 slaves); and GS No. 2, ff. 334–336 (1775; Addison's 3 plantations, 109 slaves) and Charles Carroll Account Book, Maryland Historical Society (rest of slaves). The three-generation households include grandparents and grandchildren but not the generation in between. The unknown or mixed category includes all those apparently living away from all kinfolk but perhaps living near them. Some of the slaves in this category probably belong in the others, but the sources (especially the Addison and Wardrop documents) do not permit location of them.

Carroll insisted that the inventory be "taken in Familys with their Ages," the document permits a detailed reconstruction of kinship networks.[26] Though the complexity and size of kinship groups on Carroll's quarters were probably greater than on other large plantations, the general pattern could easily have been repeated elsewhere.[27]

The ten men and three women who headed each list were probably leaders of their quarters. Five of the quarters were named for these individuals.[28] They tended to be old slaves who had been with the Carroll family for many years. While the mean age of all adults was thirty-seven years, the mean age of the leaders was forty-nine, and six of the thirteen were over fifty-five.[29] The leader often lived with many kinfolk; he or she was closely related to about 36 to 38 percent of all the other slaves on the quarter. For example, Fanny, sixty-nine years of age, was surrounded by at least forty near kinfolk on the main plantation at Doohoregan, and Mayara James, sixty-five years of age, lived with twenty-three relatives on his quarter.[30]

The two slaves' genealogies presented in Figures 2 and 3 provide detailed examples of the kinds of kinship networks that could develop on quarters after several generations of relative geographic stability. Because

TABLE II

AFRO-AMERICAN HOUSEHOLD STRUCTURES ON SMALL PLANTATIONS
(1–8 SLAVES). PRINCE GEORGE'S COUNTY, MARYLAND, 1776

Household Type	Males 15+	Females 15+	Children 0–9	Children 10–14	Percentage of Total in Household Types
Husband-wife-children	17	18	22	10	18
Mother-children	2	35	56	29	32
Father-children	2	*	4	1	2
Siblings	7	5	6	17	8
Mixed	72	42	12	43	41
Total percentage	100	100	100	100	101
Number of people	275	276	325	162	1038

Source: 1776 Census. The household types were assumed from black age structures on individual farms. The statistics must be treated as educated guesses. For a detailed explanation of the biases of this table, see the original article in *Law, Society and Politics in Early Maryland*. Land et al., eds., (Baltimore: Johns Hopkins Press, 1977).

* = less than ½%.

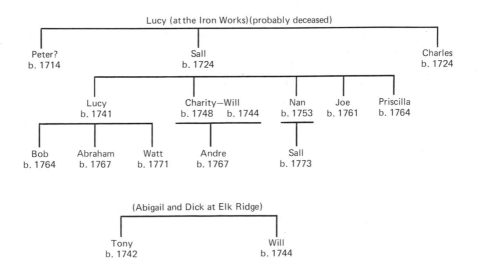

Figure 2   Kinship Ties Among Charles Carroll's Slaves at Annapolis Quarter, 1774

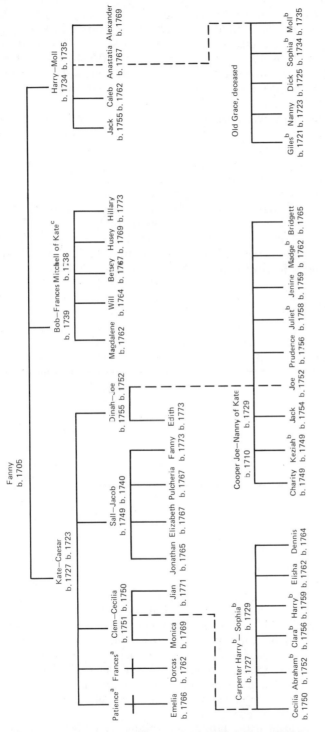

Figure 3   Fanny and Some of her Kinfolk on Doohoregan Manor, 1773

most slave quarters had between fifteen and thirty slaves, the network
included just two or three households. The kin group shown in Figure 2
may have been typical. Thirteen of the seventeen slaves who lived at
Annapolis Quarter in 1774 were descendants of Iron Works Lucy. Ten
were children and grandchildren of Sall. One of Sall's sons-in-law and his
brother also lived there. Peter and Charles, other descendants of Lucy,
lived on the quarter but had families elsewhere.

Nearly half the slaves who resided on Riggs Quarter, Carroll's main
plantation, were kinfolk (63/130). A network of this size could develop
only on the home plantation of the largest Chesapeake planters.[31] Each
of the members of the group was either a direct descendant or an affine
(in-law) of old Fanny. She was surrounded on her quarter by five children, nineteen grandchildren, nine great-grandchildren, four children-in-
law, and three grandchildren's spouses. The network grew through the
marriage of Fanny's children and grandchildren to children of other residents of the quarter. For example, Cooper Joe, his wife, and thirteen
children and grandchildren were closely related to Fanny's family. By
the early 1750s Cooper Joe had married Nanny of Kate, and about 1761
Fanny's son Bob married Frances Mitchell of Kate. Joe and Nanny's
children were first cousins of the children of Bob and Frances, and thereby
more remotely connected to all the rest of Fanny's descendants. The
alliance of the two families was cemented in 1772, when Dinah, the
daughter of Kate of Fanny married Joe, the son of Cooper Joe.[32]

The intraquarter kinship network was also a work group. Fanny's
and Lucy's adult and teenage kinfolk worked together in the fields.
Masters separated their slaves by sex, age, and strength, and determined
what each would do, but blacks judged each other in part by the reciprocal kinship obligation that bound them together. Afro-Americans
worked at their own pace and frequently thwarted their masters' desires
for increased productivity. Part of this conflict can be explained by the
Afro-American's preindustrial work discipline, but part may have been
due to the desires of kinfolk to help and protect each other from the
master's lash, the humid climate, and the malarial environment.[33]

Landon Carter's lament upon the death of his trusted old slave Jack
Lubbar suggests the dimensions of kinship solidarity in the fields. Lubbar
had been a foreman over many groups of slaves. In his old age, he worked
at the Fork quarter "with 5 hands and myself; in which service he so
gratefully discharged his duty as to make me by his care alone larger
crops of Corn, tobacco and Pease twice over than ever I have had made by
anyone. . . ." Other blacks did not share Lubbar's desire to produce a
large crop for Carter. "At this plantation," Carter writes, "he continued
till his age almost deprived him of eyesight which made him desire to be
removed because those under him, mostly his great grandchildren, by the
baseness of their Parents abused him much." Lubbar's grandchildren and
great-grandchildren, who worked together, were related in intricate
ways: parents and children, maternal and paternal cousins, uncles and
aunts, and brothers and sisters. They united against Lubbar to slow the
work pace and conserve their energy.[34]

When Afro-Americans came home each night from the fields, they broke into smaller domestic groups. Their habitat set the scene for social intercourse. On large plantations "a Negro quarter is a Number of Huts or Hovels, built at some distance from the Mansion House; where the Negroes reside with their wives and Families, and cultivate at vacant times the little spots allow'd them." [35] Four early-nineteenth-century slave houses still standing in Southern Maryland suggest that slave families living on the same quarter were very close. Each house included two rooms of about sixteen-by-sixteen feet, separated by a thin wall. In three of the homes, the two huts shared the same roof but had separate doorways. Two had separate fireplaces, the residents of one duplex shared a fireplace, and one quarter (which was over a kitchen) did not have a fireplace.[36] Neither family had much privacy, and communication between them must have been commonplace. No activity could occur on one side of the hut without those on the other knowing about it. And the two halves of the hut shared a common yard, where residents could talk, eat, or celebrate.

On the quarters the smallest local residence unit to contain kinfolk was the household. Household members were not isolated from other kinfolk; they worked with their relatives in the fields, associated with neighbors in the common yard, and cooked meals or slept near those who lived on the other side of their duplex. Nevertheless, kinfolk who lived in the same household were spatially closer when at home than any other group of kin. Who lived in typical households on slave quarters? How many husbands lived with their wives and children? How many children were separated from their parents? Did kin other than the immediate family live in many households?

Nearly half of all the Afro-Americans who lived on the three large plantations described in Table I resided in households that included both parents and at least some of their children. Over half of the young children on all three plantations lived with both parents, but a far higher proportion of adults and children ten to fourteen years of age lived in two-parent households on the Carroll quarters than on the three Addison farms and Wardrop's plantation in Prince George's. While 49 percent of the women, 51 percent of the men, and 52 percent of children between ages ten and fourteen on Carroll's farms lived in two-parent households, only 28 percent of the women, 24 percent of the men, and 30 percent of those ten to fourteen years old could be found in two-parent homes on the other farms. Almost all the other children lived with one parent, usually the mother; but over a quarter of those ten to fourteen years of age lived with siblings or with apparently unrelated people.

The differences between Carroll and the other two large slaveowners is striking. Carroll, unlike all but a few other Chesapeake gentlemen, was able to provide his people with spouses from his own plantations and chose to keep adolescent children with their parents. Over six-tenths of the men (62 percent) and 28 percent of the women on Addison's and Wardrop's plantations lived with siblings, were unmarried, or lived away from spouses and children. On Carroll's quarters only 27 percent of the men and 12 percent of the women were similarly separated from wives and children.

Many blacks on these three large farms lived with or near kin other than their parents or children. About 7 percent were in the household of a brother or sister, and over a tenth (13 percent) of parents and children shared their homes with another kinsperson. There were several types of these extended households: seven included parent(s), children, and sibling(s) of the mother; two included grandmother living with her children and grandchildren; in one household grandparents took care of two young grandchildren; and in one hut, an adult brother and sister lived with her children and one grandchild.

Far less can be learned about families on small plantations. On these farms, the slave quarter could be in an outbuilding or in a small hut.[37] All the slaves, whether kin or not, lived together, cooked together, reared children together, and slept in the same hut. Table II very roughly suggests the differences in household composition of large plantations and small farms. Only 18 percent of the blacks on small units lived in two-parent households. About a third resided in mother-child households, and that included over half the young children and three-tenths of those ten to fourteen years of age. Nearly three-quarters of the men and two fifths of the women—some unmarried—lived with neither spouse nor children. Over two-fifths of the youths ten to fourteen years of age lived away from parents and siblings.

By the 1750s, a peculiar Afro-American life cycle had developed. Afro-Americans lived in a succession of different kinds of households. Children under ten years almost always lived with their mothers, and over half on large plantations lived with both parents. Between ten and fourteen years of age, large numbers of children left their parents' home. Some stayed with siblings and their families, others were sold, the rest lived with other kin or unrelated people. Women married in their late teens, had children, and established households with their own children. Over four-tenths of the women on large plantations and a fifth on small farms lived with husbands as well as children. The same proportion of men as women lived with spouses and children, but because children of separated spouses usually lived with their mothers, large numbers of men, even on big plantations, lived with other men.

These life-cycle changes can perhaps best be approached through a study of the critical events in the lives of Afro-Americans. Those events probably included the following: infancy, leaving the matricentral cell, beginning to work in the tobacco fields, leaving home, courtship and marriage, childrearing, and old age.[38]

For the first few months of life, a newborn infant stayed in the matricentral cell, that is, received his identity and subsistence from his mother.[39] A mother would take her new infant to the fields with her "and lay it uncovered on the ground . . . while she hoed her corn-row down and up. She would then suckle it a few minutes, and return to her labor, leaving the child in the same exposure." Eventually, the child left its mother's lap and explored the world of the hut and quarter. In the evenings, he ate with his family and learned to love his parents, siblings, and other kinfolk. During the day the young child lived in an age-segregated world. While parents, other adults, and older siblings worked, children were "left, during a great portion of the day, on the ground at the doors of their huts, to their own struggles and efforts." [40] They played with age-mates or were left at home with other children and perhaps an aged grandparent. Siblings or age-mates commonly lived together or in nearby houses. On the Potomac side of Prince George's County in 1776, 86 percent of those zero to four years of age, and 82 percent of those five to nine years of age lived on plantations with at least one other child near their own age. Many children lived in little communities of five or more children their own age. Children five to nine years old, too young to work full-time, may have cared for younger siblings; in Prince George's in 1776, 83 percent of all children zero to four years of age lived on a plantation with at least one child five to nine years of age.[41]

Black children began to work in the tobacco fields between seven and ten years of age. For the first time they joined fully in the daytime activities of adults.[42] Those still living at home labored beside parents, brothers and sisters, cousins, uncles, aunts and other kinfolk. Most were trained to be field hands by white masters or overseers and by their parents. Though these young hands were forced to work for the master, they quickly learned from their kinfolk to work at the pace that black adults set and to practice the skills necessary to "put massa on."

At about the same age, some privileged boys began to learn a craft from whites or (on the larger plantations) from their skilled kinfolk. Charles Carroll's plantations provide an example of how skills were passed from one generation of Afro-Americans to another. Six of the eighteen (33 percent) artisans on his plantations under twenty-five years of age in 1773 probably learned their trade from fathers and another four (22 percent) from other kinfolk skilled in that occupation. For example, Joe, twenty-one, and Jack, nineteen, were both coopers and both sons of Cooper Joe, sixty-three. Joe also learned to be a wheelwright, and in turn probably helped train his brothers-in-law, Elisha, eleven, and Dennis, nine, as wheelwrights.[43]

Beginning to work coincided with the departure of many children from their parents, siblings, and friends. The fact that about 54 percent of all slaves in single slave households in Prince George's in 1776 were between seven and fifteen years of age suggests that children were typically forced to leave home during those ages. Young blacks were most frequently forced from large plantations to smaller farms.[44] The parents' authority was eliminated, and the child left the only community he had known. Tension and unhappiness often resulted. For example, Hagar, age fourteen, ran from her master in Baltimore in 1766. "She is supposed to be harbor'd in some Negro Quarter," he claimed, "as her Father and Mother Encourages her in Elopements, under a Pretense she is ill used at home." [45]

Courtship and marriage were highly significant *rites de passage* for many Afro-American men and women. The process began earlier for women: while men probably married in their mid- to late twenties, women usually married in their late teens.[46] Men initiated the courtship. They typically searched for wives, visiting numbers of neighboring plantations, and often found a wife near home, though not on the same quarter. Some evidence for this custom, suggestive but hardly conclusive, can be seen in the sex and age of runaways. Only 9 percent (22/233) of all

TABLE III

AGES OF RUNAWAY MEN, 1770–1779, SOUTHERN MARYLAND

Age Group	Number in Group	Percentage in Group	Percentage, 1776 Census
15–19	4	6	19
20–24	22	31	19
25–29	22	31	15
30–34	17	24	11
35–39	3	4	8
40–49	4	6	13
50–	0	0	15
Totals	72	102	100

Source: All runaway slave ads published in the *Maryland Gazette*, 1745–1779, the *Maryland Journal*, 1773–1779, and *Dunlap's Maryland Gazette*, 1775–1779, from Prince George's, Charles, Calvert, Frederick (south of Monocacy River), and Anne Arundel (south of Severn River, excluding Annapolis) counties, and any slave born in or traveling to those areas. Each slave runaway equals a single observation, but when the same slave ran away twice during the same time period, he was counted only once. The fourth column is from Prince George's County Census, 1776, and is included to provide a rough test of the likelihood that slaves of particular ages will run away.

Southern Maryland runaways, 1745–1779, were women. Few men (in terms of the total population) ran away in their late teens, but the numbers rose in the early twenties when the search for wives began, and crested between twenty-five and thirty-four when most men married and began families. Courtship on occasion ended in a marriage ceremony, sometimes performed by a Roman Catholic or Anglican clergyman, sometimes celebrated by the slaves themselves.[47] (See Table III.)

Marriage was more important for women than men. After the relationship was consummated, the woman probably stayed with her family (parents and siblings) until a child was born, unless she could form a household with her husband.[48] Once she had a child, she moved from her parents' home into her own hut. Though almost all women were field laborers, their role as wives and mothers gave them a few privileges. Masters sometimes treated pregnant women—and their children after birth —with greater than usual solicitude. For example, Richard Corbin, a Virginia planter, insisted in 1759 that his steward be "Kind and Indulgent to pregnant women, and not force them then with Child upon any service or hardship that will be injurious to them." Children were "to be well looked after."[49]

There was less change in the life of most new husbands. Many continued to live with other adult men. Able to visit his family only at night or on holidays, the nonresident husband could play only a small role in childrearing. If husband and wife lived together, however, they established a household. The resident father helped raise his children, taught them skills, and tried to protect them from the master. Landon Carter reacted violently when Manuel tried to help his daughter. "Manuel's

Sarah, who pretended to be sick a week ago, and because I found nothing ailed her and would not let her lie up she ran away above a week and was catched the night before last and locked up; but somebody broke open the door for her. It could be none but her father Manuel, and he I had whipped." [50]

On large plantations, mothers could call upon a wide variety of kin to help them raise their children: husbands, siblings, cousins, and uncles or aunts might be living in nearby huts. Peter Harbard learned from his grandmother, father, and paternal uncles how his grandmother's indentures were burned by Henry Darnall and how she was forced into bondage. He "frequently heard his grandmother Ann Joice say that if she had her just right that she ought to be free and all her children. He hath also heard his Uncles David Jones, John Wood, Thomas Crane, and also his father Francis Harbard declare as much." Peter's desire for freedom, learned from his kinfolk, never left him. In 1748, he ran away twice toward Philadelphia and freedom. He was recaptured, but later purchased his freedom. [51]

As Afro-Americans grew older, illness and lack of stamina cut into their productivity, and their kinfolk or masters were forced to provide for them. On rare occasions, masters granted special privileges to favored slaves. When Thomas Clark died in 1766, he gave his son Charles "my faithful old Negro man Jack whom I desire may be used tenderly in his old age." Charles Ball's grandfather lived as an old man by himself away from the other slaves he disliked. Similarly, John Wood, Peter Harbard's uncle, was given his own cabin in his old age. [52]

Many old slaves progressed through several stages of downward mobility. Artisans and other skilled workers became common field hands. While 10 percent of men between forty and fifty-nine years of age were craftsmen, only 3 percent of men above sixty years of age held similar positions. [53] Mulatto Ned, owned by Gabriel Parker of Calvert County, was a carpenter and cooper most of his life, but he had lost that job by 1750 when he was sixty-five. Abraham's status at Snowden's Iron Works in Anne Arundel County changed from master founder to laborer when he could not work full-time. As slaves became feeble, some masters refused to maintain them adequately, or sold them to unwary buyers. An act passed by the Maryland Assembly in 1752 complained that "sundry Persons in this Province have set disabled and superannuated Slaves free who have either perished through want or otherwise become a Burthen to others." The legislators uncovered a problem: in 1755, 20 percent of all the free Negroes in Maryland (153/895) were "past labour or cripples," while only 2 percent (637/29,141) of white men were in this category. To remedy the abuse, the assembly forbade manumission of slaves by will, and insisted that masters feed and clothe their old and ill slaves. If slaveholders failed to comply, they could be fined £4 for each offense. [54]

As Afro-American slaves moved from plantation to plantation through the life cycle, they left behind many friends and kinfolk, and established relationships with slaves on other plantations. And when young blacks married off their quarter, they gained kinfolk on other plantations. Both of these patterns can be illustrated from the Carroll plantations. Sam and Sue, who lived on Sam's quarter at Doohoregan Manor, had seven children between 1729 and 1751. In 1774, six of them were spread over four different quarters at Doohoregan: one son lived with his father (his mother had died); a daughter lived with her family in a hut near her father's; a son and daughter lived at Frost's; one son headed Moses' quarter; and a son lived at Riggs. Figure 3 shows how marriages increased the size and geographic spread of Fanny's relations. A third of the slaves (85/255) who lived away from Riggs Quarter (the main plantation) were kin to Fanny or her descendants. Two of Kate's children married into Fanny's family; Kate and one son lived at Frost's and another son lived at Jacob's. Cecilia, the daughter of Carpenter Harry and Sophia, married one of Fanny's grandchildren. Harry and Sophia lived with three of their children at Frost's, and two of their sons lived at Riggs, where they were learning to be wheelwrights with kinsperson Joe, son of Cooper Joe.[55]

Since husbands and wives, fathers and children, and friends and kinfolk were often physically separated, they had to devise ways of maintaining their close ties. At night and on Sundays and holidays, fathers and other kinfolk visited those family members who lived on other plantations. Fathers had regular visiting rights. Landon Carter's Guy, for instance, visited his wife (who lived on another quarter) every Monday evening.[56] Kinfolk, friends, and neighbors gathered in the yard around the slave cabins and talked, danced, sang, told stories, and drank rum through many an evening and special days on larger plantations.[57] These visits symbolized the solidarity of slave families and permitted kinfolk to renew their friendships but did not allow nonresident fathers to participate in the daily rearing of their children.

The forced separation of Afro-American kinfolk by masters was not entirely destructive. Slave society was characterized by hundreds of interconnected and interlocking kinship and friendship networks that stretched from plantation to plantation and from county to county. A slave who wanted to run away would find kinfolk, friends of kinfolk, or kinfolk of friends along his route who willingly would harbor him for a while.[58] As Afro-American kinship and friendship networks grew ever larger, the proportion of runaways who were harbored for significant periods of time on slave quarters seemed to have increased in both Maryland and Virginia.[59]

There were three different reasons for slaves to use this underground. Some blacks, like Harry—who left his master in 1779, stayed in the neighborhood for a few weeks and then took off for Philadelphia—used their friends' and kinfolks' hospitality to reach freedom.[60] Others wanted to visit. About 27 percent of all runaways from southern Maryland mentioned in newspaper advertisements from 1745 to 1779 (and 54 percent of all those whose destinations were described by masters) ran away to visit. For example, Page traveled back and forth between Piscataway and South River in 1749, a distance of about forty miles, and was not caught. He must have received help at many quarters along his route. And in 1756, Kate, thirty years old, ran away from her master, who lived near Georgetown on the Potomac. She went to South River about thirty miles distant, where she had formerly lived. Friends concealed her there. Her master feared that since "she had been a great Rambler, and is well known in *Calvert* and *Anne Arundel* Counties, besides other parts of the Country," Kate would "indulge herself a little in visiting her old Acquaintances," but spend most of her time with her husband at West River.[61]

Indeed, 20 of 233 Maryland runaways (9 percent) left masters to join their spouses. Sue and her child Jem, eighteen months old, went from Allen's Freshes to Port Tobacco, Charles County, a distance of about ten miles, "to go and see her husband." Sam, age thirty, lived about thirty miles from his wife in Bryantown, Charles County, when he visited her in 1755. Will had to go over a hundred miles, from Charles to Frederick County, to visit his wife, because her master had taken her from Will's neighborhood to a distant quarter.[62]

This essay has pointed to the basic cultural and demographic cleavage between African and Afro-American families. African immigrants, like free and servant immigrants from Britain, remembered their native land but had to adjust to the new conditions of the Chesapeake. As free Africans they had lived among many kinfolk; in the Chesapeake, kin ties were established with difficulty. Because most immigrants were young adult males and because plantations were small, two-parent households were rare. Mothers, by default, became the major black influence upon Afro-American children.

After immigration from Africa slowed, the sex ratio declined, and plantation sizes increased. As generation followed generation, Afro-Americans in Maryland and Virginia created an extensive kinship system. More households, especially on large plantations, included two parents and their children. Although most households did not include kinfolk other than the immediate family, other relations lived in adjacent huts. Mothers and children worked in the tobacco fields with kinfolk, ate and celebrated with many relations, and invited kin who lived elsewhere to share in the festivities. Afro-Americans forcibly separated from relatives managed to maintain contact with them. And finally, slave resistance— whether expressed in the fields or by running away—was fostered and encouraged by kinfolk.

This article has attempted to portray African and Afro-American family life among slaves in the eighteenth-century Chesapeake. It is based upon all the available evidence and upon speculations from that evidence. Many important questions about black family life in the colonial period remain to be answered. In the first place, we need to know more about household and family structure. Could the same structures be found in other parts of the region? In South Carolina? In the northern and middle colonies? Was the pattern of change described here repeated in other areas? Secondly, we must go beyond this essay and describe in greater detail the nature of the Afro-American developmental cycle and the emotional content of relationships among kinfolk in various places at different times.

NOTES

[1] Prince George's County Court Record O, f. 414, ms., Hall of Records, Annapolis, Md., hereafter cited as PG Ct. Rec.; *Maryland Gazette* (Annapolis), 12 March 1772. All manuscripts, unless otherwise noted, can be found at the Hall of Records.

[2] Pioneering essays by Russell Menard, "The Maryland Slave Population, 1658–1730: A Demographic Profile of Blacks in Four Counties," *William and Mary Quarterly*, 3d ser. 32 (1975):29–54, and Peter Wood, *Black Majority: Negroes in Colonial South Carolina through the Stono Rebellion* (New York, 1974), ch. 5, suggest some characteristics of colonial black families. Much more is known about slave families in the nineteenth century. Herbert G. Gutman, *The Black Family in Slavery and Freedom, 1750–1925* (New York, 1976) is the standard reference. Other studies include Eugene D. Genovese, *Roll, Jordan Roll: The World the Slaves Made* (New York, 1974), pp. 443–524; E. Franklin Frazier, "The Negro Slave Family," *Journal of Negro History* 15 (1930):198–266; John Blassingame, *The Slave Community: Plantation Life in the Ante-Bellum South* (New York, 1972), ch. 3; George P. Rawick, *From Sundown to Sunup: The Making of the Black Community* (New York, 1972), ch. 5.

[3] There are no standard definitions of household, domestic group, and family. I have borrowed my definitions of household and domestic group from Donald R. Bender, "A Refinement of the Concept of Household: Families, Co-residence, and Domestic Functions." *American Anthropologist* 69 (1967):493–504, quote on p. 498. The use of "immediate family," "near kin," and "distant kin" were suggested to me by Herbert Gutman.

[4] Sidney W. Mintz and Richard Price, *An Anthropological Approach to the Afro-American Past: A Caribbean Perspective*, ISHI Occasional Papers in Social Change, #2 (Philadelphia, 1976). A more systematic application of these hypotheses to the colonial Chesapeake will be found in Allan Kulikoff, "The Origins of Afro-American Society in Tidewater Maryland and Virginia, 1700–1790," *William and Mary Quarterly*, 35 (1978), 226–259.

[5] It is difficult to be more precise because most data on African kinship systems comes from twentieth-century anthropological works. The following works suggest variations in African kinship patterns: A. R. Radcliffe-Brown, "Introduction" to *African Systems of Kinship and Marriage*, ed. Radcliffe-Brown and Daryll Ford (London, 1950), pp. 1–85: Meyer Fortes, "Kinship and Marriage among the Ashanti," ibid., pp. 252–284; Jack Goody, *Comparative Studies in Kinship* (Stanford, 1969), ch. 3; Robert Bain, *Bangwa Kinship and Marriage* (Cambridge, England, 1972); William J. Goode, *World Revolutions and Family Patterns* (New York, 1963), pp. 167–200.

⁶ Mintz and Price, "Afro-American Culture History," pp. 56–78 but esp. pp. 61–62; John S. Mbiti, *African Religions and Philosophy* (New York, 1969), pp. 104–109.

⁷ Goode, *World Revolutions,* pp. 167–168, 196; Mbiti, *African Religions,* pp. 142–145. Women in polygynous societies also nursed infants for three to four years and abstained from intercourse during part of that period. If this pattern was repeated in the Chesapeake, it was partially responsible for the low gross birth rate among blacks in seventeenth-century Maryland; see Kulikoff, "Tobacco and Slaves: Population, Economy and Society in Eighteenth-Century Prince George's County. Maryland" (Ph.D. diss., Brandeis University, 1976), ch. 4; Menard, "Maryland Slave Population," p. 41; Mbiti, *African Religions,* p. 111. For polygyny on the Eastern Shore, see "Eighteenth-Century Maryland as Portrayed in the 'Itinerant Observations' of Edward Kimber," *Maryland Historical Magazine* 51 (1956):327.

⁸ For sex ratios, see Menard, "Maryland Slave Population," p. 32 and Allan Kulikoff, "A 'Prolifick' People: Black Population Growth in the Chesapeake Colonies, 1700–1790," *Southern Studies,* forthcoming; for plantation sizes, see Kulikoff, "Origins of Afro-American Society."

⁹ For the conspiracy of 1739 and evidence concerning the competition Africans faced when searching for wives, see Kulikoff, "Tobacco and Slaves," 197 and Kulikoff, "Origins of Afro-American Society."

¹⁰ Mintz and Price, *Anthropological Approach,* 22–23; Kulikoff, " 'Prolifick' People;" PG Inventories, 1730–1769, mss. Large plantations were those with ten or more adult slaves.

¹¹ Menard, "Maryland Slave Population," pp. 42–47; Kulikoff, " 'Prolifick' People," table 5 shows mean age at conception of first child of slave women born 1710–1739 to be about 17.6.

¹² These statements are based upon PG Wills, mss., for the 1730s and 1740s.

¹³ See the inventory of the plantation of Daniel Carroll of Duddington found in the Charles Carroll of Annapolis Account Book, ms. 220, Maryland Historical Society, Baltimore (the inventory was never probated). The inventory was taken in 1735, a time of high slave imports, but Carroll sold rather than bought slaves. There were only two men between 15 and 29 years of age (but twelve women) on his plantations, and seven above 60; two of the four men in their 40s, two of the three in their 50s, and six of seven in their 60s or older lived with wives and children.

¹⁴ White common-law husbands found open cohabitation with black women socially undesirable. When William Hardie of Prince George's accused Daniel Carroll of Upper Marlborough, a wealthy merchant of the same county, of buggery and of keeping mulattoes, since "he . . . could use them as he pleased," Carroll sued him for slander, finding both charges equally harmful; see

Clinton Ashley Ellefson, "The County Courts and the Provincial Courts of Maryland, 1733–1764" (Ph.D. diss., University of Maryland, 1963), pp. 544–546.

15 PG Inventories, 1730–1744.

16 Menard, "Maryland Slave Population," pp. 42–46; Kulikoff, " 'Prolifick' People."

17 These points are fully developed in Kulikoff, "Origins of Afro-American Society."

18 These statements are based upon PG Wills, 1730–1769 and court cases discussed below.

19 PG Wills, 1730–1769; mortgages in PG Land Records, libers T, Y, and PP, mss. Estate sales were sometimes advertised in the *Maryland Gazette*. Slaves could not be sold from an estate until all other moveable property had been used to pay debts. Elie Valette, *The Deputy Commissary's Guide within the Province of Maryland* (Annapolis, 1774), pp. 91, 134–35.

20 Eighteenth-century migrations of slaves are discussed in Kulikoff, "Tobacco and Slaves," ch. 6 and slave migrations in the nineteenth century are analyzed in idem, "Black Society and the Economics of Slavery," *Maryland Historical Magazine* 70 (1975): 208–10.

21 Court of Appeals of the Western Shore, BW no. 10 (1800–1801), ff. 456–583, but esp: ff. 459–460, mss.

22 Chancery Papers no. 5241 (1788) mss.; PG Wills 1:280–5; PG Original Wills, box 7, folder 66, and box 13, folder 51, mss.; PG Inventories DD no. 1, ff. 22–24; DD no. 2, ff. 379–386; GS no. 1 ff. 246–248; and ST no. 1, ff. 96–100.

23 Chancery Records 16:298–304, ms.; PG Land Record PP (second part) 4; NN, f. 407; PG Original Wills, box 7, folder 3, and box 9, folder 52; PG Inventories DD no. 1, ff. 438–441, and GS no. 2, ff. 111–112.

24 About 40 percent of Prince George's slaves lived on large units from 1750 to 1779 (estimate based upon probate inventories), and 52 percent of the slaves in that county lived on big units in 1790 (federal census); see Kulikoff, "Tobacco and Slaves," table 6–1 for references.

25 Large in-migrations of Africans to the Chesapeake region occurred in the 1670s and 1690s (see Kulikoff, "Tobacco and Slaves," ch. 4, and references there). The great-grandmother of a man born in 1755 could have immigrated from Africa as a young woman in the 1690s.

26 "A List of Negroes on Doohoregan Manor taken in Familys with their Ages Dec. 1 1773." and other lists of slaves at Popular Island, Annapolis Quarter, and Annapolis taken in February and July 1774, Carroll Account Book. There were ten quarters on the 10,500 acres of Doohoregan. I am greatly indebted to Edward Papenfuse for calling this list to my attention.

27 Only a handful of people in the Chesapeake colonies owned as

many slaves as Carroll. He could therefore afford to keep most of his slave families together, an option not open even to the very large slaveowner with several children and 100 slaves. Nevertheless, two-thirds of Carroll's slaves lived on units with less than 40 people, and 57 percent of them on quarters with less than 30. Only the 130 slaves who lived at Riggs (the main plantation at Doohoregan) developed more extensive kinship networks on a single quarter than was possible for slaves who lived on other large Chesapeake quarters of 15 to 30 slaves.

28 See Menard, "Maryland Slave Population," pp. 35–36 for seventeenth-century examples of quarters named for slave residents.

29 There were 139 married adults (all ages) and single people 21 years and over in the group. While 46 percent of the leaders were over 55, only 11 percent (15/138) of all adults were over 55. The oldest member of a quarter kin group did not necessarily head the list. For example, Carpenter Harry, 46, headed Frost's Quarter even though his mother, Battle Creek Nanny, 78, was also living there.

30 The statistics are means: 36 percent of all slaves counted together, 38 percent with each quarter counted separately (sum of means). For a complete accounting of the kin ties of quarter leaders on farms where they lived, see the original article in *Law, Society and Politics in Early Maryland*, Land et al. (eds.) Baltimore: Johns Hopkins, 1977).

31 Only a maximum of 6 percent of all slaves in Prince George's, Anne Arundel, Charles, and St. Mary's Counties, Md., in 1790, lived on units of more than 100. (The 6 percent is a maximum number because the census taker sometimes put slaves from several of the same master's quarters in the same entry.) *Heads of Families at the First Census of the United States Taken in the Year 1790;* Maryland (Washington, 1907), pp. 9–16, 47–55, 92–98, 104–109.

32 Joe married his mother's sister's husband's mother's grandchild.

33 See Kulikoff, "Tobacco and Slaves," ch. 7.

34 Jack Greene, ed., *The Diary of Landon Carter of Sabine Hall, 1752–1778* (Charlottesville, 1965), p. 840 (27 July 1775).

35 Kimber, "Itinerant Observations," p. 327. See Kulikoff, "Tobacco and Slaves," ch. 6, for a fuller description of slave quarters.

36 Three of the structures are in St. Mary's; the other one stood in Prince George's. I am indebted to Cary Carson, coordinator of research, St. Mary's City Commission, for sharing the data on St. Mary's with me, and to Margaret Cook (a local historian, who lives in Oxon Hill, Md.) for her descriptions and slides of the Prince George's hut.

37 On a small plantation a slave quarter located in a kitchen is described in Provincial Court Judgments, EI no. 4, ff. 110–112, ms.

38 For a similar perspective on the succession of households and on life cycles, see Lutz Berkner, "The Stem Family and the Develop-

mental Cycle of the Peasant Household: An Eighteenth-Century Austrian Example," *American Historical Review* 77 (1972):398–418.

³⁹ For the matricentral cell, see Meyer Fortes, "Introduction," to *The Developmental Cycle in Domestic Groups*, ed. Jack Goody, Cambridge Papers in Social Anthropology, no. 1 (Cambridge, 1958), pp. 1–14, but esp. p. 9, and Sidney W. Mintz, "A Final Note," *Social and Economic Studies* 10 (1961):528–535, but esp. pp. 532–533.

⁴⁰ Samuel Stanhope Smith, *An Essay on the Causes of the Variety of Complexion and Figure in the Human Species* (Philadelphia, 1787), p. 35; ibid., ed. Winthrop D. Jordan (Cambridge, Mass., 1965 [reprint of 1810 ed.]), pp. 61–62, 156–157.

⁴¹ Prince George's County Census, 1776, found in Gaius Marcus Brumbaugh, ed., *Maryland Records, Colonial Revolutionary, County, and Church*, 2 vols. (Lancaster, Pa., 1915–28), 1–88. For the distribution of children on plantations see the original article.

⁴² Kulikoff, "Tobacco and Slaves," pp. 251–254.

⁴³ Carroll Account Book. Elisha and Dennis were sons of Carpenter Harry and Sophia. Joe married Dinah of Kate and Caesar; her brother married Cecilia of Harry and Sophia. Elisha and Dennis were therefore Joe's wife's brother's wife's brothers.

⁴⁴ Only the children of slaveowners or those who had just bought their first slave were likely to have only one slave, so this data is a useful indicator of the age children were first sold. The transfers from large to small plantations can be seen in the fact that 12 percent of all slaves 10 to 14 years of age on large plantations, but 43 percent on small farms, lived away from parents and kinfolk (see Tables I and II). A distribution of the ages of slaves in single person households can be found in the original article.

⁴⁵ *Maryland Gazette*, 1 Oct. 1766.

⁴⁶ Kulikoff, "Tobacco and Slaves," table 4–1, shows that the median age at first conception for slave women born 1710–1759 was 17 years. Age at marriage cannot be determined with precision but can be approximated from the age differences of husbands and wives. On the Carroll, Addison, and Wardrop plantations, 47 husbands were 6.8 years (mean) older than their wives, Carroll Account Book; PG Inventories GS no. 1, f. 73; GS no. 2, ff. 334–336.

⁴⁷ Thomas Hughes, *History of the Society of Jesus in North America Colonial and Federal*, 4 vols. (London, 1910–1917), *Text, 1645–1773*, 2:560–61; William Stevens Perry, ed., *Historical Collections Relating to the American Colonial Church*, 4 vols. (Davenport, Iowa, 1870), 4:306–7; Thomas Bacon, *Four Sermons upon the Great and Indispensible Duty of All Christian Masters and Mistresses to Bring Up Their Negro Slaves in the Knowledge and Fear of God* (London, 1750), pp. v–vii.

⁴⁸ Seventy percent of all marriages of slave women, 1720–1759 birth cohorts, took place before age 20 (marriages defined as first conception). Kulikoff, " 'Prolifick' People." Substantial numbers of

these teenage girls should have been pregnant with their first children between ages 16 and 19. If they were living with husbands, then their households would include only a husband and wife. On the three large plantations analyzed in Table 1, there were only three husband–wife households, and the women in them were 19, 27, and 56 years old. There is evidence that five of the sixteen women, 16 to 19 years old, were married—three who had children lived with sisters; one lived with her husband; one was separated from her husband but had no children; and the other lived with her husband and children. Ten of the other eleven lived with their parents.

49 For female occupations, see Kulikoff, "Tobacco and Slaves," ch. 7; quote from William Kauffman Scarborough, *The Overseer: Plantation Management in the Old South* (Baton Rouge, 1966), pp. 183–184.

50 Greene, *Diary of Landon Carter*, p. 777 (22 Sept. 1773).

51 Court of Appeals of the Western Shore, BW no. 10 (1800–1801), ff. 459–460; *Maryland Gazette*, 2 Nov. 1748.

52 PG Original Wills, box 10, folder 35; Charles Ball, *Fifty Years in Chains* (1836; New York, 1970), pp. 21–22; Court of Appeals of the Western Shore, BW no. 10, f. 549 (1802). These were the only examples I found in all the wills and court records I examined.

53 Kulikoff, "Tobacco and Slaves," table 7–6. Ages were collected from PG Inventories, 1730–1769.

54 Snowden Account Book, Private Accounts, ms.; Inventories 43: 320, ms.; Chancery Records, 7:2–12, 25–34, 50–52; William Hand Browne, et al., eds., *Archives of Maryland*, 72 vols. (Baltimore, 1883), 50.76–78; *Gentleman's Magazine* 34 (1764):261. For two examples of ill slaves sold from master to master, see *Maryland Journal*, 28 Sept. 1778, and Chancery Records 16:469–78 (1789).

55 Carroll Account Book.

56 Greene, *Diary of Landon Carter*, pp. 329, 348, 648, 845, 1109–1110; *Maryland Gazette*, 11 July 1771.

57 See references cited in Kulikoff, "Tobacco and Slaves," ch. 6, note 44.

58 My work on slavery owes much to the pioneering book of Gerald Mullin, *Flight and Rebellion: Slave Resistance in Eighteenth-Century Virginia* (New York, 1972), but my perspective on runaways differs from the ones he presents in chapters 3 and 4 of his book. Mullin has, I believe, missed the significance of kin networks in helping most runaways.

59 See Kulikoff, "Tobacco and Slaves," table 6–4; Mullin, *Flight and Rebellion*, p. 129, shows that the proportion of visitors (as defined in table 8.5) increased from 29% before 1775 to 38% of all runaways whose destinations can be determined from 1776 to 1800. The major problem with this data and Mullin's is the large number of unknowns (52% in Maryland and 40% in Virginia).

60 *Maryland Gazette*, July 6, 1779. Other examples of slaves using

the underground to escape slavery are found in ibid., April 28, 1757, and July 11, 1771. A profile of slaves from Southern Maryland who ran away from 1745 to 1779 follows. A distribution of destinations of slaves broken down into five-year groups and a discussion of the method of computing the data can be found in the original article:

MOTIVE OF RUNAWAY SLAVE

	To Visit Spouse	To Visit Other Kinfolk	To Visit Friends	Number of Runaways
	20	9	34	233
% All Runaways	9	4	15	27
% All Visitors	32	14	54	100

[61] Ibid., 4 Oct. 1749; Nov. 1756; for other extensive visiting networks, see ibid., 11 Aug. 1751; 12 March 1772; 30 Jan. and 22 May 1777.

[62] Ibid., 9 March 1758; 6 Feb. 1755, and 12 Aug. 1773, table 8.7. John Woolman claimed the husbands and wives were often separated. *The Journal of John Woolman* (Corinth ed., New York, 1961), p. 59.

Religion, Communications, and the Ideological Origins of the American Revolution

HARRY S. STOUT

In the age of exploration, when Europeans reached out to conquer and colonize other parts of the world, human control over the natural environment was slight. With their power to master the awesome forces of nature severely limited by the meager extent of scientific and technological knowledge, people of all societies tended to attribute to supernatural forces what could not be understood or controlled. Religious faith, not scientific reason, governed life. This was true for Native Americans as well as Europeans, although most Indian cultures were polytheistic—worshiping many Gods to whom they attributed natural forces—while the Europeans were monotheistic—worshiping one God.

Religion, whether polytheistic or monotheistic, can be understood as a formula for living, a way of making sense out of the uncontrollable forces and events surrounding human experience, a method of giving order and meaning to one's world and one's place in it. Rather than being a ritual observed once a week, religion pervaded life every day.

While piety and self-denial were central values in the lives of most colonists in the seventeenth century, the ideas of the European Enlightenment, emphasizing "reason" over "faith," tended in the eighteenth century to dilute the importance of religion. Material success in the New World and a preoccupation with accumulating worldly goods also eroded the obsession with life after death. The countinghouse became more important than the meetinghouse. Ministers watched their flocks diminish and lamented the decline of religiosity.

Sparks of religious revival began to appear in the mid-Atlantic colonies in the late 1720s and a decade later in New England. Then, in 1739, a man appeared in America whose religious passion was so great and whose exhortatory abilities so sharply honed that he altered the social landscape from Georgia to New Hampshire. It was George Whitefield, only twenty-five years old, who began a barnstorming trip that evoked a mass religious response of dimensions never before witnessed in America. Now, two centuries later, we still lack an adequate sociological and psychological model for interpreting this outpouring of religious fervor called the Great Awakening.

This essay by Harry Stout captures the feeling of how profoundly the evangelical preachers affected the lives of thousands of colonial Americans. Stout shows that the Awakening cannot be understood solely in religious terms—as simply a return to the religion-centered life of the seventeenth century. At its core it challenged established sources of authority and spread the message that ordinary people should cast aside deference to those above them and participate in the revitalization of their communities. In its religious content the Awakening foresaw a second coming of Christ, a rebirth of godly communities.

In its social and political dimensions, Stout suggests, it mobilized masses of lower-class colonists and taught them lessons that paved the road to revolution. Perhaps more than any other change in the colonial period, it altered the everyday values and attitudes of common folk.

... I saw before me a Cloud or fogg rising; I first thought it came from the great River, but as I came nearer the Road, I heard a noise something like a low rumbling thunder and presently found it was the noise of Horses feet coming down the Road and this Cloud was a Cloud of dust made by the Horses feet; it arose some Rods into the air over the tops of Hills and trees and when I came within about 20 rods of the Road, I could see men and horses Sliping along in the Cloud like shadows and as I drew nearer it seemed like a steady Stream of horses and their riders, scarcely a horse more than his length behind another, all of a Lather and foam with sweat, their breath rolling out of their nostrils every Jump; every horse seemed to go with all his might to carry his rider to hear news from heaven for the saving of Souls, it made me tremble to see the Sight ...

Nathan Cole's description of George Whitefield's appearance before four thousand avid listeners in Middletown, Connecticut, in 1740 captures our attention at least partly because Cole's voice is one that is rare in early American literature.[1] The crude spelling and syntax signal a vernacular prose composed by an ordinary man, whose purpose is less to analyze the theological issues of the revival than to describe an exhilarating event. Lacking the literary refinements of a classical education, Cole portrayed his experience in the form of a "realistic narrative" framed against a concrete social background.[2] Although common in setting, the

[1] Michael J. Crawford, ed., "The Spiritual Travels of Nathan Cole," *William and Mary Quarterly*, 3d Ser., XXXIII (1976), 93. The crowd estimate at Middletown is taken from *George Whitefield's Journals* (Philadelphia, 1960), 479.

[2] Hans W. Frei distinguishes a "realistic narrative" in the following terms: "Realistic narrative is that kind in which subject and social setting belong together, and characters and external circumstances fitly render each other. ... [R]ealistic narrative, if it is really seriously undertaken and not merely a pleasurable or hortatory exercise, is a sort in which in style as well as content in the setting forth of didactic material, and in the depiction of characters and action, the sublime or at least serious effect mingles inextricably with the quality of what is casual, random, ordinary, and everyday" (*The Eclipse of Biblical Narrative: A Study in Eighteenth and Nineteenth Century Hermeneutics* [New Haven, Conn., 1974], 13–14).

"Religion, Communications, and the Ideological Origins of the American Revolution," by Harry S. Stout. From *William and Mary Quarterly*, 34 (1977):519–41. Reprinted by permission of the author and the publisher.

passage is hardly trivial, for it brings to life the impassioned world of the common people and conveys, in their own words, a sense of the irrepressible spontaneity that marked the revivals throughout the colonies. Thunderous noise, clouds of dust, horses in a lather, and unrecognizable shadowy figures dominate a vocabulary that manages to express, as no official account could possibly do, the powerful emotions evoked by the Great Awakening.

With Whitefield's celebrated speaking tours of the colonies there appeared an innovative style of communications that redefined the social context in which public address took place. The sheer size and heterogeneity of the audience exceeded anything in the annals of colonial popular assembly. To organize the mass meetings, both speaker and audience altered the roles and language they customarily adopted in public worship. In the process, a new model of social organization and public address developed—a model which could be applied to a broad range of social, political, and religious contexts.

Contemporary and historical accounts agree that the Awakening was the most momentous intercolonial popular movement before the Revolution. Indeed, the parallel between the popular engagement and "enthusiasm" evidenced alike in the revivals and the rebellion merits close attention. Unfortunately, however, attempts to explain the meaning those two movements had for their participants must confront the fact that the documentary evidence originates overwhelmingly from an elitist "rhetorical world" that excluded the common people from the presumed audience.[3] Although the informed writings of the Founding Fathers provide the official revolutionary vocabulary, they do not render in a realistic narrative form the ideological arousal of the common people, who by the very rhetoric of those documents, were excluded from the message. How were revolutionary sentiments communicated with ideological force to an audience unversed in the rhetorical forms of the literature? And, conversely, how did the active popular self-consciousness manifested in the popular movements energize a republican vocabulary and push it in egalitarian directions the leaders had never intended? The documents are of little help here. More to the point, they actually create the problem of interpretation.

Cole's description of the popular enthusiasm of the revival suggests a different approach to the problem of popular culture and republican ideology. If *what* was communicated is qualified by the restrictive rhetoric through which the ideas were intended to be transmitted, it may help to ask instead *how* communications were conducted and how they changed during the second half of the eighteenth century? There could be no egalitarian culture as we know it today without an ideological predisposition toward the idea that the vulgar masses ought to be reached directly. By examining the changing style of communications in the revivals it is

---

[3] The term "rhetorical world" is taken from Gordon S. Wood, "The Democratization of Mind in the American Revolution," in *Leadership in the American Revolution*, Library of Congress Symposia (Washington, D.C., 1974), 72.

possible to gain insights into the nature of an egalitarian rhetoric through which, and only through which, republican ideas could be conveyed to an unlettered audience.

David Ramsay, a noted participant in and historian of the Revolution, recognized that, to understand the meaning of the Revolution, "forms and habits" must be regarded.[4] Before a republican vocabulary could communicate radical social meanings, a new rhetoric had to appear in which familiar terms were used to express unfamiliar thoughts. And this, it is argued here, is precisely what happened in the mass assemblies inaugurated by preachers like Whitefield. Despite the differences in intellectual substance between the revivals and the rebellion, those movements exhibited a close rhetorical affinity that infused religious and political ideas with powerful social significance and ideological urgency.

The point of departure for this article is Alan Heimert's study of *Religion and the American Mind.*[5] Published in 1966, the book had a generally cool reception. Critical essays by Edmund S. Morgan and Sidney E. Mead pointed out conceptual shortcomings in the work but failed to recognize its value in suggesting a method of historical analysis that focuses on the context of communications.[6] This failure had the unfortunate effect of foreclosing a line of inquiry into the subject of religion and the ideological origins of the Revolution.

Heimert's foreward states his central thesis: religious "Liberalism was profoundly conservative, politically as well as socially, and . . . its leaders, insofar as they did in fact embrace the Revolution, were the most reluctant of rebels. Conversely, 'evangelical' religion, which had as its most notable formal expression the 'Calvinism' of Jonathan Edwards, was not the retrograde philosophy that many historians rejoice to see confounded in America's Age of Reason. Rather Calvinism, and Edwards, provided pre-Revolutionary America with a radical, even democratic, social and political ideology, and evangelical religion embodied, and inspired, a thrust toward American nationalism."[7] This assertion diverged dramatically from the conventional wisdom regarding the relations of religion and the Revolution. In demonstrating his thesis Heimert contended, in now notorious words, that it was necessary to read the sources "not between

---

[4] David Ramsay, *The History of the American Revolution* (1789), in Edmund S. Morgan, ed., *The American Revolution: Two Centuries of Interpretation* (Englewood Cliffs, N.J., 1965), 8.

[5] Alan Heimert, *Religion and the American Mind: From the Great Awakening to the Revolution* (Cambridge, Mass., 1966).

[6] Edmund S. Morgan's review in *WMQ*, 3d Ser., XXIV (1967), 454–459, and Sidney E. Mead, "Through and beyond the Lines," *Journal of Religion*, XLVIII (1968), 274–288. The prominent exception to the negativity of the reviews is William G. McLoughlin's "The American Revolution as a Religious Revival: 'The Millennium in One Country,'" *New England Quarterly*, XL (1967), 99–110.

[7] Heimert, *Religion and the American Mind*, viii.

the lines, but, as it were, through and beyond them." [8] Only by doing this would it be possible to cut through the immediate idiom of political discourse that dominated the official Revolutionary debates and discover the underlying "relationship of ideology and political commitment to modes of persuasion." [9] In Heimert's view, these "modes of persuasion" were derived from the Evangelical rather than the Liberal tradition.

Against this thesis, and the method upon which it rests, Morgan and Mead launched an impressive assault. The conceptual framework they impose on early America, and their way of reading historical documents, were molded largely by Perry Miller, and it was as an extension of Miller's work that they interpreted Heimert.[10] To them, Heimert's tactic of reading "beyond" the content of the documents to the styles they expressed smacked, in Morgan's word, of "fantasy." [11] They contended that the method not only detached the historian from the security of objective reference (that is, the content of the documents) but also ignored social and intellectual connections between revivalism and republicanism that were neither as sharp nor as consistent as Heimert supposed.

Influential as these criticisms have been in stifling consideration of *Religion and the American Mind*, we must ask whether in fact Heimert wrote the book the critics reviewed. If Heimert's study is simply an extension of Miller, then the problems with the book become insurmountable because, as the critics demonstrate, there is no clear and consistent link between revivalism and republicanism at the level of ideas. But if the book is viewed in a different context altogether—if Heimert was not seeking to establish direct intellectual links between religious thought and political rebellion—then the entire effort needs to be revaluated.

Perry Miller's fullest statement on religion and the ideological origins of the Revolution appeared in his essay "From the Covenant to the Revival," published in 1961.[12] Addressing the role of "Calvinistic" Protestantism (a term he applied indiscriminately to Liberals and Evangelicals) in the Revolution, Miller insisted that, with the exception of a few hope-

[8] *Ibid.*, 11. Heimert's terminology is not meant to imply that one reads beyond the documents by ignoring documentation (as nearly 2,000 footnotes fully attest). Rather, it is the recognition, recently articulated by Gene Wise, that to get at the meaning of verbal statements "one would have to go beyond the documents to the original experience they came out of" (*American Historical Explanations: A Strategy for Grounded Inquiry* [Homewood, Ill., 1973], 73).

[9] Heimert, *Religion and the American Mind*, vii.

[10] Mead is most explicit here in the opening comments of his review: "Essentially Mr. Heimert's work seems to me to be a 639-page expansion, with massive footnoting of some suggestions imaginatively adumbrated in 1961 by Perry Miller. . . . The voice seems to be that of Jacob, but the hand that tapped the typewriter was that of Esau" ("Through and beyond the Lines," *Jour. of Religion*, XLVIII [1968], 274).

[11] Morgan states in his review: "The world he offers us has been constructed by reading beyond the lines of what men said; and what he finds beyond the lines is so far beyond, so wrenched from the context, and so at odds with empirical evidence, that his world, to this reviewer at least, partakes more of fantasy than of history" (*WMQ*, 3d Ser., XXIV [1967], 459).

[12] In James Ward Smith and A. Leland Jamison, eds., *The Shaping of American Religion* (Princeton, N.J., 1961), 322–368.

lessly optimistic Anglicans, the American people shared a religious tradition articulated in the Reformed vocabulary of "federal" theology.[13] Under the influence of this austere covenantal tradition the colonists could never be moved by self-congratulatory appeals to natural rights and enlightened self-interest. Rather, the dynamic for revolution issued from a deep sense of moral corruption and degradation that found a target in English oppression but, more important, spoke to the sins of colonial society itself. For generations of colonists schooled in the language of covenant, judgment, and collective accountability, the jeremiad functioned as the "form of discourse" capable of driving them to a moral revolution. Considered as an intellectual movement, the Revolution represented a spiritual purge administered to a corrupt established order in the interest of restoring a pure order that would both free the colonists from a decadent oppressor and cleanse their own society. The Revolution was inspired by this highly unstable compound of pious contrition and political rebellion, moral reformation and patriotic resistance.

Miller's essay came to exert an enormous influence on assessments of the role of religion in the Revolution.[14] Yet nowhere did it reflect a recognition of the social dislocations and divisions which we now know proliferated in eighteenth-century America.[15] Miller's framework fails to show how Americans sharing the "Puritan Ethic" could have been so sharply divided over the issue of independence or why, among the patriots, such confusion and contradiction raged over the question of what the Revolution was all about.[16] Finally, it is impossible in Miller's terms to account for receptivity to rebellion on the part of a populace of limited literacy.[17] To focus solely on the ideas set forth in surviving

[13] *Ibid.*, 325.

[14] See, in particular, Edmund S. Morgan, "The Puritan Ethic and the American Revolution," *WMQ*, 3d Ser., XXIV (1967), 3–43, and Bernard Bailyn, *The Ideological Origins of the American Revolution* (Cambridge, Mass., 1967), 7, 32, 140, 193, 250. It is instructive to note exactly where Miller's "From the Covenant to the Revival" fits in Heimert's work. In *Religion and the American Mind* the essay is cited only three times, and never expanded on. Even more revealing, in his introductory essay to the volume of Great Awakening documents jointly edited with Miller (*The Great Awakening: Documents Illustrating the Crisis and Its Consequences* [Indianapolis, 1967]), Heimert includes Miller in every historiographical citation, but not one of those citations is to "From the Covenant to the Revival."

[15] See Kenneth A. Lockridge, "Social Change and the Meaning of the American Revolution," *Journal of Social History*, VI (1973), 403–439, and Jack P. Greene, "The Social Origins of the American Revolution: An Evaluation and Interpretation," *Political Science Quarterly*, LXXXVIII (1973), 1–22.

[16] See John R. Howe, Jr., "Republican Thought and the Political Violence of the 1790s," *American Quarterly*, XIX (1967), 147–165.

[17] Drawing upon a sampling of colonial will signatures, Kenneth A. Lockridge concludes that "the literacy of that American generation which took the colonies into the Revolution was less than perfect. It seems probable that one-quarter of the generation born around 1730 . . . was totally illiterate. Including New England in the total would not much alter the level of enduring illiteracy since two-thirds of the population lived outside of New England" (*Literacy in Colonial New England: An Enquiry into the Social Context of Literacy in the Early Modern West* [New York, 1974], 87).

documents as the source of ideological change is to confuse a deep cultural transformation with its subsequent manifestation in a self-conscious, theoretical vocabulary.

In opposition to Miller, Heimert describes two clearly separate and distinctive revolutionary styles in eighteenth-century America, each originating in opposing "rhetorical strategies" that crystallized after the mass revivals.[18] On the one hand, there was the rebellion itself—the movement for independence from England, which Heimert concedes may well have proceeded from Liberal assumptions. On the other hand, there emerged with the rebellion an egalitarian impulse that pointed toward the creation of a society fundamentally incompatible with traditional conceptions of order, hierarchy, and deference.[19]

Approaching the problem of popular receptivity and concentrating on the verbal forms through which ideas were presented, Heimert locates the sources of this animating egalitarianism in the Great Awakening but concludes that it can be understood only by reading beyond the religious content of evangelical ideas to the new forms of public address established in the revivals. At some point prior to the popular reception of a revolutionary vocabulary, a new rhetoric must appear in which familiar terms can be used to mean something different—and this change in the *form*, as distinguished from the *content*, of communications marks the moment of a fundamental transformation of popular consciousness. Any revolution in world-view requires a new rhetoric. The most conspicuous and revolutionary product of the revivals was not to be found in doctrine, in the creation of new ecclesiastical or academic institutions, or even in resistance to the tyranny of established religion or monarchy. Evangelicalism's enduring legacy was a new rhetoric, a new mode of persuasion that would redefine the norms of social order. In Heimert's words, "quite apart from the question of Revolution, the contrasts between Liberal and Calvinist social thought were possibly of less ultimate significance than the re-

[18] I use the term "mass revival" here intentionally to distinguish multi-community meetings addressed by itinerating preachers, who were often uneducated and of low social origins, from local revivals conducted by a settled pastor. Heimert's concentration on Jonathan Edwards and the established New England ministry tends, I believe, to work at cross-interests to his point concerning the stylistic innovation of the revivals. Historians would do better to concentrate on Whitefield and the awakening he inspired through his public addresses on unprecedented thousands of auditors. The fundamental problem raised by the revivals was not Edwards's treatises but the itinerants' practices.

[19] Heimert, *Religion and the American Mind*, 14, 532. To avoid terminological confusion I will use the term "rebellion" to refer to independence from England and "revolution" to describe the radical internal impulse to reorder American society in an egalitarian direction. Similarly, the classical (deferential) theory of republicanism richly described in Gordon S. Wood, *The Creation of the American Republic, 1776–1787* (Chapel Hill, N.C., 1969), 3–124, and J. G. A. Pocock, "The Classical Theory of Deference," *American Historical Review*, LXXXI (1976), 516–523, must be distinguished from the more radical egalitarian "republicanism" that ultimately came to mean, in Wood's terms, "nothing less than a reordering of eighteenth-century society and politics as they had known and despised them . . ." (*Creation of the American Republic*, 48).

markable differences between their oratorical strategies and rhetorical practices." [20]

Heimert's recognition of the revolutionary potentialities of the revivals suggests a closer look at evangelical oratory, particularly in relation to the forms of public worship that prevailed before the revivals. Despite differences in style and substance between Puritanism and southern Anglicanism, all churchmen believed traditionally with Samuel Willard that God did "Ordain Orders of Superiority and Inferiority among men." [21] This hierarchical world-view presupposed a society of face-to-face personal relationships in which people identified themselves with reference to those around them and acted according to their rank in the community. Forms of attire, the "seating" of public meetings, and patterns of speech were among the more conspicuous indications of a pervasive social stratification that separated the leaders from the rank and file. As Stephen Foster observes, "mutuality, subordination, and public service constituted a kind of sacred trinity of all respectable societies, Puritan or otherwise." [22]

The social institutions of colonial America were designed to sustain this prevailing perception of proper social organization. In this traditional social ethic, itinerancy was inconceivable because, in Increase Mather's words, "to say that a Wandering Levite who has no flock is a Pastor, is as good sense as to say, that he that has no children is a Father." [23] What made a pastor was not simply the preaching of the Word but also a direct, authoritarian identification with a specific flock. To ignore the personal and deferential relationships of a minister with his congregation would be to threaten the organic, hierarchical principles upon which both family and social order rested.

That ministers be "settled" was no idle proposition but rather an insistence carrying with it responsibility for the whole social order. An institution as critically important as the church could deny the forms of social hierarchy only at the peril of undermining the entire organization of social authority. In terms of communications this meant that speaker and audience were steadily reminded of their *personal* place in the community; in no context were they strangers to one another, for no public

---

[20] Heimert, *Religion and the American Mind*, 18.

[21] Perry Miller and Thomas H. Johnson, eds., *The Puritans* (New York, 1938), 251. For a discussion of the inherited social ethic which the revivals challenged see especially William G. McLoughlin, *Isaac Backus and the American Pietistic Tradition* (Boston, 1967), 1–22; Rhys Isaac, "Religion and Authority: Problems of the Anglican Establishment in Virginia in the Era of the Great Awakening and the Parsons' Cause," *WMQ*, 3d Ser., XXX (1973), 3–36; and Isaac, "Evangelical Revolt: The Nature of the Baptists' Challenge to the Traditional Order in Virginia, 1765 to 1775," *ibid.*, XXXI (1974), 345–368.

[22] Stephen Foster, *Their Solitary Way: The Puritan Social Ethic in the First Century of Settlement in New England* (New Haven, Conn., 1971), 18.

[23] Quoted in Cedric B. Cowing, *The Great Awakening and the American Revolution: Colonial Thought in the Eighteenth Century* (Chicago, 1971), 23.

gatherings took place outside of traditional associations based upon personal acquaintance and social rank.[24]

Within this world of public address Liberals and Evangelicals alike realized that something dramatically different was appearing in the revivalists' preaching performances. The problem raised by the revivals was not their message of the new birth. Indeed, it was the familiar message of regeneration that lulled leaders into an early acceptance and even endorsement of the revivals. The problem, it soon became clear, was the revolutionary setting in which the good news was proclaimed. The secret of Whitefield's success and that of other evangelists (no less than of Patrick Henry in the 1770s) was not simply a booming voice or a charismatic presence. It was a new style: a rhetoric of persuasion that was strange to the American ear. The revivalists sought to transcend both the rational manner of polite Liberal preaching and the plain style of orthodox preaching in order to speak directly to the people-at-large.[25] Repudiating both the conventions of the jeremiad and the ecclesiastical formalities, they assaulted the old preaching style no less devastatingly than they attacked the doctrines of covenant theology. Their technique of mass address to a voluntary audience forced a dialogue between speaker and hearer that disregarded social position and local setting.

Immensely significant were the separation of the revivalists from local ministerial rule and their unfamiliarity with the audience. Until then, preachers, like political leaders, had to know whom they were addressing. Because the very act of public speaking signified social authority, they were expected to communicate through the existing institutional forms. When public speakers in positions of authority communicated outside of the customary forms, they set themselves, by that act itself, in opposition to the established social order. The eighteenth-century leaders' obsession with demagogy and "enthusiasm" can only be understood in the context of a deferential world-view in which public speakers who were not attached to the local hierarchy created alternative settings that represented a threat to social stability. The frenzy raised by the itinerants was not born of madness but was derived from the self-initiated associations of the people meeting outside of regularly constituted religious or political meetings and, in so doing, creating new models of organization and authority. As the Harvard faculty clearly recognized in their censure of Whitefield, the "natural effect" of his preaching was that "the People have been thence ready to despise their own Ministers." [26]

[24] On the cultural implications of a face-to-face traditional society see Rhys Isaac, "Dramatizing the Ideology of Revolution: Popular Mobilization in Virginia, 1774 to 1776," *WMQ*, 3d Ser., XXXIII (1976), 364–367. I am indebted to Professor Isaac for sharing his article with me prior to its publication and for clarifying many of the points raised in this essay.

[25] Although Puritan rhetoric rejected the ornamental tropes and "witty" figures common to classical (Ciceronian) rhetoric, the New England plain style remained a literate rhetoric born in the schools and designed to instruct a reading public. The plain style was not intended to persuade essentially illiterate audiences unused to the logic of rational discourse. See Walter J. Ong, *Ramus: Method, and the Decay of Dialogue* (Cambridge, Mass., 1958), 212–213.

[26] Heimert and Miller, eds., *Great Awakening*, 352.

In gathering their large and unfamiliar audiences the revivalists utilized the only form of address that could be sure to impress all hearers: the spoken word proclaimed extemporaneously in everyday language. As historians immersed in printed documents, we scarcely recognize the dominance of speech and oratory in aural cultures—an orality that, by definition, never survives in the written record. Alphabetic writing and print emerged, after all, as an *imitation* of spoken words, and so they have remained ever since. Recognition of the powerful social and psychological imperatives of direct oral address has led Walter Ong to observe that "writing commits the words to space. But to do so, it makes words less real, pretends they are something they are not: quiescent marks." [27] Print and typographic culture create highly visual, sequential, and analytic patterns of thought which aural cultures, attuned to easily remembered forms of speech, cannot readily comprehend.[28] Unlike print, which is essentially passive, reflective, and learned, sound is active, immediate, and spontaneously compelling in its demand for a response. Speech remains in the deepest sense an event or psychological encounter rather than an inert record—an event that is neither detached from personal presence nor analyzed, but is intrinsically engaged and calculated to persuade. Print cannot match the persuasive power of the spoken word whose potential audience includes everyone who can understand the language. It is no wonder that literate elites have feared persuasive orators from Plato condemning the sophists to Charles Chauncy damning the demagogues of the revival. Once orators are allowed the opportunity to address the people, there is, in Chauncy's words, "no knowing how high it [their influence] may rise, nor what it may end in." [29]

To portray the word as event, as a vital indwelling principle, the revivalists employed what Miller termed a "rhetoric of sensation" [30]—a new rhetoric that, through its recognition of the singular power of the spoken word delivered to a mass audience, differed fundamentally from the Old Light or rational preaching which was written out like a lecture and was more concerned, in the revivalists' words, with "ornament" than with the "affections." The animadversions of Liberals against what they called the revivalists' "mighty noise," which not only stimulated enthusiasm but also challenged the social order, were certainly justified from their perspective.[31] Ong makes the important point that "script, and

[27] Walter J. Ong, *Why Talk? A Conversation about Language* (San Francisco, 1973), 17.

[28] On the relationship of literacy and analytical thought see Jack Goody and Ian Watt "The Consequences of Literacy," *Comparative Studies in Society and History,* V (1963), 304–345, and Jack Goody, "Evolution and communication: the domestication of the savage mind," *British Journal of Sociology,* XXIV (1973), 1–12.

[29] Heimert and Miller, eds., *Great Awakening,* 256.

[30] Perry Miller, *Errand into the Wilderness* (Cambridge, Mass., 1956), 167–183. Heimert brilliantly develops this theme in his chapter on "The Danger of an Unconverted Ministry," which he singles out as the "principal hinge" of his study (*Religion and the American Mind,* 159–236).

[31] John Caldwell, *The Nature, Folly, and Evil of rash and uncharitable Judging. A Sermon Preached at the French Meeting-House in Boston . . .* (1742), in Richard L. Bushman, ed., *The Great Awakening: Documents on the Revival of Religion, 1740–1745* (New York, 1969), 159.

particularly the alphabet, provides a heightened experience of order. The world of thought is itself a beautifully intricate world, and the world of words is likewise impressively, if mysteriously, organized. . . . To attack the printed word would be to attack *the* symbol of order." [32]

Looking to the New Testament as their model, the revivalists rediscovered the effectiveness of extemporaneous address in their struggle against the Standing Order. Recent analyses of New Testament rhetoric demonstrate the prevailing orality of the gospel. Amos Wilder, for example, notes that "Jesus never wrote a word. . . . In secular terms we could say that Jesus spoke as the birds sing, oblivious of any concern for transcription. Less romantically we can say that Jesus' use of the spoken word alone has its own theological significance." [33] Throughout the gospels the Word is the oral word, and the Good News is uttered through ordinary speech. In his classic study of the Western literary tradition Eric Auerbach pointed out that "in the last analysis the differences in style between the writers of antiquity and early Christianity are conditioned by the fact that they were composed from a different point of view and for different people." [34]

Returning not only to the social doctrine of the gospel but to its rhetoric as well, the evangelists excited the people to action by "calling them out" and exhorting them to experimental Christianity. Radical attacks on an "unconverted ministry" that acted more like "Letter-learned . . . Pharisees" than preachers of the Word take on additional meaning in the social context of eighteenth-century established religion.[35] The danger that the Liberals sensed in the revivals was rhetorical as well as doctrinal. The Anglican commissary Alexander Garden correctly, and sarcastically, identified this threat: *"What went you out*, my Brethren, *to see*, or rather to *hear?* Any *new* Gospel, or message from Heaven? Why, no? but the *old* one explained and taught in a *new* and better Manner." [36] Pointing to the spirit of this new manner, one opponent of the revivals observed that "it abhors Reason, and is always for putting out her Eyes; but loves to reign Tyrant over the Passions, which it manages by Sounds and Nonsense." [37] The identification of sight with reason, and of sound with the passions, is here obvious and comes very near to the center of the raging controversy surrounding the itinerants. At stake was nothing less than the rules and conventions governing public address and social authority.

The revivalists' repudiation of polite style and their preference for

[32] Walter J. Ong, *The Presence of the Word: Some Prolegomena for Cultural and Religious History* (New Haven, Conn., 1967), 136.

[33] Amos N. Wilder, *Early Christian Rhetoric: The Language of the Gospel* (Cambridge, Mass., 1971), 13.

[34] Eric Auerbach, *Mimesis: The Representation of Reality in Western Literature*, trans. Willard R. Trask (Princeton, N.J., 1953), 46.

[35] Gilbert Tennent, *The Danger of an Unconverted Ministry, Considered in a Sermon on Mark VI. 34* (1741), in Heimert and Miller, eds., *Great Awakening*, 73.

[36] Alexander Garden, *Regeneration, and the Testimony of the Spirit. Being the Substance of Two Sermons* . . . (1740), *ibid.*, 58.

[37] *A true and genuine Account of a WANDERING SPIRIT, raised of late* . . . , *ibid.*, 149.

extemporaneous mass address cut to the very core of colonial culture by attacking the habit of deference to the written word and to the gentlemen who mastered it. Evangelical rhetoric performed a dual function: it proclaimed the power of the spoken word directly to every individual who would hear, and it confirmed a shift in authority by organizing voluntary popular meetings and justifying them in the religious vocabulary of the day. Partly through doctrine, but even more through the rhetorical strategy necessitated by that doctrine, the popular style of the revivals challenged the assumption of hierarchy and pointed to a substitute basis for authority and order in an open voluntary system.

The popular rhetoric of the evangelists contrasted sharply with the much more formal modes of address preferred by upholders of established authority. Nowhere were the social divisions of American society more clearly reflected than in the leaders' utilization of a printed form of discourse that separated the literati from the common people. Throughout the eighteenth century, public communications were not only increasingly printed but were tuned to a genteel European literary style governed by canons of correct usage. As George Philip Krapp observed in his seminal history of the English language, "pronunciation, grammar and spelling were not then tests of respectability [in the seventeenth century] . . . in the degree to which they have since become. What seems now like illiterate speech, the speech of persons who do not reflect how they speak, was then merely the normal speech of the community." [38] With no printed dictionaries to provide authority for correct spelling and usage, seventeenth-century vernacular literature exhibited a high degree of variability. As the spread of printing in the eighteenth century gave increased importance to writing, however, there emerged a concomitant movement toward standardization of spelling and usage. Following the appearance of Samuel Johnson's dictionary in 1755, language came to be thought of as written rather than spoken, and educated elites on both sides of the ocean adopted a written style intended to communicate with their literate peers. [39] Linguistic divisions between the well-bred and the vulgar became increasingly clear to both sectors of the colonial society. One revealing example of a distinctive lower-class style is a radical essay, *The Key of Libberty*, written (though never accepted for publication) in 1797 by James Manning, an untutored Massachusetts farmer who "neaver had the advantage of six months schooling in my life." In organization, spelling, and grammar the essay stands in stark contrast to the polished style of the whig patriots. It was, as Manning recognized, "not in the language and stile of the Larned for I am not able." [40]

---

[38] George Philip Krapp, *The English Language in America*, I (New York, 1925), ix.
[39] See, for example, H. L. Mencken, *The American Language: An Inquiry into the Development of English in the United States*, 4th ed. (New York, 1936), 380, and James Root Hulbert, *Dictionaries: British and American*, rev. ed. (London, 1968), 10.
[40] Samuel Eliot Morison, ed., "William Manning's *The Key of Libberty*," *WMQ*, 3d 3d Ser., XIII (1956), 202–254.

Linguistic uniformity conspired with classical education to establish a learned discourse that effectively separated the literate elite from the common folk. Hugh Blair, whose handbook, *Lectures on Rhetoric and Belles Lettres,* came to epitomize the style for aspiring gentlemen, averred that the educated class "is now so much accustomed to a correct and ornamental style, that no writer can, with safety, neglect the study of it." [41] To encourage such a style Blair pointed to the patrician cultures of classical Greece and Rome, and urged his fellow literati "to render ourselves well acquainted with the style of the best authors. This is requisite, both in order to form a just taste in style, and to supply us with a full stock of words on every subject." [42] The classical heritage provided a vocabulary and mode of discourse which leaders had to learn if they were to communicate through the proper forms.[43]

Classical learning inculcated a set of social and cultural attitudes about the nature of speaker and audience that went far beyond the content of literature. A formal, analytical style conveyed social as well as literary prerogatives. For centuries, masters of print and the written word enjoyed social power and prestige partly because the people were awed by a sequential form of communications they could not understand. The eighteenth-century rise in learned treatises, tightly argued pamphlets, and belletristic writing reflected an effort, in Mather Byles's words, to "cultivate *polite* Writing, and form and embellish the Style of our ingenious Countrymen.—" [44] But Byles's "ingenious Countrymen" did not include the common folk.

The eighteenth-century shift in the direction of print and polite style was reflected in the growing appeal of rational religion among the educated elite. Cotton Mather typified this shift as early as 1726 in his *Manuductio ad Ministerium,* which, as Miller recognized, "in its catholicity of taste and urbanity suggests the spirit of current periodical essays

---

[41] Hugh Blair, *Lectures on Rhetoric and Belles Lettres,* I (Philadelphia, 1862), 215. Blair's lectures and essays were gathered together for publication in 1783.

[42] *Ibid.,* 214.

[43] Walter Ong observes in "Latin and the Social Fabric," that "using Latin was like playing a game whose rules could never be changed. . . . Latin was not merely one subject among many or even among several . . . Latin effected the transit from ignorance to tribal or communal wisdom. . . . Youngsters were given to understand that the treasures of all understanding were stored in the ancient tongues" (*The Barbarian Within* [New York, 1962], 206, 215). For descriptions of the classical grounding of colonial thought and education see Richard M. Gummere, *The American Colonial Mind and the Classical Tradition* (Cambridge, Mass., 1963); Robert Middlekauff, "A Persistent Tradition: The Classical Curriculum in Eighteenth-Century New England," *WMQ,* 3d Ser., XVIII (1961), 54–67; Meyer Reinhold, ed., *The Classick Pages: Classical Reading of Eighteenth-Century Americans* (University Park, Pa., 1975); and Wood, *Creation of the American Republic,* 48–53.

[44] Miller and Johnson, eds., *The Puritans,* 689. For a description of the increasingly high incidence of colonial borrowing from polite British culture see T. H. Breen, *The Character of the Good Ruler: A Study of Puritan Political Ideas in New England, 1630–1730* (New Haven, Conn., 1970), 203–239, and Jack P. Greene, "Search for Identity: An Interpretation of the Meaning of Selected Patterns of Social Response in Eighteenth-Century America," *Jour. Soc. Hist.,* III (1970), 189–200.

rather than the utilitarian aim of a preaching manual." [45] Followers of deism, which carried the Liberal print-centered rationalism to an extreme, tended, in Ong's words, "to think of God himself as no longer a communicator, one who speaks to man, but as a Great Architect . . . , a manipulator of objects in visual-tactile space." [46] Treating communications as written rather than spoken, and locking words in printed space, rational Protestantism was incapable of penetrating the soul of an aural society; its ideas set forth in printed sermons and treatises could never inform a popular mentality attuned to the spoken word.

Attached to the elitist typographic culture were social imperatives. As long as social identities depended on a traditional social order for context and location within a finely graded hierarchy, communications had to be transacted through an elitist rhetoric. Power became so closely tied to print that advanced literacy and a classical education were virtually prerequisite to authority, and a college education guaranteed rapid advance in the social hierarchy. [47] By 1776 there were nearly three thousand college graduates in the colonies who, through the remarkable improvements in post and press, were able to communicate with one another on a scale and with a frequency unimaginable in the seventeenth century. [48] The cosmopolitan "better sort" formed a close-knit community that provided both authors and audience for the wave of printed literature that began to surge in the late eighteenth century. Pamphlets written by educated gentlemen, primarily lawyers, merchants, ministers, and planters, were addressed to their peers. [49] The common people were not included in the audience, but it was assumed that they would continue to defer to the leaders. There was no recognition that the pamphleteers' impassioned celebration of republicanism would require a new rhetoric of

[45] Miller and Johnson, eds., *The Puritans*, 669. See also Johnson's discussion of Puritan rhetoric, *ibid.*, 64–79.

[46] Ong, *Presence of the Word*, 73. The same print-centered ("visual") mode of perception is apparent in the Lockean epistemology that underlay Liberal assumptions in both religious and political contexts. See Ernest Tuveson, "Locke and the 'Dissolution of the Ego,'" *Modern Philology*, LII (1955), 164–165.

[47] On the social meaning and political significance of a classical education in the colonies see James Axtell, *The School upon a Hill: Education and Society in Colonial New England* (New Haven, Conn., 1974), 201–244; James J. Walsh, *Education of the Founding Fathers of the Republic: Scholasticism in the Colonial Colleges* . . . (New York, 1935); and Robert M. Zemsky, "Power, Influence, and Status: Leadership Patterns in the Massachusetts Assembly, 1740–1755," *WMQ*, 3d Ser., XXVI (1969), 511–512.

[48] Axtell, *School upon a Hill*, 213. For classic descriptions of the expanding networks of communications in 18th-century America see Frank Luther Mott, *American Journalism: A History of Newspapers in the United States Through 250 Years, 1690–1940* (New York, 1941), 3–110, and Wesley Everett Rich, *The History of the United States Post Office to the Year 1829* (Cambridge, Mass., 1924), 3–67.

[49] Gordon S. Wood observes that "even more indicative of the limited elitist conception of the audience was the extraordinary reliance on personal correspondence for the circulation of ideas. It is often difficult to distinguish between the private correspondence and the public writings of the Revolutionaries, so much alike are they" ("Democratization of Mind," *Leadership in the American Revolution*, 67–72).

communications reflecting a profound shift in the nature of social authority—a rhetoric, in brief, that threatened to undermine the exclusive world
in which the pamphlets were originally conceived.

    With the coming of independence the American leadership could
congratulate itself on the creation of a unique republican world-view
through their publications. At the same time, however, these leaders could
neither anticipate nor appreciate an egalitarian rhetoric that would soon
compel them to relinquish their traditional claims to power and authority
in the new republic. As a model of society, the neoclassical world of the
colonial gentlemen was essentially stable; their exclusion of the common
people meant that their writings could not reflect a changing self-
consciousness initiated from below. The very outlook that created a
learned and articulate "Republic of Letters" served, at the same time, to
limit the writers' historical consciousness. Quite simply, the people were
neither heard nor understood in their own terms.
    The creation of an egalitarian rhetoric owed nothing to the classical
heritage. If we are to understand the cultural significance of the Revolution, we must move beyond the rhetorical world of informed publications
to the social world of popular assembly. We must *listen* as the "inarticulate" would have listened and determine to what extent religious and
political meetings had a common rhetorical denominator that reached a
revolutionary crescendo in the movement for independence.[50] For Philip
Davidson, whose work continues to stand as the best general description
of communications in the Revolutionary period, there was an unmistakably oral orientation to patriot "propaganda." [51] Throughout the colonies
there existed a broad range of dramatic and oral communications in which,
in William Eddis's words, "the busy voice of preparation echoes through
every settlement." [52] The mobilization of the people was accomplished

---

[50] That the revivals did, in fact, continue to grow is most clearly reflected in the
    rapid growth of the dissenter movements in the colonies. Thomas Jefferson, for
    example, observed that by the time of the Revolution "two-thirds of the people [of
    Virginia] had become dissenters" (*Notes on the State of Virginia*, ed. William
    Peden [Chapel Hill, N.C., 1955], 158). More generally, Isaac Backus noted that, by
    1795, the number of Separate Baptist preachers had grown to 1,125 (*A History of
    New England with Particular Reference to the Baptists*, ed. David Weston, 2d ed.
    [Newton, Mass, 1871], 401).
[51] Philip Davidson, *Propaganda and the American Revolution, 1763–1783* (Chapel Hill,
    N.C., 1941). Despite his penetrating description of Revolutionary communications,
    Davidson failed to recognize that the sort of mass society in which a manipulative
    propaganda could flourish did not exist in pre-Revolutionary America. What made
    the pamphlets significant was not the writers' intent to hoodwink the people but
    rather their exclusion of the people from the presumed audience. Both the term and
    the practice of mass propaganda originated after the Revolution. See David Hackett
    Fischer, *The Revolution of American Conservatism: The Federalist Party in the
    Era of Jeffersonian Democracy* (New York, 1965), 144–149.
[52] William Eddis, *Letters from America*, ed. Aubrey C. Land (Cambridge, Mass.,
    1969), 100.

through extra-institutional mass meetings which, Merrill Jensen recognizes, were "of even greater long-range importance than mob action." [53]

The Founding Fathers were reluctant, for obvious reasons, to dwell on the oral dynamic unleashed in the course of rebellion; the same cannot be said of the loyalist opposition. Jonathan Sewall recognized both the evangelical and oral connections with republicanism: "there is an Enthusiasm in politics, like that which religious notions inspire, that drives Men on with an unusual Impetuosity, that baffles and confounds all Calculation grounded upon rational principles. Liberty, among Englishmen, is a Word, whose very Sound carries a fascinating charm." [54] Loyalist literature is replete with complaints that American towns were increasingly "filled with mock orations and songs, which for composition and sentiment would disgrace the most stupid and abandoned . . ." [55]

Whigs and loyalists used against one another the same arguments from constitution, law, and natural rights, but the charge of demogogic orality was a one-way criticism. The loyalist opposition never mustered a counterattack until after 1773; and when it finally appeared, it was almost exclusively printed. Like earlier Liberal rhetoric, that of the loyalists disdained the "wild uproars" of the whigs which culminated in nothing less than a "Yell of Rebellion," and concentrated instead on pen and press.[56] In Davidson's words, "the Tory appeal was a written appeal; the dearth of oral, dramatic, and pictorial suggestions is striking." [57]

Insofar as the whig gentlemen favored traditional modes of public address, they failed to plumb the depths of a popular revolutionary spirit that was oral and egalitarian rather than printed and elitist. Bernard Bailyn, who has examined the ideological origins of the Revolution more deeply than any other scholar, relies almost exclusively on printed sources as a sufficient explanation for the development of a Revolutionary mentality. It was "the opposition press, as much as any single influence," Bailyn argues, "that shaped the political awareness of eighteenth-century Americans." [58] Although this is true for the informed populace, the link be-

[53] Merrill Jensen, "The American People and the American Revolution," *Journal of American History*, LVII (1970), 15. For suggestive descriptions of how these "mass meetings" aroused "popular enthusiasm" for independence see Davidson, *Propaganda and the American Revolution*, 173–208; Isaac, "Dramatizing the Ideology of Revolution," *WMQ*, 3d Ser., XXXIII (1976), 357–385; and Robert Middlekauff, "The Ritualization of the American Revolution," in Stanley Coben and Lorman Ratner, eds., *The Development of an American Culture* (Englewood Cliffs, N.J., 1970), 31–43.

[54] "A Letter from Jonathan Sewall to General Frederick Haldimand," May 30, 1775, in Jack P. Greene, ed., *Colonies to Nation, 1763–1789: A Documentary History of the American Revolution* (New York, 1975), 267.

[55] Margaret Wheeler Willard, ed., *Letters on the American Revolution* (New York, 1925), 81. See also Ramsay, *History of the American Revolution*, 16–17.

[56] Daniel Leonard, "To the Inhabitants of the Province of the Massachusetts-Bay," (1775), in Leslie F. S. Upton, ed., *Revolutionary Versus Loyalist: The First American Civil War, 1774–1784* (Waltham, Mass., 1968), 39.

[57] Davidson, *Propaganda and the American Revolution*, 298, 301.

[58] Bernard Bailyn, *The Origins of American Politics* (New York, 1967), 38–39. Bailyn attributes many of the ideas presented in the "opposition press" to the English

tween print culture and the people, between pamphlets and popular ideology, is assumed, not demonstrated. Despite the rhetorical incompatibility of a popular culture and tightly reasoned pamphlets, the existence of a distinctive popular ideology is denied.[59] But as Patrick Henry pointed out, "the middle and lower ranks of people have not those illumined ideas which the well-born are so happily possessed of—they cannot so readily perceive latent objects." [60] Henry's refusal to enter into "the labyrinths of syllogistic [Latin] argumentative deductions" in his public address may well account for the power of his oratory, which more than one commentator has likened to that of the revivalists in style and impact.[61]

The problem with Bailyn's analysis is not that it is wrong in the way it portrays ideology; indeed, it represents a brilliant plea for the late eighteenth century as an "age of ideology." The problem is pamphlets: although central to the rebellion and to the articulation of classical republican theory in the colonies, they are not sufficient to explain the process of an egalitarian cultural transformation. Bailyn concentrates on the pamphlets and the "real whig" country ideology as the formative sources of the rebellion. Having set the ideological background for rebellion, he describes some of the manifestations of the "transforming radicalism" unleashed by the Revolution.[62] But the instances of transforming radicalism which Bailyn isolates are described far more effectively than they are

---

"real whig" tradition. This is of some importance because, like the American whigs, the English libertarian persuasion was almost exclusively print-centered. As Caroline Robbins observes, "the Real whigs, the liberals, seem to have been associated in certain areas and institutions around a few persuasive men. They were related by a bewildering series of marriages. . . . They relied on conversation, on letters among themselves or occasionally in the public press, on the dissemination of the printed word. . . . [T]hey followed a hit-and-miss method, consistent only in their determined faith in the printed tracts and treatises continually produced by them" (*The Eighteenth-Century Commonwealthman: Studies in the Transmission, Development and Circumstance of English Liberal Thought from the Restoration of Charles II until the War with the Thirteen Colonies* [Cambridge, Mass., 1959], 381, 382, 383).

[59] Bernard Bailyn argues that "the outbreak of the Revolution was not the result of social discontent. . . . Nor was there a transformation of mob behavior or of the lives of the 'inarticulate' in the pre-Revolutionary years that accounts for the disruption of Anglo-American politics" ("The Central Themes of the American Revolution: An Interpretation," in Stephen G. Kurtz and James H. Hutson, eds., *Essays on the American Revolution* [Chapel Hill, N.C., 1973], 12).

[60] William Wirt Henry, ed., *Patrick Henry: Life, Correspondence and Speeches*, III (New York, 1891), 462.

[61] Heimert, *Religion and the American Mind*, 232, 233; Rhys Isaac, "Preachers and Patriots: Popular Culture and the Revolution in Virginia," in Alfred F. Young, ed., *The American Revolution: Explorations in the History of American Radicalism* (DeKalb, Ill., 1976), 152–154.

[62] Bailyn states that "the radicalism the Americans conveyed to the world in 1776 was a transformed as well as a transforming force. . . . Institutions were brought into question and condemned that appeared to have little if any direct bearing on the immediate issues of the Anglo-American struggle" (*Ideological Origins of the American Revolution*, 161, 232).

explained in terms of their cultural sources. Pamphlets could never represent the primary source of radical republicanism, any more than the
revivals could have issued from printed sermons or the loyalist critique
of the rebellion organize itself through oral popular appeals.

Recognizing the failure of pamphlets to capture the growing revolutionary sentiment in America, a writer for the *Pennsylvania Packet* argued
in 1776 that "our cause will never appear to advantage in a pamphlet. . . .
When you write a pamphlet you are expected to say the best, if not all
that can be said on the subject, and if it contains [only] a few weighty
arguments the author is despised and the subject suffers." [63] The writer
was referring, of course, to pamphlets generally. Not every pamphlet was
limited by the rhetorical constraints of a classical style. What made
Thomas Paine's *Common Sense* so unlike the prevailing pamphlet literature of the day was its scorn for the best literary canons and its repudiation of the language and forms of classical discourse. Coming from a
lower-class Quaker background, Paine lacked the formal Latin education
common to other pamphleteers; in its place he managed to establish a new
style that anticipated the wave of nineteenth-century literature intended
for the people generally.[64]

Another major atypical pamphlet to appear in the colonies before
independence was *An Oration on the Beauties of Liberty*, published in
1773 by the Baptist minister and linen-draper John Allen. Like Paine,
Allen was a recent arrival from England at the time *An Oration* was
printed, and, like *Common Sense*, the tract enjoyed immense popularity
in the colonies.[65] In style it bears repeated resemblances to the "enraged"
language which scholars have found throughout *Common Sense*.[66] Also,
as in *Common Sense*, the references and quotations are not drawn, as in
the other pamphlets, from classical republicanism or British constitutional
theory, but rather from the Bible. There is not one page of *An Oration*
that does not supply biblical precedent or injunction for the assault on
privilege and tyranny. Ahab, the golden calf, Zedekiah, Cain, Abel, and
Rehoboam constituted a familiar vocabulary that was "opened up" and
explained repeatedly in colonial sermons. To liken a ruler to Ahab or a
social order to Babylon was to call for a revolution.

Perhaps the most important aspect of *An Oration* is that it was
obviously meant to be heard as well as read.[67] Its full impact can be felt

[63] Quoted in Thomas R. Adams, *American Independence, the Growth of an Idea:
A Bibliographic Study of the American Political Pamphlets Printed Between 1764
and 1776* ... (Providence, R.I., 1965), xiv–xv.

[64] This point is effectively developed in Eric Foner, *Tom Paine and Revolutionary
America* (New York, 1976), xv–xvi, 80–87.

[65] *An Oration Upon the Beauties of Union* (Boston, 1773) was exceeded in separate
editions by only two pamphlets including the "runaway best seller" *Common Sense*.
For tabulations see Adams, *American Independence*, xi–xii.

[66] See, for example, Bernard Bailyn, "Common Sense," in *Fundamental Testaments
of the American Revolution*, Library of Congress Symposia (Washington, D.C.,
1973), 7–22.

[67] John M. Bumsted and Charles E. Clark, "New England's Tom Paine: John Allen
and the Spirit of Liberty," *WMQ*, 3d Ser., XXI (1964), 570.

only when one *listens* to the rhetoric. Addressing the common people, Allen repeatedly relied on a coarse prose, rather than on logical syllogisms or authorities from a printed past. Reminding the people that rulers and ministers were "servants" who must "hear" a free and "affectionate" people, Allen demanded, "Has not the voice of your father's blood cry'd yet loud enough in your ears, in your hearts? . . . Have you not heard the voice of blood in your own streets . . . ?" [68] In striking contrast to virtually all the other pamphleteers, but like Paine later, Allen aimed his rhetoric beyond the literate elite to the rank and file.

If action proceeds from a cultural perception of public events in terms of symbolic forms, then analyses of the mobilization of ideas into ideology and action must recognize, at least in part, the cultural preconditions for receptivity, particularly on the popular level. A discontinuous ("revolutionary") cultural change could, by definition, never emerge from a continuing intellectual tradition; there must be a break somewhere. Where are the sources of such a radical ideology to be discovered?

Without denying the influence of typographic culture on the leaders of the rebellion and in the formation of the new governments, it might be helpful to think of republicanism in a pluralistic context as absorbing both traditional and egalitarian perceptions of social order. The theoretical work of J. G. A. Pocock builds upon an understanding of the unavoidable "multivalency" of language that derives from the different experiences of speakers and hearers.[69] Recognizing the truism that words do not necessarily mean what either the speaker or the historian believe they mean, Pocock does not examine language and ideas as fixed entities, but rather insists that language and communications not be separated from the circumstances and comprehension of their individual users. When "conceptual and social worlds" are placed in conjunction, no singular "constellation of ideas" or "climate of opinion" appears to have embodied an identical meaning for all social ranks.[70] To get at the popular meaning of republican ideology requires moving beyond the verbal content of the documents themselves to the social world in which they were transmitted.

Pocock's insights, placed in the context of the American Revolution, reveal that not one but two ideological explosions propelled the colonies into a new nation. Both leaders and followers were possessed of an extraordinarily powerful ideology that at points converged on common antagonists and a common vocabulary, and at other points diverged dramatically. No ideology that is pieced together solely from the literate world of print can fully comprehend the radical dynamic of the Revolution. It is incapable of accounting for the enormously creative power of *vox populi* to organize a social order bound together in voluntary associations based on discussion and public address. Resisting John Adams and

[68] Allen, *An Oration on the Beauties of Liberty*, 19, 27.
[69] See, especially, J. G. A. Pocock, *Politics, Language and Time: Essays on Political Thought and History* (New York, 1971), 3–41.
[70] *Ibid.*, 15.

others who located the Revolution's *raison d'être* among the classical world view of the elite, Benjamin Rush issued the following advice to historians: "I hope with the history of this folly, some historian will convey to future generations, that many of the most active and useful characters in accomplishing this revolution, were strangers to the formalities of a Latin and Greek education." [71]

The social conditions that allowed for the popular upsurge in the revivals and rebellion did not permit unstructured public address to degenerate into "anarchy" and mass rebellion, as the Standing Order had always feared. Perhaps the enduring legacy of the Revolution lay in its demonstration that distinctive ideologies *could* work in concert. The typographic ideology of the real whig tradition was, as Bailyn and others demonstrate, an "inner accelerator" of a transforming radicalism, but only in the sense that the aroused elite were compelled by the logic of their argument for rebellion to create, in law and politics, an egalitarian vocabulary, and, in communications, the secular equivalents of the revival in voluntary political parties and free presses.[72] Beneath that impulse, however, we must also recognize typographic ideology and the rebellion as accelerating a movement *already in progress*, a movement that originated among the lower rather than the upper strata of colonial society, and that, combined with profound social strains which increased throughout the eighteenth century, opened the way for the "enchanting sound" of mass public address.[73]

While the whig justification of the rebellion pointed to an "invisible government" of ministers, cliques, and venal officials, another conspiracy, recognized as early as 1773 by the loyalist Boucher, was equally "invisible" and far more powerful. Attacking the foundations of traditional social order, this conspiracy derived its "invisibility" from its essentially extemporaneous nature. In Boucher's words: "as though there were some irrefutable charm in all extemporaneous speaking, however rude, the orators of our committees and sub-committees, like those in higher spheres, *prevail with their tongues*. To public speakers alone is the government of our country now completely committed. . . . An empire is thus completely established within an empire; and a new system of government of great power erected, even before the old one is formally abolished." [74] An empire premised on talk, wholly lacking in the formal coercive structure that kings, churches, aristocracies, standing armies, and mercantile controls provided, did indeed represent a revolutionary departure in the

[71] Quoted in Meyer Reinhold, "Opponents of Classical Learning in America during the Revolutionary Period," American Philosophical Society, *Proceedings*, CXII (1968), 230.

[72] Bailyn, *Ideological Origins of the American Revolution*, 95.

[73] Garden, *Regeneration, and the Testimony of the Spirit*, in Heimert and Miller, eds., *Great Awakening*, 47.

[74] Jonathan Boucher, *A View of the Causes and Consequences of the American Revolution in Thirteen Discourses* . . . (New York, 1967 [orig. publ. London, 1797]), 320, 321. See David Ammerman's discussion of "government by committee," in *In the Common Cause: American Response to the Coercive Acts of 1774* (Charlottesville, Va., 1974), 103–124, and Wood, *Creation of the American Republic*, 319–328.

principles of government and social order. Voluntaryism, the very linch-pin of social, religious, and political organization in the new republic, was perhaps the clearest manifestation of this revolutionary system of author-ity.[75] Of course, public address did not replace print, nor was the populace hostile to print and literacy *per se*, but only to a print culture that was elitist and hierarchical. Still, it is no accident that early republicanism represented the "Golden Age of Oratory," because mass address was, for a time, the most effective means of reaching the new audience and utiliz-ing the egalitarian style seized upon by republican orators and revivalists as the creative force within the popular ideology.[76]

The rhetorical transformation in the revivals signified an emerging popular culture asserting itself against a paternalistic social ethic. In the course of the Revolution, the social order prefigured in evangelical assemblies was suffused with secular and political meanings, articulated in the world-view of republicanism. This new order, in Michael Kam-men's description, was not so much a "seamless web" as an "unstable pluralism" defying reduction to any one ideology or social system.[77] The rhetorical division resulting from the revivals played a major role in generating subsequent tensions and conflicts in American society. These tensions, moreover, reflected not so much opposing ideas with conflicting literary traditions as entirely different social outlooks and attitudes toward social authority, all deriving legitimacy from the individualism implicit in a mass democratic society. Evangelical attacks on a settled and educated ministry may have expressed a pristine "anti-intellectualism" in the colonies,[78] but it was an anti-intellectualism that was positive and creative—indeed, revolutionary. Without it there would have been no creation of an egalitarian American republic.

[75] On the frontier the essentially oral, voluntary association was most clearly mani-fested in the revivals which, as Donald G. Matthews suggests, represented a critical "organizing process" in the new nation. See Matthews, "The Second Great Awaken-ing as an Organizing Process, 1780–1830," *Am. Qtly.*, XI (1969), 23–43. Similarly, Leonard L. Richards points out how, in the voluntary reform efforts of the "evan-gelical crusade," evangelical abolitionists effectively utilized the "revolution in com-munications and the creation of mass media" to bypass traditional social channels and organize voluntary associations within "impersonal, large-scale organizations" (*"Gentlemen of Property and Standing": Anti-Abolition Mobs in Jacksonian America* [New York, 1970], 167).

[76] Wood points this out in *Creation of the American Republic*, 621–622, and "Demo-cratization of Mind," in *Leadership in the American Revolution*, 78–82. Perhaps not sufficiently emphasized in studies of early American literature is the abrupt decline in public significance of pamphlets, letters, treatises, and printed sermons after the Revolution.

[77] Michael Kammen, *People of Paradox: An Inquiry Concerning the Origins of Amer-ican Civilization* (New York, 1972), 89–96. The social ramifications of this cultural pluralism are treated in Robert H. Wiebe, *The Segmented Society: An Introduc-tion to the Meaning of America* (New York, 1975).

[78] Richard Hofstadter, *Anti-Intellectualism in American Life* (New York, 1962), 55–141.

The oral explosion and egalitarian style evidenced in the revivals were not limited to religion, nor was the articulation of a radical ideology the conscious objective of itinerant evangelists. The primary concern of the revivals was the saving of souls, and the rhetorical innovations that lent force to the movement were not fully perceived or verbalized for what they could come to represent: a revolutionary shift in world-view. As a movement initiated from below, the social experience of the revivals existed in fact before the emergence of a literate rationale. This does not mean that the experience proceeded from irrational impulses but, rather, that the terms necessary for rational comprehension and formal legitimation had to be invented. What opponents of the revivals termed a "spirit of superstition" was, for Jonathan Edwards, a new "sense" that could not easily be rendered into the existing forms of speech: "Some Things that they are sensible of are altogether new to them, their Ideas and inward Sensations are new, and what they therefore knew not how to accommodate Language to, or to find Words to express." [79] Edwards's concern was to fit the new social experience of the revivals to its proper spiritual vocabulary, while acknowledging that no language could fully express the essence of religious faith.

What Edwards and other churchmen failed to recognize was that the "spirit of liberty" manifest in the revivals would not be contained in religious categories. In the movement for independence both leaders and followers adopted a political vocabulary that expressed the egalitarian impulse in the secular language of republicanism. This vocabulary was largely provided, as Bailyn and Caroline Robbins demonstrate, through the Commonwealth tradition. But the ethos and ideological fervor of republicanism did not derive so much from the injection of Commonwealth vocabulary into colonial pamphlets as from the translation of the evangelical experience into a secular theoretical vocabulary that more adequately embodied, for some, the revolutionary thrust first widely experienced in the revivals. Words that were abstracted from their restrictive, deferential context came to mean something else. In Tocqueville's observation, Americans had a penchant for abstract words because only by using a vocabulary lacking specificity could they communicate radical ideas that destroyed a conventional style. "An abstract word," Tocqueville noted, "is like a box with a false bottom; you may put in it what ideas you please and take them out again unobserved." [80] The "country" publicists did not provide the textbook of revolution, so much as a lexicon of revolution, the meaning of which could be grasped only within a persuasion that celebrated the sovereignty of the new political audience.

[79] Jonathan Edwards, *The Distinguishing Marks of a Work of the Spirit of God . . .* (1741), in Bushman, ed., *Great Awakening*, 123. On Edwards's use of language see Harold P. Simonson, *Jonathan Edwards: Theologian of the Heart* (Grand Rapids, Mich., 1974), 91–118.

[80] Alexis de Tocqueville, *Democracy in America,* eds. J. P. Mayer and Max Lerner (New York, 1966), 482. See also Robert E. Shalhope, "Toward a Republican Synthesis: The Emergence of an Understanding of Republicanism in American Historiography," *WMQ,* XXIX (1972), 72–73.

The Loyalties of American
Revolutionary Seamen
in British Prisons

JESSE LEMISCH

Although historians have lavished attention on political events in our history, they have seldom studied how politics affected the lives of common people, and, conversely, how common people affected politics. Yet political events were a part of the everyday lives of most colonists. This was especially true in New England, where the town meeting gave common folk an opportunity to make their opinions heard, and where most men in their lifetime were likely to occupy at least a minor office, such as, "fence viewer" or "hogreeve."

At no time are common people more important in politics than when change occurs swiftly, for rapid political alterations are almost always associated with challenges to established authority. These challenges are usually accompanied by violence. In most historical writing, however, only the leaders of political movements appear before our view. Behind the scenes operates the "mob"—a term that itself is loaded with emotional meaning. But who made up the mob, or "crowd," as we might better label a collection of individuals massed for political purposes? How did it come together? What did its members intend? How did they impose their collective will on those who held political power? Until questions of this kind are posed and answered, the political lives of ordinary people will be obscured, and those beneath the elite will remain historically voiceless.

Insofar as they have studied the political "crowd," American historians have employed several explanatory models. In the eighteenth century, upper-class targets of the crowd's wrath frequently described the mob as "frenzied," "mad," or "unthinking." This is the model of crowd behavior that historians have most often used, especially since the invention of the term "mass hysteria" by social psychologists. In this view the crowd is made up of lower-class individuals inspired by passion rather than reason. The "mob" surges through a town willy-nilly, feeding on its own emotions, and striking out recklessly and wantonly at anything in its way. A second model of crowd behavior, equally condescending, presumes that most crowds are led and controlled by middle-class or upper-class individuals who manipulate the mob for their own purposes. Peter Oliver, one of the targets of the crowd's wrath in Boston in 1765, wrote: "As for the People in general, they were like the Mobility of all Countries, perfect Machines, wound up by any Hand who might first take the Winch."

The third model of crowd dynamics, formulated by historians only recently, sees most eighteenth-century mobs in a far different way. The urban mob is not emotionally out of control. It does not strike out indiscriminately. Instead it pursues specific interests related to the lives of its members, who are often skilled artisans and small shopkeepers. Its targets are selected in advance and its goals are carefully calculated. In part this theory has only lately received attention from American historians because violent mass action has not been widely recognized in modern America as a legitimate form of protest.

Such was not the case in the eighteenth century. Popular expression of grievances, often accompanied by violence, was accepted as a proper antidote to unresponsive holders of political power. Moreover, mass disobedience often brought quick results, for in colonial America those in authority, as yet unshielded from the people by urban police forces, maintained only a frail grip on their offices. For example, mobs in Boston as early as 1709 used violence to prevent one of the town's richest merchants from shipping grain to the West Indies at a time when bread was in short supply among the town's laboring people. In the 1730s, crowds working by night destroyed the Boston public market, because it was regarded as a mechanism that enriched the affluent at the expense of the poor. In both cases the crowd acted out of calculated self-interest, and in both cases it successfully defied the authorities to take action against its members. Rather than being "irrational" or manipulated, these crowds were self-conscious and self-activating.

No American historian has done more than Jesse Lemisch, the author of this selection, to study the grievances and political consciousness of ordinary laboring people in colonial America. Of special concern to him have been the merchant seamen of the colonial seaports. Ill paid, badly treated, often incapacitated by dangerous work, they formed a kind of waterborne proletariat. Their oppressors, as his essay shows, were press gangs of the British navy before the Revolution and also some colonial masters. When revolution came, however, they hewed overwhelmingly to the patriot side. In fact, they played an important role as radical agitators in the northern port towns.

Lemisch takes us into the world of these seamen. He examines their plight as British prisoners, their values, their political awareness, and their way of struggling with their unenviable position. His essay makes it clear that even at the lowest level of society, people were in the habit of shaping an ideology that fit the circumstances of their lives.

"**O**f kings and gentlemen," wrote W. E. B. Du Bois, "we have the record ad nause[a]m and in stupid detail. . . ."[1] But of "the common

---

[1] For this and the following, see Du Bois' preface to Herbert Aptheker, ed., *A Documentary History of the Negro People in the United States* (New York, 1951), p. v.

"Listening to the 'Inarticulate': William Widger's Dream and the Loyalties of American Revolutionary Seamen in British Prisons," by Jesse Lemisch. From *Journal of Social History*, 3 (1969–70): 1–29. Reprinted by permission of the author and the publisher.

run of human beings," he went on, "and particularly of the half or wholly submerged working group, the world has saved all too little of authentic record and tried to forget or ignore even the little saved." "Who built the seven towers of Thebes?" echoed Bertolt Brecht. "The books are filled with names of kings." [2] Such appeals for what might be called a history of the inarticulate have come not only from the left, nor have they necessarily been populist in intent. A century ago, looking at history with somewhat different sympathies, Frederick Law Olmsted, a self-proclaimed "honest growler," spoke as much to the question of validity as to that of humanity:

> Men of literary taste . . . are always apt to overlook the work-
> ing-classes, and to confine the records they make of their own times,
> in a great degree, to the habits and fortunes of their own associates,
> or to those of people of superior rank to themselves, of whose say-
> ings and doings their vanity, as well as their curiosity, leads them
> to most carefully inform themselves. The dumb masses have often
> been so lost in this shadow of egotism, that, in later days, it has been
> impossible to discern the very real influence their character and
> condition has had on the fortune and fate of nations.[3]

Should the character and condition of the "dumb masses" play a minor role in historiography? *Must* they? The answer to the first ques-tion, at least, seems clear: the most conservative standards of evidence and proof require that historiography include a history of the inarticulate. No generalization has much meaning until we have actually examined the constituent parts of the entity about which we are generalizing. No contention about the people on the bottom of a society—neither that they are rebellious nor docile, neither that they defer to an authority whose legitimacy they accept nor that they curse an authority which they deem illegitimate, neither that they are noble nor that they are base—no such con-tention even approaches being proved until we have in fact attempted a history of the inarticulate. Consensus, in order to demonstrate its valid-ity, must confront the conservative rocks of evidence and sail safely through them, as must any generalization which claims to describe a society on the basis of research on only a part of that society.[4]

---

[2] *Selected Poems*, trans. H. R. Hays (New York, 1947), pp. 108–109.

[3] *A Journey in the Seabord Slave States, with Remarks on Their Economy* (New York, 1861), pp. 214–215, quoted in Stephan Thernstrom, *Poverty and Progress: Social Mobility in a Nineteenth-Century City* (Cambridge, Mass., 1964), p. 1. For Olmsted's self-description, see p. ix of *Journey*.

[4] For further remarks on inaccuracies in the historiography of early America due to elitism, see my "The American Revolution Seen From the Bottom Up," in Barton J. Bernstein, ed., *Towards A New Past: Dissenting Essays in American History* (New York, 1968), pp. 3–45. Cf. Michael Rogin, "Progressivism and the California Electorate," *Journal of American History*, LV (Sept. 1968), 298: "conclusions that progressivism was not a movement of 'the people' can hardly be sustained until the behavior of the people is actually examined."

Similar comments may be made concerning the use of the concept of ideolog-

Can we write a history of the inarticulate? It was, in part, to answer that question that I undertook my study of merchant seamen in early America. That study began in dissatisfaction with the role assigned to this group in the secondary literature of the American Revolution.[5] In that literature, seamen appear with great frequency, battling over impressment and rioting in the streets of colonial cities. But although the accounts suggest that seamen acted consistently against British authority, when historians narrate such events it seems to me that they generally evade their central task—explanation.[6] In the absence of other explanations, it frequently appears that Jack Tar rioted because he is and always has been boisterous and irresponsible, the willing victim of alcoholic fantasies, seeking merely to blow off steam. Or at best the seamen rioted because they were manipulated by certain ill-defined groups.

Even accepting a large role for the accidental and the irrational in human affairs, it seems to me that the job of the historian as social scientist is to limit as much as possible the area within which explanation must rely upon such factors. Manipulation exists and irrationality exists, and the historian must acknowledge them when he finds them. But the historian who would make his discipline a more rigorous one should have as his *working assumption* that human actions are generally purposeful and are related to some system of values as well as needs; given that assump-

---

ical hegemony. Deriving the term from Antonio Gramsci, a Marxist theoretician who was especially concerned with the role of intellectuals in twentieth-century Italian politics, Eugene D. Genovese defines ideological hegemony as "the seemingly spontaneous loyalty that a ruling class evokes from the masses through its cultural position and its ability to promote its own world view as the general will" ("Marxian Interpretations of the Slave South," in Bernstein, ed., *Towards a New Past*, p. 123). Genovese correctly contends that an understanding of "class struggle . . . presupposes a specific historical analysis of the constituent classes" (p. 98), but he draws conclusions about the hegemony of the slaveholders with very little examination of "the masses," who, he contends, accepted that hegemony (pp. 90–125; see also his *The Political Economy of Slavery: Studies in the Economy and Society of the Slave South* [New York, 1965]). Genovese's work has produced rich results for our understanding of the slaveholders, but it tells us less about the "loyalty" or otherwise of the nonslaveholders; one does not need to contend that the latter were in open, or even furtive, rebellion to note that there remain enormous complexities which prevent a definition of "to rule" as synonymous with "to evoke loyalty." The existence of hegemonic mechanisms does not demonstrate the existence of hegemony. This important area needs fuller exploration. (See also my "New Left Elitism," *Radical America*, I [Sept.–Oct. 1967], 43–53; and my "Communication," *American Historical Review*, [LXXIV (June 1969), 1766–1768]).

[5] For a partial summary of this research, see my "Jack Tar in the Streets: Merchant Seamen in the Politics of Revolutionary America," *William and Mary Quarterly*, 3d Ser., XXV (July 1968), 371–407. Except where otherwise noted, this is the source for the following statements about seamen and historiography.

[6] For some notable exceptions, see Carl Bridenbaugh, *Cities in Revolt: Urban Life in America, 1743–1776* (New York, 1955), pp. 114–117, 305–312; Richard B. Morris, *Government and Labor in Early America* (New York, 1946), pp. 188–193, 225–278; and Oliver M. Dickerson, *The Navigation Acts and the American Revolution* (Philadelphia, 1951), pp. 218–219.

tion, it is inadequate for him to "explain" the recurrent conduct of large groups of men who seem to act consistently in accord with certain values by making those groups simply the puppets of their social superiors or the victims of alcohol.

In order to explain the seamen's conduct, I found that I would have to ask of them some of the same kinds of questions which intellectual historians generally ask of an elite: questions concerning loyalties and beliefs, all examined within a context which assumed that Jack Tar, like Thomas Jefferson, had ideas and perhaps something which might be called an ideology. On the track of these ideas, I found that actions which might in themselves appear inexplicable made more sense when causality was explored: the historian decides in advance that Jack Tar is a rebel without cause when he neglects to look for cause. The rioting of the pre-Revolutionary decades, for instance, makes more sense when seen against the background of an ancient and bloody tradition of violent resistance to British authority; impressment, commented a Pennsylvania Revolutionary leader, had produced "an estrangement of the Affections of the People from the Authority" of the British, which had led in turn, "by an easy Progression . . . to open Opposition . . . and Bloodshed." [7]

I found inadequacies in the approach to the Revolution—primarily from the top down—generally taken by historians. *Of course*, British officials—insensitive as they were to grievances of the victims of the policies which they administered—could find no better explanation than manipulation for the conduct of the seamen. *Of course*, Admiralty records distorted the realities of impressment, leading those who based their research on such sources to see impressment in the context of a manning problem rather than in the context of deprivation of personal liberty.

The struggle to get inside Jack Tar's head suggested the notion of what might be called an "experimental history." One way of evaluating the contention that a crowd is manipulated is to ask, what would the crowd do in the absence of those alleged to be its manipulators? The social psychologist might devise such a condition, but the historian has no choice but to accept the data provided by the past. As it happens, in the New York Stamp Act riots of 1765, precisely such a condition existed: witnesses who are in conflict on other matters agree that at one point whatever leaders the crowd had had lost control.[8] At this point, eschewing plunder, the crowd (including some four to five hundred seamen) marched some distance in a new direction and in orderly fashion to attack the logical political target. What is of interest to us here is not that in this particular instance a crowd demonstrably had political thoughts of its own but rather that if one attempts to devise conditions under which one might evaluate the thought and conduct of crowds, one may find a historical situation which approximates these conditions.[9]

[7] Joseph Reed, President of Pa., quoted in my "Jack Tar in the Streets," p. 395.

[8] See my unpubl. diss. (Yale, 1962), "Jack Tar vs. John Bull: The Role of New York's Seamen in Precipitating the Revolution," pp. 88–91.

[9] Cf. Merle Curti's criticism of historians for their reluctance "to try to adapt experimental logic to situations where actual experimentation is impossible" (rev. of C. Vann Woodward, ed., *The Comparative Approach to American History* [New

The notion of an "experimental history" seems crucial for a history of the inarticulate. Given the absence of a laboratory and the impossibility of controlling conditions experimentally, one must sensitize oneself to seek such conditions in the existing data. In effect, the historian of the inarticulate must train himself to think as if he were an experimental social psychologist; he must try to devise experiments for testing various contentions; then he must look to history and do his best to find a "natural experiment"—a situation in which such an experiment was in fact acted out.[10]

❧

One night in 1781—which is some sixty thousand nights ago—American seaman William Widger, who was nobody,[11] dreamt this dream as sentries marched around his Revolutionary War prison:

Last night I Dreamed I was in Marblehead and See [saw] Sylvester Stevens[.] [12] after discourseing with him about his Giting

---

York, 1968] in *Journal of American History*, LV [Sept. 1968], 373). Historians are of course limited to what psychologists call "natural experiments"; their predictions are made *a posteriori*, and the experiment cannot be rerun under other conditions to determine whether the variable focused upon is in fact the decisive one.

[10] Such training might fruitfully begin with study of the imaginative and rigorous experiments on obedience and defiance devised by Stanley Milgram. See his "Behavioral Study of Obedience," *Journal of Abnormal and Social Psychology*, LXVII (1963), 371–378; "Issues in the Study of Obedience: A Reply to Baumrind," *American Psychologist*, XIX (Nov. 1964), 848–852; "Some Conditions of Obedience and Disobedience to Authority," *Human Relations*, XVIII (1965), 57–76; and "Liberating Effects of Group Pressure," *Journal of Personality and Social Psychology*, I (Feb. 1965), 127–134. Milgram's experiments were called to my attention by Prof. Naomi Weisstein of the Dept. of Psychology, Loyola Univ., Chicago. Weisstein briefly discusses Milgram's work and other experiments with broad implications for the writing of history (especially work by R. Rosenthal and by S. Schachter and J. E. Singer) in "Kinder, Küche, Kirche as Scientific Law: Psychology Constructs the Female," a paper presented at the meeting of The American Studies Association, Univ. of California, Davis, Oct. 1968 (revised version forthcoming in *Psychology Today*).

[11] Widger (1748–1823) was a Marblehead privateersman captured in the brig *Phoenix*, Feb. 12, 1779, and committed to Mill Prison, May 10, 1779. After the war Widger became master of the brig *Increase*. For his dream, see "Diary of William Widger of Marblehead, Kept at Mill Prison, England, 1781," *Essex Institute Historical Collections* (Salem, Mass.), LXXIII–LXXIV (1937–38), 347 (hereafter cited as *EIHC*). Concerning Widger, see "Diary," *ibid.*, LXXXIII, 311–312; *Boston Gazette, and the Country Journal*, July 1, 1782; Benjamin J. Lindsey, *Old Marblehead Sea Captains and the Ships in Which They Sailed* (Marblehead, 1915), p. 131; Thurlow S. Widger, "The Widger Family" (n.d.; typescript at Essex Institute), pp. 4, 9–13. I am indebted to Dorothy M. Potter, Librarian at the Essex Institute, for help in securing biographical information about Widger.

[12] One of Widger's shipmates; Stevens escaped from Mill Prison (*Boston Gazette, and the Country Journal*, July 1, 1782).

home I said to him tis Damd hard now I have Got so near home and
Cant git their. . . . he asked me What the Matter was[;] I sayes
Why you See I am this Side of the weay and the Souldiers Standing Sentrey over by Mr. Roundays house. . . . I Left him and Went
a Little further & met Georg Tucker down by the eand of Bow-
den's Lain wheir he Stouped and Shock hands with me and Said he
Was Glad to See me[;] he Said my Wife was Just Deliver'd a Boy.
. . . I Started at that and Said it was a dam'd Lye it was imposable
for I had been Gone tow [two] years and leatter [later] and it was
inposable. . . . I Left him in a Great pashan and I was Going Down
towards Nickes cove I met my Mother and Stopt and talked with
hur[.] She asked me wheir [whether] I was not a Going home to
see my wife[.] I told hur no I was dam'd if ever I desired to See
hir a Gain[.] She Said the Child was a honest begotten Child and it
was Got before I went to See and it was mine[.] I Said it was inposable for the Child to be Mine for I had been Gone Mour then
two years and it was Inpousable[.] I told hur I was a dam'd foule to
Coum home but I Could go back in the Brig I came in. . . . She
pursuaded upon me to go home but . . . I was in Such a pashan I
Swore I would Never See hur a Gain. . . . She intreated me to go
home but I Swore I would not and it was no use to ask me[;] but
before I was don talking With hur a bout it I awaked.

What did you, who are somebody, dream last night—or a thousand nights
ago? This is not an argument for dream analysis. It simply says that even
the most fragile and evanescent sort of historical evidence can be retrieved
if we will only look for it. The naval prisons of the American Revolution are
an especially rewarding place to look for evidence for the history of the
inarticulate. A rich concentration of sources from conflicting points of
view enables us to look into the mind of the common seaman; here, we
can begin to say meaningful things about what significance the Revolution
had for at least some of the inarticulate.

During the Revolution, captured American seamen found themselves
imprisoned up and down the Atlantic coast and offshore,[13] and at various

---

[13] For New York, see the numerous citations in the following pages.

For Norfolk, see "Biographical Memoir of Commodore [Richard] Dale," *The
Port Folio*, VIII, ser. 3 (June 1814), 500.

For Rhode Island: John K. Alexander, ed., "Jonathan Carpenter and the
American Revolution: The Journal of an American Naval Prisoner of War and
Vermont Indian Fighter," *Vermont History*, XXXVI (Spring 1968), 78–79; Charles
Collins to Benjamin Franklin, July 8, 1779, in Franklin Papers (American Philosophi-
cal Society), XV, 26; "Diary of George Thompson of Newburyport, Kept at
Forton Prison, England, 1777–1781," *EIHC*, LXXVI (July 1940), 222.

Quebec: "Reminiscences of the Revolution: Prison Letters and Sea Journal
of Caleb Foot," *EIHC*, XXVI (March 1889), 105–108.

Halifax: Commissioners of Sick and Hurt Seamen (hereafter abbreviated as
CSHS) to Admiralty, Feb. 25, 1777, Jan. 5, 1778, Sept. 17, 1779, Public Record
Office, Admiralty 98/11/86, 153–154, 12/176–179; Admiralty to CSHS, Aug. 1,
1777, Jan. 14, 1778, Sept. 8, 1779, March 15, 1782, National Maritime Museum,
Greenwich, Adm/M/404, 405; [Boston] *Independent Chronicle and the Universal*

places in the British Isles.[14] The three major prisons for captured seamen
were a fleet around the prison ship *Jersey* at New York and, in England,
Mill and Forton prisons on land at Plymouth and Portsmouth. During the
war these three prison complexes held upwards of ten thousand and perhaps as many as twenty or thirty thousand captured American seamen.[15]

These prisons, in many ways different, had this in common: here
thousands of American common seamen were imprisoned, most of them

Advertiser, Feb. 5, 1778; John Blatchford, *Narrative of the Life & Captivity* . . .
(New London, 1778), pp. 3–6.

St. John's: *Salem* [Mass.] *Gazette*, Oct. 17, 1782.

West Indies: Admiralty to CSHS, July 3, Dec. 7, 1780, Sept. 15, 1781, Sept. 3,
1782, Adm/M/404, 405; Account of George Ralls, Nov. 7, 1778, New-York Historical Society; Secretary of State to Admiralty, Dec. 5, 1781, Adm/1/4146.

[14] For Mill and Forton Prisons, see numerous citations in the following pages. Smaller
numbers of Americans were kept, usually temporarily, at such places as Kinsale,
Kilkenny, and the Cove of Cork in Ireland, at Edinburgh, at Liverpool, Deal, at the
Nore, off Chatham, at Bristol, Pembroke, Shrewsbury, Falmouth, Weymouth, and
Yarmouth. Mention of these is scattered throughout the correspondence between
the Admiralty and the CSHS. (Admiralty to CSHS, 1777–83, National Maritime
Museum, Greenwich, Adm/M/404–405; CSHS to Admiralty, 1777–83, Public Record Office, London, Adm 98/11–14). A fuller description of these prisons and more
specific citations will appear in my full-length study, "Jack Tar in the Darbies:
American Seamen in British Prisons during the Revolution," to be completed
shortly.

[15] For almost complete figures for Mill (1296 American prisoners) and Forton (1200)
see John Howard, *The State of the Prisons in England and Wales* . . . (4th ed.;
London, 1792), pp. 185, 187. *Jersey*'s logs list a total of 7773 (Adm 51/493 and Adm
51/4228). But more than twenty ships held captured seamen at New York during
the war, and although *Jersey* was the major prison ship, others, such as *Good Hope*,
held more than three hundred at one time (*New Hampshire Gazette*, Feb. 9, 1779),
and *Jersey* did not receive her first prisoners until June, 1779. Thus it is likely that
the total for New York will be more than doubled when figures are found for the
other prison ships. In addition, the figure for *Jersey* alone is low because there are
two gaps in the logs (Nov. 21, 1777–Aug. 2, 1778, and Dec. 25, 1780–Feb. 14, 1781)
one of them during the period of *Jersey*'s service as a prison ship, and because, as
will be seen below, those who kept *Jersey*'s logs were far from faithful record
keepers.

Mill and Forton were set up early in 1777 explicitly for Americans captured
at sea: Admiralty to CSHS, March 13, April 19, 1777, Adm/M/404; Commissioners'
Memorandum, March 14, 1777, Adm 98/11/87–88; CSHS to Admiralty, Dec. 15,
1777, Adm 98/11/149; Commissioners' Minute, April 22, 1777, Adm 99/49. The
New York prison ships primarily held soldiers after the Battle of Long Island, e.g.,
Jabez Fitch, *A Narrative of the Treatment with which the American Prisoners were
Used, Who Were Taken by the British and Hessian Troops on Long Island* . . .
[publ. as *Prison Ship Martyr, Captain Jabez Fitch: His Diary in Facsimile*] (New
York, 1903). But by the end of 1777 and for the rest of the war the prison ships
were reserved for seamen, while soldiers and their officers were kept on land: Al-
bert G. Greene, ed., *Recollections of the Jersey Prison-Ship: Taken and Prepared
for Publication from the Original Manuscript of the late Captain Thomas Dring, of
Providence, R.I., One of the Prisoners* (New York, 1961 [1st ed.: Providence,
1829]), p. 50; Danske Dandridge, ed., *American Prisoners of the Revolution*
(Charlottesville, 1911), p. 405; [New York] *Royal Gazette*, Jan. 15, 1779.

under atrocious conditions, segregated from their officers, and with little
hope of release but much opportunity to defect. They were confronted
with the necessity to make decisions which they themselves perceived as
tests of their loyalty to one another and to the new nation. Those decisions
were expressed in specific acts which can be measured quantitatively.
These preconditions, then, make our laboratory: here we find solid data
concerning the conduct of common seamen; in addition, the sources enable
us to move beyond conduct into consciousness. William Widger's dream
suggests how deeply into consciousness—some would say beyond—we
can dig. In the prisons we can observe the society which the men
construct on their own, how they govern themselves, their culture, their
values, their ethos, and their ideology.

A situation *in certain ways* similar, that of Americans in prisoner-
of-war camps in North Korea in the early 1950's, seemed not only to
military men, but also to psychiatrists, psychologists, sociologists, and
journalists, a basis for a sometimes critical re-examination of the American
as *civilian*.[16] Conduct in prison, they said, could be explained in terms of
"diverse aspects of our culture,"[17] and thus that conduct in turn illumi-
nated American culture, character, and values. (Dr. Spock himself recon-
sidered permissiveness.)[18] Although it is tempting to draw conclusions
about comparative strengths of national loyalties in the eighteenth and
twentieth centuries from an examination of the two sets of prisoners, that
is not what is intended here. (In any case, conditions were too dissimilar
for facile comparisons of the two groups.) Korea is introduced here solely
as a *methodological* analogue, that is, a recent instance in which scholars
in various disciplines felt that an examination of a war-prisoner situation
could reveal something of the culture and values of the men. Like Korea,
the British prisons of the American Revolution offer a ready-made laboratory for the examination of the degree and quality of national and group
loyalty. In the British prisons we can study the estrangement of American
popular affection from British authority and the process by which Americans came to see a new authority as legitimate.

Jersey and the other prison ships at New York were places of crowd-

---

[16] The content of that re-examination varied greatly; for conflicting interpretations,
together with summaries of the views of others, see Eugene Kinkead, *In Every War
But One* (New York, 1959) and Albert D. Biderman, *March to Calumny: The
Story of American POW's in the Korean War* (New York, 1963).

[17] The phrase appears in Kinkead, p. 18. According to Biderman, "Kinkead's book is
misleading with regard to the strengths as well as the weaknesses that may be char-
acteristically American" (p. 45). Biderman sees among the prisoners in Korea "a
noteworthy display of group organization and discipline (although not always the
traditional Army variety of organization or one that can easily be perceived by the
more traditionalistic Army officers. . . .)"; he finds the roots of certain kinds of
prisoner resistance in characteristics and "generalized dispositions" which are
"peculiarly" or "distinctively" American (pp. 43–45 and passim).

[18] "Are We Bringing Up Our Children Too 'Soft' For The Stern Realities They Must
Face?" *Ladies Home Journal*, Sept. 1960, 20–25, discussed in Betty Friedan, *The
Feminine Mystique* (New York, 1963), pp. 373–374. Both Spock and Friedan ac-
cepted Kinkead uncritically.

ing, filth, disease, and death.[19] Contemporaries estimated that close to 12,000 died there during the war.[20] Interestingly—and not unpredictably—the historian who relied only on *Jersey's* logs and other official sources would be left almost totally unaware of the realities which led Henry Steele Commager and Richard B. Morris to describe the prison ships as the Revolution's Andersonville.[21]

A few prisoners had the misfortune to spend time both in *Jersey* and in one of the old buildings used as prisons at Plymouth and Portsmouth in England; they invariably concluded that *Jersey* was worse.[22] Part of

[19] Ample documentation for this contention may be found in the various sources cited in this article. For reasons of space, I am here giving only brief attention to physical conditions in the prisons and prison ships, while focusing instead on the conduct of the men.

[20] The figure usually offered is 11,644; although it was generally offered for *Jersey* alone, it was probably intended as a total for all the twenty or so prison ships at New York, of which *Jersey* was the best known. See *Connecticut Gazette*, April 25, 1783; *Pennsylvania Packet*, April 29, 1783; *New York Packet, and the General Advertiser* [Fishkill], May 8, 1783; David Ramsay, *The History of the American Revolution* (Philadelphia, 1789), II, 285; Dring, pp. 4–5; Thomas Andros, *The Old Jersey Captive; or, A Narrative of the Captivity of Thomas Andros, (Now Pastor of the Church in Berkley,) on Board the Old Jersey Prison Ship at New York, 1781* (Boston, 1833), p. 8. (For a lower estimate, see Henry Steele Commager and Richard B. Morris, eds., *The Spirit of 'Seventy-Six: The Story of the American Revolution as Told by Participants* [2 vols.; New York, 1958], II, 854).

    Since we do not know how the figure was derived, we must distrust it. But British prison officials who were in New York after the war had ample opportunity to deny it and never did: (James Lenox Banks, *David Sproat and Naval Prisoners in the War of the Revolution* [New York, 1909], p. 107 [cf. p. 22], Charles I. Bushnell, ed., *The Adventures of Christopher Hawkins . . . first Printed from the original Manuscript. Written by Himself* [New York, 1864], p. 263). Conservative projections on the basis of known daily death rates derived from sources cited in this article produce a total over 11,000. (Almost one third of one captured crew was dead within seven weeks—Henry Onderdonk, Jr., *Revolutionary Incidents of Suffolk and Kings Counties; with an Account of the Battle of Long Island, and the British Prisons and Prison-Ships at New-York* [New York, 1849], p. 240). There may be support for a large projection in the most substantial sort of evidence: actual remains, uncovered over the years; see I. N. P. Stokes, *The Iconography of Manhattan Island, 1498–1909* (New York, 1895–1928), V, 1398, 1493; Henry R. Stiles, ed., *Account of the Interment of the Remains of American Patriots who Perished on Board the Prison Ships during the American Revolution* (New York, 1865), p. 10; and Prison Ship Martyrs' Monument Assoc., *Secretary's Report of the Obsequies of the Prison Ship Martyrs at Plymouth Church, Brooklyn, New York, June 16, 1900* (New York, 1901), p. 17; cf. Dring, pp. 60, 146.

[21] [*The Spirit of 'Seventy-Six*], II, 854. One captain stopped recording deaths in *Jersey's* log after six weeks, and the others never started; see entries for Feb. 20, March 4, April 3, 5, 1781, Adm 51/4228, and see logs, *ibid., passim*, and Adm 51/493. The only disease mentioned anywhere in the logs is smallpox, and that is mentioned only once (June 5, 1782). See also my "Jack Tar in the Streets," p. 402n. (Conversely, relying solely on accounts by prisoners would also be misleading; for some criticism of these sources, see nn. 24, 45 below.)

[22] E.g., "Journal of William Russell," in Ralph D. Paine, ed., *The Ships and Sailors of Old Salem: The Record of a Brilliant Era of American Achievement* (New

the difference between *Jersey* and the English prisons is simply the difference between imprisonment ashore and imprisonment in a ship. Another major element of difference offers sharp testimony to the cruelty of civil war. In occupied New York, the prisoners' fellow Americans could hardly bring themselves to acknowledge their presence and their troubles; [23] in England, however, people at all levels of society poured out charity, aid, and comfort, some of it open, some of it underground. "Why, Lard, neighbour," observed a surprised Sunday gawker at Forton, the Americans "be white paple; they taulk jest as us do, by my troth." [24] Englishmen filled the prisoners' charity boxes, raised several thousand pounds for them in meetings throughout England, supported them on the floor of Parliament, and finally helped them to escape and concealed them. [25]

York, 1909), p. 169. The Continental Congress agreed; see Worthington Chauncey Ford, ed., *Journals of the Continental Congress, 1774–1789* (Washington, 1904–37), XXII, 245–246. See also Dring, pp. 79–80.

Both Mill and Forton had held French and Spanish prisoners during the Seven Years War, although neither had been designed for that purpose (Admiralty to CSHS, March 13 and April 19, 1777, Adm/M/404; CSHS to Admiralty, Nov. 22, 1780, Adm 98/13/137). Forton had been built as a hospital for sick and wounded seamen at the beginning of the century and was still referred to in Admiralty correspondence early in the war as "Forton Hospital" (John S. Barnes, ed., *Fanning's Narrative: Being the Memoirs of Nathaniel Fanning, an Officer of the Revolutionary Navy* [New York, 1912], p. 9; Admiralty to CSHS, March 13, 1777, Adm/M/404). At least one of the buildings at Mill dated back to Queen Anne's time (Andrew Sherburne, *Memoirs of Andrew Sherburne: A Pensioner of the Navy of the Revolution* [2nd ed.; Providence, 1831], p. 84).

[23] For some possible minor exceptions, see Dring, pp. 74–78, and Onderdonk, p. 248.

[24] Fanning, p. 11. Although in this instance contemporary evidence almost precisely confirms Fanning's report (cf. Charles Herbert, *A Relic of the Revolution* [Boston, 1847], pp. 19–20), most reminiscences of dialogue must of course be taken with a grain of salt. (Fanning seems to have written the section of his *Narrative* dealing with his imprisonment before and/or during 1801, although he "compiled" and "copied" it from his "old journal" [pp. i, 123n., 124].) While most of the sources on which this article is based are contemporary, a few are later reminiscences. The latter must be used with caution—just as we would use the memoirs of a Benjamin Franklin, or a Henry Adams, or old former slaves. In each case we should, as Edward P. Thompson advises, hold sanctimoniousness up to "a Satanic light and read backwards"; our sources must be "critically fumigated" (*The Making of the English Working Class* [New York, 1964], p. 58, 493). At the same time, we must be certain that we are not—as so often seems to be the case—applying critical standards which vary by race or class, so that the reminiscences of an aged Franklin seem acceptable as sources, while the reminiscences of aged former slaves are dismissed. (Consider also the tendency of historians of slavery to accept plantation records while largely ignoring the rich materials contained in the Federal Writers' Project's Slave Narrative Collection.) Such sources as the latter are complex and difficult to use; rather than ignoring them, we would do better to develop methodologies for distinguishing what is genuine in them from what is later superimposition. For such an attempt, see Jesse Lemisch, J. Gordon Melton, and John R. Cory, "A Methodology of Gospel Scholarship Applied to the History of the 'Inarticulate'" (in preparation).

[25] Olive Anderson, "The Treatment of Prisoners of War in Britain during the American War of Independence," *Bulletin of the Institute of Historical Research*, XXVIII

Although never so bad as *Jersey*, the English prisons, too, had their share of bad food,[26] overcrowding, and bad health,[27] brutal guards, and harsh punishment.[28] To the prisoners, the agent who ran the prison was "the old crab," "arbitary cruel & inhuman," "as full of Spite as an Infernal fiend could bee," "divested of every human feeling." [29] When a friendly peer visiting Mill Prison was told that the agent was a "dirty fellow," he replied: "Government keeps dirty fellows, to do their dirty Work." [30] But although the Commissioners of Sick and Hurt Seamen did not succeed in securing prisoners from "every evil of captivity, but captivity itself," the story of Mill and Forton is less a story of physical deprivation than is *Jersey*.[31] This provides us with a valuable comparison,

(1955), 81; John K. Alexander, "Forton Prison during the American Revolution: A Case Study of British Prisoner of War Policy and the American Response to that Policy," *EIHC*, CIII (Oct. 1967), 378–379; Herbert, p. 85–89; Petition of two hundred prisoners to the Lords in Parliament, June, 1781, Adm/M/405; Admiralty to CSHS, Dec. 11, 1777, Adm/M/404; "Journal of Samuel Cutler," *New-England Historical and Genealogical Register*, XXXII (Jan.–Oct., 1878), 187; *Annual Register for 1778* (London, 1779), pp. 78–79. The Americans were somewhat more effective in getting help to their countrymen in England than to those imprisoned in America; see, e.g., CSHS to Admiralty, Jan. 2, 1778, Adm 98/11/152. For English help to American escapees, see n. 65 below.

[26] Widger, "Diary," LXXIII, pp. 316, 320; Herbert, pp. 60, 75, 140; Ralls Account, New-York Historical Society; Cutler, p. 396; "Humanitas" to Admiralty, Aug. 29, 1777, encl. in Admiralty to CSHS, Sept. 3, 1777, Adm/M/404; "A Yankee Privateersman in Prison in England, 1777–79 [Journal of Timothy Connor]," *New-England Historical and Genealogical Register*, XXX–XXXIII (1876–79), XXX, 352. (Connor's authorship is uncertain; see William R. Cutter to Librarian of State Dept., Jan. 31, 1893, with the original manuscript in the Library of Congress, Manuscript Div., U.S. Navy, Accession 748.)

[27] CSHS to Admiralty, July 23, 1779, Feb. 11, 1783, Adm 98/12/106–107, 14/301; Carpenter, p. 83.

[28] Widger, "Diary," LXXIII, 335; Thompson, "Diary," p. 227; Connor, XXXII, 165.

[29] Fanning, p. 10; Ralls Account, New-York Historical Society; Widger, "Diary," LXXIV, 37; *Pennsylvania Journal*, Sept. 22, 1781.

[30] Russell, p. 164. One historian who failed to find anything "recriminatory or vindictive" in the correspondence between the Admiralty and the CSHS offered this as evidence of "tolerance and good sense" in official attitudes toward the prisoners (Eunice H. Turner, "American Prisoners of War in Great Britain, 1777–1783," *Mariners' Mirror*, XLV [Aug. 1959], 200). This proves nothing of the sort and suggests the reverse: consensus among administrators should be an ominous sign for those who study the administrated. Olive Anderson—who defends prisoner policy in England as "strikingly enlightened" and dismisses harsher versions as originated by "propagandists" and perpetuated by "race-tradition"—nonetheless moves away from Turner's formalism and closer to the truth of actual decision-making when she notes that the Admiralty "rarely had enough time, knowledge or interest to take an independent line. Normally therefore they merely authorized or implemented the commissioners' proposals . . ." (pp. 65, 82, 83).

[31] The Commissioners, Sept., 1779, quoted in Anderson, 72. According to figures derived from official sources, 4.57 percent of the prisoners in Mill and Forton died (Howard, pp. 185, 187, 191). Such figures seem to be confirmed by an American source (*Boston Gazette, and the Country Journal*, June 24, July 1, 8, 1782) whose

enabling us more nearly to test the quality of the men's response to captivity itself rather than simply to physical deprivation.

There is no ambiguity about the meaning of *Jersey*: by any standard it is undoubtedly a tale of atrocity. Despite Samuel Eliot Morison's exhortation that we not "stir up" the "unpleasant subject of the treatment of American naval prisoners," [32] there would seem to be important reasons to do so. If history contains horrors, the attempt to forget them is likely to lead to the necessity to relive them. But in noting that the American Revolution was, among other things, a cruel war, we do so not only out of motives of humanity, but because we want to know the truth of the matter. Was the American Revolution different from others—say, the French Revolution? Certainly it was. Was the American Revolution peculiar in that it was primarily legalistic and not so bloody? The facts of life and death in the prison ships do not jibe with that picture; America, too, was born in bloodshed. In any case, we will never have an accurate answer so long as we study the legalisms and avoid the bloodshed.

But our aim goes beyond the telling of atrocities: our interest is in the thought and conduct of the men. In order to understand that thought and conduct, we must consider the ways in which prisoners could regain their freedom. For much of the war, exchange as prisoners of war seemed hopeless. First of all, they were *not* prisoners of war; they were rebels, candidates for hanging,[33] detained under a suspension of *habeas corpus*.[34] If informal exchanges took place, formal cartels were repeatedly delayed. We cannot explore here the intricacies of exchange policies on both sides and the tortuous discussions of the matter. It should be noted that if legal status was an obstacle to exchange on the British side, American governments were also sometimes dilatory and uninterested. In America, Washington instructed the commissary-general of prisoners "absolutely to reject every overture for exchanging" captured privateersmen, who were civilians and therefore not "proper subjects of military capture." [35] Washington took little interest in the exchange of naval prisoners in general,[36] and the civilians in the prison ships at New York were at the bottom of the heap, their fate essentially in the hands of their friends.

3.5 percent figure for deaths in Mill alone almost precisely duplicates the British source. I am indebted to John K. Alexander, a graduate student at the Univ. of Chicago, for the latter figure and for other valuable assistance in many areas, especially in connection with my research on the English prisons. (For figures for Forton, see Alexander, "Forton Prison," pp. 380, 380n.)

[32] *John Paul Jones: A Sailor's Biography* (Boston, 1959), pp. 165–166. (Morison did not want to provide "fuel for American Anglophobes . . .")

[33] Until March 25, 1782 (22 Geo. III, c. 10). See, e.g., Benjamin Franklin to John Adams, April 21, 1782, Adams Mss. Trust, Mass. Historical Society.

[34] 17 Geo. III, c. 9 ("North's Act").

[35] Washington to John Beatty, Aug. 19, 1779, John C. Fitzpatrick, ed., *The Writings of George Washington from the Original Manuscript Sources, 1745–1799* (Washington, 1931–44), XVI, 131.

[36] Washington to Major General William Heath, June 9, 1780, *Writings*, XIX, 93; Washington to Mrs. Theodosia Prevost, May 19, 1779, *Writings*, XV, 105; Washington to Board of War, June 16, 1780, *Writings*, XIX, 17.

relatives, home towns. Washington's policy stressed instead palliation of conditions in the ships, and the logic of the policy was stated most bluntly by Secretary of War Benjamin Lincoln: ". . . to reconcile them as much as possible to the miseries of a loathsome confinement until they can be exchanged—and to prevent them—from an idea that they are neglected, engaging in the service of Britain. . . ." [37]

In France, Franklin devoted more energy to trying to arrange exchanges. The British—and sometimes the French—presented obstacles.[38] The British told the prisoners that the Americans were responsible for delays.[39] In common with some officials in America, Franklin thought that the British deliberately delayed exchanges in order to influence the prisoners to go into the British navy, and there is evidence from the prisoners that, regardless of the cause, delays were often so used by recruiting officers.[40] "Where to lay the blame I'm at a loss," wrote one prisoner from Mill.[41] "If Job himself was here," wrote another, "his patience would be worn out." [42] Hopes for exchange fluctuated, many became cynical, and finally concluded, "them hopes are gone . . . ," "Out of all hopes." [43]

"There is nothing but death or entering into the British service before me," wrote a prisoner from *Jersey.*[44] The narrow limits of the choices available to captured seamen forced them to consider the alternative.[45]

[37] Banks, pp. 99–100.

[38] See, e.g., American Commissioners to Stormont, April 3, 1777, *London Chronicle,* Nov. 6, 1777; Benjamin Franklin to Wuibert, Lund, McKellar and other prisoners at Forton, Oct. 20, 1778, Library of Congress (copy); Benjamin Franklin to David Hartley, Jan. 25, 1779, Library of Congress (transcript); Alexander, "Forton Prison," p. 385.

[39] This produced some poignant letters from prisoners to Franklin, e.g., Jacob Smith to Benjamin Franklin, Jan. 24, 1783, Franklin Papers, XXVII, 47, APS; two hundred eighty American Prisoners at Forton to Benjamin Franklin, Feb. 3, 7, 1780, Historical Society of Pa.; Samuel Harris to Benjamin Franklin, June 12, 1781, Bache Collection, APS.

[40] Franklin to David Hartley, March 21, 1779, Library of Congress (letter-book copy); Franklin to S[amuel] Huntington, March 4, 1780, National Archives; Connor, XXXII, 281; *New-York Gazette; and the Weekly Mercury,* Feb. 12, 1781; Banks, pp. 79, 88–89; Dandridge, ed., *American Prisoners,* p. 403.

[41] Russell, p. 134.

[42] Herbert, p. 219.

[43] Herbert, pp. 78, 135, 164; Connor, XXXI, 20, 213, 286, XXXII, 280, 283; Thomas Smith, "Letter," *EIHC,* XLI (April 1905), 227.

[44] Onderdonk, p. 238.

[45] Some had no choice in the matter. Impressment of captured seamen in the early stages of the war brought complaint from Jefferson in the Declaration of Independence (Carl L. Becker, *The Declaration of Independence: A Study in the History of Political Ideas* [New York, 1958], p. 190). For other information concerning impressment, both before and after captives' arrival in prison, see, e.g., Admiralty to Vice-Admiral Graves, Sept. 9, 1775, Adm 2/550; Graves to Admiralty, Nov. 10, 20, 1775, Adm 1/485; John Fisher to Admiralty, Dec. 5, 1781, Adm 1/4146; *New-Jersey Gazette,* May 9, 1781; Hawkins, pp. 31–32; and George Little *et al.* to Benjamin Franklin, Aug. 25, 1781, Franklin Papers, LX, 16, APS; Ebenezer Fox, *The Adventures of Ebenezer Fox in the Revolutionary War* (Boston, 1847), pp.

There was no confusion in the prisoners' minds about the meaning of enlistment: it constituted a clear act of disloyalty, what we call "defection"—as did they. "What an honour to walk his majestey['s] Quarter deck," roared a recent captive who refused.[46] To prisoners, to join meant, in their words, to be "seduced," to "desert their country's cause." [47] They called those who refused to defect the "brave Americans," "true sons of America." [48] A seaman delivering a speech to his fellow prisoners in *Jersey* congratulated them for their refusal to be bribed into deserting "the banners of our country." [49] Defectors were coerced, "hooted at and abused," [50] and prisoners solemnly swore to remain loyal to their country.[51]

Service in the British navy meant "fighting against the liberties of their country" to Americans in Paris and back home.[52] For our purposes it is more significant, and historiographically useful, that the prisoners *themselves* saw it that way. The act of enlistment may mean different things to those who are actually faced with the choice and to those who only consider it from afar. And even among the prisoners, defection had many individual causes and consequences, some of them in conflict. Re-

---

93–94. At another point (p. 136), Fox, whose reminiscences are cast in the form of somewhat sanctimonious grandfather stories, acknowledges drawing upon Ramsay, William Gordon's *History of the Rise, Progress, and Establishment of the Independence of the United States of America* (London, 1788), and Charles Botta's *History of the War of Independence of the United States of America*, trans. George Alexander Otis (New Haven, 1840–41). He does not acknowledge that in sections dealing with *Jersey*, he often borrows and adapts from Dring (cf., e.g., Fox, pp. 100 ff., and Dring, pp. 23 ff.; Fox, p. 114, Dring, p. 38). Although his memory of certain events which occurred while he was in *Jersey* is thus strongly assisted by Dring, most of what Fox says is clearly his own.

There is also plagiarism in some of the diaries and journals of the English prisons. See Alexander's " 'American Privateersmen in the Mill Prison during 1777–1782': An Evaluation," *EIHC*, CII (Oct. 1966), pp. 322–326; cf. Howard Lewis Applegate, "American Privateersmen in the Mill Prison during 1777–1782," *EIHC*, XCVII (Oct. 1961), 303–320; Alexander, "Forton Prison," p. 366n., and "Jonathan Haskins' Mill Prison 'Diary': Can it Be Accepted at Face Value?" *New England Quarterly*, XL (Dec. 1967), 561–564. In each such case, it is only the identity of the author, not the authenticity of the information provided, which is in question. Wherever I have found plagiarism, I have attempted to use the more reliable of the two sources.

46 Robert Wilden Neeser, ed., *Letters and Papers Relating to the Cruises of Gustavus Conyngham, a Captain of the Continental Navy, 1777–1779* (New York, 1915), p. 161.

47 Andros, p. 18; Dring, p. 71; Russell, p. 127.

48 Herbert, pp. 156, 177.

49 Dring, p. 93.

50 Henry B. Dawson, ed., *Recollections of the Jersey Prison-Ship: From the Original Manuscripts of Captain Thomas Dring* (Morrisania, N.Y., 1865), p. 187. See also, e.g., Sir Thomas Pye to Admiralty, May 30, 1781, in Admiralty to CSHS, June 5, 1781, Adm/M/405

51 Herbert, p. 202.

52 American Commissioners to Lord North, Dec. 12, 1777, Library of Congress; Russell, 94–95. See also Franklin's remarks at the Constitutional Convention, quoted in my "Jack Tar in the Streets," p. 404.

gardless of the diverse and individual significances of defection, we can say that the men in the prisons had a set of beliefs, an ethos concerning defection. In that ethos, refusal to defect was seen as loyalty to the Revolution, defection as disloyalty. The adherence of the prisoners to this belief establishes one of the major preconditions for our natural experiment studying the seamen's loyalties under pressure.

The laboratory is by no means perfect. Many enlisted, or were impressed, between the time of their capture and their arrival at prison.[53] Once in prison, some enlisted because various coercions seemed to them strong enough to remove the voluntary quality of the decision, and some doubtless enlisted because they genuinely believed that that course would increase their opportunities for escape.[54] But most of the factors which make the prisons a less than ideal laboratory tend to mislead us in a conservative direction; that is, we know that defection was, if anything, a maximal measure of disloyalty; a few may have defected despite a high degree of loyalty to the American cause. Finally, an important positive feature of the prisons as laboratory is that the men were quartered separately from their captains; the officers demanded separation, protested to the British when they felt that separation was inadequate and tried to arrange it themselves.[55] In most cases our sources allow us to distinguish between seamen and captains and to be reasonably certain that we are describing the activities of common seamen.

Thus with no apparent way out, the men were offered a choice. If the conditions under which the choice was made are not so clean as they would be were we constructing an experimental situation to study the

[53] For one instance in which 25 out of a crew of 100 entered in the ship which captured them, see Connor, XXXI, 284, and Alexander, "Forton Prison," p. 368. (For some indication of the coercive circumstances under which this took place, see Fanning, pp. 2–4.) It should be noted that capturing vessels, including this one, were also the scene of resistance and escape attempts on the way in (see Fanning, 2–5). For some other instances of resistance, escape and refusal to defect between capture and imprisonment, see Carpenter, p. 79; CSHS to Admiralty, Dec. 29, 1780, Adm 98/13/166; Marion S. Coan, ed., "A Revolutionary Prison Diary: The Journal of Dr. Jonathan Haskins," *New England Quarterly*, XVII (June–Oct. 1944), 295; Cutler, p. 187; Hawkins, p. 63; and Fox, pp. 93–94. For what appears to be the commitment of almost an entire 120-man crew to Mill Prison some five months after capture and after much pressure to defect and shunting about from ship to ship, see Herbert, pp. 17–44, 258; *Boston Gazette, and the Country Journal*, June 24, 1782; and Haskins, p. 295. At present, no meaningful quantitative statements on the relative frequency of defection as opposed to escape *before* imprisonment can be made. For quantitative statements on these matters *after* imprisonment, see below.
[54] Fox, pp. 146–147, 149, 167 ff., 209; Blatchford, p. 22; Anderson, p. 71.
[55] For the separate quartering of men and officers in both prison ships and prisons ashore, see, e.g., Cutler, pp. 395, 396; Herbert, p. 92; CSHS to Admiralty, Jan. 14, 30, 1778, Adm 98/11/154–55, 164–165; Fanning, pp. 14, 15; Russell, p. 171; Dring, pp. xiv–xv, 25, 39–40. Insofar as the British were responsible for the separation, there is some indication that they did it because they felt that quartering officers and men together operated to inhibit defection by the men (*New-York Gazette; and the Weekly Mercury*, Feb. 12, 1781). See also, Conyngham, p. 171. For American officers' demands and arrangements for separation, see Dring, p. 25, and CSHS to Admiralty, Jan. 30, 1778, Adm 98/11/164–166. For a related complaint by Congress, see *Journals*, XX, 622.

choice, interpretations of the Korean prisoner-of-war experience suggest that this is nonetheless a fruitful site for the study of the loyalties of the inarticulate in the American Revolution.

၆ာ

To an extraordinary degree, captured American seamen remained Americans. In the prisons our measure of loyalty can approach precision. For *Jersey*, a generous estimate indicates that, with death more likely than exchange, for every one hundred men who arrived in the ship, only eight chose to defect.[56] Similarly, in Mill and Forton, the overall defection rate was between seven and eight percent,[57] and of the defectors it is possible that fifty percent were what the prisoners called "Old Countrymen," [58] born in the British Isles. Thus, while birthplace clearly did make a difference, the similarity of conduct under the immensely different conditions of Mill and Forton on the one hand and *Jersey* on the other suggests that the degree of physical deprivation was not relevant: the men's conduct seems to have been rooted more in who they were, and what their loyalties were, than in the material circumstances of their imprisonment.

Men escaped more often than they defected—perhaps three or four times as often: almost eight hundred escaped from Mill and Forton.[59]

[56] *Jersey*'s logs (Adm 51/493 and 51/4228) record no one entering before May 17, 1781. This presumably reflects a failure to keep records on the matter rather than an absence of defection. After that date, the tally is regular and probably reliable. Between May 17, 1781, and April 7, 1783, the log describes 487 men as "entered," "volunteered," or "enlisted" (a few in services other than the navy). The figure may be generous, since some of these were doubtless impressed. During the same period, 5995 men are listed as arriving.

[57] See my "Jack Tar in the Streets," p. 403n., where British and American sources are in close agreement. Cf. Alexander, "Forton Prison," p. 384, where an American prisoner in Forton offers information indicating a defection rate in *Forton alone* of 5.7 percent (in the period June 14, 1777–July 2, 1779).

[58] Anderson (p. 72n.) says that "a high proportion" of the defectors were "old countrymen." For some descriptions of defections by "old countrymen" see Connor, XXXI, 288, and Herbert, pp. 63, 107, 155 (where one group of 30 defectors is described as "chiefly old countrymen"). Of 64 defectors in Herbert, 243–257, 32 were from England, Scotland, or Ireland. See also n.103 below.

[59] In Mill and Forton, over-all escape figures are between 17.4 percent (derived from *Boston Gazette*, May 24–July 8, 1782) and 30.0 percent (derived from Adm 98/11–14; Howard, pp. 185, 187). The disparity may be partially explained by the fact that British figures are based simply on reports of escapees—many of whom were later retaken, and of whom many tried again—while the American figures are totals of escapees *not retaken*. Thus the higher figure is an approximate measure of the prisoners' *intent*, the lower figure a measure of their *success*. In Forton alone, Adm 98/11–14 gives a figure of 44.7 percent, while an American prisoner gives a figure of 27.0 percent (for 1777–79) (Connor, XXXIII, 36–39).

Jersey's log is almost totally silent on the matter of escapes, mentioning only two attempts (March 7, 1781, and Feb. 3, 1782, Adm 51/493 and 51/4228). Numerous references to escapes in other sources cited in this paper indicate that the captains simply did not record escapes. On the other hand, the log does list frequent repairs of ports broken open by prisoners presumably escaping or planning to do so. For repair of ports, see logs, Oct. 9, 1780, Oct. 11, 1781, May 15, 16, June 5, 12–14, Oct. 31, and Nov. 11, 1782. Several of these entries explicitly describe the repairs as

What did escape mean to the prisoners? It was a serious matter, involving great and sometimes mortal risks both for those going out and those remaining inside. Those attempting escape from *Jersey* might be shot in the act [60] or flogged in punishment.[61] In the English prisons, failure meant forty days on half allowance in the Black Hole and a plunge to the bottom of the exchange list.[62] Getting out of *Jersey* still meant a perilous swim to the shore and the possibility of recapture once ashore.[63] In England, where a large reward was offered for escaped Americans, men whom the prisoners called "five pounders"—"peasants, who were always lurking about" and who "would sell their fathers"—beat the bushes with dogs and clubs; [64] some of them had probably been tipped off by guards with whom they were in collusion.[65]

If most prisoners displayed a great deal of courage and ingenuity in their escape attempts, some were merely in collusion with guards, turnkeys, or civilians, splitting the five pound reward, somtimes after a night and a day of sex and liquor in a civilian's home on the outside.[66] Joyrides

necessary in order to prevent escapes. For prisoners' descriptions of such destruction as a necessary preliminary to escape, see, e.g., Hawkins, p. 78; Onderdonk, p. 236. Fox (p. 131) describes the apparent escape of 200 men in a three-month period (cf. Hawkins, p. 72) during which time the log lists a maximum of 68 defections (log of *Jersey*, March–May, 1782). This suggests a ratio of escape to defection of approximately 3 to 1. None of the figures offered above include escapes between the time of capture and arrival in prison.

[60] For *Jersey*, see, e.g., Andros, p. 23; Hawkins, p. 74; Dring, pp. 110–112. Even those trying to flee a shipboard fire could expect to be shot (*New-York Gazette; and the Weekly Mercury*, Feb. 12, 1781). In Mill and Forton, at least in the early part of the war, the guards did not have orders to fire at escaping prisoners (Alexander, " 'American Privateersmen,' " 336–337, and "Forton Prison," p. 381). There is indication that these orders were later revised, or that there was a difference between orders and actual execution (Herbert, p. 150; Widger, "Diary," LXXIV, 152; Russell, p. 159).

[61] *New-York Gazette; and the Weekly Mercury*, Feb. 12, 1781.

[62] Herbert, p. 54; Thompson, "Diary," p. 238; CSHS to Admiralty, June 26, 1778, Jan. 5, 1779, Oct. 31, 1781, Adm 98/11/206, 398–400, 13/493–495; Benjamin Golden to Benjamin Franklin, Dec. 2, 1781, Franklin Papers, XXIII, 94, APS; Ralls Account, New-York Historical Society.

[63] See, e.g., Hawkins, pp. 73–75, 82–87; log of *Jersey*, March 7, 1781, Adm 51/4228; Onderdonk, pp. 236–237; [N.Y.] *Royal Gazette*, Dec. 8, 1781.

[64] Connor, XXX, 347, XXXI, 19, XXXII, 165; Fanning, p. 10; Haskins, p. 299.

[65] CSHS to Admiralty, Oct. 27, 1779, Nov. 14, 1780, Adm 98/12/240–241, 13/133–134; Admiralty to CSHS, April 29, 1782, Adm/M/405. Prisoners also received a great deal of help from a kind of underground railway in which British clergymen played a major role: Thompson, "Diary," pp. 232–233, 241–242; John Thornton to American Commissioners, Memorandum, Jan. 5–8, 1778, Harvard College Library; Philip Hancock to American Commissioners, Aug. 2, 1778, Franklin Papers, L(i), 45, APS; G. Williams to Benjamin Franklin, Oct. 2, 1778, Franklin Papers, XII, 5; Cutler, p. 397.

[66] Luke Matthewman, "Narrative," *Magazine of American History*, II (March 1878), p. 182; Admiralty to CSHS, Oct. 17, 1781, Adm/M/405, Justices of Peace of Fareham to Admiralty, Sept. 29, 1779, in Admiralty to CSHS, Oct. 15, 1779, Adm/M/404, Major General Smith to Secretary [of] War, Feb. 14, 1782, in Admiralty to CSHS, March 2, 1782, Adm/M/405; CSHS to Admiralty, Nov. 22, 1780, April 12, 1782, Adm 98/13/139, 14/141.

such as these suggest some of the complexities involved in generalizing about what escape meant to prisoners.[67] We can note, however, that for the majority who were serious about it, escape meant a rejection of the most available alternative way of leaving prison: defection. Just as defection implied disloyalty, escape implied loyalty; we have evaluated the loyalties of twentieth-century prisoners in this way,[68] just as Washington did when he commended escaped seamen as he would have praised brave and loyal soldiers.[69] "We committed treason through his [Majesty's] earth," was the way one captive described his escape.[70] A seaman laughed as prisoners made it past "the grand Lobster guard"; [71] others mocked defection by using the pretense of enlisting as a mask for organized escape.[72] "Kiss my arse!" signaled an escapee, once out of *Jersey's* firing range.[73] "Do you know that it is a great crime to break one of His Majesty's locks?" asked a prison commander; [74] "I told him that I did not regard His Majesty nor his locks. What I was after was my liberty."

Underlying escape was organization and cooperation. Not only those escaping but also many of those staying behind were direct participants in escape attempts. There were tools to be gotten and concealed, locks to be picked, bars to be broken, holes to be cut or dug, dirt to be hidden.[75] Plans for the escape had to be agreed upon, contingency plans had to be made in case detection took place, signals had to be devised, and arrangements made for rendezvous. The decision had to be made that the time had come to put the plan into execution. During the escape itself, guards had to be deceived or overwhelmed, prisoners had to be assisted out through holes or broken ports. The one hundred and nine men who escaped from Mill one night in December 1778 after a month's digging had previously drawn lots to decide the order of egress, and two men checked them off a list as they entered the hole.[76] None of these decisions and plans made themselves; a historical record which presents us with

---

[67] But we can say that collusive escapes were *in addition* to such totals as the 27 percent for *successful* escapes (see n.59 above), since those in collusion with guards were returned to prison.

[68] In Korea, "not one of our men escaped from a permanent enemy prison camp and successfully made his way back to our lines" (Kinkead, pp. 16–17. For a strong qualification of this statement and disagreement about its implications, see Biderman, pp. 84–90 and *passim*.) One of the results of the Korean experience was the promulgation by President Eisenhower in 1955 of a new Code of Conduct for the Armed Forces. Article III included a pledge that, if captured, "I will make every effort to escape and aid others to escape" (Biderman, p. 279).

[69] Dring, p. 180.

[70] Conyngham, p. 194.

[71] Carpenter, p. 83.

[72] Fox, pp. 124–125.

[73] Fox, pp. 129–130.

[74] For this and the following, see Foot, p. 107.

[75] For some of the cooperative actions described here and below, see Hawkins, pp. 78–83, Dring, pp. 109–110; Fox, pp. 116, 119–120, 124; Onderdonk, p. 236; Matthewman, p. 182; Herbert, p. 52; and CSHS to Admiralty, July 24, 1781, Adm 98/13/413–414.

[76] CSHS to Admiralty, Jan. 5, 15, 1779, Adm 98/11/398–401, 411–412: Herbert, pp. 203–207.

faits accomplis, decisions made and carried out, should invite us to look beyond, into the process leading to these decisions, and to recognize that these actions could not have been taken without serious thought, much discussion, and mutual trust.

The cooperation behind escapes is one facet of the larger story of prisoner organization and self-government. What follows, although only a sampling of the material available, is intended to suggest that exploration of the specifics of the prisoners' self-government and even their culture is feasible.[77] First of all, just as prison officials posted a list of regulations to let the prisoners know, as the officials put it, "what behaviour is expected on their Part," [78] there was a parallel but in many senses more inclusive structure erected by the prisoners themselves, who, as one put it, "adventured to form themselves into a republic, framed a constitution and enacted wholesome laws, with suitable penalties." [79] Early in the war, prisoners created "a code of By-Laws . . . , for their own regulation and government. . . ." [80] These codes, or "Articles," had a quite literal existence; written copies existed, and they were posted and read aloud periodically.[81] These rules, and the behavior which *they* sanctioned, competed with the official rules for the prisoners' respect.

Legislation by prisoners ranged from health to morality to political conduct. There were rules requiring "personal cleanliness . . . , as far as . . . practicable" and forbidding smoking, "blackguarding," drunkenness and theft.[82] "Due observance of the Sabbath . . ." was honored in the breach.[83] Consider this, and consider prisoners petitioning for a clergyman,[84] and the shame of one at being overheard praying "like a minister,"[85] and consider another, complaining, "It is a great grievance to be . . .

[77] My "Jack Tar in the Darbies" will give fuller attention to these matters. For some model studies dealing with the politics and culture of lower-class groups in different environments, see, e.g., Thompson, *Making of the English Working Class,* and several excellent studies by Herbert G. Gutman (e.g., "The Worker's Search for Power: Labor in the Gilded Age," in H. Wayne Morgan, ed., *The Gilded Age: A Reappraisal* [Syracuse, 1963], pp. 38–68, and "Protestantism and the American Labor Movement: The Christian Spirit in the Gilded Age," *American Historical Review,* LXXII [Oct. 1966], 74–101). The stance and methodology of Black historiography are also rich with models and implications for the rewriting of white history "from the bottom up." See, e.g., communications by Anna Mary Wells, Vincent Harding, and Mike Thelwell, *N.Y. Rev. of Books,* Nov. 7, 1968; and John Henrik Clarke, ed., *William Styron's Nat Turner: Ten Black Writers Respond* (Boston, 1968).

[78] For the rules, see Thompson, "Diary," pp. 238–240. CSHS to Admiralty, Jan. 28, 1778, Adm 98/11/162, notes that the rules were first posted Nov. 30, 1777. Cf. Herbert, p. 82, and Howard, pp. 473–474.

[79] Sherburne, p. 83.

[80] Dring, p. 84. Cf. Herbert, pp. 145–146; Sherburne, p. 85. There is no evidence of such a written code at Forton, although there is ample evidence of organized self-government, e.g., CSHS to Admiralty, Jan. 27, 1779, Adm 98/11/442–444.

[81] Dring, p. 86, 91–94; Herbert, pp. 145–146, 148; Sherburne, p. 85.

[82] Dring, p. 85; Herbert, pp. 68, 145, Widger, "Diary," LXXIV, 144; Russell, p. 155; Sherburne, p. 83.

[83] Dring, pp. 85, 89; Andros, pp. 18–19, and n.86 below.

[84] Widger, "Diary," LXXIV, 142.

[85] Sherburne, p. 99.

debarred from hearing the gospel preached on the Lord's day. . . ." [86]
In such evidence as this, and more like it, there hangs a tale, not yet told,
of the real meaning of religion in early America. (And other untold tales,
of Franklinian virtues among the inarticulate, are to be found in men
fretting over their shipmates' "blaspheming their Maker continually," [87]
and others, keeping accounts of whittled ladles sold to visitors at a shilling
apiece,[88] and others, struggling toward literacy through diligent study,
leaving prison captains-to-be.) [89]

Survival requires that any group living together make rules on such
matters as hygiene. But just as prisoner legislation in more political areas—
to be examined shortly— expresses an active rather than a passive response
to their situation, so some of their rules for moral conduct indicate that
their culture is not fully explicable simply in terms of the minimal necessities for group survival. "No giant like man should be allowed to tyranize
over, or abuse another who was no way his equal in strength." [90] No
prisoner, when liberated, could remove his chest." [91] Many distributed
other property before escape or exchange [92] or, afterwards, tried to will
money left in the prison agent's hands to other prisoners.[93] Loyalties to
town and crew flourished,[94] and communal institutions established by
the captors—such as the mess—were imbued by the captives with a deeper
meaning than the British intended.[95]

"A secret, . . . revealed to the guard, was death." [96] Committees
were formed to deal with informers; trials were held, sentences handed
down, punishments carried out.[97] In *Jersey*, a prohibition of defection may
have been written into the by-laws.[98] An anti-defection agreement carrying harsh penalties was posted in Forton,[99] and in Mill over one hundred
signed this paper:

[86] Herbert, p. 78.
[87] Haskins, p. 425.
[88] Cutler, pp. 187, 306; Herbert, pp. 45–46.
[89] Fanning, pp. 15, 15n.; Sherburne, p. 83–84. Some of the Franklinian virtues suggest
an individualistic strain amidst what seems a predominantly collectivist ethos. Disobedience by prisoners to prisoner-made rules and norms constitutes another significant area of deviation (see n.103 below).
[90] Andros, p. 18.
[91] Dring, p. 129.
[92] Dring, p. 129; Hawkins, p. 81.
[93] CSHS to Admiralty, May 6, 1779, Adm 98/12/9–10.
[94] E.g., Sherburne, p. 82–83; Herbert, p. 161.
[95] Thompson, "Diary," p. 240; Dring, pp. 33–34, 81–82; Fox, pp. 115–120; Herbert, p.
67; Sherburne, pp. 85–86.
[96] Andros, p. 17.
[97] Thompson, "Diary," pp. 225, 226; Andros, pp. 17–18; Herbert, p. 116; Hawkins, pp.
69–71; CSHS to Admiralty, Jan. 27, 1779, Nov. 12, 1781, Adm 98/11/442–444,
13/503–505.
[98] See Andros, pp. 17–18, where prisoners' refusal to defect is described in the context
of an enumeration and discussion of the prisoners' rules; also, see Dring, pp. 91–94,
where a shipboard orator, using the rules as the "text of . . . his discourse," praised
his fellow prisoners for not defecting.
[99] Thompson, "Diary," p. 225.

> We, whose names are hereunto subscribed, do, of our own free
> and voluntary consent, agree firmly with each other, and hereby
> solemnly swear, that we are fully determined to stand, and so re-
> main as long as we live, true and loyal to our Congress, our coun-
> try, our wives, children and friends, and never to petition to enter
> on board any of His Britannic Majesty's ships or vessels, or into any
> of his services whatsoever.[100]

Those prisoners who sought to defect did so only "very slyly." [101] Even
Old Countrymen, complained a British admiral, "dare not make known
their Intentions," lest they be exposed, like the defecting Americans, "to
the Resentment of the other Prisoners, who threaten the lives of those
who offer to serve in the Navy. . . ." [102]

It is clear that some prisoners stayed only under compulsion, disobey-
ing many of the prisoner-made rules described above, and undergoing
harsh punishments at the hands of other prisoners. What stands out in
the prisons is not that there was disunity but that, in this hostile environment, there was sufficient unity to maintain effective self-government.
There were various forms of organization: there were votes and lotteries,
and other arrangements, to assure the equitable distribution of food and
clothing; there were committees for trial and punishment and committees
of correspondence which drew up, read aloud, and circulated for signatures petitions and remonstrances, addressed to Franklin, to Washington,
to the House of Lords, to "Friends and Fellow Countrymen in America."
Hundreds signed these documents, protesting prison conditions, seeking
to publicize their situation on the outside and to bring about exchange
or amelioration. Beneath the guns and bayonets of the British the prisoners
maintained a legal structure which in many ways directly contradicted
the official structure.[103]

When Captain Thomas Dring sat down in 1824 to recall his experiences as a twenty-three year old imprisoned in *Jersey* in 1782, he found it
"an astonishing fact" that the prisoners had obeyed the by-laws so long

---

[100] Herbert (p. 202) contends that more supported the document than signed it.
[101] Herbert, p. 183.
[102] Sir Thos. Pye to Admiralty, May 30, 1781, in Admiralty to CSHS, June 5, 1781, Adm/M/405.
[103] Defection and informing were of course major forms of disobedience to prisoner government. In the English prisons, in regard to defection as well as other matters, we often find that the division is between Americans and Old Countrymen: "The Americans unanimously hang together, and endeavor to keep peace in prison, but if the [Old Countrymen] were stronger than . . . [the Americans] we should have a hell upon earth" (Herbert, p. 119). For committees, trials, and punishments for theft, see Widger, "Diary," LXXIV, 144; Sherburne, pp. 83, 85; Herbert, pp. 68, 145–146; and Dring, pp. 85–86. For forms of distribution of food and clothing, see, in addition to the mess, Herbert, pp. 166 (voting), and Russell, p. 157 (lottery). For petitions and remonstrances, see Committee of Prisoners in *Jersey* to "Friends and Fellow Countrymen in America," [N.Y.] *Royal Gazette*, June 12, 1782; Peti-tion signed by 100 prisoners in *Jersey*, Aug. 15, 1782, Banks, p. 101; 280 American

and so well.[104] The prisoners were "so numerous" and, thought the old captain—by now a leading citizen of Providence—they were "of that class . . . who are not easily controlled, and usually not the most ardent supporters of good order." And yet, men so prone to disorder as Dring supposed them to be had paid what he called "a willing submission" to the rules. They mutually supported their own good order and reserved for themselves the right to decide when British authority deserved obedience and when they would reject it as unjust and therefore unworthy of obedience: ". . . if any man misbehaves and deserves punishment, we will deliver him up, or punish him ourselves, rather than he should go un-punished; but rather than see a man chastised unjustly, we will do our utmost for his rescue." [105] In this way they attempted to overrule British authority, through demonstration and direct action, based always on what Edward Thompson has called "some legitimising notion of right." [106] They had withdrawn their loyalties from the British and had given legiti-macy to their own prison government, a government deriving its just powers from the consent of the governed.

If the government of the prisoners was legitimate, that was not only because it was the prisoners' own but also because it was *American*. They were quite articulate in their nationalism. We have already seen how they viewed the decision concerning defection in the context of national loyalty. In addition, from the very beginning, they expressed contempt for what they perceived as the merely pretended legalisms by which the British attempted to define them as rebels, pirates, and traitors. "D[am]n his Majesty & his pardon too . . . what murder or treason have we done Prey [?]" [107] They damned the King and tried and punished those who

---

Prisoners in Forton Prison to Benjamin Franklin, Feb. 7, 1780, Historical Society of Pa.; Herbert, p. 62 (petition read aloud in prison yard); CSHS to Admiralty, Sept. 8, 1777, Adm 98/11/132; To the House of Lords from "upwards of two hundred American Prisoners . . . in Mill Prison . . . in behalf of themselves and others, their countrymen and Fellow Captives," June, 1781, encl. in Admiralty to CSHS, June 23, 1781, Adm/M/405; and CSHS to Admiralty, Oct. 4, 1782, Adm 98/14/254.

[104] For this and the following, see Dring, pp. iii–iv, 84–85.

[105] Herbert, p. 184; see also pp. 78, 174.

[106] P. 68. For such action, see, e.g., Widger, "Diary," LXXIII, 335, LXXIV, 41; J. How to Major General Mocher, Feb. 23, 1782, in Admiralty to CSHS, March 16, 1782, Adm/M/405; Russell, p. 162; Connor, XXX, 352, XXXI, 213 ("Our provisions not being good we condemned them. . . ."); Dring, ed. Dawson, p. 179; CSHS to Admiralty, Oct. 28, 1782, Adm 98/14/262.

[107] Carpenter, pp. 83–84. See also Mary Barney, ed., *A Biographical Memoir of the Late Commodore Joshua Barney: From Autobiographical Notes and Journals* (Boston, 1832), p. 88; Herbert, pp. 34, 44; and Haskins, p. 433. The challenge to the legitimacy of the prisoners' commitment was in many senses a just one; see CSHS to Admiralty, May 17, 1780, Adm 98/12/456 for an attempt by the Com-missioners to have some Americans sent to Mill "although we are aware they possibly cannot be legally committed to Prison for want of Evidence. . . ." And of course North's Act, under which they were committed, came under fire for its suspension of *habeas corpus* (*Annual Register for 1777* [London, 1778], pp. 53–66; *The Works of the Right Honorable Edmund Burke* [rev. ed.; Boston, 1866], II, 193).

damned the Continental Congress.[108] They delivered fiery patriotic
speeches and held contemptuous dialogues with their captors.[109] They
sang defiant and exultant songs, of the Stamp Act and the Boston Tea
Party, and Bunker Hill, along with songs of lamentation by English
widows and generals on the harshness of the war in America, longing for
peace. Their songs wished "bad luck to the King and Queen/ And all the
Royal family . . . ,"

> Success unto America likewise to Washington
> Here is a health unto America that scorns to be
>   control'd.[110]

There were frequent patriotic demonstrations and celebrations of
American victories: American flags and thirteen cheers for the French
King's birthday; cheers to commemorate the defeat of Burgoyne; huzzas
for the French, for the Spanish, and for the Dutch; for the capture of
Cornwallis, American flags in hatbands, a parade around the prison yard,
and, at night, an illumination: ". . . generale Respect agreable to the
present ability of the prison." [111] And, on the Fourth of July: stars and
stripes, cheers and songs, and, for some, bayonets and death. On their
cockades they wrote, "INDEPENDENCE" and "LIBERTY OR
DEATH." Seeing what was on their heads, but never really knowing
what was on their minds, the prison keeper doubled the guard.[112]

Unquestionably, the seamen were nationalists. That is not, however,
a mark of distinctiveness. Indeed, their nationalism might be seen as a
measure of the extent to which they shared in the consensus and did not
conceive of their interests as distinctive; [113] they rallied strongly to the
support of a government which was not theirs.[114]

[108] Haskins, p. 305.

[109] Dring, pp. 89–95; Carpenter, p. 84.

[110] Prisoners' songs are a rich source for the patriotic as well as other aspects of the
seamen's lives. See, e.g., Hawkins, pp. 63–64; Carpenter, p. 86. The songs quoted
above are part of a manuscript from Forton Prison in the Library of Congress,
containing more than fifty songs. Most songs are given a specific date (in 1778);
there is a journal entry and several notations such as "Success to the Honourable
Continental Congress. . . ." George Carey of the Dept. of English, Univ. of
Maryland, is at work on a monograph on these "Songs of Jack Tar in the Darbies."
I am grateful to him for the use of his transcript and a xerox of the songs and for
some useful advice.

[111] Connor, XXXII, 72; Herbert, p. 175; Russell, 131; Widger, "Diary," LXXIV, 43–
44, 156–157; Sherburne, pp. 88–89; Benjamin Golden to Benjamin Franklin, Dec. 2,
1781, Franklin Papers, XXIII, 94, APS.

[112] Herbert, pp. 141–142; Russell, p. 129; Widger, "Diary," LXXIV, 30; Dring, pp. 97–
105.

[113] Ironically, one way in which the seamen moved in the direction of a distinctive
definition of their own interests was on those few occasions when they tempered
their nationalism with rage over what they saw as their country's desertion of them
and threatened in turn to desert their country unless Washington and others made
stronger efforts to exchange them. See [N.Y.] Royal Gazette, June 12, 1782, and
n.44 above.

[114] See, e.g., my "Jack Tar in the Streets," pp. 378–380, 387–388, 404.

To say, simply, that the seamen were nationalists says nothing about the *content* of their nationalism—what it was they thought they were being loyal to when they were loyal to "America," the values which they fastened to their nationalism and expressed through it.

The prisoners articulated a collectivist ethical code. Their government was egalitarian, and in their culture and conduct they showed a high degree of awareness of themselves as a group and loyalty to that group. There is a distinctive flavor about this egalitarianism and collectivism, seeming to set the seamen's values apart from the individualism and hierarchism [115] of the leaders of the Revolution. But does this constitute politics? The line between politics and what has been called "pre-politics" [116] is uneven and unclear, and no law of nature nor of man dictates that the one become the other, that potentiality become actuality. Although ethical code and group conduct would seem to have both implications and potentialities for politics, they are probably closer to "pre-politics" than to politics. What of constitution-making, laws, trials, petitions, committees, votes, and the rest of the structure of self-government in the prisons? This seems more nearly to be politics, especially when we note that the seamen self-consciously connected them with the ideals of the larger struggle; they governed themselves in accord with abstract notions of liberty, justice, and right, and they associated these notions with the birth of a new and better nation. Their nationalism clearly had political dimensions.

If the seamen had politics, that does not mean that they had class politics in the prisons. "Class happens," writes Edward Thompson, "when some men, as a result of common experiences . . . , feel and articulate the identity of their interests as between themselves, and as against other men whose interests are different from . . . theirs." [117] This describes what happened in the prisons, but with the vital qualification that it happened in the *nationalist* sense.[118] If *class* happened, it would be more likely to occur after the war, when independence *per se* was no longer the predominant issue and the seamen were able to test against the new realities the ideals for which they had fought.

The decision of the inarticulate to give their loyalties to one side or another in war has been a matter of fundamental importance in history,

[115] Although the term itself is rarely applied to the political thought and conduct of the Revolution's leaders, it seems to fit the descriptions offered by recent analysts: see, e.g., studies by Roy N. Lokken, J. R. Pole, and Richard Buel, Jr., cited in my "American Revolution Seen from the Bottom Up," pp. 34–35.

[116] "*Pre-political* people . . . have not yet found, or [have] only begun to find, a specific language in which to express their aspirations about the world" (E. J. Hobsbawn, *Primitive Rebels: Studies in Archaic Forms of Social Movement in the 19th and 20th Centuries* [New York, 1965], p. 2; see *passim* for a working out of the definition in more specific terms).

[117] P. 9.

[118] I am indebted to Christopher Z. Hobson for insights into the relations between class and nationalist consciousness; see his unpubl. M.A. thesis (Univ. of Chicago, 1969), "Economic Discontent, Ghana 1951–66: A Study in the Class Dynamics of Third-World Nationalist Movements," especially chap. V. See also Staughton Lynd, *Class Conflict, Slavery, and the United States Constitution: Ten Essays* (Indianapolis, 1967), pp. 13–14.

a decision with enormous political meaning. In the Revolution, men like William Widger chose the American side. William Widger was somebody; he had individuality, dignity, and values of his own. He expressed those values, in part, in his nationalism, and he and his fellow prisoners held to their nationalism with a strength which cannot be explained by manipulation. The nationalism of the seamen was as authentic as the nationalism of a Jefferson, an Adams, or a Franklin; in this sense, the Revolution happened from the bottom up as well as from the top down.

❧

We know what William Widger dreamt sixty thousand nights ago.[119] If we can find William Widger's dream in the published *Historical Collections* of the Essex Institute; if we can find, in Yale's Franklin Collection, rich and poignant letters from seamen which even convey, through their spelling, something of the sound of the spoken language;[120] if Philip Freneau, the man who came to be called "The Poet of the American Revolution," shared some of the experiences of "The British Prison Ship" and wrote of them;[121] if the seamen themselves left us ample materials which invite us to examine their politics, their loyalties, and their culture; if sources such as these and others exist, from which it is possible to construct laboratories in which the inarticulate can be heard—then is it not time that we put "inarticulate" in quotation marks and begin to see the term more as a judgment on the failure of historians than as a description of historiographical reality? [122]

[119] For some other dreams and fever fantasies, see Russell, pp. 152–153, and Sherburne, pp. 93–94, 99–100.

[120] In addition to letters cited above from Americans in English prisons, many Americans—some of whom had been captured by the French as English—wrote Franklin from French prisons, begging his assistance, e.g., Jonathan Atkin to Benjamin Franklin, Nov. 10, 1778, Franklin Papers, LX, 3, APS; William Gardner to Benjamin Franklin, March 21, 1779, Franklin Papers, XIII, 215; and James Mathews to Benjamin Franklin, Oct. 19, 1782, Historical Society of Pa. All of the correspondence to and from Franklin cited in this article was originally examined in photocopy form at the Franklin Collection at Yale (citations are given to original repositories). I am grateful to Leonard W. Labaree and to Helen C. Boatfield in connection with these items and for innumerable other kindnesses over many years.

[121] Fred Lewis Pattee, ed., *The Poems of Philip Freneau, Poet of the American Revolution* (3 vols.; Princeton, 1902–07), 18–39, and Freneau's *Some Account of the Capture of the Ship "Aurora"* (New York, 1899).

[122] Not considered in this paper are certain ideological barriers to writing a history of the "inarticulate." Prominent among these is pluralism, aptly described by Michael Paul Rogin (*The Intellectuals and McCarthy: The Radical Specter* [Cambridge, 1967], p. 282), as "not . . . the product of science but . . . a liberal American venture into conservative political theory." Pluralism is an explicitly elitist doctrine; it praises the distribution of power among elites, and in so doing it justifies the exclusion from political power of the "illegitimate." Thus Daniel Bell writes, "Democratic politics means bargaining between *legitimate* groups and the search for consensus" ("Passion and Politics in America," *Encounter*, VI [Jan. 1956], p. 61; emphasis added). Just as pluralism as political philosophy justified the exclusion of

the "illegitimate," pluralism as historiography justified the exclusion of the past "illegitimate," which is to say the "inarticulate." Thus we have seen the past too uncritically through the eyes of such men as Olmsted's "Men of literary taste" and too little through eyes defined by pluralists as illegitimate. (See my rev. of Bernard Bailyn, *The Origins of American Politics* [New York, 1968], in *New Republic*, May 25, 1968, pp. 25–28, and also my study in progress, "Anti-Communism as a Goal of Recent American Historiography.")

Eighteenth-Century American Women in Peace and War

MARY BETH NORTON

Historical writings about the American Revolution are conspicuous for their omission of more than passing notice of the roles played by women in the upheaval and of the effect of the war on their lives. Only a few images have stuck in our historical consciousness—Betsy Ross stitching the flag, Molly Pitcher tending the wounded on the battlefield, and, perhaps, Abigail Adams lecturing her husband as he bustled about to create a new social order: "Remember the Ladies, and be more generous and favourable to them than your ancestors. Remember all Men would be tyrants if they could. If particular care and attention is not paid to the Ladies, we are determined to foment a Rebellion. . . ."

In part, the neglect of the study of women's lives during tho Revolutionary era is symptomatic of the general disregard of the importance of women in history. The current women's movement has provided the climate to develop a generation of historians who are posing questions about women in the past and who are going to the archives in search of answers. Their work is beginning to appear in print. Already it is clear that the historical sources will yield answers about women in history if only historians will ask appropriate questions. It is not the American past that has changed but our understanding of it.

Mary Beth Norton is one of the younger historians concerned with the role of women in shaping American society. Her study of loyalist women explores the revolutionary experience of her subjects, examining the lives of these women before as well as during and after the Revolution. Her essay helps us understand that revolutions may not be equally momentous for all people or affect everyone in the same ways. Women in the American Revolution, for example, took up new economic roles and managerial responsibilities, partly because of the absence of husbands, fathers, and brothers and partly because wartime disruption and the severing of ties with England created a heavy demand for the domestic manufacture of cloth, military supplies, and other items.

Counteracting this trend was the fact that many women had already been conscripted into bourgeois culture, accepting the notion that a woman's place was in the home. The roles of wife and mother were enhanced, but the wider world of business, politics, and public affairs remained in another sphere. Norton finds evidence that loyalist women perceived themselves as "helpless" creatures, greatly inferior to men. If she is correct, this internalized "cult of domesticity," which is usually associated with the nineteenth century, had permeated colonial culture by the eve of the Revolution. Readers may wish to

think back to the earlier selection, "The Planter's Wife," which described women's roles in the seventeenth century.

To what extent the Revolution altered, reversed, or accelerated
forces that were already acting on the roles and self-perceptions of
American women is a fascinating but as yet unanswered question. This
much is clear: there were few male revolutionists who believed that
this was the time to alter the increasingly rigid way in which sex roles
were being defined. They had other things on their minds. But despite
male lack of concern, women did experience the Revolution as a period
of social upheaval, new responsibilities, and tradition-breaking innovations. How they drew upon their revolutionary experiences after the
war in order to challenge existing norms is an exciting new topic of
research.

In recent years historians have come to recognize the central role of the
family in the shaping of American society. Especially in the eighteenth
century, when "household" and "family" were synonymous terms, and
when household manufactures constituted a major contribution to the
economy, the person who ran the household—the wife and mother—occupied a position of crucial significance. Yet those who have studied
eighteenth-century women have usually chosen to focus on a few outstanding, perhaps unrepresentative individuals, such as Eliza Lucas Pinck-
ney, Abigail Smith Adams, and Mercy Otis Warren. They have also
emphasized the activities of women outside the home and have concentrated on the prescriptive literature of the day. Little has been done to
examine in depth the lives actually led by the majority of colonial women
or to assess the impact of the Revolution upon them.[1]

Such a study can illuminate a number of important topics. Demographic scholars are beginning to discover the dimensions of eighteenth-
century households, but a knowledge of size alone means little without a

---

[1] See, for example, such works as Mary Sumner Benson, *Women in Eighteenth-
Century America: A Study of Opinion and Social Usage* (New York, 1935); Elisa-
beth Anthony Dexter, *Colonial Women of Affairs*, 2d ed. (New York, 1931); and
Joan Hoff Wilson, "Dancing Dogs of the Colonial Period: Women Scientists,"
Early American Literature, VII (1973), 225–235. Notable exceptions are Julia Cherry
Spruill, *Women's Life and Work in the Southern Colonies* (Chapel Hill, N.C.,
1938), and Eugenie Andruss Leonard, *The Dear-Bought Heritage* (Philadelphia,
1965). On the importance of the early American family see David Rothman, "A
Note on the Study of the Colonial Family," *William and Mary Quarterly*, 3d Ser.,
XXIII (1966), 627–634.

"Eighteenth-Century American Women in Peace and War," by Mary Beth Norton.
From *William and Mary Quarterly*, 33 (1976):386–409. Reprinted by permission of
the author and the publisher. Some footnotes have been omitted.

delineation of roles filled by husband and wife within those households.[2] Historians of nineteenth-century American women have analyzed the ideology which has been termed the "cult of true womanhood" or the "cult of domesticity," but the relationship of these ideas to the lives of women in the preceding century remains largely unexplored.[3] And although some historians of the Revolution now view the war as a socially disruptive phenomenon, they have not yet applied that insight specifically to the study of the family.[4]

Fortunately, at least one set of documents contains material relevant to an investigation of all these aspects of late eighteenth-century American family life: the 281 volumes of the loyalist claims, housed at the Public Record Office in London. Although these manuscripts have been used extensively for political and economic studies of loyalism, they have only

[2] Two recent works that deal with family size, among other topics, are Robert V. Wells, "Household Size and Composition in the British Colonies in America, 1675–1775," *Journal of Interdisciplinary History*, IV (1974), 543–570, and Daniel Scott Smith, "Population, Family and Society in Hingham, Massachusetts, 1635–1880" (Ph.D. diss., University of California, Berkeley, 1973). Internal household relationships in 17th-century New England have been analyzed by Edmund S. Morgan, *The Puritan Family: Religion & Domestic Relations in Seventeenth-Century New England* (Boston, 1944), and John Demos, *A Little Commonwealth: Family Life in Plymouth Colony* (New York, 1970).

[3] Barbara Welter, "The Cult of True Womanhood, 1820–1860," *American Quarterly*, XVII (1966), 151–174, was the first to outline the dimensions of this ideology. For writings dealing with some of the implications of the "cult of domesticity" see Carroll Smith-Rosenberg, "The Hysterical Woman: Sex Roles and Role Conflict in 19th-Century America," *Social Research*, XXXIX (1972), 652–678; Ann Douglas Wood, "Mrs. Sigourney and the Sensibility of the Inner Space," *New England Quarterly*, XLV (1972), 163–181; Kathryn Kish Sklar, *Catharine Beecher: A Study in American Domesticity* (New Haven, Conn., 1973); and Nancy Falik Cott, "In the Bonds of Womanhood: Perspectives on Female Experience and Consciousness in New England, 1780–1830" (Ph.D. diss., Brandeis University, 1974), esp. chap. 6. An explicit assertion that women were better off in 18th-century America than they were later is found in Dexter, *Colonial Women of Affairs*, vii, 189–192, and in Page Smith, *Daughters of the Promised Land* (Boston, 1970), 37–76. But two European historians have appropriately warned that it may be dangerous to assume the existence of a "golden, preindustrial age" for women, noting that the "goldenness is seen almost exclusively in terms of women's work and its presumed relationship to family power, not in terms of other vital aspects of their lives, including the physical burdens of work and child bearing." Patricia Branca and Peter N. Stearns, "On the History of Modern Women, a Research Note," *AHA Newsletter*, XII (Sept. 1974), 6.

[4] For example, John Shy, "The American Revolution: The Military Conflict Considered as a Revolutionary War," in Stephen G. Kurtz and James H. Hutson, eds., *Essays on the American Revolution* (Chapel Hill, N.C., 1973), 121–156; John Shy, "The Loyalist Problem in the Lower Hudson Valley: The British Perspective," in Robert A. East and Jacob Judd, eds., *The Loyalist Americans: A Focus on Greater New York* (Tarrytown, N.Y., 1975), 3–13; and Ronald Hoffman, *A Spirit of Dissension: Economics, Politics, and the Revolution in Maryland* (Baltimore, 1973), esp. chaps. 6, 8.

once before been utilized for an examination of colonial society.[5] What
makes the loyalist claims uniquely useful is the fact that they contain
information not only about the personal wartime experiences of thousands
of Americans but also about the modes of life the war disrupted.

Among the 3,225 loyalists who presented claims to the British government after the war were 468 American refugee women. The analysis
that follows is based upon an examination of the documents—formal
memorials, loss schedules, and private letters—submitted by these women
to the loyalist claims commission, and on the commission's nearly ver-
batim records of the women's personal appearances before them.[6] These
women cannot be said to compose a statistically reliable sample of American womanhood. It is entirely possible that loyalist families differed
demographically and economically, as well as politically, from their revolutionary neighbors, and it is highly probable that the refugee claimants
did not accurately represent even the loyalist population, much less that
of the colonies as a whole.[7] Nonetheless, the 468 claimants included white
women of all descriptions, from every colony and all social and economic
levels: they were educated and illiterate; married, widowed, single, and
deserted; rural and urban; wealthy, middling, and poverty-stricken. Accordingly, used with care, the loyalist claims can tell us much about the
varieties of female experience in America in the third quarter of the
eighteenth century.[8]

One aspect of prewar family life that is systematically revealed in the
claims documents is the economic relationship of husband and wife
within the household. All claimants, male and female alike, had to supply

[5] Catherine S. Crary, "The Humble Immigrant and the American Dream: Some Case
Histories, 1746–1776," *Mississippi Valley Historical Review*, XLVI (1959), 46–66.

[6] For a detailed examination of the claims process see Mary Beth Norton, *The British-
Americans: The Loyalist Exiles in England, 1774–1789* (Boston, 1972), 185–222. More
than 468 women appear in the claims documents; excluded from the sample selected
for this article are all female children, all English women who never lived in
America (but who were eligible for compensation as heirs of loyalists), and all
American women who did not personally pursue a claim (that is, whose husbands
took the entire responsibility for presenting the family's claims). In addition to those
requesting reimbursement for property losses, the sample includes a number of
women—mostly the very poor, who had lost only a small amount of property, if
any—who applied solely for the subsistence pensions which were also awarded by
the claims commissioners. On the allowance system see *ibid.*, 52–61, 111–121, and
225–229. [All quoted material from loyalist women, unless otherwise noted, comes
from the A.O. 12 and A.O. 13 documents, Public Record Office, London.]

[7] On the statistical biases of the loyalist claims see Eugene Fingerhut, "Uses and
Abuses of the American Loyalists' Claims: A Critique of Quantitative Analyses,"
WMQ, 3d Ser., XXV (1968), 245–258.

[8] This approach to women in the Revolutionary era differs from the traditional focus
on their public contributions to the war effort. See, for example, Elizabeth F. Ellet,
The Women of the American Revolution (New York, 1848–1850); Walter Hart
Blumenthal, *Women Camp Followers of the American Revolution* (Philadelphia,
1952); Elizabeth Cometti, "Women in the American Revolution," *NEQ*, XX (1947),
329–346; and Linda Grant DePauw, *Four Traditions: Women of New York during
the American Revolution* (Albany, 1974).

the commission with detailed estimates of property losses. Given the circumstances of the war, documentary evidence such as deeds, bills of sale, and wills was rarely available in complete form, and the commission therefore relied extensively upon the sworn testimony of the claimants and their witnesses in assessing losses. The claimants had nothing to gain by withholding information, because the amount of compensation they received depended in large part on their ability to describe their losses. Consequently, it may be assumed that what the loyalists told the commission, both orally and in writing, represented the full extent of their knowledge of their families' income and property.[9] The women's claims thus make it possible to determine the nature of their participation in the financial affairs of their households.

Strikingly, although male loyalists consistently supplied detailed assessments of the worth of their holdings, many women were unable to place precise valuations on the property for which they claimed compensation. Time after time similar phrases appear in the records of oral testimony before the commission: "She cant say what the Houses cost or what they woud have sold for" (the widow of a Norfolk merchant); "Says she is much a Stranger to the state of Her Husband's Concerns" (the widow of a storekeeper from Ninety-Six, South Carolina); "It was meadow Land, she cannot speak of the Value" (a New Jersey farmer's widow); "Her husband was a Trader and had many Debts owing to him She does not know how much they amounted to" (a widow from Ninety-Six); "She can't speak to the Value of the Stock in Trade" (a Rhode Island merchant's widow); "It was a good Tract but does not know how to value it" (the widow of a Crown Point farmer).

Even when women submitted detailed loss schedules in writing, they frequently revealed at their oral examinations that they had relied on male relatives or friends, or even on vaguely recalled statements made by their dead husbands, in arriving at the apparently knowledgeable estimates they had initially given to the commission. For example, a New Jersey woman, questioned about her husband's annual income, referred the commissioners to her father and other male witnesses, admitting that she did not know the amount he had earned. Similarly, the widow of a Charleston saddler told the commissioners that "she does not know the Amount of Her husband's Property, but she remembers to have heard him say in the year 1777 that he was worth £2,000 sterling clear of all Debts." Such statements abound in the claims records: "She is unable to speak to the value of the Plantn herself, but refers to Mr. Cassills"; "Says she cannot speak to the Value—the Valuatn was made by Capt McDonald and Major Munro"; "Says her Son in Law Capt Douglas is better acquainted with the particulars of her property than herself and she refers to him for an Account thereof."

[9] Only if they intended to commit fraud could loyalists gain by withholding information from the commission; two refugees, for example, requested compensation for property they had already sold during the war. But the commissioners found deliberately fraudulent only 10 of the claims submitted to them, and although they disallowed others for "gross prevarication," none of the claims falling into either category were submitted by women. See Norton, *British–Americans*, 217–219, on the incidence of fraud, and 203–205, 216–217, on the importance of accurate testimony.

Although many female claimants thus lacked specific knowledge of their families' finances, there were substantial variations within the general pattern. The very wealthiest women—like Isabella Logan of Virginia (who could say only that she and her husband had lived in "a new Elegant, large double Brick House with two wings all finish'd in the best taste with Articles from London") and Mrs. Egerton Leigh of South Carolina (who gave it as her opinion that her husband had "a considerable real Estate as well as personal property . . . worth more than £10,000 . . . tho' she cannot herself speak to it with accuracy")—also tended to be the ones most incapable of describing their husbands' business affairs. Yet some wealthy, well-educated women were conversant with nearly every detail of the family finances. For the most part, this latter group was composed of women who had brought the property they described to their husbands at marriage or who had been widowed before the war and had served as executrixes of the estates in question for some time. A case in point is that of Sarah Gould Troutbeck, daughter, executrix, and primary heir of John Gould, a prosperous Boston merchant. Her husband John, an Anglican clergyman, died in 1778, and so she carried the full burden of presenting the family's claim to the commission. Although she deprecatingly described herself to the board as "a poor weak Woman unused to business," she supplied the commissioners with detailed evidence of her losses and unrelentingly pursued her debtors. "Your not hearing from me for so long a time may induce you to think I have relinquished my claim to the interest due on your note," she informed one man in 1788. "If you realy entertain any such thoughts I must beg leave to undeceive you." In addition, she did what few loyalists of either sex had the courage to attempt—return to the United States to try to recover her property. When she arrived in 1785, she found her estates "in the greatest confusion" but nevertheless managed within several months to repossess one house and to collect some debts. In the end she apparently won restoration of most of her holdings.[10]

Yet not all the female loyalists who had inherited property in their own right were as familiar with it as was Sarah Troutbeck. Another Massachusetts woman admitted to the commissioners that she did not know the value of the 550 acres left her by a relative, or even how much of the land was cultivated. "Her Brother managed everything for her and gave her what Money she wanted," she explained. In the same vein, a New Yorker was aware that her father had left her some property in his will, but "she does not know what property." A Charleston resident who had owned a house jointly with her brother commented that "it was a good House," but the commission noted, "she does not know the Value of it." And twice-widowed Jane Gibbes, claiming for the farms owned by her back-country South Carolina husbands, told the commission that she had relied on neighbors to assess the worth of the property, for "she can't speak positively to the value of her Lands herself."

But if Jane Gibbes could not precisely evaluate the farms she had

[10] Sarah Troutbeck to commissioners, June 5, 1787, A.O. 13/49, pt. 2, 565; Troutbeck to Samuel Peters, May 22, 1788, Peters Papers, III, fol. 83 (microfilm), New-York Historical Society, New York City.

lived on, she still knew a good deal about them. She described the total acreage, the amount of land under cultivation, the crops planted, and the livestock that had been lost. In this she was representative of most rural female loyalists with claims that were not complicated by the existence of mortgages or outstanding debts. Although they did not always know the exact value of the land for which they requested reimbursement, they could supply the commission with many important details about the family property: the number of cattle, horses, sheep, and hogs; the types of tools used; the acreage planted, and with what crops; the amounts of grain and other foodstuffs stored for the winter; and the value of such unusual possessions as beehives or a "Covering Horse." It was when they were asked about property on which they had not lived, about debts owed by their husbands, or about details of wills or mortgages that they most often admitted ignorance.

A good example is Mary McAlpin, who had settled with her husband on a farm near Saratoga, New York, in 1767. She did not know what her husband had paid for some unimproved lands, or the acreage of another farm he had purchased, but she was well acquainted with the property on which they had lived. The farm, she told the commissioners, "had been wholly cleared and Improved and was in the most perfect State of Cultivation." There were two "Log Houses plaistered and floored," one for them and one for their hired laborers, and sufficient materials on hand to build "a large and Commodious Brick House." Her husband had planted wheat, rye, peas, oats, barley, corn, turnips, potatoes, and melons; and "the Meadows had been laid down or sown with Clover and Timothy Grass, the two kind of Grass Seeds most Valued in that Country." The McAlpins had had a kitchen garden that produced "in great abundance every Vegitable usually cultivated in that part of America." Moreover, the farm was "well Provided" with such utensils as "a Team waggon, Carts sledges Carwls [*sic*] Wheels for Waggons, Wheels for Carts, Wheelbarrows, drags for Timber Ploughs, Harrows Hay Sythes Brush Sythes Grubbling Harrows, and all sorts of Carpenters Tools Shoemakers Tools Shovels, Spades, Axes Iron Crow Barrs etc."

After offering all these details, however, Mrs. McAlpin proved unable to assess the value of the property accurately. She gave the commission a total claim of £6,000, clearly an estimate, and when asked to break down a particular item on her schedule into its component parts she could not do so, saying that "She valued the Whole in the Lump in that Sum." Moreover, she proved ignorant of the terms of her husband's will, confusedly telling the commissioners that he had "left his real personal Estate to his Son—This she supposes was his Lands" (the board's secretary noted carefully, "This is her own Expression"), when in fact she had been left a life interest in the real estate plus half the personal estate. In short, Mary McAlpin typifies the rural female claimant, though her husband's property was substantially larger than average. She knew what he had owned, but she did not know exactly how much it was worth. She was well acquainted with the day-to-day operations of the farm but understood very little about the general family finances. And she knew nothing at all about legal or business terminology.

The pattern for urban dwellers was more varied. In the first place, included in their number were most of the wealthy women mentioned earlier, both those who knew little or nothing about their husbands' estates and those who, like Sarah Troutbeck, were conversant with the family holdings. Secondly, a higher percentage of urban women engaged directly in business. Among the 468 female claimants there were forty-three who declared either that they had earned money on their own or that they had assisted their husbands in some way. Only three of these forty-three can be described as rural: a tavernkeeper's wife from Ticonderoga, a small shopkeeper from Niagara, and the housekeeper for the family of Col. Guy Johnson. All the other working women came from cities such as Boston, Philadelphia, Charleston, and New York, or from smaller but substantial towns like Williamsburg, Wilmington, N.C., and Baltimore. The urban women's occupations were as varied as the urban centers in which they resided. There were ten who took lodgers, eighteen shopkeepers and merchants of various sorts, five tavernkeepers, four milliners, two mantua makers, a seamstress, a midwife, an owner of a coffeehouse, a schoolteacher, a printer, one who did not specify an occupation, and two prostitutes who described themselves as owners of a small shop and declared that their house had been "always open" to British officers needing "aid and attention." [11]

As might be expected, the women who had managed businesses or assisted their husbands (one wrote that she was "truly his Partner" in a "steady Course of painfull Industry") were best informed about the value of their property. Those who had been grocers or milliners could usually list in detail the stock they had lost; the midwife had witnesses to support her claim to a high annual income from her profession; the boardinghouse keepers knew what they had spent for furniture and supplies; and the printer could readily value her shop's equipment. But even these working women could not give a full report on all aspects of their husbands' holdings: the widow of a Boston storekeeper, for example, could accurately list their stock in trade but admitted ignorance of the value of the property her husband had inherited from his father, and although the widow of another Boston merchant had carried on the business after her husband was wounded at Bunker Hill, she was not familiar with the overall value of their property.

It is therefore not surprising that women claimants on the average received a smaller return on their claims than did their male counterparts. Since the commissioners reimbursed only for fully proven losses, the amounts awarded are a crude indicator of the relative ability of individual refugees to describe their losses and to muster written and oral evidence on their own behalf. If women had known as much as their husbands about the family estates, there would have been little or no difference

[11] The list totals more than 40 because some women listed two enterprises. The women divided as follows: 10 each from New York City and Charleston, 7 each from Boston and Philadelphia, 2 from Baltimore, and 1 each from Savannah, Williamsburg, Wilmington, N.C., and St. Augustine. Twenty-eight were long-time widows or single, or were married but operated businesses independently of their husbands; 8 assisted their husbands; and 7 took over businesses after the death or incapacitation of their husbands.

between the average amounts granted to each sex. But of the claims heard in England for which complete information is available, 660 loyalist men received an average return of 39.5 percent, while for 71 women the figure was 34.1 percent. And this calculation does not take into account the large number of women's claims, including some submitted by business-women, which were entirely disallowed for lack of proof.[12]

In the absence of data for other time periods and populations, it is difficult to assess the significance of the figures that show that slightly less than 10 percent (9.2 percent, to be exact) of the loyalist refugee women worked outside the home. Historians have tended to stress the widespread participation of colonial women in economic enterprise, usually as a means of distinguishing them from their reputedly more confined nine-teenth-century counterparts.[13] The claims documents demonstrate that some women engaged in business, either alone or with their husbands, but 9.2 percent may be either a large or a small proportion of the total female population, depending on how one looks at it. The figures themselves must remain somewhat ambiguous, at least until additional data are ob-tained.[14] What is not at all ambiguous, however, is the distinctive pattern of the female claimants' knowledge.

For regardless of whether they came from rural or urban areas, and regardless of their background or degree of participation in business, the loyalist women testified almost exclusively on the basis of their knowledge of those parts of the family property with which their own lives brought them into regular contact. What they uniformly lacked were those pieces of information about business matters that could have been supplied only by their husbands. Evidently, late eighteenth-century American men, at least those who became loyalists, did not systematically discuss matters of family finances with their wives. From that fact it may be inferred that the men—and their wives as well, perhaps—accepted the dictum that

[12] For a general discussion of claims receipts see Norton, *British–Americans*, 216–220. Property claims submitted by 10 of the businesswomen were disallowed, and at least another 10 of them apparently did not pursue a claim for lost property. (Be-cause of the destruction and disappearance of some of the claims records it is im-possible to be more precise.)

[13] This emphasis appears to have resulted from the influence of Dexter's *Colonial Women of Affairs*. Although she was careful to explain that she had searched only for examples of women who worked outside the home, and although she did not attempt to estimate the percentage of such women in the female population as a whole, historians who draw upon her book invariably stress the wide-ranging eco-nomic interests of colonial women. See, for example, Gerda Lerner, *The Woman in American History* (Reading, Mass., 1971), 15–19, and Carol Ruth Berkin, *Within the Conjuror's Circle: Women in Colonial America* (Morristown, N.J., 1974), 8–10.

[14] If anything, the loyalist claimants tended to be more urban than other loyalists and the rest of the American population, and therefore would presumably overrepresent working women. See the analysis in Norton, *British–Americans*, 37–39, and Finger-hut, "Uses and Abuses of Loyalists' Claims," *WMQ*, 3d Ser., XXV (1968), 245–258. Further, the method of choosing the sample—including only those women who themselves submitted claims and pension applications—would also tend to bias the result in favor of working women, since they would be the most likely to act on their own.

woman's place was in the home. After all, that was where more than 90 percent of the loyalist women stayed, and their ignorance of the broader aspects of their families' economic circumstances indicates that their interest in such affairs was either minimal or else deliberately thwarted by their husbands.[15]

It would therefore appear that the 9 percent figure for working women is evidence not of a climate favorable to feminine enterprise but rather of the opposite: women were expected to remain largely within the home unless forced by necessity, such as the illness or death of their husbands, to do otherwise. The fact that fewer than one-half (seventeen, to be precise) of the working women enumerated earlier had healthy, living husbands at the time they engaged in business leads toward the same conclusion. The implication is that in mid-eighteenth-century America woman's sphere was rigidly defined at all levels of society, not merely in the wealthy households in which this phenomenon has been recognized.[16]

This tentative conclusion is supported by evidence drawn from another aspect of the claims, for a concomitant of the contention that colonial women often engaged in business endeavors has been the assertion that colonial men, as the theoretical and legal heads of household, frequently assumed a large share of domestic responsibilities.[17] Yet if men had been deeply involved in running their households—in keeping accounts and making purchases, even if not in doing day-to-day chores—they should have described household furnishings in much the same detail as their wives used. But just as female claimants were unable to delineate their husbands' business dealings accurately, so men separated from their wives—regardless of their social status—failed to submit specific lists of lost household items like furniture, dishes, or kitchen utensils. One such refugee observed to the commission in 1788, "As Household Furniture consists of a Variety of Articles, at this distance of time I cannot sufficiently recollect them so as to fix a Value on them to the Satisfaction of my mind." It is impossible to imagine a loyalist woman making a comparable statement. For her, what to a man was simply "a Variety of Articles" resolved itself into such familiar and cherished objects as "1 Compleat set blue and white Tea and Table China," "a Large new Goose feather Bed, bolster Pillows and Bedstead," "a Small painted Book Case and Desk," "1 Japan Tea Board," "2 smoothing Irons," and "1 old brass Coffee Pott." Moreover, although men usually noted losses of clothing in a general way, by listing a single undifferentiated sum, women frequently

[15] The failure of 18th-century men to discuss finances with their wives is also revealed in such letters as that of Jane Robbins to her daughter Hannah Gilman, Sept. 1799, Gilman Papers, Massachusetts Historical Society, Boston. Mrs. Robbins declared that, although her husband had made his will some years before, "I never saw it till after his death." Further, she informed her daughter, on his deathbed he told her, "I should have many debts to pay that I knew nothing about."

[16] Berkin, *Conjuror's Circle,* 12–14, and Nancy F. Cott, ed., *Root of Bitterness: Documents of the Social History of American Women* (New York, 1972), 8–10, link sex role differentiation specifically to the upper classes that were emerging in the process which has been called "Europeanization" or "Anglicization."

[17] See, for example, Spruill, *Women's Life and Work,* 78–79.

claimed for specific articles of jewelry and apparel. For example, Mary
Swords of Saratoga disclosed that she had lost to rebel plunderers a "Long
Scarlet Cloak" and a "Velvet Muff and Tippett," in addition to "One
pair of Ear Rings French paste set in Gold," "One small pair of Ear Rings
Garnets," and "one Gold Broatch with a small diamond Top."

The significance of such lists lies not only in the fact that they indicate what kinds of property the claimants knew well enough to describe
accurately and in detail, but also in the insight they provide into the
possessions which claimants thought were sufficiently important to mention individually. For example, a rural New York woman left no doubt
about her pride in "a fine large new stove"; a resident of Manhattan carefully noted that one of her lost beds was covered in "Red Damask"; and
a Rhode Islander called attention to the closets in her "large new dwelling
house." The differentiated contents of men's and women's claims thus take
on more importance, since the contrasting lists not only suggest the extent
of the claimants' knowledge but also reveal their assessments of the relative importance of their possessions. To men, furniture, dishes, and clothing could easily be lumped together under general headings; to women,
such possessions had to be carefully enumerated and described.

In the end, all of the evidence that can be drawn from the loyalist
claims points to the conclusion that the lives of the vast majority of
women in the Revolutionary era revolved around their immediate households to a notable degree. The economic function of those households in
relation to the family property largely determined the extent of their
knowledge of that property. In rural areas, where women's household
chores included caring for the stock and perhaps occasionally working in
the fields, women were conversant with a greater proportion of the
family estates than were urban women, whose knowledge was for the
most part confined to the furnishings of the houses in which they lived,
unless they had been widowed before the war or had worked outside the
home. The wealth of the family was thus a less significant determinant of
the woman's role than was the nature of the household. To be sure, at the
extreme ends of the economic scale, wealth and education, or the lack of
them, affected a woman's comprehension of her family's property, but
what the women displayed were relative degrees of ignorance. If the
loyalist claimants are at all representative, very few married colonial
women were familiar with the broader aspects of their families' financial
affairs. Regardless of where they lived, they were largely insulated from
the agricultural and business worlds in which their husbands engaged
daily. As a result, the Revolutionary War, which deprived female loyalists
of the households in which they had lived and worked, and which at the
same time forced them to confront directly the wider worlds of which
they had had little previous knowledge, was for them an undeniably
traumatic experience.

At the outbreak of the war, loyalist women expected that "their Sex
and the Humanity of a civilized People" would protect them from "dis-
respectfull Indignities." Most of them soon learned otherwise. Rebel men
may have paid lip service to the ideal that women and children should be

treated as noncombatants, but in practice they consigned female loyalists to much the same fate as their male relatives. Left behind by their fleeing husbands (either because of the anticipated difficulties of a journey to the British lines or in the hope that the family property might thereby be preserved), loyalist wives, with their children, frequently found themselves "stripped of every Thing" by American troops who, as one woman put it, "not contented with possessing themselves of her property were disposed to visit severity upon her person and Those of her friends." Female loyalists were often verbally abused, imprisoned, and threatened with bodily harm even when they had not taken an active role in opposing the rebel cause.

When they had assisted the British—and many aided prisoners or gathered intelligence—their fate was far worse. For example, the New Yorker Lorenda Holmes, who carried letters through the lines in 1776, was stripped by an angry band of committeemen and dragged "to the Drawing Room Window . . . exposing her to many Thousands of People Naked." On this occasion Mrs. Holmes admitted that she "received no wounds or bruises from them only shame and horror of the Mind," but a few months later, after she had shown some refugees the way to the British camp, an American officer came to her house and held her "right foot upon the Coals until he had burnt it in a most shocking manner," telling her "he would learn her to carry off Loyalists to the British Army."

As can readily be imagined, the women did not come through such experiences emotionally unscathed. One Massachusetts mother reported that her twelve-year-old daughter suffered from "nervous Fits" as a result of "the usage she met with from the Mobs"; and another New England woman, the wife of a merchant who was an early target of the local committee because he resisted the nonimportation movement, described to a female friend her reaction to a threatening letter they had received: "I have never injoyed one hours real Sattisfaction since the receipt of that Dreadfull Letter my mind is in continual agitation and the very rustling of the Trees alarms me." Some time later the same woman was unfortunate enough to be abused by a rebel militiaman. After that incident, she reported, "I did not recover from my fright for several days. The sound of drum or the sight of a gun put me into such a tremor that I could not command myself." [18] It was only natural for these women to look forward with longing to the day when they could escape to Canada or, better still, to England, "a land of peace, liberty and plenty." It seemed to them that their troubles would end when they finally left America. But, as one wrote later with the benefit of hindsight, their "severest trials were just begun." [19]

[18] Mary Serjeant, loss schedule, Feb. 19, 1783, A.O. 13/49, pt. 1, 285; Christian Barnes to Elizabeth Smith, July 13–28, 1770, Christian Barnes Letterbook, Library of Congress; Barnes to Elizabeth Smith Inman, Apr. [2]9, [1775], in Nina Moore Tiffany, ed., *Letters of James Murray, Loyalist* (Boston, 1901), 187–188.

[19] Louisa Susannah Wells Aikman, *The Journal of a Voyage from Charlestown, S.C., to London undertaken during the American Revolution . . .* (New York, 1906), 52; Catherine Goldthwait to Elizabeth [Inman], Mar. 27, 1780, Robbins Papers, Mass. Hist. Soc. For a discussion of the loyalists' initial optimism and subsequent dis-

Male and female refugees alike confronted difficult problems in England and Canada—finding housing, obtaining financial support, settling into a new environment. For women, especially widows with families, the difficulties were compounded. The Bostonian Hannah Winslow found the right words: it was a "cruell" truth, she told her sister-in-law, that "when a woman with a family, and Particularly a large one, looses her Husband and Protector People are afraid to keep up the Acquaintance least they may ask favrs." [20] Many of the men quickly reestablished their American friendship networks through the coffeehouses and refugee organizations; the women were deprived not only of the companionship such associations provided but also of the information about pensions and claims that was transmitted along the male networks. As a result, a higher proportion of female than male loyalists made errors in their applications for government assistance, by directing the memorials to the wrong officials and failing to meet deadlines, often because they learned too late about compensation programs. Their standard excuses—that they "had nobody to advise with" and that they "did not know how to do it"—were greeted with skepticism by the claims commission, but they were undoubtedly true. [21]

On the whole, female loyalists appear to have fared worse in England than their male counterparts, and for two major reasons. In the first place, the commissioners usually gave women annual pensions that were from £10 to £20 lower than those received by men, apparently because they believed that the women had fewer expenses, but also because in most cases the women could not claim the extra merit of having actively served the royal cause. [22] Second, fewer women than men found work to supplement the sums they received from the government. To the wealthier

---

illusionment see Mary Beth Norton, "The Loyalists' Image of England: Ideal and Reality," *Albion*, III (1971), 62–71.

[20] Hannah Winslow to [a sister-in-law], June 27, 1779, Winslow Papers, Mass. Hist. Soc. See also Rebecca Dolbeare to John Dolbeare, Aug. 30, 1780, Dolbeare Papers, Mass. Hist. Soc.; Polly Dibblee to William Jarvis, Nov. 1787, A.O. 13/41, 248. For a general discussion of the exiles' financial problems see Norton, *British–Americans*, 49–61. For another similar observation by a single woman see Louisa Oliver to Andrew Spooner, Mar. 1, 1788, Hutchinson-Oliver Papers, Mass. Hist. Soc.

[21] . . . Of course, a few men also made similar claims; see, for example, A.O. 12/43, 322–325, 328–331, and A.O. 12/46, 63. On the male networks see Norton, *British–Americans*, 63–79, 162–164, 186–196, 206–216. The memorials submitted by women were not only more prone to error but also more informal, less likely to be written in the third person, less likely to contain the sorts of ritualistic phrases and arguments used by the men, and consequently more likely to be personally revealing.

[22] Norton, *British–Americans*, 52–61, 111–121, discusses the bases for pension decisions. It was standard practice for the commission to lower a family's allotment immediately after the death of the husband, regardless of the fact that the widow usually had to meet medical and funeral expenses at exactly that time. The pension records (A.O. 12/99–105, and T. 50/11ff, Public Record Office) show that women's pensions were normally smaller than men's. In addition, T. 50/11 reveals a clear case of discrimination: in 1789 the Charleston midwife Janet Cumming . . . was, under the commission's rules, entitled to an annual pension of £200 for loss of profession (she was the only woman to qualify for one in her own right); instead, she was granted only a £50 widow's allowance.

female refugees work seemed so automatically foreclosed as an option that only a small number thought it necessary to explain to the commission why they could not contribute to their own support. Mary Serjeant, the widow of a Massachusetts clergyman, even regarded her former affluence as a sufficient reason in itself for her failure to seek employment. In 1782 she told the commissioners, "Educated as a Gentlewoman myself and brought up to no business I submit it to your [torn], Gentlemen, how very scanty must be the Subsistence which my Own Industry [can] procure us." Those who did try to earn additional income (many of whom had also worked outside the home in America) usually took in needlework or hired out as servants or housekeepers, but even they had trouble making ends meet. One orphaned young woman reported, "I can support myself with my needle: but not my two Sisters and infant Brother"; and another, who had learned the trade of mantua making, commented, "I now got Work for my self [sic]—but being oblidged to give long credit and haveing no Money of my one [sic] to go on with, I lived Cheifly upon tea which with night working brought me almost into the last stadge of a Consumtion so that when I rec'd my Money for work it went almost [all] to dockters."

Many of the loyalist women displayed a good deal of resilience. Some managed to support themselves, among them the Wells sisters of Charleston, who in 1789 opened a London boardinghouse for young ladies whose parents wished them to have a "suitable" introduction to society. Others survived what might seem an overwhelming series of setbacks—for example, Susannah Marshall of Maryland, who, after running taverns in Baltimore and Head of Elk and trying but failing to join Lord Dunmore off Norfolk in 1776, finally left the United States by sea the following year, only to have her chartered ship captured first by the Americans and then by the British. In the process she lost all the goods she had managed to salvage from her earlier moves, and when she arrived in England she not only learned of her husband's death but was unsuccessful in her application for a subsistence pension. Refusing to give up, she went to work as a nurse to support her children, and although she described herself to the commission in 1785 as "very Old and feeble," she lived long enough to be granted a permanent annual allowance of £20 in 1789.[23]

Susannah Marshall, though, had years of experience as a tavernkeeper behind her and was thus more capable of coping with her myriad difficulties than were women whose prewar experience had been restricted to their households. Such women recognized that they were "less able than many who never knew happier days to bear hardships and struggle with adversity." These women, especially those who had been, as one of them put it, *"born to better expectations"* in America, spoke despairingly of encounters with "difficultys of which she had no experience in her former

23 On the Wells sisters' enterprise see Steuart Papers, 5041, fol. 123, National Library of Scotland, Edinburgh; Ann Elmsley to James Parker [1789?], Parker Papers, Pt. IV, no. 15, Liverpool Record Office, England; and Aikman, *Journal of a Voyage,* 71. Susannah Marshall's story may be traced in A.O. 13/62, 4, 7, A.O. 12/6, 257–263, and A.O. 12/99, 244.

life," of "Adversities which not many years before she scarcely thought it possible, that in any situation, she should ever experience."

For women like these, exile in England or Canada was one long nightmare. Their relief requests have a desperate, supplicating tone that is largely absent from those submitted by men. One bewailed the impending birth of her third child, asking, "What can I do in my Condishtion deprived of helth with out Friends or mony with a helpless family to suffer with me?" Another begged the commission's secretary for assistance "with all humility" because "the merciless man I lodge with, threatens to sell the two or three trifling articles I have and put a Padlock on the Room unless I pay him the Rent amounting to near a Pound." By contrast, when a man prepared a memorial for the exceptionally distressed Mrs. Sarah Baker, he coolly told the commissioners that they should assist her because her children "as Soldiers or Sailors in his Majesty's Service may in future compensate the present Expence of saving them."

The straits to which some of the female refugees were driven were dramatically illustrated in early 1783 when a South Carolina woman appeared before the commission "in Rags," explaining that she had been "obliged to pawn her Goods." It was but the first incident of many. Time and again women revealed that they had sold or pawned their clothes—which were usually their most valuable possessions—to buy food for themselves and their children. One was literally "reduced to the last shift" when she testified before the commission; another, the New Yorker Alicia Young, pawned so much that "the want of our apparel made our situation very deplorable" until friends helped her to redeem some of her possessions. Strikingly, no man ever told the commission stories like these. Either male refugees were able to find alternatives to pawning their clothes, or, if they did not, they were too ashamed to admit it.

Such hardships took a terrible mental as well as physical toll. Evidence of extreme mental stress permeates the female loyalists' petitions and letters, while it is largely absent from the memorials of male exiles. The women speak constantly of their "Fear, Fatigue and Anxiety of Mind," their "lowness of Spirit," their "inexpressable" distress, their "accumulated anguish." They repeatedly describe themselves as "desolate and distressed," as "disconsolate, Distressed and helpless . . . with a broken Spirit Ruined health and Constitution," as "Oppressed in body and distressed in mind." "I am overwhelm'd with misfortunes," wrote one. Poverty "distracts and terrifies me," said another; and a third begged "that she may not be left a Prey to Poverty, and her constant companons [sic], Calamity and Sorrow." "My pen is unable to describe the horrors of My Mind—or the deploreable Situation of Myself and Infant family," Alicia Young told a member of the commission. "Judge then Dr Sir what is to become of me, or what we are to exist upon—I have no kind of resource. . . . oh Sir the horrors of my Situation is almost too much for me to bear." Most revealing of all was the wife of a Connecticut refugee: "Nature it self languishes," Mary Taylor wrote, "the hours that I should rest, I awake in such an aggitation of mind, as though I had to suffer for sins, that I neaver committed, I allmost shudder when I approache the Doone [doom?]—as every thing appears to be conspired against me, the

Baker, and Bucher, seams to be weary of serving me oh porvity what is its Crime, may some have Compassion on those who feeals its power—for I can doo nothing—but baith my infant with my tears—while seeing my Husbands sinking under the waight of his misfortuens, unable to afford me any release." [24]

Even taking into account the likelihood that it was more socially acceptable for women to reveal their emotions, the divergence between men's and women's memorials is too marked to be explained by that factor alone. It is necessary to probe more deeply and to examine men's and women's varying uses of language in order to delineate the full dimensions of the difference.[25] As C. Wright Mills pointed out in an influential article some years ago, actions or motives and the vocabularies utilized to describe them cannot be wholly separated, and commonly used adjectives can therefore reveal the limitations placed on one's actions by one's social role. Mills asserted that "the 'Real Attitude or Motive' is not something different in kind from the verbalization or the 'opinion,'" and that "the long acting out of a role, with its appropriate motives, will often induce a man [or, one is compelled to add, a woman] to become what at first he merely sought to appear." Furthermore, Mills noted, people perceive situations in terms of specific, "delimited" vocabularies, and thus adjectives can themselves promote or deter certain actions. When adjectives are "typical and relatively unquestioned accompaniments of typal situations," he concluded, "such words often function as directives and incentives by virtue of their being the judgements of others as anticipated by the actor." [26]

In this theoretical context the specific words used by female loyalists may be analyzed as a means of understanding the ways in which they perceived themselves and their circumstances. Their very phraseology—and the manner in which it differs from that of their male counterparts—can provide insights into the matrix of attitudes that helped to shape the way they thought and acted. If Mills is correct, the question whether the women were deliberately telling the commission what they thought it wanted to hear becomes irrelevant: it is enough to say that they were

[24] . . . In sharp contrast to such statements, Andrew Allen, a male refugee, wrote in Feb. 1783, "Notwithstanding what has happened I have the Satisfaction to feel my Spirits unbroken and my Mind prepared to look forwards without Despondency." Allen to James Hamilton, Feb. 3, 1783, Dreer Collection, Historical Society of Pennsylvania, Philadelphia.

[25] Recent articles by linguists raise provocative questions about sex differences in speech. Most of them are concerned with 20th-century oral expression, however, and it is difficult to determine how accurately they apply to 18th-century documents. Among the most interesting are Nancy Faires Conklin, "Toward a Feminist Analysis of Linguistic Behavior," *University of Michigan Papers in Women's Studies*, I (1974), 51–73; Mary Ritchie Key, "Linguistic Behavior of Male and Female," *Linguistics: An International Review*, LXXXVIII (1972), 15–31; Cheris Kramer, "Women's Speech: Separate but Unequal?," *The Quarterly Journal of Speech*, LX (1974), 14–24; and Robin Lakoff, "Language and Woman's Place," *Language in Society*, II (1974), 45–79.

[26] C. Wright Mills, "Situated Actions and Vocabularies of Motive," *American Sociological Review*, V (1940), 904–913, esp. 906–909.

acting in accordance with a prescribed role, and that that role helped to determine how they acted.[27]

With these observations in mind, the fact that the women refugees displayed an intense awareness of their own femininity assumes a crucial significance. The phrases permeate the pages of the petitions from rich and poor alike: "Though a Woman"; "perhaps no Woman in America in equal Circumstances"; "being done by a Woman"; "being a poor lame and infirm Woman." In short, in the female loyalists' minds their actions and abilities were to a certain extent defined by their sex. Femininity was the constant point of reference in measuring their achievements and making their self-assessments. Moreover, the fact of their womanhood was used in a deprecating sense. In their own eyes, they gained merit by not acting like women. Her services were "allmost Matchless, (being done by a Woman)," wrote one; "tho' a Woman, she was the first that went out of the Gates to welcome the Royal Army," declared another. Femininity also provided a ready and plausible excuse for failures of action or of knowledge. A South Carolinian said she had not signed the address to the king in Charleston in 1780 because "it was not posable for a woman to come near the office." A Pennsylvanian apologized for any errors in her loss estimate with the comment, "as far as a Woman can know, she believes the contents to be true." A Nova Scotian said she had not submitted a claim by the deadline because of "being a lone Woman in her Husband's Absence and not having any person to Advise with." A Vermonter made the ultimate argument: "had she been a man, Instead, of a poor helpless woman—should not have faild of being in the British Servace."

The pervasive implication is one of perceived inferiority, and this implication is enhanced by the word women used most often to describe themselves: "helpless." "Being a Poor helpless Widow"; "she is left a helpless Widow"; "a helpless woman advanced in life"; "being a helpless woman": such phrases appear again and again in the claims memorials. Male loyalists might term themselves "very unhappy," "wretched," "extremely distressed," or "exceedingly embarrassed," but *never* were they "helpless." For them, the most characteristic self-description was "unfortunate," a word that carried entirely different, even contrary, connotations. Male loyalists can be said to have seen their circumstances as not of their own making, as even being reversible with luck. The condition of women, however, was inherent in themselves; nothing they could do could change their circumstances. By definition, indeed, they were incapable of helping themselves.

---

[27] The only woman claimant who appears to have manipulatively assumed a "feminine" role was Sarah Troutbeck. It is also difficult to determine, first, what it was that the commission "wanted" to hear from female loyalists and, second, how the women would know what the commission wanted, given their isolation from the male information networks. It could perhaps be argued that every 18th-century woman "knew" what every 18th-century man expected of her, but the fact is that the women claimants had a great deal to gain by displaying a very "unfeminine" knowledge of their husbands' estates and by demonstrating their competence to the commission.

It should be stressed here that, although women commonly described themselves as "helpless," their use of that word did not necessarily mean that they were in fact helpless. It indicates rather that they perceived themselves thus, and that that perception in turn perhaps affected the way they acted (for example, in seeking charitable support instead of looking for work). Similarly, the fact that men failed to utilize the adjective "helpless" to refer to themselves does not mean that they were not helpless, for some of them surely were; it merely shows that—however incorrectly—they did think that they could change their circumstances. These two words, with all their connotations, encapsulate much of the divergence between male and female self-perceptions in late eighteenth-century America, even if they do not necessarily indicate much about the realities of male–female relationships in the colonies.[28]

There was, of course, more to the difference in sex roles than the sex-related ways in which colonial Americans looked at themselves. The claims documents also suggest that women and men placed varying emphases on familial ties. For women, such relationships seemed to take on a special order of magnitude. Specifically, men never said, as several women did, that after their spouses' deaths they were so "inconsolable" that they were unable to function. One woman declared that after her husband's execution by the rebels she was "bereft of her reason for near three months," and another described herself as "rendred almost totally incapable of Even writing my own Name or any assistance in any Shape that Could have the least Tendency to getting my Bread." Furthermore, although loyalist men expressed concern over the plight of the children they could not support adequately, women were much more emotionally involved in the fate of their offspring. "Your goodness will easily conceive, what I must feel for My *Children*," Alicia Young told a claims commissioner; "for myself—I care not—Misfortunes and distress have long since made me totally indifferent to everything in the World but *Them*—they have no provision—no provider—no protector—but God—and me." Women noted that their "Sorrows" were increased by the knowledge that their children were "Partners in this Scene of Indigence." Margaret Draper, widow of a Boston printer, explained that although she had been ill and suffering from a "disordered Mind," "what adds to my affliction is, my fears for my Daughter, who may soon be left a Stranger and friendless." In the same vein, a New Jersey woman commented that she had "the inexpressible mortification of seeing my Children in want of many necessaries and conveniencies. . . . and what still more distresses me, is to think that I am obliged by partaking of it, to lessen even the small portion they have."

[28] The women who were most definitely not helpless (for example, Susannah Marshall, Janet Cumming, and Sarah Troutbeck) did not use that word to describe themselves. Consequently, it appears that the term was not simply a formulaic one utilized by all women indiscriminately, but rather that it represented a real self-perception of those who did use it. At least one 18th-century woman recognized the sex-typed usage of the word "helpless." In her book of essays, Judith Sargent Murray noted that she hoped that "the term, *helpless widow*, might be rendered as unfrequent and inapplicable as that of *helpless widower*." See Judith Sargent Murray, *The Gleaner*, III (Boston, 1789), 223.

The women's emphasis on their families is entirely compatible with the earlier observation concerning the importance of their households in their lives. If their menfolk were preoccupied with the monetary consequences of adhering to the crown, the women were more aware of the human tragedy brought about by the war. They saw their plight and that of their children in much more personal terms than did their husbands. Likewise, they personalized the fact of their exile in a way that male loyalists did not, by almost invariably commenting that they were "left friendless in a strange Country." Refugee men, though they might call themselves "strangers," rarely noted a lack of friends, perhaps because of the coffeehouse networks. To women, by contrast, the fact that they were not surrounded by friends and neighbors seemed calamitous. "I am without Friends or Money," declared one; I am "a friendless, forlorn Woman . . . a Stranger to this Country, and surrounded by evils," said another. She is "far from her native Country, and numerous Friends and Relations where she formerly lived, much respected," wrote a third of her own condition.

When the female refugees talked of settling elsewhere or of returning to the United States, they spoke chiefly of the friends and relatives they would find at their intended destinations. Indeed, it appears from the claims that at least six women went into exile solely because their friends and relatives did. A loyalist woman who remained in the United States after the war explained that she did so because she chose "to reside near my relations [rather] than to carry my family to a strange Country where in case of my death they would be at the mercy of strangers." And Mary Serjeant's description of her situation in America as it would have been had her husband not been a loyalist carried the implication that she wished she too had stayed at home: "His poor Children and disconsolate Widow would now have had a House of their own and some Land adjoining to it And instead of being almost destitute in a Land of Strangers would have remained among some Relatives."

In sum, evidence drawn from the loyalist claims strongly suggests that late-eighteenth-century women had fully internalized the roles laid out for them in the polite literature of the day. Their experience was largely confined to their households, either because they chose that course or because they were forced into it. They perceived themselves as "helpless"—even if at times their actions showed that they were not—and they strongly valued ties with family and friends. When the Revolution tore them from the familiar patterns of their lives in America, they felt abandoned and adrift, far more so than did their male relatives, for whom the human contacts cherished by the women seemed to mean less or at least were more easily replaced by those friendships that persisted into exile.

The picture of the late-eighteenth-century woman that emerges from the loyalist claims, therefore, is of one who was almost wholly domestic, in the sense that that word would be used in the nineteenth-century United States. But at the same time the colonial woman's image of herself

lacked the positive attributes with which her nineteenth-century counterpart could presumably console herself. The eighteenth-century American
woman was primarily a wife and a mother, but America had not yet developed an ideology that would proclaim the social value of motherhood.
That was to come with republicanism—and loyalist women, by a final
irony, were excluded by their political allegiance from that republican
assurance.[29]

[29] On the development of republican ideology pertaining to women see Linda K.
Kerber, "Daughters of Columbia: Educating Women for the Republic, 1787–1805,"
in Stanley Elkins and Eric McKitrick, eds., *The Hofstadter Aegis* (New York,
1974), 36–59.

Suggestions for Further Reading

Religion has been a primary focus for colonial historians, and yet most scholarship in this area deals with doctrinal and institutional aspects of Puritanism, Anglicanism, or other forms of Protestant commitment. For the personal experience of religion one must turn to a few scattered books. Among the best are Ola Winslow, *Meetinghouse Hill, 1630–1783** (New York, 1952); Norman Pettit, *The Heart Prepared: Grace and Conversion in Puritan Spiritual Life* (New Haven, Conn., 1966); and Perry Miller's essays in *Errand into the Wilderness** (Cambridge, Mass., 1956). For the Great Awakening see J. M. Bumsted and John E. Van de Wetering, *What Must I Do to Be Saved: The Great Awakening in Colonial America** (Hinsdale, Ill., 1976); Alan Heimert, *Religion and the American Mind from the Great Awakening to the Revolution* (Cambridge, Mass., 1966); Rhys Isaac, "Evangelical Revolt: The Nature of the Baptists' Challenge to the Traditional Order in Virginia, 1765 to 1775," *William and Mary Quarterly*, 31 (1974): 345–68, and "Preachers and Patriots: Popular Culture and the Revolution in Virginia," in Alfred F. Young, ed., *The American Revolution: Explorations in the History of American Radicalism** (DeKalb, Ill., 1976):125–56.

The lives of indentured servants are studied in Abbot E. Smith, *Colonists in Bondage: White Servitude and Convict Labor in America, 1607–1776** (Chapel Hill, N.C., 1947); Lawrence W. Towner, "A Fondness for Freedom: Servant Protest in Puritan Society," *William and Mary Quarterly*, 19 (1962):201–19; and Russell R. Menard, "From Servant to Freeholder: Status Mobility and Property Accumulation in Seventeenth-Century Maryland," *William and Mary Quarterly*, 30 (1973):37–64. An excellent firsthand account is Edward M. Riley, ed., *The Journal of John Harrower: An Indentured Servant in Virginia, 1773–1776* (Williamsburg, Va., 1963).

Studies of slavery are legion, but the inquiring student must be selective in order to find works about slaves themselves, rather than

* Available in paperback edition.

books on slaveowners. Basil Davidson's *The African Slave Trade: Pre-Colonial History, 1450–1850** (Boston, 1961) is a good introduction to that subject. For slave life consult Gerald W. Mullin, *Flight and Rebellion: Slave Resistance in Eighteenth-Century Virginia** (New York, 1972); Peter H. Wood, *Black Majority: Negroes in Colonial South Carolina from 1670 through the Stono Rebellion** (New York, 1974); and Herbert G. Gutman, *The Black Family in Slavery and Freedom, 1750–1925** (New York, 1976).

For the role of politics in the lives of ordinary people see Jesse Lemisch, "Jack Tar in the Streets: Merchant Seamen in the Politics of the American Revolution," *William and Mary Quarterly*, 25 (1968):371–407; Pauline Maier, "Popular Uprisings and Civil Authority in Eighteenth-Century America," *William and Mary Quarterly*, 27 (1970):3–35; Rhys Isaac, "Dramatizing the Ideology of Revolution: Popular Mobilization in Virginia, 1774 to 1776," *William and Mary Quarterly*, 33 (1976):357–85; Edward Countryman, " 'Out of the Bounds of the Law': Northern Land Rioters in the Eighteenth Century," in Young, *The American Revolution**: 37–69; and Dirk Hoerder, *Crowd Action in Revolutionary Massachusetts, 1765–1780* (New York, 1977).

Women in the Revolutionary era may be studied further by reading Elizabeth Cometti, "Women in the American Revolution," *New England Quarterly*, 20 (1947):329–46; Joan Hoff Wilson, "The Illusion of Change: Women and the American Revolution," in Young, *The American Revolution**:383–445; Nancy F. Cott, "Divorce and the Changing Status of Women in Eighteenth-Century Massachusetts," *William and Mary Quarterly*, 33 (1976):586–614; and Linda K. Kerber, "Daughters of Columbia: Educating Women for the Republic, 1787–1805," in Stanley Elkins and Eric McKitrick, eds., *The Hofstadter Aegis: A Memorial, 1916–1970* (New York, 1974), pp. 36–59.

1790–1830
The Early Republic

Changing Customs
of Childbirth in America,
1760 to 1825

CATHERINE M. SCHOLTEN

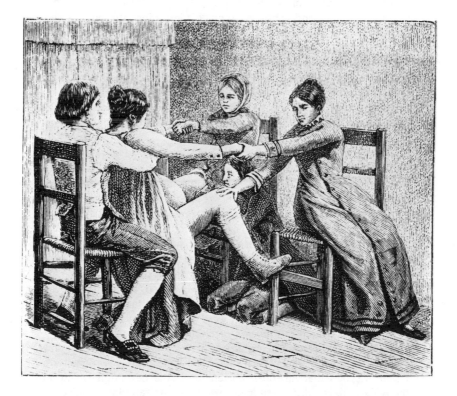

Few experiences have more meaning for most women than child-birth. Especially in the pre–industrial age, childbearing nearly dominated female life. The average American woman was pregnant or nursing infants for approximately half of the years between the ages of twenty and forty and gave birth to about seven children. Therefore, no book on everyday life in pre–industrial America is complete without a consideration of childbirth.

Living in the last quarter of the twentieth century in a modern, industrialized, medically advanced society, we may have difficulty appreciating how the rituals and practices for bringing children into the world have been transformed. The selection by Catherine Scholten transports us back to this earlier age—to a time when "the medical management of childbirth" began to change. This alteration had several components. First, the "obstetrick art," whose practitioners for centuries had been midwives, gradually became dominated by male physicians. This trend continued through the nineteenth century and reached its completion with the legal restriction of midwifery in most states by the 1930s. In New York City, for example, 37 percent of recorded live births were assisted by about 3,000 midwives in 1908. By 1929 only 1,200 midwives were practicing in the city. A decade later their number had fallen to 270. Only two remained in 1957, and six years later New York's last midwife retired. Only in the last few years have the natural-childbirth movement and the struggle for women's rights led to a revival of midwifery.

Integrally associated with this male takeover of a traditionally female sphere was the transformation of childbirth from a "communal experience" to a "private event." During the nineteenth century childbirth continued, as for time beyond recall, to be played out in the home; but by the twentieth century the hospital room, shut off from family and friends, became the new arena for bringing babies into the world. It was biologically impossible for males to assume the female reproductive function, but it proved eminently feasible to deliver over the management of the phenomenon to male obstetricians and male anesthesiologists practicing in male-administered hospitals. Heavily sedated, confined to the antiseptic delivery room, placed in the hands of male doctors, American women were almost removed, socially and psychologically, from the process of childbirth.

This radical change in obstetrical practice was accomplished only after generations of female resistance had been overcome. Scholten's research shows that American women found the new "atmosphere of the lying-in room" distasteful and that there was "an almost universal repugnance on the part of women to male assistance in time of labor." But the male medical reformers prevailed, though their drive for

hegemony over the birth process took many generations to accomplish.
It is only in the last decade that American women have begun to return to childbirth as a communal act in which midwives are valued for
their medical skill and womanly support. These new American mothers-
to-be do not wish to give up the advantages to mother and child that
modern medicine has ushered in, but they insist that such a central
act in women's lives must not be simply a "scientifically managed
event," robbed of its communal and sisterly aspects.

In October 1799, as Sally Downing of Philadelphia labored to give birth
to her sixth child, her mother, Elizabeth Drinker, watched her suffer "in
great distress." Finally, on the third day of fruitless labor, Sally's physician, William Shippen, Jr., announced that "the child must be brought
forward." Elizabeth Drinker wrote in her diary that, happily, Sally delivered naturally, although Dr. Shippen had said that "he thought he
should have had occasion for instruments" and clapped his hand on his
side, so that the forceps rattled in his pocket.[1]

Elizabeth Drinker's account of her daughter's delivery is one of the
few descriptions by an eighteenth-century American woman of a commonplace aspect of women's lives—childbirth.[2] It is of special interest to
social historians because it records the participation of a man in the
capacity of physician. Shippen was a prominent member of the first generation of American doctors trained in obstetrics and, commencing in
1763, the first to maintain a regular practice attending women in childbirth.[3] Until that time midwives managed almost all deliveries, but with
Shippen male physicians began to supplant the midwives.

The changing social customs and medical management of childbirth
from 1760 to 1825 are the subjects of this article. By analyzing the rituals

[1] Cecil K. Drinker, *Not So Long Ago: A Chronicle of Medicine and Doctors in
Colonial Philadelphia* (New York, 1937), 59–61.

[2] Although births are noted frequently in diaries and letters of the 17th, 18th, and
early 19th centuries, the event itself is rarely described. For the most part, information on the medical procedures and social customs of birth analyzed in this article is
derived from midwives' manuals, medical textbooks, and lecture notes of medical
students. This literature mingles plain observation with partisan advocacy of medical
reform. It seems reasonable to accept the physician's evaluations of midwifery as
evidence of their desire for change, and their case histories as documents of the actual circumstances of birth. Despite ambiguities, the material provides a glimpse of
social change not directly reflected in many conventional sources.

[3] Betsy Copping Corner, *William Shippen, Jr.: Pioneer in American Medical Education* (Philadelphia, 1951), 103; Irving S. Cutter and Henry R. Viets, *A Short History of Midwifery* (Philadelphia, 1964), 150.

"Changing Customs of Childbirth in America, 1760 to 1825," by Catherine M. Scholten. From *William and Mary Quarterly*, XXXIV (1977):426–45. Reprinted by permission of the author and the publisher.

of childbirth it will describe the emergence of new patterns in private and professional life. It shows that, beginning among well-to-do women in Philadelphia, New York, and Boston, childbirth became less a communal experience and more a private event confined within the intimate family. In consequence of new perceptions of urban life and of women, as well as of the development of medical science, birth became increasingly regarded as a medical problem to be managed by physicians. For when Shippen, fresh from medical studies in London, announced his intention to practice midwifery in Philadelphia in 1763, he was proposing to enter a field considered the legitimate province of women.[4] Childbearing had been viewed as the inevitable, even the divinely ordained, occasion of suffering for women; childbirth was an event shared by the female community; and delivery was supervised by a midwife.

During the colonial period childbearing occupied a central portion of the lives of women between their twentieth and fortieth years. Six to eight pregnancies were typical, and pregnant women were commonly described as "breeding" and "teeming." [5] Such was women's natural lot; though theologians attributed dignity to carrying the "living soul" of a child and saluted mothers in their congregations with "Blessed are you among women," they also depicted the pains of childbirth as the appropriate special curse of "the Travailing Daughters of Eve." [6] Two Ameri-

---

[4] Cutter and Viets, *Short History*, 148–149.

[5] For a discussion of childbearing patterns see Wilson H. Grabill, Clyde V. Kiser, and Pascal K. Whelpton, "A Long View," in Michael Gordon, ed., *The American Family in Social–Historical Perspective* (New York, 1973), 392; J. Potter, "The Growth of Population in America, 1700–1860," in D. V. Glass and D. E. C. Eversley, eds., *Population in History: Essays in Historical Demography* (Chicago, 1965), 644, 647, 663, 679; Robert V. Wells, "Demographic Change and the Life Cycle of American Families," in Theodore K. Rabb and Robert I. Rotberg, eds., *The Family in History: Interdisciplinary Essays* (New York, 1971), 85, 88.

When William Byrd II wrote in his diary in 1712, "my wife was often indisposed with breeding and very cross," he used a term common until the 19th century. Louis B. Wright and Marion Tinling, eds., *The Secret Diary of William Byrd of Westover, 1709–1712* (Richmond, Va., 1941), 548. "Breeding" was used colloquially and in popular medical literature. The use of the term to describe the hatching or birth of animals parallels its application to humans. The word lingered longest in speech in the American South, where fertile or pregnant black slaves were called "breeding women," an indication of the animality implied in the word. *The Oxford English Dictionary*, s.v. "breeding"; Mitford M. Mathews, ed., *A Dictionary of Americanisms on Historical Principles* (Chicago, 1951), s.v. "breeding." "Teeming," also considered archaic dialect by the *OED*, applied to women from the 16th through 18th centuries.

[6] Benjamin Colman, *Some of the Honours that Religion Does unto the Fruitful Mothers in Israel . . .* (Boston, 1715), 8; Cotton Mather, *Elizabeth in Her Holy Retirement. An Essay to Prepare a Pious Woman for her Lying-in. Or Maxims and Methods of Piety, to Direct and Support an Hand Maid of the Lord, Who Expects a Time of Travail* (Boston, 1710), 3; Cotton Mather, *Ornaments for the Daughters of Zion, or the Character and Happiness of a Woman: in a Discourse*, 3d ed. (Boston,

can tracts written specifically for lying-in women dwelt on the divinely ordained hazards of childbirth and advised a hearty course of meditation on death, "such as their pregnant condition must reasonably awaken them to." [7]

Cotton Mather's pamphlet, *Elizabeth in Her Holy Retirement*, which he distributed to midwives to give to the women they cared for, described pregnancy as a virtually lethal condition. "For ought you know," it warned, "your Death has entered into you, you may have conceived that which determines but about Nine Months more at the most, for you to live in the World." Pregnancy was thus intended to inspire piety.[8] John Oliver, author of *A Present for Teeming American Women*, similarly reminded expectant mothers that prayer was necessary because their dangers were many. He noted that women preparing for lying-in "get linnen and other necessaries for the child, a nurse, a midwife, entertainment for the women that are called to the labour, a warm convenient chamber, and etc." However, "all these may be miserable comforters," argued Oliver, for "they may perchance need no other linnen shortly than a Winding Sheet, and have no other chamber but a grave, no neighbors but worms." [9] Oliver counseled women to "arm themselves with patience" as well as prayer, and "abate somewhat those dreadful groans and cries which do so much to discourage their friends and relatives who hear them." [10]

Surely women did not need to be reminded of the risks of childbirth. The fears of Mary Clap, wife of Thomas Clap, president of Yale College, surface even through the ritual phrases of the elegy written by her husband after her death in childbirth at the age of twenty-four. Thomas remembered that before each of her six lyings-in his wife had asked him to pray with her that God would continue their lives together.[11] Elizabeth Drinker probably echoed the sentiments of most women when she reflected, "I have often thought that women who live to get over the time of Child-bearing, if other things are favourable to them, experience more comfort and satisfaction than at any other period of their lives." [12]

Facing the hazards of childbirth, women depended on the community of their sex for companionship and medical assistance. Women who had moved away at marriage frequently returned to their parents' home for the delivery, either because they had no neighbors or because they preferred the care of their mothers to that of their in-laws. Other women

---

1741), 2–3. Even a secular medical manual affirmed the curse of Eve: American edition of *Aristotle's Master Piece*, 1766, discussed in Otho T. Beall, Jr., *"Aristotle's Master Piece* in America: A Landmark in the Folklore of Medicine," *William and Mary Quarterly*, 3d Ser., XX (1963), 216.

[7] Mather, *Elizabeth in Her Retirement*, 1.

[8] *The Diary of Cotton Mather* (Massachusetts Historical Society, *Collections*, 7th Ser., Pt. II [1912]), VIII, 618, 700; Mather, *Elizabeth in Her Retirement*, 2, 6, 7.

[9] John Oliver, *A Present for Teeming American Women* (Boston, 1694), 3.

[10] *Ibid.*, 118.

[11] [Thomas Clap], "Memoirs of a College President: Womanhood in Early America," ed. Edwin Stanley Wells, *The Connecticut Magazine*, XII (1908), 233–239, esp. 235.

[12] Drinker, *Not So Long Ago*, 48.

summoned mothers, aunts, and sisters on both sides of the family, as well as female friends, when birth was imminent.[13] Above all, they relied on the experience of midwives to guide them through labor.

Women monopolized the practice of midwifery in America, as in Europe, through the middle of the eighteenth century. As the recognized experts in the conduct of childbirth, they advised the mother-to-be if troubles arose during pregnancy, supervised the activities of lying-in, and used their skills to assure safe delivery. Until educated male physicians began to practice obstetrics, midwives enjoyed some status in the medical profession, enhanced by their legal responsibilities in the communities they served.

English civil authorities required midwives to take oaths in order to be licensed but imposed no official test of their skills. The oaths indicate that midwives had responsibilities which were serious enough to warrant supervision. They swore not to allow any infant to be baptized outside the Church of England, and promised to help both rich and poor, to report the true parentage of a child, and to abstain from performing abortions. Oath-breaking midwives could be excommunicated or fined.[14]

Some American midwives learned their art in Europe, where midwifery was almost exclusively the professional province of women. Though barber surgeons and physicians increasingly asserted their interest in midwifery during the seventeenth century, midwives and patients resisted the intruders.[15] The midwives' levels of skill varied. Some acquired

[13] Stewart Mitchell, ed., *New Letters of Abigail Adams, 1788–1801* (Boston, 1947), 3–5, 56; Clayton Harding Chapman, "Benjamin Colman's Daughters," *New England Quarterly*, XXVI (1953), 182; Malcolm R. Lovell, ed., *Two Quaker Sisters, from the Original Diaries of Elizabeth Buffam Chace and Lucy Buffam Lovell* (New York, 1937), 1, 12; Drinker, *Not So Long Ago*, 51–60; Mary Vial Holyoke's diary, in George Francis Dow, ed., *The Holyoke Diaries, 1709–1856* (Salem, Mass., 1911), 70, 73, 75, 83, 95, 100, 101, 107; *Diary of Samuel Sewall* (Mass. Hist. Soc., *Colls.*, 5th Ser., V–VII [1878–1882]), I, 11, 40, 110, 166, 222–223, 351, 394, 426, II, 49, hereafter cited as *Diary of Sewall*; Ethel Armes, ed., *Nancy Shippen: Her Journal Book* (Philadelphia, 1935), 122–124.

[14] James Hobson Aveling, *English Midwives: Their History and Prospects* (London, 1967 [orig. publ. 1872]), 3–4, 7, 10; E. H. Carter, *The Norwich Subscription Books: A Study of the Subscription Books of the Diocese of Norwich, 1637–1800* (London, 1937), 17–18, 134; facsimile oath of 1661, in Thomas Forbes, *The Midwife and the Witch* (New Haven, Conn., 1966), 145.

[15] Cutter and Viets, *Short History*, 5–55; Isaac Flack, *Eternal Eve* (London, 1950), 218–219; Alfred McClintock, ed., *Smellie's Treatise on the Theory and Practice of Midwifery* (London, 1876–1878), II, 248–250, III, 26–27, 298, 317–319; Percival Willughby, *Observations in Midwifery*, ed. Henry Blenkinsop (Wakefield, Eng., 1972 [orig. publ. 1803]), 37, 155.

Save for midwifery, medical practice in England was divided among three guilds of physicians, surgeons, and apothecaries. Physicians, titled "doctor" and usually possessing university degrees, theoretically as gentlemen did not work with their hands. Surgeons, trained by apprenticeship and rarely holding degrees, dealt with structural emergencies. Apothecaries, also apprenticed, sold drugs. These distinctions disappeared in the rural areas and small towns of England, as well as in colonial America, where medical men, usually without formal training and indis-

their medical education in the same way as many surgeons and physicians, by apprenticeship; some read manuals by more learned midwives and physicians; and after 1739, when the first British lying-in hospital was founded, a few were taught by the physicians who directed such hospitals.[16] But more often than not, women undertook midwifery equipped only with folk knowledge and the experience of their own pregnancies.[17]

Disparity of skills also existed among American midwives. Experienced midwives practiced alongside women who were, one physician observed, "as ignorant of their business as the women they deliver." [18] By the end of the eighteenth century physicians thought that the "greater part" of the midwives in America took up the occupation by accident, "having first been *catched*, as they express it, with a woman in labour." [19] The more diligent sought help from books, probably popular medical manuals such as *Aristotle's Master Piece*.[20]

American midwives conducted their practice free, on the whole, from governmental supervision and control. Only two colonies appear to have enacted regulatory statutes, and it does not seem that these were rigorously enforced. In the seventeenth century Massachusetts and New York required midwives, together with surgeons and physicians, not to act contrary to the accepted rules of their art. More specifically, in 1716 the common council of New York City prescribed a licensing oath for midwives, which was similar to the oaths of England, though without the provision on baptism. The oath included an injunction—significant for the theme of this article—that midwives not "open any matter Appertaining to your Office in the presence of any Man unless Nessessity or Great

---

criminately called doctor, engaged in general practice. Even after 1765, the American men who were by strict definition physicians practiced general medicine. Richard Harrison Shryock, *Medicine and Society in America, 1660–1860* (Ithaca, N.Y., 1960), 2–3, 7, 10.

[16] Aveling, *English Midwives*, 138–144; Alice Clark, *Working Life of Women in the Seventeenth Century* (London, 1919), 265, 269, 270–275; *The Compleat Midwifes Practice, in the Most Weighty and High Concernments of the Birth of Man . . .* (London, 1656), 119–124; John Memis, *The Midwive's Pocket Companion: or a Practical Treatise on Midwifery* (London, 1765), v–vii; Jane Sharp, *The Compleat Midwife's Companion: or, the art of midwifery improved . . .* , 4th ed. (London, 1725), x–xii; Willughby, *Observations in Midwifery*, ed. Blenkinsop, 73.

[17] John Kobler, *The Reluctant Surgeon: A Biography of John Hunter* (New York, 1960), 31; Sharp, *Compleat Midwife's Companion*, introduction; Willughby, *Observations in Midwifery*, ed. Blenkinsop, 102.

[18] Valentine Seaman, *The Midwives Monitor, and Mothers Mirror: Being Three Concluding Lectures of a Course of Instruction of Midwifery* (New York, 1800), viii.

[19] *Ibid.* See also Joseph Brevitt, *The Female Medical Repository . . .* (Baltimore, 1810), 6.

[20] Beall, "*Aristotle's Master Piece*," WMQ, 3d Ser., XX (1963), 209–210; Seaman, *Midwives Monitor*, ix. Beall's article is the best study of the popular manuals of "Aristotle." The *Master Piece*, which was the creation of an English physician, "W. S.," and a succession of hack writers, first appeared in England in 1684. The numerous later editions were the only works on sex and gynecology widely available to 18th-century Americans.

Urgent Cause do Constrain you to do so." [21] This oath, which was regularly re-enacted until 1763, suggests the common restriction of midwifery to women, excluding male physicians or barber surgeons, who, in any case, were few and usually ill trained. There are records of male midwives in New York, Philadelphia, Charleston, and Annapolis after 1740, but only one, a Dr. Spencer of Philadelphia, had London training in midwifery, and it was said of another that "he attended very few natural labors." [22]

Though their duties were not as well defined by law, American midwives served the community in ways similar to those of their British counterparts. In addition to assisting at childbed, they testified in court in cases of bastardy, verified birthdates, and examined female prisoners who pleaded pregnancy to escape punishment.[23] Some colonials also observed the English custom of having the midwife attend the baptism and burial of infants. Samuel Sewall reported that Elizabeth Weeden brought his son John to church for christening in 1677, and at the funeral of little Henry in 1685 "Midwife Weeden and Nurse Hill carried the Corps by turns." [24]

The inclusion of the midwife in these ceremonies of birth and death shows how women's relationships with their midwives went beyond mere respect for the latters' skill. Women with gynecologic problems would freely tell a midwife things "that they had rather die than discover to the Doctor." [25] Grateful patients eulogized midwives.[26] The acknowledgment of the services of one Boston midwife, recorded on her tombstone, has inspired comment since 1761. The stone informs the curious that Mrs. Phillips was "born in Westminister in Great Britain, and Commission'd by John Laud, Bishop of London in ye Year 1718 to ye Office of a Mid-

[21] Jane B. Donegan, "Midwifery in America, 1760–1860: A Study in Medicine and Morality" (Ph.D. diss., Syracuse University, 1972), 9–10, 12; "A Law for Regulating Mid Wives Within the City of New York," Minutes of the Common Council of New York, 1716, Appendix I, in Claire E. Fox, "Pregnancy, Childbirth and Early Infancy in Anglo-American Culture, 1675–1830" (Ph.D. diss., University of Pennsylvania, 1966), 442–445; Richard Harrison Shryock, *Medical Licensing in America, 1650–1965* (Baltimore, 1967), 3, 16; James J. Walsh, *History of Medicine in New York: Three Centuries of Medical Progress*, II (New York, 1919), 22, 25.

[22] Cutter and Viets, *Short History*, 145, 150; *Maryland Gazette* (Annapolis), Sept. 30, 1747; Francis R. Packard, *History of Medicine in the United States*, I (New York, 1931), 52–53; Shryock, *Medicine and Society*, 11–12; J. Whitridge Williams, *A Sketch of the History of Obstetrics in the United States up to 1860* (Baltimore, 1903), 1.

[23] Wyndham B. Blanton, *Medicine in Virginia in the Seventeenth Century* (Richmond, 1930), 166; Packard, *History of Medicine*, I, 52; Julia C. Spruill, *Women's Life and Work in the Southern Colonies* (Chapel Hill, N.C., 1938), 272; Herbert Thoms, *Chapters in American Obstetrics* (Springfield, Ill., 1961), 10.

[24] *Diary of Sewall*, I, 40, 114; Sharp, *Compleat Midwife's Companion*, frontispiece of midwife at christening.

[25] Aristotle (pseud.), *Aristotle's Compleat and Experienc'd Midwife, in two Parts. I. Guide for Childbearing Women. II. Proper and Safe Remedies for the Curing of all those Distempers that are incident to the Female Sex . . .* , 9th ed. (London, [1700?]), iii.

[26] Broadside of elegy to Mary Broadwell, in Francisco Guerra, *American Medical Bibliography, 1639–1783* (New York, 1962), 69.

wife," came to "this Country" in 1719, and "by ye Blessing of God has brought into this world above 3000 Children." [27]

We may picture Mrs. Phillips's professional milieu as a small room, lit and warmed by a large fire, and crowded by a gathering of family and friends. In daytime, during the early stages of labor, children might be present, and while labor proceeded female friends dropped in to offer encouragement and help; securing refreshments for such visitors was a part of the preparation for childbirth, especially among the well-to-do families with which we are concerned. Men did not usually remain at the bedside. They might be summoned in to pray, but as delivery approached they waited elsewhere with the children and with women who were "not able to endure" the tension in the room.[28]

During the final stages of labor the midwife took full charge, assisted by other women. As much as possible, midwives managed deliveries by letting nature do the work; they caught the child, tied the umbilical cord, and if necessary fetched the afterbirth. In complicated cases they might turn the child and deliver it feet first, but if this failed, the fetus had to be destroyed. In all circumstances the midwife's chief duty was to comfort the woman in labor while they both waited on nature, and this task she could, as a woman, fulfill with social ease. Under the midwife's direction the woman in labor was liberally fortified with hard liquor or mulled wine. From time to time the midwife examined her cervix to gauge the progress of labor and encouraged her to walk about until the pains became too strong. There was no standard posture for giving birth, but apparently few women lay flat in bed. Some squatted on a midwife's stool, a low chair with an open seat. Others knelt on a pallet, sat on another woman's lap, or stood supported by two friends.[29]

Friends were "welcome companions," according to one manual for midwives, because they enabled the woman in labor "to bear her pains to more advantage," and "their cheerful conversation supports her spirits and inspires her with confidence." [30] Elizabeth Drinker endeavored to talk her daughter into better spirits by telling her that as she was thirty-nine "this might possibly be the last trial of this sort." [31] Some women attempted to cheer the mother-to-be by assuring her that her labor was easy compared to others they had seen, or provoked laughter by making bawdy jokes.[32]

---

[27] Packard, *History of Medicine*, I, 49.

[28] Drinker, *Not So Long Ago*, 51, 52, 54, 59; Dow, ed., *Holyoke Diaries*, 70, 73, 75, 81, 83, 95, 101, 107; *Diary of Sewall*, V, 40, 222–223, 394, VI, 49; Charles White, *A Treatise on the Management of Pregnant and Lying-in Women* (Worcester, Mass., 1793), 19–20.

[29] Aristotle (pseud.), *Compleat and Experienc'd Midwife*, 50–51, 56, 57; Nicholas Culpeper, *A Directory for Midwives: or, a Guide for Women in Their Conception, Bearing, and Suckling their Children* (London, 1651), 167; Drinker, *Not So Long Ago*, 60; *Diary of Sewall*, V, 40; Sharp, *Compleat Midwife's Companion*, 81, 82, 124, 125, 128; White, *Treatise on Pregnant Women*, 20, 74; Willughby, *Observations in Midwifery*, ed. Blenkinsop, 4, 11, 13, 19.

[30] Seaman, *Midwives Monitor*, 90–91.

[31] Drinker, *Not So Long Ago*, 59.

[32] William Buchan, *Advice to Mothers on the Subject of Their Own Health* (Charleston, S.C., 1807), 28; *The London Practice of Midwifery by an American Practi-*

For some attendants, a delivery could be a wrenching experience. Elizabeth Drinker relived her own difficult deliveries when her daughters suffered their labors, and on one such occasion she noted with irony, "This day is 38 years since I was in agonies bringing her into this world of troubles: she told me with tears that this was her birthday." [33] For others the experience of assisting the labors of friends was a reminder of their sex. Sarah Eve, an unmarried twenty-two-year-old, attended the labor of a friend in 1772 and carried the tidings of birth to the waiting father. "None but those that were like anxious could be sensible of a joy like theirs," she wrote in her journal that night. "Oh! Eve! Adam's wife I mean—who could forget her today?" [34]

After delivery, the mother was covered up snugly and confined to her bed, ideally for three to four weeks. For fear of catching cold she was not allowed to put her feet on the floor and was constantly supplied with hot drinks. Family members relieved her of household duties. Restless women, and those who could not afford weeks of idleness, got up in a week or less, but not without occasioning censure.[35]

The social and medical hold of midwives on childbirth loosened during the half century after 1770, as male physicians assumed the practice of midwifery among urban women of social rank. Initially, physicians entered the field as trained practitioners who could help women in difficult labors through the use of instruments, but ultimately they presided over normal deliveries as well. The presence of male physicians in the lying-in chamber signaled a general change in attitudes toward childbirth, including a modification of the dictum that women had to suffer. At the same time, because medical training was restricted to men, women lost their position as assistants at childbirth, and an event traditionally managed by a community of women became an experience shared primarily by a woman and her doctor.

William Shippen, the first American physician to establish a steady practice of midwifery, quietly overcame resistance to the presence of a man in the lying-in room. Casper Wistar's *Eulogies on Dr. Shippen*, published in 1809, states that when Shippen began in 1763, male practitioners were resorted to only in a crisis. "This was altogether the effect of prejudice," Wistar remarked, adding that "by Shippen this prejudice was

---

tioner (Concord, N.H., 1826), 129; Thomas Chalkey James, "Notes from Drs. Osborne's and Clark's Lectures on Midwifery taken by T. C. James, London, 1790–1791," MS, Historical Collections, College of Physicians of Philadelphia.

[33] Drinker, *Not So Long Ago*, 53, 59.

[34] Mrs. Eva Eve Jones, ed., "Extracts from the Journal of Miss Sarah Eve," *Pennsylvania Magazine of History and Biography*, V (1881), 195.

[35] Mitchell, ed., *New Letters of Adams*, 4–5; Jack P. Greene, ed., *The Diary of Colonel Landon Carter of Sabine Hall, 1752–1788*, II (Charlottesville, Va., 1965), 86; Dow, ed., *Holyoke Diaries*, 49, 56, 58, 62, 63, 65, 67, 73, 77, 78, 82, 95, 100, 107; *Diary of Sewall*, II, 51; Sharp, *Compleat Midwife's Companion*, frontispiece drawing of lying-in; McClintock, ed., *Smellie's Treatise*, I, 380.

so done away, that in the course of ten years he became very fully employed." [36] A few figures testify to the trend. The Philadelphia city directory in 1815 listed twenty-one women as midwives, and twenty-three men as practitioners of midwifery. In 1819 it listed only thirteen female midwives, while the number of men had risen to forty-two; and by 1824 only six female midwives remained in the directory.[37] "Prejudice" similarly dissolved in Boston, where in 1781 the physicians advertised that they expected immediate payment for their services in midwifery; by 1820 midwifery in Boston was almost "entirely confined" to physicians.[38] By 1826 Dr. William Dewees, professor of midwifery at the University of Pennsylvania and the outstanding American obstetrician of the early nineteenth century, could preface his textbook on midwifery with an injunction to every American medical student to study the subject because "everyone almost" must practice it. He wrote that "a change of manners within a few years" had "resulted in almost exclusive employment of the male practitioner." [39]

Dewees's statement must be qualified because the "almost exclusive" use of men actually meant almost exclusive use among upper- and middle-class urban women. Female midwives continued throughout the nineteenth century to serve both the mass of women in cities and women in the country who were "without advantage of regular practitioners." [40] During the initial years of their practice physicians shared obstetrical cases with midwives. On occasion Philadelphia women summoned Shippen together with their midwives, and Dewees reports that when he began to practice in the 1790s he depended on midwives to call him when instruments were needed.[41] It is clear, however, that by the 1820s Dewees and his colleagues had established their own practice independent of midwives.

[36] Corner, *William Shippen*, 124; Cutter and Viets, *Short History*, 150.

[37] *Kite's Philadelphia Directory for 1815* (Philadelphia, 1815), xi–xii; John Paxton, *The Philadelphia Directory and Register for 1819* (Philadelphia, 1819), n.p.; Robert Desilver, *The Philadelphia Directory and Register for 1824* (Philadelphia, 1824), n.p.

[38] Walter Channing (John Ware?), *Remarks on the Employment of Females as Practitioners in Midwifery* (Boston, 1820), 1; *Independent Chronicle and the Universal Advertiser* (Boston), Nov. 8, 1781.

[39] William Potts Dewees, *A Compendious System of Midwifery, Chiefly Designed to Facilitate the Inquiries of Those Who may be Pursuing This Branch of Study* (Philadelphia, 1826), xiv.

[40] William Buchan, *A Compend of Domestic Midwifery for the Use of Female Practitioners, Being an Appendix to Buchan's Domestic Medicine* (Charleston, S.C., 1815), 3; Frances E. Kobrin, "The American Midwife Controversy: A Crisis of Professionalization," *Bulletin of the History of Medicine*, XL (1966), 350; M. D. Learned and C. F. Brede, "An Old German Midwife's Record, Kept by Susanna Muller, of Providence Township, Lancaster County, Pennsylvania, during the years 1791–1815" (n.d.), Hist. Colls., College of Physicians of Philadelphia; Mrs. Joseph Sarber, Memorandum Kept by Mrs. Joseph Sarber, Midwife at the Falls of the Schuylkill from 1814 to 1831, MS, Historical Society of Pennsylvania, Philadelphia.

[41] Drinker, *Not So Long Ago*, 51–52; Dewees, *Compendious System of Midwifery*, 303.

On one level the change was a direct consequence of the fact that after 1750 growing numbers of American men traveled to Europe for medical education. Young men with paternal means, like Shippen, spent three to four years studying medicine, including midwifery, with leading physicians in the hospitals of London and the classrooms of Edinburgh. When they returned to the colonies they brought back not only a superior set of skills but also British ideas about hospitals, medical schools, and professional standards.[42]

In the latter part of the eighteenth century advanced medical training became available in North America. At the time of Shippen's return in 1762 there was only one hospital in the colonies, the Pennsylvania Hospital, built ten years earlier to care for the sick poor. Shippen and his London-educated colleagues saw that the hospital could be used for the clinical training of physicians, as in Europe. Within three years the Philadelphia doctors, led by John Morgan, established formal, systematic instruction at a school of medicine, supplemented by clinical work in the hospital.[43] Morgan maintained that the growth of the colonies "called aloud" for a medical school "to increase the number of those who exercise the profession of medicine and surgery." [44] Dr. Samuel Bard successfully addressed the same argument to the citizens of New York in 1768.[45]

In addition to promoting medical schools, Morgan and Bard defined the proper practitioner of medicine as a man learned in a science. To languages and liberal arts their ideal physician added anatomy, material medicine, botany, chemistry, and clinical experience. He was highly conscious not only of his duty to preserve "the life and health of mankind," [46] but also of his professional status, and this new emphasis on professionalism extended to midwifery.

The trustees of the first American medical schools recognized midwifery as a branch of medical science. From its founding in 1768, Kings College in New York devoted one professorship solely to midwifery, and the University of Pennsylvania elected Shippen professor of anatomy, surgery, and midwifery in 1791. By 1807 five reputable American medical schools provided courses in midwifery.[47] In the early years of the nine-

---

[42] Charles M. Andrews, *Colonial Folkways: A Chronicle of American Life in the Reign of the Georges* (New Haven, Conn., 1919), 147; Maurice Bear Gordon, *Aesculapius Comes to the Colonies: The Story of the Early Days of Medicine in the Thirteen Original Colonies* (Ventnor, N.J., 1949), 156–157, 460–465; Francis Packard, "How London and Edinburgh Influenced Medicine in Philadelphia in the Eighteenth Century," College of Physicians of Philadelphia, *Transactions,* 3d Ser., LIII (1931), 167.

[43] Gordon, *Aesculapius,* 465; Packard, *History of Medicine,* I, 181–230; Packard, "How London and Edinburgh Influenced Medicine," College of Physicians of Philadelphia, *Trans.,* 3d Ser., LIII (1931), 163, 166.

[44] John Morgan, *A Discourse Upon the Institution of Medical Schools in America* (Baltimore, 1937 [orig. publ. 1765]), 33.

[45] Samuel Bard, *Two Discourses Dealing with Medical Education in Early New York* (New York, 1921), 1.

[46] *Ibid.,* 10, 16, 19; Morgan, *Discourse Upon the Institution of Medical Schools,* 14–17.

[47] Packard, *History of Medicine,* II, 1125–1127; Williams, *Sketch of the History of Obstetrics,* 5–7.

teenth century some professors of midwifery began to call themselves obstetricians or professors of obstetrics, a scientific-sounding title free of the feminine connotations of the word midwife.[48] Though not compulsory for all medical students, the new field was considered worthy of detailed study along the paths pioneered by English physicians.

Dr. William Smellie contributed more to the development of obstetrics than any other eighteenth-century physician. His influence was established by his teaching career in London from 1741 to 1758, and by his treatise on midwifery, first published in 1752.[49] Through precise measurement and observation Smellie discovered the mechanics of parturition. He found that the child's head turned throughout delivery, adapting the widest part to the widest diameter of the pelvic canal. Accordingly, he defined maneuvers for manipulating an improperly presented child. He also recognized that obstetrical forceps, generally known for only twenty years when he wrote in 1754, should be used to rectify the position of an infant wedged in the mouth of the cervix, in preference to the "common method" of simply jerking the child out. He perfected the design of the forceps and taught its proper use, so that physicians could save both mother and child in difficult deliveries, instead of being forced to dismember the infant with hooks.[50]

To Smellie and the men who learned from him, the time seemed ripe to apply science to a field hitherto built on ignorance and supported by prejudice. Smellie commented on the novelty of scientific interest in midwifery. "We ought to be ashamed of ourselves," he admonished the readers of his *Treatise*, "for the little improvement we have made in so many centuries." Only recently have "we established a better method of delivering in laborious and preternatural cases."[51] Smellie's countryman Dr. Charles White reflected in his text on midwifery in 1793 that "the bringing of the art of midwifery to perfection upon scientific and medical principles seems to have been reserved for the present generation."[52]

Some American physicians shared this sense of the new "Importance of the Obstetrick Art." Midwifery was not a "trifling" matter to be left to the uneducated, Thomas Jones of the College of Medicine of Maryland wrote in 1812. Broadly defined as the care of "all the indispositions incident to women from the commencement of pregnancy to the termination of lactation," it ranked among the most important branches of medicine. "With the cultivation of this branch of science," women could now "reasonably look to men for safety in the perilous conditions" of childbirth.[53]

[48] *OED*, s.v. "obstetrics"; Packard, *History of Medicine*, II, 1125–1126.
[49] Cutter and Viets, *Short History*, 26–28.
[50] *Ibid.*, 44–59; John Glaister, *William Smellie and His Contemporaries* (Glasgow, 1894), 170, 174, 178–179, 187; McClintock, ed., *Smellie's Treatise*, II, 250–251, 339.
[51] McClintock, ed., *Smellie's Treatise*, II, 339.
[52] White, *Treatise on Pregnant Women*, viii, 70–71.
[53] Thomas Dashiell Jones, *An Essay on the Importance of the Obstetrick Art; Submitted to the Examination of Charles Alexander Warfield, M.D., President of the Medical Faculty of the College of Medicine of Maryland* ... (Baltimore, 1812), 5, 11, 21, 23.

Jones maintained, as did other physicians, that the conditions of modern urban life produced a special need for scientific aid in childbirth. Both rich and poor women in large cities presented troublesome cases to the physician. Pelvic deformities, abortions, and tedious labors Jones considered common among wealthy urban women because of their indolent habits and confining fashionable dress, and among the poor because of inadequate diet and long hours of work indoors. There was, he believed, a greater need for "well informed obstetrick practitioners in large cities than in country places." [54]

Although it cannot be established that there was an increase in difficult parturitions among urban women, social as well as medical reasons account for the innovations in the practice of midwifery in such cities as Boston, Philadelphia, and New York. Physicians received their medical education in cities, and cities offered the best opportunities to acquire patients and live comfortably. Urban families of some means could afford the $12 to $15 minimum fee which Boston physicians demanded for midwife services in 1806.[55] Obstetrics was found to be a good way to establish a successful general practice. The man who conducted himself well in the lying-in room won the gratitude and confidence of his patient and her family, and they naturally called him to serve in other medical emergencies. It was midwifery, concluded Dr. Walter Channing of Boston, that ensured doctors "the permanency and security of all their other business." [56]

The possibility of summoning a physician, who could perhaps insure a safer and faster delivery, opened first to urban women. The dramatic rescue of one mother and child given up by a midwife could be enough to convince a neighborhood of women of a physician's value and secure him their practice.[57] Doctors asserted that women increasingly hired physicians because they became convinced "that the well instructed physician is best calculated to avert danger and surmount difficulties." [58] Certainly by 1795 the women of the Drinker family believed that none but a physician should order medicine for a woman in childbed, and had no doubts that Dr. Shippen or his colleague Dr. Nicholas Way was the best help that they could summon.[59]

Although she accepted a male physician as midwife, Elizabeth Drinker still had reservations about the use of instruments to facilitate childbirth and was relieved when Shippen did not have to use forceps on

[54] Thomas Denman, *An Introduction to the Practice of Midwifery*, I (New York, 1802), 47; Jones, *Essay on Obstetrick Art*, 8, 17–19; Seaman, *Midwives Monitor*, x; White, *Treatise on Pregnant Women*, 79.

[55] Boston Medical Association, *Rules and Regulations of the Boston Medical Association* (Boston, 1806), 4–5. The minimum fee escalated to $15/day case, $20/night by 1819. Boston Med. Assoc., *Rules and Regulations* (1819 ed.).

[56] Channing, *Remarks on Employment of Females*, 19; Edward Warren, *The Life of John Collins Warren, M.D., Compiled Chiefly from his Autobiography and Journals*, I (Boston, 1860), 219.

[57] Dewees, *Compendious System of Midwifery* (Philadelphia, 1824), 307.

[58] *Ibid.* (1826), xiv.

[59] Drinker, *Not So Long Ago*, 51, 54–56, 59.

her daughter. Other women feared to call a physician because they assumed that any instruments he used would destroy the child.[60] However, once the capabilities of obstetrical forceps became known, some women may have turned to them by choice in hope of faster deliveries. Such hope stimulated a medical fashion. By about 1820 Dewees and Bard felt it necessary to condemn nervous young doctors for resorting unnecessarily to forceps.[61]

The formal education of American physicians and the development of midwifery as a science, the desire of women for the best help in childbirth, the utility of midwifery as a means of building a physician's practice, and, ultimately, the gigantic social changes labeled urbanization explain why physicians assumed the ordinary practice of midwifery among well-to-do urban women in the late eighteenth and early nineteenth centuries. This development provides insight into the changing condition of women in American society.

The development of obstetrics signified a partial rejection of the assumption that women had to suffer in childbirth and implied a new social appreciation of women, as admonitions to women for forbearance under the pain of labor turned to the desire to relieve their pain. Thus did Dr. Thomas Denman explain his life's work: "The law of a religion founded on principles of active benevolence, feelings of humanity, common interests of society, and special tenderness for women" demanded that men search for a method by which women might be conducted safely through childbirth.[62] In his doctoral dissertation in 1812 one American medical student drew a distinction between childbirth in primitive societies and his own. In the former, "women are generally looked on by their rugged lords as unworthy of any particular attention," and death or injury in childbirth is "not deemed a matter of any importance." Well-instructed assistants to women in childbirth were one sign of the value placed on women in civilized societies.[63]

The desire to relieve women in childbirth also signified a more liberal interpretation of scripture. At the University of Pennsylvania in 1804, Peter Miller, a medical student, modified the theological dictum that women must bear in sorrow. The anxieties of pregnancy and the anguish caused by the death of so many infants constituted sorrow enough for women, argued Miller. They did not need to be subjected to bodily pain as well.[64] Reiterating this argument, Dewees bluntly asked, "Why should

[60] Dewees, *Compendious System of Midwifery* (1824), 307; Drinker, *Not So Long Ago*, 60.
[61] Samuel Bard, *A Compendium of the Theory and Practice of Midwifery*, 5th ed. (New York, 1819), v, 176, 289; Dewees, *Compendious System of Midwifery* (1826), xv.
[62] Denman, *Introduction to Midwifery*, 235.
[63] Jones, *Essay on Obstetrick Art*, 8.
[64] Peter Miller, *An Essay on the Means of Lessening the Pains of Parturition* (Philadelphia, 1804), 340.

the female alone incur the penalty of God?" [65] To relieve the pain of labor Dewees and his fellows analyzed the anatomy and physiology of childbirth and defined techniques for the use of instruments.

If the development of obstetrics suggests the rise of a "special tenderness for women" on the part of men, it also meant that women's participation in medical practice was diminished and disparaged. A few American physicians instructed midwives or wrote manuals for them, but these efforts were private and sporadic, and had ceased by 1820. The increasing professionalization of medicine, in the minds of the physicians who formed medical associations that set the standards of the field, left little room for female midwives, who lacked the prescribed measure of scientific training and professional identity. [66]

William Shippen initially invited midwives as well as medical students to attend his private courses in midwifery. His advertisement in the *Pennsylvania Gazette* in January 1765 related his experience assisting women in the country in difficult labors, "most of which was made so by the unskillful old women about them," and announced that he "thought it his duty to immediately begin" courses in midwifery "in order to instruct those women who have virtue enough to own their ignorance and apply for instructions, as well as those young gentlemen now engaged in the study of that useful and necessary branch of surgery." Shippen taught these private lessons until after the Revolution, when he lectured only to the students at the University of Pennsylvania, who, of course, were male. [67]

At the turn of the century Dr. Valentine Seaman conducted the only other known formal instruction of midwives. He was distressed by the ignorance of many midwives, yet convinced that midwives ought to manage childbirth because, unlike physicians, they had time to wait out lingering labors, and, as women, they could deal easily with female patients. Seaman offered his private lectures and demonstrations at the New York Almshouse lying-in ward, and in 1800 published them as the *Midwives Monitor and Mothers Mirror*. [68] A handful of other men wrote texts at least nominally directed to midwives between 1800 and 1810; some of these, like Seaman's, discussed the use of instruments. [69] In 1817 Dr. Thomas Ewell proposed that midwives be trained at a national school of midwifery in Washington, D.C., to be supported by a collection taken up

---

[65] William Potts Dewees, *Essays on Various Subjects Connected with Midwifery* (Philadelphia, 1823), 24.

[66] Channing, *Remarks on Employment of Females*, 6–12; Jones, *Essay on Obstetrick Art*, 20; Joseph F. Kett, *The Formation of the American Medical Profession: The Role of Institutions, 1780–1860* (New Haven, Conn., 1968), 10–30.

[67] *Pennsylvania Gazette* (Philadelphia), Jan. 31, 1765.

[68] Williams, *Sketch of the History of Obstetrics*, 13; Seaman, *Midwives Monitor*, iii–vii.

[69] Bard, *Compendium of Theory and Practice of Midwifery*, iv, 289; Brevitt, *Female Medical Repository*, 149–155; Buchan, *Compend of Domestic Midwifery;* Samuel Jennings, *Married Lady's Companion, or Poor Man's Friend . . .* (New York, 1808), 135; Seaman, *Midwives Monitor*, 31–32. All of these works were directed entirely or in part to midwives.

by ministers. There is no evidence that Ewell's scheme, presented in his medical manual, *Letters to Ladies*, ever gained a hearing.[70]

Seaman and Ewell, and other authors of midwives' manuals, presumed that if women mastered some of the fundamentals of obstetrics they would be desirable assistants in ordinary midwifery cases. In 1820 Dr. Channing of Boston went further in his pamphlet, *Remarks on the Employment of Females as Practitioners of Midwifery*, in which he maintained that no one could thoroughly understand the management of labor who did not understand "thoroughly the profession of medicine as a whole." Channing's principle would have totally excluded women from midwifery, because no one favored professional medical education for women. It was generally assumed that they could not easily master the necessary languages, mathematics, and chemistry, or withstand the trials of dissecting room and hospital. Channing added that women's moral character disqualified them for medical practice: "Their feelings of sympathy are too powerful for the cool exercise of judgement" in medical emergencies, he wrote; "they do not have the power of action, nor the active power of mind which is essential to the practice of the surgeon." [71]

Denied formal medical training, midwives of the early nineteenth century could not claim any other professional or legal status. Unlike Great Britain, the United States had no extensive record of licensing laws or oaths defining the practice of midwifery. Nor were there any vocal groups of midwives who, conscious of their tradition of practice or associated with lying-in hospitals, were able to defend themselves against competition from physicians.[72] American midwives ceased practice among women of social rank with few words uttered in their defense.

The victory of the physicians produced its own problems. The doctor's sex affected the relationships between women and their attendants in childbirth, and transformed the atmosphere of the lying-in room. In his advice to his male students Dewees acknowledged that summoning a man to assist at childbed "cost females a severe struggle." [73] Other doctors knew that even the ordinary gynecologic services of a physician occasioned embarrassment and violated woman's "natural delicacy of feeling," and that every sensitive woman felt "deeply humil[i]ated" at the least bodily exposure.[74] Doctors recognized an almost universal repugnance on the part of women to male assistance in time of labor.[75] Because of "whim or false delicacy" women often refused to call a man until their condition

---

[70] Thomas Ewell, *Letters to Ladies, Detailing Important Information Concerning Themselves and Infants* (Philadelphia, 1817), vii–viii.

[71] Channing, *Remarks on Employment of Females*, 4–7.

[72] Aveling, *English Midwives*, 138–144, 153–159; Cutter and Viets, *Short History*, 43; Glaister, *William Smellie*, 32–36.

[73] Dewees, *Compendious System of Midwifery* (1826), xv.

[74] Channing, *Remarks on Employment of Females*, 16, 17; Ewell, *Letters to Ladies*, 27.

[75] Jones, *Essay on Obstetrick Art*, 11.

had become critical.[76] It is unlikely that physicians exaggerated these observations, although there is little testimony from women themselves about their childbed experience in the early nineteenth century.

The uneasiness of women who were treated by men was sometimes shared by their husbands. In 1772 the *Virginia Gazette* printed a denunciation of male midwifery as immoral. The author, probably an Englishman, attributed many cases of adultery in England to the custom of employing men at deliveries. Even in labor a woman had intervals of ease, and these, he thought, were the moments when the doctor infringed on the privileges of the husband. It would be a matter of utmost indifference to him "whether my wife had spent the night in a bagnio, or an hour of the forenoon locked up with a man midwife in her dressing room." [77] Such arguments were frequently and seriously raised in England during the eighteenth century.[78] They may seem ludicrous, but at least one American man of Dr. Ewell's acquaintance suffered emotional conflict over hiring a male midwife. He sent for a physician to help his wife in her labor, yet "very solemnly he declared to the doctor, he would demolish him if he touched or looked at his wife." [79]

Physicians dealt with the embarrassment of patients and the suspicion of husbands by observing the drawing-room behavior of "well-bred gentlemen." Dewees told his students to "endeavor, by well chosen conversation, to divert your patient's mind from the purpose of your visit." [80] All questions of a delicate nature were to be communicated through a third party, perhaps the only other person in the room, either a nurse or an elderly friend or relative. The professional man was advised "never to seem to know anything about the parts of generation, further than that there is an orifice near the rectum leading to an os." [81]

Physicians did not perform vaginal examinations unless it was absolutely important to do so, and they often had to cajole women into permitting an examination at all. Nothing could be more shocking to a woman, Shippen lectured his students, "than for a young man the moment he enters the Chamber to ask for Pomatum and proceed to examine the uterus." [82] Doctors waited until a labor pain clutched their patients and

[76] Seaman, *Midwives Monitor*, iv.

[77] *Virginia Gazette* (Purdie and Dixon), Oct. 1, 1772; reprinted in *New-London Gazette* (Conn.), Jan. 29, 1773.

[78] Elizabeth Nihill, *A Treatise on the Art of Midwifery, Setting Forth Various Abuses Therein, Especially as to the Practice With Instruments* (London, 1760), and S. W. Fores, *Man-Midwifery Dissected* (London, 1793), are outstanding examples of arguments made about the supposed immorality of man midwives. Glaister, *William Smellie*, discusses other examples of such literature.

[79] Ewell, *Letters to Ladies*, 27.

[80] Dewees, *Compendious System of Midwifery* (1826), 189; Daniel B. Smith, "Notes on lectures of Thomas Chalkey James and William Potts Dewees, University of Pennsylvania, 1826," MS, Hist. Colls., College of Physicians of Philadelphia.

[81] *London Practice of Midwifery*, 109.

[82] Bard, *Compendium of Theory and Practice of Midwifery*, 181; lecture notes from lectures of William Shippen, Jr., University of Pennsylvania, n.d., MS, Hist. Colls., College of Physicians of Philadelphia.

then suggested an examination by calling it "taking a pain." During examination and delivery the patient lay completely covered in her bed, a posture more modest, if less comfortable, than squatting on a pallet or a birth stool. The light in the room was dimmed by closing the shutters during the day and covering the lamps at night. If a physician used forceps, he had to manipulate them under the covers, using his free hand as a guide.[83] On this point doctors who read Thomas Denman's *Obstetrical Remembrancer* were reminded that "Degorges, one of the best obstetricians of his time, was blind." [84]

The crowd of supportive friends and family disappeared with the arrival of the doctor. The physician guarded against "too many attendants; where there are women, they must talk." [85] The presence of other women might increase the doctor's nervousness, and they certainly did not help the woman in labor. Medical men interpreted women's talk of other experiences with childbirth as mere gossip "of all the dangerous and difficult labours they ever heard any story about in their lives," which ought to be stopped lest it disturb the patient.[86] Especially distracting were the bawdy stories visitors told, expecting the physician to laugh, too. Medical professors recommended "grave deportment," warning that levity would "hurt your patient or yourself in her esteem." [87] Far from providing the consolation of a friend, the physician was often a stranger who needed to "get a little acquainted" with his patient. One medical text went so far as to coach him in a series of conversational ice breakers about children and the weather.[88]

Etiquette and prudery in the lying-in chamber affected medical care. Physicians were frustrated by their inability to examine their patients thoroughly, for they knew full well that learning midwifery from a book was "like learning shipbuilding without touching timber." [89] Examinations were inadequate, and the dangers of manipulating instruments without benefit of sight were tremendous. Dewees cautioned his students to take great care before pulling the forceps that "no part of the mother is included in the locking of the blades. This accident is frequent." [90] Accidental mutilation of infants was also reported, as the navel string had to be cut under the covers. Lecturers passed on the story of the incautious doctor who included the penis of an infant within the blades of his scissors.[91]

[83] Bard, *Compendium of Theory and Practice of Midwifery*, 181; Dewees, *Compendious System of Midwifery* (1826), 189–190; *London Practice of Midwifery*, 108–109.

[84] Thomas Denman, *The Obstetrical Remembrancer, or Denman's Aphorisms on Natural and Difficult Parturition* (New York, 1848 [orig. U.S. publ. 1803]), 46.

[85] *London Practice of Midwifery*, 129.

[86] *Ibid.*, 129–130.

[87] James, "Notes from Osborne's and Clark's Lectures," Hist. Colls., College of Physicians of Philadelphia; notes on Shippen lectures, *ibid.*

[88] Notes on Shippen lectures, *ibid.*; *London Practice of Midwifery*, 127.

[89] Bard, *Compendium of Theory and Practice of Midwifery*, 220; Seaman, *Midwives Monitor*, ix.

[90] Dewees, *Compendious System of Midwifery* (1826), 313.

[91] Kobler, *Reluctant Surgeon*, 32; *London Practice of Midwifery*, 132–133.

In view of such dangers, the conflict between social values and medical practice is striking. The expansion of medical knowledge brought men and women face to face with social taboos in family life. They had to ask themselves the question, Who should watch a woman give birth? For centuries the answer had unhesitatingly been female relatives and friends, and the midwife. The science of obstetrics, developing in the eighteenth century, changed the answer. Though women might socially be the most acceptable assistants at a delivery, men were potentially more useful.

In consequence of the attendance of male physicians, by 1825, for some American women, childbirth was ceasing to be an open ceremony. Though birth still took place at home, and though friends and relatives still lent a helping hand, visiting women no longer dominated the activities in the lying-in room. Birth became increasingly a private affair conducted in a quiet, darkened room. The physician limited visitors because they hindered proper medical care, but the process of birth was also concealed because it embarrassed both patient and physician.

Between 1760 and 1825 childbirth was thus transformed from an open affair to a restricted one. As one consequence of the development of obstetrics as a legitimate branch of medicine, male physicians began replacing midwives. They began to reduce childbirth to a scientifically managed event and deprived it of its folk aspects. Strengthened by the professionalization of their field, these physicians also responded to the hopes of women in Philadelphia, New York, and Boston for safe delivery. Although they helped some pregnant women, they hurt midwives, who were shut out of an area of medicine that had been traditionally their domain. All these innovations took place in the large urban centers in response to distinctly urban phenomena. They reflected the increasing privatization of family life, and they foreshadowed mid-nineteenth-century attitudes toward childbirth, mother, and woman.

Order and Disorder
Among the Youth
of the Early Republic

JOSEPH F. KETT

In modern America we think of education as the concern of schools and universities. But for the first two centuries of our history secondary schools existed for only a small minority of Americans, and universities served only a tiny fraction of that minority. This lack of schools did not mean that only the advantaged received an education. Rather, it signified that the family and the church, rather than formal institutions of instruction, were the primary means by which skills, knowledge, moral precepts, and attitudes were transmitted from one generation to another.

In nineteenth-century America public education was extended to a far broader segment of society. At the same time, schools began to perform many of the functions previously exercised by parents and religious leaders. Accordingly, not only the three Rs but religious and moral instruction fell within the schoolteacher's responsibilities. The public-school movement became an important part of the process of democratization that antebellum reformers sought to extend to every aspect of society. Before the century was over, a great majority of young Americans, for most of their formative years, would spend a significant part of their waking day within the walls of the public-school classroom. Public education, partially eclipsing the roles of family and church, became a profoundly important part of everyday life.

The educational-reform movement of the first half of the nineteenth century proclaimed the right of every child to free public education, which soon became an irreducible article of faith among virtually all reformers. A democracy, it was argued, could not stand without an educated citizenry, and a democratic society could not survive unless, through universal education, all persons were equally equipped to compete in an open marketplace of talent. Thus, we have been told, an enlightened and insistent lower class, led by humanitarian reformers, fought an entrenched upper class in antebellum America for the right to public education. And won.

Historians have recently challenged this egalitarian view, arguing that one of the primary aims, if not the central goal, of the public-school movement was to impose social control on an increasingly multiethnic, urban, and impoverished lower class. Close examination of the curriculum, pedagogical techniques, and leadership of the school-reform movement has led to the conclusion that schools were designed to inculcate values and patterns of behavior that served those whose place in society was already secure. In this sense, the main legacy of the public-school movement, as social historian Michael Katz has written in **The Irony of School Reform,** was the principle that "education was something the better part of the community did to the others to make them orderly, moral, and tractable." The research of Katz and others suggests that the public schools were widely supported by the upper classes, often against lower-class opposition, because the elite saw the public school as an instrument for arresting the social chaos and disintegration of family life that they identified as the most fearful side-effects of immigration, urbanization, and industrialization, and that together were transforming the social contours of the nation before the Civil War.

In this selection Joseph F. Kett paints a fascinating portrait of the socialization and education of American youth in the early nineteenth century. He shows how the social environment, including factors as diverse as diet and political currents, affected the maturation of the young, who made up a much larger percentage of the population than they do today. His discussion of formal education in schools and colleges gives students an opportunity to reflect on their own experiences and to compare them to an earlier age, when the boundaries of individual freedom were being broadened but were still far less expansive than today. Kett argues that student rebellions in the antebellum period were a kind of pre–political revolt against inherited modes of authoritarianism and hierarchical social structure no longer befitting a society that defined itself as democratic and egalitarian. His argument can be taken as a reminder in our study of the everyday lives of early Americans that whenever social disorder is observed, we must look beyond the unruly or violent acts themselves in order to discover the sources and inner meaning of such behavior.

THE SOCIAL EXPERIENCE OF YOUTH

To a much greater extent than now, American society between 1790 and 1840 was composed of children and youth. The median age of the population was 30.8 in 1950 but only 16 in 1800. As a corollary, there were relatively few middle-aged people in the early 19th century. Those aged 45 to 64 comprised only 9 percent of the population, a proportion which had nearly doubled by 1930.[1] In itself, the pyramidal age structure conditioned rather than determined the relations between age groups. But combined with other social factors—the gradual undermining of traditions of status and hierarchy, rapid shifts of population, and an increase in the number of towns large enough to sustain the organized activities of youth—this demographic fact led to a succession of discontinuities in the experience of young people and nurtured a kind of relationship be-

"Order and Disorder Among the Youth of the Early Republic." From *Rites of Passage: Adolescence in America, 1790 to the Present* by Joseph F. Kett, chapter 2. © 1977 by Joseph F. Kett, Basic Books, Inc., Publishers, New York. Reprinted by permission.

tween adults and youth which bears little resemblance to the rules which
have governed such relationships in the 20th century.

In general, the social life of young people followed the contours of
semidependence described earlier. As young people pushed into their
teens, they customarily experienced greater personal liberty. One aspect
of such liberty was the joining of social institutions for youth. Voluntary
associations for youth in the early decades of the 19th century were
extraordinarily diverse. Churches often had young people's societies or
special hours set aside for prayer meetings for young people.[2] But the
organized activities of youth did not have to take a pious direction. For
example, in the early 19th century most towns contained volunteer military companies which functioned simultaneously as militia, welcoming
parties for visiting dignitaries, and social clubs for young men who attired
themselves in the uniforms of hussars or dragoons, hired saber instructors
from the Continent, and paraded before the ladies on holidays.[3] By all
accounts, companies like the Richmond Light Infantry Blues or Philadelphia Lancer Guard or Brattleborough Light Infantry were high-
spirited in more ways than one. When the captain of the Brattleborough
Light Infantry ordered all cold water men to march three paces forward
during an 1830 muster, no one moved a muscle.[4] An observer described a
typical muster in Ohio as "a holyday for the lower classes, and the occasion of much intoxication and many brutal fights." [5]

The minimum age for membership in volunteer military companies
was usually set at 18, but exceptions were common. John W. Geary, later
governor of Kansas, was a lieutenant in the militia at 16.[6] At times, boys
formed their own auxiliary companies. In Alexandria, Virginia, in 1860
the "Young Riflemen," boys aged 10 to 15, paraded with neat uniforms
and knapsacks.[7] Being under age presented few real problems in the early
1800s. Since the military companies were voluntary, age requirements
could be dispensed with whenever the members felt disposed to do so.
Even during wartime, underage soldiers had little trouble joining the
army. Random references to 14- and 15-year-old soldiers during the
Revolutionary War probably reveal no more than the tip of an iceberg.[8]
Susan R. Hull was able to write a factual and meaty volume based entirely
on the exploits of teenagers in the Confederate Army, some of them as
young as 13.[9]

Somewhere between the piety of the church youth societies and the
rowdy military companies were self-improvement societies, which at
times contained specific references to young men or young people in their
titles but which, even if they did not, were usually composed of youth.
A "Young People's Total Abstinence Society" was formed in Dublin,
New Hampshire, in 1842.[10] Few towns in antebellum America were without their young men's debating or mechanics' societies, where books,
ideas, and fellowship circulated freely.[11] Lyceums, the quintessential expression of the idea of self-culture, were often outgrowths of young
men's societies. In its original form the lyceum was little more than a
young men's society for mutual instruction; only gradually did lyceums
evolve into forums for outside lecturers, and even then young men's
societies continued to play a role as sponsoring agents.[12]

By mid-century, young men's societies in the larger cities had become well-organized, prominent civic institutions with handsome budg-
ets, well-stocked libraries, and a membership drawn mainly from young
businessmen in their 20s. The constitution of the Young Men's Association
of the City of Milwaukee, organized in 1847, entitled those between 18
and 35 to become members, while limiting those under 18 to use of the
library.[13] The association's age range thus approximated that of a modern
Junior Chamber of Commerce. Prior to 1840, however, young men's
societies were less well organized and probably embraced a more youthful
age group. Apprentice associations had long carried on many of the same
functions as young men's societies, and the former certainly included
teenagers. In towns, moreover, self-improvement societies were likely to
contain a mixture of boys, girls, young men, and young ladies, even after
1840.[14] A literary club in Surry, New Hampshire, begun in 1853 with
the purpose of staging debates and theatricals, provides a good illustration
of the persistence of promiscuous age groupings outside of large cities.[15]

Members' Ages: Literary Club, Surry, N.H., 1853–1854

Males

AGE	11	12	13	14	15	16	17	18	19	20	21	22	23	24	30
Number	0	0	2	2	3	3	2	3	3	1	0	1	2	1	1

Females

AGE	11	12	13	14	15	16	17	18	19	20	21	22	23	24	30
Number	1	0	2	2	1	2	2	2	1	3	0	0	0	0	0

Loose age groupings like this one survived longer in towns than in
cities, but even in cities teenagers under 18 often formed junior append-
ages of organizations in which the majority of members were between 18
and 30. Young men in their early to middle teens served urban volunteer
fire companies in various ways, although they were too young for full
membership. The Sons of Temperance had a junior branch called the
Cadets of Temperance. Most of the members of the Young Men's Christian Association were over 18, but the minimum age was usually as low as
15.[16]

Alongside structured and organized activities a host of less formal
pursuits engaged the spare time of young people, pursuits which ranged
from firing off guns all night on the Fourth of July to dating and dancing.
When Silas Felton, who grew up in a small Massachusetts town toward
the end of the 18th century, related that he spent most of his evenings
either reading or "roving about . . . which is generally the case with
boys 10 to 21 years old," he expressed an important aspect of youthful life
experience.[17]

Two broad impulses underpinned the innumerable specific forms taken by youthful pranks before 1840: ritualized insubordination and parody. Ritualized insubordination would be a fair description of the acts of "Knotts of Riotous Young Men" who nightly serenaded Cotton Mather during the early 1700s with "profane and filthy" songs, and of the schoolboys who engaged during the 18th and early 19th centuries in the custom of "turning out" schoolmasters who refused their demands for holidays. In contrast, parody was the dominant impulse behind the mock commencements often staged by college freshmen. At times the two impulses merged. At a Pennsylvania industrial village a troop of thirty to fifty "jovial young fellows" joined in a band each New Year's Eve, equipped themselves with powder, guns, and wadding in joking imitation of militiamen, and marched from farm to farm, firing off salutes and demanding hospitality and "all manner of good cheer." This particular custom had died out by 1843, after careless shooting resulted in injuries and death to a few luckless inhabitants.[18]

Contemporary accounts of New England and southern society also abound with references to sleigh rides, chitchat, and dances among young people. Brantley York, born in 1805 in Randolph County, North Carolina, related how the youth held "disorderly and demoralizing" dances in the vicinity of his home every Wednesday and Saturday night.[19] The diary of Hezekiah Prince, a young man living in Templeton, Maine, in the 1820s, related an almost continuous round of parties and sleigh rides among the youth of Templeton and adjoining towns, with no adult chaperonage.[20] Parents, especially pious ones, often objected to youthful socializing, but there was always the recourse outlined by Amos Kendall in his autobiography.

> The family government was strict, and so far as it bore upon their eldest children, severe. They were not only prohibited from dancing, playing cards, and all like amusements, but from going to places where they were practiced. The consequence was that the elder sons deceived their parents and indulged in those forbidden recreations clandestinely.[21]

The degree of freedom rose with age. Sixteen was the usual age at which young ladies began to keep company with young men, although there were variations down to 14 and up to 18. As an example of the latter, in 1781 the 22-year-old Erkuries Beatty, an officer in the Continental Army, sent his brother Reading a kind of Baedeker to the charms of young (and some old) maidens in the vicinity of Yorktown, Virginia, where Reading was about to be sent. The list included Bekky Miller, who "rather got a sourness in her looks, but is very good Natured," and "her father will give her a very good fortune if he pleases," and fifteen other maidens, plus

> one buxom Rich widow, two old maids, three or four young girls that have got married, with a number of married ladies in the town —I could enumerate a great many more young ones to you between

ages 18 and 15, but as we were never admitted into the company of those above mentioned, being too young, it is not worth while.[22]

Whether the girls between 15 and 18 were deemed too young for dating or just too young for a bounder like Erkuries Beatty is open to question. The evidence is somewhat conflicting, but Erkuries's lack of success with girls 15 to 18 was probably atypical, especially in view of the amount of dating that went on between cousins. As Erkuries related to Reading a year earlier, "that night Cousin Polly and me set off a Slaying with a number more young People and had a pretty Clever kick-up."[23] The extent to which the social life of young people went on within the kin group or as an offshoot of kin relations probably softened prohibitions against youthful socializing.

If "dating" is defined as social meetings between young people of opposite sex who have no intention to marry, then it is a more accurate term than "courtship" to describe social engagements in the early 19th century. The presence of so many unescorted young people at social gatherings probably reduced pressures to establish formal courtship but at the same time distinguished such meetings from our own style of dating, which places a premium on physical intimacy in public and exclusive pairing.[24] The presence of adults, more as spectators than as chaperones, had the same effect. Logging bees, quilting bees, and apple bees included all ages and often ended up with "a nice supper or refreshment and the usual play or dance, kept until midnight or after."[25]

As one would expect, greater freedom marked the passage from dependence to semidependence in the social as well as economic relations of youth. But semidependence also contained a more complex element of alternation between precocious, adultlike independence and demands for childlike subordination. Young people at times experienced a halfway blend of freedom and restraint, with elements of freedom becoming more pronounced over time. But at other points they were exposed to temporally alternating opportunities for independence and adult responsibility on one side and demands for submission on the other. They grew up on a series of separate timetables, with certain elements of social maturity coming much earlier than now, and others much later.[26]

If we label one side of the ledger "precocity," the list of experiences would stretch far down the page. In the churches, for example, the presence of catechetical classes for young people did not release them from the obligation to attend regular services, nor did it exclude them from religious revivals. In the revivals of the early 1800s, teenagers usually played a more prominent role than adults, and even small children of 7 or 8 were not exempt from the religious injunction that "early piety" begin early. The fact that young people had their own self-improvement societies did not exclude them from joining societies which had no minimum or maximum age requirements. A Delaware abolition society formed in 1800 included one teenager, a 14-year-old clock and cabinet maker, three men in their 20s, one in his 30s, two in their 40s, and one in his 50s.[27] As a variation, a society originally formed by and for young men might change itself into a society without age specification. The Young Men's

New York Bible Society, established in 1823 and open to youth under 30, dropped the name "young men" in 1839 and removed its outer age limit.[28] Further, auxiliary and regular organizations could exist side by side. The presence of the Cadets of Temperance for those aged 16 to 21 did not stop the Sons of Temperance from admitting anyone 14 and over to membership, while restricting voting rights to those 18 and over.[29] Finally, in contrast to adult-sponsored youth organizations in the 20th century, the great majority of young people's societies in the early 1800s were voluntary, organized and conducted by young people themselves. Young people occasionally called in adults for assistance, but only for ceremonial or legal purposes. Apprentice associations, for example, customarily sought adult sponsorship, but simply as an expedient; adults could sign legal contracts pertaining to the use of halls and meeting places. Associations were not only of youth and for youth but by youth as well.

Political education also began at an early age. Public political gatherings were likely to attract children and youth as well as adults. The ubiquitous village debating societies were not substitutes for political involvement. Sixteen-year-old Merrill Ober of Monkton, Vermont, passed hour after hour in the village store, talking politics with adults.[30] Charles Turner Torrey attended town meetings with his grandfather when 5 or 6. Samuel Rodman, a New Bedford merchant, took his 13-year-old son to hear Wendell Phillips speak in 1837, just as he allowed his sons to accompany him on his daily business rounds.[31]

Children and young people witnessed the events surrounding death as well as life. Samuel J. May, born in Boston in 1797, related the death of his brother, when Samuel was 4 years old.

> Then they put grave-clothes upon him, and laid him upon the mattress in the best chamber, and straightened out his limbs, and folded his beautiful hands upon his breasts, and covered him only with a clear, cold, white sheet. I saw it all,—for they could not keep me away.[32]

More accurately, "they" did not want to keep him away. Responding to Samuel's desire to see where they put his brother, his uncle took him to the family vault and showed him where his brother and ancestors were entombed. Then "my kind uncle opened one of the coffins, and let me see how decayed the body had become, told me that [my brother] Edward's body was going to decay in like manner, and at last become like the dust of the earth." [33]

Necrophilia? Perhaps, but more likely Samuel's uncle was merely applying an approved psychological principle of the day, that the durability of any impression depended on the force and distinctness of the original perception. According to facultative psychology, the development of memory preceded reason, and childhood was the time to implant both strong impressions and regular habits. Death was as real as life. Everyone died, children included, and the sooner children learned about death the better. A few years later May's father was to justify a severe and probably unjust whipping that Samuel had received in school with the observation that the world was filled with injustice and that Samuel had to be inured to it.

Although evidence is difficult to recover, it seems that even in the early 19th century some parents had scruples against letting children see too many of the events surrounding a death in the family or neighborhood.[34] But even if many parents of that era had been reluctant to expose children to scenes of death, they could hardly have succeeded with any regularity, for people did not usually die in hospitals but at home, right in front of the family. Nor could parents have controlled the content of sermons aimed at youth, which were characterized by the pervasive theme of *memento mori*.

Thus, convention dictated that young people quickly be exposed to the religious, political, and emotional concerns of adults. Yet in other ways the process of maturation was slow. If we return to our ledger and label the other side "delayed development," a fairly long list of experiences can justifiably be included. For one thing, puberty came later than now. Allowing for variations between social classes and acknowledging that generalizations are no more than educated guesses based on the impressions of contemporary physicians, a reasonable estimate would put male puberty at around 16, with female puberty coming a year earlier. (Corresponding ages now would be 14 and 12, again with some qualifications.) Not only did puberty come later, but physical growth was a much more gradual process than now, with final height not attained by young men until around age 25. (Today, young people grow little beyond age 18). The gradual nature of growth helps to explain why contemporaries used terms like "youth" and "young man" to describe those in their 20s. William Gilmore Simms's description of the fictional Ralph Colleton bears comparison with Francis Lieber's description of "W——." Simms wrote: "Our traveller, on the present occasion, was a mere youth. He had probably seen twenty summers—scarcely more. Yet his person was tall and well developed; symmetrical and manly; rather slight, perhaps, as was proper to his immaturity." [35]

Delayed development was not just a matter of the timing of physical growth. Various factors, such as dependence on agriculture, the absence of graded and lubricated educational tracks, and the need to establish personal connections, all conspired to delay young men seeking to enter professions. It seems likely, too, that behind some of the foot-dragging noted earlier was a lack of intense social pressure on young men to decide on vocations. It was one thing to warn against idleness, quite another to exhort young men to break out of familiar molds, leave behind familiar scenes, and push ahead in the scramble for position. After 1840, rising in the world increasingly became a kind of moral injunction on youth; indeed, it was the major conclusion of the success philosophy. But the mandate of success philosophy was only dimly perceived in agricultural communities in the early 1800s.

A no less important feature of early 19th-century society was the emphasis on the subordination of young people. Subordination had many antecedents. It was part of a tradition that decreed that sons and daughters were inferior members of the family hierarchy. It was this tradition which led young men to recall the dignified reserve which their fathers presented to them on so many occasions, and which led boys and girls to send their "duty" rather than their love to parents.[36] The same tradition led fathers to sound like commanding officers when they addressed even mature sons. Although he was 25 years old and living in Boston, Aaron Dennison received the following advice from his father in Maine in 1837:

> I am afraid that you do not have exercise enough to keep you in good health and spirits and to remedy that difficulty as much as possible I should like to have you retire to rest by 9 and rise certainly by 5 in the morning and take a long walk in the morning air at least one hour every morning when it is suitable weather. Don't neglect this for I think it is important.[37]

Finally, the same tradition of hierarchical deference prompted the father of James Duncan to write in his will: "I also *order* my son James to live with his mother until he arrive to twenty-one years of age and to be dutiful to his mother." [38]

Hierarchical deference prevailed within families not only between parents and children but between brothers. Older brothers addressed young ones in letters with the same combination of formality and tutorial attentiveness that characterized addresses from fathers to sons. "You are now in a critical state of life," 24-year-old William Beaumont wrote to his 18-year-old brother in 1809. "Errors and improprieties will beset you on every side in spite of your precautionary efforts to evade them. . . . The strongest and most effectual barrier against these deviations is to cultivate your mind and procure a stock of familiar ideas and useful information." [39]

In the 18th century these attitudes had been rooted in the land base of society and had found their most forceful expression in the intricate provisions of wills by which fathers sought to tie sons to the land. Common in the 18th century, such provisions are less frequently encountered after 1800. But as one traditional technique to establish the subordination of youth declined, others survived, revealing themselves nowhere better than in the widespread use of humiliation and disgrace in schools.[40]

In his essay "Education," Ralph W. Emerson wrote that while many teachers of his day entered the classroom filled with idealism, the size of classes and diversity in age and preparation among students quickly put to flight the nascent aspirations of pedagogues to control their charges by moral influence alone. "Something must be done, and done speedily," Emerson continued, "and in their distress the wisest are tempted to adopt violent means, to proclaim martial law, corporal punishment, mechanical arrangements, bribes, spies, wrath, main strength and ignorance, in place of that wise and genial providential influence they had hoped, and yet hope in some future day to adopt." [41] Perhaps this is what George Moore, the Acton schoolmaster, had in mind when he told his pupils on his first day in class that he intended to " 'conquer or die.' " [42]

Although "main strength" was a popular technique of school discipline, humiliation was usually the favorite weapon of the schoolmaster's arsenal. Joseph Lancaster, originator of the Lancasterian system of education, in which the older boys taught the younger ones, spent pages denouncing corporal punishment before outlining the substitutes dear to his own heart—suspending miscreants from the ceiling in a kind of birdcage, forcing them to march backward around the room with their necks yoked, or pinning signs on their backs naming their transgressions. The birdcage does not appear to have been used in America, but most American children in district schools of the early 19th century knew that "sitting on the wall" meant sitting on thin air (squatting with only the back against the wall for balance), and that "holding nails into the floor" meant to stoop for hours. They also knew what it was like to serve as the master's footstool or to shave publicly with a wooden razor. None of this was new in the 19th century. Puritans in earlier times had been simultaneously skeptical of corporal punishment and great believers in the value of humiliation. Lancaster himself, raised as a Scottish Presbyterian, absorbed a religious tradition distinctive both for its avid belief in the importance of education and in its unshakable commitment to humiliation as a technique of discipline.[43]

Despite the persistence of certain similarities, there was a basic change in the practice of humiliation between the 17th and 19th centuries, for in the earlier period humiliation was part of a larger pattern of social control. If boys held nails into the floor, adults sat in the stocks. By 1830, in contrast, public shaming was no longer a primary method for maintaining social order among adults, but it continued to flourish in the schools—a good example of the tendency, noted by Philippe Ariès, whereby practices once generally accepted survive only among youth.[44] Perhaps because public humiliation prevailed in schools long after its disappearance elsewhere, its application after 1800 resulted increasingly in student mutinies and disruptions.

The school disruption, also called a "breaking-up," a "carrying-out" (of the master), a "turn-out," and a "barring-out," was often little more than a community ritual. This tradition, which gradually declined in the 19th century but which flourished in the small towns and villages of 150 years ago, provided a healthy outlet for pent-up energies in the dreary winter months. Spiced as it is with the flavor of the humorist, Augustus Longstreet's recounting of a fictional turn-out in *Georgia Scenes* is worth recounting. Visiting a Captain Griffen, the author learns that the local schoolboys plan to turn out the master the next day. Griffen urges that they witness the struggle, "for though the master is always upon such occasions, glad to be turned out, and only struggles long enough to present his patrons a fair apology for giving the children a holyday," the boys still will try to prove their valor, "and, in their zeal to distinguish themselves upon such memorable occasions, they sometimes become too rough, and provoke the master to wrath, and a very serious conflict ensues."

On the appointed day of the struggle, the boys arrive first and barricade themselves in the school, called an "academy" but just a long pen with a roof on top. The master, feigning ignorance of the motives of the boys, attacks with a fence rail, punctures a hole in the side of the school, and storms in, over the protests of the "largest boys," the recognized champions of the pupils. Seating himself on the desk, he leans back and puts his feet on a nearby table, thus making himself a perfect target for the next contrivance. The boys grab the master by the leg, carry him out, and wrestle with him in the yard until he finally yields to their pleas for a "holyday." [45]

Sometimes the turn-out had nothing to do with a petition for a holiday but was a forceful response to brutal and self-important masters. R. C. Stone related a local quarrel over school discipline in Rhode Island. His son, aged 15 or 16, was teaching school in Easton when "a few large scholars" grew insubordinate. Their ringleader was expelled, whereupon he appealed to his friends outside the school, young village toughs willing to take matters into their own hands. Breaking into the school, they forced young Stone out. Since it took a court decision to return Stone to his desk, we can label this as more than a community ritual. Similar turn-outs were widespread in the early 19th century, despite sustained criticism of the practice by authorities on school discipline. Horace Mann described the evil as "enormous" and blamed it on the older boys and young men aged 15 to 20, a point on which his contemporaries agreed.[46]

Even in the absence of turn-outs, disorder born of large numbers, disparate ages, late arrivers, and early leavers was routine in district schools. Confronted by a phalanx of indifferent or disgruntled plowboys in school or by their cronies outside, masters often resorted to violence in anticipation of violence, thrashing the ringleader before the trouble began.

Problems inherent to the teacher's position, moreover, exacerbated difficulties caused by the students. In theory, the authority of teachers to keep order was absolute, or nearly so, but in practice authority was conditioned by all sorts of limitations. Many of the teachers were college or academy students on vacation between terms. Often they were younger than their students. Had R. C. Stone's 16-year-old son been teaching in George Moore's Acton school, he would have been younger than more than a third of the students. Schoolmasters were often outsiders who "boarded around" in the community, living by night with the parents of students whom they taught by day. When disputes arose between pupils and teachers, townspeople were likely to remember that they were neighbors and parishioners of the students' families, forgetting their obligations to the teachers. Schoolmasters could not point consistently to any source of authority beyond themselves to sustain their actions. Law courts might help in individual cases, but in the absence of a bureaucracy to administer discipline, pressure fell mainly on the teachers. The school was theirs, to be "kept." [47]

Taken collectively, these factors exerted a number of conflicting pulls and tugs. The physical proximity of teacher and student could facilitate a friendly relationship, but it could also produce a redoubling of efforts to maintain tutorial dignity, Edward Magill, referring to his experience at a country school in 1841, aptly summarized the problem:

> From the opening of the school I was engaged with my pupils in
> games of ball, snow-balling, etc., during the recess, just as one of
> them, but was careful to put on the serious and resolute schoolmas-
> ter's face when I rang the bell for them to reassemble. This acting a
> double part as master and student, was made all the more difficult,
> because my pupils were my own personal friends, relatives, and
> near neighbors, and a number of them, both boys and girls, were
> my seniors by several years.[48]

The experiences of Silas Felton of Marlborough, Massachusetts, illustrate the connection between the proximity of age groups, insecurity
of status, and the administration of discipline. Felton's early life was
typical of New England farm boys of the period. He attended school
periodically, returning to his father whenever called, and enjoyed the
usual rounds of social visiting among the town's young people. Although
at 19 he had no advanced education and was "almost ignorant of the
English grammar," Felton was called upon to teach school in 1795. Meeting with some success in his first engagement, Felton decided to try his
luck again as a teacher. But he concluded that he needed additional
formal education, and thus sought and received permission from his
father to attend a term at Leicester Academy, then conducted by Theodore Dehon, in later life Episcopal bishop of South Carolina but at that
time on winter vacation from Harvard. Dehon and Felton were the same
age, 20, but there the resemblance ceased, for Dehon was a polished college
man, a banker's son, ignorant, according to Felton, of both human nature
and the manners of country people, and overbearing toward his students.[49]
Felton "took" a number of schools after his term at Leicester, but he
was involved in only one notable controversy, brought on by a severe
whipping which he administered to a 10- or 12-year-old boy. The occasion was a lie told by the boy, but the severity of the beating was actually
the result of the boy's refusal to admit the lie:

> I took my ruler, it was a large round ruler made of Cherry tree
> Wood, this I applied to his hand, quite moderately at first, but he
> insisted he was innocent, and they [his accusers] as strongly that he
> was guilty; I repeated the operation of the ruler again to his hand
> till I made him confess the crime and say he was sorry.[50]

After various threats and counterthreats, Felton apologized to the boy's
father. In his reminiscences, Felton justified himself on grounds that he
had administered much more severe beatings in the past. Yet he was
not a martinet by nature, nor an unthinking traditionalist, but a free
thinker of sorts who had never quite gotten over his reading of Thomas
Paine's *Age of Reason* at 16. But, as was likely true of Dehon, his mentor, Felton found that the application of main strength was one of the
few ways in which a teacher without clear and recognized authority
could force students to take him seriously. Interestingly, Felton related
one additional instance of his whipping a boy, his own brother Aaron,

who had boasted that "he wasn't going to mind Silas," until "I whipt him once or twice more and he afterwoods behaved well." [51]

School discipline fell on children and youth alike. Some masters tried to separate younger and older children in seating arrangements, but they had to be in the same room, regardless of age. A teacher who looked across his desk to see a mixture of infants, boys, girls, young men, and young ladies was unlikely to grade his discipline according to the specific age or level of development of the pupil. If anything, he was likely to note that the older boys, the 15- to 20-year-olds, usually made the most trouble and hence had to be brought into line first.

Differences in social class altered the nature but not the fact of subordination. Wealthy and well-educated parents usually held district school education in low esteem; private "select" schools, "family boarding schools," and academies flourished to suit the needs of parents who could pay for a better product. But the difference between education for ordinary people and education for the children of the rich was not that of a hard and severe regimen versus a soft and malleable one, but of the spasmodic discipline of the district school versus the more consistent but still severe discipline of a private institution. James Russell Lowell was the son of a minister who could have educated him at home but who chose instead to send young James to a preparatory boarding school characterized by harsh discipline.[52] Similarly, Samuel J. May was taken from a dame school for young children at 8 years of age and placed in a strict preparatory school, in accordance with his father's desire that he be toughened.[53] As a corollary, wealthy fathers often preferred to send their children away from home for education, just as wealthy merchants elected to send their children out as cabin boys or supercargo.[54]

Before the professionalization of teaching, a process only beginning in the 1820s and without significant effect until much later, there was little to cushion head-to-head collisions between teachers and pupils. The teacher was not the agent of some clearly recognized higher authority; he was not clothed in the panoply of certification, nor even, necessarily, of learning. With their own roles ill-defined, teachers had difficulty finding the right tone to adopt toward students. The anomalies in the teacher's position promoted the disposition to be stiff, formal, and strict, while simultaneously making the exercise of authority appear incongruous and inconsistent to the pupils. Sanctioned as they were by long-standing practice, hierarchical distance and humiliation were also nourished by the very proximity of age groups in the early Republic.[55]

DEFERENCE AND DISORDER
IN AMERICAN COLLEGES

The inconsistent administration of discipline and the alternation of freedom and submission were factors which connected the experience of students in district schools and academies with those of college students. Although they comprised only a small and declining proportion of the population, college students came from a fairly broad range of backgrounds. A few were sons of the very rich, sometimes delinquent sons shipped off to college for the same reasons that their descendants in the 20th century have been packed off to military boarding schools. But many antebellum college students were raw rubes from the villages who had abandoned farming to their less ambitious brothers in order to seek out advanced education. Others were indigents subsidized by the various evangelical benevolent societies to prepare for ministerial careers.[56] The colleges themselves were underfinanced, top-heavy with clergymen, and often intellectually sterile. Yet nowhere else in antebellum America were youth gathered in such a controlled environment, so that the 19th-century college is valuable as a kind of test tube in which to study contemporary assumptions about the behavior of young people.

Any student of antebellum college life has to confront the incongruous mixture of deference, discipline, and authority on one side and "great rout, riot, and disorder" on the other. College discipline revealed a near obsession with order at every turn. The concept of *in loco parentis* does not do justice to the traditional philosophy of college discipline, for with few exceptions those who wrote about college discipline assumed that parental discipline was too mild for the management of large groups of young men. Even Philip Lindsley, generally a humane spokesman for progressive ideals of college government, emphasized that "the government of a family is but an epitome or remote resemblance to that which obtains in a college."[57] *In loco parentis* was at most an ideal worth pursuing, at worst a corrupt philosophy, but on no count a description of the norm.[58]

Two reasons were usually given for the inadequacy of the concept of parentalism. First, in America parental discipline was too mild; it was not even good enough at home.[59] Second—and this argument had deep roots in the history of educational institutions—whatever might be said about young men as individuals, in groups they were a menace to themselves and to society. Pedagogues had associated for centuries "congregate" or "public" education, the education of youth in groups, with moral danger and had agreed on the need for strict supervision. Few administrators seriously believed that young people could be managed in colleges along parental lines, but at the same time few were willing to abandon the promotional value of advertising a mild system of discipline. The blurb of the College of East Tennessee was both a vivid expression of this dilemma and, incidentally, a classic of double-talk:

> The administration of the government of the College shall ever be mild and equitable, and as nearly parental as the nature of the establishment will admit. The reformation of the offender shall be steadily and judiciously aimed at, as far as practicable; and no severe or disgraceful penalty shall be awarded, except when the paramount interests of the Institution shall demand it, or when the flagitious character of the offence shall render it indispensable.[60]

Or, as the latitudinarian minister told his parishioners, if one sins, as it were, and does not repent, so to speak, one shall be damned, to a certain extent.

To supplement parental discipline, American colleges had issued lists of rules and regulations from their earliest days, modeled first on the statutes of English universities and later on each other. By 1800 the rule books which students were expected to sign left little to the imagination. Not content with outlining acceptable behavior, some even prescribed the curriculum. The Hamilton College laws of 1802 consisted of eleven chapters of seven to twenty-three sections each.[61] An element of exquisite detail marked some of the manuals. At Yale in the 18th century, students were forbidden to wear hats within five rods of tutors and eight rods of professors.[62] In general, the regulations had four aims. First, they prescribed behavior in chapel and classroom, often requiring daily attendance at both. Second, they limited freedom of movement from the environs of the college, prohibiting students from leaving town without the permission of the president or from going to the village during study hours. Third, they sought to safeguard students from each other by outlawing knives and guns. Finally, they forbade loud noises, the playing of musical instruments during study hours, idle conversation around doors and gates, gambling, and drinking.[63]

To ensure that the rules were obeyed, colleges provided a wide range of graduated penalties. At the bottom of the scale were private admonitions and fines, leading up to public admonition, forced public confession, suspension, rustication, and expulsion. Practices varied from college to college and between the 18th and 19th centuries. Public whippings, permissible in 17th-century and early 18th-century colleges, passed out of use in the latter part of the 18th century. At times, degradation to a lower class was added to other penalties. But at any period the college functioned in theory more like a petty despotism than like a family. The system of penalties was parental only in the sense that admonition was to precede the application of more severe penalties.

If a preoccupation with deference and authority formed one pole of antebellum college life, the other was marked by a mixture of pranks, violence, and rebellion by students. There had always been some petty harassment of college officials in the form of ringing the college bell all night, sticking dead ducks in the chapel, and snowball fights leading to broken windows. Pranks like this continued in the late 18th and early 19th centuries, with some refinements of the art. A Princeton president who commenced chapel by opening his Bible to the appropriate passage found a pack of cards staring up at him. South Carolina College students often "defiled" the pulpit, presumably with urine. At Dickinson College, Moncure Conway got even with an overbearing president by informing authorities at Staunton, Virginia, where the president was attending a church meeting, that a harmless lunatic who fancied himself the president of Dickinson College had escaped from custody, was thought to be in the Staunton area, and should be confined at once to the local asylum. A Providence farmer one morning found his horse and wood transported to the top of University Hall at Brown; later, President Asa Messer's horse made an overnight stand at the same elevation, courtesy of young Samuel Gridley Howe.[64]

The difference after 1750, however, lay less in the perfection of traditional twitting than in an increase of violence to persons and the emergence of organized student rebellions. At Yale, when President Thomas Clap—"a Tirant and a sovraign," the students said—overreacted to tormentors who wrecked his sleep by ringing the college bell, the result was continuous rebellion between 1760 and 1766, when Clap finally resigned.[65] At Brown, students stoned Messer's house almost nightly in the 1820s.[66] Harvard had a riot over bad bread in the commons in 1766, a "bread and butter riot" in 1805 over the same thing, and a "great Rebellion" in 1823.[67] During a riot at Princeton in 1807 the faculty lost control and had to call in the townspeople for help. At Virginia, Thomas Jefferson, who originally had hoped that the university would be run more or less without rules, lived long enough to see a number of students expelled for "vicious irregularities." Had he lived longer, he would have seen much worse: repeated insurrection, culminating in the murder of Professor Nathaniel Davis by a student in 1840.[68]

Student violence was not exclusively directed against people in authority. Beatings of blacks and servants and fights between students were frequent. At South Carolina College in 1833, two students fought a duel; one was killed, the other maimed for life. Two of the leading politicians in the state served as seconds, a curious example of young and old mingling in a common cause.[69] Fist and knife fights were more common than formal duels. In 1799 a North Carolina student was publicly whipped for stabbing another student, but the whipping did not deter others from similar offenses in subsequent years.[70] The long war between the rival literary societies at Chapel Hill was not always a war of words.[71] Nor were fights between students confined to the South. The rebellion of 1823 at Harvard, which ended in a confrontation between students and faculty, began as a struggle between rival student factions.

The faculty, however, being the nearest authority, received more than its share of abuse. Davis's case at Virginia was exceptional only in its outcome. Eight years before Davis was murdered, a proctor at Virginia had investigated a loud noise on the lawn, only to encounter a crowd of students parading in disguise. His remonstrances were met first by threats, then by a barrage of rocks. Professor Harrison was beaten by a student in 1830, and horsewhipped by two students in the presence of a hundred bystanders in 1839. A year earlier, Professor Blaetterman had been attacked by a student in his classroom.[72] No wonder Henry Barnard called Virginia students a "set of pretty wild fellows." At the University of North Carolina in 1850 a number of drunken students stoned two professors who presumed to interfere in their revels, forcing the teachers to take refuge in a barricaded room.[73] At Davidson in the 1850s students rioted over a difficult assignment and showered professors with stones. Amos Kendall related how Dartmouth students in the 1820s attacked professors' homes, blasting out the windows with shotguns.[74] Philip Lindsley summed up the situation crisply:

> They [students] form a party by themselves—a distinct interest of their own—view with suspicion every measure or movement of the faculty—and resolve to contravene and thwart their plans as far as it may be in their power.[75]

What was behind antebellum student disorders? Why was the period between 1790 and 1840 (or, more broadly, between 1750 and 1850) filled with such extraordinary turmoil? In the late 19th century, college officials who were familiar with past disorders often claimed that antebellum student riots were the result of attempts to apply an absurdly severe system of discipline on young men. This "argument from repression" held that antebellum students led such monkish lives and groaned under the weight of such an elaborate pyramid of rules that their human instincts drove them into periodic and desperate spasms of violence before they sank back, exhausted and defeated, into apathy. This interpretation helps to explain some aspects of antebellum student life. The petty enforcement of petty rules *was* galling, not only at pioneer universities like Indiana, where professors were determined to turn half-literate backwoodsmen into polished gentlemen, but at Harvard and Yale too. Our knowledge of the agents of discipline—professors, presidents, and tutors—lends further support to the argument from repression, for these men were often unsuited by temperament to their tasks. Too many of them were overbearing and officious, inordinately fond of the prerogatives of petty power. Probably more pious than the average person and certainly more likely to be a minister, the old-time college president often had trouble keeping perspective on student mischief. He was scandalized when others might have been indifferent or tolerantly amused. Professors and tutors often lacked the self-assurance to stay calm before taunts and indignities; indeed, they viewed themselves as islands of cultivation in a sea of barbarism. Moreover, many of those charged with the administration of discipline were young themselves, scarcely older than the students. Tutors were usually recent graduates, often younger than many of the students. To a lesser extent, the same was true of professors and presidents. Joseph Caldwell, who presided over the chaos at Chapel Hill, was only 24 when he became president. In itself, the youthfulness of the authorities could have cut either way. It might have induced tutors and professors to adopt a chummy stance toward the students, but more often it had the opposite effect, leading officials to assume the air of stiff-necked martinets.

Although the argument from repression does fit some features of antebellum student life, its defects are manifold. The argument ignores the role played in antebellum student upheavals by the changing composition of student bodies. Most of the students in 17th- and early 18th-century colleges had been teenagers, and most were preparing to become ministers. The latter part of the 18th century, in contrast, witnessed the beginning of an influx of older and poorer students, many of whom did not intend to become ministers. The presence of an abundance of young men in their 20s in colleges was the result of the same social forces that were delaying the entrance of young men into professions. The growth of towns and the pressure on available land in northern states were transforming the expectations of young men and propelling many from the plow and workbench into colleges. Changes in the student population put new kinds of stress on the traditional system of tutorial watchfulness, for economic necessity forced poor students to seek work outside the college walls. Meanwhile, the enforcement of petty rules infuriated older students, who resented the imposition of a kind of authority more suited to schoolboys than to young adults.[76]

The argument from repression also ignores the amount of real freedom experienced by the students. Because professors and presidents were much more concerned with the moral than with the intellectual development of students, for example, they usually were indifferent to the intellectual subculture that emerged at most colleges in the form of literary societies, such as the Linonian at Yale, the Jefferson at the University of Virginia, and the Philogian at Williams. Literary societies provided students with the very things that they could not find in class or commons: privacy, conviviality, and intellectual stimulation. In the literary societies, students gave speeches in the style of Webster and Choate, debated slavery and antislavery, and read romantic poets like Byron. The unofficial *Vernunft* of the literary societies flourished without really challenging the official *Verstand* which reigned in the classroom. The narrowness of the official curriculum was actually an advantage, for all the students were obliged to do was to prepare for recitation in class, an enterprise less time-consuming than working through the reading lists found in many 20th century colleges. While colleges in theory sought to become totally regulated environments, they were in practice willing to allow a significant role to self-cultivation. Throughout the antebellum period a lively extracurriculum thrived alongside a stuffy curriculum in American colleges.[77]

Antebellum students also enjoyed a respectable degree of social freedom. Unchaperoned dating was the norm, whether in the form of the parlor visit, the moonlight walk, or the sleigh ride.[78] The increasing tendency of students to board not in commons but in the town provided an added degree of social freedom. For financial reasons newer colleges often lacked residential facilities; so did some of the older colleges, such as the University of Pennsylvania.[79] Even at institutions with commons—Harvard and South Carolina, for example—students won the right to board out.[80] Like other aspects of student freedom, residential freedom lacked a theoretical justification. It just happened.

In addition, even the enforcement of moral rules was often fitful. Rule books embodying Puritan assumptions about ideal behavior also betrayed the pragmatic side of the Puritan mentality, the candid if usually unspoken recognition that gaps between real and ideal behavior were rarely bridged in this world. Puritans and pietists had always been inclined to announce a set of elevated ideals and then to assume that most individuals would miss the mark. Even President Clap of Yale, probably the most autocratic college president in 18th-century America, routinely ignored a range of petty offenses.[81] The best illustration of the dualism, however, was the rigid and detailed system of fines which prevailed in colonial colleges and survived into the early 19th century, for such a mechanical system assumed that students would go right on committing petty misdemeanors.

Dualistic assumptions about behavior were not the only mitigating factors in college discipline. Although their paper authority was nearly limitless, college officials in the early 1800s often had little practical power to respond to offenses. There were too many colleges, and they needed students more than students needed them.[82] The system of fines, whatever might be asserted in its defense, was best suited to minor infractions by individuals, not to violent felonies by student mobs. As violent disruptions increased, administrators resorted to suspensions, which students were usually willing to risk, and expulsions, which could be more costly to the college than to students. Even well-established colleges like Harvard, which responded to mass disorders with mass expulsions, found themselves on the brink of disaster.[83]

If this result was occasionally missed by professors, it did not escape trustees, who often reinstated students expelled by the faculty. Because they needed students, moreover, college officials tempered the application of authority not only by reinstating miscreants but also by widespread resort to the notorious dismission-readmission or "out-in" loophole. That is, students expelled from one university were admitted somewhere else, usually with little more than a statement of repentance or evidence, almost any sort of evidence, that they had been victimized by arbitrary authority.[84]

Merely to note that antebellum students had various types of practical freedom does not invalidate the idea that the application of rules caused disruptions, for authority administered fitfully can be more contemptible than the mailed fist. But recognition of the real limits of authority in antebellum colleges does put matters into a new perspective, and underscores similarities between the maintenance of authority in colleges and in district schools or academies. In each case discipline was inconsistent and the experience of it discontinuous.

In one respect, however, colleges were unique, for their students were more conscious of their own status as students than were their counterparts in other institutions, perhaps because colleges had virtually the only students in America for whom studentship was a chronologically continuous experience. This growing self-consciousness among college students affected the morphology of student rebellion. Usually there was an original spark, often a confrontation between students and professors over some trivial matter, but the uprisings which afflicted institutions as different as Harvard and the University of Virginia really began not with the unruly incident but with a threat by the students to leave the institution if a penalty applied to one of the original malefactors was not rescinded. The threat to quit was, in turn, usually contained in a remonstrance or petition drawn up by students and marked by lengthy declarations of their rights both as men and as students. Although not ideological in the sense that they sought to change the larger society, student remonstrants did seek to ground their case in the accepted political rhetoric of the day. An official at the University of North Carolina aptly summarized the content of the petitions and the faculty's reply to them when he complained in 1805 that

> nothing can be more ridiculous than *Boys at school* talking of "sacred regard for their rights," "the high and imposing duty of

resistance," and of "denouncing laws," etc., the genuine slang of the times, culled from the columns of newspapers.[85]

Student rebellions in the form of mass threats to leave posed a serious challenge to college authority, both in practice and in theory: in practice, because a successful rebellion could wreck an institution; in theory, because rebels, in effect, placed their horizontal allegiance to peers above their vertical allegiance to authorities. As such, the issue created by student rebellion bore on a second issue, whether a student could be held accountable for refusing to inform on another student. Few issues so well illustrated the dilemma faced by antebellum college government. College authorities had long insisted that loyalty to peers could never take precedence over loyalty to college government. Although college officials had traditionally promoted hazing and fagging, they had done so merely to develop a young man's loyalty to his class as the first step in introducing him to the hierarchical society of the college. Before freshmen could recognize the prerogatives of seniors and seniors those of professors, each group in the traditional view had to discover itself as a group.[86] Promotion of hazing had never involved acceptance of the idea that colleges should become self-governing junior republics, or tolerance for peer loyalty as such. Accordingly, officials dismissed student insistence on the absolute value of peer loyalty as no more than a "low principle of school boy ethics," while acknowledging with chagrin that students viewed it as "the depth of dishonour to testify when called upon by college authorities against the grossest violator not only of collegiate but municipal law." [87]

The intrinsic weakness of tutorial espionage in detecting infractions, coupled with the increasing number of infractions after 1800, brought the issue to a head. Tutors and professors cut preposterous figures when they went snooping. "The Old Brick resounds very frequently," a Brown student wrote, "with the breaking of glass bottles against Tudor T.'s door, if he can be called a tutor. We have given him the epithet of Weazle. He is frequently peeking through the knotholes and cracks to watch his prey." [88] If it was night, or if the student was wearing a mask or his hat over his brow, professors who gave chase to fleeting shadows might be left at the end out of breath and without a shred of evidence. Hence, the administration often told students to surrender offenders, and students often said that it was dishonorable to do so.

Both in their rebellions and in their refusal to inform on their peers, antebellum students were expressing a level of self-consciousness that had no precedent before 1750. Antebellum students continued to accept the hierarchical nature of college government, but at the same time they sought to delineate a sphere of independence for themselves. They accepted many petty rules, and even when they broke petty rules, they accepted punishment. The routine administration of discipline produced major rebellions only when the faculty tried to force students to testify against each other or when the faculty intruded in an area of student life that the students viewed as private. The rebellions at the University of

Virginia, for example, grew out of the following incidents: (1) in 1833 the faculty passed an antiriot law which provided that during any disturbance students must return to their rooms on signal from their professors and that absence from one's rooms after the signal would be proof of participation in the disturbance; (2) in 1836 the faculty sought to establish control over a student volunteer military company organized several years previously; and (3) in the spring of 1845 the faculty attempted to suppress an organization known as the Calathumpian Band, a group of students who paraded and serenaded at night. In each of these cases students perceived the intrusion of arbitrary authority. The antiriot law was ex post facto; it had not been part of the rules students signed at matriculation. In forming a volunteer military company, students were doing what young men anywhere in the country were able to do. The Calathumpian Band had been allowed by the faculty to flourish for nearly six months before action was taken.[89]

Lewis S. Feuer and others have argued that antebellum student disorders were not politically motivated.[90] This observation is correct in the sense that disputes over political issues of the day rarely occasioned student uprisings. But antebellum students often used the political ideology of human rights to establish that studentship was a limited status, or that faculty rules could go just so far and no further. A considerable distance separates the ideology of antebellum students from that of student radicals in the 1960s, but an equally great distance demarcates students between 1790 and 1840 from their predecessors in the 17th and 18th centuries.

CONCLUSION

Regardless of the type of school they attended—district school, academy, or college—young people frequently encountered alternating currents of oppression and freedom. These two poles were related in a symbiotic way. David Rothman has observed that the Draconian quality of colonial criminal law actually reflected the feebleness of police authority in the 18th century rather than the inhumanity of the lawmakers.[91] In a similar way, the practical limits of school authority reinforced the stiffness of pedagogues and contributed to the verbal despotism of the college rule books.

These observations about discipline apply directly only to schools and colleges, institutions which many young people either never attended at all or attended only sporadically. Yet there were similarities between school discipline and the sort of discipline encountered in occupations or families. The tendency of young people to shift from apprenticeship to apprenticeship, the sporadic home leavings and returns, the loose routine of the district schools, the disposition of students to shift academies every few years, and the ability of college students to defy authority were all part of a pattern of slack control over youth tempered only by occasional obtrusions of overbearing authority. Uncompromising in expression, authority was often compromised in application.

Some aspects of the social experience of youth in the early Republic were present long before 1800. The emphasis on humiliation, for example, was a feature of Puritan social discipline in the 17th century. Moreover, the necessity to leave home had long given young people certain types of practical freedom. But in the balance between freedom and oppression, the elements added after 1790 were increasingly on the side of freedom. The growing self-consciousness and radicalism of college students was as much a sign of the direction of change as was the tendency of young men after 1790 to leave home and to "start in life" at earlier ages.

After the middle of the 19th century, Americans shaped an image of the rural past as a time when young people were firmly in their place, subordinated to the wise exercise of authority and bound tightly by affective relationships to family and community. This image of the rural past became a powerful motive force behind the construction of adult-sponsored institutions for youth in the 1890s and early 1900s. So compelling was this image that the architects of institutions for city youth returned to the countryside after 1910 and sought to provide village and farm youth with surrogate experiences of the rural past. Ironically, most of the architects of adult-sponsored youth organizations at the end of the 19th century were born after 1850 and possessed little understanding of the past whose qualities they sought to recreate. Convinced that communal warmth and subordination had been characteristics of the past, they missed all the elements of tension and conflict between age groups and ignored the footloose ways of antebellum youth. Yet these misperceptions were themselves significant, for they legitimized the efforts of youth workers around 1900 to define the peripatetic habits and expressions of independence among the youth of their own day as deviant and pathological.

NOTES

[1] Warren S. Thompson and P. K. Whelpton, *Population Trends in the United States* (New York, 1933), chap. 4.

[2] Charles G. Sommers, *Memoir of the Rev. John Stanford, D.D.* (New York, 1835), p. 80; Asa Cummings, *A Memoir of the Rev. Edward Payson, D.D., Late of Portland, Maine* (New York, 1830), p. 273.

[3] Marcus Cunliffe, *Soldiers and Civilians: The Martial Spirit in America, 1775–1865* (Boston, 1968).

[4] Mary R. Cabot, ed., *Annals of Brattleboro, 1681–1895*, 2 vols. (Brattleboro, 1921–1922), vol. 1, p. 325.

[5] *The History of Warren County, Ohio* (Chicago, 1882), p. 342.

[6] Cunliffe, *Soldiers and Civilians*, p. 238.

[7] Ibid., p. 226.

[8] On youthful enlistments in the Continental Army, see *Memorial of Mr. David L. Dodge, Consisting of an Autobiography, . . . With a Few Selections From His Writings* (Boston, 1854), pp. 19–20.

9 Susan R. Hull, *Boy Soldiers of the Confederacy* (New York, 1905); see also *Ages of U.S. Volunteer Soldiery* (New York, 1886), p. 6; "The Evils of Youthful Enlistments—and Nostalgia," *American Journal of Insanity* 19 (April 1863):476.

10 Levi W. Leonard and Joseph L. Seward, *History of Dublin, New Hampshire* (Dublin, 1920), p. 547.

11 Andrew D. White, *An Autobiography*, 2 vols. (New York, 1906), vol. 1, p. 14; *The Reminiscences of Neal Dow: Recollections of Eighty Years* (Portland, Me., 1898), p. 60; James M. Miller, *The Genesis of Western Culture: The Upper Ohio Valley, 1800–1825* (Columbus, Ohio, 1938), pp. 143–144, 153–154; John L. Thomas, *The Liberator: William Lloyd Garrison—A Biography* (Boston, 1963), pp. 28–30; John S. Stone, *A Memoir of the Life of James Milnor, D.D.* (New York, 1849), p. 17.

12 Carl Bode, *The American Lyceum: Town Meeting of the Mind* (New York, 1956), pp. 64, 73, 145, 151, 172, 196–200; Paul W. Stoddard, "The American Lyceum," Ph. D. thesis, history, Yale University (1947), p. 273.

13 *Catalogue of the Library of the Young Men's Association of the City of Milwaukee* (Milwaukee, 1861), pp. 12–14.

14 *Reminiscences of Neal Dow*, p. 60; *Life and Letters of Horace Bushnell* (New York, 1880), p. 19; Wilmer Atkinson, *An Autobiography* (Philadelphia, 1920), p. 61; John S. Stone, *A Memoir of the Life of James Milnor, D.D.*, p. 17.

15 Frank B. Kingsbury, *History of the Town of Surry, Cheshire County, New Hampshire* (Surry, 1925), p. 226. I have drawn a sample of 40 of the 65 members, using family registers in Kingsbury for dates of birth.

16 Charles H. Miller, "The Order of Cadets of Temperance," in *One Hundred Years of Temperance Work* (New York, 1886), p. 527.

17 Rena L. Vassar, ed., "The Life or Biography of Silas Felton, Written by Himself," *Proceedings of the American Antiquarian Society* 19, pt. 2 (October 21, 1959):127.

18 On the European origins of the tradition of youthful parody, see John R. Gillis, *Youth and History: Tradition and Change in European Age Relations, 1770–Present* (New York, 1974), pp. 25–26; Barrett Wendell, *Cotton Mather: The Puritan Priest* (Cambridge, 1926), p. 241; Joseph Walker, *Hopewell Village: A Social and Economic History of an Iron-Making Community* (Philadelphia, 1966), pp. 386–387; Marion N. Rawson, *New Hampshire Borns a Town* (New York, 1942), pp. 244–245.

19 *The Autobiography of Brantley York* (Durham, N.C., 1910), p. 9.

20 *Journals of Hezekiah Prince, Jr., 1822–1828*, introduced by Walter M. Whitehill (New York, 1965), pp. viii–ix, 49, 311, 341.

21 William Stickney, ed., *Autobiography of Amos Kendall* (Boston, 1872), p. 3. The autobiography is written in the third person.

22 "Letters of the Four Beatty Brothers of the Continental Army,

1774–1794," *Pennsylvania Magazine of History and Biography* 44 (July 1920):225.

23 Ibid., 214.

24 *Journals of Hezekiah Prince, Jr.*, p. 49; John Frisch, "Youth Culture in America, 1790–1860," Ph.D. thesis, history, University of Missouri (1970), pt. 4.

25 Philander Stevens, *Recollections and Incidents of a Lifetime, or Men and Things I Have Seen* (Brooklyn, 1896), pp. 22–24; see also "Mrs. Ballard's Diary," in Charles E. Nash, *The History of Augusta* (Augusta, Me., 1904), p. 271.

26 I am indebted to Mr. William J. Gilmore for the timetable analogy.

27 Monte A. Calvert, "The Abolition Society of Delaware, 1801–1807," *Delaware History* 10 (October 1963):301, note 25.

28 Henry D. Dwight, *The Centennial History of the American Bible Society* (New York, 1916), pp. 93–94.

29 *Constitutions of the Order of the Sons of Temperance of North America* (Boston, 1865).

30 Wilson O. Clough, "A Journal of Village Life in Vermont in 1848," *New England Quarterly* 1 (January 1928):39.

31 J. C. Lovejoy, *Memoir of Rev. Charles T. Torrey* (Boston, 1847), p. 3; Zephaniah W. Pease, ed., *The Diary of Samuel Rodman: A New Bedford Chronicle of Thirty-Seven Years, 1821–1859* (New Bedford, 1927), pp. 170–171.

32 *Memoir of Samuel J. May* (Boston, 1873), p. 6.

33 Ibid.; Lewis O. Saum, "Death in the Popular Mind of Pre–Civil War America," *American Quarterly* 26 (December 1974):477–496.

34 Henry Ware, Jr., "Recollections of Jotham Anderson," in *The Works of Henry Ware, Jr., D.D.*, 4 vols. (Boston, 1846), vol. 1, p. 10.

35 On the estimates of physicians, see Edward H. Dixon, *Woman and Her Diseases From the Cradle to the Grave*, 10th ed. (Philadelphia, 1864), p. 19; Jonathan S. Wilson, *Woman's Home Book of Health: A Work for Mothers and for Families* (Philadelphia, 1860), pp. 5–9; James Copland, *A Dictionary of Practical Medicine*, 5 vols. (New York, 1847), vol. 5, pp. 959–960; ibid., vol. 4, p. 325. J. M. Tanner presented a series of estimates of the age of menarche in 19th-century Europe in "Sequence, Tempo, and Individual Variation in the Growth and Development of Boys and Girls Aged Twelve to Sixteen," *Daedalus* (Fall 1971):907–930. The age of menarche went as high as 18 in Scandinavia during the 19th century, but I have found no evidence in the comments of physicians that it was equally high in America. In 1900 the age of menarche was significantly lower in America than in Europe (ibid., p. 929). On attainment of height, see ibid., p. 928. As late as 1904, G. Stanley Hall was able to assemble evidence that Annapolis cadets and Amherst students did not attain final height

until their mid-20s; see his *Adolescence: Its Psychology and Its Relations to Physiology, Anthropology, Sociology, Sex, Crime, Religion and Education,* 2 vols. (New York, 1905), vol. 1, pp. 26–28; William G. Simms, *Guy Rivers, a Tale of Georgia,* rev. ed. (New York, 1860), p. 16.

[36] William C. Gannett, *Ezra Stiles Gannett, Unitarian Minister in Boston, 1824–1871* (Boston, 1875), p. 9.

[37] Quoted in Charles W. Moore, *Timing a Century: History of the Waltham Watch Company* (Cambridge, 1945), p. 5.

[38] James D. Phillips, "James Duncan of Haverhill," *Essex Institute Historical Collections* 88 (January 1952):2.

[39] Jesse S. Myer, *Life and Letters of Dr. William Beaumont,* introduced by Sir William Osler (St. Louis, 1939), p. 18.

[40] Alexis de Tocqueville, *Democracy in America,* Henry Reeve text, rev. Francis Bowen, ed. Phillips Bradley, 2 vols. (New York, 1945), vol. 2, pp. 202–208.

[41] Ralph W. Emerson, "Education," in *Complete Works,* 12 vols. in 6 (New York, 1929), vol. 10, pp. 152–153.

[42] George Moore, "Diaries," 4 vols. (Harvard College Library), vol. 1, January 1, 1829.

[43] Joseph Lancaster, *The British System of Education, Being a Complete Epitome of the Improvements and Inventions Practised by Joseph Lancaster* (Washington, D.C., 1812); Warren H. Small, *Early New England Schools* (New York, 1969), p. 388; William S. Heywood, ed., *Autobiography of Adin Ballou* (Lowell, Mass., 1890), p. 22; Henry C. Wright, *A Human Life, Illustrated in My Individual Experience As a Child, a Youth, and a Man* (Boston, 1849), p. 50.

[44] Philippe Ariès, *Centuries of Childhood: A Social History of Family Life,* trans. Robert Baldick (New York, 1962), pp. 92–99.

[45] Augustus B. Longstreet, *Georgia Scenes, Character, Incidents, Etc., in the First Half Century of the Republic,* 2nd ed. (New York, 1850), pp. 75–80. For a similar narrative of a turn-out, see Hubert M. Skinner, ed., *The Schoolmaster in Literature,* introduced by Edward Eggleston (New York, 1882), pp. 553, 557–558; see also Joseph C. Guild, *Old Times in Tennessee* (Nashville, 1878), pp. 329–336; J. E. Godbey, *Lights and Shadows of Seventy Years* (St. Louis, 1913), pp. 10–11; "Account of the 'Barring-out' of President James Blair of the College of William and Mary," in Edgar W. Knight, ed., *A Documentary History of Education in the South before 1860,* 5 vols. (Chapel Hill, 1949–1953), vol. 1, pp. 474–476; Warren Burton, *The District School As It Was* (Boston, 1833), pp. 118–123.

[46] R. C. Stone, *Life-Incidents of Home, School and Church* (St. Louis, 1874), pp. 121–125. Charles F. Moore described brutal fights between teachers and pupils at a school in Massachusetts in the 1840s in his *A Sketch of My Life* (Cambridge, 1927), p. 5; for Horace Mann's comments, see *Fourth Annual Report of the* [Massachusetts] *Board of Education, Together With the Fourth*

Annual Report of the Secretary of the Board (Boston, 1841), pp. 86–88.

47 Some progressive ideas about school government were in the air by 1840, although progressives readily acknowledged that any attempts to upgrade the position of teachers or the quality of schools would meet resistance; see Alonzo Potter and George B. Emerson, *The School and Schoolmaster* (New York, 1842).

48 Edward H. Magill, *Sixty-Five Years in the Life of a Teacher* (Boston, 1907), p. 11.

49 Vassar, ed., "Silas Felton," 142.

50 Ibid.

51 Ibid.

52 Martin Duberman, *James Russell Lowell* (Boston, 1966), pp. 14–15.

53 *Memoir of Samuel J. May*, pp. 25–26.

54 Otis P. Lord, "Memoir of Asahel Huntington," *Historical Collections of the Essex Institute* 11 (July–October 1871):83.

55 It should be added that, during the antebellum era, even spokesmen for progressive ideals of education made the establishment of order in the classroom the first priority.

56 David F. Allmendinger, Jr., *Paupers and Scholars: The Transformation of Student Life in Nineteenth-Century New England* (New York, 1975), chaps. 3–5.

57 Philip Lindsley, *An Address Delivered at Nashville, January 12, 1825, at the Inauguration of the President of Cumberland College* (Nashville, 1825), p. 40.

58 Ibid.

59 "College Instruction and Discipline," *American Quarterly Review* 9 (June 1831):231.

60 Quoted in Knight, ed., *Documentary History*, vol. 3, p. 231.

61 George P. Schmidt, *The Old Time College President* (New York, 1930), p. 79; *Documentary History of Hamilton College* (Clinton, N.Y., 1922), pp. 136–154; "Harvard College Records, Part I," *Publications of the Colonial Society of Massachusetts* 15 (1925):187.

62 Charles E. Cunningham, *Timothy Dwight, 1752–1817: A Biography* (New York, 1942), p. 253.

63 Walter W. Jennings, *Transylvania: Pioneer University of the West* (New York, 1955), pp. 116–118.

64 Thomas J. Wertenbaker, *Princeton, 1746–1896* (Princeton, 1946), pp. 155–156; James H. Morgan, *Dickinson College: The History of One Hundred and Fifty Years, 1783–1933* (Carlisle, Pa., 1933), p. 296; Maximilian La Borde, *History of South Carolina College* (Charleston, 1874), p. 130; Walter C. Bronson, *The History of Brown University, 1746–1914* (Providence, 1914), p. 184.

65 Louis L. Tucker, *Puritan Protagonist: President Thomas Clap of Yale College* (Chapel Hill, 1962), pp. 232–261.

66 Bronson, *History of Brown University*, pp. 188–189.

67 Samuel E. Morison, *Three Centuries of Harvard, 1636–1936* (Cambridge, 1965), pp. 118, 133, 208–210, 211–212, 252–254.

[68] Wertenbaker, *Princeton*, pp. 138–140; Philip A. Bruce, *History of the University of Virginia, 1819–1919: The Lengthened Shadow of One Man*, 5 vols. (New York, 1920–1922), vol. 2, pp. 306–311, 267–293.

[69] "J. Marion Simms Reports a Duel in South Carolina College, 1833," in Knight, ed., *Documentary History*, vol. 3, p. 70.

[70] Kemp P. Battle, *History of the University of North Carolina*, 2 vols. (Raleigh, 1907), vol. 1, p. 194.

[71] Ibid., pp. 266–267.

[72] Bruce, *History of the University of Virginia*, vol. 2, p. 293.

[73] Battle, *History of the University of North Carolina*, vol. 1, p. 619.

[74] Cornelius R. Shaw, *Davidson College* (New York, 1923), p. 77; Stickney, ed., *Autobiography of Amos Kendall*, p. 33.

[75] Lindsley, *Address Delivered at Nashville*, p. 41.

[76] David F. Allmendinger, Jr., "The Dangers of Ante-Bellum Student Life," *Journal of Social History* 7 (Fall 1973):75–83.

[77] Ernest Earnest, *Academic Procession: An Informal History of the American College, 1636–1953* (Indianapolis, 1953), pp. 83–96; James McLachlan, "The *Choice of Hercules:* American Student Societies in the Early 19th-Century," in Lawrence Stone, ed., *The University in Society*, 2 vols. (Princeton, 1975), vol. 1, pp. 449–494.

[78] Earnest, *Academic Procession*, pp. 108–112.

[79] Frederick Rudolph, *The American College and University: A History* (New York, 1962), pp. 98–99.

[80] La Borde, *History of South Carolina College*, p. 146.

[81] Tucker, *Puritan Protagonist*, p. 238.

[82] Frederick Rudolph, *The American College and University: A History*, pp. 218–219; Schmidt, *Old Time College President*, p. 87; Daniel W. Hollis, *University of South Carolina*, 2 vols. (Columbia, 1951), vol. 1, pp. 56–59.

[83] Morison, *Three Centuries of Harvard*, pp. 253–254.

[84] Charles Wall, "Students and Student Life at the University of Virginia, 1826–1860," Ph.D. thesis, history, University of Virginia (forthcoming), chap. 5.

[85] Quoted in Battle, *History of the University of North Carolina*, vol. 1, p. 212; see also Wall, "Students and Student Life," chap. 5; Morison, *Three Centuries of Harvard*, pp. 118, 231, and passim.

[86] Tucker, *Puritan Protagonist*, p. 79; Josiah Quincy, *History of Harvard University*, 2 vols. (Boston, 1840), vol. 2, p. 277.

[87] "College Instruction and Discipline," 295.

[88] Bronson, *History of Brown University*, p. 152.

[89] Wall, "Students and Student Life," chap. 6.

[90] Lewis S. Feuer, *The Conflict of Generations: The Character and Significance of Student Movements* (New York, 1969), chap. 7.

[91] David J. Rothman, *The Discovery of the Asylum: Social Order and Disorder in the New Republic* (Boston, 1971), pp. 50–52.

Sex Roles and Social Stress in Jacksonian America

CARROLL SMITH-ROSENBERG

As we observed in an earlier selection on childbirth practices, among the changes in American society in the eighteenth century was the transformation of women's roles. While nurturing and educating children became women's primary concern, this responsibility was invested with new importance: children were no longer regarded as miniature adults but as special creatures needing protective maternal care. The redefinition of child rearing as primarily a female responsibility also reflected a shift in the location of men's work. As America became an industrial and urban nation in the nineteenth century, the locus of men's labor changed from the farm, where men had always been in close contact with their wives and children throughout the day, to the factory or the office, where they saw nothing of their families from early morning to evening, six days a week. Domestic authority and responsibility fell more heavily upon women as a consequence of this alteration in the nature of men's work.

At the same time, women were forced into a narrower sphere of activity, especially if they rose into the middle class. Where once the family had worked together as an economic unit, now the husband was the breadwinner and the wife was guardian of the home. As the cult of domesticity grew in nineteenth-century America, middle-class women found themselves objects of admiration and praise; but at the same time they were excluded from activities in which they had once had important roles. In a society that heralded individualism, personal autonomy, and an experimental approach to life, the young married woman found herself chained to the hearth. Alexis de Tocqueville, whose observations exposed America to the Americans, put it this way in the 1830s in his extraordinary work **Democracy in America:**

In America the independence of woman is irrecoverably lost in the bonds of matrimony: if an unmarried woman is less constrained there than elsewhere, a wife is subjected to stricter obligations. The former makes her father's house an abode of freedom and of pleasure; the latter lives in the home of her husband as if it were a cloister.

Escaping "the quiet circle of domestic employments," as de Tocqueville put it, became increasingly difficult in the era of Jacksonian democracy.

It was against this trend that some middle-class women began to revolt in the 1830s. Offended by the prevailing sexual double standard, restricted and alienated in their domestic roles, unwilling to accept the passive existence to which they had been assigned, they began reform movements that were intended to change their own lives as well as society at large. Only a small number of women became actively involved, but what they did and said and wrote touched the lives of many more.

Carroll Smith-Rosenberg's essay takes us into the experiences of a few of these women—those who began the New York Female Reform Society, an organization that hoped to change the attitudes and behavior of both women and men. Through the work of such groups, which proliferated in the antebellum period, the lives of middle-class and lower-class women intersected. The double standard required that middle-class women remain chaste before marriage and virtuous afterward, while it allowed men sexual license at all times. But this social arrangement depended on the availability of lower-class prostitutes, whose sexual service to men permitted upper-class women to remain pure. The Female Reform Society brought the two kinds of women together. Nevertheless, this crossing of paths did not create a sisterhood between middle- and lower-class women, because the reformers offered prostitutes no viable economic alternative to plying their trade.

The antebellum women's movements provide a clear example of conjunction between the private and public sides of life. Many middle-class women, restricted and frustrated in their private domains, sought expanded lives and self-activation in the public sphere. Although operating in the name of religious reform, usually of the evangelical type, they were finding ways, as Smith-Rosenberg writes, "to manifest a discontent with their comparatively passive and constricted social role."

On a spring evening in May 1834, a small group of women met at the revivalist Third Presbyterian Church in New York City to found the New York Female Moral Reform Society. The Society's goals were ambitious indeed; it hoped to convert New York's prostitutes to evangeli-

"Beauty, the Beast and the Militant Woman: A Case Study in Sex Roles and Social Stress in Jacksonian America," by Carroll Smith-Rosenberg. From *American Quarterly* 23 (1971):562–84. Published by the University of Pennsylvania. Copyright, 1971, Trustees of the University of Pennsylvania. Reprinted by permission of the author and the publisher.

cal Protestantism and close forever the city's numerous brothels. This bold attack on prostitution was only one part of the Society's program. These self-assertive women hoped as well to confront that larger and more fundamental abuse, the double standard, and the male sexual license it condoned. Too many men, the Society defiantly asserted in its statement of goals, were aggressive destroyers of female innocence and happiness. No man was above suspicion. Women's only safety lay in a militant effort to reform American sexual mores—and, as we shall see, to reform sexual mores meant in practice to control man's sexual values and autonomy. The rhetoric of the Society's spokesmen consistently betrayed an unmistakable and deeply felt resentment toward a male-dominated society.[1]

Few if any members of the Society were reformed prostitutes or the victims of rape or seduction. Most came from middle-class native American backgrounds and lived quietly respectable lives as pious wives and mothers. What needs explaining is the emotional logic which underlay the Society's militant and controversial program of sexual reform. I would like to suggest that both its reform program and the anti-male sentiments it served to express reflect a neglected area of stress in mid-19th century America—that is, the nature of the role to be assumed by the middle-class American woman.

American society from the 1830s to the 1860s was marked by advances in political democracy, by a rapid increase in economic, social and geographic mobility, and by uncompromising and morally relentless reform movements. Though many aspects of Jacksonianism have been subjected to historical investigation, the possibly stressful effects of such structural change upon family and sex roles have not. The following pages constitute an attempt to glean some understanding of women and women's role in antebellum America through an analysis of a self-consciously female voluntary association dedicated to the eradication of sexual immorality.

Women in Jacksonian America had few rights and little power. Their role in society was passive and sharply limited. Women were, in general, denied formal education above the minimum required by a literate early industrial society. The female brain and nervous system, male physicians and educators agreed, were inadequate to sustained intellectual

---

[1] "Minutes of the Meeting of the Ladies' Society for the Observance of the Seventh Commandment held in Chatham Street Chapel, May 12, 1834," and "Constitution of the New York Female Moral Reform Society," both in ledger book entitled "Constitution and Minutes of the New York Female Moral Reform Society, May, 1834 to July 1839," deposited in the archives of the American Female Guardian Society (hereinafter referred to as A.F.G.S.), Woodycrest Avenue, Bronx, New York. (The Society possesses the executive committee minutes from May 1835–June 1847, and from Jan. 7, 1852–Feb. 18, 1852.) For a more detailed institutional history of the Society see Carroll Smith-Rosenberg, *Religion and the Rise of the American City* (Ithaca, N.Y.: Cornell Univ. Press, 1971), chaps. 4 and 7. The New York Female Moral Reform Society changed its name to American Female Guardian Society in 1849. The Society continues today, helping children from broken homes. Its present name is Woodycrest Youth Service.

effort. They were denied the vote in a society which placed a high value upon political participation; political activity might corrupt their pure feminine nature. All professional roles (with the exception of primary school education) were closed to women. Even so traditional a female role as midwife was undermined as male physicians began to establish professional control over obstetrics. Most economic alternatives to marriage (except such burdensome and menial tasks as those of seamstress or domestic) were closed to women. Their property rights were still restricted and females were generally considered to be the legal wards either of the state or of their nearest male relative. In the event of divorce, the mother lost custody of her children—even when the husband was conceded to be the erring party.[2] Women's universe was bounded by their homes and the career of father or husband; within the home it was woman's duty to be submissive and patient.

Yet this was a period when change was considered a self-evident good, and when nothing was believed impossible to a determined free will, be it the conquest of a continent, the reform of society or the eternal salvation of all mankind. The contrast between these generally accepted ideals and expectations and the real possibilities available to American women could not have been more sharply drawn. It is not implausible to assume that at least a minority of American women would find ways to manifest a discontent with their comparatively passive and constricted social role.

Only a few women in antebellum America were able, however, to openly criticize their socially defined sexual identity. A handful, like Fanny Wright, devoted themselves to overtly subversive criticism of the social order.[3] A scarcely more numerous group became pioneers in women's education. Others such as Elizabeth Cady Stanton, Lucretia Mott and Susan B. Anthony founded the women's rights movement. But most respectable women—even those with a sense of ill-defined grievance—were unable to explicitly defy traditional sex-role prescriptions.

I would like to suggest that many such women channeled frustration, anger and a compensatory sense of superior righteousness into the reform movements of the first half of the 19th century; and in the controversial moral reform crusade such motivations seem particularly apparent. While unassailable within the absolute categories of a pervasive evangelical world-view, the Female Moral Reform Society's crusade against illicit sexuality permitted an expression of anti-male sentiments.

[2] For a well-balanced though brief discussion of American women's role in antebellum America see Eleanor Flexner, *A Century of Struggle* (Cambridge: Harvard Univ. Press, 1959), chaps. 1–4.

[3] There are two modern biographies of Fanny Wright, both rather thin: W. R. Waterman, *Frances Wright* (New York: Columbia Univ. Press, 1924); Alice J. Perkins, *Frances Wright, Free Enquirer* (New York: Harper & Bros., 1939). Fanny Wright was one of the first women in America to speak about women's rights before large audiences of both men and women. Yet she attracted very few women into the women's rights movement, probably because her economic and political views and her emphatic rejection of Christianity seemed too radical to most American women.

And the Society's "final solution"—the right to control the mores of men—provided a logical emotional redress for those feelings of passivity which we have suggested. It should not be surprising that between 1830 and 1860 a significant number of militant women joined a crusade to establish their right to define—and limit—man's sexual behavior.

Yet adultery and prostitution were unaccustomed objects of reform even in the enthusiastic and millennial America of the 1830s. The mere discussion of these taboo subjects shocked most Americans; to undertake such a crusade implied no ordinary degree of commitment. The founders of the Female Moral Reform Society, however, were able to find both legitimization for the expression of grievance normally unspoken and an impulse to activism in the moral categories of evangelical piety. Both pious activism and sex-role anxieties shaped the early years of the Female Moral Reform Society. This conjunction of motives was hardly accidental.

The lady founders of the Moral Reform Society and their new organization represented an extreme wing of that movement within American Protestantism known as the Second Great Awakening. These women were intensely pious Christians, convinced that an era of millennial perfection awaited human effort. In this fervent generation, such deeply felt millennial possibilities made social action a moral imperative. Like many of the abolitionists, Jacksonian crusaders against sexual transgression were dedicated activists, compelled to attack sin wherever it existed and in whatever form it assumed—even the unmentionable sin of illicit sexuality.

New Yorkers' first awareness of the moral reform crusade came in the spring of 1832 when the New York Magdalen Society (an organization which sought to reform prostitutes) issued its first annual report. Written by John McDowall, their missionary and agent, the report stated unhesitatingly that 10,000 prostitutes lived and worked in New York City. Not only sailors and other transients, but men from the city's most respected families, were regular brothel patrons. Lewdness and impurity tainted all sectors of New York society. True Christians, the report concluded, must wage a thoroughgoing crusade against violators of the Seventh Commandment.[4]

The report shocked and irritated respectable New Yorkers—not only by its tone of righteous indignation and implied criticism of the city's old and established families. The report, it seemed clear to many New Yorkers, was obscene, its author a mere seeker after notoriety.[5]

[4] John R. McDowall, *Magdalen Report*, rpr. *McDowall's Journal*, 2 (May 1834), 33–38. For the history of the New York Magdalen Society see *First Annual Report of the Executive Committee of the New York Magdalen Society, Instituted January 1, 1830*. See as well, Rosenberg, *Religion*, chap. 4.

[5] Flora L. Northrup, *The Record of a Century* (New York: American Female Guardian Soc., 1934), pp. 13–14; cf. *McDowall's Defence*, 1, No. 1 (July 1836), 3; *The Trial of the Reverend John Robert McDowall by the Third Presbytery of New York in February, March, and April, 1836* (New York, 1836). [Thomas Hastings Sr.], *Missionary Labors through a Series of Years among Fallen Women by the New-York Magdalen Society* (New York: N.Y. Magdalen Soc., 1870), p. 15.

Hostility quickly spread from McDowall to the Society itself; its members were verbally abused and threatened with ostracism. The Society disbanded.

A few of the women, however, would not retreat. Working quietly, they began to found church-affiliated female moral reform societies. Within a year, they had created a number of such groups, connected for the most part with the city's more evangelical congregations. These pious women hoped to reform prostitutes, but more immediately to warn other God-fearing Christians of the pervasiveness of sexual sin and the need to oppose it. Prostitution was after all only one of many offenses against the Seventh Commandment; adultery, lewd thoughts and language, and bawdy literature were equally sinful in the eyes of God. These women at the same time continued unofficially to support their former missionary, John McDowall, using his newly established moral reform newspaper to advance their cause not only in the city, but throughout New York State.[6]

After more than a year of such discreet crusading, the women active in the moral reform cause felt sufficiently numerous and confident to organize a second city-wide moral reform society, and renew their efforts to reform the city's prostitutes. On the evening of May 12, 1834, they met at the Third Presbyterian Church to found the New York Female Moral Reform Society.[7]

Nearly four years of opposition and controversy had hardened the women's ardor into a militant determination. They proposed through their organization to extirpate sexual license and the double standard from American society. A forthright list of resolves announced their organization:

> Resolved, That immediate and vigorous efforts should be made to create a public sentiment in respect to this sin; and also in respect to the duty of parents, church members and ministers on the subject, which shall be in stricter accordance with . . . the word of God.
>
> . . . .
>
> Resolved, That the licentious man is no less guilty than his victim, and ought, therefore, to be excluded from all virtuous female society.
> Resolved, That it is the imperious duty of ladies everywhere, and of every religious denomination, to co-operate in the great work of moral reform.

[6] Northrup, *Record of a Century*, pp. 14–15; only two volumes of *McDowall's Journal* were published, covering the period Jan. 1833 to Dec. 1834. Between the demise of the New York Magdalen Society and the organization of the New York Female Moral Reform Society (hereinafter, N.Y.F.M.R.S.), McDowall was connected, as agent, with a third society, the New York Female Benevolent Society, which he had helped found in February of 1833. For a more detailed account see Carroll S. Rosenberg, "Evangelicalism and the New City," Ph.D. Diss. Columbia University, 1968, chap. 5.

[7] *McDowall's Journal*, 2 (Jan. 1834), 6–7.

A sense of urgency and spiritual absolutism marked this organizational meeting, and indeed all of the Society's official statements for years to come. "It is the duty of the virtuous to use every consistent moral means to save our country from utter destruction," the women warned. "The sin of licentiousness has made fearful havoc . . . drowning souls in perdition and exposing us to the vengeance of a holy God." Americans hopeful of witnessing the promised millennium could delay no longer.[8]

The motivating zeal which allowed the rejection of age-old proprieties and defied the criticism of pulpit and press was no casual and fashionable enthusiasm. Only an extraordinary set of legitimating values could have justified such commitment. And this was indeed the case. The women moral reformers acted in the conscious conviction that God imperiously commanded their work. As they explained soon after organizing their society: "As Christians we must view it in the light of God's word—we must enter into His feelings on the subject—engage in its overthrow just in the manner he would have us. . . . We must look away from all worldly opinions or influences, for they are perverted and wrong; and individually act only as in the presence of God." [9] Though the Society's pious activism had deep roots in the evangelicalism of the Second Great Awakening, the immediate impetus for the founding of the Moral Reform Society came from the revivals Charles G. Finney conducted in New York City between the summer of 1829 and the spring of 1834.[10]

Charles Finney, reformer, revivalist and perfectionist theologian from western New York State, remains a pivotal figure in the history of American Protestantism. The four years Finney spent in New York had a profound influence on the city's churches and reform movements, and upon the consciences generally of the thousands of New Yorkers who crowded his revival meetings and flocked to his churches. Finney insisted that his disciples end any compromise with sin or human injustice. Souls were lost and sin prevailed, Finney urged, because men chose to sin—

---

[8] "Minutes of the Meeting of the Ladies' Society for the Observance of the Seventh Commandment . . . May 12, 1834," and "Preamble," "Constitution of the New York Female Moral Reform Society."

[9] *Advocate of Moral Reform* (hereinafter, *Advocate*) 1 (Jan.–Feb. 1835), 6. The *Advocate* was the Society's official journal.

[10] Close ties connected the N.Y.F.M.R.S. with the Finney wing of American Protestantism. Finney's wife was the Society's first president. The Society's second president, Mrs. William Green, was the wife of one of Finney's closest supporters. The Society's clerical support in New York City came from Finney's disciples. Their chief financial advisers and initial sponsors were Arthur and Lewis Tappan, New York merchants who were also Charles Finney's chief financial supporters. For a list of early "male advisers" to the N.Y.F.M.R.S. see Joshua Leavitt, *Memoir and Select Remains of the Late Reverend John R. McDowall* (New York: Joshua Leavitt, Lord, 1838), p. 248, also pp. 99, 151, 192. See as well L. Nelson Nichols and Allen Knight Chalmers, *History of the Broadway Tabernacle of New York City* (New Haven: Tuttle, Morehouse & Taylor, 1940), pp. 49–67, and William G. McLoughlin, Jr., *Modern Revivalism* (New York: Ronald Press, 1959), pp. 50–53.

because they chose not to work in God's vineyard converting souls and reforming sinners.[11] Inspired by Finney's sermons, thousands of New Yorkers turned to missionary work; they distributed Bibles and tracts to the irreligious, established Sunday schools and sent ministers to the frontier.[12] A smaller, more zealous number espoused abolition as well, determined, like Garrison, never to be silent and to be heard. An even smaller number of the most zealous and determined turned—as we have seen— to moral reform.[13]

The program adopted by the Female Moral Reform Society in the spring of 1834 embraced two quite different, though to the Society's founders quite consistent, modes of attack. One was absolutist and millennial, an attempt to convert all of America to perfect moral purity. Concretely the New York women hoped to create a militant nationwide women's organization to fight the double standard and indeed any form of licentiousness—beginning of course in their own homes and neighborhoods. Only an organization of women, they contended, could be trusted with so sensitive and yet monumental a task. At the same time, the Society sponsored a parallel and somewhat more pragmatic attempt to convert and reform New York City's prostitutes. Though strikingly dissimilar in method and geographic scope, both efforts were unified by an uncompromising millennial zeal and by a strident hostility to the licentious and predatory male.

The Society began its renewed drive against prostitution in the fall of 1834 when the executive committee appointed John McDowall their missionary to New York's prostitutes and hired two young men to assist him.[14] The Society's three missionaries visited the female wards of the almshouse, the city hospital and jails, leading prayer meetings, distributing Bibles and tracts. A greater proportion of their time, however, was spent in a more controversial manner, systematically visiting—or, to be more accurate, descending upon—brothels, praying with and exhorting both the inmates and their patrons. The missionaries were specially fond of arriving early Sunday morning—catching women and customers as they awoke on the traditionally sacred day. The missionaries would

---

[11] For an excellent modern analysis of Finney's theology and his place in American Protestantism see McLoughlin, *Modern Revivalism*. McLoughlin has as well edited Finney's series of New York Revivals which were first published in 1835. Charles Grandison Finney, *Lectures on Revivals of Religion*, ed. William G. McLoughlin (Cambridge: Harvard Univ. Press, 1960). McLoughlin's introduction is excellent.

[12] Rosenberg, *Religion*, chaps. 2 and 3.

[13] These reforms were by no means mutually exclusive. Indeed there was a logical and emotional interrelation between evangelical Protestantism and its missionary aspects and such formally secular reforms as peace, abolition and temperance. The interrelation is demonstrated in the lives of such reformers as the Tappan brothers, the Grimké sisters, Theodore Dwight Weld, Charles Finney and in the overlapping membership of the many religious and "secular" reform societies of the Jacksonian period. On the other hand, the overlap was not absolute, some reformers rejecting evangelical Protestantism, others pietism, or another of the period's reforms.

[14] *Advocate*, 1 (Jan.–Feb. 1835), 4; Northrup, *Record*, p. 19.

announce their arrival by a vigorous reading of Bible passages, followed by prayer and hymns. At other times they would station themselves across the street from known brothels to observe and note the identity of customers. They soon found their simple presence had an important deterring effect, many men, with doggedly innocent expressions, pausing momentarily and then hastily walking past. Closed coaches, they also reported, were observed to circle suspiciously for upwards of an hour until, the missionary remaining, they drove away.[15]

The Female Moral Reform Society did not depend completely on paid missionaries for the success of such pious harassment. The Society's executive committee, accompanied by like-thinking male volunteers, regularly visisted the city's hapless brothels. (The executive committee minutes for January 1835, for example, contain a lengthy discussion of the properly discreet makeup of groups for such "active visiting.")[16] The members went primarily to pray and to exert moral influence. They were not unaware, however, of the financially disruptive effect that frequent visits of large groups of praying Christians would have.[17] The executive committee also aided the concerned parents (usually rural) of runaway daughters who, they feared, might have drifted to the city and been forced into prostitution. Members visited brothels asking for information about such girls; one pious volunteer even pretended to be delivering laundry in order to gain admittance to a brothel suspected of hiding such a runaway.[18]

In conjunction with their visiting, the Moral Reform Society opened a House of Reception, a would-be refuge for prostitutes seeking to reform. The Society's managers and missionaries felt that if the prostitute could be convinced of her sin, and then offered both a place of retreat and an economic alternative to prostitution, reform would surely follow. Thus they envisioned their home as a "house of industry" where the errant ones would be taught new trades and prepared for useful jobs—while being instructed in morality and religion. When the managers felt their repentant charges prepared to return to society, they attempted to find them jobs with Christian families—and, so far as possible, away from the city's temptations.[19]

Despite their efforts, however, few prostitutes reformed; fewer still appeared, to their benefactresses, to have experienced the saving grace of conversion. Indeed, the number of inmates at the Society's House of Reception was always small. In March 1835, for instance, the executive committee reported only fourteen women at the House. A year later,

---

[15] *Advocate*, 1 (Mar. 1835), 11–12; 1 (Nov. 1835), 86; N.Y.F.M.R.S., "Executive Committee Minutes, June 6, 1835 and April 30, 1836." These pious visitors received their most polite receptions at the more expensive houses, while the girls and customers of lower-class, slum brothels met them almost uniformly with curses and threats.

[16] N.Y.F.M.R.S., "Executive Committee Minutes, Jan. 24, 1835."

[17] *Advocate*, 1 (Jan.–Feb. 1835), 7.

[18] For a description of one such incident see *Advocate*, 4 (Jan. 15, 1838), 15.

[19] *Advocate*, 1 (Sept. 1, 1835), 72; Northrup, *Record*, p. 19.

total admissions had reached but thirty—only four of whom were considered saved.[20] The final debacle came that summer when the regular manager of the House left the city because of poor health. In his absence, the executive committee reported unhappily, the inmates seized control, and discipline and morality deteriorated precipitously. The managers reassembled in the fall to find their home in chaos. Bitterly discouraged, they dismissed the few remaining unruly inmates and closed the building.[21]

The moral rehabilitation of New York's streetwalkers was but one aspect of the Society's attack upon immorality. The founders of the Female Moral Reform Society saw as their principal objective the creation of a woman's crusade to combat sexual license generally and the double standard particularly. American women would no longer willingly tolerate that traditional—and role-defining—masculine ethos which allotted respect to the hearty drinker and the sexual athlete. This age-old code of masculinity was as obviously related to man's social preeminence as it was contrary to society's explicitly avowed norms of purity and domesticity. The subterranean mores of the American male must be confronted, exposed and rooted out.

The principal weapon of the Society in this crusade was its weekly, *The Advocate of Moral Reform*. In the fall of 1834, when the Society hired John McDowall as its agent, it voted as well to purchase his journal and transform it into a national women's paper with an exclusively female staff. Within three years, the *Advocate* grew into one of the nation's most widely read evangelical papers, boasting 16,500 subscribers. By the late 1830s the Society's managers pointed to this publication as their most important activity.[22]

Two themes dominated virtually every issue of the *Advocate* from its founding in January 1835, until the early 1850s. The first was an angry and emphatic insistence upon the lascivious and predatory nature of the American male. Men were the initiators in virtually every case of adultery or fornication—and the source, therefore, of that widespread immorality which endangered America's spiritual life and delayed the promised millennium. A second major theme in the *Advocate's* editorials and letters was a call for the creation of a national union of women. Through their collective action such a united group of women might ultimately control the behavior of adult males and of the members' own children, particularly their sons.

The founders and supporters of the Female Moral Reform Society entertained several primary assumptions concerning the nature of human sexuality. Perhaps most central was the conviction that women felt little

[20] *Advocate*, 1 (Mar. 1835), 11; N.Y.F.M.R.S., "Executive Committee Minutes, Apr. 5, 1836, May 30, 1835."

[21] N.Y.F.M.R.S., "Executive Committee Minutes, Oct. 4, 1836."

[22] N.Y.F.M.R.S., "Executive Committee Minutes, June 6 and June 25, 1835, June (n.d.), 1836"; N.Y.F.M.R.S., *The Guardian or Fourth Annual Report of the New York Female Moral Reform Society presented May 9, 1838*, pp. 4–6.

sexual desire; they were in almost every instance induced to violate the
Seventh Commandment by lascivious men who craftily manipulated not
their sensuality, but rather the female's trusting and affectionate nature.
A woman acted out of romantic love, not carnal desire; she was innocent and defenseless, gentle and passive.[23] "The worst crime alleged
against [the fallen woman] in the outset," the *Advocate's* editors explained, "is . . . 'She is without discretion.' She is open-hearted, sincere,
and affectionate. . . . She trusts the vows of the faithless. She commits
her all into the hands of the deceiver." [24]

The male lecher, on the other hand, was a creature controlled by
base sexual drives which he neither could nor would control. He was,
the *Advocate's* editors bitterly complained, powerful and decisive; unwilling (possibly unable) to curb his own willfulness, he callously used
it to coerce the more passive and submissive female. This was an age of
rhetorical expansiveness, and the *Advocate's* editors and correspondents
felt little constraint in their delineation of the dominant and aggressive
male. "Reckless," "bold," "mad," "drenched in sin" were terms used
commonly to describe erring males; they "robbed," "ruined" and "rioted." But one term above all others seemed most fit to describe the
lecher—"The Destroyer." [25]

A deep sense of anger and frustration characterized the *Advocate's*
discussion of such all-conquering males, a theme reiterated again and
again in the letters sent to the paper by rural sympathizers. Women saw
themselves with few defenses against the determined male; his will was
far stronger than that of woman.[26] Such letters often expressed a bitterness which seems directed not only against the specific seducer, but toward all American men. One representative rural subscriber complained,
for example: "Honorable men; they would not plunder; . . . an impu-
tation on their honour might cost a man his life's blood. And yet they
are so passingly mean, so utterly contemptible, as basely and treacherously to contrive . . . the destruction of happiness, peace, morality, and
all that is endearing in social life; they plunge into degradation, misery,
and ruin, those whom they profess to love. O let them not be trusted.
Their 'tender mercies are cruel.' " [27]

The double standard seemed thus particularly unjust; it came to
symbolize and embody for the Society and its rural sympathizers the
callous indifference—indeed at times almost sadistic pleasure—a male-

[23] "Budding," "lovely," "fresh," "joyous," "unsuspecting lamb," were frequent terms
used to describe innocent women before their seduction. The *Advocate* contained
innumerable letters and editorials on this theme. See, for example, *Advocate*, 4
(Jan. 1, 1838), 1; *Advocate*, 10 (Mar. 1, 1844), 34; *Advocate and Guardian* (the
Society changed the name of its journal in 1847), 16 (Jan. 1, 1850), 3.
[24] Letter in *Advocate*, 1 (Apr. 1835), 19.
[25] "Murderer of Virtue" was another favorite and pithy phrase. For a sample of such
references see: *Advocate*, 4 (Feb. 1, 1838), 17; *Advocate*, 10 (Jan. 1, 1844), 19–20;
Advocate, 10 (Jan. 15, 1844), 29; *Advocate*, 10 (Mar. 1, 1844), 33.
[26] *Advocate*, 1 (Jan.–Feb. 1835), 3; *Advocate*, 1 (Apr. 1835), 19; *Advocate and
Guardian*, 16 (Jan. 1, 1850), 3.
[27] Letter in *McDowall's Journal*, 2 (Apr. 1834), 26–27.

dominated society took in the misfortune of a passive and defenseless woman. The respectable harshly denied her their friendship; even parents might reject her. Often only the brothel offered food and shelter. But what of her seducer? Conventional wisdom found it easy to condone his greater sin: men will be men and right-thinking women must not inquire into such questionable matters.[28]

But it was just such matters, the Society contended, to which women must address themselves. They must enforce God's commandments despite hostility and censure. "Public opinion must be operated upon," the executive committee decided in the winter of 1835, "by endeavoring to bring the virtuous to treat the guilty of both sexes alike, and exercise toward them the same feeling." "Why should a female be trodden under foot," the executive committee's minutes questioned plaintively, "and spurned from society and driven from a parent's roof, if she but fall into sin—while common consent allows the male to habituate himself to this vice, and treats him as not guilty. Has God made a distinction in regard to the two sexes in this respect?"[29] The guilty woman too should be condemned, the Moral Reform Society's quarterly meeting resolved in 1838: "But let not the most guilty of the two—the deliberate destroyer of innocence—be afforded even an 'apron of fig leaves' to conceal the blackness of his crimes."[30]

Women must unite in a holy crusade against such sinners. The Society called upon pious women throughout the country to shun all social contact with men suspected of improper behavior—even if that behavior consisted only of reading improper books or singing indelicate songs. Churchgoing women of every village and town must organize local campaigns to outlaw such men from society and hold them up to public judgment.[31] "Admit him not to your house," the executive committee urged, "hold no converse with him, warn others of him, permit not your friends to have fellowship with him, mark as an evildoer, stamp him as a villain and exclaim, 'Behold the Seducer.'" The power of ostracism could become an effective weapon in the defense of morality.[32]

A key tactic in this campaign of public exposure was the Society's willingness to publish the names of men suspected of sexual immorality. The *Advocate's* editors announced in their first issue that they intended to pursue this policy, first begun by John McDowall in his *Journal.*[33]

[28] Many subscribers wrote to the *Advocate* complaining of the injustice of the double standard. See, for example: *Advocate*, 1 (Apr. 1835), 22; *Advocate*, 1 (Dec. 1835), 91; *Advocate and Guardian*, 16 (Jan. 1, 1850), 5.

[29] *Advocate*, 1 (Jan.–Feb. 1835), 6–7.

[30] Resolution passed at the Quarterly Meeting of the N.Y.F.M.R.S., Jan. 1838, printed in *Advocate*, 4 (Jan. 15, 1838), 14.

[31] This was one of the more important functions of the auxiliaries, and their members uniformly pledged themselves to ostracize all offending males. For an example of such pledges see *Advocate*, 4 (Jan. 15, 1838), 16.

[32] *Advocate and Guardian*, 16 (Jan. 1, 1850), 3.

[33] McDowall urged his rural subscribers to report any instances of seduction. He dutifully printed all the details, referring to the accused man by initials, but otherwise giving the names of towns, counties and dates. Male response was on occasion bitter.

"We think it proper," they stated defiantly, "even to expose names, for the same reason that the names of thieves and robbers are published, that the public may know them and govern themselves accordingly. We mean to let the licentious know, that if they are not ashamed of their debasing vice, we will not be ashamed to expose them. . . . It is a justice which we owe each other." [34] Their readers responded enthusiastically to this invitation. Letters from rural subscribers poured into the *Advocate*, recounting specific instances of seduction in their towns and warning readers to avoid the men described. The editors dutifully set them in type and printed them.[35]

Within New York City itself the executive committee of the Society actively investigated charges of seduction and immorality. A particular target of their watchfulness was the city's employment agencies —or information offices as they were then called; these were frequently fronts for the white-slave trade. The *Advocate* printed the names and addresses of suspicious agencies, warning women seeking employment to avoid them at all costs.[36] Prostitutes whom the Society's missionaries visited in brothels, in prison or in the city hospital were urged to report the names of men who had first seduced them and also of their later customers; they could then be published in the *Advocate*.[37] The executive committee undertook as well a lobbying campaign in Albany to secure the passage of a statute making seduction a crime for the male participant.[38] While awaiting the passage of this measure, the executive committee encouraged and aided victims of seduction (or where appropriate their parents or employers) to sue their seducers on the grounds of loss of services.[39]

Ostracism, exposure and statutory enactment offered immediate, if unfortunately partial, solutions to the problem of male licentiousness. But for the seduced and ruined victim such vengeance came too late. The tactic of preference, women moral reformers agreed, was to educate children, especially young male children, to a literal adherence to the Seventh Commandment. This was a mother's task. American mothers, the *Advocate's* editors repeated endlessly, must educate their sons to re-

---

[34] *Advocate*, 1 (Jan.–Feb. 1835), 2.

[35] Throughout the 1830s virtually every issue of the *Advocate* contained such letters. The *Advocate* continued to publish them throughout the 1840s.

[36] For detailed discussions of particular employment agencies and the decision to print their names see: N.Y.F.M.R.S., "Executive Committee Minutes, Feb. 12, 1845, July 8, 1846."

[37] N.Y.F.M.R.S., "Executive Committee Minutes, Mar. 1, 1838, Mar. 15, 1838"; *Advocate*, 4 (Jan. 15, 1838), 15.

[38] The Society appears to have begun its lobbying crusade in 1838. N.Y.F.M.R.S., "Executive Committee Minutes, Oct. 24, 1838, Jan. 4, 1842, Feb. 18, 1842, Apr. 25, 1844, Jan. 8, 1845"; American Female Moral Reform Society (the Society adopted this name in 1839), *Tenth Annual Report for . . . 1844*, pp. 9–11; American Female Moral Reform Soc., *Fourteenth Annual Report for . . . 1848*.

[39] The N.Y.F.M.R.S.'s Executive Committee Minutes for the years 1837, 1838, 1843 and 1844 especially are filled with instances of the committee instituting suits against seducers for damages in the case of loss of services.

ject the double standard. No child was too young, no efforts too diligent in this crucial aspect of socialization.[40] The true foundations of such a successful effort lay in an early and highly pietistic religious education and in the inculcation of a related imperative—the son's absolute and unquestioned obedience to his mother's will. "Obedience, entire and un-questioned, must be secured, or all is lost." The mother must devote herself whole-heartedly to this task for self-will in a child was an ever-recurring evil.[41] "Let us watch over them continually. . . . Let us . . . teach them when they go out and when they come in—when they lie down, and when they rise up. . . ."[42] A son must learn to confide in his mother instinctively; no thought should be hidden from her.

Explicit education in the Seventh Commandment itself should begin quite early for bitter experience had shown that no child was too young for such sensual temptation.[43] As her son grew older, his mother was urged to instill in him a love for the quiet of domesticity, a repugnance for the unnatural excitements of the theater and tavern. He should be taught to prefer home and the companionship of pious women to the temptations of bachelor life.[44] The final step in a young man's moral edu-cation would come one evening shortly before he was to leave home for the first time. That night, the *Advocate* advised its readers, the mother must spend a long earnest time at his bedside (ordinarily in the dark to hide her natural blushes) discussing the importance of maintaining his sexual purity and the temptations he would inevitably face in attempting to remain true to his mother's religious principles.[45]

Mothers, not fathers, were urged to supervise the sexual education of sons. Mothers, the Society argued, spent most time with their chil-dren; fathers were usually occupied with business concerns and found little time for their children. Sons were naturally close to their mothers and devoted maternal supervision would cement these natural ties. A mother devoted to the moral reform cause could be trusted to teach her son to reject the traditional ethos of masculinity and accept the higher —more feminine—code of Christianity. A son thus educated would be inevitably a recruit in the women's crusade against sexual license.[46]

The Society's general program of exposure and ostracism, lobbying and education depended for effectiveness upon the creation of a national association of militant and pious women. In the fall of 1834, but a few

[40] *Advocate,* 1 (Jan.–Feb. 1835), 6–7; 4 (Jan. 1, 1838), 1.
[41] *Advocate,* 10 (Feb. 1, 1844), 17–18; *Advocate and Guardian,* 16 (Jan. 1, 1850), 3–4.
[42] *Advocate,* 10 (Jan. 1, 1844), 7–8.
[43] *Advocate,* 2 (Jan. 1836), 3; *Advocate,* 4 (Jan. 15, 1838), 13.
[44] *Advocate,* 4 (Jan. 1, 1838), 1–2; *Advocate,* 10 (Feb. 15, 1844), 26; *Advocate and Guardian,* 16 (Jan. 15, 1850), 15.
[45] *Advocate,* 1 (Jan.–Feb. 1835), 5–6.
[46] An editorial in the *Advocate* typified the Society's emphasis on the importance of child rearing and religious education as an exclusively maternal role. "To a mother.—You have a child on your knee. . . . It is an immortal being; destined to live forever! . . . And who is to make it happy or miserable? You—the mother! You who gave it birth, the mother of its body, . . . its destiny is placed in your hands" (*Advocate,* 10 [Jan. 1, 1844], 8).

months after they had organized their Society, its New York officers began to create such a woman's organization. At first they worked through the *Advocate* and the small network of sympathizers John McDowall's efforts had created. By the spring of 1835, however, they were able to hire a minister to travel through western New York State "in behalf of Moral Reform causes." [47] The following year the committee sent two female missionaries, the editor of the Society's newspaper and a paid female agent, on a thousand-mile tour of the New England states. Visiting women's groups and churches in Brattleboro, Deerfield, Northampton, Pittsfield, the Stockbridges and many other towns, the ladies rallied their sisters to the moral reform cause and helped organize some forty-one new auxiliaries. Each succeeding summer saw similar trips by paid agents and managers of the Society throughout New York State and New England.[48] By 1839, the New York Female Moral Reform Society boasted some 445 female auxiliaries, principally in greater New England.[49] So successful were these efforts that within a few years the bulk of the Society's membership and financial support came from its auxiliaries. In February 1838, the executive committee voted to invite representatives of these auxiliaries to attend the Society's annual meeting. The following year the New York Society voted at its annual convention to reorganize as a national society—the American Female Moral Reform Society; the New York group would be simply one of its many constituent societies.[50]

This rural support was an indispensable part of the moral reform movement. The local auxiliaries held regular meetings in churches, persuaded hesitant ministers to preach on the Seventh Commandment, urged Sunday school teachers to confront this embarrassing but vital question. They raised money for the executive committee's ambitious projects, convinced at least some men to form male moral reform societies, and did their utmost to ostracize suspected lechers. When the American Female Moral Reform Society decided to mount a campaign to induce the New York State legislature to pass a law making seduction a criminal offense, the Society's hundreds of rural auxiliaries wrote regularly to their legislators, circulated petitions and joined their New York City sisters in Albany to lobby for the bill (which was finally passed in 1848).[51]

[47] N.Y.F.M.R.S., "Executive Committee Minutes, June 25, 1835."

[48] N.Y.F.M.R.S., "Executive Committee Minutes, Oct. 4, 1836, and May 22, 1837, and Sept. 11, 1839." Indeed, as early as 1833 a substantial portion of John McDowall's support seemed to come from rural areas. See, for example, *McDowall's Journal*, 1 (Aug. 1833), 59–62.

[49] N.Y.F.M.R.S., "Executive Committee Minutes, Oct. 4, 1838"; Northrup, *Record*, p. 22.

[50] N.Y.F.M.R.S., "Executive Committee Minutes, May 10, 1839"; N.Y.F.M.R.S., "Quarterly Meeting, July, 1839." Power within the new national organization was divided so that the president and the board of managers were members of the N.Y.F.M.R.S. while the vice-presidents were chosen from the rural auxiliaries. The annual meeting was held in New York City, the quarterly meetings in one of the towns of Greater New England.

[51] Virtually every issue of the *Advocate* is filled with letters and reports from the auxiliaries discussing their many activities.

In addition to such financial and practical aid, members of the moral reform society's rural branches contributed another crucial, if less tangible, element to the reform movement. This was their commitment to the creation of a feeling of sisterhood among all morally dedicated women. Letters from individuals to the *Advocate* and reports from auxiliaries make clear, sometimes even in the most explicit terms, that many American women experienced a depressing sense of isolation. In part, this feeling merely reflected a physical reality for women living in rural communities. But since city- and town-dwelling women voiced similar complaints, I would like to suggest that this consciousness of isolation also reflected a sense of status inferiority. Confined by their non-maleness, antebellum American women lived within the concentric structure of a family organized around the needs and status of husbands or fathers. And such social isolation within the family—or perhaps more accurately a lack of autonomy both embodied in and symbolized by such isolation—not only dramatized, but partially constituted, a differentiation in status.[52] The fact that social values and attitudes were established by men and oriented to male experiences only exacerbated women's feelings of inferiority and irrelevance. Again and again the Society's members were to express their desire for a feminine-sororial community which might help break down this isolation, lighten the monotony and harshness of life, and establish a countersystem of female values and priorities.

The New York Female Moral Reform Society quite consciously sought to inspire in its members a sense of solidarity in a cause peculiar to their sex, and demanding total commitment, to give them a sense of worthiness and autonomy outside woman's traditionally confining role. Its members, their officers forcefully declared, formed a united phalanx twenty thousand strong, "A UNION OF SENTIMENT AND EFFORT AMONG . . . VIRTUOUS FEMALES FROM MAINE TO ALABAMA."[53] The officers of the New York Society were particularly conscious of the emotional importance of female solidarity within their movement—and the significant role that they as leaders played in the lives of their rural supporters. "Thousands are looking to us," the executive committee recorded in their minutes with mingled pride and responsibility, "with the expectation that the

---

[52] The view that many women held of their role is perhaps captured in the remarks of an editorialist in the *Advocate* in 1850. Motherhood was unquestionably the most correct and important role for women. But it was a very hard role. "In their [mothers'] daily rounds of duty they may move in a retired sphere—secluded from public observation, oppressed with many cares and toils, and sometimes tempted to view their position as being adverse to the highest usefulness. The youthful group around them tax their energies to the utmost limit—the wants of each and all . . . must be watched with sleepless vigilance; improvement is perhaps less marked and rapid than is ardently desired. . . . Patience is tried, faith called into exercise; and all the graces of the Spirit demanded, to maintain equanimity and exhibit a right example. And *such* with all its weight of care and responsibility is the post at which God in his providence has placed the mothers of our land." The ultimate reward of motherhood which the writer held out to her readers, significantly, was that they would be the ones to shape the character of their children. *Advocate and Guardian*, 16 (Jan. 15, 1850), 13.

[53] N.Y.F.M.R.S., *Guardian*, p. 8.

principles we have adopted, and the example we have set before the world will continue to be held up & they reasonably expect to witness our *united onward* movements till the conflict shall end in Victory." [54]

For many of the Society's scattered members, the moral reform cause was their only contact with the world outside farm or village—the *Advocate* perhaps the only newspaper received by the family.[55] A sense of solidarity and of emotional affiliation permeated the correspondence between rural members and the executive committee. Letters and even official reports inevitably began with the salutation, "Sisters," "Dear Sisters" or "Beloved Sisters." Almost every letter and report expressed the deep affection Society members felt for their like-thinking sisters in the cause of moral reform—even if their contact came only through letters and the *Advocate*. "I now pray and will not cease to pray," a woman in Syracuse, New York, wrote, "that your hearts may be encouraged and your hands strengthened." [56] Letters to the Society's executive committee often promised unfailing loyalty and friendship; members and leaders pledged themselves ever ready to aid either local societies or an individual sister in need.[57] Many letters from geographically isolated women reported that the Society made it possible for them for the first time to communicate with like-minded women. A few, in agitated terms, wrote about painful experiences with the double standard which only their correspondence with the *Advocate* allowed them to express and share.[58]

Most significantly, the letters expressed a new consciousness of power. The moral reform society was based on the assertion of female moral superiority and the right and ability of women to reshape male behavior.[59] No longer did women have to remain passive and isolated

---

[54] N.Y.F.M.R.S., "Executive Committee Minutes, Oct. 24, 1836."

[55] See two letters, for example, to the *Advocate* from rural subscribers. Although written fifteen years apart and from quite different geographic areas (the first from Hartford, Conn., the second from Jefferson, Ill.), the sentiments expressed are remarkably similar. Letter in *Advocate*, 1 (Apr. 1835), 19; *Advocate and Guardian*, 16 (Jan. 15, 1850), 14.

[56] Letter in *Advocate*, 4 (Jan. 1, 1838), 6.

[57] Letters and reports from rural supporters expressing such sentiments dotted every issue of the *Advocate* from its founding until the mid-1850s.

[58] The editors of the *Advocate* not infrequently received (and printed) letters from rural subscribers reporting painfully how some young woman in their family had suffered social censure and ostracism because of the machinations of some lecher—who emerged from the affair with his respectability unblemished. This letter to the *Advocate* was the first time they could express the anguish and anger they felt. For one particularly pertinent example see an anonymous letter to the *Advocate*, 1 (Mar. 1835), 15–16.

[59] N.Y.F.M.R.S., "Executive Committee Minutes, Oct. 4, 1836"; *Advocate*, 1 (Apr. 1835), 19–20; *Advocate*, 3 (Jan. 15, 1837), 194; *Advocate*, 4 (Jan. 1, 1838), 5, 7–8; *Advocate*, 4 (Apr. 1838), 6–7. An integral part of this expression of power was the women's insistence that they had the right to investigate male sexual practices and norms. No longer would they permit men to tell them that particular questions were improper for women's consideration. See for example, N.Y.F.M.R.S.,

within the structuring presence of husband or father. The moral reform movement was, perhaps for the first time, a movement within which women could forge a sense of their own identity.

And its founders had no intention of relinquishing their new-found feeling of solidarity and autonomy. A few years after the Society was founded, for example, a group of male evangelicals established a Seventh Commandment Society. They promptly wrote to the Female Moral Reform Society suggesting helpfully that since men had organized, the ladies could now disband; moral reform was clearly an area of questionable propriety. The New York executive committee responded quickly, firmly—and negatively. Women throughout America, they wrote, had placed their trust in a female moral reform society and in female officers. Women, they informed the men, believed in both their own right and ability to combat the problem; it was decidedly a woman's, not a man's issue.[60] "The paper is now in the right hands," one rural subscriber wrote: "This is the appropriate work for *women*. . . . Go on Ladies, go on, in the strength of the Lord." [61]

In some ways, indeed, the New York Female Moral Reform Society could be considered a militant woman's organization. Although it was not overtly part of the woman's rights movement, it did concern itself with a number of feminist issues, especially those relating to woman's economic role. Society, the *Advocate's* editors argued, had unjustly confined women to domestic tasks. There were many jobs in society that women could and should be trained to fill. They could perform any light indoor work as well as men. In such positions—as clerks and artisans—they would receive decent wages and consequent self-respect.[62] And this economic emphasis was no arbitrary or inappropriate one, the Society contended. Thousands of women simply had to work; widows, orphaned young women, wives and mothers whose husbands could not work because of illness or intemperance had to support themselves and their children. Unfortunately, they had now to exercise these responsibilities on the pathetically inadequate salaries they received as domestics, washerwomen or seamstresses—crowded, underpaid and physically unpleasant occupations.[63] By the end of the 1840s, the Society had adopted the cause of the working woman and made it one of their principal concerns—in the 1850s even urging women to join unions and, when

---

"Circular to the Women of the United States," rpr. in *Advocate*, 1 (Jan.–Feb. 1835), 6–7, 4.

[60] N.Y.F.M.R.S., "Executive Committee Minutes, June 28, 1837."

[61] Letter in *Advocate*, 1 (Apr. 1835), 19.

[62] *Advocate and Guardian*, 16 (Jan. 15, 1850), 9.

[63] *Advocate*, 1 (May 1835), 38; N.Y.F.M.R.S., *Guardian*, pp. 5–6. The Society initially became concerned with the problems of the city's poor and working women as a result of efforts to attack some of the economic causes of prostitution. The Society feared that the low wages paid seamstresses, domestics or washerwomen (New York's three traditional female occupations) might force otherwise moral women to turn to prostitution. The Society was, for example, among the earliest critics of the low wages and bad working conditions of New York's garment industry.

mechanization came to the garment industry, helping underpaid seamstresses rent sewing machines at low rates.[64]

The Society sought consciously, moreover, to demonstrate woman's
ability to perform successfully in fields traditionally reserved for men.
Quite early in their history they adopted the policy of hiring only
women employees. From the first, of course, only women had been officers and managers of the Society. And after a few years, these officers
began to hire women in preference to men as agents and to urge other
charitable societies and government agencies to do likewise. (They did
this although the only salaried charitable positions held by women in this
period tended to be those of teachers in girls' schools or supervisors of
women's wings in hospitals and homes for juvenile delinquents.) In February 1835, for instance, the executive committee hired a woman agent
to solicit subscriptions to the *Advocate*. That summer they hired another
woman to travel through New England and New York State organizing
auxiliaries and giving speeches to women on moral reform. In October
of 1836, the executive officers appointed two women as editors of their
journal—undoubtedly among the first of their sex in this country to
hold such positions.[65] In 1841, the executive committee decided to replace their male financial agent with a woman bookkeeper. By 1843
women even set type and did the folding for the Society's journal. All
these jobs, the ladies proudly, indeed aggressively stressed, were appropriate tasks for women.[66]

The broad feminist implications of such statements and actions must
have been apparent to the officers of the New York Society. And indeed
the Society's executive committee maintained discreet but active ties
with the broader woman's rights movement of the 1830s, 40s and 50s;
at one point at least, they flirted with official endorsement of a bold
woman's rights position. Evidence of this flirtation can be seen in the
minutes of the executive committee and occasionally came to light in
articles and editorials appearing in the *Advocate*. As early as the mid-

---

[64] Significantly, the Society's editors and officers placed the responsibility for the
low wages paid seamstresses and other female workers on ruthless and exploitative
men. Much the same tone of anti-male hostility is evident in their economic
exposés as in their sexual exposés.

[65] N.Y.F.M.R.S., "Executive Committee Minutes, Feb. 20, 1835, Oct. 4 and Oct. 5,
1836"; N.Y.F.M.R.S., *Fifth Annual Report*, p. 5.

[66] A.F.G.S., *Eleventh Annual Report*, pp. 5–6. For details of replacing male employees with women and the bitterness of the male reactions, see N.Y.F.M.R.S.,
"Executive Committee Minutes," *passim*, for early 1843. Nevertheless, even these
aggressively feminist women did not feel that women could with propriety chair
public meetings, even those of their own Society. In 1838, for instance, when the
ladies discovered that men expected to attend their annual meeting, they felt that
they had to ask men to chair the meeting and read the women's reports. Their
decision was made just after the Grimké sisters had created a storm of controversy by speaking at large mixed gatherings of men and women. Northrup,
Record, pp. 21–25. For the experiences of the Grimké sisters with this same
problem, see Gerda Lerner's excellent biography, *The Grimké Sisters from South
Carolina* (Boston: Houghton Mifflin, 1967), chaps. 11–14.

1830s, for instance, the executive committee began to correspond with a number of women who were then or were later to become active in the woman's rights movement. Lucretia Mott, abolitionist and pioneer feminist, was a founder and secretary of the Philadelphia Female Moral Reform Society; as such she was in frequent communication with the New York executive committee.[67] Emma Willard, a militant advocate of women's education and founder of the Troy Female Seminary, was another of the executive committee's regular correspondents. Significantly, when Elizabeth Blackwell, the first woman doctor in either the United States or Great Britain, received her medical degree, Emma Willard wrote to the New York executive committee asking its members to use their influence to find her a job.[68] The Society did more than that. The *Advocate* featured a story dramatizing Dr. Blackwell's struggles. The door was now open for other women, the editors urged; medicine was a peculiarly appropriate profession for sensitive and sympathetic womankind. The Society offered to help interested women in securing admission to medical school.[69]

One of the most controversial aspects of the early woman's rights movement was its criticism of the subservient role of women within the American family, and of the American man's imperious and domineering behavior toward women. Much of the Society's rhetorical onslaught upon the male's lack of sexual accountability served as a screen for a more general—and less socially acceptable—resentment of masculine social preeminence. Occasionally, however, the *Advocate* expressed such resentment overtly. An editorial in 1838, for example, revealed a deeply felt antagonism toward the power asserted by husbands over their wives and children. "A portion of the inhabitants of this favored land," the Society admonished, "are groaning under a despotism, which seems to be modeled precisely after that of the Autocrat of Russia. . . . We allude to the tyranny exercised in the HOME department, where lordly man, 'clothed with a little brief authority,' rules his trembling subjects with a rod of iron, conscious of entire impunity, and exalting in his fancied superiority." The Society's editorialist continued, perhaps even more bitterly: "Instead of regarding his wife as a help-mate for him, an equal sharer in his joys and sorrows, he looks upon her as a useful article of furniture, which is valuable only for the benefit derived from it, but which may be thrown aside at pleasure." [70] Such behavior, the editorial carefully emphasized, was not only commonplace, experienced by many of the Society's own members—even the wives of "Christians" and of ministers—but was accepted and even justified by society; was it not sanctioned by the Bible?

At about the same time, indeed, the editors of the *Advocate* went

[67] N.Y.F.M.R.S., "Executive Committee Minutes, Aug. 3, 1837."

[68] N.Y.F.M.R.S., "Executive Committee Minutes, June 2, 1847, Mar. 28, 1849." The *Advocate* regularly reviewed her books, and indeed made a point of reviewing books by women authors.

[69] *Advocate and Guardian*, 16 (Jan. 15, 1850), 10.

[70] *Advocate*, 4 (Feb. 15, 1838), 28.

so far as to print an attack upon "masculine" translations and interpretations of the Bible, and especially of Paul's epistles. This appeared in a
lengthy article written by Sarah Grimké, a "notorious" feminist and abolitionist.[71] The executive committee clearly sought to associate their organization more closely with the nascent woman's rights movement.
Calling upon American women to read and interpret the Bible for themselves, Sarah Grimké asserted that God had created woman the absolute
equal of man. But throughout history, man, being stronger, had usurped
woman's natural rights. He had subjected wives and daughters to his
physical control and had evolved religious and scientific rationalizations
to justify this domination. "Men have endeavored to entice, or to drive
women from almost every sphere of moral action." Miss Grimké
charged: " 'Go home and spin' is the . . . advice of the domestic tyrant. . . . The first duty, I believe, which devolves on our sex now is
to think for themselves. . . . Until we take our stand side by side with
our brother; until we read all the precepts of the Bible as addressed to
woman as well as to man, and lose . . . the consciousness of sex, we
shall never fulfil the end of our existence." "Those who do undertake to
labor," Miss Grimké wrote from her own and her sister's bitter experiences, "are the scorn and ridicule of their own and the other sex." "We
are so little accustomed *to think for ourselves*," she continued,

> that we submit to the dictum of prejudice, and of usurped author-
> ity, almost without an effort to redeem ourselves from the unhal-
> lowed shackles which have so long bound us; almost without a de-
> sire to rise from that degradation and bondage to which we have
> been consigned by man, and by which the faculties of our minds,
> and the powers of our spiritual nature, have been prevented from
> expanding to their full growth, and are sometimes wholly crushed.

Each woman must re-evaluate her role in society; no longer could she
depend on husband or father to assume her responsibilities as a free individual. No longer, Sarah Grimké argued, could she be satisfied with
simply caring for her family or setting a handsome table.[72] The officers
of the Society, in an editorial comment following this article, admitted
that she had written a radical critique of woman's traditional role. But
they urged their members, "It is of immense importance to our sex to
possess clear and *correct* ideas of our rights and duties." [73]
Sarah Grimké's overt criticism of woman's traditional role, containing as it did an attack upon the Protestant ministry and orthodox interpretations of the Bible, went far far beyond the consensus of the *Advocate's* rural subscribers. The following issue contained several letters
sharply critical of her and of the managers, for printing her editorial.[74]
And indeed the *Advocate* never again published the work of an overt

[71] See Lerner, *The Grimké Sisters.*
[72] *Advocate*, 4 (Jan. 1, 1838), 3–5.
[73] *Ibid.*, p. 5.
[74] See, for example, *Advocate*, 4 (Apr. 1, 1838), 55; 4 (July 16, 1838), 108.

feminist. Their membership, the officers concluded, would not tolerate explicit attacks upon traditional family structure and orthodox Christianity. Anti-male resentment and anger had to be expressed covertly. It was perhaps too threatening or—realistically—too dangerous for respectable matrons in relatively close-knit semi-rural communities in New York, New England, Ohio or Wisconsin so openly to question the traditional relations of the sexes and demand a new and ominously forceful role for women.

The compromise the membership and the officers of the Society seemed to find most comfortable was one that kept the American woman within the home—but which greatly expanded her powers as pious wife and mother. In rejecting Sarah Grimké's feminist manifesto, the Society's members implicitly agreed to accept the role traditionally assigned woman: the self-sacrificing, supportive, determinedly chaste wife and mother who limited her "sphere" to domesticity and religion. But in these areas her power should be paramount. The mother, not the father, should have final control of the home and family—especially of the religious and moral education of her children. If the world of economics and public affairs was his, the home must be hers.[75]

And even outside the home, woman's peculiar moral endowment and responsibilities justified her in playing an increasingly expansive role, one which might well ultimately impair aspects of man's traditional autonomy. When man transgressed God's commandments, through licentiousness, religious apathy, the defense of slavery, or the sin of intemperance—woman had both the right and duty of leaving the confines of the home and working to purify the male world.

The membership of the New York Female Moral Reform Society chose not to openly espouse the woman's rights movement. Yet many interesting emotional parallels remain to link the moral reform crusade and the suffrage movement of Elizabeth Cady Stanton, the Grimké sisters and Susan B. Anthony. In its own way, indeed, the war for purification of sexual mores was far more fundamental in its implications for woman's traditional role than the demand for woman's education—or even the vote.

Many of the needs and attitudes, moreover, expressed by suffragette leaders at the Seneca Falls Convention and in their efforts in the generation following are found decades earlier in the letters of rural women in the *Advocate of Moral Reform*. Both groups found woman's traditionally passive role intolerable. Both wished to assert female worth and values in a heretofore entirely male world. Both welcomed the creation of a sense of feminine loyalty and sisterhood that could give emotional strength and comfort to women isolated within their homes—whether in a remote farmstead or a Gramercy Park mansion. And it can hardly be assumed that the demand for votes for women was appreciably more radical than a moral absolutism which encouraged women to invade

[75] For examples of the glorification of the maternal role see *Advocate*, 10 (Mar. 15, 1844), 47, and *Advocate and Guardian*, 16 (Jan. 15, 1850), 13–14.

bordellos, befriend harlots and publicly discuss rape, seduction and prostitution.

It is important as well to re-emphasize a more general historical perspective. When the pious women founders of the Moral Reform Society
gathered at the Third Free Presbyterian Church, it was fourteen years
before the Seneca Falls Convention—which has traditionally been accepted as the beginning of the woman's rights movement in the United
States. There simply was no woman's movement in the 1830s. The future
leaders were either still adolescents or just becoming dissatisfied with
aspects of their role. Women advocates of moral reform were among
the very first American women to challenge their completely passive,
home-oriented image. They were among the first to travel throughout
the country without male chaperones. They published, financed, even set
type for their own paper and defied a bitter and long-standing male opposition to their cause. They began, in short, to create a broader, less
constricted sense of female identity. Naturally enough, they were dependent upon the activist impulse and legitimating imperatives of evangelical religion. This was indeed a complex symbiosis, the energies of
pietism and the grievances of role discontent creating the new and activist female consciousness which characterized the history of the American Female Moral Reform Society in antebellum America. Their experience, moreover, was probably shared, though less overtly, by the thousands of women who devoted time and money to the great number of
reform causes which multiplied in Jacksonian America. Women in the
abolition and the temperance movements (and to a less extent in more
narrowly evangelical and religious causes) also developed a sense of their
ability to judge for themselves and of their right to publicly criticize
the values of the larger society. The lives and self-image of all these
women had changed—if only so little—because of their new reforming
interests.

Slave Songs and Slave Consciousness: An Exploration in Neglected Sources

LAWRENCE W. LEVINE

Explorations of the ordinary aspects of American life often require the traveling of roads unfamiliar to traditional historians. This is especially true of attempts to discover what life was like for the "historically inarticulate"—those Americans, usually at the bottom of the social scale, who left behind few diaries, autobiographies, or letters. As Lawrence W. Levine points out, such people were not, however, inarticulate. But we must go to unaccustomed sources in order to reconstruct their daily experiences, their values, their anxieties and aspirations, and, ultimately, the role they played in history.

Music has always reflected the ethos of plain people. Through music the most vibrant human emotions are often expressed—and with instruments that poor people have hand-fashioned for centuries, as well as with the voice. By employing slave music as a historical source, Levine has been able to delve into Afro-American life in the nineteenth-century South with unusual success. He shows us how slaves kept alive elements of African culture; they did so, he argues, for the good reason that African oral traditions, music, and religious outlooks provided a way of "protecting their personalities from some of the worst ravages of the slave system." Preserving cultural traits, in other words, was vital to the daily life of Afro-Americans. It kept them from becoming the "samboes" white slavemasters liked to see— and often imagined they saw—when they looked at their bondsmen and bondswomen.

In slave spirituals, Levine believes, we are admitted to many daily occurrences in the life of American slaves. Through slave songs we can glean an understanding of Southern slaves' attitudes toward work; of their feelings about resistance and accommodation to the slave system; of their innermost emotions of hope and despair; and of a religious belief in which they attempted to join the past, the present, and the future in a way that made life under slavery bearable.

Almost all of the songs on which Levine bases his analysis date from the period after the slave trade was closed. The end of the trade may have made an important difference in slaves' cultural patterns and modes of resistance, for after 1807 Afro-Americans were cut off from Africa. "Salt water slaves," as newly imported Africans were called, no longer arrived on Southern plantations, and Afro-Americans received no fresh infusions of language, music, folk art, dance, and so forth from their homelands. As Africans born in America quickly dominated the black population numerically in the nineteenth century, African cultural traditions were perpetuated with greater and greater difficulty. By reviewing Allan Kulikoff's essay, based on eighteenth-century sources, and comparing it with Levine's study, founded on

nineteenth-century sources, the student can reflect upon the daily lives
of Afro-Americans in two distinctly different eras.

Negroes in the United States, both during and after slavery, were
anything but inarticulate. They sang songs, told stories, played verbal
games, listened and responded to sermons, and expressed their aspirations,
fears, and values through the medium of an oral tradition that had characterized the West African cultures from which their ancestors had
come. By largely ignoring this tradition, much of which has been preserved, historians have rendered an articulate people historically inarticulate, and have allowed the record of their consciousness to go unexplored.

Having worked my way carefully through thousands of Negro
songs, folktales, jokes, and games, I am painfully aware of the problems
inherent in the use of such materials. They are difficult, often impossible, to date with any precision. Their geographical distribution is usually unclear. They were collected belatedly, most frequently by men
and women who had little understanding of the culture from which they
sprang, and little scruple about altering or suppressing them. Such major
collectors as John Lomax, Howard Odum, and Newman White all admitted openly that many of the songs they collected were "unprintable"
by the moral standards which guided them and presumably their readers. But historians have overcome imperfect records before. They have
learned how to deal with altered documents, with consciously or unconsciously biased firsthand accounts, with manuscript collections that were
deposited in archives only after being filtered through the overprotective
hands of fearful relatives, and with the comparative lack of contemporary sources and the need to use their materials retrospectively. The
challenge presented by the materials of folk and popular culture is
neither totally unique nor insurmountable.

In this essay I want to illustrate the possible use of materials of this
kind in discussing the contribution that an understanding of Negro songs
can make to the recent debate over slave personality. In the process I
will discuss several aspects of the literature and problems related to the
use of slave songs.

The subject of Negro music in slavery has produced a large and
varied literature, little of which has been devoted to questions of meaning and function. The one major exception is Miles Mark Fisher's 1953

study, *Negro Slave Songs in the United States*, which attempts to get at the essence of slave life through an analysis of slave songs. Unfortunately, Fisher's rich insights are too often marred by his rather loose scholarly standards, and despite its continuing value his study is in many respects an example of how *not* to use Negro songs. Asserting, correctly, that the words of slave songs "show both accidental and intentional errors of transmission," Fisher changes the words almost at will to fit his own image of their pristine form. Arguing persuasively that "transplanted Negroes continued to promote their own culture by music," Fisher makes their songs part of an "African cult" which he simply wills into existence. Maintaining (again, I think, correctly), that "slave songs preserved in joyful strains the adjustment which Negroes made to their living conditions within the United States," Fisher traces the major patterns of that adjustment by arbitrarily dating these songs, apparently unperturbed by the almost total lack of evidence pertaining to the origin and introduction of individual slave songs.[1]

Fisher aside, most other major studies of slave music have focused almost entirely upon musical structure and origin. This latter question especially has given rise to a long and heated debate.[2] The earliest collectors and students of slave music were impressed by how different that music was from anything familiar to them. Following a visit to the Sea Islands in 1862, Lucy McKim despaired of being able "to express the entire character of these negro ballads by mere musical notes and signs. The odd turns made in the throat; and that curious rhythmic effect produced by single voices chiming in at different irregular intervals, seem almost as impossible to place on score, as the singing of birds, or the tones of an Aeolian Harp."[3] Although some of these early collectors maintained, as did W. F. Allen in 1865, that much of the slave's music "might no doubt be traced to tunes which they have heard from the whites, and transformed to their own use, . . . their music . . . is rather European than African in its character,"[4] they more often stressed the distinctiveness of the Negro's music and attributed it to racial characteristics, African origins, and indigenous developments resulting from the slave's unique experience in the New World.

This tradition, which has had many influential twentieth-century adherents,[5] was increasingly challenged in the early decades of this cen-

[1] Miles Mark Fisher, *Negro Slave Songs in the United States* (New York, 1963, orig. pub. 1953), 14, 39, 132, and *passim*.

[2] The contours of this debate are judiciously outlined in D. K. Wilgus, *Anglo-American Folksong Scholarship Since 1898* (New Brunswick, 1959), App. One, "The Negro-White Spirituals."

[3] Lucy McKim, "Songs of the Port Royal Contrabands," *Dwight's Journal of Music*, XXII (November 8, 1862), 255.

[4] W. F. Allen, "The Negro Dialect," *The Nation*, I (December 14, 1865), 744–745.

[5] See, for instance, Henry Edward Krehbiel, *Afro-American Folksongs* (New York, 1963, orig. pub. 1914); James Wesley Work, *Folk Song of the American Negro* (Nashville, 1915); James Weldon Johnson, *The Book of American Negro Spirituals* (New York, 1925), and *The Second Book of Negro Spirituals* (New York, 1926); Lydia Parrish, *Slave Songs of the Georgia Sea Islands* (Hatboro, Penna., 1965, orig. pub. 1942); LeRoi Jones, *Blues People* (New York, 1963).

tury. Such scholars as Newman White, Guy Johnson, and George Pullen
Jackson argued that the earlier school lacked a comparative grounding
in Anglo-American folk song. Comparing Negro spirituals with Meth-
odist and Baptist evangelical religious music of the late eighteenth and
early nineteenth centuries, White, Johnson, and Jackson found similarities in words, subject matter, tunes, and musical structure.[6] Although
they tended to exaggerate both qualitatively and quantitatively the degrees of similarity, their comparisons were often a persuasive and important corrective to the work of their predecessors. But their studies
were inevitably weakened by their ethnocentric assumption that similarities alone settled the argument over origins. Never could they con-
template the possibility that the direction of cultural diffusion might
have been from black to white as well as the other way. In fact, insofar
as white evangelical music departed from traditional Protestant hym-
nology and embodied or approached the complex rhythmic structure,
the percussive qualities, the polymeter, the syncopation, the emphasis
on overlapping call and response patterns that characterized Negro music
both in West Africa and the New World, the possibility that it was influenced by slaves who attended and joined in the singing at religious
meetings is quite high.

These scholars tended to use the similarities between black and white
religious music to deny the significance of slave songs in still another way.
Newman White, for example, argued that since white evangelical hymns
also used such expressions as "freedom," the "Promised Land," and the
"Egyptian Bondage," "without thought of other than spiritual meaning,"
these images when they occurred in Negro spirituals could not have been
symbolic "of the Negro's longing for physical freedom."[7] The familiar
process by which different cultural groups can derive varied meanings
from identical images is enough to cast doubt on the logic of White's argument.[8] In the case of white and black religious music, however, the
problem may be much less complex, since it is quite possible that the similar images in the songs of both groups in fact served similar purposes.
Many of those whites who flocked to the camp meetings of the Methodists
and Baptists were themselves on the social and economic margins of their
society, and had psychic and emotional needs which, qualitatively, may
not have been vastly different from those of black slaves. Interestingly,
George Pullen Jackson, in his attempt to prove the white origin of Negro
spirituals, makes exactly this point: "I may mention in closing the chief remaining argument of the die-hards for the Negro source of the Negro
spirituals. . . . How could any, the argument runs, but a natively musical

---

[6] Newman I. White, *American Negro Folk-Songs* (Hatboro, Penna., 1965, orig. pub.
  1928); Guy B. Johnson, *Folk Culture on St. Helena Island, South Carolina* (Chapel
  Hill, 1930); George Pullen Jackson, *White and Negro Spirituals* (New York, 1943).
[7] White, *American Negro Folk-Songs*, 11–13.
[8] Professor John William Ward gives an excellent example of this process in his
  discussion of the different meanings which the newspapers of the United States,
  France, and India attributed to Charles Lindbergh's flight across the Atlantic in 1927.
  See "Lindbergh, Dos Passos, and History," in Ward, *Red, White, and Blue* (New
  York, 1969), 55.

and sorely oppressed race create such beautiful things as 'Swing Low,' 'Steal Away,' and 'Deep River'? . . . But were not the whites of the mountains and the hard-scrabble hill country also 'musical and oppressed'? . . . Yes, these whites were musical, and oppressed too. If their condition was any more tolerable than that of the Negroes, one certainly does not get that impression from any of their songs of release and escape." [9] If this is true, the presence of similar images in white music would merely heighten rather than detract from the significance of these images in Negro songs. Clearly, the function and meaning of white religious music during the late eighteenth and early nineteenth centuries demands far more attention than it has received. In the interim, we must be wary of allowing the mere fact of similarities to deter us from attempting to comprehend the cultural dynamics of slave music.

Contemporary scholars, tending to transcend the more simplistic lines of the old debate, have focused upon the process of syncretism to explain the development of Negro music in the United States. The rich West African musical tradition common to almost all of the specific cultures from which Negro slaves came, the comparative cultural isolation in which large numbers of slaves lived, the tolerance and even encouragement which their white masters accorded to their musical activities, and the fact that, for all its differences, nothing in the European musical tradition with which they came into contact in America was totally alien to their own traditions—all these were conducive to a situation which allowed the slaves to retain a good deal of the integrity of their own musical heritage while fusing to it compatible elements of Anglo-American music. Slaves often took over entire white hymns and folk songs, as White and Jackson maintained, but altered them significantly in terms of words, musical structure, and especially performance before making them their own. The result was a hybrid with a strong African base.[10]

One of the more interesting aspects of this debate over origins is that no one engaged in it, not even advocates of the white derivation theory, denied that the slaves possessed their own distinctive music. Newman White took particular pains to point out again and again that the notion that Negro song is purely an imitation of the white man's music "is fully as unjust and inaccurate, in the final analysis, as the Negro's assumption that his folk-song is entirely original." He observed that in the slaves' separate religious meetings they were free to do as they would with the music they first learned from the whites, with the result that their spirituals became "the greatest single outlet for the expression of the

[9] George Pullen Jackson, "The Genesis of the Negro Spiritual," *The American Mercury*, XXVI (June 1932), 248.
[10] Richard Alan Waterman, "African Influence on the Music of the Americas," in Sol Tax (ed.), *Acculturation in the Americas: Proceedings and Selected Papers of the XXIXth International Congress of Americanists* (Chicago, 1952), 207–218; Wilgus, *Anglo-American Folksong Scholarship Since 1898*, 363–364; Melville H. Herskovits, "Patterns of Negro Music" (pamphlet, no publisher, no date); Gilbert Chase, *America's Music* (New York, 1966), Chap. 12; Alan P. Merriam, "African Music," in William R. Bascom and Melville J. Herskovits (eds.), *Continuity and Change in African Cultures* (Chicago, 1959), 76–80.

Negro folk-mind." [11] Similarly, George Pullen Jackson, after admitting that he could find no white parallels for over two-thirds of the existing Negro spirituals, reasoned that these were produced by Negro singers in true folk fashion "by endless singing of heard tunes and by endless, inevitable and concomitant singing differentiation." Going even further, Jackson asserted that the lack of deep roots in Anglo-American culture left the black man "even freer than the white man to make songs over unconsciously as he sang . . . the free play has resulted in the very large number of songs which, though formed primarily in the white man's moulds, have lost all recognizable relationship to known individual white-sung melodic entities." [12] This debate over origins indicates clearly that a belief in the direct continuity of African musical traditions or in the process of syncretism is not a necessary prerequisite to the conclusion that the Negro slaves' music was their own, regardless of where they received the components out of which it was fashioned; a conclusion which is crucial to any attempt to utilize these songs as an aid in reconstructing the slaves' consciousness.

Equally important is the process by which slave songs were created and transmitted. When James McKim asked a freedman on the Sea Islands during the Civil War where the slaves got their songs, the answer was eloquently simple: "Dey make em, sah." [13] Precisely *how* they made them worried and fascinated Thomas Wentworth Higginson, who became familiar with slave music through the singing of the black Union soldiers in his Civil War regiment. Were their songs, he wondered, a "conscious and definite" product of "some leading mind," or did they grow "by gradual accretion, in an almost unconscious way"? A freedman rowing Higginson and some of his troops between the Sea Islands helped to resolve the problem when he described a spiritual which he had a hand in creating:

> Once we boys went for some rice and de nigger-driver he keep a-callin' on us; and I say, "O de ole nigger-driver!" Den anudder said, "Fust ting my mammy tole me was, notin' so bad as nigger-driver." Den I made a sing, just puttin' a word, and den anudder word.

He then began to sing his song:

> O, de ole nigger-driver!
> O, gwine away!
> Fust ting my mammy tell me,
> O, gwine away!

[11] White, *American Negro Folk-Songs*, 29, 55.
[12] Jackson, *White and Negro Spirituals*, 266–267.
[13] James Miller McKim, "Negro Songs," *Dwight's Journal of Music*, XXI (August 9, 1862), 149.

> Tell me 'bout de nigger-driver,
> O, gwine away!
> Nigger-driver second devil,
> O, gwine away!

Higginson's black soldiers, after a moment's hesitation, joined in the singing of a song they had never heard before as if they had long been
familiar with it. "I saw," Higginson concluded, "how easily a new 'sing'
took root among them." [14]

   This spontaneity, this sense of almost instantaneous community which
so impressed Higginson, constitutes a central element in every account
of slave singing. The English musician Henry Russell, who lived in the
United States in the 1830's, was forcibly struck by the ease with which
a slave congregation in Vicksburg, Mississippi, took a "fine old psalm
tune" and, by suddenly and spontaneously accelerating the tempo, transformed it "into a kind of negro melody." [15] "Us old heads," an ex-slave
told Jeanette Robinson Murphy, "use ter make 'em up on de spurn of de
moment. Notes is good enough for you people, but us likes a mixtery."
Her account of the creation of a spiritual is typical and important:

> We'd all be at the "prayer house" de Lord's day, and de white
> preacher he'd splain de word and read whar Esekial done say—
>
> *Dry bones gwine ter lib ergin.*
>
> And, honey, de Lord would come a-shinin' thoo dem pages and re-
> vive dis ole nigger's heart, and I'd jump up dar and den and holler
> and shout and sing and pat, and dey would all cotch de words and
> I'd sing it to some ole shout song I'd heard 'em sing from Africa,
> and dey'd all take it up and keep at it, and keep a-addin' to it, and
> den it would be a spiritual.[16]

   This "internal" account has been verified again and again by the
descriptions of observers, many of whom were witnessing not slave services but religious meetings of rural southern Negroes long after emancipation. The essential continuity of the Negro folk process in the more
isolated sections of the rural South through the early decades of the twentieth century makes these accounts relevant for the slave period as well.
Natalie Curtis Burlin, whose collection of spirituals is musically the most
accurate one we have, and who had a long and close acquaintance with

---

[14] Thomas Wentworth Higginson, *Army Life in a Black Regiment* (Beacon Press
edition, Boston, 1962, orig. pub. 1869), 218–219.

[15] Henry Russell, *Cheer! Boys, Cheer!*, 84–85, quoted in Chase, *America's Music*,
235–236.

[16] Jeanette Robinson Murphy, "The Survival of African Music in America," *Popular
Science Monthly*, 55 (1899), 660–672, reprinted in Bruce Jackson (ed.), *The
Negro and His Folklore in Nineteenth-Century Periodicals* (Austin, 1967), 328.

Negro music, never lost her sense of awe at the process by which these songs were molded. On a hot July Sunday in rural Virginia, she sat in a Negro meeting house listening to the preacher deliver his prayer, interrupted now and then by an "O Lord!" or "Amen, Amen" from the congregation.

> Minutes passed, long minutes of strange intensity. The mutterings, the ejaculations, grew louder, more dramatic, till suddenly I felt the creative thrill dart through the people like an electric vibration, that same half-audible hum arose,—emotion was gathering atmospherically as clouds gather—and then, up from the depths of some "sinner's" remorse and imploring came a pitiful little plea, a real "moan," sobbed in musical cadence. From somewhere in that bowed gathering another voice improvised a response: the plea sounded again, louder this time and more impassioned; then other voices joined in the answer, shaping it into a musical phrase; and so, before our ears, as one might say, from this molten metal of music a new song was smithied out, composed then and there by no one in particular and by everyone in general.[17]

Clifton Furness has given us an even more graphic description. During a visit to an isolated South Carolina plantation in 1926, he attended a prayer meeting held in the old slave cabins. The preacher began his reading of the Scriptures slowly, then increased his tempo and emotional fervor, assuring his flock that "Gawd's lightnin' gwine strike! Gawd's thunder swaller de ert!"

> Gradually moaning became audible in the shadowy corners where the women sat. Some patted their bundled babies in time to the flow of the words, and began swaying backward and forward. Several men moved their feet alternately, in strange syncopation. A rhythm was born, almost without reference to the words that were being spoken by the preacher. It seemed to take shape almost visibly, and grow. I was gripped with the feeling of a mass-intelligence, a self-conscious entity, gradually informing the crowd and taking possession of every mind there, including my own.

In the midst of this increasing intensity, a black man sitting directly in front of Furness, his head bowed, his body swaying, his feet patting up and down, suddenly cried out: "Git right—sodger! Git right—sodger! Git right—wit Gawd!"

> Instantly the crowd took it up, moulding a melody out of half-formed familiar phrases based upon a spiritual tune, hummed here and there among the crowd. A distinct melodic outline became

---

[17] Natalie Curtis Burlin, "Negro Music at Birth," *Musical Quarterly*, V (January 1919), 88. For Mrs. Burlin's excellent reproductions of Negro folk songs and spirituals, see her *Negro Folk-Songs* (New York, 1918–1919), Vol. I–IV.

more and more prominent, shaping itself around the central theme
of the words, "Git right, sodger!"

Scraps of other words and tunes were flung into the medley of
sound by individual singers from time to time, but the general trend
was carried on by a deep undercurrent, which appeared to be
stronger than the mind of any individual present, for it bore the
mass of improvised harmony and rhythms into the most effective
climax of incremental repetition that I have ever heard. I felt as if
some conscious plan or purpose were carrying us along, call it mob-
mind, communal composition, or what you will.[18]

. . . These accounts and others like them make it clear that spirituals
both during and after slavery were the product of an improvisational
communal consciousness. They were not, as some observers thought,
totally new creations, but were forged out of many preexisting bits of
old songs mixed together with snatches of new tunes and lyrics and fit
into a fairly traditional but never wholly static metrical pattern. They
were, to answer Higginson's question, *simultaneously* the result of individual and mass creativity. They were products of that folk process
which has been called "communal re-creation," through which older songs
are constantly recreated into essentially new entities.[19] Anyone who has
read through large numbers of Negro songs is familiar with this process.
Identical or slightly varied stanzas appear in song after song; identical
tunes are made to accommodate completely different sets of lyrics; the
same song appears in different collections in widely varied forms. In 1845
a traveler observed that the only permanent elements in Negro song were
the music and the chorus. "The blacks themselves leave out old stanzas,
and introduce new ones at pleasure. Travelling through the South, you
may, in passing from Virginia to Louisiana, hear the same tune a hundred
times, but seldom the same words accompanying it." [20] Another observer
noted in 1870 that during a single religious meeting the freedmen would
often sing the words of one spiritual to several different tunes, and then
take a tune that particularly pleased them and fit the words of several
different songs to it.[21] Slave songs, then, were never static; at no time did
Negroes create a "final" version of any spiritual. Always the community
felt free to alter and recreate them.

The two facts that I have attempted to establish thus far—that slave
music, regardless of its origins, was a distinctive cultural form, and that

[18] Clifton Joseph Furness, "Communal Music Among Arabians and Negroes," *Musical Quarterly*, XVI (January 1930), 49–51.
[19] Bruno Nettl, *Folk and Traditional Music of the Western Continents* (Englewood
Cliffs, 1965), 4–5; Chase, *America's Music*, 241–243.
[20] J. K., Jr., "Who Are Our National Poets?," *Knickerbocker Magazine*, 26 (October
1845), 336, quoted in Dena J. Epstein, "Slave Music in the United States Before
1860: A Survey of Sources (Part I)," *Music Library Association Notes*, XX
(Spring 1963), 208.
[21] Elizabeth Kilham, "Sketches in Color: IV," *Putnam's Monthly*, XV (March 1870),
304–311, reprinted in Jackson, *The Negro and His Folklore in Nineteenth-Century
Periodicals*, 129.

it was created or constantly recreated through a communal process—are essential if one is to justify the use of these songs as keys to slave consciousness. But these facts in themselves say a good deal about the nature and quality of slave life and personality. That black slaves could create and continually recreate songs marked by the poetic beauty, the emotional intensity, the rich imagery which characterized the spirituals—songs which even one of the most devout proponents of the white man's origins school admits are "the most impressive religious folk songs in our language" [22]—should be enough to make us seriously question recent theories which conceive of slavery as a closed system which destroyed the vitality of the Negro and left him a dependent child. For all of its horrors, slavery was never so complete a system of psychic assault that it prevented the slaves from carving out independent cultural forms. It never pervaded all of the interstices of their minds and their culture, and in those gaps they were able to create an independent art form and a distinctive voice. If North American slavery eroded the African's linguistic and institutional life, if it prevented him from preserving and developing his rich heritage of graphic and plastic art, it nevertheless allowed him to continue and to develop the patterns of verbal art which were so central to his past culture. Historians have not yet come to terms with what the continuance of the oral tradition meant to blacks in slavery.

In Africa, songs, tales, proverbs, and verbal games served the dual function of not only preserving communal values and solidarity, but also of providing occasions for the individual to transcend, at least symbolically, the inevitable restrictions of his environment and his society by permitting him to express deeply held feelings which he ordinarily was not allowed to verbalize. Among the Ashanti and the Dahomeans, for example, periods were set aside when the inhabitants were encouraged to gather together and, through the medium of song, dance, and tales, to openly express their feelings about each other. The psychological release this afforded seems to have been well understood. "You know that everyone has a *sunsum* (soul) that may get hurt or knocked about or become sick, and so make the body ill," an Ashanti high priest explained to the English anthropologist R. S. Rattray:

> Very often . . . ill health is caused by the evil and the hate that
> another has in his head against you. Again, you too may have
> hatred in your head against another, because of something that
> person has done to you, and that, too, causes your *sunsum* to fret
> and become sick. Our forbears knew this to be the case, and so they
> ordained a time, once every year, when every man and woman,
> free man and slave, should have freedom to speak out just what was
> in their head, to tell their neighbours just what they thought of
> them, and of their actions, and not only their neighbours, but also
> the king or chief. When a man has spoken freely thus, he will feel
> his *sunsum* cool and quieted, and the *sunsum* of the other person
> against whom he has now openly spoken will be quieted also.

[22] White, *American Negro Folk-Songs,* 57.

Utilization of verbal art for this purpose was widespread throughout
Africa, and was not confined to those ceremonial occasions when one
could directly state one's feelings. Through innuendo, metaphor, and
circumlocution, Africans could utilize their songs as outlets for individual
release without disturbing communal solidarity.[23]

There is abundant internal evidence that the verbal art of the slaves
in the United States served many of these traditional functions. Just as
the process by which the spirituals were created allowed for simultaneous
individual and communal creativity, so their very structure provided
simultaneous outlets for individual and communal expression. The overriding antiphonal structure of the spirituals—the call and response pattern which Negroes brought with them from Africa and which was
reinforced by the relatively similar white practice of "lining out" hymns
—placed the individual in continual dialogue with his community, allowing him at one and the same time to preserve his voice as a distinct entity
and to blend it with those of his fellows. Here again slave music con-
fronts us with evidence which indicates that however seriously the slave
system may have diminished the strong sense of community that had
bound Africans together, it never totally destroyed it or left the individual atomized and emotionally and psychically defenseless before his
white masters. In fact, the form and structure of slave music presented the
slave with a potential outlet for his individual feelings even while it continually drew him back into the communal presence and permitted him
the comfort of basking in the warmth of the shared assumptions of those
around him.

Those "shared assumptions" can be further examined by an analysis
of the content of slave songs. Our preoccupation in recent years with
the degree to which the slaves actually resembled the "Sambo" image
held by their white masters has obscured the fact that the slaves developed images of their own which must be consulted and studied before
any discussion of slave personality can be meaningful. The image of
the trickster, who through cunning and unscrupulousness prevails over
his more powerful antagonists, pervades slave tales. The trickster figure
is rarely encountered in the slave's religious songs, though its presence
is sometimes felt in the slave's many allusions to his narrow escapes from
the devil.

> The Devil's mad and I'm glad,
> He lost the soul he thought he had.[24]

23 Alan P. Merriam, "Music and the Dance," in Robert Lystad (ed.), *The African
World: A Survey of Social Research* (New York, 1965), 452–468; William Bascom,
"Folklore and Literature," in *Ibid.*, 469–488; R. S. Rattray, *Ashanti* (Oxford, 1923),
Chap. XV; Melville Herskovits, "Freudian Mechanisms in Primitive Negro Psychology," in E. E. Evans-Pritchard *et al.* (eds.), *Essays Presented to C. G. Seligman*
(London, 1934), 75–84; Alan P. Merriam, "African Music," in Bascom and Herskovits, *Continuity and Change in African Cultures*, 49–86.
24 William Francis Allen, Charles Pickard Ware, and Lucy McKim Garrison, com-
pilers, *Slave Songs of the United States* (New York, 1867, Oak Publications ed.,
1965), 164–165.

Ole Satan toss a ball at me.
O me no weary yet . . .

Him tink de ball would hit my soul.
O me no weary yet . . .

De ball for hell and I for heaven.
O me no weary yet . . .[25]

Ole Satan thought he had a mighty aim;
He missed my soul and caught my sins.
Cry Amen, cry Amen, cry Amen to God!

He took my sins upon his back;
Went muttering and grumbling down to hell.
Cry Amen, cry Amen, cry Amen to God! [26]

The single most persistent image the slave songs contain, however, is that of the chosen people. The vast majority of the spirituals identify the singers as "de people dat is born of God," "We are the people of God," "we are de people of de Lord," "I really do believe I'm a child of God," "I'm a child ob God, wid my soul sot free," "I'm born of God, I know I am." Nor is there ever any doubt that "To the promised land I'm bound to go," "I walk de heavenly road," "Heav'n shall-a be my home," "I gwine to meet my Saviour," "I seek my Lord and I find Him," "I'll hear the trumpet sound/In that morning." [27]

The force of this image cannot be diminished by the observation that similar images were present in the religious singing of white evangelical churches during the first half of the nineteenth century. White Americans could be expected to sing of triumph and salvation, given their long-standing heritage of the idea of a chosen people which was reinforced in this era by the belief in inevitable progress and manifest destiny, the spread-eagle oratory, the bombastic folklore, and, paradoxically, the deep insecurities concomitant with the tasks of taming a continent and developing an identity. But for this same message to be expressed by Negro slaves who were told endlessly that they were members of the lowliest of races *is* significant. It offers an insight into the kinds of barriers the slaves had available to them against the internalization of the

---

[25] *Ibid.*, 43.

[26] Harriet Jacobs, *Incidents in the Life of a Slave Girl* (Boston, 1861), 109.

[27] Lines like these could be quoted endlessly. For the specific ones cited, see the songs in the following collections: Higginson, *Army Life in a Black Regiment*, 206, 216–217; Allen *et al.*, *Slave Songs of the United States*, 33–34, 44, 106–108, 131, 160–161; Thomas P. Fenner, compiler, *Religious Folk Songs of the Negro as Sung on the Plantations* (Hampton, Virginia, 1909, orig. pub. 1874), 10–11, 48; J. B. T. Marsh, *The Story of the Jubilee Singers; With Their Songs* (Boston, 1880), 136, 167, 178.

stereotyped images their masters held and attempted consciously and unconsciously to foist upon them.

The question of the chosen people image leads directly into the larger problem of what role religion played in the songs of the slave. Writing in 1862, James McKim noted that the songs of the Sea Island freedmen "are all religious, barcaroles and all. I speak without exception. So far as I heard or was told of their singing, it was all religious." Others who worked with recently emancipated slaves recorded the same experience, and Colonel Higginson reported that he rarely heard his troops sing a profane or vulgar song. With a few exceptions, "all had a religious motive." [28] In spite of this testimony, there can be little doubt that the slaves sang nonreligious songs. In 1774, an English visitor to the United States, after his first encounter with slave music, wrote in his journal: "In their songs they generally relate the usage they have received from their Masters or Mistresses in a very satirical stile and manner." [29] Songs fitting this description can be found in the nineteenth-century narratives of fugitive slaves. Harriet Jacobs recorded that during the Christmas season the slaves would ridicule stingy whites by singing:

> Poor Massa, so dey say;
> Down in de heel, so dey say;
> Got no money, so dey say;
> God A'mighty bress you, so dey say.[30]

"Once in a while among a mass of nonsense and wild frolic," Frederick Douglass noted, "a sharp hit was given to the meanness of slaveholders."

> We raise de wheat,
> Dey gib us de corn;
> We bake de bread,
> Dey gib us de crust;
> We sif de meal,
> Dey gib us de huss;
> We peal de meat,
> Dey gib us de skin;
> And dat's de way
> Dey take us in;
> We skim de pot,

---

[28] McKim, "Negro Songs," 148; H. G. Spaulding, "Under the Palmetto," *Continental Monthly*, IV (1863), 188–203, reprinted in Jackson, *The Negro and His Folklore in Nineteenth-Century Periodicals*, 72; Allen, "The Negro Dialect," 744–745; Higginson, *Army Life in a Black Regiment*, 220–221.

[29] *Journal of Nicholas Cresswell, 1774–1777* (New York, 1934), 17–19, quoted in Epstein, *Music Library Association Notes*, XX (Spring 1963), 201.

[30] Jacobs, *Incidents in the Life of a Slave Girl*, 180.

> Dey gib us de liquor,
> And say dat's good enough for nigger.[31]

Both of these songs are in the African tradition of utilizing song to by-pass both internal and external censors and give vent to feelings which could be expressed in no other form. Nonreligious songs were not limited to the slave's relations with his masters, however, as these rowing songs, collected by contemporary white observers, indicate:

> We are going down to Georgia, boys,
> Aye, aye.
> To see the pretty girls, boys,
> Yoe, yoe.
> We'll give 'em a pint of brandy, boys,
> Aye, aye.
> And a hearty kiss, besides, boys,
> Yoe, yoe.[32]

> Jenny shake her toe at me,
> Jenny gone away;
> Jenny shake her toe at me,
> Jenny gone away.
> Hurrah! Miss Susy, oh!
> Jenny gone away;
> Hurrah! Miss Susy, oh!
> Jenny gone away.[33]

The variety of nonreligious songs in the slave's repertory was wide. There were songs of in-group and out-group satire, songs of nostalgia, nonsense songs, songs of play and work and love. Nevertheless, our total stock of these songs is very small. It is possible to add to these by incorporating such post-bellum secular songs which have an authentic slavery ring to them as "De Blue-Tail Fly," with its ill-concealed satisfaction at the death of a master, or the ubiquitous

> My ole Mistiss promise me,
> W'en she died, she'd set me free,

31 *Life and Times of Frederick Douglass* (rev. ed., 1892, Collier Books Edition, 1962), 146–147.

32 John Lambert, *Travels Through Canada and the United States of North America in the Years, 1806–1807 and 1808* (London, 1814), II, 253–254, quoted in Dena J. Epstein, "Slave Music in the United States Before 1860: A Survey of Sources (Part 2)," *Music Library Association Notes*, XX (Summer 1963), 377.

33 Frances Anne Kemble, *Journal of a Residence on a Georgian Plantation in 1838–1839* (New York, 1863), 128.

> She lived so long dat 'er head got bal',
> An' she give out'n de notion a dyin' at all.[34]

The number can be further expanded by following Constance Rourke's suggestion that we attempt to disentangle elements of Negro origin from those of white creation in the "Ethiopian melodies" of the white minstrel shows, many of which were similar to the songs I have just quoted.[35] Either of these possibilities, however, forces the historian to work with sources far more potentially spurious than those with which he normally is comfortable.

Spirituals, on the other hand, for all the problems associated with their being filtered through white hands before they were published, and despite the many errors in transcription that inevitably occurred, constitute a much more satisfactory source. They were collected by the hundreds directly from slaves and freedmen during the Civil War and the decades immediately following, and although they came from widely different geographical areas they share a common structure and content, which seems to have been characteristic of Negro music wherever slavery existed in the United States. It is possible that we have a greater number of religious than nonreligious songs because slaves were more willing to sing these ostensibly innocent songs to white collectors who in turn were more anxious to record them, since they fit easily with their positive and negative images of the Negro. But I would argue that the vast preponderance of spirituals over any other sort of slave music, rather than being merely the result of accident or error, is instead an accurate reflection of slave culture during the ante-bellum period. Whatever songs the slaves may have sung before their wholesale conversion to Christianity in the late eighteenth and early nineteenth centuries, by the latter century spirituals were quantitatively and qualitatively their most significant musical creation. In this form of expression slaves found a medium which

---

[34] For versions of these songs, see Dorothy Scarborough, *On the Trail of Negro Folk-Songs* (Cambridge, 1925), 194, 201–203, 223–225, and Thomas W. Talley, *Negro Folk Rhymes* (New York, 1922), 25–26. Talley claims that the majority of the songs in his large and valuable collection "were sung by Negro fathers and mothers in the dark days of American slavery to their children who listened with eyes as large as saucers and drank them down with mouths wide open," but offers no clue as to why he feels that songs collected for the most part in the twentieth century were slave songs.

[35] Constance Rourke, *The Roots of American Culture and Other Essays* (New York, 1942), 262–274. Newman White, on the contrary, has argued that although the earliest minstrel songs were Negro derived, they soon went their own way and that less than ten per cent of them were genuinely Negro. Nevertheless, these white songs "got back to the plantation, largely spurious as they were and were undoubtedly among those which the plantation-owners encouraged the Negroes to sing. They persist to-day in isolated stanzas and lines, among the songs handed down by plantation Negroes . . ." White, *American Negro Folk-Songs*, 7–10 and Appendix IV. There are probably valid elements in both theses. A similarly complex relationship between genuine Negro folk creations and their more commercialized partly white influenced imitations was to take place in the blues of the twentieth century.

resembled in many important ways the world view they had brought with them from Africa, and afforded them the possibility of both adapting to and transcending their situation.

It is significant that the most common form of slave music we know of is sacred song. I use the term "sacred" not in its present usage as something antithetical to the secular world; neither the slaves nor their African forebears ever drew modernity's clear line between the sacred and the secular. The uses to which spirituals were put are an unmistakable indication of this. They were not sung solely or even primarily in churches or praise houses, but were used as rowing songs, field songs, work songs, and social songs. On the Sea Islands during the Civil War, Lucy McKim heard the spiritual "Poor Rosy" sung in a wide variety of contexts and tempos.

> On the water, the oars dip "Poor Rosy" to an even andante; a stout boy and girl at the hominy-mill will make the same "Poor Rosy" fly, to keep up with the whirling stone; and in the evening, after the day's work is done, "Heab'n shall-a be my home" [the final line of each stanza] peals up slowly and mournfully from the distant quarters.[36]

For the slaves, then, songs of God and the mythic heroes of their religion were not confined to any specific time or place, but were appropriate to almost every situation. It is in this sense that I use the concept sacred—not to signify a rejection of the present world but to describe the process of incorporating within this world all the elements of the divine. The religious historian Mircea Eliade, whose definition of sacred has shaped my own, has maintained that for men in traditional societies religion is a means of extending the world spatially upward so that communication with the other world becomes ritually possible, and extending it temporally backward so that the paradigmatic acts of the gods and mythical ancestors can be continually reenacted and indefinitely recoverable. By creating sacred time and space, man can perpetually live in the presence of his gods, can hold on to the certainty that within one's own lifetime "rebirth" is continually possible, and can impose order on the chaos of the universe. "Life," as Eliade puts it, "is lived on a twofold plane; it takes its course as human existence and, at the same time, shares in a transhuman life, that of the cosmos or the gods." [37]

This notion of sacredness gets at the essence of the spirituals, and through them at the essence of the slave's world view. Denied the possibility of achieving an adjustment to the external world of the ante-bellum South which involved meaningful forms of personal integration, attainment of status, and feelings of individual worth that all human beings

---

[36] McKim, "Songs of the Port Royal Contrabands," 255.
[37] Mircea Eliade, *The Sacred and the Profane* (New York, 1961), Chaps. 2, 4, and *passim*. For the similarity of Eliade's concept to the world view of West Africa, see W. E. Abraham, *The Mind of Africa* (London, 1962), Chap. 2, and R. S. Rattray, *Religion and Art in Ashanti* (Oxford, 1927).

crave and need, the slaves created a new world by transcending the narrow confines of the one in which they were forced to live. They extended the boundaries of their restrictive universe backward until it fused with the world of the Old Testament, and upward until it became one with the world beyond. The spirituals are the record of a people who found the status, the harmony, the values, the order they needed to survive by internally creating an expanded universe, by literally willing themselves reborn. In this respect I agree with the anthropologist Paul Radin that

> The ante-bellum Negro was not converted to God. He converted God to himself. In the Christian God he found a fixed point and he needed a fixed point, for both within and outside of himself, he could see only vacillation and endless shifting. . . . There was no other safety for people faced on all sides by doubt and the threat of personal disintegration, by the thwarting of instincts and the annihilation of values.[38]

The confinement of much of the slave's new world to dreams and fantasies does not free us from the historical obligation of examining its contours, weighing its implications for the development of the slave's psychic and emotional structure, and eschewing the kind of facile reasoning that leads Professor Elkins to imply that, since the slaves had no alternatives open to them, their fantasy life was "limited to catfish and watermelons." [39] Their spirituals indicate clearly that there *were* alternatives open to them —alternatives which they themselves fashioned out of the fusion of their African heritage and their new religion—and that their fantasy life was so rich and so important to them that it demands understanding if we are even to begin to comprehend their inner world.

The God the slaves sang of was neither remote nor abstract, but as intimate, personal, and immediate as the gods of Africa had been. "O when I talk I talk wid God," "Mass Jesus is my bosom friend," "I'm goin' to walk with [talk with, live with, see] King Jesus by myself, by myself," were refrains that echoed through the spirituals.[40]

> In de mornin' when I rise,
>   Tell my Jesus huddy [howdy] oh,
> I wash my hands in de mornin' glory,
>   Tell my Jesus huddy oh.[41]

---

[38] Paul Radin, "Status, Phantasy, and the Christian Dogma," in Social Science Institute, Fisk University, *God Struck Me Dead: Religious Conversion Experiences and Autobiographies of Negro Ex-Slaves* (Nashville, 1945, unpublished typescript).

[39] Stanley Elkins, *Slavery* (Chicago, 1959), 136.

[40] Allen *et al.*, *Slave Songs of the United States*, 33–34, 105; William E. Barton, *Old Plantation Hymns: A Collection of Hitherto Unpublished Melodies of the Slave and the Freedmen* (Boston, 1899), 30.

[41] Allen *et al.*, *Slave Songs of the United States*, 47.

> Gwine to argue wid de Father and chatter wid de son,
> The last trumpet shall sound, I'll be there.
> Gwine talk 'bout de bright world dey des' come from.
> The last trumpet shall sound, I'll be there.[42]

> Gwine to write to Massa Jesus,
> To send some Valiant soldier
> To turn back Pharaoh's army, Hallelu![43]

The heroes of the Scriptures—"Sister Mary," "Brudder Jonah," "Brudder Moses," "Brudder Daniel"—were greeted with similar intimacy and immediacy. In the world of the spirituals, it was not the masters and mistresses but God and Jesus and the entire pantheon of Old Testament figures who set the standards, established the precedents, and defined the values; who, in short, constituted the "significant others." The world described by the slave songs was a black world in which no reference was ever made to any white contemporaries. The slave's positive reference group was composed entirely of his own peers: his mother, father, sister, brother, uncles, aunts, preacher, fellow "sinners" and "mourners" of whom he sang endlessly, to whom he sent messages via the dying, and with whom he was reunited joyfully in the next world.

The same sense of sacred time and space which shaped the slave's portraits of his gods and heroes also made his visions of the past and future immediate and compelling. Descriptions of the Crucifixion communicate a sense of the actual presence of the singers: "Dey pierced Him in the side . . . Dey nail Him to de cross . . . Dey rivet His feet . . . Dey hanged Him high . . . Dey stretch Him wide. . . ."

> Oh sometimes it causes me to tremble,—tremble,—tremble,
> Were you there when they crucified my Lord? [44]

The Slave's "shout"—that counterclockwise, shuffling dance which frequently occurred after the religious service and lasted long into the night —often became a medium through which the ecstatic dancers were transformed into actual participants in historic actions: Joshua's army marching around the walls of Jericho, the children of Israel following Moses out of Egypt.[45]

The thin line between time dimensions is nowhere better illustrated than in the slave's visions of the future, which were, of course, a direct

---

[42] Barton, *Old Plantation Hymns*, 19.

[43] Marsh, *The Story of the Jubilee Singers*, 132.

[44] Fenner, *Religious Folk Songs of the Negro*, 162; E. A. McIlhenny, *Befo' De War Spirituals: Words and Melodies* (Boston, 1933), 39.

[45] Barton, *Old Plantation Hymns*, 15; Howard W. Odum and Guy B. Johnson, *The Negro And His Songs* (Hatboro, Penn., 1964, orig. pub. 1925), 33–34; for a vivid description of the "shout" see *The Nation*, May 30, 1867, 432–433; see also Parrish, *Slave Songs of the Georgia Sea Islands*, Chap. III.

negation of his present. Among the most striking spirituals are those
which pile detail upon detail in describing the Day of Judgment: "You'll
see de world on fire . . . see de element a meltin', . . . see the stars a
fallin' . . . see the moon a bleedin' . . . see the forked lightning, . . .
Hear the rumblin' thunder . . . see the righteous marching, . . . see my
Jesus coming . . . ," and the world to come where "Dere's no sun to
burn you . . . no hard trials . . . no whips a crackin' . . . no stormy
weather . . . no tribulation . . . no evil-doers . . . All is gladness in de
Kingdom." [46] This vividness was matched by the slave's certainty that
he would partake of the triumph of judgment and the joys of the new
world:

> Dere's room enough, room enough, room enough in de heaven, my Lord
> Room enough, room enough, I can't stay behind.[47]

Continually, the slaves sang of reaching out beyond the world that confined them, of seeing Jesus "in de wilderness," of praying "in de lonesome
valley," of breathing in the freedom of the mountain peaks:

> Did yo' ever
> Stan' on mountun,
> Wash yo' han's
> In a cloud? [48]

Continually, they held out the possibility of imminent rebirth; "I look
at de worl' an' de worl' look new, . . . I look at my hands an' they look
so too . . . I looked at my feet, my feet was too." [49]

These possibilities, these certainties were not surprising. The religious revivals which swept large numbers of slaves into the Christian
fold in the late eighteenth and early nineteenth centuries were based upon
a *practical* (not necessarily theological) Arminianism: God would save all
who believed in Him; Salvation was there for all to take hold of if they
would. The effects of this message upon the slaves who were exposed
to and converted by it have been passed over too easily by historians.
Those effects are illustrated graphically in the spirituals which were the
products of these revivals and which continued to spread the evangelical
word long after the revivals had passed into history.

The religious music of the slaves is almost devoid of feelings of de-
pravity or unworthiness, but is rather, as I have tried to show, pervaded

---

[46] For examples of songs of this nature, see Fenner, *Religious Folk Songs of the
Negro*, 8, 63–65; Marsh, *The Story of the Jubilee Singers*, 240–241; Higginson,
Army Life in a Black Regiment, 205; Allen *et al.*, *Slave Songs of the United States*,
91, 100; Burlin, *Negro Folk-Songs*, I, 37–42.

[47] Allen *et al.*, *Slave Songs of the United States*, 32–33.

[48] *Ibid.*, 30–31; Burlin, *Negro Folk-Songs*, II, 8–9; Fenner, *Religious Folk Songs of the
Negro*, 12.

[49] Allen *et al.*, *Slave Songs of the United States*, 128–129; Fenner, *Religious Folk
Songs of the Negro*, 127; Barton, *Old Plantation Hymns*, 26.

by a sense of change, transcendence, ultimate justice, and personal worth. The spirituals have been referred to as "sorrow songs," and in some respects they were. The slaves sang of "rollin' thro' an unfriendly world," of being "a-trouble in de mind," of living in a world which was a "howling wilderness," "a hell to me," of feeling like a "motherless child," "a po' little orphan chile in de worl'," a "home-e-less child," of fearing that "Trouble will bury me down.' " [50]

But these feelings were rarely pervasive or permanent; almost always they were overshadowed by a triumphant note of affirmation. Even so despairing a wail as "Nobody Knows the Trouble I've Had" could suddenly have its mood transformed by lines like: "One morning I was a-walking down, . . . Saw some berries a-hanging down, . . . I pick de berry and I suck de juice, . . . Just as sweet as de honey in de comb." [51] Similarly, amid the deep sorrow of "Sometimes I feel like a Motherless chile," sudden release could come with the lines: "Sometimes I feel like/A eagle in de air. . . . Spread my wings an'/Fly, fly, fly." [52] Slaves spent little time singing of the horrors of hell or damnation. Their songs of the Devil, quoted earlier, pictured a harsh but almost semicomic figure (often, one suspects, a surrogate for the white man), over whom they triumphed with reassuring regularity. For all their inevitable sadness, slave songs were characterized more by a feeling of confidence than of despair. There was confidence that contemporary power relationships were not immutable: "Did not old Pharaoh get lost, get lost, get lost, . . . get lost in the Red Sea?"; confidence in the possibilities of instantaneous change: "Jesus make de dumb to speak. . . . Jesus make de cripple walk. . . . Jesus give de blind his sight. . . . Jesus do most anything"; confidence in the rewards of persistence: "Keep a' inching along like a poor inch-worm,/ Jesus will come by'nd bye"; confidence that nothing could stand in the way of the justice they would receive: "You kin hender me here, but you can't do it dah," "O no man, no man, no man can hinder me"; confidence in the prospects of the future: "We'll walk de golden streets/Of de New Jerusalem." Religion, the slaves sang, "is good for anything, . . . Religion make you happy, . . . Religion gib me patience . . . O member, get Religion . . . Religion is so sweet." [53]

The slaves often pursued the "sweetness" of their religion in the face of many obstacles. Becky Ilsey, who was 16 when she was emancipated, recalled many years later:

> 'Fo' de war when we'd have a meetin' at night, wuz mos' always
> 'way in de woods or de bushes some whar so de white folks

---

[50] Allen *et al., Slave Songs of the United States*, 70, 102–103, 147; Barton, *Old Plantation Hymns*, 9, 17–18, 24; Marsh, *The Story of the Jubilee Singers*, 133, 167; Odum and Johnson, *The Negro And His Songs*, 35.

[51] Allen *et al., Slave Songs of the United States*, 102–103.

[52] Mary Allen Grissom, compiler, *The Negro Sings A New Heaven* (Chapel Hill, 1930), 73.

[53] Marsh, *The Story of the Jubilee Singers*, 179, 186; Allen *et al., Slave Songs of the United States*, 40–41, 44, 146; Barton, *Old Plantation Hymns*, 30.

couldn't hear, an' when dey'd sing a spiritual an' de spirit 'gin to
shout some de elders would go 'mongst de folks an' put dey han'
over dey mouf an' some times put a clof in dey mouf an' say:
"Spirit don talk so loud or de patterol break us up." You know dey
had white patterols what went 'roun' at night to see de niggers
didn't cut up no devilment, an' den de meetin' would break up an'
some would go to one house an' some to er nudder an' dey would
groan er w'ile, den go home.[54]

Elizabeth Ross Hite testified that although she and her fellow slaves on
a Louisiana plantation were Catholics, "lots didn't like that 'ligion."

We used to hide behind some bricks and hold church ourselves.
You see, the Catholic preachers from France wouldn't let us shout,
and the Lawd done said you gotta shout if you want to be saved.
That's in the Bible.
Sometimes we held church all night long, 'til way in the
mornin'. We burned some grease in a can for the preacher to see
the Bible by. . . .
See, our master didn't like us to have much 'ligion, said it made
us lag in our work. He jest wanted us to be Catholicses on Sundays
and go to mass and not study 'bout nothin' like that on week days.
He didn't want us shoutin' and moanin' all day long, but you gotta
shout and you gotta moan if you wants to be saved.[55]

The slaves clearly craved the affirmation and promise of their religion. It would be a mistake, however, to see this urge as exclusively other-
worldly. When Thomas Wentworth Higginson observed that the spirituals exhibited "nothing but patience for this life,—nothing but triumph in
the next," he, and later observers who elaborated upon this judgment,
were indulging in hyperbole. Although Jesus was ubiquitous in the spirituals, it was not invariably the Jesus of the New Testament of whom the
slaves sang, but frequently a Jesus transformed into an Old Testament
warrior: "Mass' Jesus" who engaged in personal combat with the Devil;
"King Jesus" seated on a milk-white horse with sword and shield in
hand. "Ride on, King Jesus," "Ride on, conquering King," "The God I
serve is a man of war," the slaves sang.[56] This transformation of Jesus is
symptomatic of the slaves' selectivity in choosing those parts of the Bible
which were to serve as the basis of their religious consciousness. Howard
Thurman, a Negro minister who as a boy had the duty of reading the
Bible to his grandmother, was perplexed by her refusal to allow him to
read from the Epistles of Paul.

[54] McIlhenny, *Befo' De War Spirituals*, 31.
[55] *Gumbo Ya-Ya: A Collection of Louisiana Folk Tales*, compiled by Lyle Saxon,
Edward Dreyer, and Robert Tallant from materials gathered by workers of the
WPA, Louisiana Writer's Project (Boston, 1945), 242.
[56] For examples, see Allen *et al.*, *Slave Songs of the United States*, 40–41, 82, 97, 106–
108; Marsh, *The Story of the Jubilee Singers*, 168, 203; Burlin, *Negro Folk-Songs*,
II, 8–9; Howard Thurman, *Deep River* (New York, 1945), 19–21.

When at length I asked the reason, she told me that during the days of slavery, the minister (white) on the plantation was always preaching from the Pauline letters—"Slaves, be obedient to your masters," etc. "I vowed to myself," she said, "that if freedom ever came and I learned to read, I would never read that part of the Bible!" [57]

Nor, apparently, did this part of the Scriptures ever constitute a vital element in slave songs or sermons. The emphasis of the spirituals, as Higginson himself noted, was upon the Old Testament and the exploits of the Hebrew children.[58] It is important that Daniel and David and Joshua and Jonah and Moses and Noah, all of whom fill the lines of the spirituals, were delivered in *this* world and delivered in ways which struck the imagination of the slaves. Over and over their songs dwelt upon the spectacle of the Red Sea opening to allow the Hebrew slaves past before inundating the mighty armies of the Pharaoh. They lingered delightedly upon the image of little David humbling the great Goliath with a stone—a pretechnological victory which post-bellum Negroes were to expand upon in their songs of John Henry. They retold in endless variation the stories of the blind and humbled Samson bringing down the mansions of his conquerors; of the ridiculed Noah patiently building the ark which would deliver him from the doom of a mocking world; of the timid Jonah attaining freedom from his confinement through faith. The similarity of these tales to the situation of the slave was too clear for him not to see it; too clear for us to believe that the songs had no worldly content for the black man in bondage. "O my Lord delivered Daniel," the slaves observed, and responded logically: "O why not deliver me, too?"

> He delivered Daniel from de lion's den,
> Jonah from de belly ob de whale,
> And de Hebrew children from de fiery furnace,
> And why not every man? [59]

These lines state as clearly as anything can the manner in which the sacred world of the slaves was able to fuse the precedents of the

[57] Thurman, *Deep River*, 16–17.

[58] Higginson, *Army Life in a Black Regiment*, 202–205. Many of those northerners who came to the South to "uplift" the freedmen were deeply disturbed at the Old Testament emphasis of their religion. H. G. Spaulding complained that the ex-slaves needed to be introduced to "the light and warmth of the Gospel," and reported that a Union army officer told him: "Those people had enough of the Old Testament thrown at their heads under slavery. Now give them the glorious utterances and practical teachings of the Great Master." Spaulding, "Under the Palmetto," reprinted in Jackson, *The Negro and His Folklore in Nineteenth-Century Periodicals*, 66.

[59] Allen *et al.*, *Slave Songs of the United States*, 148; Fenner, *Religious Folk Songs of the Negro*, 21; Marsh, *The Story of the Jubilee Singers*, 134–135; McIlhenny, *Befo' De War Spirituals*, 248–249.

past, the conditions of the present, and the promise of the future into one connected reality. In this respect there was always a latent and symbolic element of protest in the slave's religious songs which frequently became overt and explicit. Frederick Douglass asserted that for him and many of his fellow slaves the song, "O Canaan, sweet Canaan,/I am bound for the land of Canaan," symbolized "something more than a hope of reaching heaven. We meant to reach the *North*, and the North was our Canaan," and he wrote that the lines of another spiritual, "Run to Jesus, shun the danger,/I don't expect to stay much longer here," had a double meaning which first suggested to him the thought of escaping from slavery.[60] Similarly, when the black troops in Higginson's regiment sang:

> We'll soon be free, [three times]
> When de Lord will call us home.

a young drummer boy explained to him, "Dey think *de Lord* mean for say *de Yankees*." [61] Nor is there any reason to doubt that slaves could have used their songs as a means of secret communication. An ex-slave told Lydia Parrish that when he and his fellow slaves "suspicioned" that one of their number was telling tales to the driver, they would sing lines like the following while working in the field:

> O Judyas he wuz a 'ceitful man
> He went an' betray a mos' innocen' man.
> Fo' thirty pieces a silver dat it wuz done
> He went in de woods an' e' self he hung.[62]

And it is possible, as many writers have argued, that such spirituals as the commonly heard "Steal away, steal away, steal away to Jesus!" were used as explicit calls to secret meetings.

But it is not necessary to invest the spirituals with a secular function only at the price of divesting them of their religious content, as Miles Mark Fisher has done.[63] While we may make such clear-cut distinctions, I have tried to show that the slaves did not. For them religion never constituted a simple escape from this world, because their conception of the world was more expansive than modern man's. Nowhere is this better illustrated than during the Civil War itself. While the war gave rise to such new spirituals as "Before I'd be a slave/I'd be buried in my grave,/ And go home to my Lord and be saved!" or the popular "Many thousand Go," with its jubilant rejection of all the facets of slave life—"No more peck o' corn for me, . . . No more driver's lash for me, . . . No more pint o' salt for me, . . . No more hundred lash for me, . . . No more

[60] *Life and Times of Frederick Douglass*, 159–160; Marsh, *The Story of the Jubilee Singers*, 188.
[61] Higginson, *Army Life in a Black Regiment*, 217.
[62] Parrish, *Slave Songs of the Georgia Sea Islands*, 247.
[63] "Actually, not one spiritual in its primary form reflected interest in anything other than a full life here and now." Fisher, *Negro Slave Songs in the United States*, 137.

mistress' call for me" [64]—the important thing was not that large numbers of slaves now could create new songs which openly expressed their views of slavery; that was to be expected. More significant was the ease with which their old songs fit their new situation. With so much of their inspiration drawn from the events of the Old Testament and the Book of Revelation, the slaves had long sung of wars, of battles, of the Army of the Lord, of Soldiers of the Cross, of trumpets summoning the faithful, of vanquishing the hosts of evil. These songs especially were, as Higginson put it, "available for camp purposes with very little strain upon their symbolism." "We'll cross de mighty river," his troops sang while marching or rowing,

> We'll cross de danger water, . . .
> O Pharaoh's army drownded!
> My army cross over.

"O blow your trumpet, Gabriel," they sang,

> Blow your trumpet louder;
> And I want dat trumpet to blow me home
> To my new Jerusalem.

But they also found their less overtly militant songs quite as appropriate to warfare. Their most popular and effective marching song was:

> Jesus call you, Go in de wilderness,
>   Go in de wilderness, go in de wilderness,
> Jesus call you. Go in de wilderness
>   To wait upon de Lord.[65]

Black Union soldiers found it no more incongruous to accompany their fight for freedom with the sacred songs of their bondage than they had found it inappropriate as slaves to sing their spirituals while picking cotton or shucking corn. Their religious songs, like their religion itself, was of this world as well as the next.

Slave songs by themselves, of course, do not present us with a definitive key to the life and mind of the slave. They have to be seen within the context of the slave's situation and examined alongside such other cultural materials as folk tales. But slave songs do indicate the need to rethink a number of assumptions that have shaped recent interpretations of slavery, such as the assumption that because slavery eroded the linguistic and institutional side of African life it wiped out almost all the more fundamental aspects of African culture. Culture, certainly, is more than merely the sum total of institutions and language. It is also expressed by something less tangible, which the anthropologist Robert Redfield has

[64] Barton, *Old Plantation Hymns*, 25; Allen *et al., Slave Songs of the United States*, 94; McKim, "Negro Songs," 149.
[65] Higginson, *Army Life in a Black Regiment*, 201–202, 211–212.

called "style of life." Peoples as different as the Lapp and the Bedouin, Redfield has argued, with diverse languages, religions, customs, and institutions, may still share an emphasis on certain virtues and ideals, certain manners of independence and hospitality, general ways of looking upon the world, which give them a similar life style.[66] This argument applies to the West African cultures from which the slaves came. Though they varied widely in language, institutions, gods, and familial patterns, they shared a fundamental outlook toward the past, present, and future and common means of cultural expression which could well have constituted the basis of a sense of community and identity capable of surviving the impact of slavery.

Slave songs present us with abundant evidence that in the structure of their music and dance, in the uses to which music was put, in the survival of the oral tradition, in the retention of such practices as spirit possession which often accompanied the creation of spirituals, and in the ways in which the slaves expressed their new religion, important elements of their shared African heritage remained alive not just as quaint cultural vestiges but as vitally creative elements of slave culture. This could never have happened if slavery was, as Professor Elkins maintains, a system which so completely closed in around the slave, so totally penetrated his personality structure as to infantalize him and reduce him to a kind of *tabula rasa* upon which the white man could write what he chose.[67]

Slave songs provide us with the beginnings of a very different kind of hypothesis: that the preliterate, premodern Africans, with their sacred world view, were so imperfectly acculturated into the secular American society into which they were thrust, were so completely denied access to the ideology and dreams which formed the core of the consciousness of other Americans, that they were forced to fall back upon the only cultural frames of reference that made any sense to them and gave them any feeling of security. I use the word "forced" advisedly. Even if the slaves had had the opportunity to enter fully into the life of the larger society, they might still have chosen to retain and perpetuate certain elements of their African heritage. But the point is that they really had no choice. True acculturation was denied to most slaves. The alternatives were either to remain in a state of cultural limbo, divested of the old cultural patterns but not allowed to adopt those of their new homeland—which in the long run is no alternative at all—or to cling to as many as possible of the old ways of thinking and acting. The slaves' oral tradition, their music, and their religious outlook served this latter function and constituted a cultural refuge at least potentially capable of protecting their personalities from some of the worst ravages of the slave system.

The argument of Professors Tannenbaum and Elkins that the Protestant churches in the United States did not act as a buffer between the slave and his master is persuasive enough, but it betrays a modern pre-

---

[66] Robert Redfield, *The Primitive World and Its Transformations* (Ithaca, 1953), 51–53.

[67] Elkins, *Slavery*, Chap. III.

occupation with purely institutional arrangements.[68] Religion is more than an institution, and because Protestant churches failed to protect the slave's inner being from the incursions of the slave system, it does not follow that the spiritual message of Protestantism failed as well. Slave songs are a testament to the ways in which Christianity provided slaves with the precedents, heroes, and future promise that allowed them to transcend the purely temporal bonds of the Peculiar Institution.

Historians have frequently failed to perceive the full importance of this because they have not taken the slave's religiosity seriously enough. A people cannot create a music as forceful and striking as slave music out of a mere uninternalized anodyne. Those who have argued that Negroes did not oppose slavery in any meaningful way are writing from a modern, political context. What they really mean is that the slaves found no *political* means to oppose slavery. But slaves, to borrow Professor Hobsbawm's term, were prepolitical beings in a prepolitical situation.[69] Within their frame of reference there were other—and from the point of view of personality development, not necessarily less effective—means of escape and opposition. If mid-twentieth-century historians have difficulty perceiving the sacred universe created by slaves as a serious alternative to the societal system created by southern slaveholders, the problem may be the historians' and not the slaves'.

Above all, the study of slave songs forces the historian to move out of his own culture, in which music plays a peripheral role, and offers him the opportunity to understand the ways in which black slaves were able to perpetuate much of the centrality and functional importance that music had for their African ancestors. In the concluding lines of his perceptive study of primitive song, C. M. Bowra has written:

> Primitive song is indispensable to those who practice it. . . . they cannot do without song, which both formulates and answers their nagging questions, enables them to pursue action with zest and confidence, brings them into touch with gods and spirits, and makes them feel less strange in the natural world. . . . it gives to them a solid centre in what otherwise would be almost chaos, and a continuity in their being, which would too easily dissolve before the calls of the implacable present . . . through its words men, who might otherwise give in to the malice of circumstances, find their old powers revived or new powers stirring in them, and through these life itself is sustained and renewed and fulfilled.[70]

This, I think, sums up concisely the function of song for the slave. Without a general understanding of that function, without a specific understanding of the content and meaning of slave song, there can be no full comprehension of the effects of slavery upon the slave or the meaning of the society from which slaves emerged at emancipation.

68 *Ibid.*, Chap. II; Frank Tannenbaum, *Slave and Citizen* (New York, 1946).
69 E. J. Hobsbawm, *Primitive Rebels* (New York, 1959), Chap. I.
70 C. M. Bowra, *Primitive Song* (London, 1962), 285–286.

Suggestions for Further Reading

Childbirth—and, more generally, attitudes toward sex and sex roles—can be studied further in G. J. Barker-Benfield, *The Horrors of the Half-Known Life: Male Attitudes Toward Women and Sexuality in Nineteenth-Century America* (New York, 1976); Nancy F. Cott, *The Bonds of Womanhood: "Women's Sphere" in New England, 1780–1835* * (New Haven, 1977); Robin M. Haller, *The Physician and Sexuality in Victorian America* (Urbana, Ill., 1974); David M. Kennedy, *Birth Control in America* (New Haven, 1970); Carroll Smith-Rosenberg, "The Hysterical Woman: Sex Roles and Role Conflict in 19th-Century America," *Social Research*, 39 (1972):652–78; and Ronald G. Walters, *Primers for Prudery: Sexual Advice to Victorian America* * (Englewood Cliffs, N.J., 1974).

Education, transmitted through either formal institutions or the daily experience of living, was woven into everyone's life. For a conceptual discussion of this see Bernard Bailyn, *Education in the Forming of American Society* * (Chapel Hill, N.C., 1964). On rearing children in the antebellum period see Robert Sunley, "Early Nineteenth-Century American Literature on Child Rearing," in Margaret Mead and Martha Wolfenstein, eds., *Childhood in Contemporary Cultures* (Chicago, 1963), pp. 150–67; and Bernard Wishy, *The Child and the Republic: The Dawn of Modern American Child Culture* (Philadelphia, 1967). For secondary education the inquiring student can turn to Michael B. Katz, *The Irony of Early School Reform: Educational Innovation in Mid-Nineteenth-Century Massachusetts* (Cambridge, Mass., 1968); Carl F. Kaestle, *The Evolution of an Urban School System: New York City, 1750–1850* (Cambridge, Mass., 1973); and Stanley K. Schultz, *The Culture Factory: Boston Public Schools, 1789–1860* (New York, 1973).

The lives of students in American colleges, which grew enormously in number between the Revolution and the Civil War, are treated extensively in David F. Allmendinger, Jr., *Paupers and Scholars: The Transformation of Student Life in Nineteenth-Century New England* (New York, 1975); Steven J. Novak, *The Rights of Youth: American Colleges and Student Revolt, 1798–1815* (Cambridge, Mass., 1977); and Robert A. McCaughey, "The Usable Past: A Study of the Harvard College Revolt of 1834," *William and Mary Law Review*, 11 (1970):587–610.

Changing women's roles in the nineteenth century are the subject of much new historical inquiry. For new female roles in an in-

* Available in paperback edition.

dustrializing work force see Edith Abbott, *Women in Industry* (New York, 1915); Hannah Josephson, *The Golden Thread: New England Mill Girls and Magnates* (New York, 1949); Caroline Ware, *Early New England Cotton Manufacturing* (Cambridge, Mass., 1931); and Gerda Lerner, "The Lady and the Mill Girl: Changes in the Status of Women in the Age of Jackson," *Midcontinent American Studies Journal*, 10 (1969):5–15. Other aspects of women's life for this period can be studied in Nancy F. Cott, "Young Women in the Second Great Awakening in New England," *Feminist Studies*, 3 (1975):15–29; Linda Kerber, "The Republic Mother: Women and the Enlightenment, An American Perspective," *American Quarterly*, 28 (1976):187–205; Carroll Smith-Rosenberg, "The Female World of Love and Ritual: Relations between Women in Nineteenth-Century America," *Signs: A Journal of Women in Society and Culture*, 1 (1975):1–30; William R. Taylor and Christopher Lasch, "Two Kindred Spirits: Sorority and Family in New England, 1839–1846," *New England Quarterly*, 36 (1963):23–41; Keith Melder, "Ladies Bountiful: Organized Benevolence in Early 19th-Century America," *New York History*, 65 (1967):231–54; and Barbara Welter, "The Cult of True Womanhood, 1820–1860," *American Quarterly*, 18 (1966):151–74.

For contrasting views of antebellum slave life the student can probe John Blassingame, *The Slave Community: Plantation Life in the Ante-Bellum South** (New York, 1972); Eugene D. Genovese, *Roll, Jordon, Roll: The World the Slaves Made** (New York, 1974); Herbert G. Gutman, *The Black Family in Slavery and Freedom** (New York, 1976); and Lawrence W. Levine, *Black Culture and Black Consciousness: Afro-American Folk Thought from Slavery to Freedom* (New York, 1977). Also valuable are Kenneth Stampp, *The Peculiar Institution: Slavery in the Ante-Bellum South** (New York, 1956); Vincent Harding, "Religion and Resistance Among Antebellum Negroes," in August Meier and Elliott Rudwick, eds., *The Making of Black America** (New York, 1969) pp. 179–97; George P. Rawick, *From Sundown to Sunup: The Making of the Black Community* (Westport, Conn., 1972); Raymond A. Bauer and Alice H. Bauer, "Day-to-Day Resistance to Slavery," *Journal of Negro History*, 27 (1942):388–419; and Robert H. Abzug, "The Black Family During Reconstruction," in Nathan I. Huggins et al., eds., *Key Issues in the Afro-American Experience,** 2 vols. (New York, 1971), 2:26–41.

1830–1877
The Expanding Nation

Factories

ALAN DAWLEY

Daily life for the lower-class American worker changed radically in the nineteenth century. In an earlier epoch most men had worked at agricultural labor. The rising and setting of the sun, the weather, the seasons, and the cycle of crops regulated their lives. When the ground lay fallow in winter, the pace of work slowed, just as it quickened at seed time and harvest time. But in the nineteenth century, with the advent of industrial capitalism, more and more people worked at machines. The clock measured out the pace of toil, and tasks were repeated again and again. They had entered a world where the rationalized, mechanized division of labor was the key to profit. The profits, however, went most often to a small number of owners rather than to the mass of workers who passed through the factory doors each morning.

The swiftness of the growth of industrialism is well illustrated by the case of Lynn, Massachusetts, the setting for the following selection. A river village of about 2,200 people on the eve of the American Revolution, Lynn grew almost tenfold in the next hundred years. By the time of the Civil War it was larger than Boston had been when the Declaration of Independence was signed. Growth and industrialization brought wholesale changes. The entrepreneur who could capitalize and organize the production and distribution of shoes, Lynn's main manufacture, replaced the independent artisan. The shift from shop craftsmanship to factory machine-labor also was accompanied by the appearance of a yawning gap between rich and poor and a redistribution of wealth that left little in the hands of the lower half of society.

The Jacksonian era is often labeled the "Age of the Common Man." Insofar as the phrase refers to broadened political participation, it has historical meaning. But in economic terms the common man was more often the victim than the beneficiary of the new order. Therein lay the central paradox of the age of industrialization: the cultural myth proclaimed that every conscientious laboring person could rise, but the social reality was that most wage earners were permanently relegated to lower-class status, and their lives were spent trying to keep poverty at bay.

Alan Dawley takes us into the streets and factories of Lynn in the antebellum period. He demonstrates that the adjustment to industrial capitalism was a long, bloody, and difficult process. In the second half of the selection, which students may want to read first, he describes the "system of the factory." After considering how preindustrial work rhythms were altered by routinized clockwork, readers may wish to think about the effects of "modernization" (of which industrialization is a central element) on everyday life. In the first part of the essay, Dawley focuses on the strike of 1860, the largest labor protest in the United States to that date. Students will want to consider the strikers' objectives and tactics and the reasons that the factory owners ultimately prevailed.

For two centuries after the initial white settlement of New England, profit hungry investors and frustrated fortune hunters encountered powerful restraints on economic development. They were impeded by Puritan strictures against profiteering, by mercantilist regulations of the economy, and by environmental backwardness. But they persevered, and by the second quarter of the nineteenth century their boundless ambition for gain had achieved significant breakthroughs in extending the principles and practices of marketplace directly into the sphere of production.

Leading the way were shoes and textiles, which stood first and second in the industrial statistics of New England from the first statistical surveys in the 1830s through the Civil War. Together these industries carved great basins of industrialization out of the hilly, rock-ribbed countryside that straddled the Merrimack and Connecticut River valleys and ran inland from the shores of Rhode Island and eastern Massachusetts. Lynn lay in one of these basins stretching from Boston to the White Mountains and including the major manufacturing cities of Lowell, Lawrence, Haverhill, Salem, Manchester, and Newburyport, plus several other smaller cities in Massachusetts, New Hampshire, and Maine. Furthermore, dozens of additional villages in the country imitated the enterprise of the more renowned urban centers, and in some of these hamlets outworkers for the shoe industry labored in the shadow of a local textile mill. Everywhere central shops, factories, and warehouses were shouldering their way in among the artisan shops, hay barns, livery stables, and grist mills that represented the vanishing era of economic restraint.

Lynn manufacturers joined the headlong rush toward unimpeded economic development. Between 1830 and 1836 they increased production by two-thirds, making this a time of "feverish excitement" when the character of the town changed "more rapidly and more essentially than at any previous period in her history." The number of streets and buildings nearly doubled in these years, and the physical strain on the community was compounded by social dislocation. The only thing that held back the rapacity of the entrepreneurs was the fearsome grip of panic, which took hold in 1837 and stopped them in their tracks. For the next seven years, they chafed at the restraints of the prolonged depression in the industry and organized through the Whig party to improve their prospects by increasing the tariff on imported shoes. But foreign competition was no longer a major factor in the industry, and when the domestic market finally responded to the proddings of the manufacturers in the mid-1840s, those who had survived congratulated themselves on being sounder and stronger than their fallen competitors and rushed ahead with renewed vigor. Another period of feverish expansion ensued

"Factories." From *Class and Community: The Industrial Revolution in Lynn* by Alan Dawley. Cambridge, Mass.: Harvard University Press, Copyright © 1976 by the President and Fellows of Harvard College. Reprinted by permission of the author and publishers.

between 1845 and 1850; boosted by the rapidly lengthening railroad network, shoe production came close to doubling. . . . Freed from the
restraints of the past, the marketplace did not produce Adam Smith's
version of stable, self-regulating progress, but manic cycles of expansion
and contraction.[1]

The main resource for expansion was labor. Increased output in the
prefactory era was directly proportional to an increase in the number of
shoemakers, and employers calculated profits in these terms: so many
hands, so many dollars. During business upturns, they hired hand over
fist; for every three employees of a Lynn firm in 1845, there were five in
1850. . . . Like the declining dominions of the Old South which were
sending slave laborers to the more profitable cotton lands of the West,
rural New England yielded up its laborers to employers who mined the
area as if it were filled with gold. Making the transfer from farming to
shoemaking was not difficult for the rural inhabitants, who had worked
with their hands from childhood. What teenage girl did not know how
to stitch and sew? What man who mended harnesses and repaired saddles
could not learn the gentle craft of shoemaking, especially now that
cutting was done by specialists? So for a quarter of a century the land
readily gave up its people.

But no resource, however abundant, is inexhaustible. Employers
quickly depleted the areas close to the cities, and they had to range ever
further afield. Driven by gold fever, shoe manufacturers ventured into
northern New Hampshire and Vermont, while textile employers pros-
pected as far away as upstate New York and Canada in search of young
female operatives. Competition among the employers was compounded by
the migration of labor out of the region; enough Massachusetts natives
moved to New York to make the number living there in 1850 almost
equal to the total number of people employed by the entire Massachusetts
boot and shoe industry.[2] The shoe industry felt these pressures in the
form of a diminishing marginal product in the branch where competition
for labor was most keen—binding. In the 1830s each binder stitched an
average of 934 pairs a year, but by 1850 the number had fallen below 700.
The rates of output appear in Table I.[3]

Because textile recruiters sent most of the ready women without
children to the factories, the boot and shoe firms had difficulty finding
full-time binders and, instead, had to rely on new recruits who bound
shoes intermittently between their other chores at home. "Women's
nimble fingers," wrote one observer, "were found inadequate to the
demand."[4]

The geographical outreach of the outwork system heightened the
manufacturers' dilemma by making production most sluggish at the
frontiers of expansion. Transportation of raw materials to the fringes of
the system 150 miles from Lynn consumed two or three weeks, and the
return trip doubled the time lost in transit. When this delay was added
to the easy going work pace logged by farmer shoemakers, the result
was a waiting time that ranged as high as six to nine months before a
pair of shoes was finished.[5] The further the system expanded without
changing its technological base the more difficulty it encountered reach-

TABLE I
AVERAGE ANNUAL OUTPUT (IN PAIRS OF SHOES) OF MEN AND
WOMEN EMPLOYED BY LYNN FIRMS, 1831–1860

Category	1831	1832	1837	1845	1850	1855	1860
Women	941	842	1018	754	689	714	1438
Men	986	1024	980	894	1154	1031	958

Source: *1831:* C. F. Lummus, *The Lynn Directory and Town Register* . . . (Lynn, 1832), p. 14; *1832:* McLane, "Documents Relative to the Manufactures in the United States," pp. 224–237; *1837:* John W. Barber, *Historical Collections* (Worcester, Mass., 1841), p. 197; *1845:* Palfrey, *Statistics,* pp. 8–38; *1850:* Shattuck, *Report,* p. 508; *1855:* DeWitt, *Information,* pp. 634–643; *1860:* author's calculations from Lynn census manuscripts.

Note: The figures were obtained by dividing total output by total employment in each category.

ing its objectives. As the distance and time between the various steps in the manufacturing process increased and as it became harder to get binding done quickly, the method of sending work out of town, originally designed as a means of raising peak seasonal output, was beginning to have just the opposite result. The gold rush was coming to a close.

DEUS EX MACHINA

The manufacturers' problem was resolved by a deus ex machina in the form of a sewing machine. Minor modifications of the original invention enabled an operator to bind the uppers in a fraction of the time it took by hand. Therefore the manufacturer no longer had to expand the geographical frontiers of his labor force and instead could cut back the total number of female employees and hire a greater proportion from among residents of Lynn. The importance of the machine was emphasized by a newspaper closely identified with the manufacturers: "The introduction of sewing machines for stitching and binding of shoes was the result of an absolute necessity." [6]

Since the uppers were made of cloth or light leather, the same machine could be used for binding uppers and mending a dress. Initially, the cost of the machines restricted their use to people with substantial savings, but their price steadily declined from the $75 to 100 range of the early 1850s to a level around $20 in the early 1860s, before Civil War inflation drove the price up again. Newspaper ads were frequently addressed to "the lady operator and the shoe manufacturer" and strained to make the point that they were for family use, as well as for manufacturing. The ads were effective, and soon "almost every house" in Lynn sported a sewing machine; the number of sewing machines per capita was more than the number of hogs had ever been in preindustrial Lynn. [7]

However, the trend in manufacturing was unmistakably away from the household and toward the factory. The first machines were tried out and proved in the shops of three of the larger manufacturers in 1852. Because they employed two to three times as many people as the average firm, these manufacturers were more deeply entangled in the contradictions of the outwork system than the smaller employers and were especially eager for a way out. Their initiative spread, and by 1855 most of the leading manufacturers had begun to use sewing machines. Sometimes smaller contractors set up independent stitching shops, but usually the manufacturers outfitted rooms of their own. From this point on through 1880 the trend in female employment was downward, even as total output rose; between 1850 and 1860 the number of women employed declined 40 percent, while their output doubled. Both speed and quality were enhanced by bringing operators and machines together under one roof, so that only one-fifth of the women employed in 1875 were left working at home.[8]

From the outset, the stitching shops looked strikingly like factories. The gathering of as many as three or four dozen women in one room and the clatter of their machines were such a contrast to the picture of a woman quietly at work in her own kitchen that everyone agreed a fundamental change had taken place.

The invention of the sewing machine opened a new frontier, which "soon transformed the old fashioned 'shoe-binders' into a new and more expansive class of 'machine girls' whose capacity for labor was only limited by the capabilities of the machines over which they presided. Iron and steel came to the aid of wearied fingers and weakened eyes. This was the beginning of a new era, which is destined to produce results big with lasting benefit to our flourishing city."[9]

Glowing enthusiasm for the factory system appeared in an 1860 federal census report on the boot and shoe industry. Describing the sewing machine as a "crowning invention," the article said that along with a sole-cutting machine it was bringing about "a silent revolution" in manufacturing. The report sensed the shoe industry was "assuming the characteristics of a factory system, being conducted in large establishments of several stories, each floor devoted to a separate part of the work, with the aid of steam-power, and all the labor-saving contrivances known to the trade. It is safe to predict that this change will go on until the little 'workshop' of the shoemaker, with its 'bench' and 'kit,' shall become a thing of the past, as the 'handcard' and the great and little 'spinning wheel' have disappeared from other branches of the clothing manufacture."[10] This report jumped the gun by a few years, but because the major forms of factory organization were fully represented in machine stitching, and because the model of [the] textile industry was so compelling, it is not surprising that the report assumed the inevitability of a full-scale factory system.

THE GREAT STRIKE

The manufacturers' enthusiasm for machines and factories did not spread to the shoemakers. Binders and journeymen looked back over a

quarter century of social dislocation, and now in the 1850s they feared
that once again the manufacturers were up to no good. The first sewing
machines introduced into the city "aroused the ire" of the binders, who
saw them as another incursion on their household independence. A dele-
gation of binders tried to block the spread of the new devices by visiting
a central shop where one had been installed and requesting the operator
to cease her work on the grounds that the machine "would ultimately be
the ruin of the poor workingwomen."¹¹ These early machines, which
cost a third to a half of a binder's annual income, were clearly implements
designed to benefit only capitalists; both the binders who went into the
stitching shops and the shrinking group of those who worked at home
continued to regard the new methods of production with extreme dis-
trust. Each binder knew that the labor the new devices saved could well
be her own, and what good, she wondered, could possibly come of something that eliminated hundreds of jobs each season.

   The binders' ire was mollified for a time by the declining price of the
sewing machine (making it more accessible for family use) and by the
persistence of high levels of employment in the shoe industry. But when
the Panic of 1857 brought the shoe business to a standstill, and workers
all over the city were given the sack, the twin pressures of depression
and displacement converged on shoemaker families to force discontent to
the surface again, as in the 1830s and 1840s. The tensions between shoemakers and their bosses were apparent at two mass meetings held on the
edge of winter in the depression's first year. As journeymen shoemakers
and other laboring men of the community filed into Lynn's rustic
Lyceum Hall, the chill November air reminded them of the blankets,
overcoats, cordwood, and provisions they would need in the coming
months, and of the long winter layover looming ahead when they would
have little or no income. They listened with growing indignation while
businessmen and politicians proposed emergency public relief, as if the
honest workingmen of Lynn were nothing but paupers. Were they not
able-bodied men willing to work?

   At a second community meeting the following week, these sentiments buried the proposals for public relief. "Would it not be better,"
asked one opponent of charity, "for the shoe manufacturers to give full
price—to say to the workman we will give you a little something to do
until business is better?" And he added, "Let the rich come forward and
say we will give you ten per cent of the profits we have made." The idea
was radical enough to prompt a quick rejoinder from a shoe manufacturer and leather dealer named John B. Alley that the purpose of the
meeting was not to degrade business for the benefit of labor. Alley was
an up-and-coming politician on his way to the House of Representatives
polishing the techniques of rhetorical compromise; he endorsed the work
ethic but argued present circumstances made public relief a practical
necessity.¹²

   Despite Alley's compromise, this debate set a tone of hostility for encounters between shoemakers and shoe manufacturers during the next
three years. Eight months later several hundred journeymen sweltered
through a July meeting in the Lyceum to consider a strike to raise wages.

No action was taken immediately, but economic distress kept up a steady pressure, and by the spring of 1859 journeymen had established the Lynn Mechanics Association and had begun publishing the *New England Mechanic*.[13] The Association and the *Mechanic* continued operation for the remainder of the year, becoming a solid core of organizational strength among the journeymen. Finally, in the winter of 1860 all the years of anxiety over the effects of machine stitching combined with the years of depression to produce a mounting frustration that burst forth in the Great Shoemakers Strike.

The biggest strike the United States had ever experienced hit the whole upper New England basin like a driving "Nor'easter." The shoe centers along the North Shore bore the full brunt of the storm, where a clear majority of shoemakers joined the strike, and it also swept inland to secondary towns and outwork villages. All in all, probably a minimum of 20,000 people quit work, somewhat more than half the employees living in this region and a third of the 60,000 employees of all Massachusetts firms. The progress of the strike was given large play in most of the region's major newspapers, and national journals sent illustrators and reporters to the scene. The experience left an indelible mark on folk memory, and for a generation it was recalled with the frequency and vividness people usually reserved for earthquakes or hurricanes. Given the scope of the strike, it is astonishing that it should have been totally ignored in the works of John Commons and several of his followers. This gap was filled by Philip Foner, who wrote an excellent overview of the strike, and later by George R. Taylor, who recognized the event as "the greatest strike in American history before the Civil War." [14]

Lynn was at the center of the storm. The strike began on Washington's Birthday, a date the journeymen picked to demonstrate they were acting in the best traditions of the Republic, They believed the producers were the bone and sinew of society, and in a community of interdependent households the producers should be able to unite and carry everyone along with them. The dimensions of their success were revealed in the scope and style of demonstrations and parades held in support of the strike. In six weeks, five processions passed through the streets of Lynn, each with 1000 or more people in the line of march, plus hundreds of sympathizers in the sidelines. The largest demonstration occurred on March 16; besides strikers from Lynn marching in ward units, the 6000 people who crowded into the procession included companies of militia and firemen, brass bands, and several out-of-town strike delegations. The order of march that day was:

> Lynn City Guards, Lynn Cornet Band; Lady stitchers, in wards; delegations of women from Swampscott and elsewhere; Fountain Engine Co. #3, Lynn; Co. #4 of Marblehead; Tiger Engine #4 of Lynn; Atlantic #1, Swampscott; Engine #5 and Chelsea Brass Band; strikers from Swampscott; Eagle #5, S. Danvers; Niagara #9, Lynn; delegations from South Danvers, Danversport, East Danvers with banners; strikers of wards 4, 5, 6 of Lynn; strikers of Saugus and South Reading; Volunteer Fire #8, Lynn; Worth #2

> Stoneham with strikers from Stoneham and East Woburn; ward 7
> strikers of Lynn; strikers from Beverly and Beverly Cornet band;
> Salem strikers; Marblehead strikers, escorted by Lafayette Guards,
> Glover Light Guards, Marblehead Band, Engine Cos. #1, #2;
> Washington Hook and Ladder #1, Gerry Co.[15]

The strikers immersed themselves in the pageantry of waving banners and brightly festooned uniforms to show that their strike had the support and expressed the will of the general community. The presence of the militia companies and firemen—themselves mostly laboring men in special uniforms—emphasized the interdependence among the householders of an artisan community. The organization of the strikers into ward units bespoke the ties of neighborhood fraternity and sorority. The joint participation of men and women expressed the solidarity of all who labored in the craft. The strike processions, therefore, emerged from the customs and traditions of preindustrial society. They were festivals of the old artisan way of life presented in the context of the new system of industrial capitalism. Influences from the past and forces leading to the future simultaneously fashioned the present event.

The presence of women was a noteworthy feature of the processions. Without the action of women, it is questionable whether the strike would have occurred at all, and certainly without them it would have been far less massive in its impact. Women's grievances helped cause it; their demands shaped its objectives; their support ratified it as a community undertaking. Whether they worked at home or in the manufacturers' shops, all women employees earned piece wages, and both home and shop workers focused their demands on an increase in wages. They held their own strike meetings, did their own canvassing in Lynn and nearby towns to win support, and turned out in strength for the big street demonstrations. The laborer, they contended, was worthy of her hire.

The demonstration on March 7 was held in their honor. Escorted by a detachment of musket-bearing militia, 800 women strikers started at Lynn Common and marched in the falling snow for several hours past the central shops on Lynn's major thoroughfares. Their action was a bold violation of the cultural code that stipulated women should not venture beyond kitchen hearth and church pew. The keepers of this code of True Womanhood were middle-class families in retreat from the disorder of urban life into their parlors, sewing circles, and church clubs. But workingwomen were bound to no such cult of domesticity. For several generations their labor had mingled with that of other producers, just as their protests had blended with the journeymen, and they were not about to renounce their own heritage of Equal Rights.[16]

At the head of their procession they carried a banner with an inscription taken from the Equal Rights philosophy: "AMERICAN LADIES WILL NOT BE SLAVES: GIVE US A FAIR COMPENSATION AND WE LABOUR CHEERFULLY." Slavery had long been the measure of the ultimate degradation of labor, the point to which the shoe bosses seemed to be driving their employees. With the execution of John Brown only three months before the strike, artisans felt the im-

mediacy of the conflict between slavery and Free Soil, and analogies
linking manufacturers to slavemasters flowed freely. One speaker at a
mass meeting declared it was not necessary to go to "bleeding Kansas" to
find oppressors of labor; there were plenty who had been "drawing the
chains of slavery, and riveting them closer and closer around the limbs of
free laboring men at home." [17] A similar note was struck by the first
stanza of the "Cordwainers' Song," written during the strike by Alonzo
Lewis.

Shoemakers of Lynn, be brave!
  Renew your resolves again;
Sink not to the state of slave,
  But stand for your rights like men!

Resolve by your native soil,
  Resolve by your fathers' graves,
You will live by your honest toil,
  But never consent to be slaves!

The workman is worthy his hire,
  No tyrant shall hold us in thrall;
They may order their soldiers to fire,
  But we'll stick to the hammer and awl.

Better days will restore us our rights,
  The future shall shine o'er the past;
We shall triumph by justice and right,
  For like men we'll hold onto the last!

The peaceable people of Lynn
  Need no rifles to keep them at peace;
By the right of our cause we shall win;
  But no rum, and no outside police.[18]

For all its resounding resolves, the song was clearly not in tune with full
sexual equality. The Equal Rights tradition countenanced a limited version
of feminism: women who worked should be accorded a place of honor
among the ranks of toilers, should be paid a fair and equal compensation,
and should take an active role in defending the rights of labor. But this
was the extent of labor feminism; when it came to critical strike strategy,
to political affairs, and to final arbitration in domestic matters, men ought
to be in charge. Thus the cultural environment of the strike was filled
with symbols of manhood which could hardly appeal to women strikers.
The call to "stand for your rights like men!" must have left women
seated in their chairs.

The "Cordwainers' Song" rallied shoemakers to the defense of the
Tree of Liberty. Striking a classic Jeffersonian pose, the brave shoemakers prepared to shed their blood, should tyrants order their soldiers
to fire. The tyrants of the song were the big shoe bosses of Lynn, especially those who practiced "dishonest competition" and affected an air
of superiority in their dealings with the masses. But some of the manu-

facturers held the trust of the shoemakers, and four bosses received "Hurrahs!" when the Washington's Birthday marchers passed their central shops. One of the four reciprocated the holiday spirit by decorating his building with flags and bunting for the occasion. This was the kind of harmony between labor and capital many strike leaders hoped for. The week before Washington's Birthday, officers in the Mechanics Association had carried a bill of wages around to the manufacturers asking for voluntary agreement to pay the advanced rates. The committee even solicited contributions from the bosses to the strike fund! Shoemakers were not surprised when several manufacturers actually subscribed to pay; leading the list was a boss who "agreed to be taxed $300." Believing they represented the general will of their community, shoemakers found nothing strange in their plan to "tax" their neighbors.[19]

Shoemakers prepared for the strike as members of the "producing classes." As producers they felt they were entitled to a fair reward for their toil, which they defined as an exchange of the goods they made for an equivalent value of food, clothing, shelter, and enjoyments. Anything less was cheating. Thus "monopolists" and "grinders" who cut their prices or cheapened their wares to increase their sales practiced "dishonest competition." In their train followed a host of unfortunate laborers forced to toil for a pittance on cheap goods until their existence approached the pauper labor of Europe. The dire result was the degradation of the earnings and reputations of "honest labor." When artisans divided their employers into "good bosses" and "bad bosses," they were not indulging in meaningless moralizing; they expressed a view of reality that conformed to the heritage of a community of householders.

Yet reality itself went well beyond this view. The central shop was no simple producer's household. The marketplace compelled manufacturers to adhere to the laws of competition, opposing the interest of those who bought labor to the interest of those who sold it. Moreover, shoemakers did not control the instruments of public authority. In the course of the strike, shoemakers were forced to face these disturbing facets of reality. The image of the artisan seemed to dissolve before their eyes, and in its place they saw an image of the industrial worker taking shape.

Shoemakers had to come to terms with the fact that manufacturers did not behave like fellow household producers. Only one came through on his pledge to the strike fund; the rest either reneged completely or paid only a trifling sum, such as a $20 contribution from the man who had agreed to be taxed $300. Worse than that, the manufacturers connived to break the back of the strike by hiring scab labor. They sent agents to ransack the surrounding states for workmen and hired "everything in the shape of a shoemaker." To the manufacturer, business was business, and the laws of the marketplace were more compelling than the will of the majority. With debts to pay, orders to fill, and customers to keep, manufacturers were not about to suspend the quest for profits just because the shoemakers desired it. But to the shoemakers, the manufacturers' effort to keep up production, after promising "to help us through, if we would strike and stick for a few weeks," was an outrageous betrayal. In a retrospective article fuming with indignation, two strike leaders snarled that the manufacturers, virtually without exception, tried to "defeat and disgrace us." One of the leaders told a group of binders in early April that the events of the past few weeks proved "the interest of capital is to get as much labor for as little money as possible." [20]

Shoemakers had interests and compulsions of their own. Money wages were the staff of life; no one could survive any longer on home-grown pork and greens. Because shoemakers were wholly dependent on their industrial income, the wages of industrial unemployment were debt and destitution. Going into debt during the winter layover was a normal experience for shoemakers, but every year since the Panic of 1857 getting out of debt in the spring had been unusually difficult. The manufacturers were "grinding us down so low that men with large families could not live within their own means." [21] Neither could young men with little experience (who were given low-paid tasks) nor women of any age and skill (whose wages were the lowest in the industry). Wage earners of all types concluded that the degradation of free labor was at hand.

In a mood of bitter determination shoemakers vowed that if the manufacturers would not willingly raise their wages, then they must be compelled to do so through a complete cessation of labor. This feeling motivated some strikers to use force to win their objectives, a marked contrast to the holiday atmosphere of the strike processions. On the morning of the day after Washington's Birthday a crowd of strikers gathered in front of the Central Square railroad depot. It was apparent that most manufacturers intended to maintain business as usual, because they continued to send cases of shoe stock to the depot for shipment to outworkers. A considerable portion of the crowd was in favor of preventing all such cases from leaving Lynn. Many who assembled that morning were piqued by a hoax played on them the previous afternoon, when they had carried what appeared to be a case of shoe stock back to its owner, only to discover it was filled with leather scraps and floor sweepings. This provocation was heightened by the local city marshal who addressed the crowd in insulting terms that "only served to increase irritation and excitement among the strikers who heard them." [22]

The marshal got another crack at the shoemakers the same afternoon. With a few deputies in tow he fell upon a handful of men who were dumping cases destined for scab outworkers off an express wagon. The marshal's force succeeded in replacing the cases on the wagon, but in the eyes of the strikers, the marshal was now firmly identified with the shoe bosses, and his office lost whatever majesty it might have had. Pursuing their own justice, the strikers attempted to cast down the cases once again, and when the marshal stood in their way, they pummeled him and his men with their fists. It was reported that one of the strikers drew a knife. Overpowered in this fracas, the marshal refrained from further adventures that afternoon, and several more cases were taken from the train depot and returned to the central shops. In addition, the pugnacious expressman who tried to defend his cargo was "badly hurt," and strikers roughed up at least one journeyman on his way home with fresh materials.[23]

In the eyes of the manufacturers the interference with the flow of

trade and the attack on the city marshal constituted a vile threat to the
social order bordering on insurrection. Through friends in city government, they prevailed upon the mayor to call out the militia. In his letter
to the commander of the Lynn Light Infantry, Co. D, Eighth Regiment
of the Massachusetts Volunteers, the mayor took note that "bodies of
men have tumultuously assembled in [Lynn], and have offered violence
to persons and property, and have, by force and violence resisted and
broken the laws of the Commonwealth; and that military force is necessary to aid the civil authority in suppressing the same." The men were
called to appear at their armory the next morning "armed, equipped with
ammunition." Then while the mayor went off to counsel moderation before a mass meeting of shoemakers, other city officials got in touch with
the state attorney general, the sheriff of Essex County, a major general in
the state militia, and the city officials and police chiefs of Boston and
South Danvers. The manufacturers were taking no chances with unruly
employees.[24]

The next day, February 24, shoemakers arose with dawning amaze-
ment to find their community occupied by outside police and armed militia. In the morning a detachment of deputies from South Danvers stood
guard at the train station to see that there was no more interference with
the shipment of shoe materials, and at 1:00 o'clock a posse of twenty uni-
formed Boston policemen arrived at the depot. These professional law
officers joined the militia at an inn named the Sagamore House, which had
been converted into command headquarters for the day. Decisions were
in the hands of the attorney general, the major general, the city marshal,
and several aldermen; conspicuously absent from the Sagamore was the
mayor, who had fallen ill, and the city councilors. Apparently with the
aim of arresting those who were disorderly the day before, the Boston
regulars were sent back into the streets. Led by the hated city marshal,
they roved through the town for two hours, stimulating near riots where
ever they went. Hounded by hoots and hisses, pelted by stones and brick-
bats, they ran the gauntlet of a hostile crowd, participated in a "general
melee in which several of the crowd were knocked down," and finally
ended their tumultuous trek through town at the railroad depot in Central Square where it had begun.[25]

Most residents of the community were outraged at this incursion on
their right of self-government, and it was a man who lived by his wits,
not his hands, that wrote:

> The peaceable people of Lynn
>   Need no rifles to keep them at peace;
> By the right of our cause we shall win;
>   But no rum and no outside police.

Widespread indignation apparently blocked the prosecution of the five
men arrested that day. Though they were spirited away to Salem for
safekeeping and arraigned and bound over to the grand jury in Lynn a
few days later, there is no record that the grand jury was ever convened
or that any of the men were ever convicted of riotous conduct. The five
benefited from community opposition to the odious actions of manufac-

turers and public officials, even though only one of the men arrested was a long-standing, propertied resident of Lynn. The others were newcomers, immigrants living in poverty, including the Irishman reported to have pulled a knife.[26]

The turmoil of the first three days of the strike was the worst fury of the storm. On the evening of the third day the outside police and state officials left town, and the temporary soldiers dismantled their rifles and went home. That was the end of violence. But the passions stirred up in these days imparted a force and momentum to the strike that carried it through six weeks of mass organizing on a scale never before seen in American industry. While manufacturers hunted for scabs, teams of strike canvassers combed the neighborhoods of Lynn and visited a score of other shoe towns to mobilize support. Thousands of people were organized into strike processions, with thousands more watching. On the days of the processions, dozens of kitchens kept up a steady outpouring of food to provide refreshment to those who marched. In addition, there were rallies in Central Square, mass meetings in Lyceum Hall, and frequent meetings of the strike leadership in the Mechanics Association and the Ladies' Association of Binders and Stitchers.

Support of nonshoemakers was also mobilized. Besides other laboring men who marched in the fire and militia companies (with the conspicuous absence of the infamous Lynn Light Infantry), the city's retail businessmen were called upon to aid the strikers. Most grocers and provisions dealers were compelled to defer collection of shoemakers' bills, regardless of their opinion of the strike, but because of neighborhood ties and revulsion against the military invasion of their community, many retailers actively sympathized with the strikers. One lumber dealer, for example, gave shoemakers free access to a stand of trees he owned so they would not have to purchase cordwood. Several politicians also came forth, though their effort to curry favor with the voters led them into some strange political contortions. Congressman John B. Alley sent a donation of $100 to the strike fund, but after bending over backwards to be identified as a friend of labor he spun around and lectured the shoemakers on the foolishness and futility of their strike, intoning the perpetual murmur of the manufacturers, "the interests of the manufacturer and the journeymen are identical." [27]

The strike was carried through March on high spirits, but by the beginning of April it was fast losing momentum, and within another two weeks it had subsided. Though a substantial number of manufacturers were paying higher wages by the end of the strike, the shoemakers were completely frustrated in their other goal of getting their employers to sign the bill of wages and thereby accede to the principle that shoemakers collectively had a voice in determining their wages. In this regard, the strikers were defeated partly by the decentralized character of bottoming (enabling manufacturers to get shoes bottomed by outworkers with less organization and militancy than Lynn artisans) and partly by the very economic factors that had caused the strike in the first place. To someone with no means of support except his labor, even low wages are better than no wages. Finally, the manufacturers' ability to lay their hands on the instruments of institutionalized violence (even though the effectiveness of the local police force on their behalf was nullified by the shoemakers) put the coercive power of the state on their side and tipped the balance of power their way. Coming after several decades of social dislocation caused by the growth of industrial capitalism, the Great Strike exposed the class fears and hatreds generated by the rising order. In the expanding marketplace, the manufacturer was both the hunter and the hunted, predator and prey. He sharpened his weapons, knowing that creditors and competitors did the same. Thus when a committee of his employees politely asked that he disarm, he politely refused, and when disorderly bands of employees broke his weapons in the street, he gave them a taste of martial law. For their part, the workers knew that the weapons of competition, though they be aimed at business competitors, struck them first. When it came to businessmen buying cheap and selling dear, employees' livelihoods could only suffer. And unless they could act collectively and effectively in their own cause, each would stand alone, the hunted and the prey.

THE SYSTEM OF THE FACTORY

Enclosed in a wooden box like a miniature casket, the vital processes of the factory time clock went on unseen behind the stark white mask and black Roman numerals of the clock face. As the hands on the front face edged toward 7:00 A.M., the hidden workings were convulsed with a spontaneous whirring of wheels and a lifting of levers that tripped the hammer that struck the bell that signaled the start of the day's work. Outside behind the factory a man pushed against an iron rod that threw a lever to engage a wheel that caught the motion generated by a steam engine. Inside the factory on the first floor, gears transmitted energy upward to the ceiling where other gears and shafts and wheels and belts began to spin and whirr until all was ready for the machines and operatives below to begin the day's production. If the clock was an emblem of the mechanical inventiveness of an earlier age, surely the factory was the crowning symbol of the mechanical arts of the nineteenth century. The factory itself was a kind of supermachine—a gross, cacophonous exaggeration of the elegant principles of the clock.

The outer shell of the shoe factory was sometimes fashioned of wood in the traditional style of the central shops and sometimes of stone, but most often it followed the functional, almost military, style of classic factory architecture—several stories of densely regimented red brick, which surfaced iron support beams that carried the weight of the structure and permitted rows of large windows to parade along the walls in brigade formation. Behind the flat, rectilinear facade lay the inner workings of the factory, a jumble of discordant sounds and motions which appeared to the self-important factory owner as a marvel of technological efficiency. In his eyes everything appeared as part of a larger system; every gear and lever, every machine and work table, every foreman and operative hastened the swift, smooth flow of production.

On the first floor the leather was cut and sorted into drawers according to size; the drawers were loaded together and set on a small cart which was wheeled on rails to an elevator and hoisted to the top floor. The uppers were taken from the drawers and prepared by the stitchers, assisted by an assortment of pasters, liners, and buttonhole sewers. Then the completed uppers were replaced in their appropriate drawer on the appropriate car and lowered to the second floor, where other operatives matched them with the appropriate soles. Back in the drawers again, the elevator rose to the third floor where, in a series of short, quick motions, each shoe was passed along a row of workmen to be lasted, bottomed, heeled, finished, and packed. This process could infatuate those who watched it: "The arrangements of this building are perfect in their way. It is a complete beehive of industry; everything is systemized, everything economized, and each part made to act in concert with every other part. There is no clashing or jar[r]ing, and the harmony that prevails speaks volumes for the master mind that planned and controls its operations." [28]

The masterminds who established the factory system had long been preoccupied with the technological and managerial problems associated with prefactory production. Simple hand-tool technology imposed labor intensive conditions on the shoe industry, and expansion in this context created an increasingly inefficient flow of materials from the central shops out and back, and out and back again. Equally significant, the manufacturers could not control the process of production at its most crucial point—in the artisan household—and this hurt their ability to compete in the marketplace. First, it hampered efforts to standardize their wares, something entrepreneurs had been trying to do since the eighteenth century. Manufacturers yearned to tell their retail customers that every shoe they sold had the same shape and overall quality, but because individual artisans had different styles of work and disparate levels of competence, their work lacked uniformity and sometimes showed poor workmanship. Second, manufacturers were stymied by the artisan control over the rhythm of production. Among outworkers, in particular, irregular work schedules meant that sometimes several months went by before finished shoes came back to Lynn. Conditions were somewhat more efficient among the resident journeymen of Lynn, but even here the manufacturers were frustrated by the absence of direct supervision over production. Journeymen sometimes neglected work they had promised to do, occasionally failed to keep the shoes clean, and were also at liberty to break off when they felt like it. Manufacturers concluded that the "employer's interests were allowed to suffer for some momentary enjoyment which was not always conducive to health or good morals." [29]

The factory system resolved the contradictions and conflicts of the household era in favor of the manufacturers. It gave them the means to make the employees act in the employers' interests. Under the new industrial discipline, workers pursued their own momentary enjoyments at the risk of a head-on collision with the boss or his foreman and the loss of a job. Order, therefore, rested on the power of the manufacturers, and harmony in the beehives of industry was founded on economic compulsion, rather than on some instinctive dronish desire on the part of wage earners to cooperate among themselves for the owners' benefit. The manufacturers were eager to take charge of the new industrial army, and, like other men on horseback, they were confident of their right to command and convinced they were astride the forces of progress: "The problem as to how best to bring in and concentrate the vast army of men and women employed in the shoe manufacture of Lynn is one that has attracted the attention of many thinking minds among our business men, but it has never been satisfactorily solved until now." [30]

The catalyst for conversion to the factory system was the adaptation of the sewing machine. Since shoe uppers were made of light leather or cloth, the original invention was quickly altered to suit the task of binding, but since sole leather was harder to sew and bottoming was a more complicated process, it took another decade for a clever inventor to figure out how to apply the sewing machine to that branch of the trade. Finally, Lyman R. Blake of South Abington, Massachusetts, hit on the right combination of moving metal parts to take the needle and thread out of the hands of journeymen cordwainers. Like many another industrious inventor, Blake was pushed aside by a hustling businessman who attached his own name to the machine and sold the first "McKay stitcher" in Lynn in 1862. [31]

The productivity of the McKay operator was far greater than the hand bottomer. The machine allowed an operator to stitch *eighty pairs* in the same time a journeyman could sew the seams on only *one*. [32] However, this ratio of eighty to one was not the final measure of the overall gain in productivity, because the McKay stitcher actually did only part of the journeyman's job. The machine did not last the uppers, position the sole, or shape the leather; for each of these steps, additional hands were necessary, so the journeyman's job was parceled out to a series of workers stationed along the factory production line. At least three other workers were required to put the uppers and bottoms in position to be sewn, and two more had to finish the bottoming process after the shoe came off the machine. Without these other workers, the machines would have been useless, no matter how fast their needles pumped up and down.

The system of the factory was built on the twin foundations of mechanization and the division of labor. The McKay stitcher divided bottoming into half-a-dozen separate steps, and, overall, mechanization broke down the process of shoemaking into thirty-five or forty discrete operations. Prior to the introduction of mechanical labor-saving devices, certain efficiencies had been realized by the specialization of hand laborers into separate branches of the trade. Besides the basic division of labor between binders and bottomers, there were cutters, finishers, and packers working in the central shops.

On the eve of conversion to the factory system, heelers appeared in the trade, and their branch carried specialization further than it had ever been. David Johnson, who was born in 1829 when plenty of men still could make a whole shoe from start to finish, described the various steps in heeling in a passage that echoes Adam Smith's famous account of pin manufacturing: "A man working exclusively at this branch of the craft soon became an expert, even though he knew nothing else of the art of shoemaking. The 'heeling' was afterward subdivided into 'nailing,' 'shaving,' 'blacking,' and 'polishing;' and from this gradually came that minute division which is now the marked feature in this business, distinguishing the new order of things from the old." [33] Of course, this minute division of labor was itself a cause of mechanization, since the simplification of a task only invited the development of a machine to perform it.

The ever finer divisions and the new high-speed machines imparted a revolutionary dynamic to the industry. As speed and efficiency increased in one branch of production, other branches strained to catch up, and to restore equilibrium it was necessary for the whole industry to move at a much faster pace. In this fashion the introduction of the first sewing machines for binding created an imbalance in the rhythm of production. Once, it had been necessary to hire more binders than bottomers to keep the latter supplied with materials. Now the reverse was true; while binding was done at great speed with fewer and fewer binders, bottoming lagged behind. Balance was restored by the McKay stitcher, which vastly increased the velocity of bottoming, but this change, in turn, created new imbalances vis-à-vis cutting, lasting, shaping, trimming, nailing, and buffing. By 1880 every operation except cutting uppers and lasting had been brought up to the faster pace by the invention of new machines. In this period of rapid technological advance, one increase in productivity beckoned forth another . . . innovation sparked further innovation . . . change begat change.

The factory system cracked the whip on production. With technological advance as the pivot, the production line swung around at an ever faster clip, so that out at the tip of the line, productivity streaked ahead at breakneck speed. Each year the average factory worker processed nearly three times as many shoes as a prefactory counterpart. On a daily basis, the increase was about the same. Comparing the statistics from 1875 and 1855, the factory system enabled approximately 2,000 fewer workers to produce 7,000,000 more shoes! There is little wonder that the manufacturers were so effusive in their praise for a system that yielded such wondrous results.[34]

Conversion to the factory system was virtually complete by 1870. Such an enormous changeover in such a short time required larger sums of capital than had ever before been necessary in the shoe industry. In one inner city ward there were half-a-dozen firms valued at $100,000 or more in 1870, whereas no firm in the entire city was worth even half that much before the factories.[35] For a short time this capital expansion could be financed on loans from the local Mechanics Bank (rechristened the First National City Bank in 1864) or from investors in other cities, but sooner or later the bill had to be paid with profits from the shoe industry itself. The manufacturers counted on two factors to provide sufficient profits: mounting productivity and soaring inflation. In terms of productivity, the factory system financed itself by reducing the unit cost of labor and generating the enormous increase in output. Concerning inflation, the manufacturers benefited from a Civil War bonus in the form of large increases in the price of shoes. Although no government contracts were let in Lynn, the inflationary effects of the Union's fiscal expenditures and greenback monetary policy drove up prices on manufactured goods at the precise moment that manufacturers needed extra funds. The average price of a pair of Lynn-made shoes zoomed up from under $1 in 1860 to $1.65 in 1865 and remained at this level through 1870. The rising price made the risk of investing large sums in buildings and machinery seem to disappear. Hoping to get in on the bonus, dozens of small entrepreneurs rushed into the shoe business during the mid-sixties, and were rushed out again just as quickly, but larger manufacturers held on more firmly and carried the conversion through successfully.[36]

The fighting itself caused a temporary loss of the vital southern market, but it was not long before the difficulties of the rebellion began to look like blessings. New orders from everywhere except the deep South arrived in Lynn with cash generated by federal financial policy, a most welcome substitute for the six to eight months credit manufacturers were accustomed to give.[37] This solidified the resources of well-established firms and boosted their capacity to build. Thus with bottlenecks in the rhythm of production breaking up, with unit labor costs dropping, and with ample cash on hand, the manufacturers had a heyday of investment. Stashing away their profits in bricks and iron, gears and machines, they embarked on a period of rapid capital accumulation, and brought Industrial Revolution to the ancient and honorable metropolis of the gentle craft of leather.

By substituting machines for simple hand tools and by eliminating the time lost in transporting the goods to and from the workers, the factory generated an intense concentration of human energy on the productive process. The factory worker did not take an afternoon off because he had a headache or wanted to go fishing; he did not postpone the completion of a case of shoes because he needed to begin the spring plowing. He worked steadily at a pace set by the external forces of the production line and enforced by the line foreman. If he slackened his pace, he threatened his own standard of living, either by risking firing or by cutting down his piece-wage for the day. Since he had no other source of livelihood, it is no wonder that a visitor to one of the factories noticed "the men and boys are working as if for life and scarcely stop to bestow a look upon the visiting party."[38] Such were the requirements of "system" in the factories.

The conversion to factory production appeared as nothing short of revolutionary. David Johnson named the period from 1855 to 1865 "The Great Revolution." It was commonly felt that the changes of those years were not confined to the shoe industry but had effects that pervaded the entire society. The sense of revolutionary change is fully conveyed in the following comment on the factory system which appeared in a local paper of 1863: "Of course, the system is yet in its infancy—the business is yet in a transition state; but the wheels of revolution are moving rapidly, and they never turn backward. Operatives are pouring in as fast as room can be made for them, buildings for "shoe factories" are going

up in every direction, the hum of machinery is heard on every hand, old
things are passing away, and all things are becoming new." [39]

NOTES

[1] [David N.] Johnson, *Sketches [of Lynn, or the Changes of Fifty
Years* (Lynn, 1880)], pp. 146, 154, describes Lynn's growth in the
1830s; *Lynn Freeman*, March 5, March 12, May 21, 1842, provides information on the demand for a higher tariff.

[2] [George R.] Taylor, *[The] Transportation Revolution [1815–
1860* (New York, 1962)], pp. 286–287; [Oliver] Warner, *Abstract
of the Census of Massachusetts, 1865* (Boston, 1867), pp. 291,
784–793; [John G.] Palfrey, *Statistics [of the Condition . . . of
Industry in Massachusetts* (Boston, 1846)], pp. 373–377; Francis
DeWitt, *Statistical Information Relating to Industry in Massachusetts . . . 1855* (Boston, 1856), pp. 634–643. The same statistical sources showed that Haverhill's shoe industry was
experiencing the same problem of declining productivity in
binding.

[3] See Appendix A, ["Tables on Population, Output, and Employment," in Dawley, *Class and Community*].

[4] *[Lynn] Reporter*, Feb. 28, 1863.

[5] *New Hampshire Statesman*, Dec. 4, 1858; *Reporter*, Nov. 21, 1863.

[6] *Reporter*, Feb. 28, 1863.

[7] Carroll D. Wright, *Census of Massachusetts, 1875* (Boston, 1876),
for 1875, II, pp. 825, 827; *[Lynn] News*, ads. June 6, 1856, Feb.
10, 1854; *Reporter*, June 21, 1862, Oct. 7, 1865; Johnson,
Sketches, p. 340.

[8] U.S., Seventh Census, Statistics on Industry in Lynn, data on the
firms of John Wooldredge and George Keene; Wright, *Census,
1875*, II, 39–41.

[9] *Reporter*, Feb. 28, 1863.

[10] U.S., Eighth Census, *Manufactures [of the United States in]
1860*, pp. lxxi–lxxii.

[11] *Reporter*, Oct. 7, 1865.

[12] *News*, Nov. 10, Nov. 16, Nov. 24, 1857, gave detailed reports on
the meetings about the effects of the depression.

[13] *News*, July 27, 1858, March 1, 1859.

[14] The strike was given extensive coverage in the Lynn papers, especially the *Bay State*, a Democratic paper, and the *News*, usually
Republican; it was also covered by the *Independent Democrat* of
Concord, N.H. March 1, March 8, 1860; and the *New Hampshire
Patriot*, Feb. 29, March 7, 1860, published in Concord; the strike
was also reported in the eastern urban press, such as the *Boston
Journal*, the *New York Illustrated News*, and *Frank Leslie's Illustrated Newspaper*. The estimate of 20,000 strikers was proposed
by Philip Foner, *History of the Labor Movement in the United
States* (New York, 1947), I, 240. George Taylor apparently followed Foner's account, in the *Transportation Revolution*, p. 284.

[15] *News*, March 21, 1860.

[16] *Bay State*, March 8, 1860, describes the women's march; Barbara Welter discusses "The Cult of True Womanhood, 1820–1860," in *The Underside of American History* (New York, Harcourt Brace Jovanovich, 1971), 2 vols., I, 205–228.

[17] *Bay State*, April 5, 1860.

[18] The "Cordwainers' Song" was printed in the March 21, 1860, *Reporter*, and reprinted a quarter century later in the *Lynn Saturday Union*, Sept. 26, 1885, in an issue commemorating the Great Strike.

[19] *News*, Feb. 22, 1860; *Bay State*, April 12, 1860.

[20] *Bay State*, April 12, 1860.

[21] Ibid., April 12, 1860.

[22] Ibid., March 8, 1860.

[23] Ibid., March 8, 1860.

[24] Ibid., March 8, 1860.

[25] Ibid., March 8, 1860.

[26] Police court proceedings are recounted in the *Bay State*, March 2, 1860; information on property ownership and birthplace of those arrested is in the U.S. Eighth Census manuscripts: the five included one Lynn native, one Irish immigrant, two Canadian immigrants who were probably of Irish ancestry, and one who escaped notice in the records.

[27] The gift of wood to the strikers was reported in the *Bay State*, April, 12 1860; Alley's contortions were depicted in the *News*, March 21, 1860.

[28] Descriptions of the factory system appeared in the *Reporter*, Nov. 21, Feb. 28, 1863, Oct. 21, 1865, June 5, 1869; the quote is from the *Reporter*, Feb. 28, 1863.

[29] Ibid., Nov. 21, 1863.

[30] Ibid., Feb. 28, 1863.

[31] [Blanche] Hazard, [*The Organization of the Boot and*] *Shoe Industry* [*in Massachusetts before 1875* (Cambridge, Mass., 1921)], pp. 245–246; Johnson, *Sketches*, pp. 342–343.

[32] Johnson, *Sketches*, p. 342.

[33] Ibid., p. 341.

[34] See Appendix A [of Dawley, *Class and Community*,] for the sources on overall employment and output; see Alan Dawley, "The Artisan Response," unpub. diss. (Harvard University, 1971), pp. 109–111, for a discussion of the changes in daily output. The factory average was 6 prs./worker/day, while the average in the 1840s was 2–3 prs./worker/day.

[35] U.S., Eighth and Ninth Census manuscripts, Industrial Statistics on Lynn.

[36] Price information for 1860 is based on calculations from the U.S., Eighth Census manuscripts, Industrial Statistics on Lynn; the 1865 price is from Warner, *Information*, p. 77; the 1870 price cannot be calculated from the census manuscripts, owing to incomplete returns; [Alonso] Lewis and [James R.] Newhall, *History* [*of*

Lynn, 2 vols. (Lynn, 1897)], II, 39, estimate $1.60, while the *Reporter*, Jan. 14, 1871, indicated an average price of $2; *Reporter*, Nov. 14, 1866, describes the high turnover in shoe firms.

[37] *Reporter*, Nov. 16, 1861, Dec. 23, 1865.

[38] Clarence Hobbs, *Lynn and Surroundings* (Lynn, 1886), p. 71.

[39] Johnson, *Sketches*, p. 16; *Reporter*, Feb. 28, 1863.

Blackface Minstrelsy
and Jacksonian Democracy

ALEXANDER SAXTON

Entertainment is a part of daily life for people in every culture. Its range is wide—from formal entertainment staged for the few to self-structured entertainment, such as banjo picking or reading, for the many. But whatever its form, entertainment fulfills a vital need for emotional release, for symbolic breaking of conventions, and for diversion from the burdens of rules and responsibilities, pain and sorrow. Since the Second World War, entertainment has become a far more important part of daily life in America, because leisure time has increased and affluence has been sufficiently widespread to subsidize a large number of professional entertainers for our pleasure. But even in the nineteenth century, when most people worked a twelve-hour day, when the population was far more dispersed, and when electronic mass communication was unknown, entertainment was an important part of life.

In addition to serving psychic and emotional needs, entertainment performs a second function, as a carrier of ideas and attitudes. The popular entertainer is a powerful figure, reflecting and feeding the fears and fantasies of his or her audience. "The subtlest and most pervasive of all influences," wrote Walter Lippmann, "are those which create and maintain the repertory of stereotypes. We are told about the world before we see it. We imagine most things before we experience them." It is this function of entertainment—the role of reflecting and shaping popular opinion—that demands our attention in any consideration of nineteenth-century history.

That Negro minstrelsy became the most important form of mass entertainment in nineteenth-century America is a fact of special poignancy. It demonstrates not only how closely related were the tragic and the comic in the public mind, but how closely entwined were the lives of white and black Americans. As Alexander Saxton emphasizes, it was the black American who became the dominant character in American humor, though white entertainers, impersonating blacks, dominated the minstrelsies that toured every city, town, and village from the 1830s to the First World War.

The appeal of the minstrelsy lay not only in the music, rhythm, and catchy phraseology of black folk songs, which white entertainers collected and imitated, but in the racist stereotypes these white minstrels concocted for the entertainment of largely white audiences. The Negro as buffoon constituted the core of the minstrel's appeal to mass audiences in nineteenth-century America. This was as true in the North or West as in the South. The popularity of the minstrelsy, which reached the remotest corners of America both before and after the Civil War, can be explained by the fact that it gave white Americans precisely what they wished to see—an impersonation of the black American as a delightfully ignorant, unthreatening, happy-go-lucky servant. The persistence of this distorted image, evidenced by the continuation of the minstrelsy's enormous popularity well into the twentieth century, reinforces the conclusion that behind the laughter of white audiences at the sight of the grinning, watermelon-eating Negro lurked the fear of the hostile, revengeful, and autonomous American black.

The stereotype perpetuated by the nineteenth-century minstrelsy died hard in America. The descendants of the minstrelsy Sambo were the blackface acts of the vaudeville stage in the first third of the twentieth century, some of the movies and stage appearances of Al Jolson and Eddie Cantor, and a whole genre of movie and radio characters from Stepin Fetchit to Amos 'n' Andy. These characters, while serving the public need for entertainment, simultaneously played their part in shaping the nation's race relations, as did the dancing Jim Crow a century before.

Blackface minstrelsy, according to the preface to one of E. P. Christy's countless "plantation songsters," marked the advent of a national American music. "After our countrymen had . . . confuted the stale cant of our European detractors that nothing original could emanate from Americans—the next cry was, that we had no NATIVE MUSIC; . . . until our countrymen found a triumphant vindicating APOLLO in the genius of E. P. Christy, who . . . was the first to catch our *native airs* as they floated wildly, or hummed in the balmy breezes of the sunny south." The verbs *floated* and *hummed* referred of course to the fact that the original "native airs" had been appropriated from music and dance of African slaves by white professional entertainers, including (among many others) E. P. Christy. A more realistic account explained later in the same preface that the minstrels had possessed skills which enabled them "to harmonize and SCORE systematically the original NEGRO SOLOS." From these somewhat discordant beginnings, the preface rose to a crescendo of national triumph. "The air of our broad, blest land, and even that of Europe, became vocal with the thousand native melodies." [1]

"If I could have the nigger show back," Mark Twain wrote in his autobiography, ". . . I should have but little further use for opera . . . I remember the first negro musical show I ever saw. It must have been in the early forties. It was a new institution. In our village of Hannibal

---

[1] Edwin P. Christy, *Christy's Plantation Melodies No. 4* (Philadelphia: Fisher, 1854), pp. v–vii.

"Blackface Minstrelsy and Jacksonian Ideology," by Alexander Saxton. From *American Quarterly*, 27 (1975): 3–28. Published by the University of Pennsylvania. Copyright, 1975, Trustees of the University of Pennsylvania. Reprinted by permission of the author and the publisher.

. . . it burst upon us as a glad and stunning surprise." [2] During the decade recalled by Mark Twain, blackface minstrelsy became the most popular form of entertainment in the United States.[3] Its spread coincided with the rise of mass political parties and mass circulation newspapers. All three manifested in part at least the urban culture of Jacksonian America. Hannibal, Missouri, for example, which in Mark Twain's childhood was a rural slaveholding community, could hardly have found fragments of African music or caricatures of black slaves particularly surprising. What made the first minstrel show a "glad surprise" was that it provided a window into the complex culture developing in the new cities. For approximately half a century after Mark Twain's experience at Hannibal, minstrel shows dominated the nation's public entertainment, and at their latter end merged through variety and vaudeville into the modern era of film.[4] Clearly blackface minstrelsy has comprised an important element of the "American experience." What follows is an exploration of the ideological significance of that element.

Underlying the choice of the adjective *ideological* are several starting assumptions which can be set forth, hypothetically, as follows: Minstrel shows expressed class identification and hostility; they conveyed ethnic satire as well as social and political commentary of wide-ranging, sometimes radical character; they often contained explicitly sexual, homosexual and pornographic messages. Taken as a whole, the genre provided a kind of underground theater where the blackface "convention" rendered permissible topics which would have been taboo on the legitimate stage or in the press. Spontaneity and ad-libbing favored a flexible approach to different audiences and regions, changing moods and times. This combination of adaptiveness and liberty of subject matter explains in part the popularity and staying power of minstrelsy as mass entertainment. It was linked from its earliest beginnings to Jacksonian democracy. The rise of the first mass party in America and the dominance of the minstrel show as mass entertainment appear to have been interrelated and mutually reinforcing sequences. Finally, the "convention" of blackface was by no means separate from minstrelsy's social content or neutral in regard to it. On the contrary it saturated that content. For a study of the ideology of minstrel shows, the interpenetration of form and content is relentlessly at the crux of the matter.

[2] Mark Twain, *The Autobiography of Mark Twain*, ed. Charles Neider (New York: Washington Square Press, 1961), p. 64.

[3] T. Allston Brown, "The Origins of Minstrelsy," in Charles H. Day, *Fun in Black or Sketches of Minstrel Life* (New York: DeWitt, 1874), pp. 5–10.

[4] Hans Nathan, *Dan Emmett and the Rise of Early Minstrelsy* (Norman, Okla.: Univ. of Oklahoma Press, 1962); Nathan Huggins, *Harlem Renaissance* (New York: Oxford Univ. Press, 1971), pp. 244–301; Robert G. Toll, "Behind the Grinning Mask: Blackface Minstrelsy in Nineteenth Century America," Diss. Univ. of California, Berkeley 1971. Toll's study, soon to be published, provides a nearly definitive survey. Two older but still useful works are: Carl Wittke, *Tambo and Bones: A History of the American Minstrel Stage* (Durham, N.C.: Duke Univ. Press, 1930) and Dailey Paskman and Sigmund Spaeth, *"Gentlemen Be Seated!" A Parade of the Old Time Minstrels* (Garden City, N.Y.: Doubleday, 1928).

The discussion which follows will deal with the first three decades of minstrelsy, roughly 1845 to 1875. Its content will be treated as a matrix within which a dominant political line becomes discernible. Attention will then be concentrated upon that political line and its racial aspects. The final section will examine the ideological product which resulted from the infusion of social content into the specific form of blackface minstrelsy.

The social content of minstrelsy was shaped in part by the social experience of its founders and purveyors. Three men, Thomas Rice, Dan Emmett and E. P. Christy, are generally recognized as founders of blackface minstrelsy. To these should be added the name of Stephen Foster, the major white innovator of minstrel music. Where did these men come from and how did they happen to launch a new mode in mass entertainment? Rice, oldest of the four, was born in New York in 1808. He tried unsuccessfully to break into New York theater, then drifted west, working as stagehand and bit player through the Mississippi Valley. In 1831, imitating a shuffle he had seen performed by a black man on the Cincinnati levee, Rice for the first time "jumped Jim Crow." Jim Crow made Rice's fortune. Adapting it to various uses—including eventually a minstrel plagiarism of Uncle Tom—Rice was applauded in London and became a perennial favorite at New York's famous Bowery Theatre. The second founder, Dan Emmett, son of a village blacksmith of Mt. Vernon, Ohio, was born in 1815. He ran away to become a drummer in the army and served briefly at posts in Kentucky and Missouri. Dismissed for being under age, Emmett followed circuses and sideshows, occasionally singing comic songs in blackface. Early in 1843 he organized the first blackface quartet as a one night fill-in at New York's Chatham Theatre. Emmett devoted the rest of his long career to minstrelsy.[5]

Edwin P. Christy, also born in 1815, was the son of "respectable" Philadelphia parents who sought to launch him on a commercial career by arranging to place him in a New Orleans countinghouse. Christy rebelled and took to the road with traveling circuses. In 1843, he and several other young men were providing musical entertainment at a theater-saloon on the Buffalo waterfront. Apparently having heard of Emmett's success in New York, the Buffalo entertainers called themselves Christy's Plantation Minstrels; later, moving down to New York City, they became a permanent fixture at Mechanics' Hall on lower Broadway. It was through Christy's Minstrels that many of Stephen Foster's early songs reached the public. Foster, eleven years younger than Christy or Emmett, was born in Pittsburgh in 1826. Like Christy, he came of parents with intimations of upward mobility who tried to provide him with a proper education, then sent him off to work as a bookkeeper for an older brother in Cincinnati. Foster meanwhile was writings songs for minstrel shows for which

[5] Nathan, pp. 98–120; Edward LeRoy Rice, *Monarchs of Minstrelsy from Daddy Rice to Date* (New York: Kenny, 1911), pp. 7–8.

he received ten or fifteen dollars apiece. His "Old Folks at Home," according to the publisher, sold 130,000 copies in three years.[6]

The careers of these four men show several similarities. All were Northerners (but none was born in New England) and all except Emmett were of urban origin. At least three came of old-stock American families and were clearly of middle-class background. They all rejected the straight ways of the Protestant ethic and sought escape into the bohemianism of the entertainment world. Three had direct contact through their wanderings in the lower Mississippi Valley with the music and dance of black slaves, and we know from their own accounts that they consciously exploited this resource. None had achieved success in theatrical or any other pursuit prior to the venture into blackface minstrelsy; and in each case that venture brought spectacular success.[7] It seems likely that the pattern suggested by these summaries approximates the experiences of many professionals active during the first three decades of minstrelsy. A sampling group composed of 43 men born before 1838 who achieved prominence as blackface performers in large Northern cities or San Francisco yields the following information: five were born south of the Mason-Dixon line (including Baltimore); seven were of European birth (English five, Irish and French one each); all the rest (31) were born in the North, but of these only five were New Englanders. With respect to urban background, New York, Brooklyn, Rochester, Utica, Troy, Philadelphia, Baltimore, Providence, New Haven and Salem (Mass.) accounted for 24 of the 43 (with London and Paris probably claiming three or four more). Regionally, upstate New York matched New York City and Brooklyn with nine each; Philadelphia came next with six.[8]

Typical purveyors of minstrelsy, then, were Northern and urban; they were neither New Englanders nor Southerners (although their parents may have been); and if of rural or small-town origin, most were likely to have come from upper New York State. Eager to break into the exclusive but inhospitable precincts of big city theater, they needed new and exciting materials. These they found during their forced marches through the Mississippi Valley South in the music and dance of slaves and in the half-man, half-alligator braggadocio of the river and the frontier. The two separate lines had merged to some extent before the minstrels took them over.

> My mammy was a wolf, my daddy was a tiger,
> And I'm what you call de old Virginia nigger;
> Half fire, half smoke, a little touch of thunder,
> I'm what dey call de eighth wonder.[9]

[6] *Christy's No. 4*, pp. v–vii; John Tasker Howard, *Stephen Foster, America's Troubadour* (New York: Crowell, 1934), pp. 65–201, 372–77.

[7] Brown, pp. 5–10; *Christy's No. 4*, p. vii; Nathan, pp. 70–71, 116–22; Howard, pp. 202–14.

[8] The biographical data is from Rice, which is indexed. See also *Bryant's Essence of Old Virginny* (New York: DeWitt, 1857), pp. vii–viii and *Buckley's Melodies* (New York: Cozans, 1853), pp. v–vii.

[9] Charley White, *White's New Illustrated Melodeon Song Book* (New York: Long, 1848), pp. 51–52; *Christy's Ram's Horn Nigga Songster* (New York: Marsh, n.d.),

Ambivalent especially toward the black component of their borrowings, the minstrels coveted the power and newness of the music, yet failed to recognize its Africanness, or to perceive in it segments of an idiom distinct and separate from the European idiom. They ascribed the impact of slave music to its being close to nature. It "floated wildly" or "hummed . . . in the breezes," to repeat the metaphor of E. P. Christy's preface, and its wildness could be taken simply as part of the general crudity of frontier style. In any case the work of white entertainers with such materials was to "turn them to shape," to Europeanize them sufficiently so that they would not offend refined ears. Thus the dual task of exploiting and suppressing African elements began from the first moments of minstrelsy. But these elements possessed great vitality. It was suggested earlier that a major factor in the popularity and staying power of minstrel entertainment was its freedom of subject matter; certainly another, perhaps *the* other, major factor was the persistence of African borrowings (especially in dance movement and sense of rhythm) throughout the entire half-century of blackface minstrelsy.[10]

Partial acceptance of these African musical elements was facilitated by the fact that they fitted logically into a portrayal of the Old South which took on a symbolic and powerful, although derivative, meaning for many white Americans during the 19th century. But before examining that somewhat removed aspect of minstrel content, it is necessary to turn to a set of meanings which were direct and immediate. For the minstrels, as for the new mass audience upon which they depended, the city was the focal experience of life. The city offered (or seemed to offer) new sorts of work, money, movement, excitement. It offered access to liquor and sex, to education, culture, progress. All this was ignored in the high culture of the established upper classes; Walt Whitman, almost alone among American 19th century poets, celebrated the city. The purveyors of minstrelsy shared in this celebration; but in order to do so, they had to impose some startling transformations upon materials whose primary reference was to frontier and plantation. Here is one of the early mutations:

> I'm de sole delight of yaller gals,
> De envy ob de men,
> Observe this nigger when he turns,
> And talk of dandies then.[11]

---

pp. 99–100; "Twill Nebber Do to Gib it up so," *Old Dan Emmit's Original Banjo Melodies* (Boston: Keith, 1843), sheet music in "Dan Emmett" folder, Theater Collection, Harvard Library. See also Nathan, pp. 50–56 and Constance Rourke, *American Humor: A Study of the National Character* (New York: Harcourt, Brace, 1931), pp. 77–103.

[10] *Christy's No. 4*, p. v; Nathan, pp. 70–97; Toll, pp. 1–19; Jean and Marshall Stearns, *Jazz Dance* (New York: Macmillan, 1968), pp. 11–60; Marshall Stearns, *The Story of Jazz* (New York: Oxford Univ. Press, 1956), pp. 3–33, 109–22; LeRoy Jones, *Blues People* (New York: Morrow, 1963), pp. 1–59, 82–86.

[11] "The Dandy Broadway Swell," *Wood's New Plantation Melodies* (New York: Garrett, n.d.), pp. 50–51.

The Broadway dandy was in one respect a transplant of the swaggering Southwest frontier hero, already widely rendered in blackface. But the dandy also caricatured a new social type in the United States—the urban free black.

Possible uses of this stereotype, which expressed an enthusiasm for city life uncloyed by nostalgia or regret, were limitless.[12] Early in 1852, one of New York's permanent minstrel companies began performing a number titled "Wake Up, Mose." The hero appeared in the first verse as the already familiar urban free black. "He used to run de railroad—he was de bulgine tender"; and it was clear from the context that "bulgine tender" meant a railroad fireman. The chorus then made an abrupt switch, followed up in subsequent verses, to a fireman of a different sort, and presumably of a different race:

> Wake up, Mose! Wake up, Mose!
> Wake up, Mose! De Fire am burning;
> Round de corner de smoke am curling.
> Wake up, Mose! the engine's coming;
> Take de rope and keep a running! [13]

So who was Mose?

Mose was an early hero of melodrama made famous through the United States by a New York actor named W. S. Chanfrau in a series of loosely structured scenes and spectacles gathered under titles such as *New York As It Is, Mose and Lize, Mose in California*. Probably a butcher by trade, or an apprentice carpenter or stonecutter, Mose was one of the city's famous "Bowery bhoys." After work he liked to dress up and go to the theater with an armful or two of his innumerable girl friends ("Bowery gals, will you come out tonight?").[14] Gallant volunteer fireman, avid participant in New York City politics, an invincible pugilist, Mose was the urban culture hero, derived from, yet standing against, older rural heroes like the New England Yankee or the half-man, half-alligator of the Southwest. Mose cared nothing for Yankees or alligators either; he breathed the fire of burning buildings; and when it came to warfare, he could tell even an old frontier fighter like Zachary Taylor how to run his campaigns. Mose, however, transcended regionalism. Essentially he stood for the new urban mass culture as against the "high" culture of the old elite.

But Mose in blackface is something else. There was of course a historical logic in rendering the Broadway dandy as Mose in blackface, since both had reached the city by different routes from a common ancestry in frontier folklore. But this hardly explains *why* it was done. The value

[12] See *Christy's Panorama Songster* (New York: Murphy, n.d. [1850?]), p. 93, for an example of ethnic satire in blackface.

[13] M. Campbell, *Wood's Minstrels' Songs* (New York: Garrett, 1852), p. 25.

[14] *Christy's Plantation Melodies No. 1* (Philadelphia: Fisher, 1851), pp. 45–46. Playbills, Theater Collection, Harvard Library: Chatham Theatre (New York, 1848), Jenny Lind (San Francisco, 1851), St. Charles (New Orleans, 1857). See also David Grimsted, *Melodrama Unveiled: American Theater and Culture, 1800–1850* (Chicago: Univ. of Chicago Press, 1968), pp. 65–75; and Alvin F. Harlow, *Old Bowery Days: Chronicles of a Famous Street* (New York: Appleton, 1931), p. 264.

of such as characterization was that it extended minstrel show content to include class satire. As minstrelsy became more formalized, it moved from separate song-dance numbers to routines including spoken repartee, and finally to elaborate composites of song, dance and drama. The original foursome of undifferentiated musicians expanded into a line in which customary position corresponded roughly to class identification. The end men, who always played tambourine and bones, were lower class. By costume and vernacular they were "plantation nigger," or "Broadway dandy,"—often one of each. The middleman, or interlocutor, served as bogus mouthpiece for the high culture.[15] His dress and speech were upper class, sometimes straight, more often burlesqued; and the plot was usually the putting down of the interlocutor by the end men. Even after the ad-lib repartee of the original line had evolved into more formal presentations, the class character and plot remained substantially the same. Blackface could thus serve to enhance the ridicule directed against upper-class pretensions.[16] More important, it had the effect of preserving the comic mood, since otherwise the role of Mose tended toward serious drama or even tragedy. The careers of real "Bowery bhoys" in politics, of John Morrissey, the prizefighter, or the proletarian congressman, Michael Walsh, and especially of David Broderick, were actings out of tragic conflict between the new urban culture and the cultures of older elites.[17] This was too serious to be fun. Blackface defused such meanings without denying them. It did so by placing social content in the background of a conventional proscenium which permitted instantaneous escape through shifts of scene and mood and which constantly intervened to discredit serious implications.

Part of the entertainment lay in skating on thin ice. Temperance, a topic taken very seriously by many mid-19th century Americans, was nearly always an object of ridicule in minstrel songs.

> Niggar, put down dat jug,
> Touch not a single drop,
> I hab gin him many a hug
> And dar you luff him stop.

Parodying the sentimental ballad, "Woodman Spare That Tree," this song, published about 1850, seemed to hint (especially in the third line) at more than the simple pleasures of alcohol. Subsequent verses elaborated in graphic detail:

> I kiss him two three time,
> And den I suck him dry

15 Mark Twain, pp. 65–66.
16 "Mose he went to college, he said he was a poet . . ." in *Wood's Minstrels*, p. 25. Minstrel burlesques of tragedy and grand opera exemplified this usage. See Harlow, p. 265, for an account of T. D. Rice in a burlesque of *Othello*.
17 "Michael Walsh," *Dictionary of American Biography* (New York: Scribners, 1936), 19:390–91; Jack Kofoed, *Brandy for Heroes: a Biography of the Honorable John Morrissey, Champion Heavyweight of America and State Senator* (New York: Dutton, 1938); David A. Williams, *David C. Broderick, a Political Portrait* (San Marino, Calif.: Huntington Library, 1969).

> Dat jug, he's none but mine
> So dar you luff him lie.[18]

The primary effect of these lines, rendered in blackface, would have been
to attribute masturbation or homosexuality to black males. However, the
prevailing stereotype of blacks (already well established in minstrelsy by
the 1850s) was of unflagging heterosexuality. This apparent contradiction
suggests that the song contained several layers of meaning and conveyed
different messages to different listeners.

Minstrelsy had become mass entertainment in the decade of war
against Mexico and the California gold rush. Until well after the Civil
War minstrel shows were performed exclusively by males, before largely
male audiences. Both in the East and West, the male population was concentrated in factories, boardinghouses, construction and mining camps.
Frontier settlements had few women, and contemporary accounts tell of
men dancing in saloons and hotel dining rooms dressed as women. Given
this context, the song quoted above appears as a permissive reference to
homosexuality and masturbation, veiled but not negated by the blackface
"convention." The point here is not the prevalence of homosexuality, but
the tolerance of sexuality in general, the realism and the flexibility of
standards which flourished behind the false façade of blackface presentation. A more typical sort of minstrel pornography would be a duet titled,
"Cuffee's Do-it," in which Cuffee was obviously typed as a Broadway
dandy:

> *He.*
>> Oh, Miss Fanny, let me in,
>> For de way I lub you is a sin . . .
> *She.*
>> (spoken) Oh no I cannot let you in . . .
> *He.*
>> Oh, when I set up an oyster cellar,
>> You shall wait upon de feller,
>> Sell hot corn and ginger pop,
>> You be de lady ob de shop.
> *She.*
>> Oh, Sam, if dat's de trufe you tell . . .
>> Oh, Sam Slufheel, you may come in.
> *He.*
>> Oh, Miss Fanny, I'se a comin' in . . .[19]

Moral permissiveness was not accidental or idiosyncratic. It was an
aspect of life-style. The life-style expressed in minstrelsy could appropriately be called "urbanity" since it had developed in middle Atlantic cities,
moved west with the Érie Canal and urbanization of the Mississippi and

---

[18] *Christy's Ram's Horn,* pp. 76–77.

[19] Ibid., pp. 109–10. Many male performers built reputations playing "wench parts."
Rice, pp. 71, 86–87. And see Frank C. Davidson, "The Rise, Development, Decline
and Influence of the American Minstrel Show," Diss. New York Univ. 1952, pp.
130–31.

its tributaries, and west again with the acquisition of California. It was both urban and frontier. During the last two major frontier decades, the 1850s and 1860s, even the frontier had become urbanized: its new cities were garrison towns and mine camps which sprang into existence before much in the way of rural hinterland had developed around them. When Charles De Long made the following entry in his diary for Christmas Eve, 1859—

> Spent the day in the office hunting up authorities . . . in the evening went to the gymnasium, and the sparring school, and then called on Elida . . . saw the Christmas tree and then went in and celebrated Christmas with Lide. Came downtown went to Nigger Festival [a minstrel show] and got supper and then went to the Catholic Church to high mass, and then down and got on a little burden and went to bed late, raining some. . . .

he might have been describing a day in the life of a moderately successful Bowery politician. Actually De Long was working out of Marysville, some fifty miles northeast of Sacramento. A political henchman of Stephen Douglas, De Long earned his living at the time by collecting the California foreign miners' tax from Chinese laborers. "Started with Dick Wade and Bob Moulthrop collecting," he wrote for October 23, 1855, ". . . supper at Hesse's Crossing went down the river in the night collected all the way had a great time, Chinamen tails cut off." [20] De Long attended performances of many of the same minstrel troupes he would have seen had he lived in New York, because minstrelsy was invading the towns and camps of the Pacific slope. So prominent was San Francisco as a minstrel city that for several years one of New York's leading companies styled itself the "San Francisco Minstrels." [21]

The dual relationship of city and frontier profoundly affected the social content of minstrelsy. Blackface singers (again like Walt Whitman) were protagonists of Manifest Destiny.

> Mose he went to Mexico, and dar he saw Santa Anna;
> He sent a message to de camp, telling Zack not to surrender.
> Says Santa Anna, "Who are you—you seem to be so witty?"
> Says Mose, "Go 'long—I'm one of de boys—I'm from de Empire City.[22]

Always the West and the westward movement were focal:

> Den I step on board de *Oregon*
> For de gemman say who bought her
> Dat she for sure's de fastest crab
> What lives upon de water.[23]

[20] Carl I. Wheat, ed., " 'California's Bantam Cock': The Journals of Charles E. De Long," *California Historical Society Quarterly*, 10 (June 1931), 185, and 8 (Dec. 1929), 346.

[21] Rice, pp. 27, 68–70.

[22] *Wood's Minstrels*, p. 25.

[23] *George Christy and Wood's Melodies* (Philadelphia: Peterson, 1854), pp. 39–40.

Stephen Foster's "Oh! Susanna" (of which the verse above was a topical variation) was first performed in the year of Scott's conquest of Mexico City and reached the height of its popularity during the California gold rush. A later cliché, perpetuated by Hollywood and television, has associated the song with westering pioneers from rural regions such as Kansas and Missouri. Kansas wagonmasters may certainly have sung "Oh! Susanna"; but its origin was at Pittsburgh and it was first popularized in New York City's minstrel halls.[24] Underlying the sociological congruency between city and frontier was a psychological identity between traveling to the city and traveling west. Each, for the individual who undertook such a transition, was a journey involving a traumatic break with a previous situation. In minstrelsy's complex matrix of social content, the *journey* became the central theme. It stood in contrast to the celebration of urban opportunity and permissiveness as a lament for what had been left behind and lost. This theme, I believe, entered minstrelsy at its earliest beginnings, not in any sense as a reflection of journeys made by black slaves, but as a projection by the white performers of their own experience. The projection was then magnified because it also expressed the psychic experience of urban audiences. The notion of a symbolic journey suggests the power of minstrelsy's impact upon white viewers. At the same time it helps to place in perspective one of the most puzzling aspects of minstrel repertory: the endless evocation of the Old South.

Early minstrels (as represented by the sampling group discussed above) had understood slave music not as African but as close to nature. Correspondingly they perceived slaves as *part* of nature, part of the nature of the South, and from this curiously ahistorical viewpoint undertook to "delineate" plantation culture. City dwellers by birth or adoption, they were strangers and interlopers in the plantation society. While they might observe and borrow from slave music, their social contacts were with whites, and it is scarcely surprising that their depiction of the South overlapped and duplicated the plantation myth which white Southerners were then bringing to perfection as part of their defense of slavery. That myth was also ahistorical because its germinating inspiration was to fix the black slave as an everlasting part of nature rather than as a figure in history. When the wandering minstrels carried their fragments of African music back to Northern and Western cities, they took them encased in a mythology of the South as a region fascinatingly different, closely wedded to nature, and above all, timeless. The word "timeless" defines the relationship which would develop between the image of the South and the anomie experienced by men and women of rural, Eastern background who lived in cities or who moved out west. The South became symbolically their old home: the place where simplicity, happiness, all the things we have left behind, exist outside of time.

> Down by the river our log hut stands
> Where father and mother once dwelt
> And the old door latch that was worn by our hands
> And the church where in prayer we knelt.[25]

[24] Howard, pp. 119, 136–39, 144–45.
[25] *Christy's Plantation Melodies No. 2* (Philadelphia: Fisher, 1853), p. 35.

What has been left behind collectively may be a rural past, but individually it is childhood. New cities and new frontiers, attractive to conspiring and perspiring adults, have little room for children; and the South, in the legend of blackface minstrelsy, became the antithesis to both.[26]

When E. P. Christy organized his first entertainments at Buffalo in 1842, he brought in a younger man, George Harrington, who adopted the name Christy and eventually became more famous than his mentor. The senior Christy retired in the mid-1850s; George Christy went into partnership with a New York theatrical promoter, Henry Wood. Under their joint direction Christy and Wood's became a metropolitan establishment and one of the best-known companies of the prewar era. Henry Wood belonged to a remarkable family. His brother Benjamin served three terms as a Democratic Congressman from the city and one term as state senator; for almost half a century he presided over the aggressively Democratic New York *Daily News*. A second brother was Fernando Wood, Copperheadish mayor of New York, fighter for control of Tammany Hall, several times Congressman.[27]

George Christy went to San Francisco in 1857. There he performed under the sponsorship of Tom Maguire, West Coast tycoon of minstrelsy, opera and varied theatricals. Maguire had spent his younger days on New York's Bowery as a saloon keeper, hack driver, fight promoter, volunteer fireman and Tammany stalwart. When David Broderick, the New York stonecutter of background substantially similar to Maguire's, abandoned the Bowery for the Golden Gate in 1849, he lived for several years as a boarder at Maguire's house, and apparently helped Maguire to escape bankruptcy by arranging the sale of his Jenny Lind Theatre for $200,000 to an obliging (Democratic) city administration of San Francisco. Maguire was soon back in business with other theaters.[28]

Dan Emmett, after launching the nation's first minstrel quartet on the New York stage, toured England with middling success, then returned to White's Minstrel Melodeon on lower Broadway. By the late 1850s, Emmett had worked out a lasting connection with Bryants' Minstrels of New York, next to Christy's the most enduring of the prewar troupes. Composer of dozens of songs and musical farces, Emmett was especially noted for his walkarounds or group finales. One of these, titled for its New York première, "Dixie's Land," became popular in the South, where it was taken by itinerant minstrels and emerged during the war as "Dixie," the *de facto* Confederate national anthem. In postwar years, the Bryants,

---

[26] Mark Twain repeatedly makes these connections. For example, *Autobiography*, pp. 5–6.

[27] Rice, p. 20; Samuel A. Pleasants, *Fernando Wood of New York* (New York: Columbia Univ. Press, 1948); Leonard Chalmers, "Fernando Wood and Tammany Hall: The First Phase," *New York Historical Society Quarterly*, 52 (Oct. 1968), 379–402. On Henry Wood, see Paskman and Spaeth, pp. 155–56.

[28] Rice, p. 20; "De Long Journals," *California Historical Society Quarterly*, 9 (Dec. 1930), 385; "Continuation of the Annals of San Francisco," *California Historical Society Quarterly*, 15 (June 1936), 178–80, 184; New York *Clipper*, May 23, 1868; Kofoed, pp. 69–86; Williams, pp. 29–31.

following the trend of theater and fashion, moved uptown to East Fourteenth Street. Emmett by this time had drifted back to the Midwest, but
the Bryants commissioned a special walkaround in honor of their uptown
location and Emmett obliged with a piece called "The Wigwam." In May
of 1868, "The Wigwam" climaxed the Bryants' opening in their new
theater at Tammany Hall's recently constructed Fourteenth Street headquarters.[29]

Stephen Foster, drinking himself to death in New York during the
Civil War, sometimes peddled his handwritten songs along Broadway, and
at least one of the buyers was Henry Wood of Wood's Minstrels. In
happier days, Foster had helped to organize the Allegheny City Bu-
chanan-for-President Club. All ardent Democrats, the Fosters were related by marriage to President Buchanan's brother, an Episcopal minister. In 1856 Stephen Foster contributed two songs to the Buchanan
Glee Club. One was a lampoon of Abolitionism; the other was a paean
to the unifying spirit of the South:

> We'll not outlaw the land that holds
> The bones of Washington,
> Where Jackson fought and Marion bled
> And the battles of the brave were won.[30]

From such fragments of evidence, several "founding" minstrels as
well as two or three of the nation's best-known minstrel companies can
be placed in a scattered but consistent pattern of pro-Southern expression
and intimate contact with Democratic Party leaders in New York and
San Francisco. The pattern points to a more general typicality when considered against the background of minstrelsy's political orientation, which
has already been defined—in a negative sense—by its social content. Temperance, hostility to recent European immigration and lack of enthusiasm
for, or direct opposition to, territorial expansion were frequently (not
always) characteristic of the Whig, Liberty, Free-Soil, Native American
and Republican parties. Regardless of mutual antagonisms, these parties
always opposed the Democratic Party, which, in turn, was nearly always
hostile to temperance, receptive to recent European immigration and
strenuously in favor of territorial expansion. The positions of the Democratic Party on these issues were congruent to the outlook expressed by
blackface minstrelsy; the positions of anti-Democratic parties generally
were not. Minstrelsy, then, appears to have been oriented toward the
Democratic Party. Since minstrels were generally Northern, as was most
of their mass audience, it would seem reasonable to pursue an inquiry into
the political line of minstrelsy by investigating its responses to major
problems confronting the Northern wing of the Democratic Party.

The Democracy was probably the world's first mass political party.
It seems to have been a loose amalgam of class and interest groups in
which the new urban working class played a significant but not dominant
role. Common goals, antipathies and aspirations which held this amalgam

---

[29] *Clipper,* Apr. 25, May 30, 1868; Nathan, pp. 135–42, 214–75.
[30] Howard, pp. 27–28, 43–45, 256–64.

together found expression through an ideology then crystallizing around the "Jacksonian" concept of the individual producer in an expanding society. Emerging cadres of professional leadership became expert at formulating political principles and programs. For the Jacksonian party the three basic principles of its period of ascendancy were: expansion (nationalism), antimonopoly (egalitarianism) and white supremacy. Without venturing further into a theory of American parties and party systems, it may be assumed that Northern Democratic leaders during the 30 years under consideration were endeavoring to perpetuate, or regain, control over the Federal government. Pursuit of this goal presented different problems before, during and after the war.[31]

Before the Civil War, the Democratic Party was dominant nationally, having controlled the Federal government without major interruption since the first election of Andrew Jackson in 1828. Continuance of such control depended upon unity among the party's regional branches. But the price of unity, as set by Southern Democrats, was that the national party must defend the institution of slavery. Consequently a major task of Northern leaders was to resist criticisms of slavery from outside the party and to prevent antislavery sentiment from infiltrating party ranks. This was no easy task as views hostile to slavery gained widening acceptance in the North and West.[32]

For blackface minstrelsy, given its Southern origins, slavery was an inescapable topic. Minstrelsy's political stance was a defense of slavery. That this should seem a statement of the obvious is in itself a revealing commentary. In a broader frame of reference, artistic endeavors aimed at "delineating" the cultural traditions of oppressed or enslaved peoples would more commonly be associated, I think, with ideologies of liberation than of oppression. Minstrelsy, however, faithfully reproduced the white slaveowners' viewpoint.

> Old Massa to us darkies am good
> Tra la la, tra la la
> For he gibs us our clothes and he gibs us our food. . . .[33]

Slaves loved the master. They dreaded freedom because, presumably, they were incapable of *self*-possession. When forced to leave the plantation

[31] The literature on parties and party systems during the Jacksonian period is extensive. Two recent essay collections with convenient bibliographies are Edward Pessen, ed., *New Perspectives on Jacksonian Parties and Politics* (Boston: Allyn and Bacon, 1969) and Joel H. Silbey, *Political Ideology and Voting Behavior in the Age of Jackson* (Englewood Cliffs, N.J.: Prentice-Hall, 1973). With respect to the "three basic principles" of the Democratic Party, see Thurman Williams, *Cherokee Tragedy* (New York: Macmillan, 1970); Richard H. Brown, "The Missouri Crisis, Slavery and the Politics of Jacksonianism," *South Atlantic Quarterly*, 65 (Winter 1966), 55–72; and James K. Paulding, *Slavery* (New York: Harpers, 1836). My own interpretation will be found in greater detail in Saxton, *The Indispensable Enemy: Labor and the Anti-Chinese Movement in California* (Berkeley: Univ. of California Press, 1971).

[32] Eric Foner, *Free Soil, Free Labor, Free Men: The Ideology of the Republican Party Before the Civil War* (New York: Oxford Univ. Press, 1970).

[33] *Christy's Panorama Songster*, p. 79; see also Toll, pp. 70–99.

they longed only to return. These themes in minstrelsy worked at several
levels. On the one hand, propagating the plantation myth, they portrayed
slavery as benign and desirable. On the other hand they reinforced the
image of the South as symbol of the collective rural past and of individual
childhood, thus acquiring an emotional impact logically unrelated to their
content. At the same time, the docility attributed to slaves, commendable
as this might seem to a Southern planter, was certain to strike Northern
audiences imbued with Jacksonian principles of upward mobility as
ridiculous and contemptible.

Was minstrelsy monolithic in its justification of slavery? Almost, but
not quite. There appeared a scattering of antislavery expressions which
entered in two different ways. First, the early borrowings of Afro-American music and dance carried antislavery connotations which sometimes
persisted subliminally in traditional verses like this from "The Raccoon
Hunt":

> My ole massa dead and gone,
> A dose of poison help him on
> De debil say he funeral song [34]

Subversive sentiments might be negated in chorus or verses, perhaps
added later. This seems to have been the case with the ballad, "De Nigga
Gineral," which referred to Nat Turner's rebellion, although parts of the
song were apparently of older origin. Here the antislavery thesis represented by a black general, "chief of the insurgents," is carefully set at rest
by antithetical verses telling of his defeat, repudiation by his own followers, and execution.

> O, Johnson Ben he drove de waggon
> Ho, boys yere most done . . .
> And dey hung him and dey swung him
> Ho, boys, yere most done.[35]

A second and later means of entry of antislavery content was through
the essentially white identity of romantic and nostalgic songs, European in
tradition and style, which quickly became a staple of minstrel repertory.
Performed in blackface, yet dealing seriously with themes of parted
lovers, lost children and so forth, these songs both invited identification
with the situation of the slave and suggested that slavery might have been
the cause of separation or loss. But to admit such a possibility was to
contradict the myth of the benign plantation and yield ground to antislavery propagandists. Thus, even when given in "darkey" vernacular,
sentimental minstrel songs seldom made direct mention of slavery. Occasional references did nonetheless break through. They were then usually
softened or disguised by shifting specific griefs to the generalized sorrows of time and distance, or by emphasizing the troubles blacks were
likely to encounter in the North.[36]

[34] *Christy's Ram's Horn*, p. 102.
[35] Ibid., p. 200; *Christy's No. 2*, pp. 44–45.
[36] Mark Twain, p. 66; Howard, pp. 210–11, 246; *White's Serenaders' Song Book: No.
4* (Philadelphia: Peterson, 1851), p. 40.

The two sorts of expressions described above represented the only penetration into minstrelsy of antislavery views. By contrast, a major trend through the 1850s and into the war years consisted of attacks against Abolitionists, who were portrayed as stupid, hypocritical, cowardly, subservient to England and practitioners of miscegenation. Minstrelsy not only conveyed explicit proslavery and anti-Abolitionist propaganda; it was in and of itself a defense of slavery because its main content stemmed from the myth of the benign plantation. Critics of slavery were well aware that the incompatibility between that myth and romantic concepts of love and family constituted a weak point in slavery's defense; and against this point was directed one of their main attacks—that slavery prevented marriage and broke up families. This was the central message of *Uncle Tom's Cabin;* and antislavery singers (never minstrels) like the Hutchinson Family of New Hampshire had been developing similar criticisms long before Harriet Beecher Stowe's novel. The counter to this attack, in which minstrelsy led the field, took the form of ridiculing the very notion of love, or any other human or humane emotion, among blacks. Within a few months after the appearance of *Uncle Tom's Cabin*, minstrels had co-opted the title and main characters, while reversing the message. The famous T. D. Rice "jumped Jim Crow" in the role of Uncle Tom.[37] Indeed all that was needed to render a serious theme ludicrous in blackface minstrelsy was to permit its dehumanizing form to overbalance the content. In an age of romantic sentiment, minstrels sang love songs like this one:

> My Susy she is handsome
> My Susy she is young . . .
> My Susy looms it bery tall
> Wid udder like a cow
> She'd give nine quarts easy
> But white gals don't know how.[38]

By 1860 the infiltration of antislavery sentiments into Northern party ranks combined with the mounting anxiety and aggressiveness of Southern Democrats had made further compromise impossible. The party split; Lincoln was elected; secession and civil war followed. Although virtually impotent at the national level, the Democracy in the North remained locally powerful in many regions. The task now facing its activists was to hold together their potentially large constituency by loyal Unionism while at the same time seeking to discredit Republican leadership.

[37] *Christy's Panorama Songster*, p. 85; *Christy's Plantation Melodies No. 3* (Philadelphia: Fisher, 1853), pp. 10–11, 40–41; *Hooley's Opera House Songster* (New York: Dick, 1864), p. 5; "Joshua" [Hutchinson], *A Brief Narrative of the Hutchinson Family: Sixteen Sons and Daughters of the "Tribe of Jesse"* (Boston: Lee and Shepard, n.d.); A. B. Hutchinson, *The Granite Songster* (Boston: Holt, 1847); George W. Clark, *The Liberty Minstrel* (New York: Saxton and Miles, 1845). On the permutations of *Uncle Tom's Cabin*: Harry Birdoff, *The World's Greatest Hit* (New York: Vanni, 1947); M. B. Leavitt, *Fifty Years of Theatrical Management* (New York: Broadway, 1912), p. 6; and Toll, pp. 104–7.

[38] *Christy's Ram's Horn*, pp. 46–47.

Once again slavery was at the heart of the matter. The South, Democrats argued, would fight to the bitter end, convinced that the Republicans intended to destroy slavery. But the war could be settled and the Union preserved, if, through ouster of the Republicans from control of the federal apparatus, the slavery issue were fully set at rest. This line was vigorously pushed in media of mass communication accessible to Democratic leadership; and these primarily were newspapers and blackface minstrelsy.

Minstrels re-adapted the plantation myth to wartime purposes, their message being that a struggle against slavery was neither necessary to save the Union nor desirable. Traditional blackface caricatures were politicized. The "plantation nigger" now lamented the inexplicable "white folks'" war which was causing everyone so much trouble; while up North the Broadway dandy thrived like the green bay tree. He conspired with Republican leaders, rejoiced in the war but dodged the draft; paraded in fancy uniform but took to his heels at the first whiff of gunpowder.

> Niggers dey can pick de cotton—dey'll do it very freely
> But when dey smell de bullets, how dey'll run for Horace Greely! [39]

To their basic paradox of lauding the plantation system in the midst of a war against the plantation South, the minstrels added a satirical and sometimes brilliant critique of Republican war policy. They questioned the competence of particular leaders (including Lincoln). They attacked political generals, profiteers and shoddy contractors. Songs like Dan Emmett's "How Are You, Greenbacks?" provided a framework for variations upon the class and ethnic sequences worked out during the 1850s.

> We're coming, Father Abram, one hundred thousand more.
> Five hundred presses printing us from morn till night is o'er . . .
> To line the fat contractor's purse, or purchase transport craft
> Whose rotten hulks shall sink before the winds begin to waft.

The bearers of true patriotism, according to minstrel repertory, were honest workingmen who battled to save the Union. Outstanding among these were regiments raised from New York's volunteer fire companies ("For I belong to the Fire Zouaves that started from New York . . ."); and the Irish ("Meagher is leading the Irish Brigade"); and, nearly always treated comically, the lager-drinking Germans ("I'm Going to Fight Mit Sigel"). General McClellan became a symbol of the straightforward Union-loving soldier as opposed to the profiteering, Abolition-tainted Republican politician. Minstrelsy in 1864 mounted an extensive campaign for McClellan, whose platform as Democratic presidential candidate called for peace on any terms of reunion acceptable to the South.

> We're willing, Father Abram, ten hundred thousand more
> Should help our Uncle Samuel to prosecute the war;

[39] Frank Converse, "Old Cremona" Songster (New York: Dick, 1863), pp. 9–10.

But then we want a chieftain true, one who can lead the van,
George B. McClellan you all know, he is the very man . . .[40]

Thus it was loyal workingmen and soldiers who were saving the
Union; but their efforts were sabotaged by profiteers and politicians, and
worst of all, their lives were needlessly expended for the benefit of the
"niggers."

Abram Linkum said to me—
Send de sojers down!
He's gwine to make de niggers free—
Send de sojers down!

At this level the entire spectrum of minstrelsy from the plantation myth
through its urban repertory of ethnic humor and class satire was permeated by the blackface form:

I wish I was a blinkin' [Abe Lincoln], a blinkin', a blinkin'
I wish I was a blinkin'
I'll tell you what I'd do . . .
Oh, if I was much bigger—some bigger—great bigger,
Oh, if I was some bigger I tell you what I'd do:
I'd buy up all de niggers—de niggers—de colored African-American citizens,
I'd buy up all de niggers, and—sell 'em, wouldn't you?[41]

This "comic-banjo" piece, as it was described, appeared in a songster
published in New York in 1863. Geographically and emotionally, it was
only a block or two from a song such as this to the maiming and lynching
of blacks on the sidewalks of New York during the draft riots of the
same year.[42]

After the war, Democratic strategy was based upon the conviction
that the old national majority could be re-created through judicious use
of Jacksonian slogans adapted to fit the new situation. Moreover it was
soon obvious that the party could count on a massive accession of strength
when (or if) the Democratic South was restored to the Union. The three
basic appeals of Jacksonianism—nationalism, egalitarianism and white supremacy—assumed the postwar form of demands for immediate readmis-
sion of the South, criticism of profiteering and monopoly, and struggle
against "black" Reconstruction. The plantation myth, always central to
minstrelsy, continued to serve Democratic needs since it softened wartime

40 Dan Bryant, *How Are You, Greenbacks* (New York: Pond, 1863), sheet music,
"Bryant's Minstrels" folder, Theater Collection, Harvard Library. *Hooley's Opera
House*, pp. 16–17; *The Little Mac Songster* (New York: Dick, 1863), pp. 11–13,
and 29, 42–43, 53.
41 Converse, "Old Cremona," pp. 47–48 and 44–45.
42 James B. Fry, *New York and the Conscription Act of 1863: A Chapter in the History of the Civil War* (New York: Putnam, 1885); A Volunteer Special [William
Osborn Stoddard], *The Volcano Under the City* (New York: Fords, Howard &
Hulbert, 1887).

hostilities and tended to favor rapid restoration of the seceded states.[43] As
during the war period, however, the minstrels' political line defined itself
most sharply in caricatures based on the Northern, urban partner of the
Tambo and Bones pair—the Broadway dandy. "Urban" blacks were portrayed as pickpockets, crooked politicians, carpetbaggers and "colored
senators"; the wartime formulae of blacks as draft dodgers and deserters
were endlessly repeated. Skits and farces came increasingly into use, and
the extent to which blackface "convention" permeated their content is
indicated by the cast of characters in a farce published in the last year of
Reconstruction: "IKEY PIKE (a gentleman of dark complexion, sometimes called an unbleached American citizen) . . . TOM (who blacks
boots, still darker) . . . DINAH (the dark daughter of a dark sire . . .)
. . . The rest of the characters are all so dark that they cannot be seen." [44]
Ridicule continued to be the basic resource of minstrelsy's political line.
Similar treatment was now extended to other minority groups which
came into the focus of national hostility. As might be expected from
previous orientations of minstrelsy, the extension was not to ethnic or
religious minorities, but to racial minorities.

Warfare against Indians in the West intensified after Appomattox.
Veterans of the Blue and Gray armies joined hands to extirpate the last
independent Indian tribes from the Great Plains and Rocky Mountains.
Minstrelsy supported this long-delayed opening up of the Western territories by blackface portrayals of Indians as drunken scalpers, and of those
who supported the Indian cause as misguided, corrupt, effete, upper class
and miscegenationist. "Oh, dear me," sighed Miss Matilda Livingston ("a
young lady of society" in *The Bogus Injun*), "I never do get tired of
reading about the noble braves in their forest homes of the far West."
Duped by a couple of con men, one of whom impersonates a visiting
Indian chief, Miss Livingston donates money to the tribal fund and ar-
ranges to have one of her friends, Miss Millefleurs, dress up as an Indian
"squaw" to make the chief feel at home. "That really is a good idea," Miss
Millefleurs enthusiastically agrees, "as it will allow me to be present at all
events, and no doubt prove very interesting to me." The bogus Indian,
stimulated by so much hospitality, draws out his tomahawk. The ladies,
terrified, run away, while: "The INDIAN . . . chases PETE [Miss
Livingston's black footman] around the stage once or twice, and finally
catches him in the centre and scalps him while PETE is on his knees." [45]

On the Pacific Coast during these same years, Chinese immigration

---

[43] For example, Franck Dumont, *Birch and Backus' Songs of the San Francisco Minstrels* (New York: DeWitt, 1881), pp. 9, 23, 53, 56, 68, 103, 105, 114, 144. And see
Toll, pp. 150–51.

[44] Harry McCarthy, *Deeds of Darkness* (New York: DeWitt, 1876), p. 2. For a few
other examples among hundreds, *Dick's Ethiopian Scenes, Variety Sketches and
Stump Speeches* (New York: Dick & Fitzgerald, 1879), esp. pp. 151–53; Bert
Richards, *Colored Senators, an Ethiopian Burlesque* (Clyde, Ohio: Ames, 1887);
Charles White, *The Recruiting Office, an Ethiopian Sketch in Two Scenes* (New
York: DeWitt, 1874).

[45] Charles White, *The Bogus Injun: A Very Laughable Sketch in Four Scenes* (New
York: DeWitt, 1875).

had been steadily increasing since the gold rush. California's Democratic Party, heavily discredited by the secessionist proclivities of its prewar leaders, focused after the war upon the Chinese menace as a means of rehabilitating the organization. Democratic platforms and oratory linked the Chinese issue directly to the party's national stance against Radical Reconstruction and black suffrage. Government of, by and for white men, on the Pacific Coast as in the South, was the gist of the party's program. San Francisco, one of the nation's leading minstrel cities since before the war, became the gateway through which stereotypes of Chinese, performed in blackface, first reached national audiences. As early as 1856 (twenty years before Bret Harte's "Heathen Chinee") "The Chinese Washerman" was performed in New York by Eph Horn, a minstrel recently returned from the Golden State. Charles Backus, who had once been Horn's partner in San Francisco, joined Billy Birch, of like background, in the 1870s to organize the San Francisco Minstrels in New York. Part of their regular repertory was "The Chinee Laundryman."

> Me workee all day in Chinee laundry
> For "Ching Chow," dat's his name;
> Me catchee all de rats in de market
> Makee pot-pie all-a-same (gong)
> All-a-same (gong) all-a-same (gong).
>
> Me soon become a cit'zen
> And votee just likee me please
> By'm by me gettee a good jobbee
> To workee on de police! (gong)
> Police! (gong) Muchee clubbee! (gong) [46]

From the outbreak of the Mexican War to the closing years of Reconstruction, blackface minstrelsy had consistently reinforced the politics of Jacksonian and neo-Jacksonian Democracy. Civil war, the industrial depression of 1873 and the final phasing out of Reconstruction altered the social and political environment in which the alliance of minstrelsy and Democracy had originally taken shape. Elements of Jacksonian ideology now filtered through both members of a changed party system. With respect to the racial components of Jacksonian ideology, what this meant may be epitomized by noting that three great Jacksonian issues—Indian removal, white supremacy in the South, and Chinese exclusion—had by the 1880s become matters of bipartisan agreement. After 1877 it would no longer be surprising to encounter a professional minstrel who was not also a Democrat. Meanwhile minstrelsy itself was changing. This was not so much a decline as a spreading out into other forms of mass entertainment. Minstrelsy bequeathed its cast of racial caricatures, along with the dehumanizing ridicule which had literally *informed* them, to the nation's popular culture. As early as 1870 a melodrama celebrating the

46 Dumont, *Birch and Backus' Songs*, p. 57. George C. D. Odell, *Annals of the New York Stage* (New York: Columbia Univ. Press, 1931), 6:585; Stuart W. Hyde, "The Chinese Stereotype in American Melodrama," *California Historical Society Quarterly*, 34 (Dec. 1955), 357–65.

transcontinental railroad predicted uses to be made of those caricatures in ten thousand westerns which would march across the landscape of dime novels, stage plays, and ultimately of films, radio and television. In *Across the Continent; or, Scenes from New York Life and the Pacific Railroad*, the minstrel roles of Tambo and Bones were filled by a black servant, "Caesar Augustus, called Coon because he is one," and "Very Tart, a Chinaman." The California-bound party, barricaded in a railroad station, is expecting attack from Indians led by the ferocious chief, Black Cloud. Very Tart, never having seen a black man before, mistakes Caesar Augustus for the chief. "Oh, Black Cloud—Black Cloud!" he cries in terror. But John (the hero) reassures him, "That ain't an injun—it's only a nigger." To which Caesar Augustus agrees: "Well, thank the Lord I'se only a nigger." The climax of course will be the arrival of a trainload of soldiers to annihilate Black Cloud and his horde. Just before the shooting starts, Very Tart finds a large empty packing crate on the station platform, and as he crawls inside informs the audience: "Melican man like fightee. Chinaman like sleepee in a box." [47]

The ideological impact of minstrelsy was programmed by its conventional blackface form. There is no possibility of escaping this relationship because the greater the interest, talent, complexity, and *humanity* embodied in its content, the more irresistible was the racist message of the form. One is tempted to borrow McLuhan's phrase: the medium was the message. Yet that would miss the point since without its content, the form would have been inconsequential. As noted earlier, the matrix of social content contained, among other elements, a style of moral permissiveness. Horizontally this style was linked to the cosmopolitanism of new urban environments and the open opportunity of the frontier. There was also a vertical linkage which went straight down under to a permissiveness to demean, ridicule and destroy all those outside the fraternity of white egalitarianism. The meaning did not reside solely in negative or ridiculous portrayals of nonwhites; it resided in the "convention" itself. Blackface performers were like puppets operated by a white puppet-master. Their physical appearance proclaimed their non-humanity; yet they could be manipulated not only to mock themselves, but also to act like human beings. They expressed human emotions such as joy and grief, love, fear, longing. The white audience then identified with the emotions, admired the skill of the puppeteer, even sympathized laughingly with the hopeless aspiration of the puppets to become human, and at the same time feasted on the assurance that they could not do so. Blackface minstrelsy's dominance of popular entertainment amounted to half a century of inurement to the uses of white supremacy.

American historians have traditionally attached a major importance to the Jacksonian era. The effects of that era have been interpreted

[47] James J. McCloskey, *Across the Continent: or, Scenes from New York Life and the Pacific Railroad*, in Isaac Goldberg and Hubert Heffner, eds., *Davy Crockett and Other Plays* (Princeton: Princeton Univ. Press, 1940), pp. 110–12.

variously in terms of nationalism, politics, social status, population movement, technological and economic growth. Each of these interpretations
assumes diffusion of new ideas and attitudes through a population which,
during the period under consideration, was moving from the Mississippi
Valley to the Pacific Coast and increasing numerically from seventeen to
fifty millions. No doubt diffusion of ideas and attitudes occurred in such
old-fashioned ways as by word of mouth and written correspondence;
but it occurred also by new methods including steam-powered presses
and popular entertainment which brought mass audiences into the tents,
town halls and theaters of new population centers. Thus gathered together, they could rejoice in what Mark Twain had described as a "glad
and stunning surprise." At other times a vitriolic critic of American society, Mark Twain's uncritical approval of minstrelsy is testimony to the
pervasiveness of its influence. He seems simply to have taken the blackface
"convention" for granted and probably had no perception of the African
elements in the music and dance. Minstrel songs, he wrote, "were a delight to me as long as the Negro show continued in existence. In the
beginning the songs were rudely comic . . . but a little later sentimental
songs were introduced, such as 'The Blue Juniata,' 'Sweet Ellen Bayne,'
'Nelly Bly,' 'A Life on the Ocean Wave,' 'The Larboard Watch,' etc." [48]
Two of the five songs mentioned were Stephen Foster's. Clearly what
Mark Twain preferred was the nostalgic, "white" voice of minstrelsy
which had already attained full expression ten years before the Civil War.

> Way down on the Swanee ribber
> Far, far away,
> Dere's wha my heart is turning ebber . . .[49]

The "darkey" dialect is transparent. The black puppets are striving
to be white, singing in white voice, while the white audience in the new
city or the new West lingers through a moment of self-pity and regret
for things past, before the rattle of tambourine and bones calls up the
clowns again. It would be a mistake to underestimate these tearjerkers.
Whatever they may or may not say to anyone in the mid-20th century,
it is clear that to the author of *Huckleberry Finn* they said a great deal.
For Mark Twain, as for many of his contemporaries, they touched the
central chords of white consciousness—the place left behind and the endless outward journey. By setting a heroic, tragic concept of human
destiny in a conventional form which denied human status to nonwhites,
blackface minstrelsy acted out the most appalling aspect of Jacksonian
ideology. It is useless to debate whether the minstrels created or merely
reflected this ideology; mass entertainment necessarily transmits as it
creates and creates in transmitting.

48 Mark Twain, p. 66.
49 [Stephen Foster], "Old Folks at Home," in *Christy's No. 1*, p. 7.

The Heart That Dared Not
Let in the Sun

O. E. RÖLVAAG

America has always been a nation of immigrants. This was especially true in the nineteenth century, when some 20 million people entered the country to pursue the American dream. In the 1820s and 1830s immigrants arrived at a rate of about 65,000 per year. But in the next two decades, when the population of the country grew from 17 to 31 million, the rate of immigration tripled. About 4.4 million immigrants left their homelands between 1840 and 1860 for a new start in the United States. American society was permanently transformed by this inundation of diverse peoples, just as each of the immigrants was transformed by the experience of starting life over in a new land.

Millions of these immigrants were peasant farmers who were fleeing crop failures or persistent poverty in northwestern Europe. America, with its vast resources of open land, seemed the answer to their despair. Even now, in the historical imagination, the romance and glamour of the pioneer experience persist. But the daily life of the immigrant was far from romantic. It has been calculated that one of every three immigrants before the Civil War died within three years of arrival in America—from the hardship of steerage passage across the ocean, from exposure to new diseases, from economic hardship after arrival, or from debilitating psychological disorientation. Instant success was very seldom achieved; in fact success at any point in life was rare for the nineteenth-century immigrant. Usually it was the sons and daughters who reaped the rewards of their parents' decision to move to America.

Giants in the Earth, the novel by the Norwegian immigrant O. E. Rölvaag, tells the story of Per Hansa, his wife Beret, and their children, Ole, Store-Hans, And-Ongen, and Peder Victorious. The scene is the Dakotas and the time is in the late 1860s and early 1870s. But the immigrants could be German, Swedish, Irish, Bohemian, or Russian. The scene could be Minnesota, Iowa, Kansas, Missouri, or anywhere else in the trans-Mississippi West. And the time could be almost any decade of the nineteenth century. For in writing about Per Hansa and his family, Rölvaag was attempting to write about the realities of daily life for all who struggled for survival on the Great Plains. The grim reality of pioneer life on the prairie is the major concern of his story. Per Hansa, the father, is a frontier hero of sorts—dauntless to the end, when he is found frozen to death in drifting snow. But his wife Beret personifies the psychological ravages the Great Plains environment inflicted on European immigrants in America. For her the reality of life in North Dakota is interminable winters, painful memories of her Norwegian village and her parents whom she left behind, fears of the wilderness, and deep de-

381

pression and suicidal urges that sweep over her as she struggles to
find her place in the new land. For her the immigrant experience is a
sustained tragedy.

The collective result of the vast human migration to America in
the nineteenth century was the peopling of the nation, the transformation of the Great Plains into the nation's granary, the "subduing
of the frontier," and the conquest of the entire continent, from east
to west, at the expense of its original inhabitants. But the thousands
of individual experiences that made up the collective result are rarely
recorded by historians. They must be sought in novels such as
Rölvaag's **Giants in the Earth,** Hamlin Garland's **A Son of the Middle
Border** and **A Daughter of the Middle Border,** and Willa Cather's
My Antonia. In these portraits of everyday frontier life the student
will find vivid examples of many crucial issues in the social history
of the westward-moving frontier.

It was well enough that winter had come at last, thought Per Hansa; he
really needed to lay off and rest awhile. After a good square meal of
ducks or fresh fish, he would light his pipe and stretch himself, saying:

"Ha!—now we're really as well off here, my Beret-girl, as anybody
could ever wish to be!" . . . He did not always expect an answer, and
seldom got one. Then he would throw himself on the bed and take a
good after-dinner nap, often sleeping continuously on into the night. . . .
Life seemed very pleasant now!

In this fashion he spent quite a number of days; the bad weather
still held out. Per Hansa continued to do full justice to the fare. When
he had eaten his fill he would point out again to Beret how well off they
were, and go to his couch to sleep the sleep of the righteous. It was almost uncanny—he could never seem to get sleep enough! He slept both
day and night; and still he felt the need of more rest. . . . Now and then
he would go to the door to look out at the weather, and glance across
toward the neighbours. No . . . nothing to do outside—the weather was
too beastly! He would come in again, and stretch himself, and yawn. . . .

The days wore on.

Yes, they wore on. . . . One exactly like the other. . . . Per Hansa
couldn't grasp the strange contradiction that had begun to impress him;
he knew that the days were actually growing shorter—were being shorn
more closely by every passing night; but—weren't they growing longer?

Indeed they were—no question about it! They finally grew so long
that he was at a dead loss to find something to do with which to end

them. He assured himself that all this leisure was very fine; that he needed
to ease up a bit; during the fall he hadn't spared himself; now it felt like
a blessing to sit around and play the gentleman. Times would be strenuous enough for him once more, when spring came with fair weather and
his great estate needed to be planted; he would just lay off and rest for a
while yet! . . .

The days only grew longer and longer.

In the end, this enforced idleness began to gall him. The landscape
showed a monotonous sameness . . . never the slightest change. . . .
Grey sky—damp, icy cold. . . . Snow fell . . . snow flew. . . . He
could only guess now where the huts of Hans Olsa lay. There wasn't a
thing to do outdoors; plenty of wood lay chopped and ready for use;
it took but a little while to do the chores. . . . Beyond this, everything
took care of itself outside.

Per Hansa sat by the table, or lay down on the bed when he got
tired of sitting up; tried to sleep as long as possible; woke up with a start;
turned over and tried to sleep again; rose and sat by the table once more,
when he grew weary of lying down.

The days wore on, and yet got nowhere. . . . Time had simply
come to a standstill! He had never seen the like; this was worse than
the deadest lay-up in Lofoten!

The boys were almost as badly off; they too sat restless and idle;
and because they had nothing at all to occupy their minds they often
came to blows, so that the father had to interfere. . . . But he was never
very rough with them; poor boys, what else could they find for amuse-
ment? . . . The mother always reminded him of their books. . . . Yes,
of course—certainly they must learn to read, the father said; no heathen
were going to grow up in his house! He tried to be stern with them
over this matter; but then . . . after all, boys were boys, he remembered!

At length he realized that this sort of life could not go on. He didn't
give a hang for the weather—put on his coat and bade the boys do the
same; then they went out and attacked the woodpile. They sawed and
they chopped; they lugged in wood and piled it up; first they stacked up
as much chopped wood as they could stow in the odd corners of the
house; then they built a curious little fort of chopped wood out in the
yard—very neatly and craftily constructed—and piled it full, too; this
work cheered them up and kept their minds occupied, though the weather
was bitterly cold and inclement. They toiled at it from early morning
until late at night, and hardly took time off to eat their dinner; the boys
began to get sick of the job and complained of being tired. The woodpile lasted exactly four days; when they had chopped up the last stick
there was nothing left for them to do outside.

Then they sat idle again.

The bad spell of weather held out interminably. A cold, piercing
wind from the northeast blew the livelong day, and moaned about the
corners at night. . . . Snow flew . . . more snow fell.

No sun. . . . No sky. . . . The air was a grey, ashen mist which
breathed a deathly chill; it hung around and above them thick and frozen.
. . . In the course of time there was a full moon at night, somewhere be-

hind the veil. Then the mist grew luminous and alive—strange to behold.
. . . Night after night the ghostly spectacle would return.

Per Hansa would gaze at it and think: Now the trolls are surely
abroad! . . .

One evening Tönseten and Kjersti came over. They sat and talked
until it grew very late. One could readily see that Syvert was out of
sorts about something; he puffed at his pipe in glum, ill humor, glared
at Per Hansa's walls, and didn't have much to say. When he did speak
his voice was unnecessarily loud.

Kjersti and Beret sat together on the bed; they seemed to be finding
a good deal to chat about.

Kjersti was in an unusually neighbourly mood; she had come over
to ask if . . . well, if she couldn't do something for Beret? She had some
woollen yarn at home in her chest, very soft and very fine. Would Beret
be offended if she knitted a pair of socks for the little newcomer they
were all awaiting? . . . It was fine yarn, the very finest! Beret must just
try to imagine how lonesome she was, sitting at home all alone with that
useless husband of hers—and no little newcomer to wait for! . . . She
had plenty of yarn; she could easily make the socks long enough to serve
as leggings, too. The work would really bring joy to her—and to Syvert,
too, poor fellow, to whom no little newcomer would ever arrive!

. . . Ah, well! . . . God pity us, Syvert wasn't so bad, after all—
far be it from her to complain! . . . At that, Kjersti happened to think
of a story she had heard, about a couple who couldn't seem to get a child
though they wanted one very badly. Here the story was, since they
happened to be talking about such matters. . . . This wife had so little
sense that she sought the aid of a witch woman, who gave her both *devil's
drink* and *beaver-geld;* she rubbed herself with the stuff and drank some
of it, too, but no change came; that is, not until one summer when a shoal
of herring come into the fjord and with it a fleet of strange fishermen.
. . . Alas! desire makes a hot fire, once it has been kindled! But what do
you suppose?—her husband became just as fond of that child as if he
had been the father of it! . . . Wasn't that a queer thing? . . . But when
the boy was a year old and was on the point of being christened—well, on
that very Sunday it happened, as they were sailing across the fjord, that
the boat capsized and the Lord took both mother and child, right there
and then! He had taken away what he had refused to give in honour, and
more besides. . . . There was something mysterious about such things,
didn't Beret think so? And wasn't it strange that the father should have
been so fond of *that* child? . . . Kjersti had known them both very well.

Beret listened attentively to this tale, putting in a word here and
there.

Over at the table, the men had pricked up their ears as the story
began; they heard it all. Per Hansa looked at Syvert and laughed; Syvert,
in turn, glared at the wall and said, angrily:

"I should think you'd be able to find something American to talk
about! . . . We're through now with all that troll business over in Norway!" . . . He got up and started to go. . . .

But Per Hansa wouldn't listen to their leaving just yet; since they had braved the weather to make a call they might as well sit awhile longer. . . . "You'll have the wind astern, Syvert, going home! . . . Come on, sit down and behave yourself!"

On another afternoon all of Hans Olsa's household came over. They stayed till dark; then they began to say that perhaps they'd better be going now—but they made no move to leave. . . . Sörine had brought a gift for Beret. There had been a few bits of cloth lying around the house, for which she could find no use; it had been rather lonesome these days and she had needed something to do, so she had made a little article for this newcomer whom everyone was waiting for! . . . At that, Sörine drew out from her ample bosom a child's cap, of red, white, and blue stripes, with long silk ribbons, all sewed with the greatest care. It was a beautiful cap; all had to see it; there were many warm words of praise. Beret received it in silence; her eyes were wet as she took the cap and laid it carefully in the big chest. . . .

To night it was Beret who refused to let the visitors leave. She abso lutely insisted. Such quantities of food lay outside around the house— far more than they would ever need—that they might as well stay for supper and help to eat it! . . . This proposal overjoyed Per Hansa. It was the plain truth, as Beret said, they had more than they needed—and there was plenty left in the Sioux River, for that matter; to-night they were going to celebrate with fresh fish for supper! . . . He went outside and brought in a generous supply of the frozen fish, which he scaled and cut up; he was in the finest of spirits—it seemed just like the good old days in Lofoten.

. . . That evening was a happy interlude for them all.

. . . No, the days would not pass! . . . Why, here it was, only the middle of November! It seemed to Per Hansa, as he sat by the table puffing his pipe and following Beret around with his eyes, that many winters must have gone by already.

He found himself watching Beret very often; during the last two weeks he had discovered many things about her which he had never noticed before. Just trifles, they were, but so many of them—one thing after another. Sitting here now with nothing else to occupy his mind, he began slowly and carefully to piece together what he had observed; the result pleased him less and less as he went on adding. He tried to wave the truth aside—to deny the plain facts; he even succeeded for a while— in the beginning. . . . Goodness! nothing but trifles—things that were always likely to happen under such circumstances! . . . Oh no! There was no danger that Beret couldn't stand her watch; things would right themselves when the time came; for it was only the law of nature, which man must obey. . . . Of course she couldn't help dreading it, poor thing!

. . . Did her face seem a good deal more wasted this time—or was he mistaken? She didn't look well at all. . . . No. . . . Then why didn't she eat more? Good Heavens! she wasn't trying to save on the food? Here

was everything—quantities of it: meat aplenty, and any amount of flour!
. . . She should help herself, this Beret-girl of his, or he would make her
dance to another tune!

One day at table he burst out with it, telling her that she mustn't
act the stranger in her own house! He made his voice sound gruff and
commanding: Now she must sit up and eat like a grown woman. . . .
"Here, help yourself!" . . . He took a big piece of fish from the platter
and put it on her plate; but she merely picked at it, and left the most of
it lying there.

"It is hard when you have to force every mouthful down," she complained.

"But look here, you've got to eat, both for yourself and— Of course
you must eat!"

"Oh, well," she said, wearily, as she got up and left the table. . . .
"It doesn't matter much about the food." . . .

Lately he had also begun to notice that she lay awake the greater
part of the night; he always dropped off to sleep before she did; yet she
would be wide awake in the morning when he first stirred, although he
was by habit an early riser. And if by chance he woke up in the night,
he would be almost certain to find her lying awake beside him. . . . One
night she had called him; she had been sitting up in bed, and must have
been crying—her voice sounded like it. And she had only wanted him to
get up and see what ailed Store-Hans; he had been moaning in his sleep
all night, she said. Per Hansa had risen to look after the boy, and had
found nothing the matter, as he had expected. . . . That night he had
been seriously frightened. When he had come back to lie down she had
started crying so despairingly; he hadn't been able to make any sense of
the few words he got out of her. . . . From that time on, he had been
scared to show her any tenderness; he had noticed that when he did so,
the tears were sure to come. And that, certainly, was not good for her!

As he sat through the long, long day observing his wife, he grew
more and more worried about Beret, poor thing. Every day there were
new trifles to be noticed.

She, who had always been so neat and could make whatever clothes
she put on look becoming, was now going about shabby and unkempt;
she didn't even bother to wash herself. He realized that he had noticed
it subconsciously for a long time. . . . But now he seldom saw her even
wash her face. And her hair, her beautiful hair which he admired so
greatly and loved to fondle when she was in good spirits, now hung
down in frowsy coils. . . . Wasn't it two days since she had touched
her hair? Well—*that* he didn't dare to mention! . . . How could he ever
speak of cleanliness at all to his Beret—his Beret who was always so prim
and often nagged him for being slovenly and careless about his own appearance? . . . Not that she wasn't pretty enough, just as she was, his
Beret-girl; this Per Hansa told himself many times. But one day as he
sat looking at her, he suddenly got up, went over to the window, and
stood there gazing out; and then he said:

"I really think you ought to go and fix up your hair, Beret-girl. . . .
I kind of feel that we're going to have company to-day."

She gave him a quick glance, blushed deeply, rose, and left the room. He heard her go into the stable, where she stayed a long time; he couldn't imagine what she was doing in there at that hour of the day. Her actions made him feel worried and uncertain. When she came in again he did not dare to look at her. . . . Then she began to tidy herself; she took some water and washed, loosened up her braids and combed her hair, and afterward coiled it very prettily. She gave herself plenty of time, and took careful pains. . . . At last he *had* to look at her; his whole self was in the gaze that he fixed upon her; he would have liked to say something kind and loving to her now. But she did not glance at him, and so he dared not speak. . . . In a little while he found an excuse to go out; passing close to her, he said in a tender, admiring voice:

"Now we've got a fine-looking lady!"

All the rest of that day he felt happier than he had been for a long while. . . . Of course his Beret-girl would be all right. . . . Indeed, she *was* all right, as far as that went! . . .

But . . . other days followed. Per Hansa remained idle and had nothing to do but look at his wife. He looked and looked, until he had to face the hard fact that something was wrong.

. . . Had she ever been so brooding and taciturn when she was with child before? He could talk to the boys about the future until they would be completely carried away by his visions; but whenever he tried to draw her into the conversation he failed completely—failed, no matter which tack he took nor how hard he tried. He understood it clearly: it wasn't because she did not want to respond—she *couldn't!* . . . The pain of it surged through him like a wave. God in Heaven, had she grown so weak and helpless! . . . She wasn't even able to take nourishment. . . . There Beret sat in the room with them, within four paces—yet she was far, far away. He spoke to her now, to her alone, but could not make her come out of the enchanted ring that lay about her. . . . When he discovered this, it hurt him so that he could have shrieked. . . .

. . . Another queer thing, she was always losing the commonest objects—completely losing them, though they were right at hand. He had seen it happen several times without taking much notice; but by and by it began to occur so frequently that he was forced to pay attention. She would put a thing down, merely turn around, and then go about searching for it in vain; and the thing would lie exactly where she had placed it, all the time. . . . This happened again and again; sometimes it struck them all as very funny. . . . "It looks as if your eyes were in your way, Mother!" Store-Hans once exclaimed, laughing so heartily that the others had to join in; but Per Hansa soon noticed that she was hurt when they made fun of her.

One day she was looking for the scissors. She had been sitting by the stove, mending a garment; had risen to put on more fuel; and when she sat down again had been unable to find her scissors, which she held all the while in her hand. She searched diligently, and asked the others to help her. Suddenly Ole discovered the scissors in his mother's hand; he ran up to her and jerked them away; the boy was roaring with laughter. . . . Then she burst into violent tears, laid her work aside, threw herself down on the bed, and buried her face in the pillow. All three menfolk felt painfully embarrassed.

And sometimes she had moments of unusual tenderness toward them all—particularly toward Per Hansa. Her concern would grow touchingly childlike; it was as if she could not do enough for him and the children. But it was a tenderness so delicate that he dared not respond to it. Nevertheless, he felt very happy when these moods came; they gave him renewed courage.

. . . Of course she would be all right again as soon as it was over! . . . And now the event could not be far away! . . .

Winter was ever tightening its grip. The drifting snow flew wildly under a low sky, and stirred up the whole universe into a whirling mass; it swept the plain like the giant broom of a witch, churning up a flurry so thick that people could scarcely open their eyes.

As soon as the weather cleared icy gusts drove through every chink and cranny, leaving white frost behind; people's breaths hung frozen in the air the moment it was out of the mouth; if one touched iron, a piece of skin would be torn away.

At intervals a day of bright sunshine came. Then the whole vast plain glittered with the flashing brilliance of diamonds; the glare was so strong that it burnt the sight; the eyes saw blackness where there was nothing but shining white. . . .

. . . Evenings . . . magic, still evenings, surpassing in beauty the most fantastic dreams of childhood! . . . Out to the westward—so surprisingly near—a blazing countenance sank to rest on a white couch . . . set it afire . . . kindled a radiance . . . a golden flame that flowed in many streams from horizon to horizon; the light played on the hundreds and thousands and millions of diamonds, and turned them into glittering points of yellow and red, green and blue fire.

. . . Such evenings were dangerous for all life. To the strong they brought reckless laughter—for who had ever seen such moon-nights? . . . To the weak they brought tears, hopeless tears. This was not life, but eternity itself. . . .

Per Hansa sat in his hut, ate, drank, puffed at his pipe, and followed his wife with his eyes in vague alarm; for the life of him he didn't know what to do. Where could he betake himself? It wouldn't do for him to go from house to house, when things were in such a bad way at home. . . . No, here he was condemned to sit! . . . His temper was growing steadily worse; he found it more and more difficult to keep his hands off things.

He would be seized by a sudden, almost irresistible desire to take Beret, his own blessed Beret, hold her on his knee like a naughty child—just *make* her sit there—and reason with her . . . talk some sense into her!

For this wasn't altogether fair play on her part! Of course it was hard for her these days; but after all, the time would soon come to an end; and *that* was something real to struggle with—something to glory

in! Besides, she had her wonted round of duties to perform. . . . But he!
. . . Here he was forced to sit in idleness, and just let his eyes wander! . . .

 . . . And it wasn't right for him to feel this way, either; but the
endless waiting had at last got on his nerves. . . . Strange, how long it
took! Hadn't the time ought to be drawing near pretty soon? . . . During
these days he often thought about the matter of a name. He immediately
decided that if it turned out to be a girl, she should be named *Beret;* that
part of it was settled. But suppose she bore him a boy? In that case he
wasn't so certain. Two boy's names were running in his mind, but—well,
time would tell. . . . If she would only hurry up and bring forth the
child, he would guarantee to find a suitable name for it!

He began to feel weak and miserable as he dragged himself about
the house. . . . Then, one day, came a fascinating thought: if he could
only make a short trip east to the Sioux River, to visit the Trönders! This
spell of cold weather was nothing to mind; it was a long way, to be sure,
but he felt that he could easily manage it. Hadn't he sailed a cockleshell of
an eight-oared boat all the way from Helgeland to West Lofoten in the
dark of winter? This would be mere child's play compared to that
journey. . . . What great sport it would be to fish with a net through the
ice! From the Trönders, who were old settlers in this region, he could
get a lot more valuable information; it was really remarkable, what they
had told him last time, about the fur trade with the Indians north at
Flandreau. . . . Whenever the thought of this journey came to him he
could hardly push it aside.

 . . . Useless even to dream of such a thing! Here was poor Beret,
pottering helplessly about—he must think only of her.

And Per Hansa tried his best to think of her to some effect. He had
noticed that she minded the cold; she never complained, but he was well
aware of it; from now on he tended the fire himself and kept the stove
red hot most of the day. In spite of that he couldn't get the house properly
warm when the cold was at its worst; the earthen floor was always cold
and Beret's feet seemed particularly sensitive.

One day Per Hansa got an idea which gave him much diversion.
While they had been busy chopping the wood he had selected a few of
the largest and straightest-grained sticks, trimmed them out square and
stood them behind the stove to dry; he had promised himself that he
would make something out of them during the winter. Now he chose
the best piece he could pick out; he had decided to make a pair of clogs
for Beret; he knew by experience that such shoes were very warm while
they were new. For a long while he couldn't think of any material to use
for the vamps; then he resolutely cut off a corner of the old sheepskin
robe which they used on their bed; he sheared the wool snug, and made
the vamps of that. . . . He did a neat, attractive job and felt rather proud
when the job was finished.

He brought the clogs to Beret and put them on her feet.

It was plain to be seen that she was touched by the gift; but then
she said something that he wished she had left unspoken:

"You might have thought of this before, it seems to me. Here I have gone with cold feet all winter." . . . The words were uttered quietly; she meant no reproach by them, but merely said what came into her mind.

He turned away and went out of the house; outside the door he paused, and stood for a long time gazing off into the evening. . . . Somewhere out there life was still happy. . . . There was no solitude. . . . Didn't it seem to call to him?

. . . Per Hansa felt that now he needed to cry. . . .

The days wore on . . . sunny days . . . bleak, gloomy days, with cold that congealed all life.

There was one who heeded not the light of the day, whether it might be grey or golden. Beret stared at the earthen floor of the hut and saw only night round about her.

Yes . . . she faced only darkness. She tried hard, but she could not let in the sun.

Ever since she had come out here a grim conviction had been taking stronger and stronger hold on her.

This was her retribution!

Now had fallen the punishment which the Lord God had meted out to her; at last His visitation had found her out and she must drink the cup of His wrath. Far away she had fled, from the rising of the sun to the going down thereof . . . so it had seemed to her . . . but the arm of His might had reached farther still. No, she could not escape—this was her retribution!

The stillness out here had given her full opportunity for reflection; all the fall she had done nothing but brood and remember. . . . Alas! she had much to remember!

She had accepted the hand of Per Hansa because she must—although no law had compelled her; she and he were the only people who had willed it thus. She had been gotten with child by him out of wedlock; nevertheless, no one had compelled her to marry him—neither father, nor mother, nor anyone in authority. It had been wholly her own doing. Her parents, in fact, had set themselves against the marriage with all their might, even after the child, Ole, had come.

. . . It had mattered nothing at all what they had said, nor what anyone else had said; for her there had been no other person in the world but Per Hansa! Whenever she had been with him she had forgotten the admonitions and prayers of her father and mother. . . . He had been life itself to her; without him there had been nothing. . . . Therefore she had given herself to him, although she had known it was a sin—had continued to give herself freely, in a spirit of abandoned joy.

Now she found plenty of time to remember how her parents had begged and threatened her to break with him; she recalled all that they had said, turning it over in her mind and examining it minutely. . . . Per Hansa was a shiftless fellow, they had told her; he drank; he fought; he was wild and reckless; he got himself tangled up in all sorts of brawls; no honourable woman could be happy with such a man. He probably had affairs with other women, too, whenever he had a chance. . . . All the other accusations she knew to be true; but not the last—no, not the last! She alone among women held his heart. The certainty of this fact had been the very sweetness of life to her. . . . What did she care for the rest of it! All was as nothing compared with this great certainty. . . . Ah, no—she knew it well enough: for him she was the only princess!

But now she understood clearly all that her parents had done to end it between them, and all the sacrifices they had been willing to make; she had not realized it at the time. . . . Oh, those kind-hearted parents on whom she had turned her back in order that she might cleave to him: how they must have suffered! The life which she and he had begotten in common guilt they had offered to take as their own, give it their name and their inheritance, and bring it up as their very child. They had freely offered to use their hard-earned savings to send her away from the scene of her shame . . . *so* precious had she been to them! But she had only said no, and no, and *no*, to all their offers of sacrifice and love! . . . Had there ever been a transgression so grievous as hers!

. . . Yet how could she ever have broken with him? Where Per Hansa was, there dwelt high summer and there it bloomed for her. How can a human forsake his very life? . . . Whenever she heard of one of his desperately reckless cruises through rough and stormy seas, on which he had played with the lives of his comrades as well as his own, her cheeks would glow and her heart would flame. This was the man her heart had chosen—this was he, and he alone! a voice would sing within her. Or when she sat among the heather on the mountain side in the fair summer night, and he came to her and laid his head in her lap—the tousled head that only she could lull to sleep—then she felt that now she was crossing the very threshold of paradise! . . . Though she had had a thousand lives, she would have thrown them all away for one such moment—and would have been glad of the bargain! . . .

. . . Yes, she remembered all that had happened in those days; it was so still out here . . . so easy to remember!

No one had ever told her, but she knew full well who it was that had persuaded Hans Olsa to leave the land and the ancient farm that had been in his family for generations, and go to America. There had been only one other person in the world whom Per Hansa loved, and that was Hans Olsa. She had been jealous of Hans Olsa because of this; it had seemed to her that he took something that rightfully belonged to her. She had even felt the same way toward Sörine, who was kindness itself; on this account she had not been able to hold her friendship as fully as she needed to, either in Norway or here. . . .

. . . But when Per Hansa had come home from Lofoten that spring and announced in his reckless, masterful way, that he was off for America: would Beret come now, or wait until later? . . . Well, there hadn't been a "no" in her mouth then! There she had sat, with three children in a nice little home which, after the manner of simple folk, they had managed to build. . . . But she had risen up, taken the children with her, and left it all as if nothing mattered but him!

. . . How her mother had wept at that time! . . . How her father

had grieved when they had left! Time after time he had come begging
to Per Hansa, offering him all that he had—boat and fishing outfit, house
and farm—if only he would settle down in Norway and not take their
daughter from them forever. . . . But Per Hansa had laughed it all aside!
There had been a power in his unflinching determination which had sent
hot waves through her. She must have led a double life at that time; she
had been sad with her parents but had rejoiced with Per Hansa. He had
raged like a storm through those days, wild and reckless—and sometimes
ruthless, too. . . . No!—he had cried—they would just make that little
trip across the ocean! America—that's the country where a poor devil
can get ahead! Besides, it was only a little way; if they didn't like it, they
could drift back on the first fair western breeze! . . . So they had sold
off everything that they had won with so much toil, had left it all like a
pair of worn-out shoes—parents, home, fatherland, and people. . . . And
she had done it gladly, even rejoicingly! . . . Was there ever a sin like
hers?

        . . . Then she had arrived in America. The country did not at all
come up to her expectations; here, too, she saw enough of poverty and
grinding toil. What did it avail, that the rich soil lay in endless stretches?
More than ever did she realize that "man liveth not by bread alone!" . . .
Even the bread was none too plentiful at times. . . .
        Beyond a doubt, it was Destiny that had brought her thither. . . .
Destiny, the inexorable law of life, which the Lord God from eternity
had laid down for every human being, according to the path He knew
would be taken. . . . Now punishment stood here awaiting her—the
punishment for having broken God's commandment of filial obedience.
. . . Throughout the fall she had been reckoning up her score, and it
came out exactly thus: Destiny had so arranged everything that the punishment should strike her all the more inevitably. Destiny had cast her
into the arms of Per Hansa—and she did not regret it! Destiny had held
up America as an enticing will-o'-the-wisp—and they had followed! . . .
        But no sooner had they reached America than the west-fever had
smitten the old settlements like a plague. Such a thing had never happened before in the history of mankind; people were intoxicated by bewildering visions; they spoke dazedly, as though under the force of a
spell. . . . "Go west! . . . Go west, folks! . . . The farther west, the
better the land!" . . . Men beheld in feverish dreams the endless plains,
teeming with fruitfulness, glowing, out there where day sank into night
—a Beulah Land of corn and wine! . . . She had never dreamed that the
good Lord would let such folly loose among men. Were it only the
young people who had been caught by the plague, she would not have
wondered; but the old had been taken even worse. . . . "Now we're
bound west!" said the young. . . . "Wait a minute—we're going along
with you!" cried the old, and followed after. . . . Human beings gathered together, in small companies and large—took whatever was movable
along, and left the old homestead without as much as a sigh! Ever westward led the course, to where the sun glowed in matchless glory as it

sank at night; people drifted about in a sort of delirium, like sea birds in mating time; then they flew toward the sunset, in small flocks and large —always toward Sunset Land. . . . Now she saw it clearly: here on the trackless plains, the thousand-year-old hunger of the poor after human happiness had been unloosed!

Into this feverish atmosphere they had come. Could Destiny have spun his web more cunningly? She remembered well how the eyes of Per Hansa had immediately begun to gleam and glow! . . . And the strange thing about this spell had been that he had become so very kind under it. How playfully affectionate he had grown toward her during the last winter and spring! It had been even more deliciously sweet to give herself to him then, than back in those days when she had first won him. Was it not worth all the care and sorrow in the world to taste such bliss, she had often asked herself—but had been unable to answer. But—then it had happened: this spring she had been gotten with child again. . . . Let no one tell her that this was not Destiny!

She had urged against this last journey; she had argued that they must tarry where they were until she had borne the child. One year more or less would make no difference, considering all the land there was in the west. . . . Hans Olsa, however, had been ready to start; and so there had been no use in trying to hold back Per Hansa. All her misgiving he had turned to sport and laughter, or playful love; he had embraced her, danced around with her, and become so roguish that she had been forced to laugh with him. . . . "Come here, *Litagod*—now we're gone!" . . . She well recalled how lovely this endearing term had sounded in her ears, the first night he had used it. . . .

But this was clear to her beyond a doubt: Per Hansa was without blame in what had happened—all the blame was hers. . . . He had never been so tender toward her as in the days since they had come out here; she could not have thought it possible for one human being to have such strong desire for another as he held. . . . Who could match him—who dared follow where he led? She remembered all that he had wrought since they had set out on their journey last spring, and felt that no one else could do it after him. He was like the north wind that sweeps the cloud banks from the heavens! . . . At these thoughts, something unspeakably soft and loving came into Beret's eyes. . . . No, not like the north wind: like the gentle breeze of a summer's night—that's how he was! . . . And this too, was only retribution! She had bound herself inseparably to this man; now she was but a hindrance to him, like chains around his feet; him, whom she loved unto madness, she burdened and impeded . . . she was only in his way!

. . . But that he could not understand it—that he could not fathom the source of her trouble; that seemed wholly incomprehensible to her. Didn't he realize that she could never be like him? . . . No one in all the world was like him! How could she be? . . .

Beret struggled with many thoughts these days.

. . . Wasn't it remarkable how ingeniously Destiny had arranged it all? For ten long years he had cast her about like a chip on the current, and then had finally washed her ashore here. *Here,* far off in the great stillness, where there was nothing to hide behind—here the punishment would fall! . . . Could a better place have been found in which to lay her low?

. . . Life was drawing to a close. One fact stood before her constantly: she would never rise again from the bed in which she was soon to lie down. . . . This was the end.

. . . Often, now, she found herself thinking of the churchyard at home. . . . It would have been so pleasant to lie down there. . . . The churchyard was enclosed by a massive stone wall, broad and heavy; one couldn't imagine anything more reliable than that wall. She had sat on it often in the years when she was still her father's little girl. . . . In the midst of the churchyard lay the church, securely protecting everything round about. No fear had ever dwelt in that place; she could well remember how the boys used to jump over the graves; it had been great fun, too—at times she had joined the game. . . . Within that wall many of her dear ones slumbered: two brothers whom she had never seen, and a little sister that she remembered quite clearly, though she had died long, long ago; her grandparents, on both her father's and her mother's side, also rested here, and one of her great-grandfathers. She knew where all these graves lay. Her whole family, generation after generation, rested there—many more than she had any knowledge of. . . . Around the churchyard stood a row of venerable trees, looking silently down on the peace and the stillness within. . . . They gave such good shelter, those old trees!

. . . She could not imagine where he would bury her out here. . . . *Now,* in the dead of winter—the ground frozen hard! . . . How would he go about it? . . . If he would only dig deep down . . . the wolves gave such unearthly howls at night! No matter what he thought of it, she would have to speak to him about the grave. . . . Well, no need to mention it just now.

One day when Beret had to go out she stayed longer than usual. Before she finally came back to the house she went to the spot where the woodpile had stood, visited the curious little fort which they had built of chopped wood, and then entered the stable. . . . It worried her to know where he would find material for a coffin. She had looked everywhere outside, but had discovered only a few bits of plank and the box in which he had mixed the lime. . . . Hadn't she better remind him of this at once? Then perhaps he could go to the Trönders, east on the Sioux River, and get some lumber from them. . . . Never mind, she wouldn't do anything about it for a few days yet.

. . . If he could only spare her the big chest! . . . Beret fell to looking at it, and grew easier in her mind. . . . That chest had belonged to her great-grandfather, but it must have been in the family long before his day; on it she could make out only the words "*Anno* 16—" . . . the rest was completely worn away. Along the edges and running twice around the middle were heavy iron bands. . . . Beret would go about looking at the chest—would lift the lid and gaze down inside. . . .

Plenty of room in there, if they would only put something under her head and back! She felt as if she could sleep safely in that bed. She would have to talk to Sörine about all these matters. . . . One day Beret began to empty the chest; she got Per Hansa to make a small cupboard out of the mortar box, and put all the things in there; but she took great care not to do this while he was around.

She realized now the great forethought he had shown last summer in building the house and stable under one roof. They undoubtedly had the warmest house in the neighbourhood; and then she enjoyed the company of the animals as she lay awake at night; it felt so cosy and secure to lie there and listen to them. . . . She could easily distinguish each animal by its particular manner of breathing and lying down. The oxen were always the last to finish munching; Rosie was the first to go to sleep; Injun's habits were entirely different from those of the others; he moved softly, almost without noise, as if engaged in some secret business. She never could hear him, except when the howl of a wolf sounded near by; then he would snort and stamp his feet. It was probably the wild blood in him that made him so different! . . . Beret had learned to love the pony.

When she was not listening to the animals she had other things to occupy her mind. . . . As a little girl, she had often been taken into bed by her grandmother. This grandmother had been a kindly woman, sunny and always happy, in spite of her great age; each night before going to sleep she would repeat to herself pious little verses from memory. Beret could not remember them all now; but she managed to patch them together little by little, inserting new lines of her own, and repeating them over and over to herself. This she would do for hours at a time, occasionally sitting up in bed to say the verses aloud:

"Thy heavy wrath avert
From me, a wretched sinner;
Thy blissful mercy grant,
Father of love eternal!

"My sins are as many
As dust in the rays of the sun,
And as sands on the shore of the sea
If by Thee requited,
I must sink benighted.

"Look with pity,
Tender Saviour,
At my wretched state!
Wounds of sin are burning;
May Thy hands, in love returning,
Heal my stinging stripes!

"Weighed by guilt I weary wander
In the desert here below;
When I measure
My transgressions,
Breaches of Thy holy law,
I must ponder
Oft, and wonder;
Canst Thou grace on me bestow?

"Gentle Saviour,
Cast my burden
Deep into the mercy-sea!
Blessed Jesus,
Mild Redeemer,
Thou Who gav'st Thy life for me!"

The day before Christmas Eve snow fell. It fell all that night and the following forenoon. . . . Still weather, and dry, powdery snow. . . . Murk without, and leaden dusk in the huts. People sat oppressed in the sombre gloom.

. . . Things were in a bad way over at Per Hansa's now; everyone knew it and feared what might befall both Beret and him. . . . No one could help; all that could be done was to bide the time; for soon a change must come!

"Listen, folks," said Tönseten, trying to comfort them as best he could. "Beret can't keep this up forever! I think you had better go over to her again, Kjersti!"

Both neighbour women were now taking turns at staying with her, each one a day at a time. They saw clearly that Per Hansa was more in need of help than Beret; there was no helping her now, while something, at least, could be done for him and the children. Christmas would soon be here, too, and the house ought to be made comfortable and cosy!

They all felt very sorry for Per Hansa. He walked about like a ragged stray dog; his eyes burned with a hunted look. Each day, the children were sent over to Hans Olsa's to stay for a while; if they remained longer than they had been told, he made no protest; at last they formed the habit of staying the whole day. He did not realize that it was bad for Beret to be without them so much; he tried to keep the talk going himself, but she had little to say; she answered in monosyllables and had grown peculiarly quiet and distant. In the shadow of a faint smile which she occasionally gave him there lay a melancholy deeper than the dusk of the Arctic Sea on a rainy, grey fall evening.

About noon of Christmas Eve the air suddenly cleared. An invisible fan was pushed in under the thick, heavy curtain that hung trembling between earth and heaven—made a giant sweep, and revealed the open, blue sky overhead. The sun shone down with powerful beams, and started a slight trickling from the eaves. Toward evening, it built a golden fairy castle for itself out yonder, just beyond Indian Hill.

The children were at Hans Olsa's; And-Ongen wanted to stay outside and watch the sunset. Sofie had told her that to-day was Christmas Eve, and that on every Christmas Jesus came down from heaven. The child asked many questions. . . . Would he come driving? Couldn't they lend him the pony? . . . Sofie hardly thought so—he probably would be driving an angel-pony!

Store-Hans, who was listening to them, thought this very silly and just like girls. He knew better! . . . Toward evening he suddenly wanted to go home, and was almost beside himself when his godfather said that he couldn't: all the children were to stay with Sofie to-night. They had to hold him back by force. . . . This was *Christmas Eve.* . . . He understood very well that something was about to go wrong at home. Why had his mother looked so wan and worn of late, and his father acted so queer that one couldn't talk to him?

That afternoon Beret was in childbed. . . . The grim struggle marked Per Hansa for life; he had fought his way through many a hard fight, but they had all been as nothing compared with this. He had ridden the frail keel of a capsized boat on the Lofoten seas, had seen the huge, combing waves snatch away his comrades one by one, and had rejoiced in the thought that the end would soon come for him also; but things of that sort had been mere child's play. . . . *This* was the uttermost darkness. Here was neither beginning nor end—only an awful void in which he groped alone. . . .

Sörine and Kjersti had both arrived a long time since. When they had come he had put on his coat and gone outside; but he hadn't been able to tear himself many steps away from the house.

Now it was evening; he had wandered into the stable to milk Rosie, forgetting that she had gone dry long ago; he had tended to Injun and the oxen, without knowing what he was about. . . . He listened to Beret wailing in the other room, and his heart shrivelled; thus a weak human being could not continue to suffer, and yet live. . . . And this was his own Beret!

He stood in the door of the stable, completely undone. Just then Kjersti ran out to find him; he must come in at once; Beret was asking for him! . . . Kjersti was gone in a flash. . . . He entered the house, took off his outdoor clothes, and washed his hands. . . .

. . . Beret sat half dressed on the edge of the bed. He looked at her, and thought that he had never seen such terror on any face. . . . God in heaven—this was beyond human endurance!

She was fully rational, and asked the neighbour women to leave the room for a moment, as she had something to say to her husband. She spoke with great composure; they obeyed immediately. When the door closed behind them Beret rose and came over to him, her face distorted. She laid a hand on each of his shoulders, and looked deep into his eyes, then clasped her hands behind his neck and pulled him violently toward her. Putting his arms firmly around her, he lifted her up gently and carried her to the bed; there he laid her down. He started to pull the covers

over her. . . . But she held on to him; his solicitous care she heeded not
at all.

When he had freed himself, she spoke brokenly, between gasps:

. . . "To-night I am leaving you. . . . Yes, I must leave you. . . . I
know this is the end! The Lord has found me out because of my sins. . . .
It is written, 'To fall into the hands of the living God!' . . . Oh!—it is
terrible! . . . I can't see how you will get along when you are left alone
. . . though I have only been a burden to you lately. . . . You had better give And-Ongen to Kjersti . . . she wants a child so badly—she is
a kind woman. . . . You must take the boys with you—and *go away
from here!* . . . How lonesome it will be for me . . . to lie here all
alone!"

Tears came to her eyes, but she did not weep; between moans she
went on strongly and collectedly:

"But promise me one thing: put me away in the big chest! . . . I
have emptied it and made it ready. . . . Promise to lay me away in the
big chest, Per Hansa! . . . And you must be sure to dig the grave deep!
. . . You haven't heard how terribly the wolves howl at night! . . .
Promise to take plenty of time and dig deep down—do you hear!"

His wife's request cut Per Hansa's heart like sharp ice; he threw
himself on his knees beside the bed and wiped the cold perspiration from
her face with a shaking hand.

. . . "There now, blessed Beret-girl of mine!" . . . His words
sounded far off—a note of frenzy in them. . . . "Can't you understand
that this will soon be over? . . . To-morrow you'll be as chipper as a
lark again!"

Her terror tore her only the worse. Without heeding his words, she
spoke with great force out of the clearness of her vision:

"I shall die to-night. . . . Take the big chest! . . . At first I thought
of asking you not to go away when spring came . . . and leave me here
alone. . . . But that would be a sin! . . . I tell you, you *must go!* . . .
Leave as soon as spring comes! Human beings cannot exist here! . . .
They grow into beasts. . . ."

The throes were tearing her so violently now that she could say no
more. But when she saw him rise she made a great effort and sat up in
bed.

. . . "Oh!—don't leave me!—don't go away! . . . Can't you see
how sorely I need you? . . . And now I shall die! . . . Love me—oh,
do love me once more, Per Hansa!" . . . She leaned her body toward
him. . . . "You must go back to Norway. . . . Take the children with
you . . . let them grow up there. Ask father and mother to forgive me!
. . . Tell father that I am lying in the big chest! . . . Can't you stay with
me to-night . . . stay with me and love me? . . . Oh!—*there they come
for me!*"

Beret gave a long shriek that rent the night. Then she sobbed violently, praying that they should not take her away from Per Hansa. . . .

Per Hansa leaped to his feet, and found his voice.

"Satan—now you shall leave her alone!" he shouted, flinging the door open and calling loudly to the women outside. Then he vanished into the darkness.

No one thought of seeking rest that night. All the evening, lights shone from the four huts; later they were extinguished in two of them; but in the house of Hans Olsa four men sat on, grieving over the way things were going at Per Hansa's. When they could bear the suspense no longer some one proposed going over to get news.

Tönseten offered to go first. . . . When he came back little sense could be gathered from what he said. He had not been allowed inside; the women were in a frenzy; the house was completely upset; Beret was wailing so loud that it was dreadful to hear. And Per Hansa himself was nowhere to be found. . . . "We must go and look for him, boys! . . . Haven't you got a Bible or something to read from, Hans Olsa? This is an awful thing!"

. . . There they sat, each occupied with his own thoughts—but all their thoughts were of the same trend. If Beret died to-night, it would go hard with Per Hansa—indeed it would. In that case he probably wouldn't stay out here very long. . . . But if he went away, the rest of them might as well pack up and go, too!

Sam ran over to inquire; then Henry; at last it was Hans Olsa's turn. He managed to get a couple of words with his wife, who said that Beret would hardly stand it. No one had seen Per Hansa.

"Can you imagine where the man can be keeping himself?" asked Tönseten, giving voice to the fear that oppressed them all. . . . "May the Lord preserve his wits, even if He chooses to take his wife away!" . . .

Per Hansa walked to and fro outside the hut all night long; when he heard some one coming he would run away into the darkness. He could not speak to a living soul to-night. As soon as the visitor had gone he would approach the hut again, circle around it, stop, and listen. Tears were streaming down his face, though he was not aware of it. . . . Every shriek that pierced the walls of the hut drove him off as if a whip had struck him; but as soon as it had died out, something would draw him back again. At intervals he went to the door and held it ajar. . . . What did Per Hansa care for custom and decency, now that his Beret lay struggling with death! . . . Each time Sörine came to the door; each time she shook her head sadly, and told him there was no change yet; it was doubtful if Beret would be able to pull through; no person could endure this much longer; God have mercy on all of them!

That was all the comfort Sörine could give him. . . . Then he would rush off into the darkness again, to continue his endless pacing; when daylight came they found a hard path tramped into the snow around the hut.

The night was well-nigh spent when the wails in there began to weaken—then died out completely, and did not come again. Per Hansa crept up to the door, laid his ear close to it, and listened. . . . So now the end had come! His breath seemed to leave him in a great sob. The whole prairie began to whirl around with him; he staggered forward a few steps and threw himself face downward on the snow.

. . . But then suddenly things didn't seem so bad to him . . . really not so bad. . . . He saw a rope . . . a rope. . . . It was a good, strong rope that would hold any thing. . . . It hung just inside the barn door —and the crossbeam ran just *there!* . . . No trick at all to find these things. Per Hansa felt almost happy at the thought; that piece of rope was good and strong—and the crossbeam ran just *there!*

. . . A door opened somewhere; a gleam of light flashed across the snow, and vanished. Some one came out of the hut quietly—then stopped, as if searching.

"Per Hansa!" a low voice called. . . . "Per Hansa, where are you?" . . . He rose and staggered toward Kjersti like a drunken man.

"You must come in at once!" she whispered, and hurried in before him.

The light was dim in there; nevertheless it blinded him so strongly that he could not see a thing. He stood a moment leaning against the door until his eyes had grown accustomed to it. . . . A snug, cosy warmth enveloped him; it carried with it an odd, pleasant odour. The light, the warmth, and the pleasant smell overcame him like sweet sleep that holds a person who has been roused, but who does not care to awaken just yet.

"How is it?" he heard a man's voice ask. Then he came back to his senses. . . . Was that he himself speaking? . . .

"You'll have to ask Sörine," Kjersti answered.

Sörine was tending something on the bed; not until now did he discover her—and wake up completely. . . . What was this? . . . the expression on her face? Wasn't it beaming with motherly goodness and kindliness?

"Yes, here's your little fellow! I have done all I know how. Come and look at him. . . . It's the greatest miracle I ever saw, Per Hansa, that you didn't lose your wife to-night, and the child too! . . . I pray the Lord *I* never have to suffer so!"

"Is there any hope?" was all Per Hansa could gasp—and then he clenched his teeth.

"It looks so, now—but you had better christen him at once. . . . We had to handle him roughly, let me tell you."

"*Christen him?*" Per Hansa repeated, unable to comprehend the words.

"Why, yes, of course. I wouldn't wait, if he were mine."

Per Hansa heard no more—for now Beret turned her head and a wave of such warm joy welled up in him that all the ice melted. He found himself crying softly, sobbing like a child. . . . He approached the bed on tiptoe, bent over it, and gazed down into the weary, pale face. It lay there so white and still; her hair, braided in two thick plaits, flowed over the pillow. All the dread, all the tormenting fear that had so long disfigured her features, had vanished completely. . . . She turned her head a little, barely opened her eyes, and said, wearily:

"Oh, leave me in peace, Per Hansa. . . . Now I was sleeping so well."

. . . The eyelids immediately closed.

Women and Their Families
on the Overland Trail
to California and Oregon,
1842-1867

JOHNNY FARAGHER AND CHRISTINE STANSELL

As twentieth-century Americans living in the automotive age we think of ourselves as a geographically mobile people. The American family, it is said, is perpetually on the move. Job transfers, searches for new careers, and just plain wanderlust seem woven into our social fabric. Little do we realize that in the nineteenth century rootlessness was also epidemic in America, so much so that everyday life for thousands of families each year centered on breaking up a homestead, taking to the road, and resettling in a distant location.

Daily life was far more affected by these relocations in the pre-automotive age because of the time they required and the conditions under which the trip was made. The transcontinental railroad was not completed until 1869, so most westward-moving Americans went by boat and wagon across the roadless plains and mountains. It was a trip that lasted not days but months. So much time elapsed that all the phases of life—birth, maturation, marriage, and death—were likely to occur at some point as a wagon caravan threaded its way from the East or the Midwest to the Rockies and the Pacific Coast.

The following selection by Johnny Faragher and Christine Stansell explores the trauma of the overland odyssey. The authors are particularly concerned with the effect of the journey on the separation of sex roles. They argue that of necessity women began to take up men's work on the overland trail, though the reverse was rarely true. Like women in the American Revolution, who were obliged to take up new tasks and assume new responsibilities, these women of the caravans shucked the cult of domesticity on the expanding frontier. Whether this alteration of sex roles, attitudes, and self-images persisted after the destination was reached is another question worth pondering.

I am not the wheatfield
nor the virgin forest

I never chose this place
yet I am of it now

—*Adrienne Rich*
"From an Old House in America"

From 1841 until 186[9], the year in which the transcontinental railroad was completed, nearly 350,000 North Americans emigrated to the Pacific coast along the western wagon road known variously as the Oregon, the California, or simply the Overland Trail. This migration was essentially a family phenomenon. Although single men constituted the majority of the party which pioneered large-scale emigration on the Overland Trail in 1841, significant numbers of women and children were already present in the wagon trains of the next season. Families made up the preponderant proportion of the migrations throughout the 1840s. In 1849, during the overwhelmingly male Gold Rush, the number dropped precipitously, but after 1851 families once again assumed dominance in the overland migration.[1] The contention that "the family was the one substantial social institution" on the frontier is too sweeping, yet it is undeniable that the white family largely mediated the incorporation of the western territories into the American nation.[2]

The emigrating families were a heterogeneous lot. Some came from farms in the midwest and upper South, many from small midwestern towns, and others from northeastern and midwestern cities. Clerks and shopkeepers as well as farmers outfitted their wagons in Independence, St. Louis, or Westport Landing on the Missouri. Since costs for supplies, travel, and settlement were not negligible,[3] few of the very poor were present, nor were the exceptionally prosperous. The dreams of fortune which lured the wagon trains into new lands were those of modest men whose hopes were pinned to small farms or larger dry-goods stores, more fertile soil or more customers, better market prospects and a steadily expanding economy.

For every member of the family, the trip West was exhausting, toilsome, and often grueling. Each year in late spring, westbound emigrants gathered for the journey at spots along the Missouri River and moved out in parties of ten to several hundred wagons. Aggregates of nuclear families, loosely attached by kinship or friendship, traveled together or joined an even larger caravan.[4] Coast-bound families traveled by ox-drawn wagons at the frustratingly slow pace of fifteen to twenty miles per day. They worked their way up the Platte River valley through what is now Kansas and Nebraska, crossing the Rockies at South Pass in southwestern Wyoming by mid-summer. The Platte route was relatively easy going, but from present-day Idaho, where the roads to California and Oregon diverged, to their final destinations, the pioneers faced disastrous conditions: scorching deserts, boggy salt flats, and rugged mountains. By this time, families had been on the road some three months and were only at the midpoint of the journey; the environment, along with the wear of the road, made the last months difficult almost beyond endurance. Finally, in late fall or early winter the pioneers straggled into their promised lands, after six months and over two thousand miles of hardship.[5]

As this journey progressed, bare necessity became the determinant of most of each day's activities. The primary task of surviving and getting to the coast gradually suspended accustomed patterns of dividing work between women and men. All able-bodied adults worked all day in one way

"Women and Their Families on the Overland Trail to California and Oregon, 1842–1867," by Johnny Faragher and Christine Stansell. From *Feminist Studies*, vol. 2, no. 2/3 (1975): 150–66. Reprinted by permission of the publisher, *Feminist Studies*, c/o Women's Studies Program, University of Maryland, College Park, Maryland 20742.

or another to keep the family moving. Women's work was no less indispensable than men's; indeed, as the summer wore on, the boundaries
dividing the work of the sexes were threatened, blurred, and transgressed.

The vicissitudes of the trail opened new possibilities for expanded
work roles for women, and in the cooperative work of the family there
existed a basis for a vigorous struggle for female–male equality. But most
women did not see the experience in this way. They viewed it as a male
enterprise from its very inception. Women experienced the breakdown
of the sexual division of labor as a dissolution of their own autonomous
"sphere." Bereft of the footing which this independent base gave them,
they lacked a cultural rationale for the work they did, and remained
estranged from the possibilities of the enlarged scope and power of family
life on the trail. Instead, women fought *against* the forces of necessity to
hold together the few fragments of female subculture left to them. We
have been bequeathed a remarkable record of this struggle in the diaries,
journals, and memories of emigrating women. In this study, we will examine a particular habit of living, or culture, in conflict with the new
material circumstances of the Trail, and the efforts of women to maintain
a place, a sphere of their own.

The overland family was not a homogeneous unit, its members imbued with identical aspirations and desires. On the contrary, the period
of westward movement was also one of multiplying schisms within those
families whose location and social status placed them in the mainstream of
national culture.[6] Child-rearing tracts, housekeeping manuals, and etiquette
books by the hundreds proscribed and rationalized to these Americans a
radical separation of the work responsibilities and social duties of mothers
and fathers; popular thought assigned unique personality traits, spiritual
capacities, and forms of experience to the respective categories of man,
woman, and child.[7] In many families, the tensions inherent in this separatist
ideology, often repressed in the everyday routines of the East, erupted
under the strain of the overland crossing. The difficulties of the emigrants,
while inextricably linked to the duress of the journey itself, also revealed
family dynamics which had been submerged in the less eventful life "back
home."

A full blown ideology of "woman's place" was absent in preindustrial
America. On farms, in artisan shops, and in town marketplaces, women
and children made essential contributions to family income and subsistence; it was the family which functioned as the basic unit of production
in the colony and the young nation. As commercial exchanges displaced
the local markets where women had sold surplus dairy products and textiles, and the workplace drifted away from the household, women and
children lost their breadwinning prerogatives.[8]

In Jacksonian America, a doctrine of "sexual spheres" arose to facilitate and justify the segregation of women into the home and men into
productive work.[9] While the latter attended to politics, economics, and
wage-earning, popular thought assigned women the refurbished and newly
professionalized tasks of child-rearing and housekeeping.[10] A host of

corollaries followed on the heels of these shifts. Men were physically strong, women naturally delicate; men were skilled in practical matters, women in moral and emotional concerns; men were prone to corruption, women to virtue; men belonged in the world, women in the home. For women, the system of sexual spheres represented a decline in social status and isolation from political and economic power. Yet it also provided them with a psychological power base of undeniable importance. The "cult of true womanhood" was more than simply a retreat. Catharine Beecher, one of the chief theorists of "woman's influence," proudly quoted Tocqueville's observation that "in no country has such constant care been taken, as in America, to trace two clearly distinct lines of action for the two sexes, and to make them keep pace with the other, but in two pathways which are always different." [11] Neither Beecher nor her sisters were simply dupes of a masculine imperialism. The supervision of child-rearing, household economy, and the moral and religious life of the family granted women a certain degree of real autonomy and control over their lives as well as those of their husbands and children.

Indeed, recent scholarship has indicated that a distinctly female subculture emerged from "woman's sphere." By "subculture" we simply mean a "habit of living"—as we have used "culture" above—of a minority group which is self-consciously distinct from the dominant activities, expectations, and values of a society. Historians have seen female church groups, reform associations, and philanthropic activity as expressions of this subculture in actual behavior, while a large and rich body of writing by and for women articulated the subcultural impulses on the ideational level. Both behavior and thought point to child-rearing, religious activity, education, home life, associationism, and female communality as components of women's subculture. Female friendships, strikingly intimate and deep in this period, formed the actual bonds.[12] Within their tight and atomized family households, women carved out a life of their own.

At its very inception, the western emigration sent tremors through the foundations of this carefully compartmentalized family structure. The rationale behind pulling up stakes was nearly always economic advancement; [13] since breadwinning was a masculine concern, the husband and father introduced the idea of going West and made the final decision. Family participation in the intervening time ran the gamut from enthusiastic support to stolid resistance. Many women cooperated with their ambitious spouses: "The motive that induced us to part with pleasant associations and the dear friends of our childhood days, was to obtain from the government of the United States a grant of land that 'Uncle Sam' had promised to give to the head of each family who settled in this new country." [14] Others, however, only acquiesced. "Poor Ma said only this morning, 'Oh, I wish we never had started,' " Lucy Cooke wrote her first day on the trail, "and she looks so sorrowful and dejected. I think if Pa had not passengers to take through she would urge him to return; not that he should be so inclined." [15] Huddled with her children in a cold, damp wagon, trying to calm them despite the ominous chanting of visiting Indians, another woman wondered "what had possessed my husband, anyway, that he should have thought of bringing us away out through this

God forsaken country." [16] Similar alienation from the "pioneer spirit"
haunted Lavinia Porter's leave-taking:

> I never recall that sad parting from my dear sister on the plains of
> Kansas without the tears flowing fast and free. . . . We were the eld-
> est of a large family, and the bond of affection and love that existed
> between us was strong indeed . . . as she with the other friends
> turned to leave me for the ferry which was to take them back to
> home and civilization, I stood alone on that wild prairie. Looking
> westward I saw my husband driving slowly over the plain; turn-
> ing my face once more to the east, my dear sister's footsteps were
> fast widening the distance between us. For the time I knew not
> which way to go, nor whom to follow. But in a few moments I
> rallied my forces . . . and soon overtook the slowly moving oxen
> who were bearing my husband and child over the green prairie . . .
> the unbidden tears would flow in spite of my brave resolve to be
> the courageous and valiant frontierswoman.[17]

Her dazed vacillation soon gave way to a private conviction that the
family had made a dire mistake: "I would make a brave effort to be cheerful and patient until the camp work was done. Then starting out ahead
of the team and my men folks, when I thought I had gone beyond hearing
distance, I would throw myself down on the unfriendly desert and give
way like a child to sobs and tears, wishing myself back home with my
friends and chiding myself for consenting to take this wild goose chase." [18]
Men viewed drudgery, calamity, and privation as trials along the road to
prosperity, unfortunate but inevitable corollaries of the rational decision
they had made. But to those women who were unable to appropriate the
vision of the upwardly mobile pilgrimage, hardship and loss only testified
to the inherent folly of the emigration, "this wild goose chase."

If women were reluctant to accompany their men, however, they
were often equally unwilling to let them go alone. In the late 1840s, the
conflict between wives and their gold-crazed husbands reveals the determination with which women enforced the cohesion of the nuclear family.
In the name of family unity, some obdurate wives simply chose to block-
bust the sexually segregated Gold Rush: "My husband grew enthusiastic
and wanted to start immediately," one woman recalled, "but I would not
be left behind. I thought where he could go I could and where I went I
could take my two little toddling babies." [19] Her family departed intact.
Other women used their moral authority to smash the enterprise in its
planning stages. "We were married to live together," a wife acidly reminded her spouse when he informed her of his intention to join the
Rush: "I am willing to go with you to any part of *God's Foot Stool* where
you think you can do best, and under these circumstances you have no
right to go where I cannot, and if you do you need never return for I
shall look upon you as dead." [20] Roundly chastised, the man postponed his
journey until the next season, when his family could leave with him. When
included in the plans, women seldom wrote of their husbands' decisions to
emigrate in their diaries or memoirs. A breadwinner who tried to leave
alone, however, threatened the family unity upon which his authority

was based; only then did a wife challenge his dominance in worldly affairs.[21]

There was an economic reason for the preponderance of families on the Trail. Women and children, but especially women, formed an essential supplementary work force in the settlements. The ideal wife in the West resembled a hired hand more than a nurturant Christian housekeeper.[22] Narcissa Whitman wrote frankly to aspiring settlers of the functional necessity of women on the new farms: "Let every young man bring a wife, for he will want one after he gets here, if he never did before."[23] In a letter from California, another seasoned woman warned a friend in Missouri that in the West women became "hewers of wood and drawers of water everywhere."[24] Mrs. Whitman's fellow missionary Elkanah Walker was unabashedly practical in beseeching his wife to join him: "I am tired of keeping an old bachelor's hall. I want someone to get me a good supper and let me take my ease and when I am very tired in the morning I want someone to get up and get breakfast and let me lay in bed and take my rest."[25] It would be both simplistic and harsh to argue that men brought their families West or married because of the labor power of women and children; there is no doubt, however, that the new Westerners appreciated the advantages of familial labor. Women were not superfluous; they were workers. The migration of women helped to solve the problem of labor scarcity, not only in the early years of the American settlement on the coast, but throughout the history of the continental frontier.[26]

In the first days of the overland trip, new work requirements were not yet pressing and the division of labor among family members still replicated familiar patterns. Esther Hanna reported in one of her first diary entries that "our men have gone to build a bridge across the stream, which is impassable," while she baked her first bread on the prairie.[27] Elizabeth Smith similarly described her party's day: "rainy . . . Men making rafts. Women cooking and washing. Children crying."[28] When travel was suspended, "the men were generally busy mending wagons, harnesses, yokes, shoeing the animals etc., and the women washed clothes, boiled a big mess of beans, to warm over for several meals, or perhaps mended clothes."[29] At first, even in emergencies, women and men hardly considered integrating their work. "None but those who have cooked for a family of eight, crossing the plains, have any idea of what it takes," a disgruntled woman recalled: "My sister-in-law was sick, my niece was much younger than I, and consequently I had the management of all the cooking and planning on my young shoulders."[30] To ask a man to help was a possibility she was unable even to consider.[31]

The relegation of women to purely domestic duties, however, soon broke down under the vicissitudes of the Trail. Within the first few weeks, the unladylike task of gathering buffalo dung for fuel (little firewood was available *en route*) became women's work.[32] As one traveler astutely noted, "force of surroundings was a greater leveler";[33] miles of grass, dust, glare, and mud erased some of the most rudimentary distinctions between female and male responsibilities. By summer, women often helped drive the wagons and the livestock.[34] At one Platte crossing, "the men drawed the wagons over by hand and the women all crossed in safety"; but at the next, calamity struck when the bridge collapsed, "and then commenced the hurry and bustle of repairing; all were at work, even the women and children." [35] Such crises, which compounded daily as the wagons moved past the Platte up the long stretches of desert and coastal mountains, generated equity in work; at times of Indian threats, for example, both women and men made bullets and stood guard.[36] When mountain fever struck the Pengra family as they crossed the Rockies, Charlotte relieved her incapacitated husband of the driving while he took care of the youngest child.[37] Only such severe afflictions forced men to take on traditionally female chores. While women did men's work, there is little evidence that men reciprocated.

Following a few days in the life of an overland woman discloses the magnitude of her work. During the hours her party traveled, Charlotte Pengra walked beside the wagons, driving the cattle and gathering buffalo chips. At night she cooked, baked bread for the next noon meal, and washed clothes. Three successive summer days illustrate how trying these small chores could be. Her train pulled out early on a Monday morning, only to be halted by rain and a flash flood; Mrs. Pengra washed and dried her family's wet clothes in the afternoon while doing her daily baking. On Tuesday the wagons pushed hard to make up for lost time, forcing her to trot all day to keep up. In camp that night there was no time to rest. Before going to bed, she wrote, "Kept busy in preparing tea and doing other things preparatory for the morrow. I baked a cracker pudding, warm biscuits and made tea, and after supper stewed two pans of dried apples, and made two loaves of bread, got my work done up, beds made, and child asleep, and have written in my journal. Pretty tired of course." The same routine devoured the next day and evening: "I have done a washing. Stewed apples, made pies and baked a rice pudding, and mended our wagon cover. Rather tired." And the next: "baked biscuits, stewed berries, fried meat, boiled and mashed potatoes, and made tea for supper, afterward baked bread. Thus you see I have not much rest." [38] Children also burdened women's work and leisure. During one quiet time, Helen Stewart retreated in mild defiance from her small charges to a tent in order to salvage some private time: "It exceeding hot . . . some of the men is out hunting and some of them sleeping. The children is grumbling and crying and laughing and howling and playing all around." [39] Although children are notably absent in women's journals, they do appear, frightened and imploring, during an Indian scare or a storm, or intrude into a rare and precious moment of relaxation, "grumbling and crying." [40]

Because the rhythm of their chores was out of phase with that of the men, the division of labor could be especially taxing to women. Men's days were toilsome but broken up at regular intervals with periods of rest. Men hitched the teams, drove or walked until noon, relaxed at dinner, traveled until the evening camp, unhitched the oxen, ate supper, and in the evening sat at the campfire, mended equipment, or stood guard. They also provided most of the labor in emergencies, pulling the wagons through mires, across treacherous river crossings, up long grades, and down precipitous slopes. In the pandemonium of a steep descent, you would see the women and children in advance seeking the best way, some of them slipping down, or holding on to the rocks, now taking an "otter slide," and then a run til some natural obstacle presented itself to stop their accelerated progress and those who get down safely without a hurt or a bruise, are fortunate indeed. Looking back to the train, you would see some of the men holding on to the wagons, others slipping under the oxen's feet, some throwing articles out of the way that had fallen out, and all have enough to do to keep them busily occupied.[41]

Women were responsible for staying out of the way and getting themselves and the children to safety, men for getting the wagons down. Women's work, far less demanding of brute strength and endurance, was nevertheless distributed without significant respite over all waking hours: mealtimes offered no leisure to the cooks. "The plain fact of the matter is," a young woman complained,

> we *have no time for sociability*. From the time we get up in the morning, until we are on the road, it is hurry scurry to get breakfast and put away the things that necessarily had to be pulled out last night—while under way there is no room in the wagon for a visitor, nooning is barely long enough to eat a cold bite—and at night all the cooking utensils and provisions are to be gotten about the camp fire, and cooking enough to last until the next night.[42]

After supper, the men gathered together, "lolling and smoking their pipes and guessing, or maybe betting, how many miles we had covered during the day," [43] while the women baked, washed, and put the children to bed before they finally sat down. Charlotte Pengra found "as I was told before I started that there is no rest in such a journey." [44]

Unaccustomed tasks beset the travelers, who were equipped with only the familiar expectation that work was divided along gender lines. The solutions which sexual "spheres" offered were usually irrelevant to the new problems facing families. Women, for example, could not afford to be delicate: their new duties demanded far greater stamina and hardiness than their traditional domestic tasks. With no tradition to deal with the new exigencies of fuel-gathering, cattle-driving, and cooking, families found that "the division of labor in a party . . . was a prolific cause of quarrel." [45] Within the Vincent party, "assignments to duty were not accomplished without grumbling and objection . . . there were occasional angry debates while the various burdens were being adjusted," while in "the camps of others who sometimes jogged along the trail in our company . . . we saw not a little fighting . . . and these bloody fisticuffs were invariably the outcome of disputes over division of labor." [46] At home, these assignments were familiar and accepted, not subject to questioning. New work opened the division of labor to debate and conflict.

By midjourney, most women worked at male tasks. The men still retained dominance within their "sphere," despite the fact that it was no longer exclusively masculine. Like most women, Lavinia Porter was responsible for gathering buffalo chips for fuel. One afternoon, spying a grove of cottonwoods half a mile away, she asked her husband to branch off the trail so that the party could fell trees for firewood, thus easing her work. "But men on the plains I had found were not so accomodating, nor so ready to wait upon women as they were in more civilized communities." Her husband refused and Porter fought back: "I was feeling somewhat under the weather and unusually tired, and crawling into the wagon told them if they wanted fuel for the evening meal they could get it themselves and cook the meal also, and laying my head down on a pillow, I cried myself to sleep." [47] Later that evening her husband awakened her with a belated dinner he had prepared himself, but despite his conciliatory spirit their relations were strained for weeks: "James and I had gradually grown silent and taciturn and had unwittingly partaken of the gloom and somberness of the dreary landscape." [48] No longer a housewife or a domestic ornament, but a laborer in a male arena, Porter was still subordinate to her husband in practical matters.

Lydia Waters recorded another clash between new work and old consciousness: "I had learned to drive an ox team on the Platte and my driving was admired by an officer and his wife who were going with the mail to Salt Lake City." Pleased with the compliment, she later overheard them "laughing at the thought of a woman driving oxen." [49] By no means did censure come only from men. The officer's wife as well as the officer derided Lydia Waters, while her own mother indirectly reprimanded teenaged Mary Ellen Todd. "All along our journey, I had tried to crack that big whip," Mary Ellen remembered years later:

> Now while out at the wagon we kept trying until I was fairly successful. How my heart bounded a few days later when I chanced to hear father say to mother, "Do you know that Mary Ellen is beginning to crack the whip." Then how it fell again when mother replied, "I am afraid it isn't a very lady-like thing for a girl to do." After this, while I felt a secret joy in being able to have a power that set things going, there was also a sense of shame over this new accomplishment. [50]

To understand Mrs. Todd's primness, so incongruous in the rugged setting of the Trail, we must see it in the context of a broader struggle on the part of women to preserve the home in transit. Against the leveling forces of the Plains, women tried to maintain the standards of cleanliness and order that had prevailed in their homes back East:

> Our caravan had a good many women and children and although we were probably longer on the journey owing to their presence— they exerted a good influence, as the men did not take such risks with Indians . . . were more alert about the care of teams and seldom had accidents; more attention was paid to cleanliness and sanitation and, lastly, but not of less importance, meals were more regular and better cooked thus preventing much sickness and there was less waste of food. [51]

Sarah Royce remembered that family wagons "were easily distinguished by the greater number of conveniences, and household articles they carried." [52] In the evenings, or when the trains stopped for a day, women had a chance to create with these few props a flimsy facsimile of the home.

Even in camp women had little leisure time, but within the "hurry scurry" of work they managed to recreate the routine of the home. Indeed, a female subculture, central to the communities women had left behind, reemerged in these settings. At night, women often clustered together, chatting, working, or commiserating, instead of joining the men: "High teas were not popular, but tatting, knitting, crochetting, exchanging recipes for cooking beans or dried apples or swopping food for the sake of variety kept us in practice of feminine occupations and diversions." [53] Besides using the domestic concerns of the Trail to reconstruct a female sphere, women also consciously invoked fantasy: "Mrs. Fox and her daughter are with us and everything is so still and quiet we can almost imagine ourselves at home again. We took out our Daguerrotypes and tried to live over again some of the happy days of 'Auld Lang Syne.' " [54] Sisterly contact kept "feminine occupations" from withering away from disuse: "In the evening the young ladies came over to our house and we had a concert with both guitars. Indeed it seemed almost like a pleasant evening at home. We could none of us realize that we were almost at the summit of the Rocky Mountains." [55] The hostess added with somewhat strained sanguinity that her young daughter seemed "just as happy sitting on the ground playing her guitar as she was at home, although she does not love it as much as her piano." [56] Although a guitar was no substitute for the more refined instrument, it at least kept the girl "in practice with feminine occupations and diversions": unlike Mary Ellen Todd, no big whip would tempt her to unwomanly pleasure in the power to "set things going."

But books, furniture, knick-knacks, china, the daguerrotypes that Mrs. Fox shared, or the guitars of young musicians—the "various articles of ornament and convenience"—were among the first things discarded on the epic trash heap which trailed over the mountains. On long uphill grades and over sandy deserts, the wagons had to be lightened; any materials not essential to survival were fair game for disposal. Such commodities of woman's sphere, although functionally useless, provided women with a psychological lifeline to their abandoned homes and communities, as well as to elements of their identities which the westward journey threatened to mutilate or entirely extinguish. [57] Losing homely treasures and memorabilia was yet another defeat within an accelerating process of dispossession.

The male-directed venture likewise encroached upon the Sabbath, another female preserve. Through the influence of women's magazines, by mid-century Sunday had become a veritable ladies' day; women zealously exercised their religious influence and moral skill on the day of their families' retirement from the world. Although parties on the Trail often suspended travel on Sundays, the time only provided the opportunity to unload and dry the precious cargo of the wagons—seeds, food, and clothing—which otherwise would rot from dampness. For women whose creed forbade any worldly activity on the Sabbath, the work was not only irksome and tedious but profane.

> This is Sabath it is a beautiful day but indeed we do not use it as
> such for we have not traveled far when we stop in a most lovely
> place oh it is such a beautiful spot and take everything out of our
> wagon to air them and it is well we done it as the flower was damp
> and there was some of the other ones flower was rotten . . . and we
> baked and boiled and washed oh dear me I did not think we would
> have abused the sabeth in such a manner. I do not see how we can
> expect to get along but we did not intend to do so before we
> started.[58]

Denied a voice in the male sphere that surrounded them, women were also unable to partake of the limited yet meaningful power of women with homes. On almost every Sunday, Helen Stewart lamented the disruption of a familiar and sustaining order of life, symbolized by the household goods strewn about the ground to dry: "We took everything out the wagons and the side of the hill is covered with flower biscut meat rice oat meal clothes and such a quantity of articles of all discertions to many to mention and childre[n] included in the number. And hobos that is neather men nor yet boys being in and out hang about." [59]

The disintegration of the physical base of domesticity was symptomatic of an even more serious disruption in the female subculture. Because the wagon trains so often broke into smaller units, many women were stranded in parties without other women. Since there were usually two or more men in the same family party, some male friendships and bonds remained intact for the duration of the journey. But by midway in the trip, female companionship, so valued by nineteenth-century women, was unavailable to the solitary wife in a party of hired men, husband, and children that had broken away from a larger train. Emergencies and quarrels, usually between men, broke up the parties. Dr. Powers, a particularly ill-tempered man, decided after many disagreements with others in his train to make the crossing alone with his family. His wife shared neither his misanthropy nor his grim independence. On the day they separated from the others, she wrote in her journal: "The women came over to bid me goodbye, for we were to go alone, all alone. They said there was no color in my face. I felt as if there was none." She perceived the separation as a banishment, almost a death sentence: "There is something peculiar in such a parting on the Plains, one there realizes what a goodbye is. Miss Turner and Mrs. Hendricks were the last to leave, and they bade me adieu the tears running down their sunburnt cheeks. I felt as though my last friends were leaving me, for what—as I thought then— was a Maniac." [60] Charlotte Pengra likewise left Missouri with her family in a large train. Several weeks out, mechanical problems detained some of the wagons, including those of the other three women. During the month they were separated, Pengra became increasingly dispirited and anxious: "The roads have been good today—I feel lonely and almost disheartened. . . . Can hear the wolves howl very distinctly. Rather ominis, perhaps you think. . . . Feel very tird and lonely—our folks not having come—I fear some of them ar sick." Having waited as long as possible for the others, the advance group made a major river crossing. "Then I felt that indeed I had left all my friends," Pengra wrote, "save my husband and his brother, to journey over the dreaded Plains, without one female acquaintance even for a companion—of course I wept and grieved about it but to no purpose." [61]

Others echoed her mourning. "The whipporwills are chirping," Helen Stewart wrote, "they bring me in mind of our old farm in pensillvania the home of my childhood where I have spent the happiest days I will ever see again. . . . I feel rather lonesome today oh solitude how I love it if I had about a dozen of my companions to enjoy it with me." [62] Uprootedness took its toll in debilitation and numbness. After a hard week, men "lolled around in the tents and on their blankets seeming to realize that the 'Sabbath was made for man,' " [63] resting on the palpable achievements of miles covered and rivers crossed. In contrast, the women "could not fully appreciate physical rest, and were rendered more uneasy by the continual passing of emigrant trains all day long. . . . To me, much of the day was spent in meditating over the past and in forebodings for the future." [64]

The ultimate expression of this alienation was the pressure to turn back, to retrace steps to the old life. Occasionally anxiety or bewilderment erupted into open revolt against going on.

> This morning our company moved on, except one family. The woman got mad and wouldn't budge or let the children go. He had the cattle hitched on for three hours and coaxed her to go, but she wouldn't stir. I told my husband the circumstances and he and Adam Polk and Mr. Kimball went and each one took a young one and crammed them in the wagon, and the husband drove off and left her sitting. . . . She cut across and overtook her husband. Meantime he sent his boy back to camp after a horse he had left, and when she came up her husband said, "Did you meet John?" "Yes," was the reply, "and I picked up a stone and knocked out his brains." Her husband went back to ascertain the truth and while he was gone she set fire to one of the wagons. . . . He saw the flames and came running and put it out, and then mustered spunk enough to give her a good flogging.[65]

Short of violent resistance, it was always possible that circumstances would force a family to reconsider and turn back. During a cholera scare in 1852, "women cried, begging their men to take them back." [66] When the men reluctantly relented, the writer observed that "they did the hooking up of their oxen in a spiritless sort of way," while "some of the girls and women were laughing." [67] There was little lost and much regained for women in a decision to abandon the migration.

Both sexes worked, and both sexes suffered. Yet women lacked a sense of inclusion and a cultural rationale to give meaning to the suffering and the work; no augmented sense of self or role emerged from augmented

privation. Both women and men also complained, but women expanded
their caviling to a generalized critique of the whole enterprise. Margaret
Chambers felt "as if we had left all civilization behind us" [68] after crossing
the Missouri, and Harriet Ward's cry from South Pass—"Oh, shall we
ever live like civilized beings again?" [69]—reverbated through the thoughts
of many of her sisters. Civilization was far more to these women than law,
books, and municipal government; it was pianos, church societies, daguerrotypes, mirrors—in short, their homes. At their most hopeful, the exiles
perceived the Trail as a hellish but necessary transition to a land where
they could renew their domestic mission: "Each advanced step of the
slow, plodding cattle carried us farther and farther from civilization into
a desolate, barbarous country. . . . But our new home lay beyond all this
and was a shining beacon that beckoned us on, inspiring our hearts with
hope and courage." [70] At worse, temporary exigencies became in the
minds of the dispossessed the omens of an irrevocable exile: "We have
been travelling with 25–18–14–129–64–3 wagons—now all alone—how
dreary it seems. Can it be that I have left my quiet little home and taken
this dreary land of solitude in exchange?" [71]

Only a minority of the women who emigrated over the Overland
Trail were from the northeastern middle classes where the cult of true
womanhood reached its fullest bloom. Yet their responses to the labor
demands of the Trail indicate that "womanliness" had penetrated the
values, expectations, and personalities of midwestern farm women as well
as New England "ladies." "Woman's sphere" provided them with companionship, a sense of self-worth, and most important, independence from
men in a patriarchal world. The Trail, in breaking down sexual segregation, offered women the opportunities of socially essential work. Yet this
work was performed in a male arena, and many women saw themselves
as draftees rather than partners.

Historians have generally associated "positive work roles" [72] for
women with the absence of narrowly defined notions of "woman's place."
In the best summary of literature on colonial women, for example, the
authors of *Women in American Society* write: "In general, neither men
nor women seemed concerned with defining what women were or what
their unique contribution to society should be. . . . Abstract theories about
the proper role of women did not stand in the way of meeting familial
and social needs." [73] Conversely, the ascendancy of "true womanhood"
and the doctrine of sexual spheres coincided with the declining importance
of the labor of middle- and upper-class women in a rapidly expanding
market economy. On the Overland Trail, cultural roles and self-definitions
conflicted with the immediate necessities of the socioeconomic situation.
Women themselves fought to preserve a circumscribed role when material circumstances rendered it dysfunctional. Like their colonial great-
grandmothers on premarket subsistence farms, they labored at socially indispensable tasks. Yet they refused to appropriate their new work to their
own ends and advantage. In their deepest sense of themselves they remained estranged from their function as "able bodies."

It could be argued that the time span of the trip was not long enough to alter cultural values. Yet there is evidence that the tensions of the Trail haunted the small and isolated market farms at the journey's end.[74] Women in the western settlements continued to try to reinstate a culture of domesticity, although their work as virtual hired hands rendered obsolete the material base of separate arenas for women and men.

The notion of subculture employed in this and other studies of nineteenth-century women is hazy and ill-defined. We need to develop more rigorous conceptions of society, culture, and subculture, and to clarify the paradoxes of women's position, both isolated and integrated, in the dominant social and cultural movements of their time. Nonetheless, the journals of overland women are irrefutable testimony to the importance of a separate female province. Such theorists as Catharine Beecher were acutely aware of the advantages in keeping life divvied up, in maintaining "two pathways which are always different" for women and men.[75] The women who traveled on the Overland Trail experienced first hand the tribulations of integration which Beecher and her colleagues could predict in theory.

NOTES

1 The 1841 Bidwell-Bartelson party of about fifty people included only five women—three of them wives—and ten children. Contemporary figures for the forties' migrations indicate that men made up roughly 50 percent of the parties, women and children the other 50 percent. These proportions prevailed until the Gold Rush. In contrast, the composition of the 1849 emigration was men–92 percent, women–6 percent, and children–2 percent; in 1850, men–97 percent, women and children–3 percent. In 1852 the proportions shifted toward the pre-1849 norm: men–70 percent, women–13 percent, children–20 percent. These percentages are rough estimates, and indicate no more than trends.

For overall figures see Merrill Mattes, *The Great Platte River Road* (Lincoln, Nebraska: Nebraska State Historical Society, 1969), p. 23. For the early forties' on the Oregon Trail, see David Lavender, *Westward Vision: The Story of the Oregon Trail* (New York: McGraw-Hill, 1963), pp. 349–50, 365. For the California branch: George R. Stewart, *The California Trail: An Epic With Many Heroes* (New York: McGraw-Hill, 1962), pp. 8, 54–55, 85, 147, 187, 195, 232, 303, 310. For the Gold Rush: Georgia Willis Read, "Women and Children on the Oregon–California Trail in the Gold-Rush Years," *Missouri Historical Review* 34 (1944–1945):6.

2 Arthur W. Calhoun, *A Social History of the American Family from Colonial Times to the Present* 3 vols. (New York: Barnes & Noble, 1945) 2:11. Calhoun's statement has stood up well to demographic tests; after analysis of nineteenth-century census data, Jack Eblen concludes that "the deeply entrenched ideal and institution of the family provided the mechanism by which people were

bound together during the process of cultural transplantation and adaptation" ("An Analysis of Nineteenth Century Frontier Populations," *Demography* 2, no. 4 [1965]:341).

³ A simple enumeration of the special equipment necessary for the trip indicates the expense. Each family needed a light wagon, harnesses, and a team, usually oxen; the team alone could easily cost two hundred dollars. Arms and ammunition were purchased specially for the trip; such weapons as shotguns and rifles cost around twenty-five dollars. Since there was practically no chance for resupply along the route, a family had to stock for the entire six-month trip, a considerable investment that only the economically stable could afford. For discussion and details see Mattes, *Great Platte River Road*, pp. 37–50; Stewart, *The California Trail*, pp. 106–26.

⁴ Neighbors and friends often moved as a "party," later joining a larger train. Brothers, cousins, and their families, or parents and one or two married children and their families, might set out together. Conjugal and parental ties usually survived under stress, while other relations disintegrated or exploded. Interestingly, the most enduring extrafamilial bonds may have been between nuclear families and the single men who traveled with them. The latter saved money by attaching themselves to family parties rather than outfitting a wagon alone. Some paid for their passage, while others worked as drivers or cattle drovers. For examples of various groupings, see Phoebe Goodell Judson, *A Pioneer's Search for an Ideal Home* (Bellingham, Washington: United Printing, Binding and Stationery Co., 1925), pp. 15–17; Mary E. Ackley, *Crossing the Plains and Early Days in California* (San Francisco: the author, 1928), p. 17; Sarah J. Cummins, *Autobiography and Reminiscences* (Walla Walla, [Wash.]: The Walla Walla Bulletin, 1920), p. 22; Mrs. J. T. Gowdy, *Crossing the Plains: Personal Recollections of the Journey to Oregon in 1852* (Dayton, Oregon: n.p., 1906), p. 1; Nancy A. Hunt, "By Ox Team to California," *Overland Monthly* 67 (April 1916):10; Mrs. M. A. Looney, *A Trip Across the Plains in the Year of 1852 with Ox Teams* (McMinnville, Oregon: n.p., 1915), p. 8; and Mrs. Lee Whipple-Halsam, *Early Days in California: Scenes and Events of the '60s as I Remember Them* (Jamestown, California: n.p., 1923), p. 8.

⁵ For a recent revision of work on the Overland Trail see Mattes, *The Great Platte River Road*.

⁶ Most of the research on the Victorian family has been based on middle- and upper-class northeastern and midwestern families. We do not yet know to what extent the ideology of domesticity affected poor, proletarianized, or southern families.

Although our suggestions about the geographic and class composition of the migrations are generally accepted ones, they remain hypothetical in the absence of demographic research. An overwhelming majority of the women who kept the journals upon which much of our research is based *did* come from the northeastern and midwestern middle class. Nevertheless, until we know much more about the inarticulate families from backwoods Missouri, we cannot pretend to describe the "normative" experience of the overland family. Our interpretation is limited to families whose structure and consciousness were rooted in American bourgeois culture.

[7] The ten volumes of Sarah Hale's *Ladies' Magazine* (1828–1837) are rich primary sources for antebellum ideals of sex roles and the family. For secondary works see the introductory pieces in Nancy Cott, ed., *Root of Bitterness* (Boston: E. C. Dutton, 1972), and Kathryn Kish Sklar, *Catharine Beecher* (New Haven: Yale University Press, 1973). A relatively inaccessible essay remains one of the most illuminating treatments of the period: Nancy Osterud, "Sarah Josepha Hale: A Study of the History of Women in Nineteenth Century America" (unpublished honors thesis, Harvard College, 1971).

[8] See Cott, *Root of Bitterness,* pp. 11–14; Alice Clark, *Working Life of Women in the Seventeenth Century* (London: G. Routledge & Sons, 1919); Elisabeth Dexter, *Colonial Women of Affairs: Women in Business and Professions in America Before 1776* (Boston: Houghton Mifflin Co., 1924); Alice M. Earle, *Home Life in Colonial Days* (New York: McMillian Co., 1899); and Nancy Osterud, "The New England Family, 1790–1840" (unpublished manuscript, Old Sturbridge Village Education Department; Sturbridge, Mass., n.d.).

[9] We do not use "productive" as a value judgment but as a historically specific concept: labor which produces surplus value within the capitalist mode of production. Within the work process itself, both men's *and* women's labor was "useful," but only men's, in the accepted sex-division, resulted in the creation of commodities. For a provocative discussion of this problem see Ian Gough, "Marx's Theory of Productive and Unproductive Labor," *New Left Review* 76 (November–December 1972):47–72, and Lise Vogel, "The Earthly Family," *Radical America* 7 (July–October 1973):9–50.

[10] See Sklar, *Catharine Beecher,* and Ann D. Gordon, Mari Jo Buhle, and Nancy E. Schrom, "Women in American Society," *Radical America* (1972):25–33.

[11] Quoted in Catharine Beecher, *A Treatise on Domestic Economy* (New York: Harper Brothers, 1858), p. 28.

[12] The most comprehensive account to date of domesticity, culture, and sexual spheres is Sklar, *Catharine Beecher;* see especially pp. 151–67 and 204–16. For the cultural importance of reform to women, see Carroll Smith-Rosenberg, "Beauty, the Beast, and the Militant Woman: A Case Study in Sex Roles in Jacksonian America," *American Quarterly* 23 (Fall 1971):562–84 and Gail Parker, *The Oven Birds: American Women on Womanhood 1820–1920* (New York: Doubleday and Co., 1972), pp. 1–56. Nancy Cott's argument in *Root of Bitterness,* pp. 3–4, is a concise summary of

the subculture argument. See Ann Douglas Wood, "The 'Scribbling Women' and Fanny Fern: Why Women Wrote," *American Quarterly* 23 (Spring 1971):1–24, and "Mrs. Sigourney and the Sensibility of the Inner Space," *New England Quarterly* 45 (June 1972):163–81 for women's cultural impulses in literature.

13 The Great Pacific migration began in the wake of the depression of 1837–40. The Pacific Northwest and California seemed to offer unfailing markets at Hudson's Bay forts, Russian settlements, even the massive Orient. The Pacific itself was to be the great transportation network that backwoods farmers needed so desperately. The 1841 migration was the result of the work of the Western Emigration Society, specifically organized to overcome the economic problems of the depressed Midwest. In short, the coast was rich in fertile, free land and unlimited chances for economic success. See Lavender, *Westward Vision*, pp. 327–28. The major exception to this generalization is the Mormon emigration.

14 Judson, *A Pioneer's Search*, p. 9.

15 Lucy Rutledge Cooke, *Crossing the Plains in 1852 . . . as told in Letters Written During the Journey* (Modesto, California: the author, 1923), p. 5. See also James Robertson, *A Few Months in America* (London: n.p., 1855), p. 150; Nancy A. Hunt, "By Ox-Team," p. 9; and Elias Johnson Draper, *An Autobiography* (Fresno, California: the author, 1904), p. 9.

16 Margaret M. Hecox, *California Caravan: the 1846 Overland Trail Memoir of Margaret M. Hecox* (San Jose, California: Harlan-Young Press, 1966), p. 31.

17 Lavinia Honeyman Porter, *By Ox Team to California: A Narrative of Crossing the Plains in 1860* (Oakland, California: author, 1910), p. 7; see also Margaret White Chambers, *Reminiscences* (n.p.: n.p. 1903), pp. 5–7.

18 Porter, *By Ox Team*, p. 41.

19 Luzena Stanley Wilson, *Luzena Stanley Wilson, '49er* (Oakland, California: The Eucalyptus Press, 1937), p. 1.

20 Mary Jane Hayden, *Pioneer Days* (San Jose, California: Murgotten's Press, 1915), pp. 7–8.

21 Our sample of women's diaries and memoirs is by definition biased toward those women who successfully challenged their husbands. A more comprehensive view requires reading another set of journals—those of men who left their families behind. This work, as a part of a general history of the family, women, and men on the Overland Trail, is now in progress: John Faragher, "Women, Men and Their Families on the Overland Trail" (Ph.D. thesis, Yale University, in progress).

22 For a particularly striking record of marriage proposals, see *Mollie: The Journal of Mollie Dorsey Sanford in Nebraska and Colorado Territories, 1857–66* (Lincoln, Nebraska: University of Nebraska Press, 1959), pp. 20, 58, 59, 74, 91.

23 Quoted in Nancy Ross, *Westward the Women* (New York: Alfred A. Knopf, 1944), p. 110.

[24] Mrs. John Wilson, quoted in Read, "Women and Children on the Oregon-California Trail in the Gold-Rush Years," p. 7.

[25] Ross, *Westward the Women,* p. 111.

[26] See Mari Sandoz's biography of her father, *Old Jules* (Lincoln, Nebraska: University of Nebraska Press, 1955) for a dramatic illustration of a male homesteader's functional view of wives and children.

The conventional view that the American west was predominantly male dies hard. Jack Eblen, in "Nineteenth Century Frontier Populations," conclusively demonstrates that the sex ratio in the West was little different from that in the East: women were nearly always present in numbers equal to men. See Christine Stansell, "Women on the Plains." *Women's Studies* (forthcoming).

[27] Esther Allen, *Canvas Caravans: Based on the Journal of Esther Belle McMillan Hanna* (Portland, Oregon: Binfords & Mort, 1946), p. 18.

[28] Mrs. Elizabeth Dixon Smith Geer, "Diary," in Oregon Pioneer Association, *Transactions of the Thirty-fifth Annual Reunion* (1907), p. 169.

[29] Catherine Margaret Haun, quoted in Read, "Women and Children on the Oregon-California Trail in the Gold-Rush Years," p. 9.

[30] Chambers, *Reminiscences,* p. 8.

[31] See Adrietta Applegate Hixon, *On to Oregon! A True Story of a Young Girl's Journey Into the West* (Wesler, Idaho: Signal-American Printers, 1947), p. 17, for one of the few instances in the diaries when men took on women's work.

[32] See Charles Howard Crawford, *Scenes of Earlier Days: In Crossing the Plains to Oregon, and Experiences of Western Life* (Chicago: Quadrangle, 1962), p. 9, for an account of women's resistance to assuming this particular responsibility.

[33] Cummins, *Autobiography and Reminiscences,* p. 28.

[34] See Gowdy, *Crossing the Plains,* p. 2; John Barnett, *Long Trip in a Prairie Schooner* (Whittier, California: Western Stationery Co., 1928), p. 105; and Lydia Milner Waters, "A Trip Across the Plains in 1855," *Quarterly of the Society of California Pioneers* 6 (June 1929):66.

[35] Charlotte Emily Pengra, "Diary of Mrs. Byron J. Pengra," (unpublished typescript in Lane County Historical Society, Eugene, Oregon, n.d.), p. 8.

[36] Mary Burrell, "Mary Burrell's Book" (manuscript diary, Beinecke Library, Yale University), no pagination; Cummins, *Autobiography,* p. 27; E. Allene Dunham, *Across the Plains in a Covered Wagon* (Milton, Iowa: n.p., n.d.), p. 10.

[37] Pengra, "Diary," p. 5.

[38] Ibid., pp. 6, 8–9, 12.

[39] Helen Marnie Stewart, "Diary," (unpublished typescript at Lane County Historical Society, Eugene, Oregon, 1961), p. 13.

[40] The place of children in the structure of the overland family is an intriguing question that we are reserving for more research and reflection. On the basis of their infrequent appearance in the journals, it seems that in this area, too, nineteenth-century patterns were modified. Many historians have pointed to the antebellum period as the time when "the child" emerged from obscurity to a special social status. In the overland sources, however, children over the age of five are rarely discussed except as younger and more vulnerable members of the working group, requiring little extra or special attention.

[41] Elizabeth Wood, "Journal of a Trip to Oregon, 1851," *Oregon Historical Society Quarterly* 17 (1926):4.

[42] Helen M. Carpenter, "A Trip Across the Plains in an Ox Wagon, 1857" (manuscript diary, Huntington Library, San Marino, California), pp. 27–28.

[43] Hixon, *On to Oregon!* p. 17.

[44] Pengra, "Diary," p. 5.

[45] Emery T. Bray, ed., *Bray Family Geneology and History* (n.p.: n.p., 1927), p. 10.

[46] Ibid.

[47] Porter, *By Ox Team to California*, p. 43.

[48] Ibid., p. 118.

[49] Waters, "A Trip Across the Plains in 1855," p. 77.

[50] Hixon, *On to Oregon!* p. 45.

[51] Catherine Haun in Read, "Women and Children During the Gold-Rush Years," p. 9. See also Hixon, *On to Oregon!* p. 15 and *passim;* and William Smedley, "Across the Plains in Sixty-two," *The Trail* 19 (March 1927):11.

[52] Sarah Royce, *A Frontier Lady: Recollections of the Gold Rush and Early California* (New Haven: Yale University Press, 1932), pp. 8–9.

[53] Haun in Read, "Women and Children During the Gold-Rush Years," p. 9.

[54] Harriet Sherril Ward, *Prairie Schooner Lady: The Journal of Harriet Sherril Ward* (Los Angeles: Westernlore Press, 1959), p. 60.

[55] Ibid., p. 95. See also Celinda E. Hines, "Diary of Celinda E. Hines," in Oregon Pioneer Association, *Transactions of the Forty-sixth Annual Reunion* (1918), pp. 82–83 and *passim.*

[56] Ward, *Prairie Schooner Lady*, p. 69.

[57] See Narcissa Whitman, "Diary," (manuscript, Beinecke Library, Yale University), p. 18, or in any one of its many published versions—e.g., *Oregon Historical Quarterly* 35 (1936). Also Esther and Joseph Lyman, "Letters About the Lost Wagon Train of 1853" (unpublished typescript in Lane County Historical Society, Eugene, Oregon), p. 6; and Georgia Read and Ruth Gaines, eds., *Gold Rush: the Journals, Drawings, and Other Papers of J. Goldsborough Bruff . . . April 2, 1849–July 20, 1851* (New York: n.p., 1949), p. 45 and *passim.*

[58] Stewart, "Diary," entry for June 6, 1853. See also Whitman, "Diary," p. 21; Pengra, "Diary," p. 3; and Royce, *Frontier Lady*, p. 11.

[59] Stewart, "Diary," entry for June 12, 1853.

[60] Mrs. Mary Rockwood Power, "The Overland Route: Leaves from the Journal of a California Emigrant," *Amateur Book Collector* 1 (November 1950):6.

[61] Pengra, "Diary," entries for May 2, 3, 8, and 10, and entries for June 5, 24, and July 7, 1853. See also, Royce, *Frontier Lady*, p. 9; and Mrs. Mary A. Frink, *Journal of the Adventures of a Party of California Gold-Seekers* (Oakland, California: n.p., 1897), p. 67.

[62] Stewart, "Diary," entry for May 1, 1853.

[63] Judson, *A Pioneer's Search*, p. 23.

[64] Ibid.

[65] Geer, "Diary," pp. 165–66.

[66] Hixon, *On to Oregon!* p. 18.

[67] Ibid.

[68] Chambers, *Reminiscences*, p. 7.

[69] Ward, *Prairie Schooner Lady*, p. 128. See also Allen, *Canvas Caravans*, p. 28.

[70] Judson, *A Pioneer's Search*, p. 18.

[71] Maria Parsons Belshaw, "Diary of a Bride Written on the Trail in 1853," *Oregon Historical Society Quarterly* 33 (March–December 1932):334.

[72] Cott, *Root of Bitterness*, p. 5.

[73] Gordon, Buhle, and Schrom, *Women in American Society*, p. 22.

[74] Stansell, "Women on the Plains."

[75] Catharine Beecher, *Domestic Economy*, p. 28.

Heroes and Cowards

BELL WILEY

By the mid–nineteenth century Americans were largely unaccustomed to wholesale bloodshed. The war against Mexico (1846–48) and campaigns against the Indian tribes of the West were largely left to the small military establishment. Average citizens knew far less about combat and the agonies of the battlefield than their forbears who had fought against the Indians in the seventeenth and eighteenth centuries or against the British in the American Revolution and the War of 1812. The Civil War thus came as a shocking experience. It not only involved an unprecedented proportion of the population in military service, but because it was the first "modern" war in our history, it introduced Americans to sophisticated death-dealing weapons, scorched-earth policies, wretched concentration camps, and the employment of a large part of the civilian population. The Civil War touched the daily lives of almost everyone in one way or another. Its horrors have yet to be washed from the national consciousness.

The history of the war is usually told in terms of battle tactics and strategies, epic victories and defeats, exploits of military heroes, and the policies of statesmen and diplomats. But just as the social history of politics can be written by shifting our focus from the statehouse to the street, the social history of war can be portrayed by moving from the maproom to the trench. Bell Wiley is one of those historians who have peered behind the curtain of official military history to examine the lives of common soldiers. He concerns himself with their day-to-day existence as they endured the rigors of training camp, reveled in the camaraderie of camp life, recoiled from the stench of the field hospital and the carnage of the blood-soaked battlefield. Students may wish to reconsider Francis Jennings' essay "Savage War" in Part 1 as they read Wiley's account in order to reflect on changes in American attitudes toward war over a period of two centuries.

W hile it may be granted that there were significant changes in the reactions of soldiers as they became accustomed to combat, the fact remains that the experiences and behavior of those taking part in Confederate battles followed the same general pattern. These more or less common characteristics must be described in some detail.

When an encounter with the Yankees was expected certain preliminaries were necessary. One of these was the issue of extra provisions, accompanied by the order to "cook up" from three to five days' rations, so that time would not have to be taken for the preparation of food during the anticipated action. This judicious measure generally fell short of its object because of Johnny Reb's own characteristics: he was always hungry, he had a definite prejudice against baggage, and he was the soul of improvidence. Sometimes the whole of the extra ration would be consumed as it was cooked, and rarely did any part of it last for the full period intended. About the same time that food was dispensed the general in command would address his men for the purpose of firing their spirit and inspiring them to deeds of valor. Soldiers en route to Shiloh, for example, were thus charged by Albert Sidney Johnston:

> "I have put you in motion to offer battle to the invaders of your country. With the resolution and disciplined valor becoming men fighting, as you are, for all worth living or dying for, you can but march to a decisive victory over the agrarian mercenaries sent to subjugate and despoil you of your liberties, property, and honor. Remember the precious stake involved; remember the dependence of your mothers, your wives, your sisters, and your children on the result; remember the fair, broad, abounding land, the happy homes, and the ties that would be desolated by your defeat.
>
> "The eyes and the hopes of eight millions of people rest upon you. You are expected to show yourselves worthy of your race and lineage; worthy of the women of the South, whose noble devotion in this war has never been exceeded in any time. With such incentives to brave deeds and with the trust that God is with us, your general will lead you confidently to the combat, assured of success." [1]

Presently each man would be given a supply of ammunition. This was delayed as long as possible, so that the powder would not become dampened through carelessness of the men. If Confederates held the initiative, the issue of ammunition would take place the night before the attack; but if the Rebs were on the defensive, without any definite knowledge of the time of assault, the issue of cartridges had to take place at an earlier stage. The customary allotment to each fighter was from forty to sixty rounds, a round being a ball and enough powder for a single shot. [2]

Prior to their issue lead and powder for each load had, for convenience, been wrapped in a piece of paper with the bullet at one end, the powder behind it, and the other end closed with a twist or a plug to hold the powder in place. This improvised cartridge was cylindrical in shape, somewhat resembling a section of crayon. When Johnny Reb loaded his gun—usually a muzzle loader—he bit off the twisted end so that the powder would be exploded by the spark when the trigger was pulled, dropped the cartridge in the muzzle, rammed in a piece of wadding and waited for the opportunity to draw bead on a Yankee. Surplus rounds were kept in a cartridge box—a leather or metal container that hung from the belt—or in a haversack, or in trouser pockets.

Knapsacks and other baggage not actually needed on the field were supposed to be left in the rear with the quartermaster, but officers always had trouble preventing their men from throwing aside their equipment at random. After Bull Run and Shiloh most soldiers did not have to be cautioned about their canteens, as the acute suffering from thirst experienced in those engagements was a sufficient reminder to carry well-filled water tins into subsequent fights.

The day of battle finally comes. The men are roused from sleep at a very early hour, perhaps two or three o'clock. The well-known call to arms is an extended beat of the snare drum known as the "long roll." After the lines are drawn up officers inspect equipment, giving particular attention to ammunition, to see that all is in readiness.

Then a few words of advice and instruction: Do not shoot until you are within effective musket range of the enemy; fire deliberately, taking care to aim low, and thus avoid the overshooting to which you have been so markedly susceptible in previous battles. If you merely wound a man so much the better, as injured men have to be taken from the field by sound ones; single out a particular adversary for your fire, after the example of your sharpshooting forefathers at Bunker Hill and New Orleans. When possible pick off the enemy's officers, particularly the mounted ones, and his artillery horses. Under all conditions hold your ranks; avoid the natural but costly inclination to huddle together under heavy fire. When ordered to charge, do so at once and move forward rapidly; you are much less apt to be killed while going steadily forward than if you hesitate or retreat; but in case you have to fall back, do so gradually and in order; more men are killed during disorganized retreat than at any other time; if your objective is a battery, do not be terrorized—artillery is never as deadly as it seems; a rapid forward movement reduces the battery's effectiveness and hastens the end of its power to destroy. Do not pause or turn aside to plunder the dead or to pick up spoils; battles have been lost by indulgence in this temptation. Do not heed the calls for assistance of wounded comrades or stop to take them to the rear; details have been made to care for casualties, and the best way of protecting your wounded friends is to drive the enemy from the field. Straggling under any guise will be severely punished. Cowards will be shot. Do your duty in a manner that becomes the heroic example your regiment has already set on earlier fields of combat.[3]

Orders to march are now given, and to the waving of colors and the stirring rhythm of fife and drum the regiments proceed to their appointed place in the line of battle. As the dawn mist clears away, a scene of intense activity is revealed on all sides. Surgeons are preparing their kits; litter bearers and ambulances are ominously waiting.[4] Arrived at their place in line, the men wait for what seem interminable hours while other units are brought into position. There is some talk while they wait, though less than earlier in the war. Comrades quietly renew mutual pledges to seek out those who are missing at the battle's end—for help if they are wounded and for protection of belongings and notification of homefolk if they are dead. A few men read their testaments, some mutter soft prayers—a devout captain is observed standing with Bible in hand reading aloud to his Mississippians, but this scene is unusual.[5] Here and there a soldier bites off a chew of tobacco and joins a host of comrades whose jaws are already working. Very rarely an officer or a private sneaks a swig of "How Come You So" to bolster his spirit for the ordeal ahead.[6] Everywhere suspense bears down with crushing force, but is indicated largely by silence.

Presently the rattle of musketry is heard in front. Skirmishers must have made contact with enemy pickets. All are alert. A signal gun is fired and the artillery joins in with accumulating fury. At last the command—"Forward!"—and an overpowering urge to make contact with the enemy. Soon lines of blue are discernible. Comrades begin to fall in increasing numbers. Now the shout, lost perhaps in the din of battle—"Charge!"—accompanied by a forward wave of officer's saber and the line leaps forward with the famous "Rebel yell."

This yell itself is an interesting thing. It was heard at First Manassas and was repeated in hundreds of charges throughout the war. It came to be as much a part of a Rebel's fighting equipment as his musket. Once, indeed, more so. Toward the end of an engagement near Richmond in May 1864, General Early rode up to a group of soldiers and said, "Well, men, we must charge them once more and then we'll be through." The response came back, "General, we are all out of ammunition." Early's ready retort was, "Damn it, holler them across." And, according to the narrator, the order was literally executed.[7]

The Confederate yell is hard to describe. An attempt to reproduce it was made a few years ago when Confederate veterans re-enacted battle scenes in Virginia. But this, by the very nature of things, was an inadequate representation. Old voices were too weak and incentive too feeble to create again the true battle cry. As it flourished on the field of combat, the Rebel yell was an unpremeditated, unrestrained and utterly informal "hollering." It had in it a mixture of fright, pent-up nervousness, exultation, hatred and a pinch of pure deviltry. Yelling in attack was not peculiar to Confederates, for Yanks went at Rebels more than once with "furious" shouts on their lips.[8] But the battle cry of Southerners was admittedly different. General "Jube" Early, who well understood the spirit of his soldiers, made a comparison of Federal and Confederate shouting as a sort of aside to his official report of the battle of Fredericksburg. "Lawton's Brigade, without hesitating, at once dashed upon the enemy," he said, "with the cheering peculiar to the Confederate soldier, and which is never mistaken for the studied hurrahs of the Yankees, and drove the column opposed to it down the hill." Though obviously invidious, the general's observation is not wholly inaccurate.[9]

The primary function of the rousing yell was the relief of the shouter. As one Reb observed after a fight in 1864, "I always said if I ever went into a charge, I wouldn't holler! But the very first time I fired off my gun I hollered as loud as I could, and I hollered every breath till we stopped."[10] At first there was no intention of inspiring terror in the enemy, but the practice soon attained such a reputation as a demoralizing agent that men were encouraged by the officers to shout as they assaulted Yankee positions. In the battle of Lovejoy's Station, for instance, Colonel

Clark cried out to his Mississippians, "Fire and charge with a yell." [11] Yankees may not have been scared by this Rebel throat-splitting, but they were enough impressed to set down in their official reports that the enemy advanced "yelling like fiends," or other words to the same effect.[12]

Naturally a thing of such informal character as the Rebel yell varied considerably with the time and circumstance. Mississippians had a note quite different from that of Virginians. Rebs attacking Negro troops injected so much hatred into their cry as to modify its tonal qualities. A most interesting variant was that of the trans-Mississippi Indians organized by the Confederacy. Colonel Tandy Walker, commander of the Second Indian Brigade, reporting an action of his troops in Arkansas, said that when the Federals retreated Private Dickson Wallace was the first man to reach their artillery, "and mounting astride one of the guns gave a whoop, which was followed by such a succession of whoops from his comrades as made the woods reverberate for miles around." [13]

But those Rebs who are now charging at the Yankees know that yelling is only a small part of their business. Yankee lines loom larger as the boys in gray surge forward. Now there is a pause for aiming, and the roar of countless muskets, but the individual soldier is hardly conscious of the noise or the kick of his weapon. Rarely does he have time to consider the effectiveness of his shot. He knows that scores of Yankees are falling, and his comrades as well, but he cannot attend to details of slaughter on either side. He drops to his knee, fumblingly bites off and inserts a cartridge, rams it home with a quick thrust of the rod, then rises and dashes forward with his fellows. On they go, these charging Rebs, feeling now that exaltation which comes after the fight gets under way. "There is something grand about it—it is magnificent," said Robert Gill of his experience under fire near Atlanta. "I feel elated as borne along with the tide of battle." [14]

Presently there is an obvious slowing down of the advance, as resistance increases and attacking ranks become thin. Artillery fire comes in such force as to shatter good-sized trees, and men are actually killed by falling limbs.[15] The lines of gray seem literally to bend beneath the weight of canister and grape, and yelling soldiers lean forward while walking as if pushing against the force of a wind.[16] Slaughter becomes so terrible that ditches run with blood.[17] The deafening noise is likened by one Reb to "a large cane brake on fire and a thunder storm with repeated loud thunder claps." The flight of shells (called "lamp posts" and "wash kettles" according to their size and shape) reminds Robert Gill of "frying on a large scale only a little more so"; and Maurice Simons thinks of a partridge flying by, "only we would suppose that the little bird had grown to the size of an Eagle." [18] Some of the men, unable to confront this holocaust, seek the protection of rocks, trees and gullies. Others of stronger nerve close the gaps and push onward.

The overwhelming urge to get quickly to the source of danger brings an end to loading and shooting. With one last spurt the charging troops throw themselves among their adversaries, gouging with bayonets, swinging with clubbed muskets, or even striking with rocks, fence rails and sticks.[19] Presently one side or the other gives way, and the charge is over.

But not the battle. Before the day's fighting is completed there will be several charges, each followed by lulls for reorganization. And perhaps the conflict, as at Gettysburg, will extend to a second and third day, each characterized by repetitions of attack over various portions of the field; or perhaps the main action, as at Fredericksburg, will be defensive, staving off repeated Federal assaults.

Moving to the charge, though by far the most dramatic part of the fighting, actually made up only a small portion of a soldier's experience in battle. There were hours of lying on the ground or of standing in line, perhaps under the heat of a broiling sun, while troops on other parts of the field carried out the tasks assigned them. Then there was endless shifting, to bolster a weak spot here, to cut off an enemy salient there, or to replenish ammunition. These and many other activities, coupled with repeated advances on enemy positions, took a heavy toll of the soldier's strength.

As the day wore on he was increasingly conscious of exhaustion. Though accustomed before the war to long hours of labor on the farm or extended jaunts in pursuit of game, he found fighting the hardest work he had ever done. Fatigue was sharpened by the fact that rest and food had been scarce during the days before the battle. By midafternoon his strength was often so depleted that he could hardly load and fire his gun, if indeed he was able to stand at all.[20] Those who fought at Shiloh may have joined in the postwar criticism of Beauregard for not pushing the battle as Sunday's sun sank in the west, but officers' reports made soon after the fight show that most of the men were so exhausted that further aggression was impossible.[21]

Increasing with the combatant's fatigue came intolerable thirst. Sweating in the grime and dust, he had emptied his canteen early in the day, hoping to refill it from some stream. But rarely was there any such chance. If he were lucky enough to reach a pond he was apt to find it so choked with the dead and wounded as to be unfit for use. But even so, that soldier considered himself lucky who could sweep aside the gory scum and quench his thirst by greedy draughts of the muddy water underneath.[22]

If the battle happened to be in winter, as at Murfreesboro, Fredericksburg, or Nashville, the suffering from thirst was not so intense. But the exposure to cold was hardly less severe. Discomfort was increased by damp weather, scarcity of clothing, and the inability to make fires. At Murfreesboro, for instance, soldiers lay in line of battle for nearly a week under a cold rain without fire.[23]

When the combat extended over several days, as was frequently the case, hunger was added to other discomforts. At Gettysburg Washington Artillerymen became so famished that a captain sent a detail to gather food from the haversacks of Federal dead.[24] Many other hungry soldiers were not so fortunate as to have this opportunity.

The coming of night usually brought a rest from fighting, but not from suffering. The disorganization which characterized Confederate battles often separated the soldier from his regiment.[25] The command of duty, plus a desire to know the lot of his friends, would cause him, tired

to the point of prostration though he was, to set out on a tedious search
for his fellows. When he found the scattered remnants of his company he
would probably discover that some messmate, committed to his care by
mutual pledge before the battle, was missing. Then he must make a round
of the battlefield and the emergency hospitals, inquiring patiently, calling
out the name of his friend, and scanning by candlelight the ghastly faces
of dead and wounded. The quest might end in happy discovery, but more
likely it would prove futile. At last the weary soldier would fall down
on the ground. And in spite of the piteous cries of the wounded he would
sink at once into heavy slumber.

The morrow of a battle, whether its duration was for one or several
days, was in some respects more trying than the conflict itself. Scenes
encountered in the burial of the dead were strange and appalling: there
a dead Yankee lying on his back "with a biscuit in his hand and with one
mouthful bitten off and that mouthful still between his teeth"; here "the
top of a man's Skull Hanging by the Hair to a Limb some 8 or 9 feet
from the ground"; yonder another "man Siting behind a large oak tree his
head . . . shot off"; to the right a small, whining dog curled up in the
arms of a dead Yankee, refusing to be coaxed from its erstwhile master;
to the left a lifeless Reb sprawled across the body of a well-dressed Federal, the gray-clad's hand in the Northerner's pocket—a gruesome warning to those who are tempted to plunder during battle; farther on, the field
is strewn with nude figures blackened and mutilated by a fire that swept
across the dry foliage in the wake of the fight.[26] One of the burying
party working in Federal-traversed territory is shocked to find that before his arrival "the hogs got a holt of some of the Yankey dead." [27] In
any direction one chances to gaze lie heaps of disfigured bodies; to a
rural-bred Georgian the scene following Fredericksburg suggested "an
immense hog pen and them all killed." [28]

After a prolonged summer encounter the task was unusually repul-
sive. Wrote a soldier who helped in the burial of the Gettysburg dead:

> "The sights and smells that assailed us were simply indescrib-
> able—corpses swollen to twice their original size, some of them
> actually burst asunder with the pressure of foul gases and vapors.
> . . . The odors were nauseating and so deadly that in a short time
> we all sickened and were lying with our mouths close to the
> ground, most of us vomiting profusely." [29]

While some were burying the dead, others were walking about picking up spoils. Trinkets of all sorts, such as Yankee letters, diaries, photo-
graphs, and pocket knives are much in demand as souvenirs to be sent
home to relatives. "I am going to send you a trophie that come off the
battle field at Gettysburg," wrote a Reb to his sister. "I got three pictures
out of a dead Yankees knapsack and I am going to send you one. . . .
The pictures are wraped up in a letter from the person whose image they
are. . . . She signed her name A. D. Spears and she lived in Main somewhere, but I could not make out where she lived." [30] Occasionally Rebs
laughed over the sentimental contents of such letters. Some soldiers

profited financially from their plundering of battlefields. Following the
Franklin engagement of December 1864 George Athey wrote:

> "I got agood knapsack fuol of tricks whitch I sold $4.5 dolars
> worth out of it and cepe as mutch as I wanted." [31]

Articles essential to personal comfort were eagerly gathered up.
After the Seven Days' Battles a Reb wrote exultantly:

> "We have had a glorious victory with its rich Booty A many
> one of our boys now have a pair of Briches a nice Rubber cloth
> & a pair of Blankets also a pair or more of Small Tent Cloths." [32]

The avidity with which an impoverished Confederate might pounce
upon the riches left in the wake of Federal defeat, as well as the unhappy
consequence of overenthusiasm, is evidenced by an entry in a Tennessean's
diary following the battle of Seven Pines:

> "I awoke quite early yesterday morning, and everything
> seemed very quiet, I went over the field seeing what I could see.
> Here were Sutlers' tents, filled with luxuries, oranges, lemons,
> oysters, pineapples, sardines, in fact, almost everything that I could
> think of. My first business was to eat just as much as I possibly
> could, and that was no small amount, for I had been living on hard
> tack several days. I then picked out a lot of stationery, paper, en-
> velopes, ink, pens and enough to fill one haversack, then I found
> a lot of puff bosomed linen shirts, and laid in a half dozen together
> with some white gloves and other little extras enough to fill another
> haversack. Then I filled another with nuts and candies and still an-
> other with cheese. With this load, I wandered around picking up
> some canteens to carry back to the boys. Then adding to my load
> such articles as a sword, an overcoat, etc. . . . I quickened my pace
> and before I had gone twenty steps, the Yankees opened fire . . .
> and the balls whistled around me in a perfect shower. I had about
> two hundred yards to go before reaching my regiment, and by the
> time I reached it, I had thrown away all my plunder." [33]

If the battle ended in defeat, falling back might be so hurried as to
leave the dead and wounded in Federal hands. This, added to the increased hardships of retreat and the disappointment of being whipped,
caused the soldier's cup to overflow with bitterness.

But whether victorious or not, Johnny Reb began within a remark-
ably short time to recall and to enjoy the interesting and humorous detail
of the combat. Campfire groups must have delighted in teasing Private
Joseph Adams about losing his pants when a shell exploded near him at
Murfreesboro; and there was doubtless plenty of laughter when M. D.
Martin told how a shell cut off his two well-stocked haversacks and

scattered hardtack so promiscuously that "several of the boys were struck by the biscuits, and more than one thought he was wounded." [34]

James Mabley could always get a good laugh with his story of the Reb at Chancellorsville who while in the act of drawing a bead on a Yank was distracted by a wild turkey lighting in a tree before him; the Federal was immediately forgotten, and in an instant the crack of this Reb's gun brought the turkey to the ground. [35]

The men of Gilmor's Battalion never tired of asking their colonel after a valley engagement of 1864 "if spades are trumps"; for during this fight a ball went all the way through an unopened deck of cards that he was carrying in his inside coat pocket, stopping only at the last card, the ace of spades. [36]

Almost everyone could tell of a "close shave" when a bullet hit a knapsack, perforated a hat, or spent itself by passing through a bush immediately in front, to fall harmlessly to the ground in plain view. One soldier marveled at hearing through the din of battle the cry of John Childress as he fell: "I am killed, tell Ma and Pa goodbye for me." [37]

Then someone may have mentioned the tragic case of Jud and Cary Smith, Yale-educated brothers from Mississippi. While in the act of lying down under fire, the younger, Cary, putting his hand under his coat found his inner garments covered with blood; and with only the exclamation "What does this mean?" he died. Jud was so overwhelmed with grief that he spent the entire night muttering affectionate words over his brother's corpse. He passed the next day and night in unconsolable solitude. The third day was that of Malvern Hill, and when the first charge took place Jud kept on going after his comrades fell back under the murderous fire, and he was never seen or heard of again. After the father learned of the fate of his two sons he joined Price's army as a private soldier; when his regiment charged at Iuka, he followed the example set by Jud at Malvern Hill, and he likewise was never heard of again. [38]

But there was not much lingering on tragic notes. It was more pleasant to talk of how Jeb Stuart at Second Manassas beguiled the Yankees into exaggerated ideas of Rebel strength by having his men drag brush along the roads to stir up huge clouds of dust; or of how the Yankee General Banks was duped into abandoning several strong positions during his Red River campaign by such Confederate ruses as sending drummers out to beat calls, lighting superfluous campfires, blowing bugles, and "rolling empty wagons over fence rails"; or of how George Cagle, while lying on a ridge at Chickamauga, kept at work four or five muskets gathered from incapacitated comrades, and as Yankee bullets whistled overhead he simulated the activity of an artillery unit, giving such commands as "attention Cagle's Battery, make ready, load, take aim, fire"; of how Sergeant Nabors scared nervous Yankee prisoners who asked him at Atlanta if he were going to kill them by replying, "That's our calculation; we came out for that purpose." [39]

By no means was all of the fighting in the open field. Warring in trenches—Johnny Reb usually called them "ditches"—made its appearance in the spring of 1862 on the Virginia peninsula where Magruder's army

was entrenched for a month. At Vicksburg, where Pemberton's troops
were under siege for forty-seven days, soldiers spent most of the time in
earthworks along the line, or in caves to the rear. During the Atlanta
campaign Rebs of the Army of Tennessee saw considerable trench warfare. But by far the longest stretch of this sort of campaigning was done
by Lee's troops, who spent the greater part of the war's last year in the
ditches around Petersburg.

Occasionally the routine of trench fighting was broken by an assault
of one army or the other, but the time was mostly spent in desultory
exchanges of artillery and musket fire. The Federals, being the besiegers
and having vastly superior resources, did the larger part of the firing. So
unlimited, indeed, were their supplies of ammunition that they could
make the countryside reverberate with repeated discharges of their heavy
cannon.[40]

The defenders of Vicksburg were subjected to heavier fire than any
other trench fighters in the war. Back of them lay the Mississippi, dotted
with gunboats, and before them were the troops of Grant and Sherman
well equipped with artillery. The besieged were deficient in both guns
and ammunition. Hemmed in thus by superior forces and equipment, conscious of their inability to give effective retaliation, living on ever dwindling rations, suffering from a shortage of drinking water, and cut off
largely from their friends, they were subjected day after day and night
after night to a cannonading that was so severe at times as to make heads
ache from the concussion.[41] One of the defenders wrote in his diary at
the midpoint of siege:

> "The fighting is now carried on quite systematically . . . in the
> morning there seems to be time allowed for breakfast, when all at
> once the work of destruction is renewed. There is about an hour at
> noon & about the same at sunset, taking these three intervals out the
> work goes on just as regularly as . . . on a well regulated farm & the
> noise is not unlike the clearing up of new ground when much
> heavy timber is cut down! Add to that the nailing on of shingles by
> several men & one has a pretty good idea of the noise. It might be
> supposed that a score of villages had sprung up all round him & that
> the inhabitants were vieing with each other to see who could be
> the most industrious." [42]

The caves dug in the hillside were poor protection against the heavy
shells that came screeching through the air with varying notes of terror.
If one lifted his head ever so little above the earthworks, the crack of a
sharpshooter's rifle, followed instantly by a dull thud, would announce
the doom of another Reb. A man who was slightly wounded in the
trenches stood in considerable danger of being more seriously injured, if
not killed outright, as he traversed the open space between battle line and
hospital. Life under such conditions became a torturing ordeal, and the
situation was not helped by jesting speculation as to the prospective comforts of Johnson's Island, Camp Chase and Camp Douglas.[43]

In the trenches before Atlanta and Petersburg existence was not so perilous nor so gloomy as at Vicksburg. Common to all, however, was the intolerable heat of the summer sun. Some men sought alleviation by building little brush arbors along the trenches. The sultriness of the ditches became so unbearable at night that some of the men resorted to sleeping on the edge—and when the Federal batteries opened they would simply roll over to safety. But immunity from danger in the Atlanta and Petersburg trenches was only comparative. The killing and wounding of men by Federal sharpshooting and artillery fire were of such common occurrence as hardly to elicit notice save by the company to which the casualty belonged.[44]

The number of killed and wounded would have been much greater but for the skill of the men in side-stepping arched shots. "The mortars are thrown up a great height," wrote an Alabamian from Petersburg, "and fall down in the trenches like throwing a ball over a house—we have become very perfect in dodging them and unless they are thrown too thick I think I can always escape them at least at night." He added that the dugouts which they contrived at intervals along the trenches and which they were wont to call bombproofs were not impervious at all to mortar shells, and that "we always prefer to be out in the ditches—where by using strategy and skill we get out of their way." [45] So confident did the troops become of their ability to escape these lobbed shots of the Yankees that they would keep up a derisive yelling throughout a bombardment.[46]

During periods of truce ladies from Petersburg made several visits to the lines, walking down the ditches in their cumbersome hoop skirts to see how bombproofs were made, climbing upon the parapets to get a look at the Yankees, giggling and oh-ing at the strange sights confronting them. Both Federals and Rebs enjoyed these interludes in crinoline but some of the latter could not refrain from mischievously expressing the wish that the Yanks would throw a few shells over to see if the fair visitors woud shake with terror or raise the Rebel yell.[47]

But these tantalizing glimpses of Petersburg belles afforded only brief respite from the terrible filth, the smothering heat of summer and the cold of winter, the rain and mud of all seasons, the restricted movement and the countless other deprivations that made trench warfare the most unpleasant aspect of Confederate soldierhood. Open fighting with all its dangers was immeasurably preferable to such existence as this.

But what of valor and of cowardice on the field of battle? There were numerous manifestations of both, though many more of the former than of the latter. Deeds of Rebel bravery, individual and collective, were of such common occurrence as to be quite beyond all estimation. A few definite instances will serve as examples of the glory that lighted up the fields of Manassas, of Shiloh, of Antietam, of Gettysburg, of Spottsylvania —and of countless others.

At Shiloh Private Samuel Evans refused to go to the rear when a ball passed through both cheeks, "but remained and fought for a considerable length of time, cheering on the men and loading and shooting as fast as he could." An officer who saw his men reduced from twenty-eight to twelve as he led them into the ravaging fire at Seven Pines cried out as he fell pierced through the heart, "Boys, I am killed, but you press on." [48] Private Ike Stone was severely wounded at the beginning of the Murfreesboro fight, but he paused only to bind up his injuries, and when his captain was incapacitated Stone took charge of the company and led it valorously through the battle, this despite a second wound. In the thick of this same fight Sergeant Joe Thompson was overwhelmed with the impulse to take a prisoner; leaping ahead of his comrades he overtook the retreating Federal column, seized a Yank and started to the rear with him; but this man having been shot down in his grasp, Thompson ran back to the still-retreating lines, seized a second Federal and brought him away safely. When Private Mattix's left arm was so seriously injured that he could no longer fire his musket, he went to his commanding officer and said, "Colonel, I am too badly wounded to use my gun but can carry the flag; may I?" Before this three standard-bearers had been shot down in succession, but when the requested permission was given him, Mattix seized the staff, stepped boldly in front of the regiment, and carried the colors throughout the remainder of the contest.[49]

In his official report of Second Manassas Major J. D. Waddell, commanding Toombs' Georgians, said that he "carried into the fight over 100 men who were barefoot, many of whom left bloody foot-prints among the thorns and briars through which they rushed, with Spartan courage and really jubilant impetuosity, upon the serried ranks of the foe." Colonel E. C. Cook of the Thirty-second Tennessee Infantry reported after Chickamauga that one of his men, J. W. Ellis, who had marched for six weeks without shoes, "went thus into battle and kept up with his company at all times till wounded." [50]

At Chickamauga Private Mayfield was wounded in the thigh by a Minié ball and at the same time dazed by a shell. Litter bearers picked him up and were carrying him to the rear when he recovered from the shock and sprang to the ground with the remark, "This will not do for me," and rushed back to continue the fight. In this same engagement Private McCann fought gallantly until his ammunition was exhausted; then he picked up cartridge boxes of the dead and wounded and coolly distributed ammunition among his comrades. When the colonel commended his heroic conduct McCann asked that his bravery be cited in the official report of the battle. Shortly afterward he received a mortal wound and as he was borne dying to the rear, he turned smiling to his colonel and reminded him of the promise of honorable mention.[51]

Of all the brave those who were entrusted with the colors had the most consistent record. Almost every official report of regimental commanders mentions the courageous action of standard-bearers. To keep the flag flying was a matter of inestimable pride, and its loss to the enemy was an incalculable disgrace. Consequently men vied with each other for the honor of holding the cherished emblem aloft in the thickest of the fight.[52] The Federals, knowing the close association of morale and colors, and being easily able to single out standard-bearers because of their conspicuousness, were wont to concentrate an unusually heavy fire upon them. Literally thousands of those who aspired to the honor of carrying and guarding the flags paid for the privilege with their lives.

"In my two color companies," reported Colonel Jenkins of the Palmetto Sharpshooters after Seven Pines, "out of 80 men who entered 40 were killed and wounded, and out of 11 in the color guard, 10 were shot down, and my colors pierced by nine balls passed through four hands without touching the ground." At Antietam the First Texas Infantry lost eight standard-bearers in succession, and at Gettysburg, the Twenty-sixth North Carolina lost fourteen.[53] At Antietam also, the flag of the Tenth Georgia—which regiment lost fifty-seven per cent of its men and officers in this one engagement—received forty-six shots. The standard of Lyle's Regiment was torn to tatters at Corinth, and color-bearer Sloan when last seen by his comrades was "going over the breast works waving a piece over his head and shouting for the Southern Confederacy." [54]

Color Sergeant Rice of the Twenty-eighth Tennessee Infantry, downed by a bullet at Murfreesboro, still clung to the flag, holding it aloft as he crawled on his knees until a second shot brought death and delivered him of his trust. On another part of this bloody field Color Sergeant Cameron advanced too far ahead of his comrades and was captured. He tore the flag from its staff, concealed it on his person, carried it to prison with him, escaped, and brought it back to be unfurled anew above its proud followers.[55]

Murfreesboro likewise afforded the setting for perhaps the most extraordinary of all color-bearer feats. While this contest raged at its greatest fury the opposing lines came very near each other in that portion of the field occupied by the Nineteenth Texas Cavalry (dismounted). A Yankee standard carrier stood immediately to the front of the Texas Color Sergeant, A. Sims, waving his flag and urging the blue column forward. Sergeant Sims, construing this as something of a personal insult, rushed forward, planted his own flag staff firmly on the ground with one hand and made a lunge for that of his exhorting adversary with the other. At the moment of contact, both color-bearers, Yankee and Rebel, "fell in the agonies of death waving their banners above their heads until their last expiring moments." The Texas standard was rescued, but not until one who rushed forward to retrieve it had also been shot down.[56]

Confederate authorities sought to stimulate the men by offering medals and badges to those who were cited by officers. Unable to supply these emblems, Congress passed an act in October 1862 providing for the publication of a Roll of Honor after each battle which should include the names of those who had best displayed their courage and devotion. Such lists were read at dress parades, published in newspapers and filed in the adjutant general's office. As a further inducement commissions were offered to those who should distinguish themselves, and special inscriptions were placed on flags of those regiments that captured artillery or gave other proof of unusual achievement.[57] But the most effective incentive was probably that of personal and family pride. This was strikingly evidenced by the remark of a Georgian to his brother after Franklin: "I am proud to say that there was no one between me and the Yankees when I was wounded." [58]

Cowardice under fire, being a less gratifying subject than heroism, has not received much attention from those who have written or talked of the Confederate Army. Of the various sources of information on this obscure point the most fertile are the official reports of battles by commanders of units ranging from regiments to armies. But the most numerous of these reports—those submitted by regimental commanders—are characterized by a reluctance to admit wholesale cowardice because of possible reflections on the conduct of the commanders themselves. This reluctance sometimes resulted in misrepresentation of the rankest sort, as in the following case: After the attack on Battery Wagner, Morris Island, South Carolina, July 18, 1863, Colonel Charles W. Knight, commanding the Thirty-first North Carolina Regiment, said in closing his report, "It is useless to mention any officer or man, when all were acting coolly and bravely." In the body of his report he mentioned being repulsed, but there is absolutely no suggestion of bad conduct on the part of the regiment. But when Knight's superior, General William B. Taliaferro, reported the battle, he said: "The Thirty-first North Carolina could not be induced to occupy their position, and ingloriously deserted the ramparts. . . . I feel it my duty to mention . . . [their] disgraceful conduct." [59]

In the reports of higher ranking officers, who could admit bad conduct of portions of their commands with more impunity than colonels, and in the wartime letters and diaries of the common soldiers, much testimony on the subject may be found. This evidence shows clearly that Confederate soldiers were by no means immune to panic and cowardice.

At First Manassas a few Rebs fled into the woods when shells began to fly. There was disgraceful conduct at the beginning of McClellan's peninsula campaign, when General D. H. Hill wrote that "several thousand soldiers . . . have fled to Richmond under pretext of sickness. They have even thrown away their arms that their flight might not be impeded." At Seven Pines there were a few regiments that "disgracefully left the battle field with their colors." General W. H. C. Whiting in reporting the battle of Gaines's Mill said: "Men were leaving the field in every direction and in great disorder . . . men were skulking from the front in a shameful manner; the woods on our left and rear were full of troops in safe cover from which they never stirred." At Malvern Hill, General Jubal Early encountered "a large number of men retreating from the battle-field," saw "a very deep ditch filled with skulkers," and found a "wood filled with a large number of men retreating in confusion." [60]

Men ran, skulked and straggled by the hundreds at Shiloh. A Tennessee regiment took fright during an advance, ran back on supporting lines crying, "Retreat! Retreat!" and caused great confusion; but they were rallied and set in motion toward the Federal position; again they were overcome with fear, and this time they rushed back so precipitately that they ran over and trampled in the mud the color-bearer of the regiment behind them. A Texas regiment behaved in the same manner; placed in line of battle it began firing, but before the guns had all been discharged, "it broke and fled disgracefully from the field." An officer who attempted to bring back the fugitives and threatened to report them as "a pack of cowards" was told that "they did not care a damn" what they were called, they would not follow him. When General W. J. Hardee tried to rally another demoralized regiment he was fired on by its members. Some of the straggling for which Shiloh was notorious was due to circumstances that exonerate those involved, but there can be no doubt that a large part of those who found various pretexts for leaving the firing line were playing the coward. Said Colonel O. F. Strahl in his official report: "On Monday morning we . . . had a great number of stragglers attached to us. The stragglers demonstrated very clearly this morning that they had strayed from their own regiments because they did not want to fight. My men fought gallantly until the stragglers ran and left them and began firing from the rear over their heads. They were then compelled to fall to the rear. I rallied them several times and . . . finally left out the stragglers." General Beauregard clinched this evidence in his official report: "Some officers, non-commissioned officers, and men abandoned their colors early in the first day to pillage the captured encampments; others retired shamefully from the field on both days while the thunder of cannon and the roar and rattle of musketry told them that their brothers were being slaughtered by the fresh legions of the enemy." [61]

General Bushrod Johnson reported that at Murfreesboro troops on his right became demoralized and "men of different regiments, brigades, divisions, were scattered all over the fields," and that he was almost run over, so precipitate was their flight. Captain Felix Robertson said that he had never seen troops so completely broken as those demoralized at Murfreesboro. "They seemed actuated only by a desire for safety," he added. "I saw the colors of many regiments pass, and though repeated calls were made for men of the different regiments, no attention was paid to them." [62]

At Chancellorsville and Gettysburg the conduct of the soldiers seems to have been exceptionally good. This may have been due in some part to vigorous efforts of General Lee and of the War Department early in 1863 to tighten up the discipline of the Army of Northern Virginia. The fighting before Vicksburg was marred by shameful conduct in the action of May 16, 1863, of which General Pemberton said: "We lost a large amount of artillery. The army was much demoralized; many regiments behaved badly," and Colonel Edward Goodwin reported of a small number of troops immediately in front of him:

> "At this time our friends gave way and came rushing to the rear panic-stricken. . . . I brought my regiment to the charge bayonets, but even this could not check them in their flight. The colors of three regiments passed through. . . . We collared them, begged them, and abused them in vain." [63]

The wholesale panic which seized Confederate troops at Missionary Ridge was as notorious as it was mystifying. A soldier who took part in the battle wrote in his diary, "In a few minutes the whole left gave way and a regular run commenced." After a retreat of several hundred yards, this Reb's battalion rallied momentarily, "but it was in such a confused mass that we made but a feeble resistance, when all broke again in a perfect stampede." His conviction was that the troops acted disgracefully, that they "did not half fight." [64]

General Bragg in his official report of the fight said that "a panic which I had never before witnessed seemed to have seized upon officers and men, and each seemed to be struggling for his personal safety, regardless of his duty or his character." He added that "no satisfactory excuse can possibly be given for the shameful conduct of the troops on our left in allowing their line to be penetrated. The position was one which ought to have been held by a line of skirmishers against any assaulting column, and wherever resistance was made the enemy fled in disorder after suffering heavy loss. Those who reached the ridge did so in a condition of exhaustion from the great physical exertion in climbing, which rendered them powerless, and the slightest effort would have destroyed them." What stronger indictment could there be of any soldiery by its general-in-command! [65]

But the woeful tale is not ended. In connection with Early's campaign of 1864 in the Shenandoah Valley occurred some of the most disgraceful running of Confederate history. After an engagement near Winchester on July 23, General Stephen Ramseur wrote his wife:

> "My men behaved shamefully— They ran from the enemy. . . .
> The entire command stampeded. I tried in vain to rally them & even
> after the Yankees were checked by a few men I posted behind a
> stone wall, they continued to run all the way to the breastworks at
> Winchester—& many of them threw away their guns & ran on to
> Newtown 6 miles beyond. They acted cowardly and I told them
> so." [66]

On September 19, 1864, during another hard fight near Winchester, a panic of unprecedented proportions struck the ranks of Early's army. Regiment after regiment broke and fled back toward the town. General Bryan Grimes, appalled by the demoralization and fearful that his brigade would succumb to it, threatened "to blow the brains out of the first man who left ranks," and then moved over to confront the fugitives, waving his sword and giving many a Reb the full weight of its flashing blade.[67] But fleeing regiments, increasing now in number, could not be stopped. They poured into the town, out the valley pike, and some continued their disordered course for miles beyond. "The Ladies of Winchester came into the streets and beged them crying bitterly to make a stand for their sakes if not for their own honor," wrote a captain who witnessed the rout; but "the cowards did not have the shame to make a pretense of halting." [68]

A month later at Cedar Creek, plunder combined with cowardice to inflict upon Early's veterans one of the most shameful defeats of the war. In the morning, by brilliant action, the Confederates pounced upon the Federals and drove them from their camps. As the Southern lines advanced large numbers of soldiers and officers turned aside, against positive orders, and began to ransack the rich stores abandoned by the foe. While the victors were absorbed in pillage, the Federals rallied, and in the afternoon they counterattacked. The disorganized Confederates broke first on the left, and then all along the line. Efforts of division commanders and of others who attempted to stay the tide of panic was to no avail, and the field was utterly abandoned.

"It was the hardest day's work I ever engaged in," Grimes said, "trying to rally the men. Took over flags at different times, begging, commanding, entreating the men to rally—would ride up and down the lines, beseeching them by all they held sacred and dear, to stop and fight, but without any success. I don't mean my Brigade only, but all." [69]

Price's Missouri expedition of 1864 was marked by an instance of large-scale panic. When the Federals attacked the Confederate rear on October 25, near Carthage, Missouri, demoralization set in. As Price rode rapidly to the point of danger he "met the divisions of Major-Generals Fagan and Marmaduke retreating in utter and indescribable confusion, many of them having thrown away their arms. They were deaf to all entreaties or commands, and in vain were all efforts to rally them." [70]

While the Atlanta campaign seems to have been remarkably free of demoralization under fire, there were at least two instances involving a considerable number of men. In a skirmish on June 9, 1864, a Texas cavalry unit that had a distinguished record in battle broke upon slight contact with the Federal cavalry, and fled in a manner described as disorderly and shameful by General Ross. Later, in the Battle of Jonesboro, August 31, 1864, an advancing brigade of Confederates halted without orders when it came to the Federal picket line, the men seeking shelter behind piles of rails. They seemed "possessed of some great horror of charging breastworks," reported Colonel Bushrod Jones, "which no power of persuasion or example could dispel." [71]

The last instance of large-scale panic during the war was at Nashville, December 16, 1864. On this occasion the division of General Bate, when assaulted about four o'clock in the afternoon by the Federals, began to fall back in great confusion and disorder. In a few moments the entire Confederate line was broken, and masses of troops fled down the pike toward Franklin. All efforts to rally the troops proved fruitless. General Bate in his official report leaves the impression that the rout, due to extenuating circumstances, cast little if any reproach upon his men. But General Hood, in chief command, was evidently of contrary opinion, as he says that Confederate loss in killed and wounded was small, implying that withdrawal took place without much resistance. He says further that the break came so suddenly that artillery guns could not be brought away.[72] Captain Thomas J. Key says in his diary that "General Bate's division . . . shamefully broke and fled before the Yankees were within 200 yards of them," and that there "then ensued one of the most disgraceful routs" that it had ever been his misfortune to witness.[73]

There were innumerable cases of individual cowardice under fire. When men are assembled in such large numbers, especially when many of them are forced into service, a certain proportion are inevitably worthless as fighters. Some of those who fled wanted earnestly to act bravely, but they had not the power to endure fire unflinchingly. This type is well exemplified by the Reb who covered his face with his hat during the battle of Fredericksburg, and who later, when told that his turn at the rifle pits was imminent, "made a proposition that he would go out from camp and strip" and let his comrades "get switches and whip him as much as they wanted" if they would obtain his release from the impending proximity to Federal fire.[74] A similar case was encountered by Colonel C. Irvine Walker. A man had been reported for cowardly behavior on the field. Walker called him to task and told him that he would be watched closely during the next engagement. When the time came the colonel went over to check his performance as the regiment advanced. "I found him in his place," reported Walker, "his rifle on his shoulder, and holding up in front of him a frying pan." The man was so scared that he sought this meager protection, yet he moved forward with his company and was killed.[75]

Another case of infamy converted to valor was cited by Colonel William Stiles, of the Sixtieth Georgia Infantry. During a charge this officer saw a robust Reb drop out of line and crouch behind a tree; the colonel slipped up and gave him a resounding whack across the back with the flat of his sword, and shouted, "Up there, you coward!"

The skulker, thinking evidently that he was the mortal victim of a Yankee shot, "clasped his hands, and keeled over backwards, devoutly ejaculating, 'Lord, receive my spirit!' "

After momentary bafflement, Stiles kicked the prostrate soldier violently in the ribs, exclaiming simultaneously, "Get up, sir! The Lord wouldn't receive the spirit of such an infernal coward."

The man sprang up with the joyful exclamation, "Ain't I killed? The Lord be praised," grabbed his musket, rejoined his comrades, and henceforth conducted himself with courage.[76]

Other officers had less success. Men who had no shoes were often excused from fighting, and a good many soldiers took advantage of this rule by throwing away their shoes on the eve of conflict. Others left the field under pretext of helping the wounded to the rear, and this in spite of strict orders against removal of casualties by anyone except those specifically detailed for the purpose. Still others feigned sickness or injury. A favorite ruse was to leave one's own regiment during the confusion of battle, and then to evade duty by a pretense of endless and futile searching for the outfit intentionally abandoned.[77]

Infuriated officers would curse these shirkers, beat them with swords and even threaten them with shooting, and on occasion carry out their threats on the spot. Commanders would place file-closers in the rear with instructions to arrest, and in some instances to shoot down, those who refused to do their duty.[78] Courts-martial sentenced great numbers to hard and disgraceful punishments. Private soldiers covered spineless comrades with scorn and ridicule.[79] But these measures were only partially effective.

There can be no doubt that the trying conditions under which Confederate soldiers fought contributed to the bad performance of some on the field of battle. Men often went into combat hungry and remained long under fire with little or nothing to eat. Sometimes, as at Antietam and Gettysburg, they fought after exhausting marches. Many of those who participated in the routs at Chattanooga and at Nashville were without shoes. Often the Confederate artillery protection was inadequate. The superior number of the Federals made Rebel flanks unduly vulnerable, and flank sensitiveness was the cause of more than one panic. Casualties among line officers were unusually heavy, and replacement with capable men was increasingly difficult after 1863.

When all of these factors are considered, it is rather remarkable that defection under fire was not more frequent than it actually was. Those soldiers who played the coward, even granting that the offenders totaled well up in the thousands, were a very small proportion of the Confederate Army. Taken on the whole of his record under fire, the Confederate private was a soldier of such mettle as to claim a high place among the world's fighting men. It may be doubted that anyone else deserves to outrank him.

NOTES

1 [*Official Records of the Union and Confederate Armies* (Washington, D.C., 1880–1901)], series 1, X, part 2, 389 [to be cited hereinafter as *O. R.*].

2 Forty rounds was evidently the capacity of an ordinary cartridge box. After the battle of Gettysburg the War Department sent out a circular to army and departmental commanders enjoining the practice, except on special order of the general commanding, of issuing on the eve of battle twenty rounds of ammunition, "over and above the capacity of the cartridge boxes." *O. R.*, series 1, XXVII, part 3, 1091.

3 This summary of pre-battle instructions is derived from various sources. For examples, See *O. R.*, series 1, X, part 2, 325–326, 535, and XI, part 3, 410–411. State pride was sometimes appealed to in these addresses. George Whitaker Wills to his sister, June 28, 1862, manuscript, University of North Carolina. General T. C. Hindman sought on one occasion to invoke hatred of the enemy as a pre-battle conditioner: "Remember that the enemy you engage has no feeling of mercy," he said. "His ranks are made up of Pin Indians, Free Negroes, Southern Tories, Kansas Jayhawkers, and hired Dutch cutthroats. These bloody ruffians have invaded your country, stolen and destroyed your property, murdered your neighbors, outraged your women, driven your children from their homes, and defiled the graves of your kindred." Broadside, dated Dec. 4, 1862, Emory University.

4 T. W. Montfort wrote to his wife from Ft. Pulaski, April 5, 1862: "There is something sad and melancholy in the preparation for Battle. To see so many healthy men prepareing for the worst by disposing of their property by will—to see the surgeon sharping his instruments & whetting his saw . . . men engaged in carding up & prepareing lint to stop the flow of human blood." Typescript, Georgia Archives.

⁵ Journal of William P. Chambers, entry of May 18, 1864, Mississippi Historical Society *Publications*, Centenary Series, V, 321. This source will be cited hereinafter as P.M.H.S.

⁶ Robert M. Gill wrote to his wife from line of battle in Georgia, June 23, 1864: "I saw a canteen upon which a heavy run was made during and after the charge—I still like whisky but I do not want any when going into action for I am or at least was drunk enough yesterday without drinking a drop." Manuscript in author's possession.

⁷ J. H. Belo, *Memoirs* (Boston, 1904), 40.

⁸ For example, see *O. R.*, series 1, XXX, part 2, 237.

⁹ *O. R.*, series 1, XXI, 664. A Virginia veteran attributed the greater resonance of the Southern battle cry to the rural background of most Confederates. In isolated areas, he said, hallooing was a necessary means of communication, while in the cities and towns from which a substantial portion of Yankees came, there was hardly ever an occasion for shouting. In comparing the sounds of the two yells, he said that the Federal cheer was a repeated "hoo-ray," with prolonged emphasis on the second syllable, while the Confederate cry was a series of "woh-who—eys" with a heavy subsiding accent on the blended "who" and "ey," the effect being a sort of "whee." J. Harvey Dew, "The Yankee and Rebel Yells," *Century Magazine*, XLIII (1892), 953–955. Other veterans referred to the Yankee shout as a practiced "hurrah," or a concerted "hip, hip, huzza, huzza, huzza," and to the Rebel Yell as a "yai, yai, yi, yai, yi," but nearly all stress the individual informal quality of the latter. W. H. Morgan, *Personal Reminiscences of the War of 1861–1865* (Lynchburg, 1911), 70; A. P. Ford, *Life in the Confederate Army* (New York, 1905), 58. Douglas Freeman told the writer in an interview that the Confederate cheer was a battle-field adaptation of the fox hunter's cry, which cry the Richmond *News Leader* designated in the Aug. 17, 1936, issue as a wild "y-yo yo-wo-wo." The writer leans toward the theory that the "who-ey" version was the one most commonly used.

¹⁰ Journal of William P. Chambers, entry of Aug. 4, 1864, *P.M.H.S.*, Centenary Series, V, 332.

¹¹ *O. R.*, series 1, XXXVIII, part 3, 922.

¹² For example, see *ibid.*, series 1, XXXIV, part 1, 752.

¹³ *Ibid.*, series 1, XXXIV, part 1, 849.

¹⁴ Robert M. Gill to his wife, July 28, 1864.

¹⁵ *O. R.*, series 1, X, part 1, 583; XXXVI, part 1, 1093–1094.

¹⁶ Morgan, *op. cit.*, 200; E. D. Patterson, in his diary entry of June 28, 1862, says that at Gaines's Mill when he and his comrade went over a ridge they encountered such heavy fire "that the whole brigade literally *staggered* backward several paces as though pushed back by a tornado." Typescript in private possession.

¹⁷ *O. R.*, series 1, XXXVI, part 1, 1093–1094, General Samuel McGowan's report of the "Bloody Angle" phase of Spottsylvania Court House; McGowan says further that a 22-inch oak tree was

cut down by the heavy musket fire, injuring several soldiers when it fell. *Ibid.*

18 John L. G. Wood to his aunt, May 10, 1863, typescript, Georgia Archives; Robert M. Gill to his wife, Oct. 6, 1863; diary of Maurice K. Simons, entry of May 31, 1863, manuscript photostat, University of Texas.

19 *O. R.*, series 1, XXX, part 2, 305, Gen. T. C. Hindman's official report of Chickamauga; XXXIX, part 1, 821, Maj. E. H. Hampton's report of Allatoona; XXXI, part 2, 726, 750–757, Gen. John C. Brown's and Gen. P. R. Cleburne's reports of Lookout Mountain; XXVII, part 2, 486–487, Maj. Samuel Tate to Gov. Z. B. Vance, July 8, 1863, concerning Gettysburg; A. C. Redwood, "Jackson's Foot Cavalry at the Second Bull Run," *Battles and Leaders of the Civil War* (New York, 1887–1888), II, 535–536; Walter Clark, editor, *North Carolina Regiments, 1861–1865* (Raleigh and Goldsboro, 1901), II, 376.

20 *O. R.*, series 1, XXXVIII, part 3, 689.

21 For condition of troops before and during the Shiloh fight see *O. R.*, series 1, X, part 1, 454, 464, 498, 499, 522, 547, 569–570, 586; and XVII, part 2, 641.

22 A young Georgian, writing of his experience at Manassas, said, "As we were retiring I stopped to take a mouthful of mud— scarcely could it be called water—my mouth was awfully hot and dry." New Orleans *Daily Crescent*, Aug. 8, 1861.

23 Thomas Warrick to his wife, Jan. 11–13, 1863, manuscript, Alabama Archives.

24 [Napier Bartlett, *A Soldier's Story of the War, Including the Marches and Battles of the Washington Artillery* (New Orleans, 1874)], 192–193.

25 For instances of scattering of regiments under fire, see *O. R.*, series 1, X, part 1, 467, 584; XXV, part 1, 984–985; LI, part 2, 199. Also John Crittenden to J. S. Bryant, Jan. 29, 1863, typescript, University of Texas; and J. E. Hall to his father, June 3, 1862, manuscript, Alabama Archives.

26 [W. W.] Heartsill, [*Fourteen Hundred and 91 Days in the Confederate Army* (Marshall, Texas, 1876)], 159; [O. T.] Hanks, ["Account of Civil War Experiences,"] 29, manuscript photostat, University of Texas; Henry L. Graves to his aunt, Aug. 7, 1862, typescript, Georgia Archives; G. A. Hanson, *Minor Incidents of the Late War* (Bartow, Florida, 1887), 36; *O. R.*, series 1, XXX, part 2, 418.

27 J. W. Rabb to his mother, Jan. 14, 1863, manuscript photostat, University of Texas.

28 John L. G. Wood to his wife, Dec. 18, 1862, typescript, Georgia Archives.

29 Robert Stiles, *Four Years Under Marse Robert* (New York, 1903), 219–220.

30 Harmon Martin to his sister, Aug. 25, 1863, typescript, Georgia Archives.

[31] George W. Athey to his sister, (no date, but Dec., 1864), manuscript, Alabama Archives.

[32] Hanks, *op. cit.*, 35.

[33] Diary of E. D. Patterson, entry of June 2, 1862.

[34] *O. R.*, series 1, XX, part 1, 957; M. D. Martin to his parents, May 8, 1863, typescript in private possession.

[35] James Mabley to his sister, May 16, 1863, manuscript, Emory University.

[36] Harry Gilmor, *Four Years in the Saddle* (New York, 1866), 141.

[37] Diary of E. D. Patterson, entry of Aug. 31, 1863.

[38] Stiles, *op. cit.*, 116–117.

[39] *O. R.*, series 1, XII, part 2, 736; W. W. Heartsill, *op. cit.*, 159; Robert M. Gill to his wife, July 25, 1864.

[40] Diary of Maurice K. Simons, various entries, May 17–July 3, 1863.

[41] *Ibid*. River water next to the east bank became contaminated with maggots from the great number of dead animals thrown in, and cisterns were either polluted or exhausted. *O. R.*, series 1, XXIV, part 2, 392.

[42] Diary of Maurice K. Simons, entry of June 13, 1863.

[43] *Ibid.*, entries of May 27, 31, 1863.

[44] Diary of James J. Kirkpatrick, entry of Aug. 5, 1864; Robert M. Gill to his wife, July 9, Aug. 16, 1864; Bolling Hall to his sister, Laura, Sept. 20, 1864, manuscript, Alabama Archives.

[45] Crenshaw Hall to his father, Oct. 16, 1864, manuscript, Alabama Archives.

[46] Crenshaw Hall to Laura Hall, Feb. 20, 1865. A Virginia officer charged with building a redoubt on the Petersburg line kept a man posted to call out the Yankee shots. At each flash of their guns he would call out "down" and the men would fall flat in the trench. The Federals got on to the trick and resorted to the device of setting off a blaze of powder to deceive the Rebs, and then giving them the real load as they rose up from their shelter. C. G. Chamberlayne, editor, *Ham Chamberlayne—Virginian* (Richmond, 1932), 267–268.

[47] J. E. Hall to Laura Hall, Oct. 15, 1864, Feb. 8, 1865; Crenshaw Hall to Laura Hall, Feb. 20, 1865.

[48] *O. R.*, series 1, X, part 1, 589; XI, part 1, 950.

[49] *Ibid.*, XX, part 1, 730, 747, 867.

[50] *Ibid.*, XII, part 2, 593; XXX, part 2, 379.

[51] *Ibid.*, XXX, part 2, 190, 379–380.

[52] *Ibid.*, XXV, part 1, 1003.

[53] *Ibid.*, XI, part 1, 950; XIX, part 1, 933; Clark, *op. cit.*, II, 350–354.

[54] *Ibid.*, XVII, part 1, 400; XIX, part 1, 875.

[55] *Ibid.*, XX, part 1, 719, 852.

[56] *Ibid.*, 931.

[57] *Ibid.*, X, part 2, 528; XI, part 2, 992–993; XX, part 2, 494; Robert Ames Jarman, "History of Co. K, 27th Mississippi Infantry," 10, typescript in private possession.

[58] James A. McCord to his brother, Dec. 3, 1864, manuscript photostat in private possession.

[59] *O. R.*, series 1, XXVIII, part 1, 418–419, 524.

[60] [Samuel E.] Mays, [compiler, *Genealogical Notes on the Family of Mays and Reminiscences of the War Between the States* (Plant City, Fla., 1927)], 36; *O. R.*, series 1, XI, part 2, 563, 612; part 3, 506, 571.

[61] *O. R.*, series 1, X, part 1, 391, 432, 571–572, 576–577. For other evidences of reprehensible conduct under fire at Shiloh see *ibid.*, 401, 501, 507, 546, 570, 589.

[62] *Ibid.*, XX, part 1, 761, 879.

[63] *Ibid.*, XXIV, part 2, 88.

[64] Anonymous diary of a Louisiana soldier, entry of Nov. 25, 1863, manuscript, Confederate Memorial Hall, New Orleans.

[65] *O. R.*, series 1, XXXI, part 2, 665–666; see also Bate's General Order of Nov. 28, 1863, *ibid.*, 744. News correspondent "Sallust" wrote from a point near the battlefield at midnight of November 25: "The Confederates have sustained today the most ignominious defeat of the whole war—a defeat for which there is but little excuse or palliation. For the first time during our struggle for national independence, our defeat is chargeable to the troops themselves and not to the blunder or incompetency of their leaders. It is difficult for one to realize how a defeat so complete could have occurred on ground so favorable." Richmond *Daily Dispatch*, Dec. 4, 1863.

[66] Stephen Ramseur to his wife, July 23, Aug. 3, 1864, manuscript, University of North Carolina.

[67] Pulaski Cowper, compiler, *Extracts of Letters of Maj. Gen. Bryan Grimes* (Raleigh, 1883), 69–70.

[68] G. P. Ring to "My own Darling," Sept. 21, 1864, manuscript, Confederate Memorial Hall, New Orleans. General Grimes also mentions the pleading of the women. Cowper, *op. cit.*, p. 70.

[69] Cowper, *op. cit.*, 77–78; *O. R.*, series 1, XLIII, part 1, 598–600; R. W. Waldrop to his father, Oct. 21, 1864, manuscript, University of North Carolina.

[70] *O. R.*, series 1, XLI, part 1, 637, official report of General Price.

[71] *Ibid.*, XXXVIII, part 3, 835; part 4, 766–767.

[72] *Ibid.*, XLV, part 1, 660, 747, 749, 750.

[73] [Wirt A.] Cate, [editor, *Two Soldiers* (Chapel Hill, 1938)], 169.

[74] [W. A.] Fletcher, [*Rebel Private Front and Rear* (Beaumont, Texas, 1908)], 84.

[75] C. Irvine Walker to Ada Sinclair, July 28, 1864, typescript, University of Texas.

[76] Stiles, *op. cit.*, 135.

[77] *O. R.*, series 1, XXX, part 2, 183–184; part 4, 715.

[78] *Ibid.*, LI, part 1, 273; William R. Stillwell to his wife, May 2–3, 1863, manuscript, Georgia Archives; Thomas Caffey to his sister, Feb. 16, 1863, "War Letters of Thomas Caffey," Montgomery *Advertiser*, April 25, 1909.

[79] For example, see Fletcher, *op. cit.*, 84.

Suggestions for Further Reading

With industrialization and the growth of cities in the early nineteenth century, the life of the urban worker changed dramatically. The dynamics of this change can be approached through several important articles: E. P. Thompson, "Time, Work-Discipline, and Industrial Capitalism," *Past and Present*, 38 (1967):56–97; David Montgomery, "The Working Classes of the Pre–Industrial American City, 1780–1830," *Labor History*, 9 (1968):3–22; and Herbert G. Gutman, "Work, Culture, and Society in Industrializing America, 1815–1919," *American Historical Review*, 78 (1973):531–87. Also important are Walter Hugins, *Jacksonian Democracy and the Working Class* (Stanford, Cal., 1960); Norman Ware, *The Industrial Worker, 1840–1860: The Reaction of American Industrial Society to the Advance of the Industrial Revolution* (New York, 1924); Paul Faler, "Cultural Aspects of the Industrial Revolution: Lynn, Massachusetts, Shoemakers and Industrial Morality, 1826–1860," *Labor History*, 15 (1974):367–94; Bruce Laurie, " 'Nothing on Compulsion': Life Styles of Philadelphia Artisans," *Labor History*, 15 (1974):337–66; and David Montgomery, "The Shuttle and the Cross: Weavers and Artisans in the Kensington Riots of 1844," *Journal of Social History*, 5 (1972):411–46.

The western frontier experience, both for old-stock Americans and immigrants, is well described in Richard A. Bartlett, *The New Country: A Social History of the American Frontier, 1776–1890** (New York, 1974); Everett Dick, *The Sod-House Frontier, 1854–1890* (New York, 1937); Merle Curti, *The Making of an American Community: A Case Study of Democracy in a Frontier County** (Stanford, Cal., 1959); and Rodman W. Paul, *Mining Frontiers of the Far West, 1848–1880** (New York, 1963). But the most poignant views of frontier life are those available in novels such as Willa Cather's *My Antonia** (Boston, 1926), and Hamlin Garland's *A Son of the Middle Border** (New York, 1917) and *A Daughter of the Middle Border* (New York, 1921). For the eastern immigrant experience in the nineteenth century, the inquiring student is advised to begin with Oscar Handlin, *Boston's Immigrants, 1790–1865: A Study in Acculturation** (Cambridge, Mass., 1941); Robert Ernst, *Immigrant Life in New York City, 1825–1863* (New York, 1949); Barbara M. Solomon, *Ancestors and Immigrants: A Changing New England Tradition* (Cambridge, Mass., 1956); and Maldwyn Jones, *Destination America* (New York, 1976).

Entertainment in the lives of nineteenth-century Americans is

* Available in paperback edition.

explored in David Grimsted, *Melodrama Unveiled: American Theatre and Culture, 1800–1850* (Chicago, 1968), and Constance Rourke, *The Roots of American Culture* (New York, 1942).

The experience of Americans during the Civil War can be probed in George W. Smith and Charles Judah, eds., *Life in the North during the Civil War: A Source History* (Albuquerque, N.M., 1966); Bell Wiley, *The Life of Billy Yankee: The Common Soldier of the Union* (Indianapolis, 1952) and *Southern Negroes, 1861–1865** (New Haven, 1938); Frank Owsley, *Plain Folk of the Old South* (Baton Rouge, 1949); Mary E. Massey, *Ersatz in the Confederacy* (Columbia, S.C., 1952); and Charles W. Ramsdell, *Behind the Lines in the Southern Confederacy* (Baton Rouge, 1944).

A 9
B 0
C 1
D 2
E 3
F 4
G 5
H 6
I 7
J 8